A History of Women

IN THE WEST

Georges Duby and Michelle Perrot, General Editors

IV. Emerging Feminism from Revolution to World War

A HISTORY OF WOMEN

IN THE WEST

IV. Emerging Feminism from Revolution to World War

Geneviève Fraisse
and Michelle Perrot, Editors

The Belknap Press of
Harvard University Press
Cambridge, Massachusetts
London, England

Writing the History of Women

Georges Duby and Michelle Perrot

WOMEN WERE LONG RELEGATED to the shadows of history. The development of anthropology and the new emphasis on the family, on a history of *mentalités* centered on everyday life, on what was private and individual, have helped to dispel those shadows. The women's movement and the questions it has raised have done even more. "Where have we come from? Where are we going?" These are questions women have begun asking themselves. Both inside and outside the university they have set out in search of their forebears and attempted to understand the roots of their domination and the evolution of male-female relations.

"The History of Women" is a convenient and attractive title, but the idea that women in themselves are an object of history must be rejected firmly. What we want to understand is the place of women, the "condition" of women, women's roles and powers. We want to investigate how women acted. We want to examine their words and their silences. We want to look at their many images: goddess, madonna, witch. Our history is fundamentally relational; we look at society as a whole, and our history of women is just as much a history of men.

It is a history of the *longue durée*: five volumes cover the history of the West from antiquity to the present. And our history covers only the West, from the Mediterranean to the Atlantic.

Histories of the women of the Orient, Latin America, and Africa are sorely needed, and we hope that one day the women and men of those regions will write them.

Our history is "feminist" in that its outlook is egalitarian; its intention is to be open to a variety of interpretations. We want to raise questions, but we have no formulaic answers. Ours is a plural history: a history of *women* as seen from many different points of view.

It is also the work of a team. Georges Duby and Michelle Perrot are responsible for the overall coordination. Each volume has one or two editors: Pauline Schmitt Pantel (antiquity), Christiane Klapisch-Zuber (Middle Ages), Natalie Zemon Davis and Arlette Farge (early modern), Geneviève Fraisse and Michelle Perrot (nineteenth century), and Françoise Thébaud (twentieth century) have chosen their own collaborators—some sixty-eight scholars in all, a representative sample of those working in this field in Europe and the United States.

We hope that this series will provide a handy summary of the results achieved to date as well as serve as a guide to further research. We also hope it will bring the pleasures of history to new readers and act as a stimulus to memory.

A History of Women

IN THE WEST

Emerging Feminism from Revolution to World War

Orders and Liberties

Geneviève Fraisse and Michelle Perrot

THE IMAGE OF THE nineteenth century as a sad and somber time, an austere, confining period for women, is one that arose spontaneously. Granted, it was during this century that women's lives were conceptualized in a new way, as the unfolding of a personal history subject to a precisely defined, socially elaborated set of rules. Yet it would be a mistake to think of the period from 1789 to 1914 solely as a time of domination, of women's absolute subjugation. For this was a century (actually a century and a quarter) that also witnessed the birth of feminism, an emblematic term that refers just as much to important changes in the social structure (such as wage labor, individual civil rights, and a woman's right to an education) as to the emergence of women as a collective force in the political arena. Thus it might be better to say that the nineteenth century was the moment in history when the lives of women changed, or, more precisely, when the perspective of women's lives changed: the advent of modernity made it possible to posit the female as subject, woman as a full-fledged individual and participant in political life and, ultimately, as a citizen. Despite the constraints of a strict code of rules governing women's daily lives, the range of possibilities had begun to expand, and bold new prospects lay ahead.

The period begins and ends with major events: a revolution and a war. Yet neither the French Revolution nor World War I provides the key to understanding the intervening 125 years. Revolutions and wars have been known to press women into service only to dismiss them the moment they cease to be needed. The interplay between invitation and rejection, between the inclusion and the exclusion of women from the affairs of state and nation, can be subtle, and we shall have more to say about how men used this strategy of alternation.

If modernity opened opportunities for women, it was because they benefited from the economic, political, social, and cultural changes that took place in the nineteenth century. Several factors proved crucial.

First, in a century of historicism it followed that if the human race had a history, women too had one; their status as man's helpmate and as the reproductive agent of the species might prove to be less immutable than it appeared, and the so-called eternal essence of the feminine might be subject to manifold variations, each containing the promise of a new life. Socialist utopias (though realized, as the etymology suggests, "nowhere" in actual history) nevertheless implied the possibility of a future different from the present. Their theorists made imaginative efforts to rethink the workings of the family, the nature of love and motherhood, and the social role of women. From another angle, evolutionary theories pondered the origins of society and in particular of the family and of patriarchy (or matriarchy). For women, the fact that the human race has a history (an origin, a past, a future) was surely a hopeful discovery.

Second, although the industrial revolution, along with the gradual expansion of democratic politics, created problems for women, it also broke the bonds of economic and symbolic dependency that had previously tethered them to fathers or husbands. The individual gained priority over society, and in this sense the female individual more nearly resembled the male than in the past. This image was not without its share of illusion: it was not until the twentieth century, for example, that women gained the right to spend their earnings as they saw fit. But the ambivalence of liberation itself is something we must try to explain: why was women's work as much an occasion for hyperexploitation as for emancipation, and why were women excluded from the political sphere for so long?

This brings us to our third point: the democratic era was not *a priori* favorable to women.[1] At first it was argued that women ought to be excluded from public affairs and confined to the domestic sphere. The reason for this is easy to surmise: under the feudal regime, the fact that a few people enjoyed certain rights, or rather privileges, did not mean that those rights or privileges extended to all; conversely, under the democratic regime it was implied that what was valid for one was valid for all. Hence it was better not to grant rights to any one category of women than to grant them to virtually all and thereby, as people at the time believed, initiate a stupid rivalry between the sexes. From now on the debate on the nature of woman in general involved all women, not just a few.

But democracy did not exclude women in a systematic way. The principle of exclusion was an internal contradiction of the democratic system, which affirmed the equality of rights and established a republican form of politics. Throughout the West this gave rise to feminism, which aimed at achieving equality of the sexes through a collective social and political movement. Feminist acts and texts can of course be found prior to the nineteenth century, but the feminism that emerged as a subtext in the revolutionary practice of 1789 came to the fore only after 1830.

The nineteenth century therefore appears to have been a turning point in the long history of women, as if the traditional deck had been reshuffled. The old tensions were still present—between work (at home or in the shop) and family, between the domestic ideal and social utility, between the world of appearances, dress, and pleasure and the world of subsistence, apprenticeship, and the practice of a profession, and between religious practice as spiritual exercise and social regulator and the new realm of education in secular schools. But the cards were dealt out differently, and new stakes had been added to the game. If women's lives were transformed, how can we find out what they thought about the transformation? Did they abide by the new rules? Did they give their assent to the new order that was imposed on them? It is difficult to say, just as it is difficult to identify the various forms of resistance, rejection, and transgression. If, moreover, the modern woman relinquished certain powers, such as those associated with rank or with the ownership of land, a family business, or a dwelling—and if in some respects the life of the Victorian housewife seems infinitely more constricted than that of the Enlightenment aristocrat, whose loss of freedom Mme de Staël lamented—she gained new powers in return, in particular those associated with motherhood. The nineteenth century overrated maternity and not simply as a reproductive function. It was a matter, as Joseph de Maistre put it, of "making men," that "great giving of life that was not cursed like the other." Women, whether in obedience or emancipation, learned to avail themselves of the power of maternity, sometimes as a refuge but also as a way of obtaining still other powers in the social realm. The image of the schoolteacher offering society her maternal qualities clearly reflects the transition from the "mother as teacher" to the "teacher as mother."

The stakes for women also changed over time. The norms enunciated early in the century were collective norms defining a social function, that of wife and mother, establishing the rights of women as a function of their duties and defining women as a social group whose role and behavior were to be standardized and therefore idealized. But this comprehensive formulation gradually disintegrated, and female identities seemed to proliferate: mother, worker, spinster, emancipated woman, and so on. Some women partook of more than one of these sometimes contradictory roles, thus giving rise to tensions not unfamiliar to the women of the twentieth century. The various forms of female solitude thus reflected the complex interaction of chance, necessity, and free choice.

No single model of the woman's role could possibly have prevailed. It was inevitable that the locks confining women within the home would be broken, that the taboos on participation in civic life would be violated, that the prohibitions on the political activities of women would be challenged. With varying degrees of naïveté or self-consciousness, women refused to accept as normal a life that was presented to them as an ideal. And even when they believed in that ideal and sought to live by it, they transformed its nature. Some cultivated their minds, and not only to dazzle society with their wit. Others left on missionary voyages or simply went off in a spirit of adventure. Still others went to town in search of work, thereby losing the support of their families. And others, finally, took to the streets to protest injustices against their sex or class or to decry slavery. Furthermore, there is reason to doubt that life in the nineteenth century was as prudish as it was claimed to be, or that sexual life was as simplified as the public may have wished. If disorder, even organized disorder, was the result of men using women—from the pregnant working girl to the tubercular prostitute—women were more than just victims, even if free love was often a trap and marginal sexual lives, such as that of the homosexual, were dangerous to lead.

In emphasizing the relation between subjection and freedom, we surely have not given an accurate portrait of nineteenth-century women's lives or done justice to the variety of social and occupational groups. What, for example, of the large number of peasant women, whose daily lives changed little over the course of the century? They probably accounted for no less than three-quarters of the total female population—a fact we ought to bear in mind. But the history we tell is not that of works and days; it is not the social history of women. We are interested, rather, in the things that changed, in that which makes a "history of women" pertinent, in the ways in which women showed themselves to be not mere walk-ons but actresses in the drama of history.

Another lacuna that the reader will notice is more difficult to explain: let us call it the concrete reality, the material and social facts of women's lives. Economic structures, the workings of institutions (such as religious institutions), and the interaction of social classes are frequently omitted from the analyses or else are mentioned along with ideas that clearly belong to the realm of symbols, images, and discourse. This is not an accident, nor is it a reflection of the current research interest in the mechanisms of the perception of women by men and by women themselves. It appears to be an inherent characteristic of the history of women: because woman never exists without her image, the history of women always involves a figurative dimension. Women are symbols: Marianne symbolizes the French Republic; the muses are women; women appeared in illustrations, popular engravings, and as characters in novels; and the philosophers tell us that they were reflections or mirrors of "the Other." And it was by starting to change these images that they changed themselves, for they knew that the image was a trap: feminism invariably called forth, in caricature, denunciation of its extremes of expression and behavior, its masculinity, its crudeness, its fury. Our illustrated chapter is therefore accompanied by a detailed commentary as distant as possible from the usual interpretations of the imagery.

The "history of women" is thus too simple a title: if this history wants to distinguish itself from a necessary history of representations, it must also be a history of men, of relations between the sexes, of the difference between the sexes. As we shall see, the formulation of this connection varies from one chapter to another, depending not only on the interests of the author but also on the subject under consideration. The body and heart of a woman are described in relation to man; law and philosophy necessarily conceptualize sexual relations. Religious codes, literary descriptions, and iconographies are also examined from the standpoint of sexual difference. So is the discourse of political economy, which is especially symptomatic of a confusion between the natural and the social order, between the sexual division of labor and the labor market for male and female workers. It will emerge that female occupations that appear to be defined by their "natural" qualities are in fact shaped exclusively by language.

Accordingly, a critique of language becomes an essential, if not the essential, element of the history of women. More than in other disciplines, it is crucial here to reflect on the way in which "the facts" and the narratives that exhibit them have been fitted together. This could, moreover, be the specific contribution that this "women's history" has to make to general history, with its ever keener concern to investigate itself as a cognitive process.

The fact that this book is centrally concerned with "the West" may seem amply justified, especially for the nineteenth century, yet it is also open to challenge on the grounds that national histories were different, as much recent work has demonstrated. Over the past two decades a considerable body of work has focused on this aspect, and new works appear literally every day. The West that concerns us here consists not only of Europe—from the Atlantic to the Urals, from the Baltic to the Mediterranean—but also of North America. There are relevant historical and cultural differences between, say, England and France, Italy and Germany, and the United States and Belgium or Switzerland. The first experiments with political transformations took place in France, with its revolutions and its secular republic. So did the great religious changes that redefined, among other things, the Catholic woman. Conversely, certain cultural transformations seem to have been more specifically British or German: for example, feminism in England and Germany was highly innovative in practice even if sometimes less political than elsewhere. And while the French Civil Code seems to have been a model of modern legislation, in philosophy the Germans set the tone throughout the century. Already the center of innovation was shifting from Europe to North America: the United States, innovative since the Revolutionary War, gave rise to early feminist models based on Protestant revival meetings and other novel forms of democratic practice. Westward expansion and the influence of immigrants soon contributed other sources. The North American continent was a new world with respect to relations between the sexes. The New Woman was born of the experiences of the Bostonians as well as of the Jewish women of New York. She returned in glory to Europe, where she became a constant presence in debates over sexual identity.

In the West, understood in this broad sense as a zone at once more homogeneous and more diverse than in centuries past, there were disparities of behavior and subtle differences of expression which the variety of feminisms made glaringly apparent, all the more so given feminism's surprising international dimensions and intensity of communication. In this ferment began a fundamental change in gender relations that persists to this day, a continuing and perhaps interminable shift in the ways men and women relate to the opposite sex that is obviously still an issue for our own time just as it was an issue for the turn of the century, which was also a time of crisis, a period of intense sexual anxiety.

TRANSLATED FROM THE FRENCH BY ARTHUR GOLDHAMMER

one

The Political Rupture and the New Order of Discourse

Defining the Essence of Femininity

Between the event, the Revolution, and the text, the Civil Code, a rupture occurred in history, and even countries in which the change cannot be dated as precisely as it can in France and the United States were marked by this transition to modernity, by the end of monarchy and the advent of democracy, and by the definition of a civil society outside the sphere of politics.

What was the nature of this rupture? In the first place, it was not a single break but many, and the changes thus set in motion had conflicting effects on women. Both the French and American revolutions carved out a realm in which women felt free to participate in collective action; individuals of the same sex were permitted to gather outside the private spaces where they generally congregated. Although women in France played a more political role than in the United States, their actions were by no means more radical. In any case, it was the event that created the possibility for women to assemble, and the women who did so began to think of themselves as gendered individuals. But these precursors of nineteenth-century feminist practices soon died out, and they were followed by decades of silence. The rupture that took place at the turn of the century also provided the justification for excluding women from civic life, an exclusion far more radical than that which had been in effect under feudalism. Modern revolutions allowed women to take to the streets and establish political clubs, but the builders of the new order could also close those clubs and call women back to their hearths. To put it in a nutshell, another consequence of revolution was that the separation between public and private space became more pronounced: a careful distinction was drawn between private life and public life, between civil society and political society. Ultimately it was through this distinction that women were kept out of politics and reduced to dependence in civil society.

The ambivalence introduced by the Revolution in France is not as apparent in other countries, but it does exist. The event alone, however, does not explain why the advent of modernity led to only modest progress for women. The text completed what political action had begun: the inception of the Civil Code, like the Revolution, was equally unprecedented and of crucial importance, as its influence throughout Europe attests. Some have called the Code a monument consecrating the subservience of women. And that is what it was, although an ambiguity exists there too: while women were in concrete ways made subservient not only to their fathers and husbands but to their families generally, daughters acquired equality vis-à-vis sons in the sense that primogeniture was abolished in favor of equal inheritance. And the Code contained many other contradictions as well: for example, unmarried daughters above the age of majority were not covered by many of the Code's provisions, whereas married women, the principal object of the legislators' concern, were hobbled in a variety of ways. The evolution of the law in several areas clearly shows the disintegration of the fundamental idea of the Civil Code, namely, that because women are inferior to men, they are and deserve to be subservient.

Throughout the nineteenth century the laws were amended, subjected to local changes and innovative interpretations, and modified as a result of feminist agitation—all signs that the law can never be definitive or static. In this respect the study of philosophy is enlightening: reading the works of those generally considered to be the great philosophers (all men, by the way), it is clear that there was a fundamental change in what philosophical texts defined as the norm. Early in the century it was held that all women ought to have the same destiny, the same unique task, that of wife and mother ("all women" here being reminiscent of "all women" as conceived by democratic thinkers, but now as reproductive agents rather than citizens). But by the end of the century, thinkers aware of exceptions, transgressions, and the actual diversity of women's choices proposed a subtler norm, according to which each woman's history was to demonstrate a particular disciplining of fate. This might be interpreted as a restoration of freedom to individual women, who were henceforth permitted to make choices affecting their own lives. But is that interpretation really correct? There is reason to doubt it: a woman's fate was now like a carefully composed score, in which medicine, sociology, psychoanalysis, and aesthetics joined forces to define the essence of femininity.

G.F.—M.P.

1

Daughters of Liberty and Revolutionary Citizens

Dominique Godineau

The end of the eighteenth century was marked by a series of ruptures. Revolution followed revolution, though not all had the same meaning or importance. It is not enough merely to observe that women either did or did not participate. Nor is it enough to examine the influence of the male/female factor. We must also study history to discover how gender relations interacted with events: how male-female relations shaped events, and what effect the events had on male-female relations. How did institutional, political, social, and ideological upheavals affect the actual and desired roles and representations of the sexes in society? (Economic changes, whose impact should not be neglected, are not considered here.)

Women and Men in Rebellion

Comparative history can help us to answer these questions. The convulsions that affected Europe and North America occurred in different contexts. Despite the common heritage of the Enlightenment, debates on the two continents revolved around different issues. The French attempted to rebuild and "regenerate" society from top to bottom; they created a new space for politics, a political arena in which both men and women participated in a powerful popular movement. The Americans, after fighting for independence, refrained from tampering with the country's social foundations. The Belgians rose up in protest against the reforms of an "enlightened despot" and insisted on a restoration of their former autonomy. While it is impossible to give an exhaustive account of all the complexities, I shall attempt to point out changes in gender relations common to a number of different countries as well as certain significant differences. My hope is that this will shed light on the linkage between a society—its evolution, its values—and the way in which it constructs male-female relations.

The "Firebrands"

There can be no revolution without rebellious crowds. In early modern Europe it is well known that women traditionally participated in riots.[1] Thus it should come as no surprise that we find women in the forefront of certain Parisian insurrections. On the morning of October 5, 1789, women were the first to band together and march on Versailles, followed in the afternoon by the National Guard. The uprisings in the spring of 1795 began with women's demonstrations. Women sounded the tocsin, beat drums in the streets of the city, mocked the authorities and the military, enlisted bystanders, invaded stores and workshops, and climbed up the stairs of houses to force reluctant sisters to march with them on the Convention, to which they came in wave after wave, soon joined by men in arms. They played "the role of firebrands," as one official later wrote.[2]

In 1795, as in 1789 and May 1793, women occupied the streets in the weeks before insurrections. They assembled in force (on May 23, 1795, the deputies prohibited them from gathering in groups of more than five on pain of arrest) and called men to action, branding those who refused as "cowards." When men hesitated, women proclaimed that if they "led the dance," the men would "follow." Before the insurrection of May–June 1793 broke out, one deputy told the Convention that "women will begin the movement . . . [and] men will come to their assistance." In fact, the uprising was not initiated by women, but the observation, which was by no means isolated, shows clearly what women were thought to be capable of in tumultuous times. In explosive situations political activists sometimes turned to women in the hope of igniting the powderkeg. Was this just because women could serve as a protective shield? No; women were seen as necessary mediators between activists and the populace. Their actions and their voices could spark a rebellion. Once this was under way, however, the roles of the sexes were reversed: when the crowd consisted of both men and women, the latter by their own admission were there to "support the men." Male citizens, after all, were organized as a National Guard and armed with cannon. In the heat of action the women still served as "firebrands." "The agitators work mainly on the women, who convey their frenzy to the men, inflaming them with seditious words and sparking the most violent upheaval," one policeman observed during the May 1795 insurrection. Although women kept an eye on their men and if necessary rekindled their ardor, it was the men who, thanks to their weaponry, led the action. Men first followed the lead of women, and then women supported their men: behind the apparent disorder and spontaneity of the crowd we clearly discern an unequal distribution of sexual roles that people took for granted as typical of any popular uprising.

Tradition and Innovation

The revolutionary period is fascinating because the old and the new were intimately intertwined. Because the legacy of past centuries was combined with rudimentary forerunners of future forms of political action, we can gain a clearer idea of how relations between the sexes evolved or turned in new directions. The pattern described above reflected an old world, not yet dead: for three centuries, from 1500 to 1800, women had called men to rebellion all across Europe, from Amsterdam to Naples. The insurrectional rhetoric of the French Revolution was rooted in a long tradition: the beating of drums, the mockery of authority through carnivalesque ritual, the invocation of maternity to legitimate a woman's action—none of this was new, and all of it stemmed from ancient practice. But if the female rebel of the French Revolution still wore the same old rags as her forerunners, she was nevertheless a different woman. She led the invasion of the Convention brandishing the Declaration of the Rights of Man and declaring that the sovereign people were "at home" in the legislative chamber—innovations which indicate that, despite her traditional role and behavior, she had entered the new political arena opened up by the Revolution. Yet this new arena had been constructed by and for men; its very structure reserved it for men alone. So that even though women in France were able for a time to make themselves heard as citizens, they soon ran up against the same restrictions on their citizenship as women in other countries.

A revolution is more than a mere rebellion—people had already begun to realize this in 1789. A revolution requires an organizing structure. And women were excluded from revolutionary institutions of all kinds: from the armed nation (whether the French National Guard, the Batavian *vrijcorps,* or the American militia), from deliberative assemblies (section meetings and townships), and from local committees and political groups. Thus relations between the sexes changed as the insurrection evolved: whereas women played a galvanizing role in more or less spontaneous uprisings, they were relegated to the sidelines as soon as revolutionary associations took control of events. In the 1784–1787 civil war between Orangemen and Patriots in the Netherlands, women were in evidence primarily in the ranks of the Orange: was this perhaps a consequence of the alleged reactionary tendency in the female nature? In fact, the Orangemen, by relying on ancient forms of mobilization (riots, appeals to the mob), allowed women to play their traditional role and push their way to the front ranks; Kaat Mussel, the mussel vendor who led the Rotterdam rebellion of 1784, is an example. There were women on the Patriot side as well, but their role was less visible, for they worked in the shadow of the organizations guiding the revolution. After 1787 the Orangemen acquired a political organization of their own, and in the second revolutionary episode of 1795 women were no longer as prominent in their ranks.[3]

In France the insurrection of 1–4 *prairial,* Year III (May 20–23, 1795), eloquently attests to the influence of political organizations in constructing relations between the sexes. Although abundant testimony confirms that women played a leading role in the events of the first day, they are absent from accounts of the following day's action, which was dominated by the sectional assemblies and the National Guard. Obliged to quit the limelight, women subsequently returned only for specific purposes, such as demanding the release of a prisoner or inciting resistance. In the initial riot there had been room for both sexes, neither being organized; but once one of them succeeded in establishing an effective political structure, a structure that excluded women even though it was supposed to represent the sovereign people from whom it drew its legitimacy, the new insurrectional economy could afford to dispense with the earlier balance of gender relations.

The Revolution from Day to Day

The participation of women in the revolutions of the late eighteenth century was not limited to insurrectional upheavals. Their daily involvement varied from country to country, depending on the local situation and traditions. Participation was undoubtedly most extensive in France, where the female *sans-culottes* who thronged the political arena managed to give a national dimension to their activities. Their practice as militants depended in large part on their ambiguous status as citizens without citizenship. Some women chose forms of political behavior explicitly to compensate for their legal exclusion from the body politic and to declare their membership in the sovereign people.

Forums, Clubs, and Salons

Though unable to take part in the deliberations of political bodies, many women nevertheless flocked to the public galleries. Contemporaries remarked on the large number of females in the audience and criticized their "fever to frequent [political] assemblies." And these women by no means kept silent. Debates were frequently interrupted by shouting, pandemonium, and applause. The women who attended these sessions were first called *tricoteuses* in 1795, and described as women "posted in the galleries [who] with their hoarse voices influence the assembled legislators." Their presence at such legislative meetings was a way for women to enter the political arena both concretely and symbolically. In the popular mind the galleries performed an essential political function: they monitored the activities of elected officials. The woman who sat in a public gallery indicated that she enjoyed a share of sovereignty even without the legal prerogatives.

Despite this participation, and despite the existence of a few mixed popular societies, women were not admitted to full membership in revolutionary organizations. In at least thirty cities some women did form their own political clubs. The members of these clubs, many of whom were relatives of prominent revolutionaries, met regularly to discuss the laws and newspapers, to debate local and national political issues, to engage in philanthropic activities, and to defend the constitutional clergy to other female citizens. After 1792 these societies became increasingly radicalized and took an active part in local political struggles, usually as allies of the Jacobins. In Paris two women's clubs came to the fore in quick succession. Founded by Etta Palm d'Aelders, the Société Patriotique et de Bienfaisance des Amies de la Vérité (1791–92) took an interest in the education of poor girls and favored divorce and political rights for women. The Club des Citoyennes Républicaines Révolutionnaires (May 10–October 30, 1793) was an association of militant women of the people (shopgirls, seamstresses, and industrial workers); closely associated with the sans-culotte movement, the club was intensely active in the conflict between Girondins and Montagnards and in the political debate of the summer of 1793 before being proscribed, along with other women's clubs, by the Convention on October 30, 1793. In the report that introduced the decree outlawing these clubs, one deputy, Amar, raised the question of the social and political division of roles between the sexes. His conclusion was peremptory: "It is not possible for women to exercise political rights." Despite this imperious dismissal, women continued to play a political role in the streets and galleries, as well as in the antigovernment conspiracies of 1795 and various insurrectional movements.

Militant practice in revolutionary times is frequently shaped by social practice in ordinary times. Social life in the popular quarters in the eighteenth century was characterized by the prominence and intensity of social interchange among women. Women gathered to gossip and exchange news (and sometimes blows), and in so doing they defined the outlines of a woman's world that was relatively autonomous. During the Revolution these encounters took on a political coloration: the laundresses who met in taverns when their day's work was done together deciphered the speeches of revolutionary orators. Neighbors who had set their chairs on their doorsteps to savor a sweet summer's night came to blows when one championed the cause of the Girondins, the other of the Montagnards. Women were apt to share their political views with women neighbors rather than with their husbands; sometimes neighbors went arm in arm, chatting gaily or "fiercely," to the legislative galleries. Militant couples did not always work together.

This situation, which war only compounded, was nothing other than the reflection in the political sphere of prevailing male-female relations. When questioned about the political conduct of their wives, some men responded by saying that "politics is none of their business." They paid little attention to "women's concerns," some disdainfully added. Women's statements, on the other hand, often reflect a certain concern for independence; their affairs were their own and no concern of men. When women of opposing opinions clashed in the streets, as often happened, men looked on without intervening, knowing full well that they were not expected to take a hand in a dispute among women regardless of whether the issue was private or political. The way chores were distributed within the family also influenced the revolutionary practice of both sexes. Thus, whereas the typical male militant was a family man in his forties, the typical female militant was a woman not yet thirty or else past the age of fifty—in other words, a woman without several children to take care of.

The militancy that claimed a place for women in the theater of urban life was primarily popular and Parisian. If we leave the revolutionary capital, plunged into turmoil with each new wave of enthusiasm or outrage, and wend our way down the dusty paths of rural villages, we cease to encounter groups of women discussing politics in smoke-filled taverns. Rural women chose less visible means of registering their commitment to the Revolution: some sent gifts or purchased rifles for National Guardsmen, while others took oaths along with men. Women in the opposing camp gathered in angry groups to protect the local priest or to prevent the removal of church bells or to demand that churches be reopened.

Women belonging to ruling circles engaged in politics in a different arena altogether, one on the borderline between private and public. It was private in the sense that meetings were held in private homes, to which admittance was restricted. But it was also public in the sense that it was a place where public officials met. Deputies saw one another not only at the Jacobin Club but also in private salons, where they prepared in an informal way for future meetings of the Assembly. Salons run by such women as Mme Roland and Mme de Condorcet were also places where men and women could discuss politics. Politicians from opposing camps could argue with one another in a relaxed setting. Before the gulf between Girondins and Montagnards became too wide, for example, Robespierre (a Montagnard) frequented the salon of

Manon Roland, "egeria of the Girondins." Because of its semi-private, semi-public character, the salon could play a strategic role. In the early stages of the Belgian revolution of 1789, the salon of the celebrated Comtesse d'Yves served as a place where guild leaders, nobles, democrats, and traditionalists could come together and talk.

Spinning for the Common Cause

The desire for political commitment on the part of American women had to take account of the available possibilities just as it did in France, but those possibilities were different there. Shaped by the male-female relations of colonial society, women's activities point up the formal and ideological differences between the two revolutions. In eighteenth-century America women did not take part in political life. Religion afforded the only available space for public affirmation. Influenced in particular by Methodism, women did not hesitate to express themselves in prayer meetings, and a few even founded new sects. In America, moreover, the revolutionary rupture did not take on the same popular and political dimensions as in France. Therefore American women were not in the forefront of revolutionary crowds; they did not join clubs or attend legislative meetings even as spectators, for the public played no supervisory role in the legislative process.

As early as 1765 people in the rebellious colonies were exhorted to boycott merchandise imported from England, to "buy American." The Sons of Liberty called, in the name of patriotism, upon women—the linchpin of this strategy—to stop ordering from importers, to give up drinking tea, and to renounce the elegant luxuries of the old continent in favor of goods cruder and simpler but made in America. Indeed, women were even urged to make their own substitutes for imported goods; to be an American woman was to spin wool for the patriotic cause. Working alone or in groups, they gathered in the home of a patriot, usually a minister, to spin yarn while listening to sermons or singing hymns, in keeping with the tradition, then flourishing in colonial America, of female prayer meetings. Always important, the religious sociability of women thus took on a political meaning. Whereas militant practice in France found its voice in a political language proclaimed in the public arena, the commitment of American women manifested itself in the private sphere, the public one remaining masculine. Learning the art of spinning, wearing American clothes, and not drinking tea were individual decisions overlaid with political meaning, civic acts that bestowed on individual women a sense of being Daughters of Liberty acting in a common cause.

This domestic aspect is also evident in one of the principal chores women assumed during the American Revolution: tending to family farms and businesses abandoned by men gone to fight the British. Those who supported the Revolution more directly also made commitments that were primarily individual: they gathered intelligence for the patriotic armies, served the troops as cooks and washerwomen, and bought war bonds. The only significant collective action by women was the collection of funds for the troops in 1780 by the members of the Philadelphia Ladies' Association, a group chiefly made up of female relatives of politicians.

Writing and Speaking in the Feminine

Wherever there were revolutions, women expressed their opinions about unfolding events. But here again national differences in how men and women divided space and chores among themselves had an impact on the way women voiced their views.

Correspondence, Pamphlets, and Petitions

Some American women, such as Mercy Otis Warren, Judith Sargent Murray, and the slave Phillis Wheatley, chose to speak out in public, but most saved their opinions for family and friends. Women of the elite wrote to brothers, fathers, or husbands serving in the legislature or to friends related to political figures. Although Abigail Adams was left to run the family farm alone, she nevertheless found time to engage in regular correspondence with her husband, John (who became the second president of the United States), and her friend Mercy. Tired of recounting local affairs, she frequently indulged in political reflection, at times with feminist overtones. In March 1776 she advised her husband, then a congressman, not to forget women in the new legal code, for otherwise the new nation might have to confront a rebellion of its women. Yet while this admonition tells us something about one woman's state of mind, it was never voiced publicly and remained a private matter between a woman and her husband. Also private and individual were the petitions of widows and other women who had supported the war only to find themselves in precarious circumstances and in need of support. Their style is subservient and imploring rather than insistent, and their requests address individual cases of material need rather than matters of general policy.

In France most women with something to say about the Revolution did so publicly. In printed and handwritten texts and public speeches they aimed at reaching a fairly broad audience, in any case beyond the narrow circle of family and friends. Whether collective or individual, their expression was seldom limited to the particular case but inserted in a broader context embracing the revolutionary phenomenon as a whole. In brochures and petitions women proclaimed their hopes, demands, and proposals for reform. Their Addresses to the Nation, whether cautious or radical, all reflect a desire not to be excluded from political life, a wish to add one's brick to the rising edifice of the city even when deprived of formal citizenship. Some of these texts by women speak in the name of their sex. They were intended to be and were political in both content (themes and language) and audience (fellow citizens, male and female, or, more frequently, legislators). Their political nature was reinforced by the manner of their distribution. Many of the texts were vetted by revolutionary organizations before being circulated. Those that were printed were hawked in the streets by news vendors and bought by militants who passed them on to others. Some authors, such as the solitary Olympe de Gouges or the "Democrat Dubois," who called for the people to rise up in the spring of 1795, posted their Notices on the walls of houses, where passersby could read them aloud.

Petitions were much used during the Revolution by both men and women. Often backed by many signatures, these petitions asked the government, frequently in menacing tones, to take various steps. Some of the documents were sent from the provinces to the National Assembly, while others were read to the deputies by the petitioners themselves. An entire volume would not be enough to consider revolutionary petitions in all their variety. But some are worth examining in greater detail because of what they tell us about how women went about seeking a place for themselves within the body politic. Sometimes their approaches were wrongheaded, yet illustrative of attempts to overcome the political inequality of the sexes. How could women assert themselves as citizens when they lacked the prerogatives of citizenship? What half-opened doors would have to be completely staved in before they could share in sovereignty? These were the questions that some women's petitions addressed.

Symbolic Language

On March 6, 1792, Pauline Léon came to the bar of the Legislative Assembly to read a petition signed by more than 300 Parisian women demanding the "natural right" to organize themselves into a unit of the National Guard. To be a part of the armed organization of the sovereign people was one of the fundamental elements of citizenship. The welcome accorded to the petitioners is an indication of the ambitiousness of their demands: the president of the Assembly quickly reminded them of the different functions assigned to each sex. "Let us not invert the order of nature," he admonished, thereby invoking a theme familiar to adversaries of political equality for men and women, an argument that had already been used to justify the banning of women's political clubs. With this demand, which would be repeated several times by 1793, these militant women laid claim to one of the rights of citizenship and thus to a place for themselves in the political sphere. Their wish to bear arms was not simply a matter of patriotic sentiment, as in the case of the hundred or so women who enlisted individually in the army; it transcended sentiment to become a matter of power, of citizenship, and of equal rights for women.

The Constitution approved by the Convention on June 24, 1793, was subsequently submitted to a referendum vote extended to men by universal male suffrage. Some women rejected this attempt to create a nation divided. They joined together to vote, to swear an oath, and to inform the representatives of the people (the nation) that they subscribed to the "constitutional act." Although it did not become an overwhelming movement, there were significant numbers of such women's petitions. The texts expressed no outright feminism: only two female citizens and three clubs disapproved of political inequality between the sexes. Yet this wave of petitions did not simply reflect the support of militant women for the Montagnards. By coming together and informing the Convention of their consent, they transformed a private act—acceptance of the Constitution by individual women deprived of political rights—into a public act whereby female citizens declared themselves to be members of the body politic. Their insistence on formally notifying the lawmakers that even if "the law deprived them of the precious right to vote," they too would ratify the Constitution "submitted to the sovereign people for approval," reflected their desire to exercise popular sovereignty despite the masculinization of the electorate.

Another collective action touching on the symbols that influenced relations between the sexes erupted in the "war of cockades." In September 1793 sans-culotte women launched a campaign in favor of a law to force all women to wear the tricolor cockade. Before being submitted to the Convention, a petition drafted by the female members of a political society with mixed membership was read and approved in sectional assemblies and clubs; likewise, the Club des Cordeliers acknowledged that "the *citoyennes* who share our labors ought also to share this advantage." Women who favored the law clashed in the streets and marketplaces with women who opposed it. Worried by the extent of the agitation, the Convention gave in and approved the law on September 21. Since July of 1789 the cockade had been one of the identifying symbols of citizenship, and to compel women to wear it was to regard them as citizens. During the summer of 1793 women had gained considerable influence in the sans-culotte movement. At the same time, growing numbers of women and men were concerned about the persistence of political inequality in a "state where the law consecrates equality." Under the circumstances the decree of September 21 can be seen as a first challenge to the status quo. As the Cordeliers recognized, the question was indeed one of sharing—a symbol of citizenship in the particular short run, perhaps power in the long run. Comment on the law suggests that a majority of men saw the issue in these terms: after the cockade, women would ask for the red cap, weapons, and the right to vote. The talk in the taverns and the speeches of Fabre d'Eglantine both sound the same note of fear, namely, that a society destabilized by a confusion of the sexes leads inevitably to chaos. Given equal rights women would become men, wearing their hair short, donning trousers, and brazenly smoking pipes. And could power be shared between the sexes? To some men such a thing was unthinkable, unimaginable. The only thing they could imagine happening—and it understandably frightened them—was an exchange of roles ("inverting the natural order," "trading one's sex"). If women were successful in winning their demands, they would slit the throats of their companions and inaugurate the reign of "a Catherine de Médicis who would put men in chains." Following the law on cockades tavern clients frightened one another with apocalyptic visions of women arming to murder men in a sort of sexual Saint Bartholomew's Day Massacre. Such visions periodically resurfaced, revealing the importance of the symbolic and imaginary in constructing political relations between the sexes in periods of radical upheaval. In fighting for the right to wear a small tricolored ribbon on their hats, militant women were thus not debating a "typically feminine" issue of fashion; they were attempting to revamp the fundamental sexual axioms of political life.

New Relations between the Sexes

Letters, articles, brochures, and speeches all added their touches to the portrait of a mythical woman clothed in the dreams of actual women who hoped that the revolutionary rupture, which had defined a before and an after, an old and a new, would also leave its mark on their place in society and their relations with men.

American Penelopes

"I expect to see our young women forming a new era in female history," wrote Judith Sargent Murray in 1798. Like the young American Republic itself, the republican woman had been born in the Revolutionary War, which had undermined rules, brutalized lives, and exploded the frivolous, carefree attitudes of women suddenly faced with the need to provide for families after their men had gone to fight. An important religious dissident, Judith Sargent belonged to a "generation of survivors,"[4] of women who had become aware of their individual strength and courage in a time of torment. It was in the light of her own experience that she created her model of the new American woman, whom she named Penelope after that other Penelope who had similarly been obliged to take care of her family's needs and keep the home fires burning during her husband's long absence. Through essays published in newspapers in the 1790s, she tried to convince people of women's intellectual capacity and their need for an education to prepare them for living in a world where sudden reversals of fortune were not unknown. Accordingly, her Penelope was a pragmatic young woman, contemptuous of fashion and frivolity, who did not tailor her personality to suit a future husband. Rather than lie on a soft bed dreaming of Prince Charming and cultivating the art of physical seduction, she chose to rise with the sun and devote her day to study, from which she derived both pleasure and independence. Thus she made herself ready to confront fate's blows, whatever they might be, and her marriage would be all the more harmonious as a result. The war, which men and women experienced in different ways, reinforced women's allegiance to qualities typical of the Protestant ethic: to cultivate one's own talents and to maintain one's "noble ardor for independence" and self-respect. The certainty that only such Penelopes could survive in troubled times is common to several literary works. Among the heroines of M. O. Warren's *The Ladies of Castille* (1790) and C. Brown's *Ormond* (1799), those that are ignorant and preoccupied exclusively with their love lives are reduced to suicide by an adversity they are incapable of mastering, whereas those that are educated, proud, strong, "self-respecting," and "self-reliant" emerge from their troubles more mature than they were. America needed the latter kind of women.

But—the country needed them at home, in the midst of their families. For that was their place, and no one, male or female, proposed changing it. The model republican woman was a mother. Her competence and the strength she derived from self-respect were placed at the service of her family; they did not extend to public decisionmaking. Nevertheless, the republican mother did have a civic role to play. By raising her sons to be good citizens, she "strengthens the civic order in which she lives."[5] Although absent from the political arena, she had political responsibilities, even if they were confined within the domestic sphere. American women did not claim a public function but reminded their men, who regarded them as negligible quantities, that the revolutionary break had given a new meaning to their familial role. They brought politics into private life, giving a civic essence to the domestic function.

Another task in building the new nation was also reserved to women: safeguarding virtue and morality, qualities that enabled the Republic to win the war and without which it could not endure. In this context morality and virtue were private qualities, individual and religious, for which each person answered to God, and not, as they were understood to be in the French Revolution, political qualities that were exercised publicly and that made each individual responsible to the community as a whole. In a society founded by Puritans this moral role was essential, and it was included in the model of the republican mother: her virtue served as a constant reminder to her husband and sons of the moral dimension of good citizenship. The conception of roles was even more radical in a pamphlet entitled *Women Invited to War.*[6] Although it starts out in the manner of a political text, this tract soon takes on a religious tone, asserting that the young nation's chief enemy is still Satan. Women being less inclined to sin (and specifically to sins such as drinking and swearing) than men, it was up to them to make war on the diabolical enemy. The civic combat of men was political and public; they laid the foundations of the city and made sure that its institutions functioned, while women fought spiritual battles. Theirs was a war waged in the private sphere, and their mission was to save the soul of the city by praying for the community's sins, by purifying their conduct, and inviting men to do the same. The text even takes on feminist religious overtones when it affirms that men and women are equals in Christ and that Eve was not created only to be trampled underfoot. Although American women did not form political clubs during the Revolution, afterwards they joined together in organizations often associated with churches and intended to provide relief to widows and orphans. Public, collective practice originated in these groups, thus laying the foundations for the abolitionist and feminist movements of the nineteenth century. In later years American women would invoke their religious and moral responsibilities to justify their political activity.

Female Citizens

The "republican mother" was the feminine ideal in French society as well: the role of women was to raise their children to be good republicans by instilling in them a love of freedom and equality. Hence women were permitted to attend political assemblies in order to learn revolutionary principles, even if they were not allowed to take part in debate. Their place was neither entirely outside political society nor entirely within it, but on the periphery. Because they were citizens without political rights, finding a proper place for them was not easy, and some women took advantage of this conceptual ambiguity to justify their political activity. The sexual separation of roles was not rejected, but it was felt that the compartmentalization of political tasks was too strict: women were indeed destined to serve in the family, but as citizens it was incumbent upon them to reach beyond the family to concern themselves with the common good. In April 1793 Deputy Guyomar wrote that woman "concerns herself with the affairs of the inside, while man pursues affairs of the outside. . . . But the greater family ought to take precedence over the lesser family of each individual, for otherwise private interest would soon undermine the general interest." The revolutionary concept of subordinating the private (or particular) to the general interest justified the assertion that political commitments and rights in the new society ought to involve both sexes. Women were therefore defined as members of the community—the human, social, and political community. In order to demonstrate the need for women's clubs, the president of one such club in Dijon used the argument that in a republic "every individual is an integral part of the whole" and must cooperate in "public affairs."

The Republic brought with it a new approach to individual relations between men and women, and women were now different from what they had been before. In one aspect the aspirations of French women resembled those of American women: gone was the time when woman was "debased and degraded by a false and frivolous cult" worthy of the "courts of despots." Republican women disposed of the ribbons and jewelry that had been signs of their subjugation and, more than that, signs of the subjugation of an entire people. The effort they had expended in the past on seducing the opposite sex had been misdirected; nor would they now seek, as in America, to assert individual qualities but to contribute actively to the public good. Here again, French women thought of themselves as part of a group rather than as individuals. This gave rise to the fiction of the "free woman," member of a "free people," acting in the general interest and thereby participating in the conquest of liberty for all. The opposite of the free woman was the "slave woman," member of a "slave people" (that is, a people without rights), whose only role was to bring pleasure to men who were themselves slaves. The goal for women was no longer to "barter their sex" but to develop the whole spectrum of their human qualities, to evolve in a space open to everyone. The image of the free woman also made it possible to play with a paradox: women were members of a free people yet subject to the "despotism" of men. A parallel was drawn between this despotism and that exercised by the king and aristocrats against the people of the Ancien Régime. American women used the same rhetoric to reject the tyranny of husband over wife as analogous to that of England over its colonies. But the slavery criticized by French women was not only private but also political: so long as women did not enjoy their full rights as citizens, they would be slaves. And "wherever women are slaves, men will be bent under despotism's yoke" (according to the president of the Women's Club of Dijon). Conceived in terms of reciprocity, the question of masculine oppression was linked to that of the freedom of humankind in general, and always understood as one of the crucial features of a society's political makeup: either democracy for all or despotism for all.

If we thus compare the places, roles, and imaginative lives of women on either side of the Atlantic, we find that they were not identical, which proves that relations between the sexes are reflections of the society in which they occur. In both cases, however, those who were interested in the question saw it as a fundamental issue in the construction of the body politic.

Independence of the individual is a central tenet of American ideology. The body politic is conceived as a sum of individual members, not a fusion of individuals into a collectivity. The strength of each personality ensures that of the Republic, but at the same time society allows individuals to work toward their own material and spiritual fulfillment (self-reliance and self-respect). Traditionally excluded from the public sphere, American women became aware of their individual capacities during the Revolutionary War. And developing a role first defined during this period of rupture made it possible for their descendants to intervene in political life.

By contrast, revolutionaries in France perceived power in terms of "collective appropriation."[7] Hence it should come as no surprise that French women thought of themselves primarily not as distinct individuals but as members of a community in which the general was supposed to take precedence over the particular. Although this way of thinking was typical of their country, they found a way to turn it to their advantage. Active in the public arena during the eighteenth century, they did not abandon that arena when it turned political. Though denied citizenship, they were nevertheless called *citoyennes*. This linguistic contradiction, which grew out of a relation between the sexes inimical to the founding principles of the Republic, revealed the essence and originality of the French Revolution: so long as the nation was declared to be sovereign, it was impossible to give women any other title. And nineteenth-century feminists would refer to the Revolution as the founding act of democracy.

TRANSLATED FROM THE FRENCH BY ARTHUR GOLDHAMMER

2

The French Revolution as the Turning Point

Elisabeth G. Sledziewski

IT IS OFTEN SAID that women gained nothing from the French Revolution, either because the Revolution failed to change their status or, on the contrary, because it did change their status but in a negative way. Yet both of these convergent albeit contradictory views neglect the importance of the revolutionary upheaval, which was too profound not to have affected all social sectors and actors and too fruitful not to have brought hope despite its ravages.

We shall therefore consider the French Revolution as a time of decisive change in the history of women—in the first place because it was a time of decisive change in the history of man and of men. Furthermore, it was a time when relations between the sexes were questioned in unprecedented ways. But the condition of women did not change simply because everything else changed—because the revolutionary tempest left nothing untouched. In a deeper sense, the condition of women changed because the Revolution raised the issue of women as a central tenet of its *political* thinking.

Therein lies the major innovation. Those who made the Revolution or fought against it or merely observed it in France or abroad could not conceive of a revolutionary polity or even a revolutionary act without defining the role of women. That this was so is a sure sign that the upheaval was of vast scope, shaking an entire civilization right down to its domestic underpinnings: the French Revolution was concerned with relations between the sexes just as early Christianity, the Reformation, and state rationalism had been before. New questions were raised, including that of women's place not just in the domestic order but in the body politic. The French Revolution was the historical moment when Western civilization discovered that women could play a civic role. Neither the European Enlightenment nor the American Revolution had politicized the age-old "woman question" in quite this way, making it a political rather than just a moral issue.

But why this discovery at this moment? What was it about the French Revolution that challenged the sexist grip on politics? How was that challenge mounted, and what came of it?

The revolutionary questioning of the civic role of women did not necessarily lead to revolutionary outcomes. To discover that women can play a political role is not the same as to give them one. Such a scandalous possibility may even have made those who raised it recoil in horror, thus inspiring a reactionary discourse on women rather than the innovations one might have expected.

Thus there is reason to stress both the audacity of the Revolution and its abdication of its historical mission. It refused to face squarely the issue of gender relations in the public sphere, as if frightened to have raised the matter at all. Yet it did put the issue on the agenda.

Women and the Political Order

Enemies of the Revolution, both at the time and later, charged that by emancipating women it introduced vice into the very heart of the social order. Fantasies of female subversion—from the *tricoteuses* and other furies of the guillotine to the *citoyenne* who divorced her husband, carried arms, participated in debate, and wielded a quill—have been a staple of counterrevolutionary discourse. It is as if the sudden admission of the weaker sex to previously forbidden places and roles epitomized the advancement of the weak in general; as if the attribution of new capabilities to women were enough by itself to symbolize a world turned upside down.

Subversive Women

The monarchist theoretician Bonald rightly blamed the revolutionaries for having destroyed "natural society," in which woman "is subject and man is power." Here, the terms "man" and "woman" are understood to be opposites, and the female "subject" is said to be subservient, incapable of independent action, and therefore properly devoid of legal rights. Everything is in order, Bonald argues, "so long as man, power in this society, remains in the place its nature assigns him; if out of weakness he descends from that place, if he obeys her whom he ought to command, he disobeys him whom he ought to obey." In other words, the man who allows a woman to have her way fails in his natural duties to God and king. Worse yet, he signals the commencement of generalized subversion: "What lessons the deplorable consequences of the weakness of power and pride of the subject teach the universe! By making the deceptive glimmer of freedom and equality shine in the eyes of the weakest segments of society, an evil genius induces people to rise up against legitimate authority."[1] For Bonald, everything is clear: the French Revolution would not have been as revolutionary if women had been kept out of it.

The English Whig Edmund Burke was no less staunch an adversary of the Revolution than Bonald. The Revolution, he wrote in 1796, had established the most licentious and depraved, as well as the most bestial, savage, and fierce moral system the world had ever known. In particular, it was a system that emancipated women. It had relaxed the marriage bond and violated the immutable laws of the sexual division of labor to a point that even "the prostitutes of London, who trade in infamy," might find shameful. Indeed, the Revolution had effaced the very boundaries of civilization, "summoning five or six hundred drunken women to the bar of the Assembly to call for their children's blood," debasing marriage to the status of a civil contract, and facilitating divorce. Among the Jacobins, Burke noted with outrage, the mingling of the sexes was abandoned to chance. And he railed against the "filthy equity" called for by a system that "gives women the right to be as licentious as we are."

Such spleen indicates the depths of the scandal. No other regime had dared overturn the hierarchy of the sexes by political fiat. Even if this was, as some adversaries believed, no more than a stratagem for disrupting society that much more effectively, the effect had been imprudent, granting women an unlimited line of credit on which all those whose natural place was subjugation would henceforth be able to draw. "It is said that women have been too long under the domination of their husbands. There is no point in my expatiating further on the possible unfortunate consequences of a law that removes half of our species from under the protection of the other half."[2] Those consequences were unfortunate not only for marital harmony but for society as a whole.

Civil Women

Burke was right. The Revolution gave women the idea that they were not children. It accorded them a civil personality that the Ancien Régime had denied, and they became human beings in the full sense, capable of enjoying their rights and exercising them. How? By becoming individuals.

The Declaration of the Rights of Man (1789) recognized that every individual enjoys an inalienable right to "liberty, property, security, and resistance to oppression."[3] Hence every woman, like every man, has a right to form her own opinions and make her own decisions and to enjoy security of her person and property. Accordingly, daughters were no longer to be at a disadvantage in the division of estates. "Did my mother not carry me in her womb as she did her other children?" asked Mère Duchêne in March 1791, while the Constituent Assembly passed a law guaranteeing equal shares of the estates of persons who died intestate as it prepared to abolish the privilege of masculinity.[4] The Constitution of September 1791 defined civil majority in identical terms for men and women. Women were also acknowledged to possess sufficient reason and independence to serve as witnesses to public documents and to contract obligations as they saw fit (1792). They were also allowed to share in communal properties (1793). In the first version of a new Civil Code proposed to the Convention by Cambacérès in 1793, mothers enjoyed the same prerogatives as fathers in the exercise of parental authority.

But it was above all the important laws of September 1792, concerning civil status and divorce, that treated husband and wife in strictly symmetrical terms, establishing both equal rights and a common set of procedures. The civil marriage contract that so horrified Burke was based on the idea that both parties to a marriage were equally responsible and capable of verifying whether the obligations created by mutual consent were properly executed. If not, and provided they could agree to disagree, they could dissolve the marriage without even going to court. The law provided for divorce on grounds of mutual incompatibility or mutual consent; contested divorces were also possible, but only after attempts to reach agreement proved futile. In other words, society would intervene in marital disputes only when the parties could not resolve their differences, and then only at their explicit request. Marriage was not an end in itself but a means to individual happiness. If it ceased to serve as such or became an obstacle to happiness, it was meaningless.

Why were these legislative measures important? In what sense did they constitute a turning point in the history of women?

As a result of these new laws French women for the first time enjoyed a true civil status, and this constituted a major change in their condition. They acquired the stature, if not the rights, of complete citizens, in the sense that they were now looked upon as free, rational individuals capable of self-government. Of course this acquisition of civil liberties did not include civic, that is, political rights, but it was a necessary condition of such rights and made their absence that much more unacceptable. As full-fledged members of a civil society under a government of laws, women logically came to believe that they also had a place in the body politic. And of course they behaved as though they did have such a place. The visible participation of militant women in public debate during the Revolution is evidence of this. Indeed, it was hard to tell the difference between social and political activism, so that when housewives called for economic controls and women congratulated lawmakers on instituting divorce, the whole community looked upon them as taking part in politics.

Nineteenth-century antifeminists were therefore not wrong to point out that the Revolution, by destabilizing marriage and the domestic order, had opened a Pandora's box of women's political demands. A woman who was free to choose her own husband or to divorce him if she saw fit probably also felt entitled to choose her own government. The Revolution taught women bad habits, something the drafters of the Civil Code deplored just ten years after the progressive legislation of 1792 and 1793. In response to Napoleon's fiercely "macho" tirades, the Conseil d'Etat became obsessed with the decline of women's morals and the collapse of marital authority. On 5 *vendémiaire*, Year X (September 27,

1801), for example, Portalis argued that the obedience of wives and daughters is not a matter of political subjugation but a law of nature. Since the inferior social status of women was a matter of physical necessity, it in no way meant that they were oppressed or deprived of legitimate authority. On the contrary, society, reasserting its rights, was now restoring women to the natural place from which the Revolution had hastily expelled them: "Hence it is not to our injustice but to their natural vocation that women ought to look for the source of the more austere duties imposed on them for their own greater advantage and for the benefit of society." A great deal of water had flowed under the bridge since the deputies had abolished the privilege of masculinity, revolutionized marriage, and accepted the petitions of revolutionary *citoyennes*. Although those deputies had hardly been feminists, they had at least believed that women had something to gain from the Revolution and naturally would want to take part in it.

Civic Women

The Revolution inaugurated a period during which politics touched every aspect of life. Within the space of a few weeks in the spring of 1789, a nation earlier ignorant of political life had developed a passion for it. One German traveler, Joachim Campe, writing from Paris to his compatriots, expressed surprise at the "warm interest that these people take in public affairs, when most of them cannot read or write." He also described certain unusual customs of a nation in which it appeared that the "participation of all" was required for the discussion of any subject: everywhere "large groups . . . of men and women of the most diverse sort" gathered to listen as posters, brochures, and penny broadsheets were read aloud. Women too were present, "from fishwives to elegant ladies." From the beginning they had a place in the modern agora, a distinctive place of their own even though they mingled with citizens of the other sex. Our Prussian observer had no doubt at all about what he was witnessing: it was a school of civics, in which an entire nation was improving itself. "Imagine for a moment the effect of . . . this participation by all in public affairs on the development of the intellectual faculties, intelligence, and reason!"[5] Clearly the Revolution had made a place for women in the public forum, a decisive step forward, and it was because of this that the reaction against "civic woman" was as vehement as it was. Even during the revolutionary period itself the desire to force women back into their previous confinement was uncompromising. It was bad enough that the common people should suddenly acquire intelligence and reason, but women? Many men who fought heroically for public education and universal suffrage so that the humblest of peasants might become enlightened citizens categorically refused to make the same benefits available to women and expressed horror at the idea that the progress of events might one day confer power on them. For to admit female citizens into the body politic was to allow them to make decisions, to become active subjects of the Revolution on a footing of equality with men. To many contemporaries this was simply intolerable. By contrast, the idea that men should pass civil laws to emancipate women was more comforting, for women were thereby in the position of objects: objects of progressive legislation to be sure, but still objects.

The vast majority of revolutionaries, including the Jacobins, favored the withdrawal of women from the public arena into the home. Farther to the left, simultaneously praising divorce and the charms of a woman in the home, the agitator Chaumette pulled no punches in castigating women's clubs, which had been outlawed for two weeks: "Since when is it considered normal for a woman to abandon the pious care of her home, the cradle of her children, to listen to speeches in the public forum?"[6] A year and a half later, on April 13, 1792, Santerre, a brewer by trade and a highly popular figure in the democratic movement, complained in similar terms of the civic zeal of Parisian women: "The men of this *faubourg*, upon returning from work, would rather find their houses in order than see their women return from an assembly where they do not always acquire a gentleness of spirit, and that is why they have looked askance at these assemblies that meet three times a week."

But we must go back to September 1791, to the time of the constitutional monarchy and triumphant moderation, to discover the common inspiration of all these partisans of the sexist status quo. France had just given itself a government whose aim was to secure the happiness of all. Were women included in that "all"? Yes, according to Talleyrand, "women above all," provided that "they do not aspire to exercise political rights and functions." Although "in abstract principle it seems impossible to explain" why "half of the human race [was] excluded by the other from participation in government" in the name of liberty and equality, or why all those women, revolutionaries from the beginning, were deprived of political rights, there was, Talleyrand assured his audience, "an order of ideas within which the issue is transformed." That order was the order of nature, or rather, what the men of the French Revolution tirelessly invoked as nature in their bewilderment at the effects of a civil emancipation of women that nearly all of them had favored. Nature, they said, required those effects to remain strictly "civil" (as opposed to "civic" or political). Nature was there to remind overenthusiastic *citoyennes* that it was in their own homes that they would enjoy, fully and honorably, the benefits of the Revolution.

The advent of the civic woman therefore seems at once implicit in and excluded by the revolutionary advent of the civil woman. Implicit in, because—make no mistake—the French women who at last came of age while making the Revolution alongside their husbands acquired historical consciousness once and for all and knew they had a role to play in the city. In any case no one thought of denying them a role, though it remained to be seen what it would be, and whether citizenship limited in the political sphere to advice and consent was still citizenship. In this sense, the development of civil rights for women could be the means of making the exclusion of women from politics acceptable to a civilization based on the "rights of man and of the citizen." Female citizens, Talleyrand said, were to be instructed, heeded, respected, and placed "under the empire of liberty and equality." For that they had to assert their civil personality. "At the moment they renounced all political rights, they gained the certainty that their civil rights would be consolidated and even expanded."[7]

Helots of the Republic

It was in response to this 1791 report of Talleyrand's that Mary Wollstonecraft dedicated to him her *Vindication of the Rights of Woman,* which was published in 1792. This "deathless book," as Flora Tristan would call it a century later, echoed Olympe de Gouges's *Declaration of the Rights of Woman and the Citizen,* written in September 1791, and Condorcet's brochure "On the Admission of Women to the Rights of the City," which dated from July 1790. All three texts deserve close examination. They develop three different arguments in favor of women's rights. All three invoke the principles of liberty and equality and are critical of institutions that mock those principles. But their fundamental preoccupations are different and reveal distinct attitudes toward the revolution in relations between men and women—for in the end all three authors agree that such a revolution must take place.

Two Briefs on Behalf of Woman

What were the priorities? If one had to characterize each of the three positions, one could say that Condorcet was primarily interested in the juridical status of women; Gouges, in their political role; and Wollstonecraft, in their social existence. All three agreed on the urgent need for an explicit formulation of the rights of women. This reflected a common feature of revolutionary discourse: nearly every aspect of the French Revolution involved the idea of winning new rights. But the meaning of "rights" varied with each of our three authors. Whereas Condorcet saw rights as required by political rationality and as a corrective to an unfortunate asymmetry in the geometry of the Constitution, Olympe de Gouges saw the objective as the historical mobilization of women, while Mary Wollstonecraft believed that by insisting on its rights, the "oppressed sex" could transform itself. Condorcet's views were purely theoretical and never issued in any specific legislative proposal to end the exclusion of women from politics. Olympe de Gouges called for militant commitment to a struggle for liberation from the tyranny of men. More radically but also more programmatically, Mary Wollstonecraft focused on the cultural dimension of women's oppression and rights and remained aloof from political conflict. All three approaches—the philosophical, the political, and the ethical—can be found in today's debates on the rights of women.

In the analysis that Condorcet published on July 3, 1790, in the fifth number of the *Journal de la Société de 1789,* he raised the question of the exclusion of women from the rights of citizenship, which he treated as a special case of the more general problem of inequality: "Either no individual of the human species has genuine rights, or all have the same rights; and he who votes against the rights of another, whatever that person's religion, color, or sex, thereby forgoes his own rights." The refusal to integrate women into the civic community was thus no different from racial or ideological ostracism and subject to the same criticism: the objection against any form of discrimination that continued, owing to habit and prejudice, to flourish without incurring the wrath of people working to make equality of rights "the sole foundation of all political institutions." Had not Condorcet himself been a proponent of property qualifications for voting until 1789?

The exclusion of women was therefore an oversight, a delay in consciousness. If enlightened men had been able to thwart their own principles "by calmly depriving half the human race" of rights acknowledged to belong to all rational creatures, it was because they had failed in their vigilance. This failure was perhaps excusable, since legal inequality between men and women had existed in all nations known to history, and the world cannot be remade in a day. Yet the philosopher was optimistic. There was no reason why women should not be accorded equal rights, because no reasoning could justify the perpetuation of inequality. In other words, an intellectually untenable position was historically condemned to disappear within a short period of time. This disarming argument might make us smile were it not that Condorcet paid with his life for his political commitment. It should be noted, in any case, that his argument, which is both courageous and idealistic, also contains a paradox: it explicitly raises an issue that all the founders of a social order based on the rights of man had repressed without the slightest remorse, but the issue is brought up in order to demonstrate that it should not be separated from the more general one of equal rights; hence women's rights are not to be covered by a specific doctrine. The problem of relations between the sexes would be solved when equal rights ceased to be a problem. Because Condorcet was arguing on a purely conceptual level and knew nothing of the specific nature of actual sexism, he ultimately defused the feminist bomb he had helped to arm. His arguments in favor of women are above all briefs against the imbecility of discrimination generally: "Why should individuals subject to pregnancies and to brief periods of indisposition not be able to exercise rights that no one ever thought of denying to people who suffer from gout every winter or who easily catch cold?" The revolutionary academician was wrong to treat the problem solely as a matter of legal logic, but he deserves credit for having raised it.

Olympe de Gouges's proposals were quite different in tone and content. She was not interested in revising the new laws governing political participation. Her purpose was to enlist women in a war on the injustices that men stubbornly insisted on perpetuating and that the Revolution had only made more glaring. Women against men: the revelation of the rights of rational human beings had disclosed the scandal of the battle between the sexes, which, having raged in the world, must now come to its final hour. In contrast to Condorcet, for whom sexism was just another form of inequality, Olympe de Gouges believed that the tyranny of men over women was the true wellspring of all forms of inequality. Accordingly, the French Revolution had failed to strike at the roots of the "bastilles" it knocked down. It had left the very principle of despotism intact. And since the Revolution had given power to men, they had made use of that principle even as they combated its effects, which they could no longer tolerate. They had therefore perpetuated and even revived the war between the sexes at the same time as they smashed their social and political chains—not, one might add, without the aid of women. So many struggles, so many hopes, only to arrive in the end at a displacement of tyranny rather than its suppression! Olympe de Gouges was outraged.

The revolutionary struggle would therefore have to continue on a new front, the defense of women against men. This was to be the new postrevolutionary battleground. Gouges's first shot was a denunciation of the Revolution's inadequacies and failures: "O, Women! Women, when will you cease to be blind? What advantages have you gained from this Revolution? A more blatant contempt, a more outright disdain. In the centuries of corruption you reigned only over the weakness of men. Your empire is destroyed. What is left? The conviction of man's injustices. The claim on your patrimony, which is based on nature's wise decrees."

In much the same way that Marx would describe the exploitation of man by man fifty years later, Olympe de Gouges characterized the French Revolution as having put an end to illusions concerning the exploitation of woman by man. She called attention to both the moral brutality and historical wholesomeness of the transition from amorous idyll to an age of contempt. The time had come for mobilization. "Woman, awake! The tocsin of reason is making itself heard the world over. Assert your rights." And the first of those rights was that of demanding an accounting from the enemy: "Man, are you capable of being just? . . . Who gave you the sovereign empire to oppress my sex?" In truth, no response was expected. How could despotism defend itself, since under it blind force usurped the place of law? It was up to *citoyennes* to respond for themselves by declaring the "rights of woman and the citizen" and insisting that these be embodied in law.

Framed by calls to battle against the male enemy, the preamble and seventeen articles of the Declaration of the Rights of Woman and the [Female] Citizen faithfully followed the model laid down by the Declaration of the Rights of Man and the Citizen of August 26, 1789. Olympe de Gouges simply bestowed the advantages of a government of laws on women by insisting on the bisexual character of the civil and political community. Thus there was nothing very original about this provocative text except for the spirit of provocation that motivated it. To point out that the rights of man could be couched in the feminine as well as the masculine gender and to urge that those rights be extended to women in law was to assert in no uncertain terms that universal rights were a fraud and that men who pretended to speak for all humankind were in fact speaking only for the male sex. By explicitly and almost obsessively feminizing the Declaration of 1789, Gouges attacked men's policy, unmasked the exclusions implicit in it, and exposed the pernicious ambiguities of a universalism held to be above suspicion. "The torch of truth has dispelled the clouds of foolishness and usurpation," Gouges proclaimed, for though she may have been a mediocre poet she was nonetheless a true woman of the Enlightenment. To allow oneself to be duped was no longer permissible. Only the political vigilance of women could prevent men from appropriating the Revolution. It was up to women to reveal the liberating significance of the event.

In Article X of her Declaration Gouges stated: "Woman has the right to mount the scaffold. She must also have the right to mount to the podium." Two years later she herself was guillotined as a Girondin, a few days before Mme Roland's execution. Her commitment was political to the end.

With Mary Wollstonecraft the tone changes again. For her as for Thomas Paine, the enthusiasm aroused by the Declaration of 1789 was above all moral, as was the rejection of the aristocratic values of English civilization. Despite her continuing interest in the French Revolution, of which she published a history in 1794, the political sphere was not the primary arena in which she believed the emancipation of women would take place. The Constituent Assembly's exclusion of the female sex was unacceptable, and Wollstonecraft made the point eloquently, accusing Talleyrand of "inconsistency" and "injustice" for having tolerated such a shortcoming in the new Constitution. But the denial of political rights to women was only a symptom, indeed a minor symptom, of a much more serious tendency: namely, that of treating man as the only true representative of the human race, "considering creatures of the female sex as women rather than as human beings." A whole civilization of denial was erected on this foundation of segregation, a civilization that repeatedly behaved as though women were not rational beings. The fundamental insult lay in the refusal to admit that humankind could embrace two types of being, could exist in two sexualized forms, both equally human. And it was perpetuated by a society organized in keeping with the principle that a single sex monopolized all reason. As a result, all of society's institutions functioned to exclude and dehumanize women and to prove that they lacked something essential.

A Vindication of the Rights of Woman was more a treatise on the status of sexual difference in evolving Western societies than it was a militant political program. Its principal objective was not to make women participants in the political process on an equal footing with men but to win recognition of their civic responsibilities. It was up to them to choose their own fate, and it was up to them to decide how they wished to contribute to the efforts of the community. That contribution was to be specifically feminine, in accordance with nature. But even though Mary Wollstonecraft called for a sharing of tasks and exalted motherhood in terms reminiscent of Rousseau, she insisted on the need to justify in rational terms the willingness of women to specialize in occupations in the private sphere. Thus there was a world of difference between the domestic slave shut up in the home and convinced that this was the reward of her ignorance, and the enlightened citizeness discharging the duties of a mistress of the household and republican mother. Maternity was to be experienced as a civic chore, not as something antithetical to learning and intelligence. It was, moreover, a misunderstanding of the domestic mission that estranged some women from their families. But men were responsible for this, because they had never been willing to take the risk of allowing women to reason about their own vocation and had rather imposed it on them as a punishment.

Mary Wollstonecraft's position might seem somewhat old-fashioned compared with the conquering militancy of Olympe de Gouges. All she wanted was the right for women to understand their place rather than servilely fill it. That place remained what it had always been. But her most important contribution was the idea that the emancipation of the oppressed sex did not require denial of its identity. For Wollstonecraft there could be no authentic liberation if women were required to renounce their nature, that is, their being as rational *and* sexual subjects. "Who made man the sole judge, if woman shares with him the gift of reason?" This question, raised at the beginning of the *Vindication,* is double-edged: at the same time that it challenges male tyranny, it also opens up a new horizon of feminine rationality, of a feminine form of judgment—in a word, a *rationalist* alternative to the male logic that had previously dominated civilization. Wollstonecraft is a revolutionary because she saw this opening, and the subsequent feminist movement is greatly in her debt.

A Brief on Behalf of Democracy

The idea that humanity encompasses two kinds of beings and that, owing to its subtle ambiguity, the word "man" ought to be eschewed by true political humanism underlies the analysis put forward by the Montagnard deputy Guyomar in the spring of 1793. The title of his admirable brief was a program in itself: "The Partisan of Political Equality among Individuals, or the Very Important Problem of Equality in Rights and Inequality in Fact." This was, for the revolutionary period, probably the most profound as well as the most modern treatise on the need to integrate women into a democratic political system. Speaking to the Convention, Guyomar rehearsed the main arguments already put forward by others in favor of political rights for women. His originality—apart from the fact of his speaking as a deputy (Condorcet was not one at the time he published his *Admission des femmes*)—lay in the proposition that participation of female citizens in politics was a necessary condition of democracy. Conversely, their exclusion was not only a failure to live up to the principles of the Declaration of 1789 and the new declaration being drafted in late April of 1793; it was also a negation of democracy, a simple and straightforward obstruction of its operation. Women, Guyomar declared, were the "helots of the Republic." Since the existence of helots, the pariahs of Spartan society, was incompatible with democracy, it was inconceivable that a nation which claimed to be laying the foundations of modern democratic civilization should allow such an obvious cause of malfunction to remain in the system. Was the justification for excluding women that their presence was required in the home? Well, then, Guyomar ironically remarked, "it may also be necessary to exclude all men whose presence in the workshop is equally essential." Wherever there was democracy, wherever there were active citizens, he concluded, "the larger family must take precedence over the smaller." This was true for both men and women. For democracy was not only the equality of rights advocated by Condorcet but even more the effective exercise of power by the *demos,* the most dynamic possible exercise of its *kratos,* the full range of its capacities. In order to have a truly effective democracy, therefore, all the people must participate. "The number of children of the fatherland ought to be doubled" by including women, thereby "augmenting the mass of enlightenment in the city."

Guyomar's position, while less abstract than Condorcet's, was not quite the feminist stand of Olympe de Gouges and Mary Wollstonecraft, taken even before the age of feminism had begun. Guyomar reasoned in terms of political demography. He conceived of democracy as a battle requiring a maximum commitment from all citizens, maximum in quality as well as quantity—and that meant including women. A hemiplegic democracy made no sense. No political humanism could seriously invoke its example. For Guyomar, if women were excluded from politics, then they should not be called citizens: "Call them *wives* or *daughters* of *citoyens,* but not *citoyennes.* Either get rid of the word or grant its substance." Eventually, political humanism would do battle with this pseudo-democracy, and that battle would be part of the struggle for democracy—which logically required the participation of women. In that sense, founding the Club des Citoyennes Révolutionnaires was the response of women to Guyomar's speech of April 29.

Translated from the French by Arthur Goldhammer

3

A Philosophical History of Sexual Difference

Geneviève Fraisse

PHILOSOPHICAL DISCOURSE about women and sexual difference necessarily stands at the crossroads of history (in this case, the political rupture and economic transformation characteristic of the modern era) and the eternal philosophical questions of mind-body duality, nature versus civilization, and private-public equilibrium. My purpose is to examine in detail how these ancient and traditional issues were treated by philosophers working in the period between Kant's last years and the publication of Freud's first papers.[1] The nineteenth century discovered that humanity has a history in two senses: people saw that revolutionary transformation was possible, and they realized that the human species itself changed over time. Certain well-established ways of understanding the relation between man and the world broke down; as a result, conceptualizations of women, though strongly resistant to change, were destabilized, and philosophers reacted to this. Thus, between the reformulation of male-female relations made necessary by historical change and the possibility of an emancipation of women, that is, of mounting a challenge to sexual inequality, a body of philosophical reflection laid down certain allegedly incontrovertible truths (or voiced certain crude judgments). This was done, moreover, in the language of metaphysics: the Same and the Other assumed the guise of sexual difference for the purpose of interrogation.

The challenge to sexual inequality was made possible by the belief that a new era had dawned, an era of individual freedom and autonomy of the subject. Because men and women are rational beings, it was assumed by some, yet denied by others, that they could potentially be viewed as "subjects" in the philosophical sense. But thinking in terms of autonomous individual subjects requires looking at male-female relations in new ways and reformulating the mind-body relation for each sex. It also leads to new questions about nature's place in the human world and about the role of "otherness" in philosophical thought.

In more concrete terms, the representation of the female subject was constructed around three central themes. All three elicited a considerable volume of commentary: first, the family, understood both as a product of marriage and as the fundamental cell of society; second, the species, the perpetuation of which was said to be the purpose of human life; and third, property, with its corollaries, work and liberty.

Philosophers (all men, of course) were naturally obsessed with the prospect of women's emancipation as a necessary consequence of the emergence of the individual subject. But male-female relations formed the context within which the issue of emancipation was discussed. Philosophers divided into two camps: some assumed that relations between the sexes would be peaceable and harmonious, while others expected war. The adversarial camps both pondered the definition of love, the focal point of life's supreme joys and most abject suffering. As Fichte observed, a reconsideration of sexual inequality seemed a matter of some urgency as the nineteenth century dawned.

Accordingly, the period produced a considerable volume of original thinking about both women and sexual difference (the two subjects overlapped but did not coincide). I hope that the reader will come to share my own astonishment at the texts I am about to discuss, which were selected with two criteria in mind. As to the choice of authors, I was obliged, given the number of texts pertinent to these issues, to give priority to the works of those generally considered to be "great" philosophers. As to the choice of themes, I had to confine my attention to the concrete issue of sexual difference (the female subject and her relation to the male), avoiding the larger issue of how sexual difference relates to the overall structure of each philosopher's thought. To simplify matters, moreover, I focus on the intersection of the political with the metaphysical.

The Family, the Subject, and the Sexual Division of the World

Early nineteenth-century philosophers, taking up where postrevolutionary texts left off, were primarily concerned with questions of law: not directly with the law as it pertained to women but rather with the status, juridical or otherwise, of the relationship between men and women (marriage). The question of whether woman should be regarded as a "subject" in the legal sense or as subservient to man—that is, as a free juridical individual or a dependent—was a secondary issue. Fichte, Kant, and Hegel may be taken as representing the principal positions in the debate.

Fichte accurately put his finger on the crux of the matter: marriage was not "a juridical association like the state" but "a natural and moral association." Therefore, natural law was not enough to determine what was "necessary" in marriage.

Marriage, Fichte argued, is a "perfect union" based on the sexual instinct of both sexes and has no end outside itself. It creates a "bond" between two individuals, and nothing more. That bond is love, and "love is the point where nature and reason join most intimately." It is this relation between nature and reason that creates the "space of law." Law intervenes only when marriage exists. Thus, prior to any law, the woman submits to the man of her own free will.

Fichte thus differed sharply from his contemporary, Kant, who saw marriage as a "contract." Marriage, for Kant, was not simply "natural intercourse between the sexes" or the expression of "simple animal nature." It was governed by law. It was permissible for the female to enjoy the male's sexual organs and vice versa only because there was reciprocity in the relation of legal possession, which established a contract. The law further stated that the man commands and the woman obeys.

A few years later, Hegel expressed "horror" at Kant's theory and described marriage as "an immediate moral act" whereby natural life is transformed into spiritual unity, "conscious love."

Neither a union nor a contract, marriage is the constitution of "one person" out of two consenting partners. Marriage is therefore above all a moral bond. Law intervenes only when the family, also a unique legal "person," dissolves and each of its members becomes an "independent person." The essence of marriage takes place within the sphere of morality; it is "a free moral act and not an immediate union of natural individuals and their instincts." The head of the family, the man, is the "juridical person."

Our three philosophers do not ascribe the same place to sexual nature, to the role of the legal system in defining male-female relations, or to morality, which somehow insinuates itself into the natural relationship of man and woman. Yet all three accept the woman's dependency and sacrifice of herself for marriage and family. Even so, Kant and Fichte attempt to strengthen their case by asserting that men and women are equally free and rational. For Kant, this equality is guaranteed by the reciprocity of legal marital possession, which is itself based on the consent of both parties, proof of their freedom. A free being is necessarily rational. Elsewhere, in the *Anthropology,* Kant says that it is through rationality that a woman discovers that her specific mission in life is to reproduce the species. A woman's marital dependency and subordination to the preservation of the species are thus in no way incompatible with liberty or reason; indeed, they are compatible with the equality of all human beings, and specifically with equality between men and women.

Fichte pursues his argument with the rigor of a man confronting a problem head on. He would not deal with the difficulty, as other philosophers did, merely in passing. Woman, he says, asserts (and preserves) her dignity qua human being by becoming the means to an end (the end being to satisfy the man), that is, by ceasing to be an end unto herself, and she does this of her own free will. The name for this action is *love,* the "form in which the sexual instinct manifests itself in woman," because, unlike man, woman cannot admit to herself that she has a sexual instinct. To do so would be to renounce her dignity. The dignity of reason requires the woman to become "the means of her own end." It would be a mistake to regard this reasoning as circular. It was on sexuality, and sexuality alone, that Fichte "grounded all that distinguishes the two sexes."

From the foregoing it follows that a woman's dependence

prevents her from having a "civil personality" (Kant). If, moreover, a woman was (as Fichte maintained) a "citizen," then she necessarily entrusted representation of that citizenship to a man. Both philosophers acknowledged the existence of unmarried women, spinsters and widows. Although Fichte conceded that such women could be citizens without delegating their citizenship to a man, he refused to allow them to hold public office. For a woman, a public existence was worse than participating in government. Women had their place in the family; their sphere was the domestic.

Hegel dwelt at length on the division between the domestic and the public spheres, which coincided with a division between two kinds of rationality, one of which aspired to autonomy and universality, while the other remained passive and attached to concrete individuality; one that was directed toward the state, science, and work, while the other turned toward family and moral upbringing. Antigone, a favorite example of Hegel's, symbolized the difference between two kinds of law: man's law and woman's law; the concrete law of the state and the eternal law of family piety; human law and divine law. Depending on the dialectical moment, the balance between them could be either harmonious or contentious. It was in any case a product of interaction between the two laws, when family and civic values clashed, that gave rise to the moral person through sublation of the contingent individual in a social context.

At this point I want to pause to consider sexual inequality. A woman could be a daughter, wife, mother, or sister. The only role in which she was man's equal was that of sister (remember Antigone). Only men straddled the divide between family and city. A man could know both the universality of citizenship and the singularity of desire, and from that duality he gained an advantage, a freedom and self-knowledge that woman did not possess. She had only the universality of her family situation (wife, mother) without the singularity of her desire. Finally, in the dialectic opposing family and civic values, the very foundation of the civic community depended on the positive repression of femininity. Yet femininity could not simply disappear; it survived, rather, as "the eternal irony of the community."

Reflecting on how men and women divided space led Fichte to what he called the "law of the separation of the two sexes." Other philosophers used this "law" to ground their discussion of the male-female dichotomy. Consider, for example, Hegel's use of sexual difference. Starting with the sexual relation, copulation and reproduction, he elaborated a dialectic of self and other whereby the male recognized himself in the female and vice versa; working with the logic of difference, he defined meaning as the production of unity through difference. All philosophies of nature, and most notably that of Hegel's contemporary Schelling, are based on the idea of duality and its resolution in unity, in particular that of the tension between the finite and the infinite. The division of nature into two sexes reflected the fact that the (finite) individual was in the service of the (infinite) species. This duality, essential for the continuation of life and nature, was antithetical to idealist principles, whence the necessity for a dialectic. Nineteenth-century metaphysics thrived on concepts of duality, relation, and the unity of opposites, for which sexual difference was one representation and perhaps even a fundamental metaphor.

In contrast to the philosophers discussed thus far, the German Romantics of the turn of the nineteenth century, particularly Friedrich Schlegel, seem to have felt the blast of the winds of freedom. Schlegel's *Letter on Philosophy,* written to his wife, Dorothea, rejected the normative precepts of the day, as did his novel *Lucinde.* Because he denounced prejudices concerning women and marriage and questioned the traditional characterization of female intellect, he was also able to broach the subject of women's pleasure (of the flesh as well as the spirit) and to consider the disparity between the sexes in regard to freedom. His very modern approach to these issues caused a scandal in his own day and afterward. The philosopher and theologian Schleiermacher defended Schlegel's stand and expressed the hope that women might win "independence from the limits of sex," while Kierkegaard, writing forty years later, attacked the immorality of a Romantic text that continued to elicit enthusiastic responses long after it was written. It was not only the "rehabilitation of the flesh" that offended the Danish philosopher. It was the self-avowedly poetic character of the Romantic attitude that posed the greatest threat. Kierkegaard was actually quite astute in detecting the importance that Schlegel attached to intellectual intercourse between the sexes, which blurred the distinction between sensuality and thought and thus, in Kierkegaard's eyes, rendered marriage immoral and irreligious.

To blunt the contradiction between flesh and spirit and to wish that a man and a woman might together explore "all the degrees of humanity, from the most exuberant sensuality to the most spiritualized spirituality" was a far more serious matter than simply to exalt the flesh on the one hand and express enthusiasm for the spirit on the other. To say that parity in the exchange between a man and a woman might come about as a result of their sexual difference (to give or receive a form, to make poetry or philosophy) was more bewildering than to assert the absolute and egalitarian identity of the sexes. And finally, to assert that "the difference between the sexes is merely an external characteristic," an "innate, natural profession," and that this difference must be consciously subverted ("only a gentle masculinity, only an independent femininity are just, true, [and] beautiful") made the scandal complete.

In France it was not Schlegel but Charles Fourier who caused a scandal, though he never achieved the notoriety of the German Romantics. Until 1830 Fourier's works remained virtually unknown. Yet no subsequent theory of women's liberation failed to pay tribute to his pioneer efforts. Fourier's thought was concerned more with liberty than with equality, more with liberation than with emancipation. He refused to take the rights of man as his starting place and declined to view the social contract as offering protection to the modern individual. In his view, the rights of man only masked the crucial realities: the economy first of all, and obviously the right to work. The "oppression and debasement" of women in civilization were epitomized by marriage, of which Fourier was a vehement critic. He prefaced his moral critique of marriage and the prejudices surrounding it in modern society with an exposé of its mercenary reality and economic foundation (money and property). In this respect Fourier was a profound innovator, and Marx would be in his debt. Fourier never missed an opportunity to denounce philosophers "who concern themselves with the Domestic Order only to tighten the chains of the weaker sex." The German philosophers of law had nothing to say that could refute him, nor did others such as the Idéologues, among them Cabanis, who had developed a scientific theory of sexual inequality (the influence of the physical on the moral essentially determining woman's social role).

Fourier's utopia was thus one of freedom: freedom of the female individual (only a quarter of women being fit, according to Fourier, for domestic life); freedom to emulate men (rivalry being healthy, according to Fourier, who disagreed with most of his contemporaries on this point); and freedom for "passional attraction" and "association" between men and women. Sexual relations, according to Fourier, lead neither to contract nor to union, and if nature is present in them, it is in the spontaneity of desire and not as the foundation of the family.

Fourier's utopia was also social, for the progress and prosperity of all humankind depended on the degree of women's freedom. His formulation was important for the nineteenth century: it was all a question of determining whether the progress of modernity would or would not include women. In the wake of the Revolution women were included in principle yet excluded in fact, and it was with that contradiction that the history of women's emancipation began.

The views of the English philosophers also lacked uniformity. The Utilitarian Jeremy Bentham was in some doubt about granting citizenship to women. If individual interests were more fundamental than human rights, then universal suffrage (the crux of the controversy) could no longer be taken for granted, because one person could represent the interests of several others. The natural subordination of women was as much a reason to deny them political equality as it was to grant it. Although Bentham hesitated, he gradually came to subscribe to the democratic principle of universal suffrage. By contrast, James Mill, initially more democratic than Bentham, wrote in 1820 that individuals whose interests were incontrovertibly subsumed by those of other individuals should be excluded from voting. The interests of a wife (or child) were subsumed by those of her husband (or father) and therefore she did not require the right to vote. Philosophies based on utility and interest were more flexible when it came to denying equality of the sexes than philosophies based on rights. Reacting to Mill, William Thompson, a friend of Bentham and Robert Owen, published an *Appeal of One Half of the Human Race, Women, against the Pretensions of the Other Half, Men, to retain them in political, and thence in civil and domestic slavery.* The era of feminism thus began with the utopians and later with a new voice, that of James Mill's son John Stuart, whose philosophical commitment to equality between the sexes we will come to in a moment.

Love, Conflict, and the Metaphysics of Sex

Before philosophers came to treat the emancipation of women explicitly, whether to refute it with argument or ill-tempered rhetoric or to support it on theoretical grounds, they paused to speak of love, seduction, and chastity, of the metaphysics of sexuality and the duality of sexes, and of an ontological complementarity rooted in social as well as biological life. In the background lurked the topical issue of feminism. Among them at least Schopenhauer, Kierkegaard, and Auguste Comte thought it worth their while to denounce it as absurd or inane. For them, apparently, the real problems lay elsewhere.

Interestingly, the biographies of these philosophers reveal that their entry into the philosophical arena coincides exactly with their emergence as sexual beings. Indeed, the biographical sources of their respective quarrels with women are frequently incorporated into their texts. Schopenhauer broke irrevocably with his mother after his father's death; Kierkegaard broke off his engagement in spectacular fashion. The presence of private life in the philosophical domain is of more than anecdotal interest, however. Strangely enough, philosophers are sexual beings. Stranger still, they themselves reveal their sexual existence. The case of Auguste Comte is exemplary: first his wife, Clotilde de Vaux, and later his servant explicitly contributed not only to his thoughts about women but to his philosophical system as a whole. Are sexual relations intrinsic to philosophical investigation?

Kierkegaard's numerous texts on love, engagement, marriage, married life, and the like might suggest that the answer to this question is yes. This conclusion is reinforced by the fact that his thinking reflects the point of view not only of the species or of humankind generally but also of the subjective individual in the uniqueness of a sexual relationship. One might refer to this as the existential dimension of a philosophy that would never again revert to the Hegelian absolute. Schopenhauer was fully conscious of the novelty of this view: "Rather than express surprise that a philosopher has for once made his own a theme that has always preoccupied poets, one should be astonished that a subject that generally plays so remarkable a role in human life has virtually never been taken into account by philosophers."

Schopenhauer wrote a metaphysics of love. Arising out of the sexual instinct, love develops and expresses itself in the consciousness of the individual. It flourishes between two extremes, the frivolity of the relationship, the amorous affair, and the imperative interest of the species, the imperturbable will of nature. More precisely, love is the mask of the sexual instinct, nature's stratagem or ruse for achieving its ends. And the individual is the dupe, taken in by the illusion. In this metaphysical text the question of the individual is left in suspense by Schopenhauer's well-known pessimism. In other texts the individual, male or female, is treated differently: although man can go beyond the will of nature to achieve a state of chaste asceticism pregnant with possibilities, woman was created solely for the propagation of the species.

The metaphysics of love is nevertheless a reflection on the relation between the two sexes, on the correspondence or complementarity of man and woman. Beyond the ruse of nature that perpetuates the will-to-live (the fundamental principle of Schopenhauer's metaphysics generally), the sexes divide responsibility for heredity: the father determines the child's character or will, the mother its intellect. It may come as a surprise that the rational faculty is ascribed to woman, given how frequently philosophers in the past had questioned whether women even possessed reason and justified the inferior status of women on the grounds that their rational faculties were weak. Schopenhauer himself remarked on the point: "All the philosophers have been mistaken, in that they located the metaphysical principle, that which is indestructible and eternal in man, in the intellect." In fact, the intellect, which is conditioned by the brain, lives and dies with it. Only will is transmissible; only the will of nature, the will to live, is spared by death. Thus Schopenhauer, who sought his metaphysics not in the empyrean of ideas but in the principle of eternal life through reproduction, gave his thought on sexual difference a surprising turn by granting women what many other philosophers denied.

Yet when Schopenhauer turns from love to sexual difference, to the metaphysics of the world's sexualization, when he speaks of women as objects of a man's discourse, his tone changes, and misogyny takes over. Woman, situated between the man and the child, possesses at best an ephemeral beauty, which is nothing more than nature's ruse to seduce man and perpetuate the species. Woman may be the fair sex, but she has no claim on Beauty as such. She is the second sex, without parity of any kind with the first. And her feeble reason lives in a state of immediacy, between frivolity and pertinence. "Germano-Christianity" had erred, Schopenhauer argued, by placing woman in the position of "lady" instead of assigning her a master and instituting polygamy. He thus divorced, in a way that proved highly influential, the metaphysics of sex from mere opinion about women. In this metaphysical system woman's role was reduced to perpetuating the species, thus neatly obviating the earlier legal-philosophical analysis of sexual difference. In this manner the problem was depoliticized, and certain safeguards, such as belief in sexual equality in the abstract, which had seemed self-evident within the legal-philosophical framework, now disappeared. Naked misogyny (later admixed with ideology) was thus free to develop unfettered.

Kierkegaard's philosophical investigations revolved around marriage. He meditated on love, first love of the other, then love of the true (and beyond truth, of God), as well as carnal and philosophical eroticism. Desire, sexualized and sexual, was questioned, described, and illuminated with remarkable thoroughness. Kierkegaard approached philosophy subjectively, transposing his own history and dramatizing other subjectivities (even to the point of using a variety of pseudonyms), and his work must be understood above all as recognizing the existence of desire in man. In this respect he was remarkably innovative, both in the choice of his subject and in the style of its treatment.

Kierkegaard was critical of Schlegel's advocacy (in *Lucinde*) of romantic love, for this kind of love, based on sensuality, distorts eternal values and may inspire a reprehensible desire for emancipation among women. What was misleading about romantic love, according to Kierkegaard, was that it deliberately ignored Christianity's fundamental impact on civilization, which was to make enemies of flesh and spirit. This tension between the sensual and the spiritual conditions all our attitudes toward love, and to ignore this would be pointless. Through a lengthy analysis of engagement and marriage Kierkegaard came to distinguish three different levels on which love could unfold: the aesthetic, where love is associated with the moment; the ethical, where it is associated with time; and the religious, where it is associated with eternity. Clearly, man cannot renounce his relation to eternity without doing damage to himself; his finitude is bearable only in relation to the infinite, a paradox that finds concrete expression in the conflict between flesh and spirit. One can thus find eternity in the aesthetic and the ethical (often the stage of marriage), and the aesthetic in the religious, but only after lengthy discussion of the kind that makes the *Diary of the Seducer,* for example, an exhaustively detailed textbook on the strategy of love. It will come as no surprise, moreover, that one way of reconciling these contradictory impulses is to choose chastity.

And what about the difference between man and woman? While it can be apprehended philosophically through reflection on desire (though not prescribed by any fixed rule), it is more easily perceived in its changing reality. Thus the presence of the female in the male, the bisexuality of the human being, is part of the interplay between the sexes. Nor can there be seduction without reciprocal freedom, or possession of the Other without recognition. Kierkegaard's amorous dialectic departed from the traditional representation of woman in only one respect: the survival of the species was but one of several purposes of marriage, so that woman was not reduced to her reproductive role. Instead she became "man's dream," "perfection in imperfection," nature, appearance, immediacy—everything that stands in man's way and prevents direct contact with the absolute. "Woman explains the finite; man pursues the infinite." Then, says the man, if the serpent of emancipation strikes his woman, "my courage would fail me, my soul's passion for freedom would wane. But I know what I would do. I would go to the marketplace and I would cry, I would cry like that artist whose work was destroyed and who could not remember what it represented."

Sexual difference implies the existence of the other, and since man is the subject of philosophical discourse, the object of that discourse, the other, must necessarily be woman.

The couple—the one and the other, man and woman—regained a central place in metaphysical thought. It should come as no surprise that the thought of doubleness—of the dualism in man between spirit and flesh and outside man between nature and God—should have its root in the idea of sexual difference. Hegel's dialectic had already underscored this point.

Let us turn now from metaphysics to Ludwig Feuerbach and Auguste Comte, in whose respective critiques of metaphysics sexual difference played a fundamental role, indeed as fundamental a role as it played in the metaphysical school the two men were attacking. Feuerbach was a critic of Christianity, Comte the prophet of a new religion, yet both based their critiques on the man/woman dichotomy.

In the *Essence of Christianity* Feuerbach contrasted the human being, necessarily sexual, with the Christian man, who, he said, was always asexual or castrated. He criticized religion as a human product in which God was created in the image of man, an image from which specific differences, and sexual differences in particular, were eliminated in favor of an empty universality: "The celibate life, the ascetic life in general, is the direct path to immortal life, because heaven is nothing other than absolutely subjective, supernatural life, liberated from gender and sex. Underlying the belief in personal immortality is the belief that the distinction between the sexes is merely an exterior epiphenomenon of individuality, the individual being *in itself* an *absolute* asexual and self-sufficient being."

Now, sexual determinacy is "an intimate, chemical constituent" of man's essence. Furthermore, the human being is nothing without the body, which is "the ground, the subject of the personality." But "the body is nothing *without flesh and blood*. . . . But flesh and blood are nothing without the *oxygen of sexual difference*. Sexual difference is not superficial or limited to only certain parts of the body. It suffuses *marrow* and *bones*. . . . The personality is divided *in an essential way* into a masculine and a feminine personality. Where there is no Thou, there is no I."

In opposition to Christianity, with its fear of sexual difference and of the flesh, Feuerbach believed in "true difference" and its correlate, the complementarity of I and Thou, of masculine and feminine. Clearly, he did not look upon chastity as a virtue when he made ironic remarks about Christianity's choice of celibacy for a few (priests) and marriage for the rest. Marriage made it possible to deny nature while satisfying its demands, and that is why "the mystery of original sin is the mystery of sexual pleasure. All men are conceived in sin because they were conceived in pleasure and sensual joy." Without marriage Christians could not tolerate this contradiction. We are a long way from love and marriage as reproductive functions, and if Feuerbach stressed the importance of sensuality and pleasure, he also placed great emphasis on the complementarity of the two sexes. He availed himself of the traditional opposition of masculine and feminine, active and passive, thought and emotional intuition, but mainly to show that the difference cannot endure without union and completion for the sake of future harmony. The idea of sexual duality is limited by that of complementarity, so that the freedom of both sexes is circumscribed by a strictly regulated game.

This idea of a complementary pair can also be found in the thought of Auguste Comte, where it occurs in both social and religious contexts, with biology as the crucial underpinning of the argument. It is not surprising to find positivist philosophy invoking the authority of science, but it should be noted that biology was not actually considered a science until the 1840s. As Comte wrote to John Stuart Mill in 1843, biology definitively confirmed "the hierarchy of the sexes." Against the backdrop of an immutable nature in which women are endowed with emotion and men with intellect, Comte rang the changes on the masculine-feminine theme. At each stage in the evolution of his thought he gave different definitions of woman without making any real modifications in his differential system: in Comte's final plan for society, women (according to Stuart Mill) were not treated as overgrown children but honored as goddesses. Mill was then working on his own book on the subjection of women, some twenty-five years after his important correspondence with Comte had been interrupted by a difference of opinion over the issue of equality between the sexes.

For Comte, women live in a "state of radical childhood." Their place is with the family, with a domestic life based on the hierarchy of the sexes. They are not the equals but rather the companions of men. Apart from their maternal functions, they are the source of social sentiments. They have a mission to fulfill in the advent of positivism, as ministers of the spiritual. They represent the "emotional sex." In that respect their lives are not entirely confined to the domestic sphere, because they have a role to play in the future religion. Indeed, positivism can be approached equally well through the head as through the heart.

Comte's relationship with Clotilde de Vaux, followed by her death and the foundation of a cult in her honor, did not alter this structure in any fundamental way except to give it new magnitude. The change primarily affected language: woman—daughter, mother, sister—became an "angel" for man and a goddess for humankind. The new religion, which dethroned the old Christianity, placed the virgin mother at center stage. Thus the idea of sexual complementarity could also lead to extremely exaggerated representations of the feminine.

Auguste Comte brought his private life into his writings, and no postmortem analysis was needed to make this clear: women were at the heart of his philosophical reflection. The fact is once again of more than merely anecdotal interest. It affected the status of Comte's utterances. The philosopher himself spoke of "the fundamental connection between my private life and my public life." More than the presence of women and the feminine, it was the union of man and woman that made itself felt in his thought. The point bears emphasizing: when Saint-Simon said "man and woman—that is the social individual," he paved the way for the utopian socialist ideas of the 1830s as well as those of Auguste Comte, who was then his secretary. As it happens, the representation of the positivist couple was as strictly regulated as that of the couple in dualist philosophy; any change was unthinkable. Comte thus became an apologist for marriage, an opponent of any public role for women, and an approving witness of their "salutary exclusion" from social and political life, to which their only access was to be through "indirect participation." He also thanked Molière for giving such apt expression to the case for limiting the education of women and denounced nascent feminism as a form of "civil disturbance" without a future.

Autonomy, Emancipation, and Justice

By the middle of the nineteenth century the issues appeared to have been clarified. Political history and philosophical history changed the nature of the problem. In the aftermath of the Revolution thinking about women was shaped by the realm of rights on the one hand and the sphere of nature on the other. Later it took the form of a discourse on love, human desire and transcendence in some quarters and on the metaphysics of difference in other quarters. Still later it returned to questions of the family and civil society and to immanence in general. Social pressure and the critique of religion took center stage, and concern with the reproduction of the species was relegated to the background.

At the same time, the nature of the philosophers' misogyny changed, no doubt because it was now possible to have a concrete sense of what the emancipation of women would mean and because feminism as a social and political movement was becoming a public reality. While certain philosophers such as Pierre Leroux, Karl Marx, and John Stuart Mill spoke of women with benevolence, others, such as Proudhon, worked in the tradition of Kant and Schopenhauer (and the ideology of the French Revolution), uncertain whether to exclude women from politics altogether or to brand them a harmful force. The critique of metaphysics had ambivalent and contradictory effects on representations of sexual difference.

Pierre Leroux, one of the theorists of emancipation, discussed rights as well as love, sexual identity as well as difference. He can be seen as a transitional figure between the earlier utopians, the Saint-Simonians and Fourierists, and the theorists of the revolution to come, Marx and Proudhon. Through his support for religion Leroux was still a man of the beginning of the century, but his call for justice placed him alongside the successful militants. *Love* was the central term to which he attempted to link certain new topics of discussion.

Leroux did not conceive of love either in terms of its sexual and reproductive reality or as a relation of desire and seduction. He defined it, rather, as "justice in its most divine form." Divine justice, unwilling to settle for mere equilibrium, inevitably strove for something more: love. God was neither male nor female (despite the suggestions of the Saint-Simonians): "God is manifest only when the *he* and the *she,* which exist virtually in it, are united by a third principle, love. And it is then, and only then, that the two principles we distinguish reveal themselves. And similarly, man and woman are revealed as distinct sexes only when love unites them. Before love and the couple, woman does not exist, in a sense; for she does not exist *qua* woman, she is only a human person."

This passage makes it clear that for Leroux, the pertinent metaphysics is not that of the pair but that of the triad. Therein lies his answer to the question of the century, the question of the dialectic, the pair eventually being subsumed in a third term. With the triad Leroux is able to conceptualize both sexual identity and sexual difference. He can also affirm the possibility of real equality between man and woman. This is what makes his thought novel and interesting. He identifies two spheres of male-female relations: the sexual/amorous sphere, and the sphere of the social condition of individual females. One is characterized by sexual difference; the other is not. Femininity is one distinguishing characteristic of the individual among others. It is a possibility, which a woman may or may not realize; if she does, she may eventually express that femininity by becoming a wife and mother. Hence a distinction is to be made between the woman, the wife, and the human being: the first is marked by sexual difference in the classic complementarity of the amorous relationship; the second manifests the social reality of the completed relationship yet respects the "parity" between male and female; the third recognizes only the similarity of the two sexes insofar as both constitute individual human beings.

These subtle distinctions are interesting for two reasons. First, they permit Leroux to criticize the day's misleading promises of equality, both the formal equality of the Civil Code, which in fact codified the wife's dependence, and equality as practiced by the Saint-Simonians, whose advocacy of free love actually led to the subjugation of women. True equality is just, and equity does not stem from empty abstractions. Sexual difference and the continuing influence of women's traditional servitude made simplistic affirmations worthless and specificity essential.

Since love is the third term that transcends sexual duality, Leroux could not accept the war of the sexes, which in his day had begun to take the form of "insurrection." Woman, he said, would emancipate man and vice versa. That was the egalitarian horizon that lay in store for both sexes: for the sexual being "woman" equality was unimportant, but for the "wife" and "human being" it was essential.

Max Stirner launched an all-out attack on Pierre Leroux's position, which he believed was shared by his compatriot and debating partner Feuerbach. What he objected to in both men's work was the sacralization of love, the restoration of the divine notwithstanding the critique of God and religion—in other words, a humanism that simply brought down to man values that had previously been vested in God. Among these were concepts such as love, the family, man, virility, and femininity. If, as Stirner proposed, one began instead with the concept of the individual, it became clear that the individual was at once unique and selfish, that is, defined by the self before being defined by masculine and feminine values.

Human beings have a sex, but men and women are not always "truly virile" or "truly feminine." Sex is a characteristic determined by nature, not an ideal to be attained. In each individual it is simply unique and incomparable. Feuerbach could not understand this, and in his debates with Stirner he treated the Ego proposed by the latter as an "Ego consequently asexual." But Stirner knew exactly where he wanted to go: he rejected so-called values and emphasized instead the unique will of the individual. Neither the species nor the family imposes its purpose on the individual. Individuals belong more to themselves than to any transcendent entity. Individuals do not constitute societies, whether through marriage, family, or state. Societies, moreover, create relations of dependence, and Stirner therefore proposed "association" as the only useful way of bringing individuals together.

This emphasis on the status of the independent individual shifted the focus of discussion to sexual difference. Individuals are sexed, even in their manner of thinking, but this sexual character does not express itself in the form of complementarity or in the assignment of places. Dualist representations were no longer appropriate, but that did not mean that humanism's "abstract man" would do as a substitute. Once again a change had taken place in the terms in which relations between the sexes were discussed: in this new discussion the family rather than the couple or marriage intervened between the individual and society as a central element of the problem. In fact, the question of relations between the sexes could be formulated in terms of the autonomous individual or in terms of the individual who, as a member of the family, is the integrating unit of society.

In his early writings Karl Marx rejected both Feuerbach's essentialism and Stirner's individualism. In Marx's view both thinkers toyed with concepts when the real need was to return to facts or, more precisely, to social facts. One fact, for example, was that the bourgeois family was not the same as the proletarian family. The family that Stirner criticized was the dominant bourgeois family, but there was another kind, the proletarian family, which was in the process of being destroyed by capitalism. The latter exhibited a different set of relations from the former. In particular, ownership and commerce were the driving elements in the bourgeois family (in regard to women and children as well as possessions).

Marx hailed Fourier as the man who had first attacked marriage and the family as a system of property relations in which women were treated as commodities.

For Marx, the family was always a historical reality. In *The German Ideology* he criticized Stirner's concept of the family for being abstract rather than historical. The family evolved as times changed, and to call for its abolition was absurd. In his earliest writings, dating from 1842, Marx declared himself in favor of monogamy and divorce (as opposed to the "sacralization" of the family found in Hegel), and he repeatedly repudiated primitive communism and its "community of wives." Indeed, such a community existed already, and it was called "prostitution," the commodity form of the circulation of women among men who possessed them as objects.

By dissolving the proletarian family and placing women on the labor market (making them productive workers as well as reproductive mothers), modern capitalism removed women from the realm of private family property and thus unwittingly initiated the process of women's liberation. In effect, wage labor was the first step toward autonomy for women, which communism was supposed to complete by putting an end to private property and changing the system of production. The economy, not the law, was the root of women's liberation and the foundation of a new family structure.

In the *1844 Manuscripts* Marx tried to define the family philosophically as the primary social relation and woman as the natural being who made it possible for man to create this primary social relation. The human relationship developed above and beyond what nature had provided, and the family was a bridge from nature to society, the primary component of every society. In the process woman became man's first possession (his slave, along with his children). It was therefore logical that in capitalist society she should have been reduced to a commodity. Originally a natural being, woman then became a market commodity: her only hope of regaining her humanity was through evolution of the family and of social relations generally.

Engels returned to this theme, the evolution of the family, its origin and its future, a little later, when the history of the social cell had been developed more fully. When Marx wrote at mid-century, the family was still viewed as an immutable essence, and only Fourier was able to imagine anything else. Fourier was also an innovator in the economic analysis of marriage and the family, and here too Marx made the debate concrete by stating that woman could cease to be an instrument of (family and social) production to become a worker in a system of production and an independent individual in private life.

In fact, the time was not yet quite ripe for a history of the family. Proudhon, Marx's contemporary and adversary, treated the family and marriage as the very embodiment of the immutable relationship between man and woman. Meanwhile, economic reality, not merely metaphysical arguments, reaffirmed the changeless status of the family and of relations between the sexes. Analysis would therefore have to begin again with the relationship between the family and society.

If Proudhon's aim was to put an end to economic and social injustice, his first objective was to define the sphere of justice. Dualism, he argued, is an organic condition of justice, and the primary form of dualism is the couple basic to the family. Derivative forms included economic dualism—production and consumption—and the dualism of labor itself, with reproduction (housekeeping, consumption, saving) delegated to the woman and production (workshop, manufacture, exchange) reserved for the man.

The family was the incarnation of justice, but that did not mean that it was the fundamental cell of society. Unlike Marx and Bonald (who exerted a powerful influence on his thinking despite their political differences), Proudhon reserved that role for the workshop. The family differed from the rest of society. In it reigned a peace based on inequality and an absence of conflict based on respect for the duality of the sexes. Conflict and competition belonged to the economic and political spheres and would cease only if justice came into being elsewhere, through sexual duality. The couple was therefore a union (and certainly not an association) of two individuals who together formed a single (social) individual that might well be androgynous.

Justice joined what should not be opposed, but not through love, a dangerous force: "Change, modify, or invert this relation between the sexes by any means whatsoever and you will destroy the essence of marriage. You will take a society in which justice predominates and make it into a society in which love predominates." Unlike Pierre Leroux, Proudhon distinguished between love and justice. And he subtly wove a tissue of connections between economics and metaphysics to confirm his contention that the female sex is inferior to the male.

Some commentators mention the women in Proudhon's life (his mother, wife, and daughters), but I prefer to call attention to his lengthy polemics with the feminists of his day (Jeanne Deroin, Juliette Lamber, and above all Jenny d'Héricourt), because the consequences of his theory of justice for his representation of women were catastrophic. "Housewife or courtesan (and not servant)"—this Proudhonian precept became popular with the highly antifeminist French workers' movement. It is to be interpreted as follows: at home the housewife performs unpaid but nonservile labor; in public woman is caught up in the cash nexus and virtually reduced to a commodity. By contrast, the sexual dualism of the married couple is based, despite the inequality of man and woman, on mutual respect.

Yet instead of developing his discourse on the complementarity and equivalence of the sexes, in which the female sex, granted, generally came out the loser (in equality as well as liberty) even though the discussion was animated by an appearance of equity, Proudhon gradually shifted to what seemed outright misogyny. Woman, he said, is a "complement" to man, adding her beauty to the man's strength, but beauty marks an end to development, so that a woman is scarcely better off than her children. She is consequently a minor, an inferior being, matter that according to Aristotle stands in need of form, and so the female seeks out the male. Last but not least, woman, according to Proudhon, is a middle term between man and animal, a variant on her usual position between nature and society, but a variant of ominous significance: "Between woman and man there can be love, passion, habitual bonds, and whatever you like, but there can never be true society. Man and woman do not go together. The difference between the sexes establishes a division between them of the same nature as that which the difference of breeds establishes between animals. Hence far from applauding what people today call the liberation of women, I would sooner, if it were to come to such an extremity, place women in confinement."

John Stuart Mill's position, of course, could not have been farther from Proudhon's. We know this from his correspondence with Comte, whose antifeminism caused the two men to break off relations. But other details of his life are equally illuminating. He recounts in his *Autobiography* how he disagreed with his father, who wanted to deny women the right to vote, and how his encounter with Harriet Taylor proved a decisive influence on him. They were close friends for twenty years before the death of Taylor's husband made marriage possible, and their wedding provided Mill with the occasion to promise never to make use of the husband's "unjust rights" over his wife. Their intellectual collaboration was especially noteworthy: they produced three works, one on marriage and divorce (1832), another on the liberation of women (1851), and a third on the subjugation of women (1869). Each influenced the other's writing. Still more remarkable was what Mill claimed he owed to their collaboration: more than a shared concern to prove the possibility of equality between the sexes, it was a guiding influence in the elaboration of his entire philosophical oeuvre (with the exception of his work on logic). In short, they enjoyed an intellectual communion that went beyond a shared commitment to ideas to include the very process of philosophical creation.

Despite the interest and importance of the question of intellectual production in relation to sexual difference, I shall confine my attention here to Mill's ideas about sexual equality. These may be grouped under three heads: the history of relations between the sexes and their present inequality; modern politics, along with the issues of suffrage and self-determination of male and female citizens; and marital rights, that is, the rights of individuals in marriage.

Mill's disagreement with Comte had to do with the first set of ideas. Biology, according to Mill, could not hold the ultimate truth about relations between the sexes. Women as they are today are the product of education, and education is subject to change. This was a standard argument (used long before Mill by Condorcet and others), based on a distinction between women as they existed in history and what was supposed to be their permanent nature. But with Mill the tone of the argument became more insistent: he used words such as "subjugation" and "liberation" and described the condition of women as a form of "slavery." Fourier and Marx also used the term, but it horrified Comte, as it would later horrify Freud (who as a young man translated several of Mill's texts). Now, the opposite of slavery is freedom, and John Stuart Mill was a philosopher of freedom. That is why he criticized his father's assertion that a woman's interest is identical with her husband's and that therefore only he ought to take part in public affairs. If freedom exists, it cannot be delegated, and each individual has a share: men as well as women, in politics as well as in civil society, in the public sphere as well as the home. Hence marriage cannot nullify a woman's rights. The end of slavery heralded emancipation and freedom for all individuals. By thus championing individual freedom, Stuart Mill set himself apart from many of his contemporaries, the metaphysicians of love and the analysts of the family as social microcosm. Sexual love and reproductive maternity were of little interest to him. His thought focused on the individual (as did Stirner's) and the citizen. But this champion of liberty was also a logician. He was determined to prove equality, and the task seemed difficult. Could there be such a thing as a proof of equality, and particularly sexual equality? Mill had his doubts, and he scrupulously confessed them to his readers.

Somewhat later the Swiss Charles Secrétan was led to similar conclusions on the basis of a moral philosophy derived from the so-called Protestant Awakening: "Woman is a person, because she has duties." Although the notion of "personality" was still vague, it was certainly meant to contrast with the contemporary "slavery of woman." And the evident differences between the sexes (which no theorist of women's rights since Condorcet had denied) posed no insuperable obstacle: "Cerebral inferiority is no more grounds than muscular inferiority for distinguishing between juridical and moral personality so as to deny the former to beings elevated by nature to the latter. If woman is a person, she is juridically her own end: the law ought to treat her as such and recognize her rights. If she is a person, she is a citizen. We demand the suffrage for woman so that she may at last obtain justice."

The Individual, the History of the Family, and the Menace of the Feminine

In the later nineteenth century the individual was examined in a variety of guises: as social actor, moral and political being, Nietzschean man, psychological subject—in one way or another men and women became all these things. The sexes were generally not considered in terms of complementarity, even if the obligatory male-female bipolarity remained. The question of the family, so pressing throughout the century, underwent a profound change as the family was acknowledged to have a history. Old certitudes about the essential nature of men and women collapsed, while real men and women were subjected to increasingly subtle analysis. Psychoanalysis marked a major break with the past, because it placed the sexes and sexuality at the center of its conceptual scheme. But as sexual difference became more visible, it also gave rise to more and more fantastic and anxious interpretations. Perhaps women were a negative influence in society, sowers of decadence. Misogyny took a belligerent view of the world.

The "destination" that women had been offered at the beginning of the century may have been lackluster, but it was less ambiguous than the "destiny" they were offered on the eve of the twentieth century.

Paradoxically, the affirmation of the individual was related in a complex way to new ideas about the family. The family was given a historical representation that offered both sexes greater freedom. Previous discussion of the origins of the family had been based on the Bible, and the patriarchal form had seemed immutable. But Engels, in his book on the subject, dated the emergence of the new history of the family from the publication of Bachofen's *Das Mutterrecht* in 1861. If the family was subject to historical evolution, then it might at one time have been matriarchal, or what Bachofen called a "gynecocracy." The history of the family could then be seen as a struggle for power between men and women.

Although some of Bachofen's latter-day readers have proposed matriarchy as a political goal, an alternative to the status quo, to the late nineteenth century it appeared more as an origin, at once real and mythical, a primitive form eventually defeated by patriarchy: "Preceding patriarchy, succeeding chaotic hetairism, Demetric gynecocracy thus occupies an intermediate position between the most primitive and the highest organization of human society." The transition from one to the other is described in the *Oresteia* of Aeschylus, in which Orestes' right to kill his mother Clytemnestra clashes with Clytemnestra's right to kill her husband Agamemnon. The conflict there is between the right of a man and the right of a woman. Bachofen was less interested in gynecocracy, women's power, than in matriarchy, or maternal law. Law rather than power: the domination of women is an extreme experiment, whereas maternal law, based as it is on the obvious fact of female filiation, is simply the first application of rule to a primitive disorder. Marriage, which succeeded this form of legitimation, validated paternity, and women thereby lost credit. But since maternal law is a part of history, women can refer to it in claiming their rights (to individual autonomy and social emancipation).

Engels clearly saw the consequences of this line of argument. The relativization of patriarchal law undermined its foundations. If it had not existed since the beginning of time, then one day it might end. Obviously Engels's vision was more realistic, more "materialistic" than that of Bachofen, from whom he borrowed his "facts" and certain preliminary interpretations: "One of the most absurd of the ideas that the Enlightenment has left us is that woman, at the inception of society, was man's slave. Among all savage tribes and all barbarian peoples of the inferior or middling stage and even among some of the higher stage, women are not only free but highly respected."

Progress thereafter was linear, although there were occasional reverses. Maternal law admittedly gave women a powerful position in society. But the sexual division of labor between production and reproduction, along with women's desire for monogamy, put an end to it. Economics and law combined to establish "conjugal marriage," which marked the transition to patriarchy. Under patriarchy, certitude of masculine filiation was combined with the possibility of a man's passing his accumulated wealth on to his offspring. The date of this revolution is unknown, although it marked *"the great historical defeat of the female sex."* Clearly, then, conjugal marriage was not an ideal; it "did not enter history as the reconciliation of man and woman, much less as the supreme form of marriage. On the contrary, it came into being as the subjugation of one sex by the other, as the proclamation of a conflict between the two sexes not previously seen at any point in the prehistoric period."

The dissolution of the family as a result of capitalism not only determined the final form of this conflict, according to Engels, but pointed the way to its possible resolution through the conquest of new legal rights and wage labor. Engels shared certain of these ideas with Marx and other socialists such as August Bebel (*Woman and Socialism,* 1883). He ended his analysis with the image of a new family created by the revolution to come. Although he had virtually no idea what this would look like, he was sure that sexual love would be essential.

The history of the family and of male-female relations introduced two important new ideas: the projections of an origin and a future distinct from and unlike the present, and the idea of a conflict between the sexes as a problem to be resolved. The discourse of complementarity no doubt lost favor because it neglected the dialectic of desire and power and the dynamic of male-female relations. Before long a number of writers had produced a range of analyses of the history of sexual conflict. These drew on such new theories as social evolution and natural or sexual selection, although it appears that neither Herbert Spencer nor Charles Darwin attached much importance to the gender issue. Nevertheless, their ideas were used by a number of thinkers determined to prove that sexual equality was a scientific impossibility. Themes culled from the work of philosophical physicians earlier in the century now found fresh support, as the fashionable new theories were invoked to prove that woman's role in perpetuating the species made it difficult if not impossible for her to have access to the higher functions. According to Herbert Spencer, the laws of evolution described a process of conflicting forces tending toward an equilibrium between the size of a population and the quantity of supplies on which it subsisted, in other words, an equilibrium between production and reproduction. Those same laws also applied to relations between the sexes: there is a conflict between reproduction and individuation or self-realization and another between fertility and mental activity in women. Clearly, therefore, every woman was trapped by her role within the species; she could not develop her self or her mind. Although dedicated to the work of perpetuating the species, she might nevertheless improve herself: education would one day allow her to obtain the right to vote. Although a proponent of sexual equality early in life when he was still a friend of John Stuart Mill's, Spencer changed his mind when he encountered the movement for the emancipation of women.

In *The Descent of Man* Darwin, despite obvious discomfort with the subject, does not mince his words: natural selection, reinforced by sexual selection, had favored man, who "became superior to woman." As to the question whether this inequality could be resolved by the development of humanity, his response was negative: according to the (false) theory of the heredity of acquired characteristics, taken from Lamarck, progress made in adulthood can be transmitted only within the sex. Hence women would always trail behind men, and the inequality would remain.

Thinkers who based their approach to the subject on history offered no more guarantee of sexual equality than those who based their work on rights. Initially, each of these "spaces of meaning" had seemed to offer women an opportunity, to open the way to sexual equality. But in the end those hopes were disappointed. Law and history were the two central axes of nineteenth-century thought, but when it came to equality between the sexes there was nothing to choose between the two.

The end of the century left the question of equality in suspense and focused instead on ideas of sexual difference. Nietzsche's work was deeply concerned with this issue. And Freud (insofar as he was a philosopher) was the first to take sexual difference as his object of inquiry, his central philosophical problem. Since psychoanalysis was a practice as well as a theory, it also brought speculation back to reality in a dramatic way. Now, testing theory against the facts was the central theme of the new human sciences such as sociology, which Durkheim helped to found. We thus come to the dawn of the twentieth century and its claims of "scientific" knowledge of sexuality. And antifeminism found its thinker in Otto Weininger, about whom it is difficult to decide whether he was an exemplar of the past or a harbinger of the future.

Sexual metaphors provided the fabric out of which Nietzsche wove a number of his themes. Indeed, for Nietzsche, sexual difference was more than a metaphor, it was a mode of thought that employed images of masculine and feminine, man and woman. He describes an epoch as "virile" or calls truth "a woman" without ever defining virility or womanhood. But difficulty of definition does not stop him from using these as qualifiers. For example, Nietzsche speaks of beauty and intelligence, and we know how the ancients divided these qualities between men and women. Yet the specific essence of each sex only becomes more confused. One might also say that men and women no longer exist in general, only certain men and certain women. The binary system of sexuality grows more supple when the argument abandons categories and hews to the individual: "This woman is beautiful and intelligent. Alas! how much more intelligent she would have become had she not been beautiful" (*Daybreak,* § 282). One individual is just as true as another, and one woman is as much Woman as any other, for it is always possible to go further: "This is how I want man and woman: the one a good warrior, the other a good mother, but both good dancers with the head and legs" (*Thus Spoke Zarathustra,* III, § 23).

The "law of the sexes" exists, however, and it is a "hard law for woman" (*The Gay Science,* § 68). Nietzsche prefers lucidity to illusion and recognition of sexual inequality to an impossible identity: "The passion of woman in its unconditional renunciation of its own rights presupposes in fact that there does not exist on the other side an equal pathos, an equal desire for renunciation: for if both renounced themselves out of love, there would result—well, I don't know what, perhaps a *horror vacui*?" (§ 363). That is the law of love, which, like the fact of conflict between the sexes itself, makes any idea of equality unthinkable and improbable. What remains is "indulgence" for women taken in by love and wariness of their emancipation: "In the three or four civilized countries of Europe women can through a few centuries of education be made into anything, even into men: not in the sexual sense, to be sure, but in every other sense. This will be the age in which the actual masculine affect will be anger: anger at the fact that all the arts and sciences have been choked and deluged by an unheard-of dilettantism, philosophy talked to death by mind-bewildering babble, politics more fantastic and partisan than ever, society in full dissolution" (*Human, All Too Human,* § 425). The reason for this, Nietzsche explains, is that women have great power "in morality and custom." But where will they gain comparable power if they renounce these? The identity of the sexes and the power of one or the other are the two keys to thinking about these issues. Nietzsche confronts these questions with rare acuity, no doubt thanks to his ability to see women from many angles—as if he were not afraid of them.

Truth is female—and so are nature and life. Because man produces the discourse, woman plays the role of the other in that discourse. But woman does not therefore become an object; rather, she becomes a substitute for that forever inaccessible object, the truth. Nietzsche was also interested in the intelligence of women. Intelligence can play a part in love, and marriage may be a "long conversation" (*Human, All Too Human,* § 406). Nietzsche adopts

Schopenhauer's distinction between the feminine understanding and the masculine will (§ 411) but endlessly mixes up the qualities of the two sexes. He is forever crossing boundaries, perhaps because he was fascinated by the image of pregnancy (indeed of "intellectual pregnancy"), a violent image for the transcendence of the individual.

He draws a contrast between the virilization of Europe, from Napoleon's campaigns to the wars of the future, and "the dangerous notion of the 'artist,' in which actors, Jews, and women recognize their common weakness and falseness." This conceptual parallel of Jew and woman was a characteristic feature of Germanic thought in this period, most notably that of the Austrian Otto Weininger. Both woman and Jew became something more than what they were in themselves, the embodiment of a precise yet somehow diffuse menace—a symbolic role that would prove tragic for the Jews in reality and for women at the level of the imagination.

Turning now from these vertiginous speculations to the reality of women's lives brings us to the new sciences of sociology and psychoanalysis, which were concerned with concrete facts and individuals. Durkheim's purpose was to bring rigor to the description of social facts. The same insistence on rigor is evident in his work on the family and divorce—the "crisis of the family." Because it was by now established that the family had a history, Durkheim analyzed the contemporary social cell, the "conjugal family," which was built around marriage. In earlier times the family had been a "domestic society," a place of production and transmission of wealth. Now, however, marriage and "matrimonial society" called attention to the "public" character of the union. "Community property" might establish a kind of equality between husband and wife, but that equality was ephemeral and without a future. Because the family no longer fulfilled its economic and moral functions, the occupational group would, Durkheim thought, become a kind of substitute for it. Similarly, equality of the sexes implied that women would lead more of their lives outside the home.

"Marriage establishes the family and at the same time derives from it." Without the matrimonial bond no moral society was possible. Durkheim rejected divorce by mutual consent, as opposed to divorce "on definite grounds," which he believed ought to be the only legal form. Divorce on specific grounds was based on justice and law, whereas divorce by consent was based on nothing but the will of the parties involved. It therefore struck at the roots of the institution of matrimony and of social morality and could lead to "a serious social malady." This analysis, which was contemporary with Engels's diametrically opposite understanding of the situation, reflected Durkheim's social vision, just as Engels's did his. Yet it would be a mistake to ascribe the divergence in their views to the difference between a man of science and a revolutionary. Some sociologists were perfectly capable of utopian views: Georg Simmel, for example, who in the early twentieth century pondered the possibility of a "feminine culture" in the modern world.

Concern with another sort of malady gave rise to psychoanalysis, specifically, the malady of hysteria, which was an affliction of women but also of the relation between mind and body. Psychoanalysis broke new philosophical ground in two respects: it proposed a new theory of sexuality, a coherent set of propositions on sexual difference, as well as a new theory of knowledge based on the notion of the unconscious. Indeed, the idea of the unconscious profoundly altered man's understanding of himself and the world. By contrast, the theory of sexuality is perhaps less original than it appears. In places it seems strangely reminiscent of the philosophical medicine of the early nineteenth century and of other attempts to assign women a "destination." Yet by shifting the ground of the discussion from "sex" to "sexuality," psychoanalysis added important new terms to the debate: it introduced the notion that sexuality is shared by all human beings, women as well as men, children as well as adults; it introduced a distinction between sexuality and reproduction; it proposed the hypothesis that all human beings are bisexual; and it gave us the notion of a nonbiological sexual life in which instincts are called drives. All of this was still but a dim outline in 1900, but what was at stake was already clear. History would have to expand to include the history of the individual. Family life could now be analyzed in such depth that it revealed the distinctive character of every family group, the "family romance." Women ceased to be the "fair sex." They not only had a history but also a "destiny," determined, according to Freud, by their sexual anatomy. The word is ambiguous: was it richer than the "social destination" that women had been offered a hundred years earlier, rich with the uniqueness of each individual? Or was it poorer than the social role supposedly attached to it, offering a prospect of a life less than entirely free?

When it came to questions of women's equality or liberty, all the learning in the world was not enough to achieve certainty, as Otto Weininger learned to his sorrow, and his suicide soon after the publication of *Sex and Character* tells us something about the risks inherent in his philosophical venture. He called what he was doing philosophy: "I am studying not facts but principles." And the purpose of his philosophy was to "deny the existence" of women, to be "antifeminist." This, he realized, would be to no one's liking: "Men will never willingly support antifeminist theses: their sexual selfishness causes them to prefer woman as they wish her to be." In this seeming paradox, that men are fundamentally feminists, lay the secret of his thought: it was better, he believed, to acknowledge than to deny that women (and Jews) are castrated creatures. "Can one ask woman to give up being a slave in order to be *unhappy*?" he asked. Certainly not, unless the emancipation of women, which preoccupied him above all, brought about a Kantian return to man's categorical imperative: the renunciation of sex in favor of chastity. Woman being nothing but sex, she could never free herself from it, but man could.

Sex or sexuality: Weininger was one of the few to make the distinction. He could therefore speak of one or the other without confusing the issue and was one of the few philosophers prepared to discuss sexual difference.

His theory of sexuality is a theory of bisexuality, not unlike that of Freud's early collaborator, Wilhelm Fliess. For Weininger, bisexuality was not the exception but the rule: "Experience shows us not men or women but only the masculine and the feminine" in each man and each woman. "The laws of sexual attraction" (including homosexual attraction) were thus based on the proportion in every individual of M and F components. Emancipation was to be understood in terms of the masculine portion of the female. Weininger was not content merely to reject women's liberation; he created a theory against it. No doubt that was why he fascinated his contemporaries: he gave reasons for what others all too easily dismissed as folly.

His antifeminism was not unalloyed: "I am not speaking of a woman's desire to be treated externally on the same footing as a man but rather of her wish to be like him inwardly, to achieve the same freedom of thought and morality, to take an interest in the same things, to exhibit the same creative force." In other words, legal equality is necessary while moral and intellectual equality are intolerable. An irreducible difference between the sexes must be maintained at all cost, even if that causes misogyny to be mistaken for antifeminism. "Masculine" women in this view represent progress and not, as Möbius suggested in *On the Physiological Imbecility of Woman,* a sign of social degeneration. Evil is feminine; it comes from the feminine in woman. The woman is a being without moral capacity: "Woman is man's SIN."

From a social destination born of responsibility to the species to an individual destiny worked out in sexual and family life: this was how the representation of woman evolved in a period that witnessed the invention of feminism. In general, then, the representation of women followed the overall evolution of nineteenth-century thought, but it was also marked by reactions to the possibility of autonomy for the female subject.

TRANSLATED FROM THE FRENCH BY ARTHUR GOLDHAMMER

4

The Law's Contradictions

Nicole Arnaud-Duc

LEGAL AND MORAL DISCOURSE together define the rational limits of male and female spheres. Through its symbolic regulatory role law sets social norms and determines social roles. On this prime battleground women won many victories in the nineteenth century. Were these sufficient to mark a historic change in male-female relations? Law is of course itself subject to internal disputes, and its enforcement may meet with popular resistance. It is the private preserve of specialists, owing to the majority's ignorance or lack of interest in its inner workings. The social and legal systems are involved in a constant tug of war, in which the balance of power between male and female is one factor, if not a central contradiction.

Ever since Aristotle the question of legal equality had come up against the assumption that certain inequalities were natural: among the supposed natural deficiencies of women were physical inferiority and weakness of the rational faculty. The dominant theory of law in the nineteenth century was based on individual free will. In France, however, legislation was authoritarian. The fiction of an independent will by which individualist liberalism set such great store gave rise to the idea that women, insofar as the law was concerned, existed only in relation to others, that is, as daughters, wives, or mothers, secondary figures defined by their relation to a man who alone was the true subject of law. Nevertheless, the law had to alter its discourse, if not its content, to adapt to changes in custom stemming from economic and political changes. Jurists therefore attempted to justify the unequal treatment of men and women by arguing that ultimately women wish to be protected from their own nature. This left open the possibility of reforms once women acquired the capacity to manage their own affairs (although they were excluded from acquiring the necessary experience). It is not hard to see why women who demanded their rights claimed to be doing so only in order to be better wives and mothers.

New contradictions emerged. Most women still felt allegiance to an imposed ideal, a model of gentleness and compassion based on the "bourgeois" mother, who looked upon the law as belonging to her man's world and not her own. Well-off women felt no need to give up their secure status, and when they did emancipate themselves at the end of the century they did so only to reject certain constraints on their behavior. The majority of women, however, belonged to the lower strata of society and had no interest in laws not intended for their kind. Oppressed by the burden of work, worn down at an early age, they were caught up in momentous economic changes, often treated as assets, occasionally emerging as victims. What did it matter to them that they could not vote or that they were not allowed to administer property they did not own in the first place? While the law arbitrarily overprotected the married woman, it left those who lived outside a family setting to their own devices. Thus women were at the center of the law's ambiguities, which resulted from the gap between legal discourse and the social reality the law claimed to regulate. What rights did women have in the nineteenth century? And how did they exercise them within the family, at the intersection of public and private, the focal point of relations between the sexes and foundation of the social order?

The Forbidden City

To take one's place in public life means not only to participate in collective sovereignty through exercise of the right to vote but also to claim the right to an education, a job, and the protection of the laws.

Citizeness or Citizen's Wife and Daughter?

Political rights empower citizens to influence the state's priorities and hold public office. Suffrage may be national (or federal), local, or limited to particular offices. Because such hierarchies existed, women could only work their way gradually toward full citizenship. At the end of the eighteenth century no woman enjoyed political equality. At the end of World War I, emancipation had yet to come to Central and South America, Greece, Austria, Italy, Spain, or Quebec. France would wait until 1946 and Switzerland until 1971 to grant women the right to vote. In Switzerland the battle lasted more than a hundred years and required more than eighty-two referenda.

The French Revolution recognized women as individuals and raised the issue of their political rights. Historically, the behavior of men in power toward women has been disappointing, yet the shock caused by the breach in the male monopoly of power would continue to fuel reactionary—in particular legal reactionary discourse—throughout the nineteenth century. Women had obtained legal status under civil law, but they apparently paid a price for the fears aroused by the image of the female revolutionary forcing her way into what had been regarded as the exclusively male province of politics. Women were excluded from political life along with the lower classes: both got in the way of the new bourgeois order. Medical and religious writers fostered fears that if women gained power they would become uncontrollable, and those fears were echoed by legal theorists. Why were women excluded from politics? The answer to the question is complex and touches on the most profound aspects of relations between the sexes. Male writers could adopt a protective attitude toward women, portraying them as fragile and helpless, and yet at the same time fear them irrationally. In secularized countries it was alleged that unworldly women, working in close association with the Church, encouraged the conservative vote. Women were barred from politics yet simultaneously exalted as mothers (Muse and Madonna), and while attempts were made to justify their exclusion on rational grounds, it must be seen in the context of the new public order.

Women in feudal Europe were represented in the order of the

nobility, but this was a property right, not a political one. In the eighteenth century feminist demands issued from an avant-garde, a group of active, bold, well-educated women of moderately well-to-do background. Female workers saw wage labor as just another form of exploitation, and nascent socialism fought primarily for social revolution and universal suffrage. Since women did not participate in the drafting of laws, they could only attempt to persuade those who did through demonstrations, petitions, and newspaper articles. They sought allies among those who defined themselves in terms of political and religious debate. In France they joined forces with free thinkers, Freemasons, and republicans. In Germany the so-called free churches played a leading role. Broadly speaking, secular democrats, republicans, and left-wing liberals supported their demands.

French women first made their demands heard when universal manhood suffrage was established in 1848. But these demands were not granted, and Pierre Leroux was shouted down when he asked that women be given the right to vote in municipal elections.[1] When the Third Republic was finally established in 1879, women's demands were rejected on the grounds that the regime was too fragile to permit radical changes. By the end of the century women had learned to count on no one but themselves. They were ideologically divided into two rough groupings: radicals, who wanted total equality, and moderates, who held, in the name of "complementarity" of the sexes, that women must first prepare themselves to hold public office, although no comparable requirement was imposed on men. Suffragism was never popular, and Hubertine Auclert had no real success. Attempts to inscribc women's names on electoral lists met with little sympathy. Rebuffed by the legislature, women turned to the courts and proposed that civil laws couched in terms of the neutral masculine be extended to all citizens; they were wasting their time.[2] Yet magistrates had no compunctions about sentencing a female "procurer"[3] or a news vendor who did not claim to have been deprived by her sentence of political rights she did not possess.[4] A celebrated professor of law attempted to solve the problem by applying a legal formula intended to distinguish between "null" and "nonexistent" legal acts; in this way he distinguished cases in which inequality was arguable from those in which it was blatant: a woman was a "nonexistent citizen who has not even the substance of a citizen . . . the sex of a candidate [being], in our customs, a fact not open to challenge."[5] Nevertheless, the year 1914 seemed full of promise. The feminist movement had regrouped tactically, having won the support of some three hundred deputies. But suddenly the lawmakers had other things on their minds. It was not until after World War II that French women obtained the right to vote, and in the event the opinion of the legislature was not consulted.

All the Latin countries with their Catholic heritage proved particularly resistant to recognizing women's political rights. By contrast, in those countries where reformist, moralistic liberalism of Protestant and especially Quaker inspiration was influential, women obtained local political power much sooner. England was a case in point, and its former colonies offer even better examples. The English Reform Bill of 1832 marked the beginning of suffragist agitation. The term "person" was used instead of "male" in the law to create new categories of electors. In 1835 a law on the election of municipal councillors specified "males," thereby depriving women of rights they possessed under certain local charters. In 1851 John Stuart Mill reported in the *Westminster Review* on discussions of the issue at the Worcester Conference in the United States in 1850. That same year, the Sheffield Women's Association submitted the first petition on women's suffrage to the House of Lords. Parliament was much agitated by the question until 1873, especially after the publication of John Stuart Mill's influential *Subjection of Women* in 1869. Mill was elected to the House of Commons, where he became the spokesman for the feminists, and the agitation increased when his amendment was rejected. At the local level women who paid taxes exercised the same functions as men in the areas of hygiene, welfare, education, and parish affairs. They were authorized to draft official documents and held posts of responsibility, particularly on the London hospital commission. Yet Parliament remained steadfastly opposed to granting women the right to vote at the national level. When, moreover, the right to vote was extended to male heads of household and tenants in the counties as well as the towns, women deemed themselves insulted by a law that made electors out of illiterate agricultural laborers. Meanwhile, Englishwomen continued to gain important rights: municipal suffrage (1869; 1882 in Scotland), the right to vote and eligibility for school boards and boards of guardians, and the right to vote for county councils, to which they became eligible to stand for election in 1907. Exasperated by repeated denials of the right to vote at the national level, feminists, especially those of the middle class, turned to violent tactics. In 1903 Emmeline Pankhurst founded the Women's Social and Political Union. When the Labor Party was formed in 1906, however, its first objectives, like those of socialist parties elsewhere, were social.

The Conservatives returned to Parliament and stepped up repression of the suffragettes (Black Friday, 1911). Until 1914 militant women were repeatedly jailed (Cat and Mouse Act). In 1913 a suffrage bill was rejected for the fiftieth time—but this would be the last. In the territories that would become the Australian confederation in 1900, municipal suffrage was granted in 1867. In 1895 women voted in numerous local parliaments there, and in 1902 they obtained the right to vote and hold office at the federal level. The same prerogatives were granted to landowners in New Zealand in 1886 and 1893. In Canada women were highly active in philanthropy, but suffragism made little headway. They did vote in municipal and school board elections, where they were also eligible to hold office, albeit with certain restrictions.

In the United States, where developments were closely monitored by European and especially English feminists, different strategies were needed. In the West the pioneer spirit tended to favor women. Around 1850 a reform-minded feminism set out to reconstruct American institutions on an egalitarian and cooperative basis. Middle-class clubs had promoted political rights for women without ending separation of the sexes. From the earliest days of the Union women had demanded the right to vote, but in 1808 a law was passed limiting it to men, although each state retained the right to set its own voting requirements. The suffragist movement came into being in New York. In 1833 feminists joined their cause to that of blacks, but the American women's delegation was denied a place at the London antislavery conference because of its sex. Women then turned their efforts toward influencing the press. The first International Women's Congress was held in Worcester, Massachusetts, in 1850. At the end of the Civil War women who had fought for the rights of slaves keenly felt the injustice of granting political rights to freed slaves while continuing to exclude women. They were no longer willing to settle for the right to serve on local councils or for limited powers in the areas of welfare, education, and the granting of liquor licenses. From 1870 on women intervened regularly in local meetings and in Congress. Henry James's ambiguous novel *The Bostonians* paints a marvelous portrait of male reactions to feminist determination.

Despite favorable popular majorities, state legislatures defeated attempts to amend the Constitution. Antifeminist masses were stirred up by tavernkeepers and distillers outraged by women's attacks on the ravages of alcoholism. The veritable social crusades waged by the Temperance Societies had a great impact in Europe. For a while women found most of their allies in the legislature among representatives of groups that had come to America long ago. This trend was reversed in Wyoming, in a compromise designed to win the votes necessary for statehood. From 1869 on Wyoming became a model, a laboratory, and an object of curiosity for European newspaper readers. By the eve of World War I women had won political rights in many states, particularly in the West. They enjoyed the right to vote and hold office at all levels of government almost everywhere. At the municipal level they played an active part in drafting most humanitarian laws. In 1889 only twelve states still denied them the right to vote in school elections. There was no law to prevent a woman from being elected president, and French commentators were overjoyed in 1884, when "a pretty, forty-year-old widow lawyer riding a bicycle and holding a briefcase and snuffbox . . . [a woman] with silver hair and gold glasses" waged a dynamic campaign. But the comments reveal the mind-set of French males: they mocked, but they also felt an obscure sense of anxiety at the emergence in these new roles not of masculinized monsters but of women endowed with all the requisite feminine qualities. Had not the lady in question "learned to sew, knit, wash, iron, bake bread, and do her own hair before learning her ABCs?"[6] A third period began around 1890, when women were invited to express their grievances before legislative committees and other official bodies. Celebrated orators like Elizabeth Cady Stanton (who had spent many of her seventy-five years fighting the good fight) distinguished themselves in these settings. Finally, in 1919, the Nineteenth Amendment to the Constitution consecrated woman's right to vote.

In northern Europe the women of Iceland made their island into a showcase of feminism after the country gained its independence in 1872. Granted the right to vote in municipal elections in 1882 and to hold office in 1902, women over forty obtained full rights in 1915 and all women in 1920. In Sweden women gained the right to participate in municipal government in the middle of the nineteenth century. In 1909 they won the right to hold office, and in 1924 they acquired full rights in the political sphere. In Denmark, where the rural population was remarkably enlightened, women voted in municipal elections from 1883 on and in parliamentary elections after 1915. Norway was the first European nation to establish political equality. The movement was launched there in 1830. Universal suffrage was established in 1910, and women enjoyed full political rights. In 1912 they gained the right to be elected to any state post with the exception of the Royal Council, the corps of dignitaries of the church, diplomatic posts, and certain other exclusively male offices. In Finland, which had been annexed to Russia in the middle of the eighteenth century, women fought against the czar. In 1906 the Finnish Diet was elected by universal suffrage of both sexes. To be sure, its powers were limited, but nineteen women held seats in 1910.

In the Latin and Germanic countries women's conquests were meager, as we have seen, and Roman law left its mark. To take the French case, which is by no means unusual, we note that women could vote for members of the Superior Council of Public Instruction in 1880, and they could vote for and hold office in the Departmental Councils of Primary Education in 1886, the Superior Council of Mutuality in 1898, the Superior Council of Labor in 1903, the Communal Assistance Commissions in 1905, the Superior Council of the Conservatory in 1905, the Labor Advisory Boards (right to vote in 1907, to hold office in 1908), and the Committees on Art and Manufacturing in 1908. It was not until 1898, however, that female merchants were allowed to vote for, but not hold office in, the Tribunals of Commerce.

Furthermore, in continental Europe generally, and most of all in countries that had been under Roman domination, women suffered from a further restriction on what were called "virile offices." These were activities that might involve a person if not in public life then at least in life outside the domestic sphere. French women were allowed to serve as witnesses (to document signings, for example) in 1792, but that right was withdrawn in 1803. In a flagrant contradiction, however, women continued to be called as witnesses in court. Similarly, in lieu of a birth certificate, a person could produce an affidavit of public knowledge issued by a judge and corroborated by seven witnesses of either sex. After a ten-year campaign women finally won back the right to serve as witnesses in 1897. Similar changes occurred in Italy in 1877, Geneva in 1897, and Germany in 1900. Austria accepted women as witnesses for wills drawn up at sea, and Spain for wills drawn up during periods of epidemic.

For a long time women were excluded from serving on juries in criminal cases, except in certain American states. Nor could women be chosen as guardians or trustees. In France they were granted the right to serve as guardians of their own natural children in 1907, at which time it was noted that they were chosen by nature for the task: a woman without legal rights was good enough for a bastard. In 1917 a temporary law allowed them to serve as guardians in a nonlegal sense. In Germany the restriction on women's guardianship was lifted in 1900, in Belgium in 1909, in the Netherlands and Switzerland in 1901. This prohibition had been coupled with a ban on women sitting on family councils.

Inequality in Education and Work

To pose the issue in terms of a right to work or to an education would be anachronistic. Yet everywhere education for young women was a fundamental feminist demand. The French revolutionaries had been unable to enforce their egalitarian program. An advisory law of June 28, 1836, suggested that municipalities establish schools for girls. But most mayors preferred the traditional parish schools, because they did not have to pay the teachers' salaries. It was not until the Falloux Law was passed on March 15, 1850, and reinforced by the Duruy Law of April 10, 1867, that every commune of more than 500 residents was obliged to maintain a primary school for girls. In 1863 an effort was made to provide for secondary education. The law of August 8, 1879, created sixty-seven normal schools for women, and the Camille Sée Law of December 21, 1881, established lycées and preparatory schools for women, followed by the Ecole Normale of Sèvres in 1883. Not until 1925 was the principle of identical instruction for boys and girls recognized by French law.

In Latin Europe the education of women was also an issue in the struggle for power between church and state. In Germany and England public elementary schools had few takers, and secondary and college education was essentially private, as in the United States, although there mixed primary schools were established quite early. Russia concentrated on education for the bourgeoisie. When the universities were closed to the daughters of the bourgeoisie for political reasons, young Russians joined women from all over Europe at the University of Zurich. Few families felt the need to make their daughters more competitive on the labor market by reducing their ignorance; at any rate such notions, when not actively rejected, were not acted on. Some advanced circles expressed concern about allowing women access to competitive examinations and universities.

As for labor legislation, we must keep in mind that one of the golden rules of nineteenth-century liberalism was not to interfere in employer-employee relations. In the final third of the century, however, Europe discovered the welfare state, and campaigns were waged in favor of legislation to protect women and children from exploitation by industry. In the name of equality certain feminists challenged these measures as discriminatory; they favored continuing women's traditional legal disabilities and limiting their opportunities for employment. Some workers saw women as potential rivals in the labor market. In this men surely also betrayed their desire to have women remain at home, but at the same time they were fighting employers who exploited female workers by underpaying them and using the threat of women substitutes to force the hand of male workers. Serious legal tomes gave almost mathematical proofs that women need less food than men and that they are incapable of performing outdoor work, although their authors were fully aware of the realities of women's work. Some proponents of protective legislation were moved more by philanthropy than by justice. In a later stage of the workers' movement (in France under the movement called *solidarisme*), the same protections would be extended to men.[7] Although legislation to protect women on the job was important, it was not the same as true equality in the workplace. The new laws were limited by their very nature: they concerned only the factory, where the "dangerous classes" were found. The peasantry, a far larger group, was ignored, as was labor at home, in the workshop, in large retail stores, and in domestic service.

In France the law of June 3, 1874, prohibited women and children from working underground. But it was the law of November 2, 1892, that really introduced the first discrimination by sex in labor law: it applied to children under eighteen and to all female industrial workers. In principle, the law was to protect working women and children from unhealthy or dangerous environments. Those who worked in print shops were not to be allowed access to licentious texts or drawings. Altogether, the aim of the law was to organize the working day differently for each sex. In the interest of the family women were thus to be given an "advantage," which as it happens deprived them of employment as skilled laborers. They were not allowed to work at night, and later laws, such as that of July 15, 1908, ratifying the decisions of the International Convention of Berne of September 26, 1906, as well as the law of December 22, 1911, further elaborated this principle.

When the newspaper *La Fronde* launched a campaign in favor of new protective legislation that would be the same for both sexes, female workers did not support it and called instead for better enforcement of existing laws. True, there were serious obstacles to drafting good legislation in this area. The law always permitted exceptions, usually having to do with night and overtime work, which was common in the fashion industry. Theoretically, the law of 1911 prohibited night work for women after ten in the evening. But enforcement was notoriously lax, particularly in charity workshops such as the Bon-Pasteur, where there was little oversight before 1902. Corps of male and female inspectors were established, but they were too few to do the job. What is more, female workers fearful of unemployment promised their employers not to reveal abuses, and work done at home after the regular working day had ended made the whole business of factory inspection a sham. In 1892 female labor inspectors were allowed to visit only shops that employed women exclusively and contained no motorized machinery (although their mandate was expanded in 1908). The law of November 2, 1892, provided for more time off on weekends and holidays, matching the longer vacations already given to schoolchildren. The law of July 13, 1906, which made Sundays off compulsory, was the first nondiscriminatory labor law, but numerous exceptions were allowed. As for the working day, a regulation adopted in 1848 theoretically covered all adult workers: the duration of the working day was initially set at ten hours in Paris and eleven in the provinces, but it was later increased to twelve hours for all workers, with one hour of rest daily. But the organization of the day was disrupted, and women's wages were reduced as a result, for payment was generally by the piece. Factory women were often replaced by home workers, who were not protected by law and whose labor was generally approved by their husbands. The law of March 30, 1900, likewise reinforced the subjugation of women to their families by structuring work time so that "rest periods" could be used for cooking family meals. A law of December 29, 1900, was known as the "chair law," because it required employers to provide chairs for their female employees.

Among the other measures that applied exclusively to women, those dealing with maternity deserve special mention. France lagged well behind the rest of Europe in granting maternity leave of four weeks, a step recommended by the International Conference that met in Berlin on March 15, 1890, and its newborns and working mothers suffered under the difficult circumstances. In 1886 feminists initiated a campaign. The law of November 27, 1909, finally recognized that a French woman did not violate her labor contract by taking unpaid leave for eight weeks prior to or following delivery of a child. In 1910 and 1911 the state granted paid maternity leave to schoolteachers, arsenal workers, and post-office employees. On March 27, 1913, an appellate court ruled that such leaves were also to be granted to unwed mothers. But the court also pointed out that an employer reserves the right to cancel a contract in case an employee's pregnancy threatens to damage the reputation of the business. The laws of June 17 and July 30, 1913, authorized expectant mothers to stop work prior to delivery and required them not to work for four weeks afterward, even in the case of home work. It was not until July 30, 1915, that a daily allowance was provided for recent mothers. The allowance was canceled in case of miscarriage, and it was in any case much less than the going wage.

Rather than exclude women from the workplace, the legislature invoked family protection as a pretext for structuring the work day in such a way as to channel female workers into what can only be described as ghettos where there was little oversight of working conditions. These measures created unemployment and encouraged discrimination in hiring. In particular they penalized unmarried women, for whom the excuse that low wages were justifiable because women's earnings were only a supplement to family income made no sense. Despite all its shortcomings, this early protective legislation was significant in that it broke with the principle that the state has no right to intervene in matters of private contract.

In the professions women had to fight for recognition of their status in one field after another, turning to the courts and the legislature to overcome masculine resistance. Two examples will suffice. In 1908 the courts dismissed a suit brought by medical students demanding nullification of a decision by the Paris welfare authorities to allow women to take the competitive examination for places as nonresident practitioners in state hospitals.[8] As for the legal profession, the issue of women's access was a matter of considerable controversy throughout Europe. All the usual arguments against women in the workplace were mobilized for the occasion, from the "*pudicitia* imposed by nature"[9] to lack of discretion and incurable garrulousness. Every imaginable allegation was raised: women lack physical stamina; they have a hard time pleading in Latin (which hardly mattered in America, where women were admitted to the bar); judges might be vulnerable to feminine wiles, women being flirtatious by nature. It comes as something of a surprise, therefore, to learn that France admitted women to the bar on December 1, 1900.[10] Numerous precedents were cited from around the world: Russia, Japan, Romania, Switzerland, Finland, Norway, New Zealand, and the United States, where the first woman lawyer set up practice in Iowa in 1869 and women were allowed to plead before federal courts in 1879. In some states women served as justices of the peace, and in many places they were court clerks.

Women and the Penal Code

Although doubts about their capacity were voiced in many areas, women generally were not deemed incapable of committing crimes and answering for them in court. In England, however, husbands were responsible for their wives' crimes until 1870, when women gained legal personhood. Although few people agreed with Michelet that women were so fragile that they ought to be considered legally irresponsible for their crimes, they were exempt from certain provisions of common law. Women were rarely put to death for one thing, and pregnant women were not incarcerated until they had delivered. In France the Penal Code of 1791 substituted forfeiture of civil rights for the iron collar and imprisonment for iron fetters. Even under the old law female prisoners had been hidden away in work houses. The law of July 19, 1907, amended that of May 27, 1885, by exempting recidivist women from banishment to a penal colony (French Guiana or New Caledonia). In general, French women, along with minors and men over seventy, were exempt from imprisonment in enforcement of a court order (law of 15 *germinal,* Year IV). This exemption did not apply to female merchants or to those guilty of selling or mortgaging a property they did not own or represented as unencumbered by any lien. In practice, this provision made it extremely difficult for women to obtain credit or to sign promissory notes of any kind. What is more, until passage of the law of April 17, 1832, and the more general measure of July 22, 1867, women were not allowed to handle public funds, which excluded them from many positions.

We come now to the matter of prostitution. Although universally practiced in the many countries with laws against free exercise of the profession, prostitution was treated particularly hypocritically in France. From the time of the Consulate (and the relative freedom of sexual behavior that developed after the Terror) up to 1946, prostitution was not illegal in France. It was "tolerated," which is quite a different thing from saying it was regulated. Deemed indispensable to men and necessary for maintaining public order and protecting other young women, prostitution nevertheless had to be carried on in secret, outside the purview of decent women yet within the "panoptic" supervision of the administration. Granted official status as "public women," prostitutes worked either on their own or in a licensed brothel. The government refrained from issuing regulations on such matters as where prostitutes could stand to solicit. The profession was obliged to remain hidden and ashamed of itself. This "French system" constituted nothing less than an attack on the female sex, which alone suffered the consequences of the "debauch" practiced by both sexes together. Even in England and the United States, which witnessed vigorous campaigns against prostitution, there was nothing like France's minute regulation, so humiliating to women. The French way of dealing with this social problem was thus legalistic, hypocritical, and contemptuous. Hospitals, prisons, "refuges of repentance," and houses of prostitution were subject to the arbitrary authority of the police and the medical and religious authorities. Legal prostitutes were subject to many forms of harassment by officials who answered to no one, although the law still frowned on dealings with "houses of debauch" even if they were officially regulated.[11]

In the period 1876–1884 the growth of unregulated prostitution, together with the proliferation of publications dealing with sexually transmitted diseases and with often fantastic notions of female sexual behavior, elicited a wave of compassion for prostitutes as victims of poverty and led to a series of investigations and a rethinking of social policy. A number of different arguments were advanced in support of the abolition of prostitution. The French system was challenged by Protestants in England and Switzerland (Geneva and Neuchâtel). In England the Contagious Diseases Acts of 1866, 1867, and 1869 had introduced a modicum of regulation by creating cities and ports in which prostitution was officially monitored. Josephine Butler, along with various British physicians and Quakers, launched an international protest modeled on developments in the United States. The movement was moralistic and sought to ban extramarital sex in all its forms: between 1870 and 1879 some 9,667 petitions gathered 2,150, 941 signatures.[12] By contrast, feminists and radicals, mainly in Paris, invoked liberty and the rights of man in their battles with the vice squad and protests against the jailing of prostitutes. Various petitions were rejected by the Chamber of Deputies. When the Bloc des Gauches (United Left) came to power in 1902, health concerns reinforced worries about public order and strengthened the belief in regulation. The law of April 11, 1908, ordered that prostitutes under the age of eighteen be placed in asylums.

In the late nineteenth century the problem of the "white slave trade" fired the imagination of newspaper readers and sold papers everywhere. Thorough parliamentary investigations were conducted in England and Belgium. The Hungarian and Austrian governments also worried about the problem. In 1881 the traffic in women was officially denounced in Geneva. In 1895 the French Senate approved a bill directed against people who forced women into prostitution, but the Chamber of Deputies failed to consider it. Only Germany took concrete steps. In 1897 traffickers became liable to fines and imprisonment, and extradition treaties were signed. Representatives of many European nations (Spain and Italy did not attend) met in a congress to consider the issue in 1899. From the work of this group it became clear that a veritable myth had been constructed, a myth fed by the press and by anxiety born of the most virulent fears of women's sexual liberation, xenophobia, and racism. The "white slave trade" was not nearly as extensive as people imagined, and many women were perfectly aware of the nature of the "contract" they signed before being shipped off to America, Australia, the Orient, or South Africa at the time of the Boer War. Only Sweden seems to have been exempt from this trade. The report, of course, did not intend to obscure the social aspect of the problem or to deny its causes. Another congress held in Paris in 1902 did not condemn the regulatory approach taken by the French. On April 3, 1903, the legislature passed a law condemning only trade in women forced into prostitution by violence, deceit, or threats. The international convention of May 4, 1910, borrowed the language of the French law, while the international accord of May 8, 1904, promulgated in France on February 7, 1905, provided for legal defense and repatriation of victims.

Victimization marginalized women. To state falsely that a woman had been raped was considered an attack on her honor and grounds for compensatory payment.[13] In French *attentat aux moeurs* (literally: attack on mores) is the expression for lewd or indecent behavior, indicating that the offense is more against the public order than against the victim of the crime. The French Penal Code of 1791 specified only two kinds of rape: simple rape (punishable by six years in irons) and aggravated rape, which was distinguished from the former by the age of the victim, the use of violence, and the involvement of confederates (and punishable by up to twelve years in irons). The abduction of a minor female under the age of fifteen for the purpose of rape or prostitution was subject to the same punishment. The Penal Code of 1810 did not distinguish between rape and "attacks on chastity accompanied by violence," a crime punishable by imprisonment (Article 330). If the victim was under fifteen, the sentence could include a term at hard labor or even life at hard labor if the criminal held a position of authority over the victim or there was an accomplice (Article 332). Anyone encouraging the prostitution of a minor under the age of twenty-one was liable to a prison term of six months to two years plus a fine, and the term could be increased to five years if the accused exercised paternal authority over the victim (articles 332–334). The law of April 28, 1832, which remained all but unchanged until December 23, 1984, modified Article 331: any "attack on the chastity" of a child under the age of eleven was subject to imprisonment (thirteen years as of May 13, 1863). Above all, the law focused on the crime of rape, although rape was never really defined. For the courts rape was an act of male violence involving penile penetration of the vagina, and judges were particularly interested in the seriousness of the violence, for there was always suspicion that a woman was lying when she claimed to have given in to force.[14] The punishment was a term of imprisonment at hard labor, longer if the victim was under fifteen.

Another form of criminal conduct that was of particular concern to women related to abortion and infanticide. French women took a dim view of the neo-Malthusian movement that flourished in the late nineteenth century, particularly in England, Germany, and the United States, all countries of Protestant tradition. One reason for this was that French women had worked out forms of cooperation outside the boundaries of morality and law. By word of mouth relatives, friends, and neighbors exchanged information about what to do and where to go to save the "honor" of a compromised woman. Methods of birth control were also passed around, especially among women who had already given birth to several children.[15] At the turn of the century, a time when many governments were concerned with keeping up the birth rate, the number of abortions increased, perhaps as an expression of popular feminism.[16] The Penal Code of 1791 provided a punishment of twenty years in irons for anyone who performed an abortion. Article 317 of the Penal Code of 1810 specified a term in prison for both the person who performed the abortion and the woman, whether or not she consented to the operation. Infanticide, which the code defined as the murder of a newborn, was punishable by death. In reality, however, juries of ordinary people were reluctant to impose punishments that were widely regarded as too harsh. Accordingly, the law of November 21, 1901, reclassified infanticide from crime to misdemeanor, which meant that cases would be heard not by juries in the *cours d'assises* but by magistrates in the *tribunaux correctionels*. The legislature's intention was thereby to reduce the number of acquittals or findings of mitigating circumstances to avoid the death penalty. In France no distinction was made between the murder of a bastard or a legitimate child, whereas most other modern European codes provided for reduced punishment when the motive for infanticide was to save the mother's honor. The fact is that most of the women accused of this crime were poor and unwed, usually servants.

The Family Trap

In the late nineteenth century the question of women's civil-legal competence exercised legislators, writers, playwrights, and feminists more than it did the man or woman in the street or on the factory floor. Throughout Europe and America women were under the legal authority of their husbands. How could it be that as soon as a fully capable woman of legal age married, she became legally incompetent, as if she were a minor or insane? What justified the role of the state in this realm of law, which regulated relations between individuals? To be sure, the importance attached to the family as the foundation of the social order played a part: "It is through the lesser fatherland of the family that one is attached to the greater. Good fathers, good husbands, and good sons make good citizens."[17] In France it was impossible to circumvent the rules governing marriage and the family, for those rules were enshrined in law.

There is a distinction between having a right and exercising it: it was an important subtlety of the law that women had rights that they were nevertheless incompetent to exercise. The justification of marital authority must be counted among the finest flowers of legal rhetoric. The husband's authority, we learn, has a practical purpose: to administer the "conjugal society," to govern wife and children in carrying out their traditional roles. Late-eighteenth-century philosophers held this authority to be in conformity with natural law, although some, such as Burlamaqui, felt that it ought to be moderated by natural equity. By contrast, Rousseau could not imagine woman as being anything other than dependent on man. In this area the contribution of the Revolution was ambiguous: while women were recognized as individuals and the tyranny of the husband was abolished, equality was not established between husband and wife. This French solution of the problem remained in practice until the appearance of modern legal codes, which in some ways took a different tack, because the role assigned to the wife is roughly the same in all societies of the patriarchal type. This was especially true in France, where the legal system was of mixed origin, even if the Code of 1804 incorporated large parts of the prerevolutionary customary law in force in the Paris region. The wife's dependent status and legal incompetence were based in part on Roman maxims as revised by eighteenth-century jurists and in part on Germanic custom. The married woman (model for all women) exists only in and through the family. Everywhere the law was conceived in terms of bourgeois women. Its purpose was to regulate a woman's person and property even after marriage.

Submission to the Ends of Marriage

The supremacy of the husband "is a homage rendered by the wife to the power that protects her."[18] The husband in effect derived his superiority from the idea of women's fragility. Taken from Roman law, the concept of *fragilitas* referred not so much to natural infirmity as to the grounds for the protection of minors. The inconsistency of the law is all the more glaring, for there was no unequivocal declaration of the husband's supremacy. His supremacy was justified on grounds of the marriage partner's physical inferiority, from which presumably only married women suffered. The husband was to be "regarded as the sovereign and absolute judge of the family honor."[19]

Thus it was considered grounds for divorce if it could be proved that a wife had transmitted syphilis to her husband, because the disease in that case was necessarily the product of adultery. In contrast, a husband was not deemed culpable even if he knowingly and repeatedly transmitted syphilis to an irreproachable woman. Similarly, allegations that a woman had concealed certain facts prior to her marriage (such as pregnancy or having been listed as a prostitute) could be used against her.

The Duty to Obey "A husband owes protection to his wife, a wife, obedience to her husband," according to Article 213 of the French Civil Code—and there are others just as bad. In some, such as the Norwegian code or the Italian and German codes of the late nineteenth century, the style is less direct. Whether explicit or not, however, the same idea underlies legislation everywhere. "These words are harsh, but they are taken from Saint Paul, and that authority is as good as any other," according to one of the drafters of the Civil Code.[20] In countries of Judeo-Christian tradition, the creation myth that tells of man's having been created first and of woman's culpability in the original sin has done serious harm. Napoleon said that Article 213 ought to be read aloud at weddings, for in a century when women "forget the sense of their inferiority" it was important "to remind them frankly of the submission they owe to the man who is to become the arbiter of their fate."[21] The First Consul's antifeminism is well known. Yet it would be misleading to see this remark as nothing more than an aberration, the vengeance of a vain, cuckolded general. In fact, his statement is a crisply military formulation of what men believed and nearly all women accepted.

In principle a woman took the nationality of her husband unless it conflicted with some state interest. This was the case after 1899 in France, where there were fears about the purity of the race. In England the laws were also tightened in the wake of "abuses" associated with prostitution. A French wife gave up her maiden name, although there was no explicit law requiring her to do so. After a divorce a husband could forbid his wife to use his name: he had only lent it to her, as it were. But the opposite was the rule in English-speaking countries. In still other places husband and wife combined both families' names.

The husband was charged with the noble duty of keeping his wife's conduct under surveillance. The "domestic magistrate [must be able] to combine . . . force with authority so as to command respect."[22] "A husband's corrective actions and outbursts of temper" are not always to be condemned, because "the authority that nature and law give the husband is for the purpose of guiding the conduct of the wife."[23] While English husbands were probably no crueler than husbands elsewhere, they enjoyed, until 1870, an impunity derived from the married woman's absolute helplessness. In 1840 a judge, quoting Bacon, authorized a husband to beat his wife and hold her prisoner so long as he did so without cruelty.[24] After publication of the article "Wife Torture in England" and years of propaganda from the *English Women's Review*, Parliament in 1878 passed an act allowing English women to petition for separation on grounds of assault. An 1893 statute extended this to include "persistent cruelty," which the courts interpreted fairly broadly as grounds for divorce, much as the French courts did for *injure grave* or the Spanish courts for *faltas*.

A husband was supposed to be "informed of the general spirit of conversations held and influences felt" by his wife outside his presence and control. An exchange of letters, for instance, was "an infraction of the contract, a sort of moral infidelity," and a husband could "place obstacles in the way of independent acts."[25] He could therefore intercept letters sent or received by his wife and could even order the post office to return letters to him rather than deliver them. If a husband obtained letters to or from his wife by legal or surreptitious means, he could use them in divorce proceedings, but his wife could not make use of his letters. A woman could not order a servant to intercept her husband's mail or make use of any correspondence between her husband and a third party.[26] There was, however, some evolution in French case law: the courts refused, for example, to consider letters written by a woman to a female friend, who had solicited them for the purpose of turning them over to the woman's husband, a transaction that the court deemed improper. Privacy of correspondence was also an issue for female lawyers, doctors, merchants, and functionaries. In this respect French law had little in common with English law: in England, after 1870 at any rate, a woman's correspondence was considered private because the law recognized her as an individual. Many French jurists felt that such rules undermined authority and threatened family unity.[27]

Husband and wife were supposed to support and assist each other. While the woman owed him submission, the man's duty was to supply his wife with the necessities of life: food, lodging, clothing, medicine. This included pocket money (variously known as *Nadelgeld, épingles,* or "pin money"). Even after a separation of property, the wife's income went to defray household expenses. In England a woman could not bring suit against her husband for nonsupport until 1857, when abandoned wives were given the right to live on the proceeds of property that would eventually be awarded to them by the court. After 1886 a husband could be forced to pay his estranged wife a modest weekly allowance. After 1895 divorce courts were granted the power to impose such alimony in cases of "persistent cruelty" or nonsupport. The United States had similar laws. In France abandonment was not subject to criminal sanction until 1924.

A woman was obliged to live in the home chosen by her husband, provided that it suited the family's social status. This was to allow her "at least to maintain her dignity outside, even though she forfeit all happiness inside."[28] A man could use force to compel his wife to return home. Countless court orders were issued to return women to their homes *manu militari,* that is, under escort by a bailiff, who was authorized to call on armed force "so as not to place at the mercy of the wife's whim, not to say crime, a new kind of marital separation subversive of the general rights of the body social."[29] Judges could order the garnishment of a woman's income or even seizure of her clothing on the simple request of her husband, without examination of the grounds. The husband, for his part, was permitted to deny his wife "nourishment" if she refused to return home. In Germany coercion was permitted until 1900, when it was supplanted by a right to sue for restoration of marital life. In one way or another husbands possessed the means to compel their wives to reside in the homes they chose.

Upholding the Legitimate Family "Conjugal duty" permitted a man to use violence, within limits laid down by "nature," custom, and law and so long as it was not for purposes contrary to "the legitimate end of marriage."[30] If, therefore, a man forced his wife to have normal sexual relations not involving "serious assault," there was no possibility of charging him with rape, lewdness, or indecency.[31] By the end of the century the courts were insisting that men not treat their wives "like prostitutes," defiling them by "unnatural contact."[32] On these grounds repeated use of a condom over a period of years and against the wife's will was judged to be an offense.[33]

To make sure that reproduction was legitimate, female infidelity was punished harshly. The law was in any case suspicious of extramarital affection: a passionate friendship between a married man and another man was acknowledged to be a purely "spiritual communion," except when the friend exhibited an "unhealthy sensibility," "a sort of hysteria of the brain," and this was deemed to be a "serious injury."[34] Obviously the law mistrusted deviant male sexuality. But a woman's infidelity raised the prospect of introducing a stranger into the family, disrupting the just distribution of family property. Hence it was punished far more severely than male infidelity. Only a partner in marriage could file a charge of adultery. Nevertheless, when adultery was grounds for divorce or separation, the magistrate could impose a sentence as in a criminal case—the only such instance in French civil law. Adultery was recognized almost everywhere as grounds for legal separation, but only in Latin countries was it considered a crime. In Germany (1900), England, the United States, and Scandinavia, the tendency was to decriminalize it.

In adultery cases the mode of proof and punishment of the guilty party and his or her accomplice was relative to the sex of the party, and the husband possessed certain rights that the wife lacked. Up to 1884 in France, for example, a wife's adultery was a single act that could be proved by any available means (including purloined letters). But a husband was guilty of adultery only if the offense continued for a certain period of time, and punishment was possible only if he kept his concubine under the same roof as his wife—in which case the crime was in a sense almost that of defiling a sacred place with the sacrilege of bigamy. The only admissible proof was to catch him in the act or to produce letters that somehow came into the possession of the wife. There was controversy over whether the keeping of the concubine had to be contemporaneous with the wife's complaint or not. Here, the "conjugal domicile" was strictly interpreted to mean the home that a man shared with his wife; if he kept a woman in a secret place, he was not subject to punishment, although the law viewed such behavior as constituting a "serious injury." In all Latin countries the husband's sin was discounted by the law unless it constituted a public scandal or included some aggravating circumstance. In England a man could be charged with adultery only if combined with bigamy, incest, a "crime against nature," an abduction, or a rape.

Article 337 of the French Penal Code provided for a prison term of three months to two years for women found guilty of adultery. Although the maximum sentence was imposed frequently throughout much of the nineteenth century,[35] the average sentence fell between fifteen days and four months in 1880; by 1890 it had decreased to fifteen days, and by 1910 it was usually just a simple fine.[36] Until Article 463 of the Penal Code was amended in 1870, it was held that the minimum sentence of three months could not be reduced, it being impossible to find mitigating circumstances for a crime that was an offense to law, morality, and religion. As in any crime, the prosecutor was empowered to appeal the sentence if he deemed it too light.

An adulterous husband risked no more than a fine of 100 to 2,000 francs (Article 339). An adulterous woman's male accomplice who was caught in the act or convicted by his own letters risked the same prison term as the woman along with a fine of 100 to 2,000 francs (Article 338). In theory the prosecutor was not allowed to bring charges if the cuckolded husband failed to file a complaint against his wife, but this was a controversial area. Furthermore, in the absence of written evidence many authors held that a concubine could not be punished. But fine calculations determined whose honor had suffered more, that of the concubine's husband or that of the deceived wife, in cases where the adulterous woman's husband opposed prosecution of his wife. The answer was, that of the deceived wife. In contrast, the concubine lacked "the usual excuse of the adulterous woman, seduction or an isolated offense, her life being devoted to the neglect of her duties."[37] The "sovereign power to pardon" was delegated to the deceived husband, who could nullify the sentence by taking his wife back into his home.[38] This pardon did not extend to the accomplice.

In addition to all these inequalities, there was one scandalous fact: if a man murdered his wife or her lover, caught in the act in the "conjugal domicile" (which the courts interpreted to mean the *de facto* domicile), the crime was excusable under the "red article" of the French Penal Code (Article 324). This meant that legally the husband risked nothing. "More unfortunate than guilty," the murderer was to receive only "light punishment," which accorded well with the prevalent attitude in Mediterranean countries.[39] Under the Colombian Civil Code of 1893, the father or husband was similarly free of guilt: witness the affair in Gabriel García Márquez's *Chronicle of a Death Foretold.* Alone among European countries France maintained this provision of its Code until 1975.[40] In Belgium, Italy, Spain, Portugal, and Ticino (a Swiss canton), both husband and wife could avail themselves of the excuse of justifiable homicide. Since the law in many countries prohibited adulterous couples from marrying, the fact that it is easier for husbands to prove adultery than for wives constituted an additional punishment for women. This provision was eliminated from French law in 1904.

The Rights of Parenthood Although liberated bourgeois, intellectuals, and artists promoted free love on the eve of World War I, there was little support for it from other segments of society. Cohabitation had no place in law. Since wives were assumed to be faithful, there was a presumption of paternity in favor of a woman's lawful husband. A man or his heirs could legally disavow a child, but that right was limited to cases in which the impossibility of paternity was evident, not to say a matter of public notoriety. The paterfamilias was thus the "owner" of any child born to his wife. Until 1964 France and several other countries availed itself of a procedure known as "guardianship in the womb," the intention being to protect a man's posthumous child from its own mother. Likewise, a man might choose not to disavow a child in order to prevent his wife and the real father from adopting the child and making it legitimate after divorce and remarriage. The presumption of marital paternity was so strong that if a man officially recognized a child born to an adulterous woman as his, the recognition was considered to be proof of adultery but not of paternity.[41] This paradoxical situation was a consequence of the rights accorded to the head of the family; although it is true that parental authority belonged to both parents, it was exercised by the father alone so long as the marriage lasted—yet another subtle legal distinction. If the father was absent, banished, or deprived of his rights, the mother replaced him. If he died, she became the legal guardian in the absence of any specific provision to the contrary in the will of the deceased. In France and elsewhere a man could name an adviser to assist his widow, and if she remarried, the family council (made up entirely of men) had to consent to her continuing as guardian of her children by appointing her new husband as subrogate guardian. French law limited the powers of the mother, whose authority over her children was less than their father's had been. If she was granted custody after a divorce, the father retained the right to oversee the children's education, and his consent was necessary before the children could marry. In Germany a father found guilty in a divorce proceeding did not forfeit his right to administer the property of his minor children. In England prior to 1870 paternal omnipotence placed women in a desperate situation, without rights in regard to their children and vulnerable to their husband's blackmail (see Thackeray's *Barry Lyndon*). The father had the absolute right to take the children from their mother and entrust them to whomever he wished. When, in 1839, a cautious early bill authorized a judge to order an investigation, it caused a scandal.

Because of the high value placed on the family, illegitimacy was thoroughly condemned. Feminists demanded criminal and civil penalties against men who seduced young women; they also wanted to remove impediments to the determination of a child's paternity. In the United States, thanks to political action by women who made use of the political rights they had acquired, seduction was severely punished, and a man who committed adultery with an unmarried woman was required to marry her. In France a one-sided interpretation of judicial procedures under prerevolutionary law led to a ban on investigations of paternity at the time of the Revolution. Prior to 1789, when a seduced woman named the "father" of her child, judges did not recognize full kinship and the child did not become a member of the father's family. If there was presumptive proof of paternity, the child might be awarded a modest pension, payment of which was difficult to enforce. During the nineteenth century, in cases where the evidence of paternity was overwhelming, the courts gradually moved toward allowing the mother to recover damages from her seducer under Article 1382 of the Civil Code. By the end of the century it was possible to file paternity suits in most European countries, including even Spain. In France it was not until November 16, 1912, that a restrictive new law was adopted. The pregnancy had to be the result of rape, kidnapping, flagrant cohabitation, misrepresentation, or obvious abuse of authority, and it had to be followed by either unambiguous written acknowledgment of paternity or clear evidence of support of the child. The law did not apply to the colonies (which tells us a great deal about the treatment of "native wives"). Paternity suits were automatically dismissed, moreover, if the mother's morality was not beyond reproach.

The Civil Incompetence of Married Women

Until the eve of World War II (and in France until 1965) a woman who wished to work had to obtain her husband's permission, "because no one in the world has better knowledge of the extent of her intelligence."[42] Whether this permission had to be explicit (as in France at the turn of the century) or tacit (the husband being required to file suit to prevent his wife from working), a woman whose husband refused to allow her to work could petition the courts or some supervisory authority to overrule the disapproving spouse, but judges were quick to invoke the interests of the family to deny such requests. Without her husband's authorization a woman could not take an examination, enroll in a university, open a bank account, obtain a passport or a driver's license, or seek treatment in a hospital, to name only a few of her disabilities. Nor could she file suit. French law went so far as to insist that a woman who wished to annul her marriage could not be exempt from "this act of deference and submission."[43] A woman could not even file a criminal complaint against her husband. To sign a legal document she needed special authorization unless she ran a business of her own with her husband's consent. In Italy after 1896 a man could grant his wife blanket authorization, and women were entitled to bring suit (not so in Spain). In Portugal from 1867 on husband and wife signed most legal documents jointly. If the man was incapacitated, banished, or absent for some other reason, his wife was competent to act in his place.

Western European countries had long known two types of patrimonial relations between husband and wife: customary practices of Germanic inspiration under which all property was placed under the husband's control, and Roman law, which theoretically recognized the wife's independence but placed so many restrictions on it as to render that independence all but meaningless in many cases.[44] The laws of matrimonial property were thus based on two distinct principles: either community property or (partial or complete) separation of property. Just as the law distinguished between having a right and exercising it, so too were legal acts distinguished as either acts of *disposition* (which could alter the value of a patrimony) or acts of *administration* (which were intended to preserve the value of a property). To exercise one's rights of ownership was to have the power to dispose of or to administer one's property, to receive income from that property, or even to destroy the property's income-producing potential. Under the system of "nonuniversal community property" neither spouse relinquished ownership of real property owned before the marriage or inherited or received as a gift afterward. The fund of common property included revenue from real estate, movable property, negotiable securities, and earnings. Under the system of separate property, each spouse retained ownership and shared household costs. The dowry system *(régime dotal)* was a system of separate property intended to preserve intact a portion of the wife's wealth for the duration of the marriage.

Generally, one system was adopted by most couples, thereby avoiding the need for a marriage contract. In the community property system adopted in France under the Napoleonic Code, the husband became the head of the family with full power over all community property (although his power over gifts was sometimes restricted). He also administered his wife's patrimony but could dispose of her property only with her authorization. In Sweden and Scotland the wife had the power to administer community property. In Italy and Russia (under the Code of 1833) as well as in most English-speaking countries, separation of property was the general rule.

England was an exception, however, and one that is worth pausing to examine more closely. Until 1870 a woman under common law lost her legal personhood, which was subsumed in that of her husband *(feme covert)*. In Blackstone's words, "the husband and wife are one and that one is the husband." The husband assumed ownership of his wife's personal property and was not obliged to render accounts. But there was also, distinct from the common law, the law of equity, which was established by the courts. The woman enjoyed equitable ownership (use) of her property, over which she retained full rights (separate use). She could increase her powers by extending the amount of property thus subject to equity, rather than by limiting her husband's powers over their joint property. The continental idea of a woman's having rights that she could exercise only under her husband's authority was unknown in English law. Feminists nevertheless waged a vigorous campaign to change the law, because the law of equity benefited only the wealthy. The Matrimonial Causes Act of 1857 awarded legal ownership to a woman separated from or abandoned by her husband under a so-called protection order intended to ensure "statutory separate property." A French woman separated from her husband did not enjoy an equivalent right until 1894.[45] After the passage of new laws in 1870 and 1874, the patrimonial independence of English couples became complete. In 1893 English women obtained the right to make wills, a right already enjoyed by women in most other countries.

In the United States the principles of common law were modified without recourse to equity. A far-reaching New York state law awarded married women full powers over their property and professional earnings. One by one, most states passed similar laws. Women had full rights under the system of separate property. Only states that had known a Spanish or French influence retained a measure of community property, most notably Louisiana, where the customary law of Paris as modified by the Napoleonic Code was enforced, just as it was in Quebec.

In the dowry system widely used in Italy, Chile, Peru, and southern France, the husband often administered his wife's property. Property acquired after marriage, however, was sometimes treated as community property (in contrast to the usual practice); this was the case in southwestern France and the Swiss canton of Ticino. The fact that the dowry was inalienable impeded commercial transactions. Hence marriage contracts or court orders sometimes allowed for exceptions in the name of prudent administration and family interest. In France, however, the courts made matters worse by extending inalienability to include movable property and even negotiable securities. Clearly the Napoleonic Code limited the competence of married women under the dowry system, which wealthy women, particularly in Provence, had learned to use shrewdly under the Ancien Régime.

The system of joint ownership was peculiar to Switzerland and parts of Germany (Prussia, Saxony, Oldenburg, and the Baltic provinces). It was officially sanctioned by the codes of 1900 and 1907. The husband, as the head of the family, administered all property and received all revenues, but ownership remained separate. He needed his wife's approval to dispose of property she brought into the marriage, and the wife retained full competence with respect to her personal property. In case of disagreement, either spouse could appeal to the trusteeship court, and from 1900 on a wife could charge her husband with abusing his rights under the system.

Because of the way sex roles were distributed, a woman needed the wherewithal to provide for the daily needs of her family. For this purpose, the law granted her what was called a *mandat* in France or an "agency of necessity" in England, a power of attorney allowing her to represent her husband and borrow against his property as well as their property in common in amounts proportionate to the income of the household, a fundamental limitation that allowed the courts to deny expenses deemed excessive. The husband could of course revoke this power, although this raised the thorny issue of how third parties were to be notified. In fact, it was generally the woman in working-class households who held the family cash and dispensed pocket money to her husband. But this was merely a social practice and not a right, even if wives sometimes negotiated with employers to have their husbands' pay remitted directly to them.[46] The law recognized the wife as the keeper of the family savings in the middle classes. As of April 9, 1881, in France women were authorized to deposit money in savings accounts; it took longer to gain the right to withdraw money, but that too eventually came almost everywhere. Some saw these laws as "feminist" in inspiration, but governments were also keen to encourage savings banks so as to funnel cash that would otherwise lie idle back into circulation. The same logic applies to retirement savings programs.

Feminists insisted that women be allowed to retain the fruits of their labor. In France the law of July 13, 1907, established a system of *biens réservés* (earnings, savings, and interest accrued therefrom).[47] This money was to be used primarily for household needs, but a woman was free to spend it as she saw fit, although her husband could appeal to the courts if he felt she was abusing this privilege. Unfortunately, this statute is a perfect example of the limitation of the law when it becomes logically incoherent. Nothing was done about the legal incompetence of women in general, so there was no zeal to implement the law in practice. Similar laws were passed in many countries at the end of the nineteenth century, and they were more effectively enforced in countries that took a less restrictive attitude toward women's rights than did France. Italy adopted such a law in 1865 and Switzerland in 1894.

Women without Men

"Women without men": it was indeed in such terms that the issue was framed. It was exceptional for a woman never to marry, although the number of unmarried women in the nineteenth century was relatively high. The woman without a husband was therefore of no interest in the eyes of the law. Minor girls were dependents of their fathers. Single adult women, although legally competent, were socially marginal, apart from the rare intellectual or artist. Life for unmarried women was generally rather bleak, although in the United States some single women banded together in organizations that gave them a certain influence. In some places women who did not marry remained, at least in principle, the wards of a guardian throughout their lives; this was the case until the final third of the century in parts of Scandinavia, Germany, and Switzerland. When a marriage dissolved as a result of divorce or death (annulment was rare), the wife regained her legal freedom. In Catholic countries for a long time there was no divorce but only legal separation, which left many marital obligations including that of fidelity intact, even though this conflicted with the natalist policies of certain governments. Divorce was not allowed in France from 1816 to 1884, or in Spain, Portugal, Italy, or Central and South America. Elsewhere divorce was legal.

The French Constitution of 1791 had secularized marriage and legally freed women from the weight of the Christian tradition. Girls as well as boys had been recognized as adults at twenty-one and had been entitled to an equal share of their parents' estate; now women won the right to make and break contracts. The divorce law of September 20–25, 1792, is remarkable for recognizing absolute equality between husband and wife, particularly in regard to divorce by mutual consent. But divorce was soon deemed a threat to the family, and in practice it was so severely restricted that it virtually vanished until 1975. Revolutionary law recognized two grounds for divorce other than mutual consent: incompatibility of mood or character and specific conditions or offenses such as dementia, conviction of a serious crime, assault, cruelty, flagrant moral turpitude, abandonment for more than two years, and emigration. Although adultery was not mentioned, it was covered by "moral turpitude" and "cruelty" and invoked primarily against women. The Civil Code all but eliminated divorce by mutual consent and recognized only these grounds: adultery, assault, cruelty, and conviction of a serious crime. Codes in other countries either specified all permissible grounds for divorce or left it to the discretion of the judge to decide what complaints were serious enough to justify ending a marriage.

The nineteenth century took a rather strict view of divorce, not only legally but also socially. Obstacles were placed in the way, and the parties were obliged to go to court. In some places a husband and wife who divorced were not permitted to remarry each other, and an adulterous spouse could not marry his or her partner. Women were forbidden to remarry within three hundred days of either a divorce or the death of a husband, a measure intended to ensure the legitimacy of their offspring.

In Italy divorce was permitted from 1796 to 1815. In France it was made illegal for religious reasons on May 8, 1816. After a long battle it was reinstated by the Naquet Law of July 27, 1884. The grounds (other than mutual consent) were the same as those in the Civil Code of 1804, except that henceforth cases of adultery were treated equally for both sexes. The law of June 6, 1908, allowed a separation that continued for more than three years to be turned into a divorce. In England divorce was not permitted until 1857; there was religiously sanctioned separation, however, and the wealthy could pay for a divorce by special act of Parliament. The Divorce Act of 1857 legalized divorce, and its influence was felt in England's former colonies, although divorce laws in the United States varied considerably from state to state. In France it was mainly women who resorted to divorce proceedings for abandonment or assault, especially during the Revolution and, later, after 1851, when legal aid was instituted (at the time only separations were legal, not divorce). Divorce remained rare, however. It was virtually unknown in the countryside and took place chiefly within the middle class. Although divorce freed women from tyrannical husbands, it left them alone, without a place of their own in society even when they received alimony. This was one of the paradoxes of a situation where the legal consequences of divorce were not adequate to cope with the social consequences.

One would expect that widows would be treated better than divorcées. Although the grasping widow is a figure familiar from literature, the reality was quite different. While a few wealthy widows may have carried on in a high-handed manner in the countryside, and others might have carried on the family business after the death of an artisan or merchant husband, most lived in straitened circumstances, protected but also constrained by their families. A widow might suddenly find herself confronted by greedy heirs and insistent creditors. Under prerevolutionary French law and certain modern legal codes widows enjoyed certain advantages (such as the right to income from their husbands' or community property). But the French Civil Code, unlike all other nineteenth-century codes, did not concern itself with survivor's rights. Until 1891 the surviving spouse was the residuary legatee, ahead of the state. Survivors had rights to the retirement pensions of functionaries and to authors' royalties under the law of July 14, 1866. A widow was entitled to "sustenance," housing, and clothing for three months and forty days. She also inherited the income from her husband's property for life, and full ownership if there were no children.

How could a married woman protect herself from an all-powerful husband's dishonest or incompetent management? It was generally accepted that she could go to court or to a supervisory authority to ask, often too late, for protective measures, such as the appointment of a trustee or a separation of property. A woman could place a lien on her husband's property if the law did not prohibit it. But such a step could hinder her husband's business. A woman was therefore allowed to drop her lien in favor of the buyers of her husband's property or his creditors (laws of March 23, 1855, and February 13, 1889), and as a result notaries began demanding that both spouses sign any contract involving the husband's property. In England a woman could stipulate a "restraint on anticipation" to prevent any transaction involving a specified property. If the marriage dissolved, she could insist on liquidation of community property.

By the eve of World War I most modern legal codes continued to favor the husband over the wife, but they also sought to promote greater legal cooperation. Given the extraordinary expansion of credit, the increased mobility of wealth, the speed with which transactions could be concluded, and the increase in the number of women who worked, the law could not remain unchanged. But the changes did not affect the poor, and work was considered a necessity only for unmarried women; for wives it was considered a source of supplementary income. Legally speaking, the problem seems to have been resolved most equitably in the English-speaking countries, where property was kept separate. But socially it was another matter, for it was difficult for women to survive in a competitive society that denied them the weapons needed to fight on a footing of equality with men. In other countries, and most notably France, the problem has only been nibbled away at, and married women are likely to suffer from legal handicaps for a long time to come.

In public law the internal contradictions are obvious. Women have been most successful in winning political rights in Scandinavia and in the former English colonies, which went much further in this direction than England itself.

The legal status of women is an excellent indicator of tensions between society and government. Legal controversies also reveal internal inconsistencies, reflecting the doubts of a conservative and nervous group. Admittedly, the legal inferiority of women is shocking at a time when large numbers of females are moving into the work force at the lowest levels, while a few educated women are finding their access to the professions denied on no other grounds but sex. Most women carry on the struggle in their everyday lives, far removed from the precincts of the law. While many women must work hard to survive without a husband or inherited wealth, the majority do not come into contact with the law except insofar as it defines the conditions of their lives. The fate of women cannot be separated from that of men, if only because the law is common to both. But the law is also the regulator of social, and therefore of sexual, relations. As society has evolved, the idea of complementarity rather than equality between the sexes has made headway. As the American example reminds us, the much-denounced "matriarchal power" is nothing other than a consequence of sexual segregation, which leads, in the name of specific sex roles under conditions of legal equality, to a kind of social inequality that reveals the pernicious consequences of divorcing law from social and economic reality.

Translated from the French by Arthur Goldhammer

two

The Production of Women, Real and Imaginary

The term "production" will be used here in two senses, one passive (how are women produced?), the other active (what do they produce?). In other words, women are not mere agents of reproduction but subjects as well as objects of production. They are not only creatures but also creators, constantly influencing the processes that make them.

Throughout the nineteenth century women were "fabricated" by religious precepts and rituals as well as by a system of education more interested in good breeding than in good teaching; what teaching there was, was concentrated on practical knowledge, etiquette, social graces, and the art of self-presentation. The "finishing" of young ladies remained fairly constant, its nature dictated by the duties of wife, mother, and housekeeper, tirelessly inculcated by a choir in unison of preachers, philosophers, moralists, and statesmen. Formal schooling was less predictable, because the curriculum depended on the general level of culture to which women were expected to adapt and on political choices that varied from place to place and time to time.

A great age of pedagogy, the nineteenth century learned to appreciate the power of education and the childrearing role of the family in general and of mothers in particular. Theories and programs for the education of young women proliferated. Public schools, boarding schools, and courses sprang up everywhere. Sometimes girls' schools competed with one another, but they remained exclusively female, because it was felt strongly that women needed a separate education. Although progress in women's literacy probably ceased for a time after the Revolution, it made great strides later on. Girls' education was at first private and mainly religious, but later it became a matter of public concern, at least in countries such as France and Belgium where a secular model that allowed for the advancement of women gradually took hold. The most interesting consequence of this was an emphasis on a more stringent code of female behavior: "virtue" took the place of God.

The education of women was a religious and political issue as well as an ethnic one in a Europe of growing nationalist aspirations. All over the Continent, from Athens to Budapest, from the Austro-Hungarian Empire to the Russia of the czars (which was the first country, by the way, to open its universities to women), hotly contested reforms resulted in new curricula, higher educational standards, and broader fields of study. Yet reforms were sometimes hampered by recurrent fears that overeducated women would abandon the family hearth and pose as rivals to men. The frontiers—institutional as well as theoretical—of knowledge shifted but never disappeared.

Because the nineteenth century recognized the power of images to encourage imitation and transgression, women, looked upon as nervous, excitable creatures, were denied full access to the culture of print. The Battle of the Book had been raging since the Renaissance. Yet we would do well to be sensitive to certain cultural differences. Protestants, particularly those of the so-called Awakening, showed much greater confidence in the judgment of women than did Catholics; thus women in countries where the Reformation dominated were more advanced than their counterparts elsewhere. In France, Protestants played a well-known role in creating the model for a system of secular education. Religious and lay authorities competed for the right to define what women should be allowed to read: they gave their blessing to certain genres and withheld it from others; they offered advice and assembled collections of "good books" and newspapers for women, and we must acknowledge that on the whole they helped to expand women's horizons.

They also had the effect of heightening age distinctions: little girls, adolescents, young ladies, and young married women were distinct groups to be molded as well as disciplined, and "molding" could have positive connotations involving greater awareness of the world and the things in it. Because translation was looked upon as a female chore, women learned foreign languages and studied other cultures, for which they were able to serve as intermediaries. And because it was considered more legitimate for women to write travel books than to try their hands at writing novels, many conceived a desire to travel. As secretaries to "great men," moreover, they made their way into the creative circle.

Thus they were able to take advantage of what was given—or left—to them for their benefit and pleasure and eventually became producers of knowledge in their own right. We must pay very close attention to the diversions and appropriations and modest forms of tinkering whereby oppressed people lay claim to words and things, for without sensitivity to such things no gender-aware history of cultural practices is possible. We must find out how and what women read if we hope to flesh out the image of the "female reader," whose thoughts were a compound of religious reverie, domestic daydream, and erotic fantasy. We must find out how women became writers and what they wrote—often letters, in an age that emphasized correspondence as a primary means of communication, but sometimes books as well. We must find out how women became artists and what they produced. While music, the language of the gods, remained largely out of reach of creative women, some wielded the paintbrush as professional illustrators, designers, and even talented painters who showed their works, some of them masterpieces, in public. Yet the obstacles to creativity were formidable, so formidable that if the unthinkable happened and a truly "great" woman painter or writer arrived on the scene, she was likely to be classified as a genre artist (Berthe Morisot as a "nursery painter," George Sand as a "rural writer") or denounced or even locked up (Camille Claudel): for genius, whether a divine or biological mystery, could only be masculine.

In any case, ambition, which made men miserable, made women even more so. Was not woman's genius directed toward life—to live in harmony and unity? Some thought so, and they were among the greatest minds of their time. No doubt the obstacle to creativity lay partly in woman's acceptance of a separate role and of the representations on which it was based, both in the symbolic order, which governs such separateness, and in the linguistic order that permits it to be expressed.

G.F.—M.P.

5

Artistic and Literary Idolatries

Stéphane Michaud

NEVER WERE WOMEN TALKED about so much as in the nineteenth century. To the consternation of even the most lucid minds, the subject was ubiquitous: in catechisms, legal codes, manuals of etiquette, works of philosophy, medical texts, treatises in theology, and of course literature. Has there ever been, before or since, so much legislation, dogma, or just plain dreaming about women? The progressive French Revolution celebrated woman as "the deity of the domestic temple," while the Catholic Church, drawing upon its vast treasury, established the Immaculate Conception as an article of faith. On December 8, 1854, Pius IX solemnly declared that alone among God's creatures Mary, the Mother of God, had been preserved from original sin. This step moved the Church closer to the secular state, and this convergence of institutions supposed to be antagonistic is certainly striking. Signs of it could be glimpsed even earlier in republican engravings that portrayed the goddess of Reason as a Madonna, borrowing from the paintings of the Italian Renaissance, or that depicted women with four breasts, symbolizing the four seasons of the year. What kind of force vanquished ideology and removed woman from the realm of fact? Although contemporaries forthrightly insisted that it was Nature, we cannot take them at their word. No, it was the force of the *image*. The women in these representations are *imaginary*. For the nineteenth century, woman was an idol.

The Cult of Images

If literature and the arts were central to the transformation of woman, perhaps no literature devoted more attention than that of the nineteenth century to the power, seductive potential, and autonomy of the image. Images can threaten identity or influence behavior. From Romantic Germany to Oscar Wilde's England by way of the France of Offenbach and Villiers de l'Isle-Adam in the 1880s, the century abounds with tales of the dangerous power of images to deceive. Material or immaterial, images were anything but insignificant. They spoke to man of his desire and of his inability to attain the object of that desire. Woe unto him who dared defy the law. Peter Schlemihl paid with endless roving for having rid himself of his shadow, and Dorian Gray paid with his soul for having appropriated his own portrait's changeless beauty. More common though no less poignant was the tragedy of the female doll or statue whose illusory loveliness somehow provokes a death. *The Tales of Hoffmann* made the point in exemplary fashion on the lyric stage. How could the image have failed to exercise a mysterious psychological power in a century that opened with a sumptuous celebration of the imagination, that primary faculty of the artist and source of his sacred aura? To believe Goethe and Novalis, Coleridge and Baudelaire, the imagination is the royal gift that kindles and epitomizes all the rest: it exalts the artist to the rank of demiurge, attuned to the harmonies of the spheres and the symphony of the senses. English and German distinguish between imagination and fancy, *Einbildungskraft* and *Fantasie*, yet no words could adequately describe this royal road to the infinite. And in *The Interpretation of Dreams* Freud taught us that the unconscious energy that courses secretly through our souls draws upon a primitive reservoir of images (*Wunschbild* or *Urfantasie*) without which we would have no access to the enigma of our own existence.

Strictly speaking, however, is it correct to describe the models that society offered to women as images? A vital relation had somehow been degraded to the status of a fixed representation. So brutal was the tyranny that reduced the infinite possibility of the image to the fixed servitude of fact, and so cynical was the trick of raising women onto a pedestal in order to win their acquiescence in their own subjugation, that all the energy of the image was sapped by the foolish equation that men in their smugness sought to establish: that woman *equals* Madonna, angel, or demon. Madonna above all: the perfection of Raphael's paintings, admired throughout Europe, wreathed mother and child in an aura of sensual plenitude: woman found her most sublime fulfillment in exhibiting the spectacle of her maternity. Exalted as mothers in the privacy of their homes, women paid the price of Restoration. The Revolution was able to depose the king and invent the *citoyen,* but not the *citoyenne.* The Church's teachings were clearer still. From the Counter-Reformation forward the celebration of Mary was a militant gesture; it signified a desire to reconquer lost territory, a refusal to compromise with the secular world. The decision to proclaim the Immaculate Conception, taken after mature reflection, was in many respects a "media coup." Pius IX had suffered a loss of prestige because of growing religious indifference, and a loss of political authority because of the first stirrings of Italian unity—for a time he was driven out of his Papal States. The Pope then restored the luster of the papal escutcheon by emulating the lavishness of the Baroque: the exaltation of Mary's glory would redound to the benefit of her Son and the blessed Church. The symbolic woman became a prize and an instrument in a struggle for power. She drove women out of their own lives until, under the new tyranny, nothing remained in its proper place.

A calm, pragmatic approach to the "woman question" was impossible. To believe contemporaries, merely raising the issue was enough to shake civilization to its very foundation. This anxiety tells us a great deal about the weakness of the edifice. When Olympe de Gouges, Mary Wollstonecraft, and Flora Tristan proposed that human nature transcends the difference between the sexes, their powerful voices were as nothing in the face of an established order that clung jealously to its privileges. "Let us consider women in the grand light of human creatures, who in common with men are placed on earth to unfold their faculties" pleaded Mary Wollstonecraft in *A Vindication of the Rights of Woman* (1792)—a plea that remained without effect yet retained its power to scandalize throughout the century. Woman was a silent idol, created by man; she could not be allowed her freedom. Balzac put it bluntly: "Woman is a slave whom we must be clever enough to set upon a throne."

Society chose its course. Exerting all its influence to impede an emancipation then in its early stages, deaf to the voices that were raised in 1789, 1848, and the 1870s when women took to the streets and climbed the barricades, it drew a veil of poetry over a strategy of repression effectively supported by such respectable institutions as medicine, law, and religion. All three took upon themselves the same pastoral mission: to protect women in their infirmity.

Literature influenced the social imagination, yet consciousness of its own powers kept it aloof from a society that turned a deaf ear to life. Like Baudelaire, who confided to his *Journaux intimes* the secret motive of his art, "to glorify the cult of images (my great, my unique, my primitive passion)," his contemporaries knew that a part of literature was dedicated to the imaginary. "The highest (and most difficult) thing in Art," according to Flaubert, the acknowledged leader of a whole generation of realist and naturalist writers, is to "stimulate dreams." For this literary mystic, salvation lay in restoring the shimmering power of the word so that like a wingèd arrow it might pierce the mind to the very core of being. Writing that took as its object the *absent* woman—that eminently receptive and no doubt overdetermined symbol in whom men, in spite of themselves, invested their contradictions and dreams—introduced movement into an otherwise static world. In this role, of course, writing was invariably masculine, accentuating woman's internal exile. Bound up with the imagination, the beloved woman became the matrix of all magic, all metamorphosis. She enlarged her partner's ego, crystallized his childhood dreams and wildest adult desires, and gave life to the law so deeply felt by Mme de Staël: "the passions fasten with all their might only on objects that one has lost." Nineteenth-century literature was able to reveal the keys of the most ancient dreams because it recognized them for what they were: dreams. Having sparked a conflagration in the mind, woman reopened a wound that would not heal. She returned life to the mystery of its source.

The idealization had another side: a glance—at times the coldest of glances—was enough to raise issues that society was reluctant to deal with and transform them into proofs of fate. To display or stage not only the poignant ubiquity of male desire but the freedom of women and the reefs upon which that freedom came to grief (or, conversely, the incredible challenge female freedom posed to those who still doubted its existence) was to open (in opposition to institutions that were hastening to close it) a space of lucidity, of sympathy, even of tenderness. And here women had their place alongside men, even if they were obliged to defend that territory inch by inch—and the energy they were obliged to divert into arguing their own case sapped their development.

The mirror of literature (which reveals the artist behind the mirror, whose "framing" selects what is considered real) thus suggested an unsuspected truth that some would have preferred to keep hidden. Perhaps more than in any previous period literature taught society about itself. This was not simply because of the significant growth of the reading public, a consequence in turn of expanded educational opportunities and ever wider availability of the printed word—all important subjects in their own right and worth looking into. A more profound change was that writers now knew that through nothing more than the creative power of language they governed a world. Their freedom challenged society by exposing its paltry ruses, by eliciting an involuntary grimace from its carefully composed mask. And society's ways of dealing with this intrusion proved mediocre or ineffective. Artists were accused of immorality to discredit them or, conversely, exalted to the point of caricature. But genius cannot be domesticated: criticism can never oblige it to trot along well-worn paths. When art is untamable, scandal is inevitable. Flaubert and Baudelaire illustrate the point for Second Empire France, and in their wake, from 1880 on, a whole generation launched an attack on hypocrisy across the Continent, from Stockholm to London to Paris to Madrid and Vienna.

Already in 1793 Blake had emblazoned an insolent judgment on the century's portals: "Brothels [are built] with the bricks of Religion."[1] He had lashed out at captive and degraded love and at the falseness of sexual relations. Surely it is not too much to compare his remark with Flaubert's famous cry: "Madame Bovary, c'est moi." To be sure, the point remains enigmatic, and the failure of the novel's ending is patent. Nevertheless, Mme Bovary, guilty of adultery and disabused of her dreams, remains superior to the meanness that does her in. Her creator does not avoid the issue: rather than abandon her to the wrath of the righteous, he identifies with her fate.

Only in recent years, however, has criticism begun to reveal literature's incredible bad faith, which was probably worse at the end of the century than at the beginning. To borrow the words of one of the best observers of the period, the examples are legion in which "women, who are victims, actually seem guilty and lack the words to make themselves heard."[2] Literature bestowed its blessing on a system of deceptions and mirages; it set traps that were all the more dangerous because they were cleverly constructed. Who can say how much damage was done by the image of woman—angel or Madonna—that dominated the century? Yet why are the heroines of the nineteenth century still capable of moving us despite profound changes in our mores? Why are they brought back to life so frequently on our screens? Perhaps because they want happiness yet are full of contradictions and forced to struggle against fate. Freedom being indivisible, we are not strangers to their aspirations.

The mean and illusory compromises of bourgeois morality were often transformed by the spell of the lyric stage. The most illustrious example is Verdi's *La Traviata,* which made a saint of the touching prostitute created a few years earlier by Alexandre Dumas *fils* in *La Dame aux camélias.* The scenario of redemption through love, so common in the theater of the period, worked its magic once again, only this time the criminal is saved not by the intercession of a pure woman but by the sinful lady's improbable submission to the laws of the family. The need for renunciation impresses itself on the consciousness of Violetta, enlightened by the revelations of the father and lover. The sacrifice of the courtesan on the altar of family and patrimony, which her past threatens, seals the redemption. "She is in heaven," the final chorus chants victoriously.

It is difficult to imagine a more apt response to the expectations of an audience enamored of pleasure and order, a public that was continually offered a mythic rejoinder to one of the most pressing problems of a great industrial age indifferent to the fate of the legions of people it uprooted—indifferent, at any rate, as long as they posed no threat to stability. Seduced innocents (modeled perhaps after Marguerite of Gounod's *Faust*) and man-eating temptresses (Strauss's Salomé, for example, faithfully copied from the figure brought to the stage by Oscar Wilde) trooped before the audience, docile or terrifying as the case may be, but in any case pure reflections of male fantasy. At the time Wagner was the century's reigning monarch. His ascendancy stemmed from more than just the novelty of his musical style. "Wagner is a neurosis,"

Nietzsche once remarked. His music, according to Thomas Mann, had the effect of a "theatrical Lourdes." His characters were all of a piece, angels or witches draped in cumbersome mythological trappings and set in motion by the artifices of a venomous music. For every Brünnhilde, the martial virgin who renounces immortality, becomes a woman, and risks betrayal and abandonment to accompany Siegfried in his earthly tribulations, how many Sentas, Elisabeths, and Kundrys were there, blindly, single-mindedly intent on saving or corrupting a man? Isolde, perhaps the noblest of all the lovers in a drama that reduces the world to two enraptured minds, is so completely identified with the dangers of narcissistic love that she lures her prey into the void and, intoxicated with leitmotifs, succumbs in ecstasy.

All these examples are fashioned of male desire. The self-intoxication of romantic passion and the moralizing of myth teach us less about the reality of women's lives than do the voices of disillusionment, expressed in works dating back to the early part of the century and gaining in power and thematic richness over time. Happiness, by which I mean self-fulfillment and individual achievement, not the simulacrum that supposedly comes from self-denial and devoted service, remained beyond the reach of women. But what adventure could be more personal than the quest for happiness? It mobilized the myriad resources of the female spirit. Even defeat, whether rebelliously resisted or accepted in silent submission, turns out to be a vast field of inquiry. When victory lies with the established order, when it can be won only through vile intrigue, then defeat may be the mark of an extraordinary destiny. And so the novel explored defeat in its many guises, even if fin-de-siècle pessimism spoke in a more somber voice to disparage both sexes and to depict their absence of communication as a permanent fixture.

Although the unity of the period is plain to see (and better delineated by the turbulences of 1789 and 1914 than by the strict chronology of years evenly divisible by one hundred), it is nevertheless risky to attempt to describe the literary images and representations of the Western world over such a time span, especially if one is reluctant to detach literature arbitrarily from its natural surroundings and allied arts. Such an undertaking flies in the face of literary history's customary categorizations; scholars are justly afraid of vast syntheses of this sort and certainly unaccustomed to dealing with the radical questions that women are putting to them. The period is rife with contradictions, many of which are still with us, for better or for worse, and there is little firm ground on which we can stand to survey them. The notion of progress, which lulled the century's critical faculties to sleep, is of no use. By contrast, the fears that transcended national boundaries and knew no literary schools have a history. They form a subtle and permanent matrix out of which came some of the models on which portraits of women were based. New mores associated with social and political changes were also decisive. Thus the end of the century was aquiver with the discovery of sexual energy, whereas a contempt for the body (which claimed Christian roots even though it was incautiously borrowed from Stoic and Gnostic traditions that struck at the very heart of what was supposed to be a religion of incarnation) had tightly constrained expression in an earlier period.

In seeking to understand the period, how can we possibly grasp the often vivid contrasts between generations or respect the particularity of different languages (and dialects) on which the "presence" of literary characters depends? Fontane's heroines are rooted in Brandenburg, Hardy's in the rural south of England, and it is the nuances that differentiate America from Europe (even English Europe) that lie behind the torment of the characters of Henry James. The only safeguard is to hew as closely as possible to life, to reject any preconceived theory, to try to identify the lines of force and the way they interact, and (who knows?) perhaps even to fall under the spell of one of these imaginary women.

Primacy of the Imaginary Woman

> Women are silver chalices, into which we place golden apples. My idea of women is not abstracted from the phenomena of reality; I was born with it, or perhaps it grew up with me.
>
> —Goethe to Eckermann, October 22, 1828[3]

> Woman is the being that casts the largest shadow or projects the most light in our dreams. . . . She lives spiritually in the imaginations she haunts and blesses with fruit.
>
> —Baudelaire, *Les Paradis artificiels* (1861), included by André Breton and Pierre Eluard in the *Dictionnaire abrégé du surréalisme* (1938)

When Rousseau, in the century of Enlightenment, first plucked women out of life's myriad contingencies and situations and placed them in the empyrean of the imagination, he was also the first to gauge, by personally paying the price, the danger of losing oneself in one's dreams. In effect succumbing to the charms of the fictional heroine he created in *La Nouvelle Héloïse* (1761), the enchanter, ravished by that Julie whom he had endowed with all that his heart deemed perfect, briefly dreamed that she had come to him in the form of Mme d'Houdetot. For this sweet fantasy he would pay a heavy price. In a sense he repeated the adventure in *Emile.* Jean-Jacques, conquered by the charms of Sophie, Emile's female counterpart in this vast treatise on education, shed the reserved demeanor of the educator. He not only arranged the plot so that Sophie's fate was to marry, but intervened on her behalf and celebrated her perfections. The philosopher thus revealed the power that images held over him. This was an affliction from which he would never recover. Woman for him was essentially an image: she attracted male energy like a magnet, stimulated it like an electric shock. She was at once the cause of society's degeneration and the agency for restoring its health.

Abounding in all the paradoxes that the idea of happiness conjures up, Saint-Preux's lyrical flight, like a firefly, casts a flickering light on woman's spells:

> Women, women! Cherished and deadly objects that nature has embellished to torture us, who punish us when we defy you, who pursue us when we fear you, whose hatred and love are equally harmful, and whom we cannot either seek or flee with impunity! Beauty, charm, attraction, sympathy! Inconceivable creature or chimera, abyss of pain and desire! Beauty more terrible to mortals than the element in which you were born, unhappy is he who surrenders to your deceptive calm! You are responsible for the tempests that torment the human race.

Did the eloquence of the passions succeed in deceiving the reader as to the unusual nature of the undertaking described in the novel and fortunately saved from failure by Julie's death? She dies before frankly admitting to herself that it is illusory to treat love as a purely spiritual principle, entrusted to the guardianship of virtue. Although *La Nouvelle Héloïse* thus left entirely open the question of a spiritual ministry of life and happiness that Rousseau, in opposition to his century, had bestowed upon woman, it also gave currency to fantasies that would continue to fascinate readers down to the Surrealists. Its effects were insidious, all the more so because Rousseau's thought, by virtue of its range and magnitude as well as conceptual and musical power, inaugurated a new world. The disease of humanity, he claimed, was deep-seated: it affected life itself. Responsibility could be laid at the door of society, whose state represented a fall from the state of nature. Any remedy would therefore need to affect the very source of existence. Since it is impossible to return to a state of nature, restoration implies building on a foundation of firm values. And what more potent remedy was available than femininity? Woman was more than "the antidote in the poison" (Jean Starobinski's expression). She was a saving Otherness (fully deserving of the capital letter): in Woman lay a promise of salvation. And even in our own century André Breton could write that she "embodies man's highest chance and, according to Goethe, asks to be taken as the keystone of the edifice."

Even as Romanticism faded into the past, the era continued to live by romantic illusions, for the otherness of woman was a pure invention, a construction of man. Rousseau did not hide that fact when, in *Emile,* he elaborated a theory of woman's subservience to nature and to the conservative instincts of society. He thus filled an arsenal with dangerous weapons, which his successors were quick to put to use. Only men could possibly disclose woman's true nature: "Eva, who are you? Do you truly know your own nature?" Alfred de Vigny asked his female companion in *La Maison du berger* (1844). But to reveal woman to herself was in fact to invent her, to shape her (preferably docile and childlike), even to protect her from obscure forces within herself (weakness, impurity, hysteria). Baudelaire knew this better than anyone when he said that "woman is natural, that is, abominable." She was scarcely distinguishable from an ape! But let jewels, perfumes, and cosmetics make her over, and the metamorphosis was total. Even her foolishness encouraged idolatry. Thus drained of her own substance, woman lifted the unbearable lid of existence and restored the poet to the paradise of his dreams. Baudelaire's short story *La Fanfarlo* (1847) is a good illustration of this: even as the lover takes possession of his beloved, a dancer superb in her abandon, he asks her to return to the theater for the dress in which she had appeared on stage a few hours earlier and reminds her not to forget the rouge she wore either. For the dandy, the object of love was an image, an artifice.

Make no mistake: poetry used these devices to plumb the depths of human nature. The quest was eccentric, even painful, but in it woman became something less mediocre than man's natural helpmate, something less convenient and deceitful than the messianic figure to which socialism briefly warmed. Cruel if need be, she escaped every attempt to hold her, the symbol of a transcendent infinity—an abyss of Evil or a token of life's unpredictability, capable of giving but not of holding back. Male desire, which was forever reviving the dream of woman as a reflection of itself (whether as fantasy or automaton), burned in the flame it could never touch. The greatest artists were not content merely to chastise the century for its smugness. In its most extreme form, I am tempted to suggest, literature's consciousness of its desperate need of artifice raised it to new heights, in blasphemous homage to indomitable freedom: what would Baudelaire be, for example, without the dogma of original sin, which left him trapped in the curse of a bad conscience?

But this was a game in which women were at best pretexts and always victims. In such circumstances how could women of flesh and blood fail to come to grief? Baudelaire, who, following a night of love, courted Mme Sabatier with a series of mystical sonnets, dismissed her in these terms: "A few days ago, you were a goddess. . . . Now you are a woman again." The fall was sudden and irreversible and scarcely softened by the warning he had issued while still devoted to his beloved: "I am a selfish man; I am using you."

Yet it was at the price of such extreme experimentation that the era made its revolutionary breakthroughs in the most diverse realms of creation and thought: for if, with Hölderlin, poetry became the critical consciousness of the age and, in the words of the poet's friend Hegel, "the schoolmistress of mankind" *(Lehrerin der Menschheit)*, and if, with Baudelaire and Nerval, it transgressed previously inviolable boundaries, it did so by worshiping a supreme feminine ideal, a pure image essentially identical with poetry itself. The old society celebrated itself in desperate cults even as it made way for the new, whose confidence was sapped by the collapse of ancient values.

Even the novel, whose great masters (such as Balzac, Dickens, and Zola, to toss out a few names at random) took as their goal the depiction of social realities (at times vying with scientists in cold exactitude), fell into the clutches of the century's demons. Dickens was an extreme case, proof of the degree to which acute observation of social misery was a talent separate from the ability to portray women. If Dickens excelled at describing the social landscape, his portraits of women are incredible stereotypes. Like so many others, Balzac quailed at the idea of anything so monstrous as a female author: she would defy the laws of nature and terrify by way of "something virginal and untamed." Marking his distance from the biblical model, he added: "The strong women must be only a symbol; in reality she is frightening to behold."

The nightmares that tormented the theologians and their lay disciples (such as Proudhon) at the mere suggestion of woman not entirely subjugated to man also visited the Goncourt brothers, yet in the depiction of women they were able to explore new territory. In fact, the Goncourts violated one of the last literary taboos by making a place for fiction for fallen women such as Germinie Lacerteux (1865), an unwed mother who succumbs to "ancillary hysteria" and dies of tuberculosis, and criminal prostitutes such as the heroine of *La Fille Elisa* (1877), who, broken by the inhumane regime of silence in women's prisons, is reduced to blithering idiocy and ultimately death. The brothers were careful investigators whose documentary researches were spurred by first-hand experience, in this instance their shock at visiting the state prison in Clermont-de-l'Oise. They were the initiators of the grand tour through the land of working women, female criminals, and demimondaines that laid the groundwork for Gervaise's self-destructive epic in Zola's *L'Assommoir* and were the precursors of the many portraits of women of toil in plays and naturalist novels across Europe; more than recording shock, however, the Goncourts attested to the contempt that attached to women cruelly reduced to exhibiting themselves as sexual objects, not to say commodities. Their *Journal* abounds with the antifeminist vituperation so common at the time. It is sprinkled with vicious remarks on the alleged inhumanity of women, creatures whom the brothers described as reduced by nature "to mere wombs." Already the days when woman represented the allure of the infinite for Baudelaire seem to belong to the distant past.

Zola, whose influence was felt throughout Europe in the 1880s, took up where the Goncourts left off. Nana, that filthy, devouring beast, is not so much social history as myth. From her start as a kept woman who gratifies the desires of a society bent on pleasure, she rises to the rank of a symbol. She illustrates the destructiveness of sexuality divorced from procreation and represents the social decomposition that undermined the Second Empire. Even the impassive Maupassant expressed horror of maternity while utterly surrendering to the image of an inaccessible dream woman, a symbol of the writer's own obsessions. And what is there to say about the aestheticism of Joris-Karl Huysmans? The novelist had a field day mocking "the old-fogeyish idealism" and "emptiness of a celibacy-maddened spinster" that he found even in naturalist literature, yet he was unable to purge his own work of images like that of Salomé in *A Rebours* (1884), which comes close to revealing a cosmic fear of women.

The other countries of Europe yielded nothing to France in this regard. The image of woman as sphinx or chimera haunted Heine before it influenced the imagination of late-nineteenth-century painters like Gustave Moreau and Félicien Rops. The implacable virgin sowed terror in the plays of Hauptmann and Hofmannsthal, as did the courtesan in Wedekind, the creator of the fearsome Lulu whom Berg would introduce to the opera in 1935. The Pre-Raphaelites in England, Klimt in Vienna, and Edvard Munch in Norway and Alfred Kubin in the Austro-Hungarian Empire evoked equally disturbing visions with their paintings. But France perhaps earlier and more clearly than any other country manifested the degree to which one whole area of intellectual and artistic production drew upon a sexualized representation of the world according to which man's purpose is to quell the troubling strangeness of woman. Michelet's powerful and intuitive genius fed a strongly lyrical prose with crude concepts. His masculine mind invaded the territory of history, which it made abundantly fertile yet ruled with loving tyranny, much as the man himself ruled his second wife's private life. A visionary, he deciphered the destiny of France and its people and celebrated the benevolent energies of the witch and mother, yet portrayed the influence of women as one of the crucial factors that turned the Revolution from its true course (*Les Femmes de la Révolution,* 1854). Paradoxically it was science, whether it called itself sociology with Comte or history of religion with Renan, that carried the logic of the century to its natural conclusion: it dreamed of the advent of a superior form of humanity in which parthenogenesis would at last put an end to the scandalous need to entrust the survival of the species to a sex as imperfect as the female.

The "dark continent" of Woman was a frightening thing, and

madness in any of its forms was preferable to her scandalous and naked presence. German idealism wore out this theme, as Wagner would later in the century. Fortunately the music overwhelmed the composer's flimsy dogma, which sought in vain to confine "the eternal woman" *(das ewige Weib)* within a subservient nature tied to man. Wagner's ill-conceived attempt to set himself above Goethe and his work only underscored the model's uniqueness. As masculine as Goethe's spirit was, even he could not exhaust woman's genius in love. His contemporary Rahel Varnhagen, an enlightened Romantic who kept a salon in Berlin, remarked that it was no accident that among the many women who figure in *Wilhelm Meister's Apprenticeship,* those who devote themselves exclusively to love end in death. To be sure, the eternal feminine, the supreme value with which Part Two of *Faust* ends, represents a coronation. The poet entrusts his wisdom to the wingèd escort of music and symbolism. "Das Ewig-Weibliche/Zieht uns hinan" (The eternal feminine/draws us upward), the choir intones. The spareness of these final lines, tied together only by the brevity of the meter and the crossed rhyme scheme, sums up a destiny. It registers the continuity of time and eternity. Faust has known more than one woman: Margaret, the *petite bourgeoise* whom he leads on to ruin, and Helen, the ancient heroine briefly brought back to life in her changeless perfection. Along with Mary, the mother of God (to whom Margaret prays in the final scene, which depicts the ascension of the immortal part of Faust against a background of high mountains populated by angels and mystics), the women nevertheless constitute only a part of the symbol whose miracle the poet inscribes in an audacious stylistic medley. In fact, the symbol exists only when suffused with the shifting energies of the dream, of beauty, and of nature. The energies that have guided Faust throughout his journey now unite in a final fulfillment. Detached from all possession, restored to the freedom of an unfettered existence open to the kind of meditation that jettisons the ballast of the soul, Faust rightfully belongs to Being. Goethe celebrates a desire docile to the laws of life.

How could such loftiness be maintained when the century preached a pallid hypocrisy? The official truth, according to which humanity had reached a pinnacle and was triumphantly enjoying the fruits of civilization, was belied by the disintegration of consciousnesses and individuals. Ibsen's *A Doll's House* (1879), which enjoyed tremendous success in theaters all across Europe, ends with a scene of parting: Nora slams the door on married life to live at last on her own. Devoted to her husband, she had saved him from death and given him two children. Yet he is too insubstantial, too incapable of seeing his wife as anything other than the doll-woman he required. Nora's only salvation is to flee: life begins outside the home and family. What remained of certitude was questioned in turn by Arthur Schnitzler in the early part of this century. His plays and stories explore in depth the hidden shadows of the soul and dwell on its anxieties and eternal indecision. By leaving the reality of actual experience in doubt (and, since people are undeniably governed by fantasy and caught up in foolish social mechanisms, experience is of little interest in any case), Schnitzler in his own inimitable fashion illustrated once again the powerful influence of the imaginary as well as its bankrupt condition. Man and woman dissolve in the imagination, carried off on the tides of the unconscious. Meanwhile, another Viennese, Sigmund Freud, saw a reflection of his own ideas in Schnitzler's somber lucidity.

Fates

> Existence must begin with the self . . . and, without ever being the center, one must always be the driving force behind one's own destiny.
>
> —Mme de Staël, *De l'influence des passions*

> When she saw this rigid system close about her . . . that sense of darkness and suffocation . . . took possession of her.
>
> —Henry James, *The Portrait of a Lady* (1881)

How was a person to be born into freedom in a society that did not tolerate it? How was happiness to be achieved in a world in which the sphere of female activity was constantly shrinking? Woman's confinement in the home, Victorian treatises tell us, was the foundation of her moral authority: "You have deep responsibilities; you have urgent claims; a nation's moral worth is in your keeping," Sarah Ellis told the readers of *The Women of England* (1839), one of countless tracts in which the triumphant industrial bourgeoisie laid down its law. Of course the power granted to women depended on their subscribing to a contract renouncing all personal social or political ambition. The moment women tore up the contract, men dropped their chivalrous pose, chivalry being a quixotic ideal to be flashed about like a shiny bauble. This was war.

Literature became the immediate battlefield. As late as the end of the eighteenth century literature had still been an instrument of feminine freedom. Letter writing, an activity particularly well suited to the broken rhythm of days devoted to the care of family and household, had gained recognition as literature and influenced the novel. But with the turn of the nineteenth century tensions arose. Maintaining the status quo became problematic. Paradoxically, England was perhaps the country most tolerant of women writers. But wasn't that tolerance (which seems so only in comparison with other places) a consequence of the attitude of writers like Jane Austen, the Brontë sisters, and George Eliot of never confronting the established order head on? For them marriage was still the essential thing. Jane Austen could still be optimistic, and the Brontë sisters could depict the triumph of Jane Eyre: a disinherited orphan, she ultimately obligates her seducer to marry her and thus achieves something of what she had hoped for (her dreams having been cruelly diminished by a hard life).

Elsewhere the struggle was fierce. In 1800 it drew from Mme de Staël the anguished recognition that the life of the woman of letters was as wretched as that of "the Pariahs of India." Rejected and cursed, she paid for having violated the taboo: she had ventured onto man's terrain by daring to exist in her own right. George Sand, who like many others of her generation was haunted by a "rage to write" as the quickest route to emancipation, found it difficult to make her mark. Given the volume of her output and the power of her genius, the century was obliged to tolerate her but not to spare her the pain of persecution; it may have been too late to stop Sand, who had already done her harm, but no effort was spared to make sure that no other writer of her ilk would appear on the scene. The picture was scarcely brighter in the German-speaking countries: Metternich's Restoration had squelched earlier initiatives. Rahel Varnhagen, who had tasted freedom, drew back. Her correspondence would remain private: to have published it would have required her to don a mask, to accept the roles men controlled. There is no better illustration of the prevailing inequality than the story of a brother and sister, the writers Clemens and Bettina Brentano. He was a celebrated poet.

But she refrained from publishing until around 1835, by which time she was fifty, a widow, the mother of seven children, and a noted Berlin personality; nevertheless she incurred her brother's reproach for having immodestly placed herself on public display. True, Bettina compounded the offense by investigating the wretched conditions in poor neighborhoods of Berlin. The ensuing social scandal intensified the literary scandal, and her book was banned. Earlier, an unhappy Caroline von Günderode had asked *"Warum war ich kein Mann?"* (Why was I not a man?). The irresponsibility of her partners ultimately drove this ardent woman to suicide.

Women's novels naturally portrayed disillusionment and shattered happiness. Consider the work of Mme de Staël. Abundantly gifted as a poet, Corinne (heroine of the novel that bears her name, published in 1807) can imagine no fulfillment other than to lay the glory she has acquired at the feet of her lover, Oswald. But Oswald leaves her in the mistaken belief that it is his duty. Death is the only thing left for Corinne. In *Delphine,* Mme de Staël's previous novel, we read: "A woman's fate has run out when she fails to marry the man she loves. Society allows women only one hope. When the lots are drawn and one has lost, that is the end of it." This judgment reflects a terrible truth of the period. In a misogynistic world there was no way for a woman to flourish. At best she could associate with other pariahs and join the redemptive wandering of a people chosen to triumph in the end: George Sand's *Consuelo* opened new possibilities for excluded women. At the time (1844) the skies had briefly cleared. Solidarity with the oppressed had begun to take concrete form through the social action of Flora Tristan, for example, who organized workers on her tour of France. But fragile hopes were dashed with the bloody repression of the 1848 uprisings.

Take the most secluded place in the world, the sheltered refuge of the aristocrat Clochegourde in a valley bordering the Indre River in Touraine, and take a woman utterly devoted to her maternal vocation and possibly exalted by an inner religion of the sort known only to the purest souls, and you have the ingredients for a novel about the drama of private life. There is not a place in the world without its secret wounds. Is Balzac's *Le Lys dans la vallée* (The Lily of the Valley, 1836) truly a novel of sacrifice? Mme de Mortsauf is aquiver with passion for Felix, a man she loves but mistakenly feels compelled to treat as a son. The terrible jealousy that overwhelms her at the sight of her rival's success reveals a profound truth: Felix's infidelity leaves her alone with her unsatisfied desires. True, Balzac censored himself. The rebellious feelings that rack the woman on her deathbed as she thinks back on her fruitless life were more explicit in the manuscript. The novelist cut the heart out of his story to satisfy his mistress, who was no doubt frightened at what the exploration of such abysses might stir up. As it is, however, the text is eloquent enough, and it is illuminated by the related stories that make up the novel. If *Le Lys* is a moral lesson, it certainly is not a lesson addressed to women. In fact a woman ends up lecturing the narrator, who has had the gall to transform his own adventure into a declaration of love: Nathalie de Mannerville dismisses the inglorious suitor who had failed to recognize Mme de Mortsauf's desire. Having shattered one woman, she tells him, is hardly a warrant for seducing another.

While Balzac reined himself in, by the 1860s many obstacles had fallen. The last decades of the century gave wide currency to the spectacle of women's implacable fate. Painterly realism was one vehicle for this: witness the scandal caused by two of Manet's paintings, *Le Déjeuner sur l'herbe* (1863) and *Olympia* (1865). The painter dared to portray a contemporary prostitute in the nude in a straightforward representation of Second Empire mores. First in France with Zola, then throughout Europe, literature began to represent all social classes and attack the last remaining taboos, such as the church, whose appetite for power and failure to understand the problems of women aroused the ire of Pérez Galdós and Clarín in Spain and, in a more restrained manner, of Thomas Hardy in England. The religious authorities were interested not so much in morality as in joining couples in religious ceremony. A multitude of new aspirations and desires came to the fore. The "woman question" could not be divorced from other issues in a society in ferment, nor could women be summed up in an archetype: in Galdós's novel *Fortunata and Jacinta* (1887) the eponymous heroines belong to two different worlds. Both hail from Madrid, and both are victims of the same man. But one was born to the lower class, from which she inherited robust health, passion, and the jealous pride that causes her to regard herself as the wife of the man whose child she bears, whereas the other enjoys money and respectability, those devastating privileges of the bourgeoisie which mean little to a woman who cannot hold on to her husband or have children. Conditions varied in other countries. From Tolstoy's Russia to the Portugal of Eça de Queirós (the creator of the memorable Luisa, the respectable matron who stumbles into adultery in *Cousin Basilio* [1874]), novels were filled with aspirations that at last declared themselves in the feminine gender and present tense, namely, happiness, desire (for sensual and intellectual fulfillment), and control of one's own life (as opposed to enduring the guardianship of an absent or indifferent husband). Literature also reverberated with the call of the flesh, on behalf of which women, when necessary, spoke out against the ambient idealism. Take, for example, Juan Valera's *Pepita Jiménez* (1874). In this work a young widow won the love of a seminarian and induced him to marry her, taking him away from the priesthood he had been about to join. The novel has a happy ending, but many others ended in disaster brought on by society's implacable conservatism. Maupassant withheld judgment yet coldly stressed the ferocity of social forces, while August Strindberg's *Miss Julie* (1888) and other plays emphasized the limits to progress. Love is an illusion, and there is no hope of ever resolving class and sexual conflict. *The Dream* (1901) held that it was better not to be born.

The novel was undeniably the most vital literary genre of the nineteenth century as well as the one that offered the best view of women's aspirations for happiness and the obstacles they encountered. Let us therefore pause briefly in this all too rapid survey to consider the novelists Thomas Hardy and Henry James. To a large extent our world begins with them. What were the obstacles against which the proud righteousness of Tess of the d'Urbervilles (1891) and the noble independence of Sue Bridehead (in *Jude the Obscure* [1895]) came to grief? In the view of the characters themselves, they succumbed to a fate inscribed in their ancestry, or simply to the way things are: they evoke life's wretchedness in the words of Job. They are too sensitive, too far in advance of their time in their desire to live in accordance with an inner law defiant of the conventions, not to fall into traps laid for those who would assert their freedom, against whom all the rest conspire. Only Bathsheba, the heroine of *Far from the Madding Crowd,* overcomes the demon and frees herself from the grip of fate, and she is able to do so only because she can count on the absolute loyalty of Gabriel Oak, a man made of the same stuff as she is. The waste implicit in the failure of Tess and the renunciations of Sue (whom society forces to return to the falseness she had hoped to flee) leaves a bitter taste: what promise was sacrificed to a moribund social order!

Henry James was no less perspicacious in his observation of the upper classes than Hardy was in his depiction of the peasantry. The love of independence and the gifts of intelligence and beauty prove dangerous to women whose extreme self-confidence causes them to reject all offers of aid. *The Bostonians* is a ferocious satire of feminism in the American capital of the intellect. Perhaps it was inevitable that life would avenge itself on these rigid, abstract, unworldly, fanatical, yet somehow uneasy believers in the cause of liberation. But the moral prison that closes in on Isabel Archer in *The Portrait of a Lady* (1882), which she feels in her very flesh, and the death that punishes Daisy Miller for her extreme insouciance, shrewdly signal a danger: given the novel and intoxicating challenges of freedom and happiness, an error of judgment might well prove fatal. How could such an error be avoided when the old Continent so effectively confounded New World rules governing the pursuit of happiness?

Welcoming Life: Lou Andreas-Salomé

> Believe me, the world won't give you any gifts. If you want to have a life, steal it.
>
> —Lou Andreas-Salomé, *Looking Back: Memoirs*[4]

> To tell the truth, I'd rather not talk any more about virtues and achievements but about what I feel more competent to discuss, namely, happiness.
>
> —Lou Andreas-Salomé, *On the Female Type* (1914)[5]

While it is true that James could bring a thoroughly feminine sympathy to the conception of his characters, it is time to leave fiction behind and turn our attention to women themselves, to observe how they gradually became aware of themselves and, no longer hindered by the spirit-dampening burden of protest, asserted their independence. More than any other woman, Lou Andreas-Salomé was involved in all the great debates of the nineteenth century. She was disconcerting in her willingness to assume all the risks of freedom and enigmatic even to her own friends, whom she often surprised. She was in love with happiness, whose secret had something to do with her extraordinary zest for life. If by chance she showed the way to follow, it was not so much because of the brilliance of a personality radiating independence, cultivation, and beauty as because of an inner discipline that allowed her to face with sovereign detachment what could only be experienced as a gift, namely, life itself:

> I am incapable of modeling my life on anyone else's and will never stand as a model for anybody. But what I surely will do, whatever the cost, is fashion my life according to my own model. In acting this way, I am defending no principle but something far more marvelous, something jubilant in the heart of every individual, warm with life, and burning only to be free. . . . It is surely impossible to be happier than I am now.[6]

The young woman who wrote this letter was just twenty-one years old. She was living in Rome, where she had gone for the sake of her precarious health. She dreamed of founding a sort of community with two brilliant but much older intellectuals whose acquaintance she had made: Friedrich Nietzsche and Paul Rée. Calmly steadfast, she answered the outraged objections of her mother and even of other feminists, conveyed from her native Russia by Reverend Gillot, the man who had been her first teacher and whom she had loved in a way he could not reciprocate. But Lou never wavered from her path, not then or at any other time in her life. The force that drove her and made her immune to what people said was not that of rebellion, for even rebellion has its conformists. Later, speaking of Ibsen's heroines, she would say that any call to freedom is doomed if it fails to get beyond the stage of negation, if it fails to rise to the level of defining its own rules of behavior. An inner certitude that I am tempted to call Stendhalian persuaded the young woman that her choice was correct. Lou would devastate more than one partner by this behavior, starting with Nietzsche and Rée, both madly in love with a woman who wanted them not as lovers but only as intellectual partners and life companions, the kind of man she finally found in her husband Andreas, with whom she enjoyed a marriage without sex. Yet she also sought a life of sexual fulfillment, which she found in her love of the young Rilke in 1897, and from it she drew the strength to support the future poet of the *Duino Elegies* and to nurture his genius, though the exclusiveness of that attachment strained relations to the breaking point.

Lou brought her rigorous training in philosophy and medicine and familiarity with the major European literary trends to the study of the promising new field of psychoanalysis. Before World War I she became one of Freud's primary collaborators. To the work of psychoanalysis she brought a creative, enthusiastic, and poetic intelligence, which enabled her to overcome obstacles and attain a higher level of synthesis than Freud, who was perhaps held back by his adherence to the scientific method of dissection and analysis. By the turn of the century Lou had taken an interest in the relation of mind to body in the experience of love, drawing upon the latest discoveries in biology to shed new light on the matter. How could psychic life possibly remain unaffected by energies welling up from the depths of the body? How could the mind remain fixed on a romanticized ideal based on the fusion of two souls when sexual frenzy struck perhaps at the very root of being, with all the possibility for self-deception this entailed? To the consternation of feminists, she looked not only to biology but also to the symbolism that exerted such powerful influence over women's lives (most notably the figure of the Madonna, which, as we have seen, dominated the imagination) for clues to understanding woman. Society's cynical misappropriation of certain values implicit in language, a misappropriation that degraded feminine wholeness into hysterical submission and the woman into the female, should nevertheless not be used as a pretext for rejecting those values altogether. Properly interpreted, they could save women and society in general from chaos and loss of orientation.

Lou's was an ambitious intellectual program, aimed at reconciling women with themselves and exploring their hitherto unexamined relation to their bodies, to language, to poetry. Having delved into images of woman (those of Ibsen and Strindberg as well as of her sister feminists), she made a major contribution in extending, in brilliant fashion, Freud's concept of narcissism. For her, narcissism was a structural principle denoting not only love of one's own image but love of one's self. It perpetuated into adulthood some of the desires of early childhood, before the infant distinguished between itself and its environment. Artists know how to capture this benevolent energy better than anyone, because in the creative act they draw on sources to which most of us only rarely have access. What better way to end the segregation of a sex associated with the insubstantiality of certain images than to point out the psychological significance of those very images for human beings generally?

Granted, Lou was not the greatest woman writer of the nineteenth century. As lively as her sensibility was, as decisive a role as she played in the inception of Rilke's poetry (which might not exist but for the support he received in letters from Lou), she made her mark primarily in philosophy and psychoanalysis. It would be to judge her hastily, however, not to recognize her extraordinary generosity as well as her gifts as a stylist and poet, so evident in her memoirs, *Looking Back,* which she wrote toward the end of her life in 1933–34. Here, this woman, who more than any other chose her own life, set aside all vanity (if she ever had any) to recount the extraordinary encounters that made her what she was and the way in which her life became a poetic work *(Dichtung),* not because she was somehow its "master" but because she knew how to use the energy that is in, and transcends, all of us.

Women artists did not have an easy time of it and often saw their work sacrificed. Alice James's journals, for example, met with indifference if not downright hostility from her brother Henry, who was largely responsible for delaying their publication until 1934, more than forty years after the death of their author; Camille Claudel's career as a sculptor was destroyed by the combined cowardice of her lover Rodin and her brother, the writer Paul Claudel. Under the prevailing conditions women had little control over the image that literature and art presented of them. And our description has of necessity alternated between masculine and feminine voices—distinct and impossible to confuse. Despite the adverse conditions, however, some remarkable developments took place. The little girl emerged as a distinct literary being, a child with a life not based on some supposedly universal male model. This figure emerged in the 1860s in the guise of a victim like Cosette or an orphan exploited by the Thénardiers in Victor Hugo's *Les Misérables.* But above all there was Sophie, the mischievous little girl created by the Comtesse de Ségur in *Les Malheurs de Sophie,* and even more, the charming and remarkably unfettered little Alice in Lewis Carroll's *Alice in Wonderland,* a clever, rebellious, dreamy little girl who earned her independence.[7]

Born at the same time as Alice, did Lou Andreas-Salomé rush into the breach that Carroll's character had opened? A woman of flesh and blood as well as philosophy and cultivation, she introduced an element of youthful vigor into the portrait of the lady.

TRANSLATED FROM THE FRENCH BY ARTHUR GOLDHAMMER

6

Reading and Writing in Germany

Marie-Claire Hoock-Demarle

IT HAS LONG BEEN DIFFICULT to determine the degree of literacy of the women of Germany, France, or any other country. The sources are hard to interpret. A glance at a late-eighteenth-century statistical table or legislative document shows why: the texts may refer to "youth" as a whole, or to various age groups or social categories, but seldom is there any allusion to the distinction between the sexes. And the few forward-looking texts that do raise the issue simply note, in regard to literacy, that the inequality between the sexes is plain to see.

It is no easier to approach the question of the "woman writer." Here the problem is not that the subject resists inquiry, but rather that the nineteenth century treated the phenomenon as shameful and inappropriate, and this moralistic overlay obscures the reality. If a woman had a gift for poetry, she might well beg forgiveness for the sin of writing in terms reminiscent of a repentant adulteress: "My husband," Louise Ackermann confessed in 1885, "never had any idea that I wrote verse, and I never told him of my poetic accomplishments."[1]

Yet between 1780 and 1880 (by which time

the major European countries had established or were in the process of establishing a system of girls' primary and secondary education[2]), women made remarkable progress, evident in political as well as autobiographical texts. Learning to read and write was a first, relatively easy step. The difficulties really began when it came to choosing what to read and how to think about the content. As for investing oneself personally in writing, that was a step that few were prepared to take. But reading and writing were also instruments for integrating women into the modern world. Reading implied social organization, and writing implied a privileged relation to an audience; both gave rise to forms of sociability that led women to reflect on themselves, their means of self-expression, and their perception of time and space.

In this essay I will be paying particular attention to the period between two revolutions, that of 1789 and that of 1848. The effects of both were felt on a European scale, and the period is long enough to encompass several generations of women yet brief enough to reveal the force and at times the violence of changes in their behavior and ways of thinking. Germany will serve as an illustration of a crucial stage in the history of women. To be sure, the same developments took place elsewhere, although often under very different auspices. But the German case allows us to concentrate on certain unique aspects. Social, political, and above all religious factors did not have the same impact in Germany as elsewhere. Furthermore, research on literacy in Germany has focused on sources different from those used in France, thus raising the level of historical debate above mere methodological controversy.[3]

The "German case" is interesting in part because the history of the country was so fragmented. By looking at different regions, we can gain an idea of the influence of different political systems and of religious controversy. In some ways Germany was a microcosm that reflected what was happening elsewhere. It epitomized developments affecting women's education and literacy all across Europe. In some German states, moreover, instruction in reading and writing was made compulsory at a very early date, allowing us to measure the effect of state policy on the progress of literacy.

The study of women's literacy raises issues of two kinds. First, how did women avail themselves of their new skills to enter what we call the modern world? Second, what obstacles did they face, and what strategies did they develop for getting around or confronting them?

Learning

Literacy means, in the first place, the acquisition of certain basic skills: the ability to read fluently, to write, and, to a lesser degree, to count. But this sort of definition, as vague as it is modest, lends itself to controversy. Do we count people as "literate" if they can sign their name or only if they can read with ease? Whichever criterion we choose, unpredictable factors intervene when we attempt to determine the literacy rate in a specific group such as conscripts, servants, or women. If our source is marriage records, for instance, it may be that only one spouse was required to sign. If the criterion is reading fluency, familiarity with the text can make a difference: religious texts in particular were read and reread countless times and scrutinized in minute detail.

By any measure, however, the participation of women in literacy-promoting processes grew steadily. In late-eighteenth-century France it increased from 14 to 27 percent, leading one author to note an "equalization of the rate of access to print culture for men and women."[4] In Germany, statistical surveys do not become available until later, and they are compiled in such a way that different criteria must be used to measure literacy. In any case, the records show that in certain parts of northern Germany as many as 86.5 percent of girls attended school in 1750. In other words, we are dealing with a veritable social phenomenon, a cultural revolution whose consequences would prove long-lasting for the entire Continent.

In Germany, and especially the northern part of the country, this revolution through learning was the result of various factors, all related in one way or another to the Enlightenment.[5] One of these was government policy: certain states, most notably Prussia, set out to establish a system of compulsory education for all children between the ages of six and fourteen. In Prussia education was made compulsory in 1717, but (Catholic) Bavaria did not adopt a similar measure until 1802. This contrast points up another key element in the education of a population: the religious factor. In Protestant countries where the ruler was also the supreme religious authority, educational reform ran far in advance of the Catholic countries of southern Europe, where for the most part only boys attended regular schools, while girls were limited to convent schools that taught chiefly prayer and so-called feminine skills.

"Compulsory" meant just what it said: church ministers saw to it that the law was enforced. In the duchy of Oldenburg, for example, which at the time was part of the kingdom of Denmark, local pastors were required to make two annual "home visits" *(Hausvistationen)*, during which they noted whether there were books in the house and the children attended school regularly. In 1750, 1.5 percent of women were still illiterate, 98.5 percent could read, but only 43.8 percent could both read and write and, what is more remarkable, only 6.6 percent could do arithmetic. It was not only the daughters of the privileged (government functionaries and well-to-do peasants) who acquired these skills; 64 percent of female servants knew how to read, and 2 percent knew numbers. This level of female literacy was remarkably high for the mid-eighteenth-century, particularly since girls in rural areas frequently attended school for shorter periods than boys: they started typically a year later, at around age seven (because they had to help their mothers), and left school at age eleven to enter domestic service. Although instruction in reading began in the first year, writing lessons started at age eight. The teaching of arithmetic was delayed until students were twelve or thirteen; moreover, it was not free of charge. Hence the fact that it was deemed worthwhile to teach arithmetic to nearly 7 percent of the girls of this region bears emphasizing. When these girls grew up, they would have the skills needed to manage household finances.

Wilhelm Norden has done research about schooling in rural areas relatively unaffected by eighteenth-century wars and famines. It is considerably more difficult to determine what proportion of girls in urban areas attended school in the late eighteenth and, even more, the early nineteenth century.

Social mobility, the displacement of the poor to the urban periphery, the difficulty of access to working-class ghettos, and the anonymity of the individual in an increasingly dense urban population—all these factors complicate the problem of compiling useful statistics on the progress of literacy and education in the nineteenth century.

Under the combined influence of triumphant Lutheranism and

Enlightenment philosophy with its emphasis on learning, education had made great strides in the eighteenth century, but by the first half of the nineteenth the reforming zeal had cooled. It is probably misleading to assert that literacy lost ground, but progress definitely ceased. For example, Prussian statistics for 1818 show that 30 percent of Berlin children did not attend school even though it was compulsory. In Bremen, which had been a bastion of Enlightenment pedagogy in the eighteenth century and where Pietism had exerted a powerful influence on the education of women,[6] 35 of 107 school-age girls were already working in factories rather than attending school in 1838. It was not until March 1839 that a decree regulating child labor prohibited factory work before the age of nine and required certification of three years' school attendance as a condition of employment—and it would be some time before that decree was effectively enforced. If expanded educational opportunity had been a reality in the eighteenth century, it was now a fond hope, something to be achieved in the better world of tomorrow. This was a leitmotif of Bettina von Arnim's study of the peripheral Vogtland sector of Berlin in the concluding section of *This Book Belongs to the King* (1843): "Holding the smallest of her boys on her lap, the mother wound her bobbins. She told me that two of her children were attending school and learning a great deal. Once again it was clear that the poor derive their greatest joys from their children and fervently hope that they will escape poverty through education."[7]

But education, especially of little girls, cannot be measured solely in terms of school attendance rates, which in any case tell us only about elementary and middle-school populations *(Volkschulen, Mittelschulen)*. The first girls' high schools in Prussia were not established until 1872, in Berlin. When the Victoria High School, named for the future empress of Germany, was dedicated in 1870, Fanny Lewald, one of the small group of women authors, raised her voice in protest: "The Victoria School, I must insist, is a very fine institution, but it is for the elite. What we lack is not the top of the tower but a solid foundation. We need schools, secondary schools for women as well as men."[8]

The baccalaureate degree, the ticket to university admission, did not become available to German women until after 1900. Women had been seeking admission to the teaching profession since the late eighteenth century, but they had been allowed in only as primary school teachers and then only on condition that they were single and did not intend to marry. It was not until 1890 (except for a brief period around 1849) that Helen Lange founded the General Association of German Schoolmistresses, which by the turn of the century boasted some 15,000 members.

The contradiction in policy is striking. On the one hand all girls, in urban as well as rural areas, from poor as well as wealthy families, had the opportunity to read, write, and (to a lesser extent) learn their sums. On the other hand, it was the nineteenth century's peculiar hypocrisy to exclude the vast majority of the female population from access to higher levels of education. In fact, one can say that, owing in part to Metternich's Restoration and the ensuing return to private pursuits, the first half of the nineteenth century was particularly regressive on this issue. Any proposal advocating equal education for all met with opposition from men who scarcely bothered to conceal their hostility to women. When, for example, the Prussian Süvern proposed a progressive plan of education in 1818, he was accused of undermining "the foundation of natural and therefore inalienable difference, namely, inequality." In other words, to favor egalitarian education was to weaken the very underpinnings of society.

Faced with this hostile attitude, women had long since understood that true learning could be acquired by alternative means. The most determined became autodidacts, and some women who proudly proclaimed themselves as such went on to write. Louise Karsch, one of the great poets of the eighteenth century, had shown the way. A woman of very humble origins, she had taught herself to read while tending animals in the fields. Any number of early-nineteenth-century female novelists boasted of having learned to read by studying Bibles and religious tracts in parsonage attics.[9] And if their style sometimes savors of this illicit learning, who is to blame?

For most girls the true source of education was the home. It was there, rather than in primary or convent schools, that they discovered themselves and learned to ask questions about the world they lived in. Some male educators insisted that the best way to prevent girls from learning too much was to keep them confined within the home's four walls. Contemporary feminists such as Mary Wollstonecraft and Betty Gleim did not fail to note the contradiction inherent in that thinking: women, though denied the right to cultivate themselves, were charged with the sacred task of educating young children of both sexes for a time and girls even longer. Appointed "natural educators" despite their total lack of experience, mothers worked hard at the task. Wilhelm von Kügelgen looked back on his own early education (1806–7): "My mother was diligent about her children's education. She thoroughly studied the day's most reputable works on education, from which she could scarcely have learned much, for a mother, even a half-educated one, instinctively knows how to raise her children. And if she does not, she will not learn anything about it from Campe or Pestalozzi."[10]

Think of women like George Sand or Bettina Brentano, the "daughters of grandmothers" in the sense that they acquired their real education not from the convents they attended in early childhood but from the grandmothers who raised them. This kind of education, although sometimes chaotic and often anachronistic, also created continuities in women's history, a kind of "female lineage." A modern author like Christa Wolf confesses her debt to such a lineage when she speaks warmly and admiringly of her path-breaking ancestors, the "women of 1800."[11] Of course when a pedagogical grandmother took charge of a child's education, the pupil was in for a rude shock. An adolescent just out of the convent would barely have known how to read, write, and above all recite prayers, while her grandmother, influenced by Enlightenment philosophy, might dream of using a universal history, a Latin Plutarch, or Mme de Sévigné's *Letters* as her sole educational tools. For George Sand and Bettina Brentano (and perhaps one should add Germaine de Staël, although she belonged to an earlier generation and was educated by her mother, not her grandmother), the result was a curious mélange of ancient and modern, of Latin exercises and Mirabeau's speeches, of cumbrous historical compilations and the day's newspapers. Indeed, these rare and fortunate women received educations more liberal than that of most boys, who were obliged to adhere to a strict curriculum, to Latin, and to an iron discipline. These women enjoyed a freedom that would foster the development of a feminine sensibility and, ultimately, world view.

The major fear of educators, men and women alike, was the specter of erudition. The *Weekly Moral Reviews*, an educational journal addressed to women, warned its readers against excesses of erudition. Sophie von La Roche, Bettina Brentano's grandmother and teacher, wrote articles for "German girls" in which she repeatedly warned that "knowing too much" could lead to neurosis and spinsterhood. People were afraid of a learned woman.

She was an "anomaly" or, to a man's eye, an absurdity capable of provoking "feverish shivers."

Pietism was a major factor in promoting private forms of education for girls. Pietist men and women met in "conventicles" for the purpose of confession and meditation, and there they developed common interests and discussed cultural matters. Little by little the autobiographical element began to outweigh the religious. The classic instance of Pietism's influence on women is that of the Beautiful Soul whose confessions Goethe recorded in *Wilhelm Meister's Apprenticeship* (1796). Although Fraülein von Klettenberg, an old Frankfurt acquaintance of the author who served as his model, was indeed a deeply religious woman, she expressed her wish to avoid a conventional woman's life in words that have an astonishingly modern ring: "I realized that I was imprisoned in an airless bell jar. All it took to break it was a little energy, and I was saved."[12]

Such attitudes were not exclusively Protestant. There was a Catholic variant of Pietism whose female adherents played an equally innovative role. The Münster circle around Princess Gallitzine and the later works of the poet Annette von Droste-Hülshoff exemplify its influence.

Pietism was not a strictly upper-class phenomenon. Numerous texts mention "the most powerful and beneficial effects of the preacher on the intellectual and moral development" of women in general and mothers in particular.[13] And since mothers were the educators of very young children of both sexes, the influence of Pietism on the education of the German nation is clear. It also affected attitudes toward the printed word: if Pietists invariably began by reading the Bible and other sacred texts, they often moved on to secular literature, which became a basis for meditation and discussions in which women were free to participate. The sense of belonging to a spiritual community was a new intellectual experience, and it initiated a process of acculturation that relied to a surprising degree on introspection. This gave rise to a literature of intimacy—journals, correspondence, and dialogues—whose liveliness and quality were in no small part the work of women: "I decided to keep a private diary in which I would answer, as to my conscience, for my innermost life, passing judgment on the ideas and feelings that arose within me both to further my education and to deepen my scrutiny of my conscience."[14] Such experiences far transcended the ordinary school curriculum.

Reading: From Escape to Meditation

For girls, as we have seen, the Bible was the primary means of acquiring knowledge at all levels. Children learned to read by spelling out the words of the Bible and learned to behave by deriving moral lessons from the sacred texts. To be sure, the catalogues of fairs such as the one at Leipzig reveal a declining though still high proportion of religious texts. In 1770 religious works accounted for 25 percent of all publications, but by 1800 the figure had dropped to just 13.5 percent. Works categorized as *belles lettres* increased from 16.5 percent in 1770 to 21.5 percent in 1800. These figures clearly point to what one contemporary bookseller and shrewd businessman called "the great publishing revolution."[15]

Frequently it was women who more or less consciously served as agents of this "revolution." Some women developed an insatiable appetite for reading. The governess of one prominent Pietist family wrote in her letters of eight kinds of daily reading: "They read the way some people stuff geese with noodles."

After learning to read and meditate on religious texts at all hours of the day and night, women around the turn of the nineteenth century began to make personal use of their recently acquired freedom. Male contemporaries were critical of what they saw as a "rage to read" in certain women.[16] When an adolescent girl lost herself in novels, they said, she lost her innocence and concocted an artificial paradise. And poetry could be just as damaging. But some men argued that the use of novels by young women to imagine what life would be like when they were older was not nearly as harmful as the abuse of literature by married women. There were Madame Bovarys in every province and every country. Books ceased to be a mere escape and became a substitute for life, a way of fleeing the everyday that spelled an end to domestic tranquility. When this happened, society was in danger, because the woman who read no longer fulfilled her duties as wife and mother; she failed in her mission as a woman, which was to maintain order within the home and family. To read was to dream, hence to escape, to flout norms and conventions—precisely the opposite of what was expected of a woman of good family in the nineteenth century.

Women did not share this view. In the solitude of private life reading was often compensation for a disastrous, arranged early marriage. Caroline Schlegel-Schelling, one of the leading figures of early German Romanticism, started out as the young wife of a stalwart provincial physician. Her only links to the wider world were the books sent her from her native city, the university town of Göttingen. If a book failed to arrive, she pleaded and fumed: "I have been dying of thirst for some time now because my source of books has dried up."[17] She dispatched lists of books to be sent her at once, ranging "from those that you read lying on the sofa" to "those that you read seated on the same sofa with a work table in front of you." The lists did not include the Bible or other religious works but rather a diverse assortment of fiction and nonfiction ranging from newspapers to ponderous historical tomes. As the content of women's reading changed, so did their attitude toward the activity. Once the Bible had been read aloud and served as the focus of moral and religious meditation, but now reading was more diverse and eclectic as well as private. Caroline had not yet reached the point of reading political tracts, but she did explore the literature of other countries: she read Shakespeare, whose plays she would later translate, as well as Mirabeau's *Letters from the Prison of Vincennes* and, later on, some essays of Condorcet. In 1796 she wrote her brother-in-law Friedrich Schlegel: "Fritz! There are two things you absolutely must read. One is by Condorcet: do not fail to read it. And read all the works of a man named Fulda, who must have been a teacher with a very original notion of the human."[18]

A fiancé or husband might well take pride in a "cultivated" woman, so long as she was content to embellish her mind and collect pleasant quotes for her poetry albums. But the moment she sought to expand her knowledge, analyze the content of what she read, or compare her reading with what she saw around her, the specter of the "learned woman" reared its head. This carries an interesting revolutionary connotation, as in Barbey d'Aurevilly's comment that "bluestockingism" was "the revolution in literature, for the blue stocking is for women what the red cap is for men."[19] Indeed, German women of the early nineteenth century were no longer content to read the sentimental novels shrewdly imported from England by some of their sisters. The German imitations of Richardson's *Pamela* and *Clarissa* now seemed dated, and even a best-seller like *The History of Fraülein von Sternheim,* which had made Sophie von La Roche's reputation in the 1770s, had gone out of fashion.

Two factors influenced the changes in women's reading habits. First, women became curious about topical matters: current events, science, innovations, and inventions. References to the *Encyclopedia* are a leitmotif of women's writing in this period. The *Encyclopedia* was looked upon as a treasure trove to be preserved at all cost and consulted on every imaginable subject, from how to build a cabin upon settling in the New World to understanding one's Indian neighbors to giving birth alone and raising one's children without a husband.

The second factor corroborates the first: with the French Revolution, women for perhaps the first time found themselves confronting history directly and permanently. For a quarter of a century, from 1790 to 1815, they frequently had to cope unaided with family, educational, and economic responsibilities in a world for which nothing had prepared them. Curiosity about topical matters and interest in current events converged to bring about a veritable "cultural revolution" for women, particularly in Germany. Yet no German woman produced a manifesto comparable to Mary Wollstonecraft's *Vindication of the Rights of Woman* (1792) or Olympe de Gouges's *Declaration of the Rights of Woman and the Citizen* (1790). Reading and literature served as messengers across international boundaries, however. The reading of newspapers and the writing of what might be called "novels of current events" were two aspects of a single process. The novel reflected the actual experience of women in France and Germany: it was no longer a vehicle for escape but just the opposite, a token of awareness of a common set of problems shared by women across Europe. Reading gave rise to a solidarity among women of all classes and all generations. At seventy-five, Goethe's mother expressed her delight with novels written by women and dealing with the most up-to-the-minute issues; in a letter to her son she wrote: "You cannot do anything kinder or more praiseworthy for your loving mother, in her poverty of spirit, than to be so kind as to share such pleasant things with me whenever you receive them."[20] Books, once read for private pleasure, spiritual improvement, or escape, now became stimuli to thinking about oneself and others.

Because books structured reading in a certain way, they initially served as efficient instruments of a kind of socialization that some readers desired. A reading public did exist, and the flourishing publishing industry worked hard to meet its ever growing demands. The latest catalogues featured new categories and genres aimed especially at women: there were histories of brigands and of convents, stories modeled on the adventures of Robinson Crusoe, novels of emigration, and novels about the French Revolution, as well as novels on "philosophical, moral, and pedagogical" themes.[21] Some commentators regretted the change and longed for the not-so-distant past when women read only "edifying works, the occasional tale, and cookbooks."

Such eclecticism restructured the act of reading. "Intensive" reading—the repeated study of a single text—gave way to "extensive" reading.[22] Women read many books, and read them only once. This required the development of a publishing industry capable of steadily increasing its output. Reading began to function as a veritable social institution. This was a second factor of socialization through reading. Like other European countries at the time, Germany experienced a vast expansion of its readership. Reading groups sprang up literally everywhere, along with lending libraries, reading rooms, and other semi-private institutions. Interestingly enough, many of these were open to women. And this was not a strictly urban phenomenon: there were reading groups in small towns and even villages.[23] They were not for the most part exclusive establishments. Of course some private libraries enjoyed sumptuous accommodations, like the *Harmonie* of Hamburg, but many were simply collections of books opened up to neighbors by doctors, lawyers, and philosophers.[24]

Books circulated at all levels. Friedrich Schlegel made fun of the servant bent under the weight of books that his wife had borrowed from the Jena library, but he knew that such circulation of printed matter was the force behind the new forms of sociability that revolved around women. Even letters, that unchallenged form of women's literature, reflected the change by venturing outside the domestic sphere and daring to express literary judgments. The Romantic circles of Jena and the salons of Berlin directed by Jewish women such as Rahel Varnhagen and Henriette Herz thrived on the discussion of recently published books. Mme de Staël, though herself an expert on the subject of literary salons, was astonished by the intensity of cultural life in Berlin, an otherwise provincial city "in the sandy wastes of Brandenburg." Reading led by stages to greater conviviality, as Henriette Herz aptly described in her memoirs: "I have spent a number of years among the most sophisticated people in Berlin. . . . At first we all met in a small *Teekränzchen*. Later there was the Fessler reading society, which brought together artists, statesmen, scholars, and women."[25] Reading societies were "revolutionary" in the sense that they were virtually the only public place apart from the theater and certain salons where men and women could meet to discuss common interests. A reading group was a secular "conventicle" in which women were full-fledged participants, and their authoritative judgments were frequently consulted.

The contemporary historical situation stimulated the readers' interest in politics, and women soon began to reflect on political subjects. Through books they thus ventured onto terrain that had once been exclusively masculine. Their incursion was brief but important.

In the first decade of the nineteenth century women's letters frequently mentioned Mirabeau, Condorcet, and Sieyès. Gazettes were astonishingly widely read. Newspapers for women sprang up throughout Europe, among them the *Journal des Luxus und der Moden,* which was published from 1786 to 1816, and the review *London und Paris,* whose Paris correspondent was Helmina von Chézy. But female readers also liked to read the major newspapers of the day, such as the *Hamburger Correspondent* and the *Moniteur.* The language was of little importance: "Lafayette! Mirabeau! Pétion! Bailly! Oh, how enthusiasm put fire in my cheeks when of a quiet evening hour I read to my husband and two or three of his close friends the speeches that the *Moniteur* so faithfully reported," remarked Joanna Schopenhauer, the philosopher's mother, in memoirs published in 1839.[26]

The period 1790–1815, during which women gained access to a number of fields previously limited almost exclusively to men, was a unique moment in German history. It was a time when compulsory education, tenuous as it may have been, began to bear fruit, and when a first generation of women chose reading as a way of compensating for the higher education they were still denied. Books, distributed through increasingly organized channels, gave women access to new social networks, so that reading served women as a true instrument of social integration. Some were satisfied with the de facto intellectual equality they enjoyed in the reading societies. But others availed themselves of the opportunities that books afforded for communication to establish the circles and salons of the Romantic period.

Some women, still few in number, were so driven by curiosity about current events as to make the activity of reading and the choice of what to read the means to a political emancipation that neither laws nor men were prepared to grant them. That is why certain male commentators felt compelled to paint somber portraits of women who fell prey to the disease of reading: "I am by no means critical of the fact that a woman should seek to refine her writing and conversation through appropriate study and the reading of decent works, or that she should wish not to remain totally without scientific knowledge. But she must not make literature her profession or venture into the realm of erudition."[27] Although the tone was intended to be judicious, the argument is hopelessly traditional: a little learning is *not* a dangerous thing, but a woman had better not drink deep at this particular spring.

The same type of argument was proposed in much more vehement terms after 1815. In a time of sweeping social change (a mass exodus from the countryside and a dramatic increase in child labor), progress in the education of girls slowed, and the "rage to read" once so prevalent among women began to encounter increasingly substantial impediments. In the order that Metternich and the Restoration established, what to read was no longer a matter of individual choice. Regulated, distributed, and censored, reading, even in private, became an activity subject to close and inescapable scrutiny. Women who read were reduced to a silence that would not be denounced until mid-century, and then only by a few marginal figures.

Toward the end of the century, however, the "voice of women" was once again heard, abetted by certain male writers such as August Bebel, the author of *Woman and Socialism* (1879). But the German women's movement, divided along bourgeois and proletarian lines, was largely confined to the narrow arena of politics and no longer elicited the same response from its "public." Indeed, the term "public" seems rather incongruous, since what mattered to and affected women belonged to the "private" sphere. Still, statistically at any rate, a female public existed, but its interests had changed considerably. Cheap, escapist fiction, strictly monitored by authorities both public and private, had carried the day: the market was flooded with historical novels that avoided any reference to the present, with pulp fiction and serializations promoted by women's magazines like *Gartenlaube*. Writers such as Eugenie Marlitt and Hedwig Courths-Mahler enjoyed tremendous success. One novel by Marlitt, first serialized in *Gartenlaube* in 1866, went through twenty-three editions in twenty years.

Other women, however, were casting about for adequate ways to express questions they were just beginning to formulate. By the middle of the century, at a time when the Restoration and censorship upheld bourgeois virtues and conventions, what women read and wrote already revealed a growing division between escapist literature and works of more serious intent.

Cultural history is full of such contradictions: at a time when books "ostensibly avoided controversial subjects such as religion,"[28] and most female readers seemed satisfied with the pulp they were offered, a few women who refused to be muzzled by censorship or slander or indifference or the dismal failure of the revolution of 1848 in Germany began to make themselves heard. By 1850 they were daring to disrupt the general "calm" with what they themselves called "the voice of women."

Writing: For Oneself, for Others

German women first took up their pens around 1800, at the beginning of what Christa Wolf has called the *Zwischenzeit* (literally: in-between time), the interregnum not only between two centuries but between two worlds fundamentally different as to their politics, society, and culture. To be sure, a woman's literature already existed in German, consisting essentially of moral, pedagogical, and sentimental works. But a very different kind of woman's literature grew out of the need to express the shattering impact of the French Revolution, and before long women found that they also felt a new need to express themselves. Over the course of the nineteenth century, the new literature evolved along with society to become an organ for the expression of realities affecting all women.

Curiously, it was precisely where political expression was absent or forbidden that a political event sparked a desire for public self-expression through literature. No German woman in this period composed a manifesto like Theodor von Hippel's demanding "the civic improvement of women." Yet between 1790 and 1815 a number of women wrote novels dealing with topical issues such as the French Revolution and its immediate consequences. Although access to the public arena would remain difficult for women throughout the century, to enter the male preserves of politics and history indirectly by way of literature was at least a first step.

The number of women who took that first step and ventured to participate in such rapidly evolving genres as the novel and theater was certainly small, and they were apt to be greeted with sarcasm by male writers: "Of the forty to fifty woman writers in Germany today (not counting the legions who do not bother to publish the foolish things they produce), there are scarcely half a dozen who, blessed as they are with a superior sort of genius, truly have a calling to venture into a realm . . . that neither nature nor the civic constitution has prepared them for."[29] This comment, made at the turn of the century, admirably captures what would remain the general attitude toward "women writers" for the next hundred years: criticism, not to say scorn, awaited those who violated a taboo enforced by the culture and the society. This positivist, pseudo-scientific age added a further taboo based on the presumed inferiority of the female body and brain: "The woman author does not exist. She is a contradiction in terms. The role of women in letters is the same as in manufacturing: she is of use when genius is no longer required."[30]

Misogyny clearly knew no bounds, and the genius or talent of women writers went unrecognized. When the elderly poet Clemens Brentano learned that his sister had tried her own hand at the literary game, he was indignant: "It is a sad thing. This creature . . . Bettina would have been admirable in the role of angel had she not made a public display of what was best and most intimate in her."[31] The favorite target of scorn was George Sand: "We find, in Madame Dudevant's pipe as in her novels, nothing but the most frightful and contemptible vulgarity."[32]

If the prevailing climate was increasingly uncongenial to women's writing, few women took up their pens unless forced to do so by material want ("to feed the family") or the vagaries of emigration, even if the kind of education they had received was not often well suited to the demands of earning a living. But some were driven by an imperious need to write: many used pseudonyms or borrowed their husbands' names, sparking countless family arguments. Some authors eventually disclosed their true identity, justifying the decision with some rather curious arguments. Theresa Huber, for instance, made this confession in 1820: "The public would have found it difficult to believe that the author [of a collection of stories published in 1803] was a mother in her prime. That is why I kept my literary activities quiet. The aging matron has no further household responsibilities. Today she can fulfill rather than neglect her maternal duties by writing."[33]

Translation was one of the best avenues open to women who wished to write. For obvious reasons work of this kind was considered ideal for women. The translator toiled at home, in private. She was not exposed to the indecent publicity of the literary market. Though well paid at times, the work was anonymous: there was no prostituting of the husband's name, no danger to the family. Last but not least, translation was compatible with a woman's duties: the work could be interrupted as necessary to fit the rhythms of the household. But there was also something else, something that those who look upon translation as a harmless woman's pastime do not always clearly perceive: to translate was to make concrete use of the knowledge one had acquired, and some female translators found a measure of freedom in choosing what texts to translate and perhaps even an occasional opportunity to slip in a thought or accent of their own that might otherwise find no outlet. Why did women who started out as translators before becoming writers deliberately choose to translate such works as the correspondence of Ninon de Lenclos or plays and novels dealing with the French Revolution?[34] Theresa Huber reveals the secret link between translation and writing in reminiscing about her translation of the fashionable author Louvet de Couvray: "I wrote an end to *Necessary Divorce.* Thoughts flowed easily from my brimming imagination straight to my pen. . . . And at night, while keeping vigil at Huber's sickbed, more than once with a child at my breast, I became a writer."

If translating was what Proudhon called a "service activity," it nevertheless gave women the encouragement they needed to move on to other forms of writing. Few women writers in either France or Germany tried their hand at theater, and those who did stood little chance of success, as the example of Marie von Ebner-Eschenbach suggests: a well-known novelist of the end of the century, she dared to write a play about Mme Roland but never managed to have it produced.[35] The story and the novel offered women the best chance of success, with the predictable consequence that these genres were dismissed as a form of "mass-produced literature": "It is women who consume the most novels, and they also produce the most. I am therefore of the opinion that they should make their own novels as they make their own frills."[36]

Bear in mind that some women's novels lent credence to such clichés. Breathless emulators of Walter Scott, indefatigable producers of Romantic and Gothic fiction, some female writers exploited the fashionable genres and turned out endless series of ever more insipid books that nevertheless found a ready audience when serialized in magazines such as *Gartenlaube*. Although this kind of fiction became, with the blessing of the authorities, synonymous with women's literature in the nineteenth century, it should not be allowed to obscure those other forms of women's writing that were subjected to censorship, sarcasm, and scorn.

Letters, the primary means of literary expression for women, provided an alternative forum where women of talent and wit could distinguish themselves. Outwardly disguised as private correspondence, letters were in fact widely diffused; they not only disseminated information but offered opportunities for reflection and experimentation with the whole gamut of literary genres. The most subtle example of this is the correspondence of Rahel Varnhagen, but there was no want of creative genius in Bettina von Arnim's poetic transformation of her earlier correspondence into a genre subsuming all the rest.[37] Significantly, much of this private literature—journals, memoirs, autobiographies—was published in the 1840s, encouraging nostalgia among women who still remembered that brief but intense interlude at the turn of the century in which they had passed their adolescence.[38] But new prospects were already looming on the horizon, and courageous women braved all opposition to voice new political demands. Bettina von Arnim's literary career, for example, did not really begin until 1837, when she took up the cause of the "Göttinger Seven," seven professors dismissed from the University of Göttingen for having been presumptuous enough to remind the duke of Hanover of his promise to promulgate a constitution. In the end, it was the increasing importance of the "social question" that revealed a hitherto latent fissure in women's literature.

Social commitment brought a new dimension and force to the writings of certain women in the 1840s. A few female authors, having made a name for themselves in literature, now abandoned the field to try their hand at sociological research.

The publication in 1839 of Flora Tristan's *London Journal* and in 1843 of Bettina von Arnim's *This Book Belongs to the King* attests that the interest of women in the social realities of the day was a Europe-wide phenomenon. Because the ongoing social changes were so far-reaching and profound, the socially engaged literature of the day gradually abandoned the use of fiction, high style, and invented characters in favor of statistics, lists of paupers, and undigested documentation. The resulting works were powerful but not much noticed by contemporaries; their style was documentary, and their social and political message one that, according to certain male writers reduced to silence by the censorship, only women could still communicate. Confirmation of this claim can be found in this excerpt from a conversation between author Louise Aston and the chief of the Berlin police in March 1846:

> *Aston:* In the interests of my literary career, it is desirable that I remain in Berlin, where I am constantly finding new inspiration.
>
> *Chief:* It is certainly not in our interest for you to publish your future writings here, for they will surely be as liberal as your other remarks.
>
> *Aston:* Well, then, Your Excellency, if the Prussian government is beginning to be afraid of a woman, then it is in a sad pass indeed![39]

The failure of the revolution of 1848 in Germany marks a crucial turning point. The socially engaged literature characteristic of the *Vormärz*[40] began to lose favor. Some women authors renounced their former commitment and took refuge in turning out safer commodities: Louise Mühlbach, whose novel *Aphra Behn,* a biography of the first professional woman writer in England, was a forceful plea in favor of a genuine emancipation of women, now published only glittering bagatelles like the *Stories of the Court of Sans-Souci in the Time of Frederick II* and other pseudo-historical works. Even the most emancipated women were still afraid of writing as a public act. In the *Story of My Life* (1861–62), Fanny Lewald, an emancipated Jew and darling of the Berlin literary establishment, offered this confession: "More accustomed than I myself suspected to a certain dependency and submission, I always regarded my literary activity as something that would be granted to me, something I would be permitted to do with all sorts of restrictions, so that I always felt obliged to do needlework on the side."[41]

If there was an awakening of certain kinds of women's literature in the second half of the nineteenth century, we must look outside the sphere of the aristocracy and the well-to-do to find its traces. To be sure, women of the upper classes continued to publish, among them Louise Otto-Peters, who in 1849 founded the *Women's Journal for Higher Female Interests;* Lily Braun, née von

Kretschman, the author of the remarkable *Memoirs of a Socialist;* and Hedwig Dohm, who fought for the right to vote.[42] But an equally powerful and much newer movement was taking shape among the women of the proletariat. The two different approaches to what was called the *Frauenfrage,* or "woman question," came to a parting of the ways in 1894. This resulted in a series of working-class autobiographies, the most famous of which remains that of Adelheid Popp, *The Youth of a Working Woman.* This book was an example of what Goethe called "autobiography from below," and the author states immediately that her intention is to represent not just herself but other women in similar circumstances: "I have written the story of my youth because it resembles that of thousands of other proletarian women and girls."[43] A family of fifteen children, three years of sporadic schooling, factory work at age ten, a hospital stay at age thirteen, and the discovery of the great classics of literature—this itinerary was recounted not for its individual value but because it exemplified that of many others. Autobiography took on the purpose of serving others, and women's literature at the end of the century assumed a role not unlike that of the pedagogical and ethical texts, "moral reviews," and sentimental novels of a century earlier. Only now the texts advised their readers not about moral issues but about social ones.

Hence the history, however brief and incomplete, of how women progressed from their first steps toward education to public political commitment by way of literature stands as a kind of parable for social history in general: "If style is the expression of a man, literature is no less the expression of a society," wrote Louis de Bonald in 1812. Woman's irresistible rise in the public domain of culture was achieved through steady progress in literacy that no legislation could truly impede.

It was much more difficult, however, to become a writer in the full sense of the word. Although those who produced fairy tales and escapist literature were well received by that portion of the female population docile to the restored order, those who hoped to make literature into a true "voice of women" capable of expressing the anxieties and doubts of the age encountered ever more powerful opposition and scorn. But instead of becoming discouraged they turned their writing in new directions[44] and did not hesitate to take a fresh look at the cultural history of mankind, which they insisted was that of womankind as well:

Women were so often told that "men will do your thinking for you" that in the end they stopped thinking. For long generations women grew up with the burden of having their intelligence held in contempt, and it is plain to see that they often helped justify that contempt. . . . Women have been denied the ability to accomplish anything important or significant in art, science, or politics. . . . But the book that has exerted the greatest influence on society was written by a woman: *Uncle Tom's Cabin*. Lincoln's presidency was a direct consequence of this book. Perhaps the greatest prose writer of our time is a woman: George Sand. The greatest contemporary novelist, in my opinion at least, is a woman: George Eliot. . . . The time for clinging sentimentally to the ruins and vestiges of the past is over. We must expose the old, crumbling pyramids, yellowing thoughts, and fossilized ideas to the light of truth.[45]

TRANSLATED FROM THE FRENCH BY ARTHUR GOLDHAMMER

7

The Catholic Model

Michela De Giorgio

Femininity and Counter-Revolution

The Virtue of the Noble Sex

In 1866 Anna Maria Mozzoni, the most renowned representative of Italian feminism, adapted to ideals of emancipation the aristocratic genealogy that was the inspiration of the Catholic feminine model under the Restoration. The "noble bravery" of Marie Antoinette of France, the valor of the Duchess of Angoulême, and the energy of Maria Carolina of Berry became the pillars of proof of women's "superior character." The pure feminist dream—"women in place of men" because they are "more deserving due to their moral virtues"—calls on History, which is above the "passions of the partisans," to "assign to each its true role."[1] The Theatine priest, Gioacchino Ventura, was equally convinced of the superiority of women. The Bourbons, by comparison, showed their true selves, "worthless men," the rock bottom of masculine moral force.

The priest and the feminist were united in their ennoblement of women. Although Father Ventura was an atypical representative of the nineteenth-century clergy, having been a follower of Lamennais and exiled to France after 1848 because of disputes with Pius IX, he was author of the noted *La donna cattolica* (1855),[2] cornerstone of the moral education of the feminine sex. This strong argument in support of the moral virtues of women ("nowadays one must not only elevate woman in the eyes of man, one must even elevate her in her own eyes") was close in style to the edifying tone common to the European cultural history of the nineteenth century, in which one can recognize the positions of very diverse political and religious credos. Ventura's model is akin to the "mother-teacher" archetype born of the debates about feminine education at the time of the Revolution. The "new" mother developed and strengthened, first in her children and then in men, the social and individual virtues; this was a classic model of revolutionary pedagogical thought from Lakanal to the Italian, Buonarrotti.

Catholic culture of the Restoration easily accepted this model, an inheritance backed by the contributions of scientific research. In France, at the end of the eighteenth century, the influence of the writings of George Stahl promoted the credo of the superiority of the soul over the body. The *Système physique et moral de la femme,* written by Pierre Roussel in 1775 and for more than a century a fundamental theoretical referent, identified the essence of the female sex as more than the physiological limitations conferred by the sexual organ. Women's fragility and sensitivity were far from negative effects of the relationship between the physical and the ethical; rather, they became positive attributes of the type. Even the soul benefited from the *extension* of the signs of femininity, from muscle fibers to moral behavior.[3]

By the first decades of the nineteenth century, many Catholic authors had already theorized a special "historical" propensity of Christianity to guide these sentimental characteristics of femininity, ultimately detached from their bodily, almost carnal, manifestations.[4] Freed from dependent link between physiological structure and psychological substance, this ideal of femininity spread through postrevolutionary Europe. The feminine soul, different and complementary to the masculine one, became for the Church of the Restoration a reservoir of civilizing resources and of conversion possibilities. Similarly, for classical idealism, the feminine soul was necessary for the full attainment of "humanity" (the family as nucleus of *Sittlichkeit* in Hegel's *Philosophy of Law*), as it was for romanticism with its ideal of the harmonious reciprocity of love.

"This sex, which seems to have been endowed as its portion only with sweetness and patience, has often shown the most active zeal, the most intrepid devotion, and the most astonishing self-possession," wrote the Catholic daily *L'Ami* in the early 1820s. In its pages the supremacy of feminine lives over masculine ones was accepted as fact.[5] In the eyes of the Catholics of the Restoration, the dialectic of feminine force and weakness revealed by the Revolution was one of the few merits of that event. This new social subject appeared uncontaminated by political passions: the Christian sentiments imbued in it made it already perfectly exemplary. At the apex, as an immediate political referent, shone the strategic valor of the women of the royal family, but underneath there was an inexhaustible web of feminine resources, without class barriers.

"Prayers, tenderness, laments, caresses" were their arms of persuasion, the intimate way by which, in France, women managed to have a powerful influence on public life. Joseph de Maistre theorized that "for good and evil, the influence of your sex has been great" (but not beyond the limit of an enlarged family nucleus: "Her children, friends, servants are more or less her subjects"). His words sum up perfectly the point of view of the epoch. An "experimental" example was that of Father Pierre Alexandre Mercier who, at Fourvières, was confessor of 20,000 penitents between 1850 and 1857, an average of 14 a day, although we do not know the percentage of females. He collected from his experience the tales of virtues and sins in a series of lectures entitled "De l'influence salutaire ou pernicieuse qu'exerce la femme dans la société." The text was recommended as a model for preachers.[6]

God Changes Gender

The Catholic formulation of a feminine counterforce using sentimental resources as a moral corrective vis-à-vis men was easier to accomplish in the French literary tradition in which "the femininity of the heart" could invoke outstanding literary names—from Madame de Sévigné to Madame de Lafayette—recounting the wise and light feminine touch in the web of private relationships. In Italy, the lack of a national society manifested itself in the spread of general handbooks of social manners. "The mere lack of society . . . naturally functions so that in Italy there is no set Italian manner or tone," Leopardi lamented.[7] It was the Church that accomplished this unification of manners—from which came a ruling civilizing tradition—blending the inherent virtues of aristocratic behavior with the virtues of the good Christian.[8] In the first decades of the nineteenth century, the tradition of the insolent treatises on women of Boccaccio or Filippo of Bergamo had definitely been superseded. The hegemony of the Church continued in the total colonization of the French Catholic handbooks with Italian authors of exemplary women's lives. The effect of this influence was lasting. At the end of the 1880s the *Civiltà Cattolica* raged against the ungodly juxtaposition in the same pantheon of such illustrious Italians (proposed by a women's magazine) as Mathilda of Canossa and Catherine of Siena with two martyrs of the Neapolitan revolution of 1789, Eleanora Fonseca Pimentel and Luisa Sanfelice.[9] The feminine social identity could not be complete without the models offered by a Catholic literary iconography and its abundance of saints.[10]

The nineteenth century's estrangement from the Church, its militant or passive anticlericalism, were exclusively masculine phenomena. It was the general complaint of the parish priests that the men were wandering off. Their religion was not *lost* but had visibly changed its content. From a global absolutist state of mind, it came to assume the relativistic outlines of a religious opinion. Men placed their faith more in "political positions," while the belief of women kept intact its character of "state of mind" of which, more than anything else, the "acts of behavior" were the signs of a robust faith. Catholicism of the nineteenth century was expressed in the female gender. The feminization of religious practices, of piety, of the clergy, was evident. "God has changed sex," Michelet pronounced in mid-century. He was the pioneer of a gendered lexicon applied to a religious credo that continues to the present.

Women hardly figured in the map of dominant vices reported by the French curates after the revolutionary torment: working on the Sabbath, skipping Mass, and failing to make the obligatory communion on Easter. The religious practices of women were more fervent and women were more observant than men. The synthesis on the national level of quite varied regional behaviors could have confirmed the hypothesis that three out of four practicing Catholics were women.[11] At the beginning of the nineteenth century Aegidius Jais noted that, in ten years of caring for souls in the countryside of Salzburg, he found only a single locality in which the stream of penitents was not predominately female.[12] Even if often one cannot verify gender differences in religious practices except through the impressionistic accounts of the curates, devotional books showed a dominant feminine presence. "Religion, as far as it is a sentimental matter, is nearer to women than to men," wrote the German Benedictine monk, C. Gartner, in 1814 in a book of readings directed specifically toward women. In mid-century *Civiltà Cattolica* confirmed as "certain and confessed" the feminization of devotional practices. Everywhere in church the "womanly sex" outnumbers the "virile."[13] In Rome, for the 1825 Holy Year, only 38 percent of the pilgrims were women.[14] But in the crowds of the faithful from all over France who went to Ars, the first and most visited shrine in the mid-nineteenth century (60,000–80,000 pilgrims a year), the predominance of women was clear: of the 397 identified, 64.5 percent were women, a majority which signaled not only their religious practice but also the fervor that sustained them.

Identification of the Catholic Woman

Gendered "Psychology of Peoples"

Clergymen in the first half of the nineteenth century, lacking statistical methods, described their flocks without differentiating by sex. In addition, their categories of identification were vague and imprecise. A "psychology of the people" was miniaturized at the parish level: the village "temperament"—devout, hard-working, indifferent or indolent—excused the clergy from having to describe the specific virtues of the faithful. This anthro-psychological *enclosure,* which Philippe Boutry observed in the diocese of Ars,[15] expanded to national boundaries, could be generalized to permit *all* sociomoral identification of the "typical" female. And it was not solely a clerical propensity: Stendhal, Michelet—and their Italian followers of various religious denominations and different disciplines, the man of letters Tommaseo as well as the anthropologist Mantegazza—all classified women into "national types." From these they derived specific moral behaviors: degrees of passion, sentimentality, willingness to sacrifice, marital obedience, and so on.

Only in the last decades of the nineteenth century, under the combined effects of industrialization, urbanization, literacy, and politicizing of women, was the Church forced to conform to the standards of classification of lay social science and to define the undifferentiated feminine cosmogony by more precise types, by class, marital state, age group, occupation.[16] The decrease of the clearly antagonistic distinctions between Catholic and non-Catholic women was one of the merits of this more comprehensive identification. "We must divest ourselves of the habit of inventing distinct and absolute types, and as far as possible not say in the singular: 'the Christian woman' or 'the non-Christian woman'," wrote Father Gabriel d'Azambuja at the end of the century.[17]

Likewise, the nineteenth-century conceptualization of "temperamental" degrees of Catholicism—by nations and not by villages—was just as unscientific and impressionistic. In 1828, Elisabeth Galitzin, traveling through Italy toward Rome in the entourage of Mother Sophie Barat, "feels" herself crossing the country of Catholicism. In the Holy City she was transported with joy: even the air was "perfumed by the proximity of the throne of Saint Peter." The streets planted with crosses and decorated with images of Mary at whose feet men and women kneel ("Mary is the châtelaine before which all Italy kneels" Taine wrote), the cities and villages strewn with statues of saints were proof of Italian devotion.[18] In those same years Félicité de Lamennais described, in that sanctified topography, "a system of followers" which included almost the entire population of the Papal States.

The political viewpoint was shared by women. In 1862, in the Duomo of Milan, Louise Colet, unquestionably emancipated, felt immersed in "a heavenly native atmosphere . . . inseparable from the soul of this people."[19] Her inalterable pro-Risorgimento vocation (as a child she fell in love with Silvio Pellico after reading *Le mie prigioni*) helped confirm her certainty that the highest degree of Catholicism was that of Italian men and women.

The national Catholic *Italian woman* was born in the 1830s, encouraged by pro-liberal political ideals. It was a cultural model without a hinterland of national common "traits." For it was difficult, in Italy, to put side by side the derisive and aggressive behavior toward the clergy of the young Neapolitan aristocrats encountered by Goethe,[20] and the keen sense of fidelity to the Catholic faith and to the sovereign of the Piedmont nobility, so conscious of its separateness from the Italian aristocracies "faithfully depicted in the Florindos and Rosauras of Goldoni."[21] The first ideal typifying of the national *Italian woman* was that of Niccolò Tommaseo: "the Italian woman, capable of inspiring others, wisely obedient and commanding when necessary, is the guarantee for us of a less harsh destiny. Wherever men are more corrupt and weak, there women are less weak and less debased."[22] *Civiltà Cattolica* condemned the text as too liberal ("though it contains some good") and recommended for the Christian formation of feminine souls more reliable authors, all of them from the ranks of the clergy. But Tommaseo's model, the "new" patriotic and very Catholic Italian woman, was adopted and reproduced in the constant stream of manuals and moral tracts of the second half of the nineteenth century.

The Church even constructed its own "psychology of peoples" upon squarely religious foundations. English women, dethroned from the pedestal of moral authority where Catholicism had placed them, became a *topos* of the polemic with Protestantism. "The English woman . . . no longer elicits admiration; she barely earns the respect due her sex," wrote the Abbé Gaume in 1844, comparing how the different religious credos safeguarded the exercise of the family authority and countered the authority of women.[23]

The nineteenth century was the century of the primacy of male discourse, and its rhetoric was not inconsistent with this copious production of models. Women were left with a "counter-discourse" essentially based on the character of their piety, a "sentimental" piety which spread from the places of devotion to the everyday life of the family. The feeling of self-satisfaction (so typical of the nineteenth-century feminine role) came from the knowing exercise of moral sovereignty over domestic life and the education of children. Obviously, the many deficiencies of real life existed. But they were softened by the certain knowledge that human sentiments are merely commonly deceptive reflections of religious sentiments, which are the valid models and instruments of any earthly sentiment.

The advance in the nineteenth century of religious sentimentality was closely linked to family sentimentalism: the feminine Catholic model was exclusively that of the wife and mother. The Church demanded from the wife submission and the spirit of self-denial. If the world is a vale of tears for all, it is especially so for women. The affective aspects—much less the sexual ones—of conjugal love were not taken up in the chaste nineteenth-century Catholic literature. The silence lasted until the first decades of the twentieth century. Rarely, and only in a few lines, was there any reference to the "matrimonial duties" which must be fulfilled, without ever abstaining, not even for "the practice of virtue." The husband was a gift of God, who brings the woman sanctity through her sacrifice.[24]

The Sentimental Code

In 1880, with the encyclical *Arcanum,* the Church responded to the lay attacks against marriage. Leo XIII confirmed marital authority: "the man is the head of the woman, as Christ is the head of the Church." The wife "must be subject and obedient to her husband, not as a handmaid, but as a companion, such that the subjection that she shows him is not devoid of decorum and dignity."[25]

The encyclical of Leo XIII affirmed and restored female dignity in marriage, although the marital protection was at times bloodthirsty. The severe condemnation of husbands' killing adulterous wives revealed the dramatic behind-the-scenes and across-classes activities of that indissoluble institution. For the majority of bourgeois and aristocratic Italian women born in the middle of the nineteenth century a marriage that yielded to family wishes was still the norm. Independent sentimental choice existed in the mythical horizons of the feminist pamphlets: "the free America" of the equality of marital exchange. In the novels of the Catholic women writers of the end of the nineteenth century, the favorite theme of marriage contained many of the suggestions of moral reform which impassioned the international militants of the nascent sociology of marital relations (Legouvé, Letourneau, Mantegazza, Lombroso, Lhotzky, Werner, Carpenter, and so on). The passive acceptance by women of marriages to much older men, one of the most debated preconditions of moral revival—that unequal trade between feminine esthetic capital and male economic capital that was a thorn in the sides of the believers in eugenics—lost, in the pages of Catholic women writers, any accusatory tone deploring the double standard of the matrimonial marketplace. And the difficulties about the age of the husband are resolved in tales with happy endings.[26] It should be recalled that women's desire for the marital state, during the whole of the nineteenth century and until the First World War, derived from the world's equating the dignity of female social existence with matrimony. This was not limited only to Catholic publications. But the marriages of reason—not of passion nor of consolation—which the presses of the Gioventù Femminile of the Italian Azione Cattolica still advised in the 1920s had a long tradition of antisentimental pedagogy. The outcomes of marital choices guided by the eyes or the heart were unstable and ephemeral. One asked of the husband of the militant Catholic woman merely that he be a good Christian.

"Far from murmuring in feminine circles about the iniquity of men," stated the panegyric of Rita da Cascia, which was read in Rome during the sanctification ceremony in 1900. The long expiation of marital pains imposed by a "savage beast" of a husband and the dignified withdrawal from other victims of matrimony played a large part in the nineteenth-century biographies of the saint.[27] It was the devout side of the overflowing lay literature about the *bad marriage,* revealing the details of the sufferings of the marital life of Rita. It was a sanctified model by which the Church recognized that for women marital life could be a burden or a martyrdom. With the new century, sexuality also appeared in rare Catholic autobiographies about marital unhappiness. Jacqueline Vincent—for twenty-five years the servant and lover of a brutal and atheistic husband and afterwards, in 1925, a Carmelite tertiary—wrote a disturbing *Livre de l'amour* in which she said that conjugal relations were like mystical torture.[28]

Hortus Clausus

Vocations

The wife and mother overshadowed the unmarried woman, whose place outside the family—a social question that would worry the *fin de siècle*—was related to the triumphant expansion of the "feminization of the clergy." In France, from 1808 to 1880, the number of women entering old and new religious congregations rose from less than 13,000 to more than 130,000. In 1830 the ratio of men to women was three to two. In 1878 the ratio was inverted, with two men to three women. Two thirds of the women founders of new congregations came from the upper classes. Before the Revolution, 29 percent came from the nobility and 33 percent from the bourgeoisie. In the nineteenth century, the bourgeois predominance was absolute: 46 percent compared to 19 percent of aristocrats. The remainder of this mighty army was drawn from the families of small farmers, artisans, and salaried workers.[29] Claude Langlois emphasized the particular novelty of the phenomenon of the feminization of the clergy. The new congregations were under the authority of the bishop or founder, but above all of the female founder and general mother superior. This institutional autonomy applied particularly to feminine education. In 1876, 80 percent of the 500,000 French children in nursery school were in the care of religious congregations. It is more difficult to translate into numbers the Catholic supremacy in boarding schools (in France as well as in Italy). In 1872, the first Italian national calculation showed an absolute monopoly of religious orders and congregations in the 570 boarding schools included in the statistics. Thirty years later, the state could show only 86 public institutions against 1,420 private boarding schools—800 of which were charitable institutions with 48,677 female boarders and 59,179 female day students,[30] proof of the absolute faith the lay elites placed in the formalization of the feminine role as it was defined by the Catholic girls' boarding schools.[31]

The impressive feminization of the French clergy was a truly national phenomenon; it touched other Catholic countries with different speeds and intensity. While in France the founding of new religious establishments with general mother superiors reached its peak during the decade 1820–1830, in Italy, where ecclesiastical politics in the preunification states precluded the definition of a comprehensive picture, the increase in the founding of female religious institutions was delayed a decade. In 1861 the first census of the kingdom of Italy—which, however, did not distinguish between "cloistered nuns" and "sisters," or between cloistered convents, convent schools, oblate houses and new centralized institutions—counted 42,664 "nuns." Even in Italy, the feminization of the clergy is a noted fact, for there were 30,632 brothers. For every 1,000 inhabitants there were 1.95 nuns: less than the 2.7 of Belgium but more than the 1.2 of Spain. The percentage was highest in Umbria and the Marches, two provinces of the former Papal States. But the great majority of nuns—22,619 of them—were found in the South, in the Neapolitan provinces (13,651) and in Sicily (8,968).[32]

It was from a Neapolitan convent that Enrichetta Caracciolo reflected on her forced taking of the veil. The *Misteri del chiostro napoletano* (1864)[33]—the private and political autobiography of an aristocratic lady consigned by the iron will of her mother to the greed of the "Levite country par excellence"—is the antihagiographic, patriotic, and Risorgimento reverse of the monastic autobiography.[34] These *mysteries* were well known, besides, to the upper echelons of the Roman clergy, who blamed them on the Bourbon royalty. The *Reports of the Bishops to the Holy See* described the taking of vows as carnival-like parades with dances and parties, unruly acclamations upon the election of a mother superior, and unsupervised comings and goings by doctors, servants, and priests.[35]

All the suppositions about the extremes of Sicilian "religious sumptuousness" can be glimpsed in the pages of a widely circulated manual of monastic behavior. The body is the evident model of sin and the place where sin is born and *enclosed*. There are sins of the tongue (slander), of the eyes (envy: *in-video*), and of the throat.[36] Encouraged to the analogic imitation of the sanctifying bodily form, the body in this teaching is never conceptual. In reality, the absolute dominance of realistic representation diminished the force of the pedagogical attempt to strengthen the will aimed at disembodiment, as Odile Arnold discovered in the French convents, beginning in the second half of the century.[37]

Entrepreneurial Mother Superiors

A high degree of emancipation—that of the English being second only to that of the Americans at the end of the century—allowed the founders of new religious orders of the English Terra Incognita to use "fictional and non-fictional 'Catholic' literature" as a means of conversion and fundraising. Lady Georgiana Fullerton (*Ellen Middleton,* 1844) and Fanny Taylor (*Tyborne,* 1857) used the proceeds from their bestsellers to develop the Poor Servants of the Mother of God. This first "industrial self-supporting" congregation had a commercial laundry as a source of funds.[38] In England and in America[39] the feminization of the clergy derived from a practical and charitable faith which acted directly in the field of social misery. The high "sense of self" of the English nuns was also tied to a practice of charity which knowingly challenged the ambulatory limitations on women mendicants based on the rules protecting feminine honor. Even Jeanne Jugan built her charisma by begging for alms along the roads of western France, seeking vagabonds to house in the institutions of her congregation. The founder, in 1843, of the Petites Soeurs des Pauvres (which in the 1880s became the second most important congregation for its real estate holdings after the Sacré Coeur), she went from door to door saying, "I am Jeanne Jugan." Her wanderings lasted thirteen years, until in 1852 the Bishop of Rennes granted recognition to the congregation and imposed on the Petites Soeurs des Pauvres the monastic virtue of stable residence.[40]

The idea of opening feminine social action to the world continued to be troubling for a long time. The belief that moral integrity could be contaminated *outside* the protection of family and domestic hearth was reflected in customary behaviors such as the strict surveillance of women in Catholic and lay families. Even immediately after World War I, Armida Barelli, the founder of the women's branch of the Italian Catholic youth group, Gioventù of Azione Cattolica, had a great deal of trouble breaking down the very Catholic resistance of thirty-two-year-old Teresa Pallavicino's father from the Marches: "Papa will absolutely not let me travel alone." Parma (Pallavicino's city) was no different from Palermo: "In Sicily, young married women do not go out alone, and you want to send them to other countries to advertise and establish associations?" was the objection of Palermo's hierarchy to Barelli's organizational enthusiasm. No doubt the intensive traveling of the militant directors of the Gioventù Femminile—victoriously overturning a social prohibition extended to the entire female sex—contributed to their dynamic charisma. The automobile of Armida Barelli (the president) and Teresa Pallavicino (vice president), new Catholic women traveling through Italy, was greeted with triumph as a symbol of their high degree of emancipation and self-determination "of gender," impressing the rank and file members who were far from such innovative behavior.[41]

Excluded from the official political scene, Catholic women found their field of action in charity. The aristocratic women—and for some of them, in Italy as in Spain,[42] the laws of Mediterranean honor were mitigated for this purpose—were the pioneers of direct immersion in social misery. From this absolute "passion governed by virtue" issued passionate exchanges of letters and lasting friendships—immortalized later in biographies—such as those of the international charity workers Paolina Craven and Georgiana Fullerton. This inexhaustible desire to help the disinherited is documented with historical reconstructions such as that compiled by Teresa Ravaschieri, the famous founder of Neapolitan works of charity of the second half of the nineteenth century, in her monumental work, *Storia della carità napoletana*. Even an ideal for a husband was composed in terms of these aspirations: "I would still like that he be rich to be able to do more good for the poor." In addition to the healing that came from comparing one's own pain with those of others (often the benefactresses named hospitals or welfare institutions after children who died at an early age), this sort of social practice made a purposeful attempt to establish alternative values to the masculine use of power. This was the meaning that the younger generation of donors gave to Ravaschieri's work at her death. "It is because of her tact and sense of independence from the crowd . . . that women today, even before calling themselves feminists, were able to begin at home to become involved in works of charity."[43]

In Paris, during the time of Jules Ferry, Miss David-Nillet was carefully supervised by her uncle and only allowed out of the house to attend Mass on Sundays. When she married, she became Albertine Duhamel. The change in her marital status revealed organizational capacities unimaginable in a former recluse. During the 1910s her itinerary of social activities described a national map of 3,400 charities. It was unmatched even by the *cursus honorarum* of the very active nineteenth-century ladies of charity.[44] To compete with feminism and its lay social service activities, Catholics began in this century to update the values and experience on which they could build a new sense of identity for women. The "militant woman"—a term invented by Pius XI—replaced the lady of charity. The women's chapters of the Azione Cattolica gathered a broad consensus in all of Europe. These were highly hierarchical structures that enhanced the national prestige of their directors. In 1910 the Patriotic League of French Women had 450,000 members. The UDACI (the Unione donne di Azione Cattolica Italiana), founded in 1908, formed more than a hundred committees with 15,000 members.[45] The "new woman" of militant Catholicism was a woman of action without the manlike traits which the Catholic leaflet (in *Civiltà Cattolica!*) ascribed to the feminist.[46]

The monumental sense of self of the Catholic leadership—kept under control among the militant women but commonly outstanding in the higher offices—stemmed from the difficulties of personal "emancipation." "As for me, I am too upright to be an opportunist, for as long as my conscience allows me to be conciliatory, I will be so, but beyond that I could never be . . . Your Eminence has also mentioned my bad character and in this Your Eminence may be right. My character is indivisible," wrote Princess Cristina Giustiniani Bandini to Pius X in 1914. She was the founder (in 1909) and the tireless president of the Union of the Catholic Women of Italy until 1917. Educated, naturally, at the Sacré Coeur, she entered a convent at eighteen. Ten years later she left it against her father's will, and she had to work for her living. The old Roman nobility did not give in to the autonomous choices of its daughters, other than what was required by marriage or the convent.[47]

Bans and Reading

Read Little, Read Well

During the whole of the nineteenth century—and for a good part of the twentieth, until after the First World War—female reading was carefully controlled. Most dangerous of all was the novel. The Church administered penalties following a code of moral judgment originating with Rousseau—"An honest girl does not read books about love"—with which both Catholics and the laity identified with equal vehemence. The young Milanese woman who, in October 1787, confessed to Goethe on a visit to Italy, "They do not teach us to write lest we use our pens to write love letters, and they would not even allow us to read had we not need to use a prayer book," did not identify "them"[48] because, on the education of women, the laity had the same viewpoint as the Church. And yet the distressed semiliterate woman acted according to the canons of her contemporaries; she traveled, conversed, and seduced (she was one of Goethe's Italian loves). But books were strictly forbidden.

We can suppose that many feminine strategies existed for circumventing the rigorous bans. The novel embodied sin to such a degree that the reader was already guilty when she simply first got it into her hands. At the end of the eighteenth century, Harlowe's *Clarissa* invaded the countryside of Burgundy. Not even the watchful eye of her Jansenist mother protected Sophie Barat (born to a well-off farming family and later founder of the congregation of the Sacred Heart) from the novel. The blame could not be placed on external causes, given the pervasive tentacles of that kind of diffusion. Remorse at having read it would remain with her to the end of her life. But in the first decades of the nineteenth century the teachings about surveillance give an indication of the original source of the contagion. The worried look with which the nineteenth century watched adolescence indicated that temptation was born precisely in that age, via friends, older sisters, or brothers (less closely watched by their parents). The intensity of female friendships was based also on the exchange of forbidden books.

In 1831 Paolina Leopardi, fleeing the control of her "ultrarigorous, truly excessive Christian perfection" of a mother, asked a friend from Bologna for Stendhal and Walter Scott.

The social honor which nineteenth-century bourgeois society accorded the role of wife bent the rigor of these rules and greatly softened them after marriage. In France the writers of manuals, followers of Baroness de Staffe or Madame de Genlis, relaxed their surveillance of the readings of married women. But in Italy, even at the end of the century, the manuals of Catholic living showed dismay that the prohibition of banned readings was no longer an unshakable matter of conscience in the married state.

The amount of feminine reading, recommended or banned, is more difficult to define. The huge quantity of Catholic reading material produced in the nineteenth century and through the first decades of the twentieth has not been correlated with research measuring the "quantity" of feminine reading. The titles are repetitive, but one of the rare pieces of data about the libraries of the Italian urban middle classes is suggestive: in the 1870s in Naples (the most populous city in Italy, whose daily newspapers had a circulation of 50,000), homes without books were in the majority.[49] In Italy, in the first half of the century, a woman with a book in her hand—which was not a devotional book—was far from a socially approved figure representing esthetic and cultural values. Few were the liberal and enlightened Catholics who dreamed of books "expressly written to arouse the intellect of women" that were not devotional tracts. Silvio Pellico wanted books about "sweet affection" and "domestic cares," and "heroic enthusiasm for love, for private virtues and for religion." They would be based on female genealogies, that is, the family lives of daughters, wives, and mothers.[50] Such materials were unthinkable in the bookstores of devotional and ascetic books which dominated the production of the early nineteenth century.[51] It was not until the 1870s that the Italian press received from its first generation of national novelists "pictures of private affections." Before that, Italy was a land of translations of (besides devotional books) mostly novels and manuals of behavior from France.

Far ahead of Italian women writers, French and English Catholic women writers traveled the dual paths of didactic educational manuals and novels. For the Church, that literary genre was still sinful, which explains the frequent precautionary explanations of the authors. The well-known Madame Bourdon (Mathilde Froment, 1817–1888) drew a distinction between her *Souvenirs d'une institutrice* (1869)—"ordinary scenes of the real world"—and a *real* novel, such as *Jane Eyre* by the much-admired Charlotte Brontë. In this way she helped to blur the rigid separation between "good" and "bad" novels. And in addition to promulgating the glorious examples of a feminine literary tradition, she looked forward to a transition from a passion for reading to a passion for writing. The teacher protagonist of the *Souvenirs* receives a banned book from a pupil, handed to her in obedience to the rules of the boarding school. It is *Corinne,* by Madame de Staël. Inflamed by the desire for literary glory—"dangerous perhaps, but seductive!"—she imagines herself a writer who turns into lasting forms "the imaginary beings floating in our imagination."[52] The feminine "fantasy" which nineteenth-century Catholic education tried to bridle could no longer be repressed: it was the golden substance on which feminine literary writing will be built.

In Italy, in mid-century, the works recommended to Catholic women readers—Plutarch's philosophical treatises, Socratic dialogues, and works of Cicero, Augustin Thierry, or Muratori—did not offer sexual role models.[53] This serious classical reading was meant to serve an antiromantic purpose, similar to that suggested by Monsignor Dupanloup in 1879 to a much younger age group. "In order to fortify the female mind" the Bishop of Orleans prescribed the great French authors of the seventeenth century—Pascal, Bossuet, Fénelon, Racine, Corneille, La Bruyère, Madame de Sévigné. He skipped the eighteenth century and from the nineteenth added only some Christian poets. Banished were the exact sciences and literature; even in his innovative program the literary disciplines reigned.

Read little and read well was the motto.[54] Reread, go back over the pages ("never leave a book without having finished it"), summarize them and copy the most important passages. Entertainment is not desirable: reading is an examination of conscience through the intermediary of a text. Through books one can construct and modify—more than learn about character traits. The instruments of the spiritual orthopedics of Madame Swetchine, who admits she was "born with little force of character," were a pencil and some sheets of paper. "Writing with a pencil . . . is like speaking in a soft voice." One marked the pages and reread them, copied summaries, and wrote (this time in pen) criticisms and reflections.[55]

Styles of Reading and Strategies for Autonomy

More convincing than the precepts of Dupanloup were the feminine intellectual autobiographies which promulgated the way of life of the true "studious woman," opportunities which only a few aristocratic women managed to carve out for themselves in nonhostile family situations. At the beginning of the century female instruction consisted mostly of learning by rote, the outward appearance of an explanation used as an antidote against the interior distraction of the "imagination." Knowing a text well made it easier to read it aloud, a form of family and living-room entertainment in which, until the end of the century, women of the upper classes were allowed to play a role. It was a method of learning that the sixteen-year-old Baroness Olimpia Savio of Turin (1816–1889) applied exclusively to French authors such as "Racine, Corneille, Mignet, Marmontel, Bouilly, Berquin, Bossuet, Fénelon, Madame de Maintenon and de Sévigné, Massillon," but "nothing Italian." In the 1830s, in the kingdom of Sardegna and Piedmont, this is an example of "higher" maternal education, "being an only daughter and thus educated always at my mother's side." It is a rare example, especially in a woman, of obstinate desire for cultural freedom. Olimpia's mother was a pioneer, self-taught at night—with books hidden under the mattress—struggling against her mother and grandmother who sought to limit her reading to devotional books.[56]

It was only at the end of the century, when women scholars began to cross the thresholds of higher institutions (at the beginning of the twentieth century female enrollment in Italian state high schools was 233, compared to a male enrollment of 12,605), that Catholic hagiography discovered, retrospectively, the value of the perseverance of the self-taught women. The rigors of their style of work delivered them from the taint of disobedience. Blessed Elena Guerra (1835–1914), founder of a school for girls in Lucca, studied Latin at night, by the light of small lamps which burned nut shells, so as not to be found out by her consumption of candles.[57] The exceptional character of such models, not compromised by a large number of imitators, allowed them to remain quietly hagiographic.

In the early twentieth century, however, the daily labors of scholastic life to which an ever increasing number of female students subjected themselves, their ambition to get a diploma, and the stressful consequences of competition reduced the girls to a state that alarmed the medical establishment and religious educators as well. The pathologic sequence of the nineteenth-century psycho-physical model of womanly frailty—bronchioceles, chlorosis, curvature of the spine, hysteria—located the external cause of all these in book learning. The theory found support, even in the twentieth century, in the Catholic press, which was in no way inclined to recommend a compensatory antidote of female physical education. This attitude persisted despite the appearance, at the dawn of the new century, of the first Catholic theorists of a "new" feminine education—foremost among them the Spanish Jesuit Ramon Ruiz Amado. They appropriated the teaching of the American hygienic school and, from their pulpits, swept away the nineteenth-century forms of feminine detention ("the prolonged sessions at the piano, so common in Spanish girls") proposing instead intense sports activities even for girls.[58]

The custom of reading devotional books aloud persisted longer in the countryside, until after the First World War. It was the training for learning the catechism and, from the beginning of the twentieth century, the banner of proselytizing of Catholic feminists. In Nivernais, at the end of the 1850s, one learned to read and write through the prayer book, trying to find (and copy) the vowels of the symbols of the apostles.[59] The evening reading of the prayers ended up as a form of learning. These prayers were "guided" more by the rhythm of the pages religiously turned than by the content of the message.

The Church continued to divide books into good and bad, keeping its eye on a continually growing production of popular novels. In 1905, Abbot Bethléem's work, *Romans à lire et à proscrire* (Books to Read and to Forbid), put some order to the copious flowering of French popular novels. The Bonne Presse concentrated most of its efforts on young girls. However, the cheap Saturday *feuilleton* soon ceased to be a hidden pleasure; girls lay across their beds reading all Sunday, charmed away from their religious duties.[60] The degree of feminine shame attached to reading bad things grew more feeble. The innocent surprise of confessants penalized for reading things deemed indecent by the confessor reveals the difficulty of self-control in a society where the book had lost its character of moral educator and had become the companion of free time.

For the militant Catholic, a new social type of the twentieth century, books became obligatory instruments of educational formation. In 1927, on the occasion of the marriage of the niece of the Marchesa Maddalena Patrizi, president of the UDACI (Unione donne di Azione Cattolica Italiana), Pius XI sent the bride a wedding gift of the ideal book collection of about 80 books, "books for her alone," as Dupanloup would have wished. Of the 37 authors, 25 were French (Dupanloup, Gratry, Tissier, and so on). The Italian works included one history of art, a manual of proper behavior, Manzoni (all of his works), and the *Sillabario del Cristianesimo* of Olgiati, of the Milanese group of the Catholic University.[61] It was a sign of the continuing Italian cultural dependence on France for spiritual works, as well as of the rigidity of the religious press. According to Claude Savart, this attitude continued (also outside France) even beyond the limits of the nineteenth century.[62]

Piety: Practices and Attitudes

The Feminine Privatization of Worship

Prayers, *vocal* prayers, more easily depicted than the impregnable *mental* prayers—the distinction is Brèmond's—formed the rhythm of feminine daily life. The Restoration altered the tonality of prayer. The dominant feelings of fear and sense of divine vengeance that were the basis of prayer in the preceding century began to disappear. Directed prayers for divine protection and benevolence regarding health, prosperity in one's affairs, safe journeys, or victorious wars that were characteristic of nineteenth-century devotion reflected either the victorious individualism of the period or the desire for theology to arm itself against mystical experience.

In the interclass system of double standards on which many nineteenth-century marriages were based, prayer had a function of pacification. The synchronic prayers of Maria Adelaide of Savoy, regal model of conjugal resignation (rewarded by Pius IX in 1847 with the Rosa d'oro, a papal honor conferred on the most virtuous Catholic sovereigns and princesses) ennobled an imperfect marital situation. Overlooking known and flaunted marital betrayals, her prayer in time of war reconstructed the peace of the relationship in the spatio-temporal unity of petitions granted. "If I could know the day when you will be going to battle, that morning I would say prayers for you," the duchess wrote. Victor

Emmanuel confirms that, at Peschiera, the enemy bullets were turned aside by her prayers.[63]

Italian devotion as influenced by the moral philosophy of Alfonso de Liguori established a different kind of familiarity with the sacred, completely modifying religious sensitivity. Excessive sentimentalism, morbid intensity, uncontrolled mysticism, or, on the other hand, merely repetitive habit and short household prayers, all distinctive characteristics of nineteenth-century prayer, were also signs of progressive feminization of the army of the faithful. The Church, taking cognizance of this phenomenon, formally promoted the maternal figure as initiator. Abbé Pichenot wanted her to be like a "priest of the hearth." Marie-Françoise Lévy showed how even the nineteenth-century manuals of devotion directed at mothers encouraged them to prefer love of God to fear.[64]

God, the object of love, had a personal relationship with the pious from childhood. The Baby Jesus of Romantic iconography was an image of suffering, with his little heart surrounded by thorns. In the second half of the century, the Virgin and child were images not of unhappy but rather of familial maternity. The heart pierced with a sword and surrounded with spines moved from its organic center to Jesus' hand like an apple or a toy; it was no longer an open accusatory wound.

A precocious propensity to prayer, the happy result of maternal initiation, is found in much of the hagiography (without any suspicion about the natural disposition of children to playful repetition). At the age of six months Jean-Baptiste Marie Vianney (the future holy curate of Ars) was the watchful conscience of his mother; she taught him to make the sign of the cross before eating, and he reminded her if she forgot.[65] Spiritual advice for young believers counseled moderation. Monsignor Dufêtre emphasized that the relationship between devotion and exterior acts was not quantitative and advised not to overdo prayers and acts of piety.[66] In the second half of the century acts of devotion for girls became more active and elaborate, inspired by the overly elaborate adult faith encouraged by the Marian cult. The age of individual religious acts was lowered, and in May even children and young girls erected little shrines in their bedrooms. Many, such as Caroline Brame, had a personal "little oratory."[67] Sacred images became feminized. The passionate obsession with furnishings in general spilled over to *canivets,* very fine paper lace which enveloped the faces of the Madonna and Jesus. The pages of missals became thicker. Missals themselves became doubly desirous for devout collectors as proof of faith and tokens of friendship. The pontifical decree *Quam singulari* of 1910 authorized private communion, which then became more widespread. A sacred image—with the name and passage from the Gospels chosen appropriately for the young age of the communicant—was witness to the event. It was not only the first conscious stage of spiritual life but of an entire socio-sentimental existence: "Feminine life in its first period unfolds between two white veils: the veil of the first communion and the nuptial veil." This is one example among many (I am quoting the most noted Italian manual of the early 1900s) of such chromato-literary imagery, even in spheres that are not strictly confessional.[68]

Matrimonial Temple and Immaculate Adolescence

The emblems of religious devotion crowded the bedroom. In the second half of the nineteenth century, the Neapolitan bourgeois protected its temple of marriage by crucifixes, statues of the Madonna, and paintings of religious subjects (sometimes as many as eleven in the same room).[69] It is not easy to judge the intensity of devotion toward such customary iconographic models, which formed part of the most ordinary decorative tradition. This translated, for children and adolescent girls, into a personal living iconography, in deferential imitation of the angelic position of prayer. This is the first level of personal self-discipline by which Catholic teaching dictated the rules of female moral bearing. Such evidently signifying models—body clothed in white, posed like the Ascension and looking on high, denoting fervor, or with eyes lowered, denoting modesty—formed the basis of a dogma of leading "dogmatic angelography" (thus did Paolo Mantegazza describe the obsessive social reverence for the rules defending feminine purity).

Sixteen-year-old Marie Bashkirtseff was a Russian aristocrat, the incarnation in life, as in death (she died of consumption at age twenty-six in 1884), of the cosmopolitan young woman who added to the late Romantic existential banner, "to live, suffer, weep and fight," a resolute "be somewhat ambitious." At prayer in the church of Saint Peter in Nice, with her chin resting on her lovely white hands, she rejected the temptation to ritualize femininity in angelic forms: "I manage to make myself ugly as a form of penitence."[70] She was a pioneer even in this because the manuals of etiquette continued, up until the twentieth century, to represent churches and religious functions as the best vantage points for social appraisal (for matrimonial reasons) of feminine virtues. The Our Father, Ave Maria, Credo, Act of Faith, Hope and Charity were the morning and evening prayers of girls (from seven or eight years old) and of young women. Once the maternal initiation was over, the ritual continued with personal requests. Petitions "of necessity" for a nineteenth-century adolescent included a pretty face, a beautiful voice, and a happy marriage. May the prayer keep away smallpox and her mother's death. Thus Marie Bashkirtseff, knowing it to be "more than what was necessary," added an inevitable coda to her orations: "to be able to meet her latest sweetheart."

The discovery in the nineteenth century that female adolescents concealed an inner life of fantasies that were difficult to control worried the clergy (no less than the laymen). Not without reason did the Church select the month of May to dedicate to the Virgin. The protection of the Madonna for the preservation of feminine innocence was most needed "in the midst of the temptations which come in droves in the fair season." The cult of Mary in the month of May, first proposed at the beginning of the eighteenth century by the Italian Jesuits (Dionisi in 1726, de Liguori in 1750, and Lalomia and Muzzarelli in 1785), spread throughout Catholic Europe in the first half of the nineteenth century. It was a preventive religious practice which sought to achieve the transcendence of adolescent love, difficult to bring about in peasant communities. The purity of the Virgin became the model of identity and the center of feminine education. After first Communion, the supervision of young Catholic girls passed to the congregations of the Daughters of Mary. In France, the first Congregation of the Children of Mary of the Sacred Heart was formed in Paris in 1820. In Italy, in addition to the congregations of the Daughters of Mary, feminine associations dedicated to the Immaculate Virgin were established after 1854 (year of the dogma).

The explosive diffusion of this cult reveals a complex specific correspondence with feminine desires and projections. In the suggestive analysis of Luisa Accati, the symbolic power of the Immaculate Virgin comes from its "being a staging of the (female) desire to seduce." Girls dream of and desire love but they fear the social prohibition and the physical pain associated with deflowering. Devotion to the Immaculate Virgin allows them to "acknowledge sexual desire without accepting it." It is not only "a desire to enjoy the pleasure without feeling the blame" (as Isidor Sadger claims) but a "search for pleasure without pain." Thus the cult consolidates narcissistic feminine self-sufficiency by linking it with the primary feeling of the age of puberty.[71]

Virtue and Appearance

Virginity Made Visible

In the villages of the French countryside, the *rosières* provided evidence of social quantification of feminine virtues. The young girls crowned with wreaths of roses in May (about a thousand in the nineteenth century) were the example of youth engaged in a proper struggle to improve its own condition, without abjuring its asset of virginity. Before a commission comprised of the mayor, the curate, and the school teacher, each must demonstrate (with a medical certificate) that she is virginal, of modest situation, and with a good attitude toward work. The prize of 1,500 francs was the clerical-state dowry which the jury awarded the *rosière* two months before her marriage.[72] This would have been unthinkable in societies other than France which, more than any other in Europe, had turned to the "allegory of sex" for political and pedagogical ends. The *rosière* had become the demonstrated antidote to the social alarm about female purity raised by inquiries and literary reports at the end of the century, such as *Les Demi-Vierges* of Marcel Prévost (1895) or *Les Jeunes Filles peintes par elles-mêmes* of Remy de Gourmont (1901). In Italy, the same concern was raised after translations of these books, but the dawn of young sexual throbbing is confirmed by Antonio Marro's studies of adolescence.[73] At exactly the same time as the triumph of physiologic realism of the *scientia sexualis,* Italian Catholic treatises avoid naming virginity in its concise bodily definition.

With the second half of the century, the regulation of feminine honor changed, as it moved away from the combined aegis of State, Church, and Family. It should be remembered that in Naples, before unification, women interned in convent schools, single and widowed alike, made up 3.8 percent of the female population. Ranked according to their varying degrees of respectability—honest, endangered, at risk, prostitute—they were enclosed in rigidly separated groups.[74]

The feminine model of virginal perfection was built on the value of purity—an individual virtue, determined internally, and founded on principles of moral autonomy intensified by confession. But the entrance of large numbers of women into the industrial labor market multiplied temptations. The value and moral duty of purity is measured in places of risk and danger. Social strata formerly excluded from normative teaching about honor encircled each other in interclass temptation. Even for aristocratic and bourgeois women, feminine virtue was above all one of "show": in the street, at theaters, balls, charity fair booths, and in the progressively more promiscuous meeting places of youthful society. Rodolfo Bettazzi, founder (in Turin, in 1894) of the Catholic League for Public Morality, suggested that at balls (finally allowed in 1915) women wear a white rose at the waist like an explicit and decorative scapular—recalling the Marian devotions no longer practiced by young ladies of the city—and that "they make sure to come out with the rose intact."[75]

The Threat of Mixed Company

In the early twentieth century the value of virginity was measured against the temptations of a more secularly determined social morality. The stimulus to imitate more emancipated behavior (clothing, social life, reading, and so on) came from living models in the street or from news items reported in the lay press. There were tragedies of passion resulting in suicides or crimes, symptoms of resistance to changes in the code of feminine honor. The Catholic press explicitly condemned them as the "accursed and bloody note which dishonors our country." Yet, in 1902 the murder of twelve-year-old Maria Goretti who resisted an attempted rape—the common theme of the condemned "crime reporting"—became a sensational case of hagiographic promotion in the mass media.[76]

The modern redemption of young debauchées, close to or already in the spiral of child prostitution was—as Annarita Buttafuoco has shown—grounds for Italian lay feminists to challenge the Catholics,[77] who were unable to find innovative arguments for the operational dilemma between the greatest degree of corruption (such as found in the penal institutions run by religious personnel) and its presumed origins. The segregation of the sexes—continuing that of the boarding schools—was the female Catholic organizations' trusted guarantee for insuring feminine purity. It was a way of conduct that would last in Italy until the mid-twentieth century.

To keep the barrier between the sexes high, women's Catholic press emphasized the merits of separate social lives. "Girls have more heart's content and spiritual rest when they have fun among themselves. When, however, there are boys present, they experience pain, envy, anxiety and recklessness," writes *Vita femminile,* a biweekly for working women, in 1912. Mixed social life was one of the contested occasions where the modernization of feminine social conduct was measured and practiced. Under the uneasy eye of Catholic supervision the defensive structures of sexual dimorphism were being undermined, both the appearance and substance, the covering and the soul of Christian femininity. Catholic organizations of women blamed the unstoppable mechanism of social imitation, spread by means of mass education, for the end of fixed public and private roles and the chaos of feminine social identity. Peasant women want to become teachers, the teachers doctors, and "from doctors and professors they are clamoring to become, as far as possible, the same as men, at least as far as social rights are concerned. That is the genesis and the beginnings of the feminist movement in Italy," according to the Union of Catholic Women of Italy (1911).[78]

The Lost Crusade against Fashion

Even Catholic women were forced to recognize the social dimension of bodily behavior when clothing became a miraculous key to social mobility. Against a fashion which imposed the ethic of change and the cult of modernity and which became, more than a right available to all classes, a social categorical imperative, feminine Catholic organizations launched, after the First World War, "crusades against indecent fashion" and "contests for proper fashion." Though ineffective (despite the support of Benedict XV),[79] the mobilization against corruption in feminine appearance spread through Europe and determined the integrity of those enrolled by the length of their skirts and of their hair. In the 1920s the lay press identified (and derided) the militants of the Gioventù Femminile Cattolica by the unmistakable signs of their severe, plain, and neglected dress.[80] Theirs was a "Puritan" type (as J. C. Flugel described them)[81] of traditional *beguinage* ripe for ridicule.

Female Catholic militants needed to invent a visible model which was no longer isolated and enclosed within the family sphere, their own autonomous esthetic "appearance" as an alternative to the extreme of the often condemned feminist "masculinization."

The "esthetic of devotion," faithful to the dogmas of rigid nineteenth-century sexual dimorphism, disappeared in the twentieth century. Tears were its shiny tinsel. Through them feminine devout behavior maintained a continuity with the tearful eighteenth century, which practiced, without distinction between the sexes, a widespread rhetoric of tears. Marcelline Pauper, one of the first Sisters of Charity of Nevers in the first half of the nineteenth century, writes of being comforted by the divine gift of tears which flooded her prayers, proof of holy union with the divine. G. Thuillier recalls that Bernadette Soubirous cried a great deal.[82] A proof of true faith was the implicit public testimony of popular devotion alive in the tears of the poor ignorant girl; it was a typical referent of the manifestations of sightings of Mary in the nineteenth century. In the upper classes the spiritual value of tears risked becoming merely an exterior gesture. "Girls love tears so much that I have seen them cry before a mirror to double their enjoyment of that state," noted Monsignor Dupanloup. With pedagogic farsightedness, the Congregation of the Sacred Heart was the first to start up a "tears police." Before the homologous emotive expressions—abundant and unrestrained—of the nineteenth-century stereotype of femininity, the congregation applied the Jesuit diffidence toward excessive artificial sentimentality.

Time and Order

The Rationalization of Virtues

Prayer infused the temporal fabric of household discipline with a new legitimacy of feminine existence. In 1810, when Giulia Manzoni returned to the sacraments, she sent her spiritual adviser, the Jansenist Father Tosi, a "questionnaire about how to pass the day." She confessed the difficulty of synchronizing daily life and prayer. The priest specified in hours and minutes (with a few extra concessions) the severe practices which Giulia read in the *Regulations*. "Reverend Sir, you have suggested for me a Christian and penitent practice of rising from bed at night to pray at least for a few minutes; I have never had the courage to do it except for a few times." And Father Tosi replied, "Even that practice of rising at night, though it is not necessary, is very appropriate for you. Begin to do it one or two nights a week, not getting out of bed when it is cold, but only sitting up well covered or at least in such a posture as to allow you to put your Crucifix in your hand." This elastic dosage of prayers and little flowers—chocolate is allowed, coffee is banned—showed the tractable substance of devotion, which one could soften or reinforce depending on the individual's capacity for absorption.[83]

The ideal of the peaceful, perfect cohabitation of the sexes (as between classes) which marks the theories of behavior based on temporal discipline—a theme of nineteenth-century civilization from Fourier's utopian communities to Payot's *selphism* of the will—crept into the manuals of behavior. In France, as in Italy, Catholic authors promoted a discipline which, with more competent precision than a confessor, combined household alacrity with spiritual conscientiousness. The cosmic maxim "God is order and rule" regulated the daily feminine microactivities of the *Journée chrétienne de la jeune fille* (Christian Day of the Young Girl) of Madame Bourdon (1867, reprinted many times and translated into Italian). Everything, even the inessential and the futile, was redeemed in this order, which had the imprint of a supreme holy exactitude.

The golden age of industry coincided with a vast literature on the use of the day. "In our times one lives in a hurry: the days are not sufficient for everything one undertakes, business, relations, travel, pleasure, and even studies," wrote Madame Bourdon.[84] It was one of the favorite books of the female sector of the population engaged in the great textile industry of the North of France. These women were the vestals of an industrious domestic morality applied to the running of household business, including budgets, organization of the servants, and the care of children (their birthrate rose from 1840 to 1900 from 5 to 7 children).[85]

The letter which Giulietta Manzoni, the oldest child of Alessandro and Enrichetta Blondel, received in October 1833 from her mother-in-law, Marchesa Cristina D'Azeglio, is a clear example of how the perfect mix of devotional and household duties was the ethical measure of a woman's social value. Giulietta's apathetic care of her ailing mother, her bad choice of readings, her rash purchases of readymade clothes for her daughter ("material can be bought, but it should be sewn at home"), of furniture, carpets, excessive trinkets—all these are examples of an untrustworthy household management, the opposite of that "ostentatious underconsumption" and distrust of the superfluous characteristic of the frugal rich and which the daughter of a converted Calvinist ought to have in her blood.[86] There is no doubt about the cause of this going astray: "You go to church like the Protestants to temple, once a week and that's all."[87]

The Self-Directed Beautiful Death

The new moral theology of Alfonso de Liguori and of Saint Francis of Sales acted as a brake to the fearful identification of death with the sufferings of Christ. In the manuals of devotion and the ascetic treatises on the good death—of which Francis of Sales's *Filotea* was the most frequently followed model—the *memento mori* was detailed in questionnaires about the time, place, season, and the hour of the exit of the soul from the body. The novices educated at the congregations of the Sacred Heart expressed familiarity with death as an intelligible reality (sentiments that found easy affinities with the romantic feminine sensibility). They were serene about leave-taking and had happy expectations about celestial meetings with their fellow sisters, testimony to the effectiveness of Francis de Sales's preparation. Such a "thirst for dying" (endemic in many novices, as O. Arnold observed) explained the vital teaching of Mother Barat, founder of the order: "To live in order to suffer and to win hearts for Jesus Christ is a far more generous thing than to wish to suffer in order to enjoy" (1829).[88]

This culture of death manifest in the serenity of the language of farewell was not exclusively limited to the professionals of prayer, those who prayed "as a duty of their state." The lay manifestation was the sequence of beautiful deaths—of which Philippe Ariès[89] spoke—in the La Ferronnays family (their complicity with death is not sexually determined). Eugénie, for example, died very young of consumption and, in a classical Lamartine scene of Naples in the 1830s, with roses, orange trees, and starlit nights, she sang for her friends "as gay as a bird, brilliant like a ray of sunshine." For her, death is an incomparable good. "Oh . . . how beautiful life is! What then will heaven be? *Is death worth more than all that?*" she glibly asked her sister, Pauline.[90]

The nineteenth-century last farewell was seldom taciturn. "I am happy with my state," said the twenty-six-year-old Cristina

Manzoni, embracing her husband just before dying (1841), in a stereotypical representation of the good death. But before that, she had refused to see her confessor or to receive last sacraments, and it was only her father's intercession which could overcome her horror of holy unction. It is difficult to suggest what were specifically feminine responses in the hour of death, for the conduct of dying women had been stylized according to interior codes of family experience. More than the manuals about the good death of Francis of Sales, it was the intimate experience with early deaths, the despairing expectation of orphan children, which constituted feminine *manners* in ceremonies of farewell. But no narratives remain about the bereavements of the Manzonis—devastated like their contemporaries, the La Ferronnays, by six deaths in a little more than ten years—that are equivalent to the *Récit d'une soeur* by Pauline Craven La Ferronnays. There, as Ariès notes, births and marriages are barely indicated as points of reference in the continual series of deaths.

The correspondence of the Manzoni women tells of illnesses and deaths without anticipated aspirations beyond the tomb. It contains faithful descriptions of blood-lettings (a common and fatal therapeutic practice in Italy), medicines, and diets. The epitaphs were concise: for Enrichetta Manzoni née Blondel, "Unequaled Daughter-in-Law Wife Mother Mother-in-law/husband sons, pray, with warm tears but with living faith/for the glory of heaven" (1833), and for Giulia d'Azeglio Manzoni, "Died in the peace of the Lord/sorrowful husband and relatives commend her to the mercy of Him/and to the prayers of the faithful" (1834). After the macabre eighteenth-century eroticism of Giulia Manzoni Beccaria, who alleviated her pain at the death of her lover, Carlo Imbonati (1805), by having him embalmed, there followed, without literary sublimations about the "blessed passage"—as Enrichetta Blondel called it—the classical and composed canons of nineteenth-century cemetery epitaphs.

Mothers

Maternal Authority Threatened

The nineteenth century is known as the century of the mother. The family and the roles of family members were transformed.

Fathers and husbands remained preeminent, but the social distance between spouses and between parents and children diminished. In the second half of the century, Ernest Legouvé attributed that unheard of rebelliousness of "gentlemen's sons" resisting the rules pertaining to their age group and lacking respect for ritual passages on the new feelings awakened by the more intense relationships between parents and sons, and on "increased security" and "weakness and relaxed authority."[91] Were the "new sons" also the result of the femininization of familial education? At the beginning of the century an attentive (lay) observer of Italian customs had already thought so. Mothers did not constitute strong models for their daughters. They had "broken the mainspring of respect" without securing greater obedience: "Nowadays a girl reaching the age of reason, uses the familiar '*tu*' with her mother and, instead of addressing her as mother, calls her *friend*."[92] Nineteenth-century Catholic culture based the maternal role on behaviors of sentimental piety typical of feminine devotion. The maternity of the Virgin had erased the stain of Eve. This image was the wellspring of Marian devotion as well as of the revaluation of maternity. In Italy, the mother of Don Bosco represented the ideal model for the Church. In 1846 she followed her son to Valdocco and organized the practical life of the oratory. "She thought of and provided for everything," proof that domestic abilities can go beyond the narrow bounds of the family.[93] At the beginning of the century, even authoritarian fathers spread the seeds of spiritual maternity: "How mistaken you are, my dear child," wrote Joseph de Maistre to his second child, Constance, "when speaking to me of the slightly vulgar merit of having children! Feminine merit consists in administering the household, making the husband happy by consoling him and encouraging him, and in raising his children: that is to say, *making men;* that is the great delivery, which is not accursed like the other."[94]

What was really *cursed* for women? The high maternal death rate in childbirth and the infant mortality rate made maternity at once a natural and a fearfully risky condition. In the Veneto region under the Hapsburgs, during the period 1839–1845, the birthrate was around 40 per thousand, the death rate 31, and infant mortality accounted for more than a third of the deaths, so that the faithful made sure to ask for baptism on the first or second day after birth. The nineteenth-century duties of a Catholic mother—

those of submission, sacrifice, and religious education—were carried out with the knowledge that the maternal filial relationship was based on a fragile thread of existence.

> I knew intimately a mother of a family who was not at all superstitious, but very strong and conscientious in her Christian beliefs and in the exercise of her religion. She not only did not pity those parents who lost their children very young but she secretly and sincerely envied them because the children had flown to paradise without danger and had freed their parents of the burden of raising them. Several times, when she found herself in danger of losing her own children at the same age, she did not pray God to have them die, for her religion did not allow this, but she cordially rejoiced, and seeing her husband cry or grieve, she withdrew into herself and felt a real and perceptible annoyance.[95]

This Italian antimother, as Giacomo Leopardi describes her in *Zibaldone,* cannot serve as a basis for any generalization about the affective nature of mother-child relationships. It is a case of maternal pathology overwhelmed by a statistical expectation of death; the reference is to that obsessive neurotic of domestic administration, the Marchesa Adelaide Antici Leopardi (1778–1857). Melania d'Azeglio (of the upper nobility of Piedmont) who died in 1841 at a young age, overcame her fear of death by writing to her daughter Costanza a letter of good-by in which she repeated the epistolary farewell left to her by her maternal grandmother in 1805. She made two recommendations to her little daughter: always dress modestly and read a chapter of Christian doctrine every day. The ability to refer to a familial epistolary source was a comfort in the face of the inevitable; it also strengthened the feminine consciousness of the tenuous earthly ties to one's children.[96]

For Thérèse Martin (Saint Teresa of Lisieux, 1873–1897), the youngest of nine children of a couple who lost two sons and two daughters, early death was a concrete lived experience since childhood. On the mystic level, Teresa was her mother's favorite. An orphan at four years old, she constructed her model of sainthood on her brief maternal bonding.[97] Nineteenth-century Catholic culture ascribed to the mother the functions of religious formation and moral correction, under the banner of an unlimited spirit of sacrifice. The most persistent example of this culture (it lasted until

1917) was the journal *Femme et la famille. Journal de la vie domestique,* founded in 1862 in Genoa by Felicita Bottaro, then transferred to Paris in 1867. The education of the woman and of children, the exaltation of the family as the sole place of happiness and, beginning in the 1870s, the polemic against public instruction were its recurrent themes. Against the "poor deluded" emancipationists who abandoned their children in order to break down "the hated system" of the division of roles, they opposed the good, hardworking, and beneficent women, capable of "sacrificing themselves in silence for an idea or a misfortune," invincible in the force of their love and suffering.[98]

The Power of Love

This ideology of the natural feminine sense of giving, as formulated by laymen and Catholics, admits of subtle distinctions. Michelet called that boundless vocation "amour." "She is the altar," he said of woman. She lives for the others; "it is this relative characteristic which puts her higher than the man and makes of her a religion."[99] This common nineteenth-century quality of women—giving and sacrifice of self for others—was the foundation for a series of "concepts," "ideal types," and "intuitive abstractions" of the feminine, many of which still inhabit the cultural history of the twentieth century. How many women did the French feminist, Nelly Roussel, address in her *L'Eternelle sacrifiée?* (1906). "Your devotion must be voluntary," she recommends, but it is the form that is contested, not the substance of sacrificial devotion. After the First World War the Italian Gina Lombroso proposed the concept of the "other-centered" woman. In it altruism, as exemplified in the profession of nursing, figured as the dominant characteristic of feminine psychology.[100] In the words of the German theologian Gertrud von le Fort, to whom Pius XII often referred (*La Femme eternelle,* 1936), the same *other-centeredness* is translated into the existential maxim "be the other, for the other, through the other": the "social" essence of the feminine as proof of a privileged relationship of women with God.

TRANSLATED FROM THE ITALIAN BY JOAN BOND SAX

8

The Protestant Woman

Jean Baubérot

Is there a distinctive "Protestant type" of woman? If the term is taken to imply that Protestantism is somehow the principal determinant of a woman's personality, the answer is certainly no. But that does not mean that religion was not an important factor in shaping the women of the nineteenth as of other centuries, just that its influence cannot be isolated from that of other inextricably related factors such as social class, nationality, and even regional origin.

The Reformation implied a conception of woman in some ways antithetical to the Catholic ideal: no special value attached to virginity or the cloistered life, for example. From the beginning, Protestantism viewed marriage (and the secular life) as the context within which "Christian fidelity" was best achieved. Yet a patriarchal system survived in Protestant countries, and women had to find their place in it. Just as "universal suffrage" long referred in practice to "universal manhood suffrage," the doctrine of "universal priesthood" (according to which every believer becomes a priest at the moment of baptism) until recently meant above all that the father in every family also served as a religious leader, even if his wife played a far from negligible (and in some circumstances essential) role in the transmission of religious beliefs.

In fact, the doctrine of universal priesthood was intended to reconcile a fundamental equality with functional distinctions. As Luther said, every baptized Christian "may take pride in being consecrated priest, bishop and pope, although it is not appropriate for everyone to discharge the duties of such offices." This shift from essence to function could signify a possibility of social mobility and advancement, but it could also lead, in practice and in the absence of a distinct clerical class, to the reproduction in ecclesiastical society of distinctions existing in the wider society.

Protestant women therefore found themselves in an ambivalent situation. On the one hand, the importance ascribed to laymen and -women, to ordinary Christians, fostered an early interest in the education of women, and not only women of the elite (although social differences did matter). As a result, Protestant regions and countries were often relatively advanced in providing educational opportunities for women in the nineteenth century. On the other hand, Protestants to a large extent shared prevailing attitudes concerning the division of social roles between men and women. This conception of society blocked women's access to certain positions, and in particular to pastoral offices.

In many cases this contradiction was resolved by making it the mission of the Protestant woman to assist her husband and serve as his partner. The married couple and family therefore proved both emotionally appealing and culturally and socially ascendant. These attitudes were particularly prevalent among English Puritans and German and Scandinavian Pietists.

The Awakening: An Opportunity for Women

Perhaps the most interesting signs of change in the religious position of Protestant woman at the dawn of the nineteenth century occurred in the Awakening, and in Methodism in particular. Yet in many respects the founder of Methodism, John Wesley (1703–1791), was a man of tradition and order. For a long time it seemed unthinkable to him that women might exercise religious authority. Initially, most male revivalists of the late-eighteenth and nineteenth century shared his views, which appeared to be justified by various passages in Paul's epistles concerning women. But several factors led many revivalists to ascribe a greater role to women.

The purpose of the Awakening was not to encourage schism or lead to the establishment of new Protestant denominations. It was rather to breathe new spirit—the spirit of the Reformation—into existing Protestant churches, especially the Anglican and Presbyterian, or Reformed, churches. The term "Awakening" is in itself evocative. But of course revivalism caused a split between those who accepted and those who rejected it. The former group included many socially marginal or dependent individuals. Many married and single women were thus among the first adepts.

Husbands and fathers of humble background did not always look favorably on religious enthusiasm. It was an act of insubordination. Some women were beaten when they defied warnings and went to hear revivalist preachers or gave money to the cause. To avoid such consequences women often participated in "God's work" without telling their husbands or fathers. Yet revivalist preaching was not socially subversive; it did not tacitly encourage women to defy the "authority" of fathers and husbands. In some revivalist communities, however, "sisters" and "brothers" were treated as equals, and this no doubt heightened the suspicions of vigilant husbands and fathers.

Even in wealthier strata of society women were often more attracted to the Awakening than were their male companions. Some men came to the movement through the influence of women they knew. The Awakening thus offered women an opportunity to exercise independence and influence, in some ways encouraging them to take responsibility.

More generally, women benefited from the relative importance of laypeople in the religious movement. Because of its opposition to the establishment, the Awakening tended to value fervor above ecclesiastical rank. Lay preachers played a role from the first, especially in England as rivals to Anglican pastors. This was particularly important insofar as the clerical structure of the Church of England was closer to that of Catholicism than was that of other Protestant churches. The theological notion of an "extraordinary call" of God was invoked to justify the use of lay preachers in the face of hostility from the authorities. Even the unordained could receive a special call, and thus women too could serve in a role traditionally closed to them: testifying publicly to their faith and preaching.

The quasi-pastoral role of certain women was particularly clear in the New World, where the pressing need for more preachers overcame the caution of many adepts of the Awakening. In England Lady Huntington lent the movement official support and Lady Maxwell helped to bring it to Scotland in the eighteenth century. Despite the lack of such social prominence, Barbara Ruckle Heck helped to establish several new churches in the St. Lawrence Valley and was considered the "mother of American Methodism." Although Heck herself did not preach, by the end of the eighteenth century other women did mount the pulpit and serve as "itinerant ministers." Women continued in these roles in the following century: among the best known were Hannah Pearce Reeves, Lydia Sexton, and the first black women preachers, Jarena Lee and Rebecca Gould Stewart.

Wherever women assumed authority, however, there was trouble and controversy. Transgressing the boundaries of a social role always entails risk. In nineteenth-century families the most common situation was that in which the wife aided her husband in his work. In revivalism, especially in the United States, some wives served as "hostesses," for example. They did everything necessary to organize prayer meetings but did not preach. Although their role was subordinate to that of preacher (and therefore more readily acceptable to men), its importance bears emphasizing. The success of a visit, the size of crowd that a preacher was able to draw, and the durability of his influence all depended to a large extent on the hostess's organizational abilities and spiritual appeal. One of the best known was Catherine Livingston Garretson, who established a sort of headquarters for itinerant preachers working the Hudson Valley in addition to keeping a remarkable diary of her religious experience.

Pastors' Wives

The situation of pastors' wives in many Protestant churches was not fundamentally different from that of hostesses in the Awakening. The wife was generally intimately involved in her husband's ministry, and his success, in turn, depended in part on his wife's qualities. Yet the preacher's wife enjoyed no official status, no institutional legitimacy. Certain duties were generally recognized as theirs, however: they received guests and visited parishioners, taught pupils, and cared for the sick. And they could go without danger or impropriety to places where women ordinarily did not set foot.

The extent of their labor and influence depended on a variety of factors, among them the size of the parish and the density of its population. When the pastor was obliged to make frequent visits to outlying chapels, his wife might become the spiritual guide in his absence. As a self-taught theologian, she could offer comfort and advice, explain the Bible, and even lead prayer meetings. It would have seemed even more natural for her to assume this role if she was educated and genteel while her parishioners were of more modest background, but that was not always the case.

Teaching and caring for the sick were more common duties than filling in for an absent minister. Whether certified as a teacher or not, the pastor's wife not only taught children but also, in many places, ran classes for adults as well. She frequently administered certain kinds of medical or nursing treatment to women. Prevailing notions of decency and morality, particularly in the first half of the century, required women to perform tasks that might involve contact or intimacy with other women. This gave women some degree of power, and ministers' wives were not the only beneficiaries. Since schools were often segregated by sex and associated with religious sects, many young Protestant women, particularly daughters of ministers, became schoolteachers. It was also common for the minister's housemaid or maids to assist his wife in her teaching and nursing activities. A striking example of this can be seen in the case of Mme Oberlin, the wife of the pastor of Le Ban-de-la-Roche in Alsace. Assisted by her maid Louise Scheppler, she founded the first kindergartens in France. When she died, Louise Scheppler took over responsibility for these classes.

Thus the women around the pastor—his wife, his daughters, and possibly his maids—educated other women and set an example in taking initiative. They served as positive role models for other Protestant women, substituting an image of the "energetic" woman for that of the woman subject to "languor" and "the vapors." This new model was all the more appealing in that it did not seem (unduly) worrisome to the average man (in general it aroused little conflict). Here was proof that it was possible for women to venture outside the home without offense to the "modesty appropriate to [their] sex" or danger to their "irreproachable morality."

The Deaconess

The possibility for middle-class Protestants to demonstrate their piety in public and engage in charitable and social activities also led to the creation of a new kind of ministry, that of the "deaconess." Deaconesses were a product of the social vigor of Protestant Pietism, especially in Germany. They grew out of the Ladies' Society for the Care of the Poor and Sick founded in 1832 by Amalie Sieveking (1794–1859), the daughter of a Hamburg senator. But the first House of Deaconesses was founded by Rev. Theodore Fliedner of Kaiserwerth in the Prussian Rhineland. In the following year the Elizabeth Clinic, where deaconesses cared for the sick, opened its doors in Berlin. In France, Rev. Antoine Vermeil founded the House of Deaconesses of Reuilly in 1841, and Rev. François Haerter established another in Strasbourg in 1842. Many such houses sprang up in Germany and other countries.

The founding of houses of deaconesses was related to the growing belief that society must provide health care and education for the poor. Through its many religious orders the Catholic Church commanded the services of a large number of dedicated people capable of meeting these new social needs. Despite the existence of certain charitable organizations, the Protestant churches possessed nothing comparable, as some Catholics were quick to point out. Dr. Sulzer, for example, wrote that "charity, that flower of heaven, cannot grow on the dry and sandy terrain of the Protestant church." In addition, the establishment of a ministry of deaconesses made it possible to meet the need of some Protestant women for total religious commitment without allowing women to become pastors. Calling themselves "servants of the poor," the first deaconesses declared: "We long ago gave ourselves to the Lord. It is about time for us to return the love He showed us in saving our souls from sin and death by serving suffering humanity."

The House of Kaiserwerth took in "novices" from other establishments. Rev. Fliedner described what happened during their stay: "In our view, the best possible training for these sisters is to gain practical experience in all aspects of treating the sick and keeping house, including instruction in medicine by a doctor, instruction in the cure of souls by myself, and instruction in patient care by my wife." The training for deaconesses who would go on to teach the poor was naturally somewhat different.

The regulations of the newly founded houses of deaconesses stressed the Protestant theology of "salvation by grace alone" rather than good works. In devoting themselves to the service of "suffering humanity," deaconesses acquired no merit and contributed nothing to their salvation. In some respects, however, there were similarities between the position of a deaconess and that of a nun belonging to one of the charitable orders. As one might expect, this gave rise to debates among Protestants.

Some houses of deaconesses such as the ones at Kaiserwerth and Reuilly were placed under the authority of a pastor, who served as a full-time director and chaplain. By contrast, others established a kind of woman's democracy. Such was the case in Strasbourg, where the House of Deaconesses was run jointly by an executive committee (consisting of women who were not deaconesses), which concerned itself with administrative matters, and a Private Council (consisting of a "sister superior" and "lead sisters" elected by the other deaconesses), which sought to maintain order, peace, and good relations among the members of the community. A woman became a deaconess after a novitiate of one year. The community offered its members room and board but no salary. Deaconesses owed obedience to the sister superior and were required to give a year's notice before leaving the community. They were unmarried and wore a distinctive habit.

In some ways the life of a deaconess was at variance with the traditional Protestant view of the Christian life, according to which devotion through love does not require any special way of life. Numerous criticisms of the new institution were voiced. One of the most elaborate was written by Mme de Gasparin, a Swiss Reformed Protestant, who published a two-volume work, *On Monastic Corporations Within Protestantism,* in 1854 and 1855. The communities of deaconesses, she argued, were not based on any biblical example. Some words of Jesus about conversion and fidelity of all Christians had been distorted to justify an institution reminiscent of the medieval convents that Luther had abolished. The danger of such an institution was that it might lead to a depreciation of the value of marriage and the secular life. The central idea "is quite clear: it is the glorification of celibacy; it is sanctification through monastic profession; it is exclusive consecration as opposed to partial consecration; it is the separation of the world that Jesus did not want; it is Rome unveiled."

These criticisms were regularly repeated later on. For some nineteenth- and twentieth-century Protestants the deaconesses with their vows and habits looked like a potentially dangerous form of crypto-Catholicism. In general, however, the deaconesses quickly found a place in the always diverse Protestant world. Although some of their principles may have seemed curiously at odds with Protestant tenets, the value of their "witness" and the depth of their spiritual commitment were widely recognized.

Protestants against Slavery

If some Protestants viewed the institution of the deaconess's ministry as a step backward, others were frightened by the audacity of active Protestant participation in major movements of social reform. The role of women in the antislavery movement had this effect, and Protestant feminism was born of the ensuing conflicts.

The Boston journalist William Lloyd Garrison and his newspaper, *The Liberator,* led the antislavery campaign in the United States. A strict Calvinist, Garrison held that the racial prejudices of the North were as sinful in the eyes of God as the slavery of the South. He demanded the immediate and total emancipation of all black slaves. He addressed himself specifically to women, calling upon them to fight for the freedom of black women abandoned to the cruelty and lust of men. His call was soon answered by a handful of upper-class women, who devoted themselves to the battle against slavery and used their social position to further the cause.

Three women's abolitionist societies were established. From the beginning two of these enlisted both black and white women in the common struggle and encouraged female members to take independent initiatives. The Boston Society was founded by Maria Weston Chapman and three of her sisters. It recruited Protestants of various denominations, primarily Unitarians, Episcopalians, and Quakers. One member, Lydia Maria Child, the well-known author of some rather romantic short stories, wrote the first attack on slavery in the United States: *An Appeal on Behalf of That Class of Americans Called Africans* (1833). The book also attacked the treatment of free black men in schools and churches and called for the legalization of interracial marriage. The Philadelphia Society, founded by the Quaker Lucretia Coffin Mott, consisted primarily of other Quakers. It was notable for the talent of its black members: Sarah Mapps Douglas and the three Forten sisters, Sarah, Margaretta, and Harriet, who belonged to a family that remained active throughout the century in the battle against slavery, for the rights of women, and on behalf of other important social issues.

New York was the third center of the women's antislavery movement. The group there consisted mainly of Presbyterians, and its organization was less advanced than that of the other two groups: the women's committee was subordinate to the men's, and black and white women organized separately.

In 1837 the first women's antislavery congress was held in New York. A round of lectures was organized that same year in a number of New England cities. For six months Sarah and Angelina Grimké, two militant lecturers from South Carolina, spoke before large audiences of men and women, often at meetings held in churches. They criticized the religious community for its complicity in perpetuating the inferior status of black slaves and even of free blacks. The audacity of the women's attacks and much of its content did not fail to antagonize a large part of the Protestant clergy. The association of Congregationalist pastors subsequently published a pastoral letter arguing, on the strength of New Testament citations, that it was not appropriate for women to speak out on public affairs.

The slavery issue was thus linked to the controversy over the rights of women. The connection between the two issues was important, because some women activists might have found the pastors' arguments persuasive if only their own interests had been involved. But they felt they were fighting in God's cause, and that helped them resist the religious arguments raised against them. The most farsighted women understood, however, that from now on they would have to do battle on many fronts to bring about "a new order of things." Angelina Grimké wrote: "It is not only the cause of slaves that we are championing but also the cause of women as responsible, moral individuals." In 1838 her sister Sarah published her *Letters on the Equality of the Sexes and the Condition of Woman,* the first manifesto of contemporary Protestant feminism.

Protestant Feminism

According to Sarah Grimké, the Bible, correctly translated and interpreted, does not teach that men and women are unequal. On the contrary, it states that both sexes were created with the same rights and duties. For example, Genesis 3:16 ("and thy desire shall be to thy husband, and he shall rule over thee"), which was often cited to justify woman's dependence on man, was to Grimké nothing more than a prediction of the consequences of original sin and not an order from God legitimating male superiority. This was a first step toward a feminist exegesis of the Bible. During the nineteenth century a number of feminists became theologians, especially in the English-speaking countries. Among them was Elizabeth Cady Stanton, the theorist and propagandist of American feminism, who in the 1890s published her *Women's Bible,* a compilation of exegetical commentaries refuting traditional Christian formulations of the relations between men and women and on woman's place in society. The century's most committed Protestant feminists in England and America had a favorite slogan: "Pray to God that She may grant your wishes."

More generally, Protestant feminists pointed to Genesis 2:18: "It is not good that the man should be alone; I will make him an help meet for him." Man's companion was therefore his equal, or perhaps, as the French Protestant Eugénie Niboyet suggested, even his superior. Niboyet cleverly stood the traditional arguments for male superiority on their head. Was Eve created from Adam's rib? Well, then, that rib was part of a human body, a nobler material than the clay and dust out of which God made Adam. But wasn't man created first, woman second? Of course, and the order of creation represents a progression: first sea monsters, then animals, then man, and finally woman, the highest of all. When Eve was created, the creation had achieved its ultimate fullness, and God could rest on the seventh day.

But most Protestants concerned in one way or another with the evolution of male-female relations did not share Niboyet's cleverly radical views. The deaconess Sarah Monod, who edited the newspaper *La Femme* at the end of the century, said she often felt offended "in [her] dignity as a woman" by the way in which feminists defended "the rights, or alleged rights," of women. In her view, feminism "ought to have the virtues of woman herself: dignity without stiffness, tenacity without impudence, perseverance without ruthlessness, warmth without passion. The best feminism will be the most feminine." Like her, many Protestant women did not want to marginalize themselves and fought to maintain their respectability. These principles did not preclude certain initiatives, however. Mme Necker de Saussure, for example, founded an innovative school on Lake Leman near Geneva, and in 1828 she published *L'Education progressive.* This frequently reprinted work advocated teaching independence to both girls and boys and stressed the need for girls to wait to marry long enough to give themselves a chance to become "enlightened spirits" and "intelligent creatures."

A number of Protestant women of the middle and upper classes shared this interest in education. In substance, their message to other women was this: the alleged "inferiority" of women is a product not of "nature" but of the inferior education available to girls, so inadequate that they are unable to develop their intelligence sufficiently to equal that of men. Working-class women must rise above the "dregs of the populace"—"depraved women" who, ignorant of the name of the "drunken" man who had gotten them with child, "dropped" their babies in public shelters; they must become true mothers and take the maximum possible interest in the education of their children. Women of the upper classes must not be "indolent" or "plaster themselves with cosmetics to the point of hideousness" in order to hide a few premature wrinkles; rather, they should accept their "social duties," such acceptance being, along with prayer, the mark of "true piety."

The charitable Protestant women of the nineteenth century were imbued with a consciousness of "social duty." Along with the many women who founded charitable organizations on a local, regional, or national level, a few great names stand out as having achieved international prominence: among them are Josephine Butler, who helped prostitutes; Elizabeth Fry, the prison reformer; and Florence Nightingale, who helped to organize the nursing profession.

Feminism and Moralism

Josephine Butler was perhaps the most significant of female Protestant voices to speak out on moral and social issues. Born into the middle class, Butler set out in 1870 to combat the system of regulated prostitution that Britain had adopted a few years earlier. Justified on grounds of public health and social control, the regulation made it almost impossible for prostitutes to escape from their condition. "Fallen women" were thus condemned to "life terms at degrading forced labor."

Josephine Butler's efforts quickly garnered support from English Protestants (the newspaper *The Shield* was founded to support the campaign), as well as from other countries such as Switzerland, where Mme de Gasparin published a book entitled *La Lèpre sociale* (Social Leprosy). The International Abolitionist Federation (working to abolish prostitution) was established in Geneva in 1877. Its French branch would be known as the Ligue Française pour le Relèvement de la Moralité Publique (French League for the Improvement of Public Morality), and it included not only Protestants but also free thinkers and even some Catholics.

Although the movement was not exclusively Protestant, it was thoroughly imbued with moral and religious concerns of Protestant origin. Even a woman who had fallen into the "depths of vice" retained an inalienable right to salvation. Most such women, it was argued, were less "guilty" than "victims" of man's "bestiality" and of the "misery" caused by society. The battle against regulated prostitution was waged in the name of both the Holy Bible and the "political Bible" (that is, the English Bill of Rights). And it was waged simultaneously on several related fronts. In the first place, the freedom of women was threatened by "medical-legal tyranny" and "state fetishism." Second, it was essential to fight for morality and the "sanctity" of the family ("vice" was not an "inevitable fate"). And last but not least, the battle against prostitution was sometimes combined with elements of social reform, especially in France and Switzerland. Rev. Tommy Fallot, the founder of the Christian social movement, launched a "crusade" on behalf of "slave women" in the 1880s. The principal causes of prostitution, its activists alleged, included neglect of education, low wages, and the absence of civil rights for women—in short, a series of "social iniquities." The French League called for legal and educational reform and a certain transformation "of the relation between capital and labor." Louis Bridel, the Swiss Protestant jurist who wrote *La Femme et le droit* (Woman and Law, 1884), was particularly active in this campaign.

The range of action was quite vast. It combined what we would now call a kind of moralism with a kind of feminism. The battle against "debauchery," for example, along with the insistence that "impurity is as reprehensible in man as it is in woman" (Congress of Geneva, 1877), led to advocacy of "a single morality for both sexes." The concerns of these campaigners linked up with those of other Protestant men and women interested in promoting "intersexual fraternity." One of the most ardent champions of such "fraternity," Mme Pieczynska, suggested ways in which it could be achieved: "judicious" sexual education for young people, mixed schooling, gymnastics for girls, and replacement of the sexual division of labor with what she called a "community of labor." In Scandinavia and the English-speaking countries mixed schools were a reality by century's end. In some Swedish boarding schools, mixing of the sexes was seen as a way of "improving morals" rather than as a "source of immorality."

Two international congresses on Women's Works and Institutions were largely dominated by Protestants. Mme Legrand-Priestley noted that the "woman question" was "infinitely more advanced" in America, England, Denmark, and Sweden than it was in France. These two congresses were quite typical of what might be called the Protestant women's movement. They were characterized by "calm" and "decorum." Although certain women's demands were heard, the accent was on philanthropy, which, it was alleged, enabled women to pursue their "social mission" and contributed to a necessary "rapprochement of classes."

Access to the Ministry

Feminism at this time absorbed a variety of influences and developed into a largely secular movement. Yet there was a parallel between the insistence on political rights for women (especially the right to vote) and the desire of Protestant women to share in all forms of religious authority, including the pastorate. At the famous Woman's Rights Convention of 1848 in Seneca Falls, New York, a resolution was adopted urging an end to the male monopoly on preaching. If women with an "extraordinary vocation" had occasionally been permitted to preach to revivalist meetings, now it was hoped that women might become regular preachers and ultimately pastors in Protestant churches.

Such hopes met with powerful opposition. According to church authorities, no passage of the Old or New Testament so much as hinted that God wanted women to serve as ministers. Men and women would do best to stick to the places that God had assigned them. After the Civil War, however, organizations controlled by women, especially those concerned with missionary activities, gained power within several Protestant denominations, especially the Baptists, Methodists, and Episcopalians. The financial resources (managed, in the North, by women themselves) and influence of these organizations increased the pressure that women were able to bring to bear.

That pressure initially focused on the issue of the power of laywomen within the church. Why did laymen enjoy more power than laywomen? In the 1880s women were first elected to represent local churches and regional synods at national synods, but they were denied the right to speak publicly or at best were restricted to speeches no longer than a few minutes' duration. By the turn of the century, however, some churches were granting equal rights to all delegates, male or female.

The issue of women preaching from the pulpit was seriously broached for the first time in the 1870s. The Quakers had traditionally allowed women to preach. The Quaker preacher Sarah Smiley was invited to preach in several Presbyterian churches in Brooklyn. A "suffragette" by the name of Anna Howard Shaw, a graduate of a Boston school of theology, obtained permission to preach in several Methodist churches. A few other women followed in the footsteps of these pioneers. To be successful, a woman preacher had to speak with the authority of a man and the modesty of a woman. In 1888 Frances Willard, head of the Woman's Christian Temperance Union, discussed the issue in her book *Woman in the Pulpit.*

Despite these difficulties, progress was made in the United States. There was no comparable evolution in Europe, where the issue of "female ministries" was not seriously considered until World War I placed it on the agenda. The war took many pastors away from their pulpits for extended periods and thus spurred a demand for new preachers.

Although the problems were similar everywhere, more is known about the French case thanks to a report prepared by Mme de Witt-Schlumberger (president of the French Union for Women's Suffrage). In a general wartime atmosphere of sacrifice and pooling of energies (and thus without an explicit political agenda), the wives of some pastors assumed their husbands' duties. Necessary though this transgression was, some of the women involved found it troubling (shocking, but also fascinating).

Broadly speaking, church women encountered three types of situation. First, a woman might partially replace (or substitute for) her husband. She would continue alone to discharge duties that she had previously discharged under his supervision. She might also assume new responsibilities that did not seem incompatible with her being a woman. For example, she might teach catechism classes, preside over various weekday religious meetings, supervise youth groups, visit the sick, aid the poor, and so on. But preaching and other pastoral duties would still be discharged by a minister (generally an elderly man not mobilized because of his age) from a nearby parish. This was probably the most common situation.

A second possibility was that the pastor's wife might replace him on an interim basis. She might begin by reading some of his old sermons, only to conclude that it was essential "to speak more directly to [parishioners'] souls." She would then begin preaching—albeit not without "considerable misgivings." Out of necessity some women were compelled to perform "pastoral acts," such as marriages and funeral services. That still left the sacraments. Mme de Witt-Schlumberger's report says nothing on the subject, but other sources suggest that women did in some instances discreetly administer the two Protestant sacraments (baptism and communion). Despite the lack of theological justification, the sacraments were, in most Protestant churches, the last bastion of the sacred that women would be obliged to conquer.

The third possibility was for the pastor's wife to take his place and introduce innovations into the parish routine. Could a woman settle for being a mere interim replacement when she had a personality of her own and when the circumstances were so extraordinary? Her sermons had to take account of the stress of living in difficult times. New ways of dealing with the needs of the mobilized, the wounded, and their families had to be found. The wives of pastors drew on their own resources to come up with novel ideas and methods. These, in the end, might influence the general direction of parish life. When the pastor returned home, he found a different church from the one he had left and a wife who had proven her capabilities as minister. In the long run, this was not without effect.

Thus the nineteenth century (broadly understood) was a period of change for Protestant women. Their condition evolved along with the broader society, though at a pace that varied according to the country, denomination, and social class. Some women were actively involved in bringing about these changes. And while the battle for the right of women to serve as ministers was not yet won, it was well under way.

TRANSLATED FROM THE FRENCH BY ARTHUR GOLDHAMMER

9

The Making of the Modern Jewish Woman

Nancy L. Green

"It may be hard to be a Jew, but it's even harder to be a Jewish woman."[1] But does the Jewish woman even exist? It is impossible to construct a single model for Jewish women that would include both the salon Jewess of early nineteenth-century Berlin and the "Yidishe mame" born in the *shtetlekh* (villages) of Eastern Europe and transplanted to America after the 1880s. For one thing, even in its most traditional form, the theoretical religious definition of the woman's place in Judaism and Jewish society has not always corresponded to reality. As the whole body of rabbinical *responsa* has forcefully shown, daily life has always been reinterpreted in each period and in each place where Jews have lived. Furthermore, the religious model itself was transformed during the nineteenth century. Under the impact of the Reform movement, the new synthesis between tradition and modernity produced, among other things, changing attitudes toward women's role in Jewish life. Moreover, the modern Diaspora, the mass migration of Jews from East to West in the late nineteenth and early twentieth century, carried along with it the seeds of ideological change with regard to gender relationships. Different national contexts then provided different educational possibilities and new models for the Jewish woman.

After delineating the ideal type of the religious model, I will look at three examples of Jewish women and their education in the nineteenth century—the salon Jewess of Berlin, the "traditional" woman of the Russian shtetl, and the immigrant Jewish woman in America—in order to explore the emergence of the modern Jewish woman and its impact on gender relations within the Jewish community. In keeping with the geographic scope of this volume, we will deal here with Ashkenazic (Western) women only. Sephardic (Oriental) women would merit a chapter unto themselves.

Gender in Religious Life

A Jewish man begins his daily prayers by thanking God that he was not made a woman. Judaism prescribes a clearly separate role for women, within the synagogue and within Jewish culture in general, based upon the concept that men are obliged by God to carry out a certain number of commandments *(mitzvot)* from which women are exempt. Thus men only are counted in constituting a *minyan,* the quorum necessary for public prayer. Women are generally not initiated into the holy language, Hebrew. They are seated separately, in an upper balcony of the synagogue, and have fewer obligations of formal worship. Their role is to prepare the Sabbath meal rather than attend Friday evening services.

The separation of men and women into public (synagogue) and private (home) spheres corresponds not only to a religious division of labor but also to a strict interpretation of the relationship between the two sexes. Jewish law seeks to protect both the sanctity of the family and the virtue of (male) learning. Men ought not to be distracted from their devotion to God and to prayer by thoughts of women, and sexual relations and daily interaction of the two sexes are thus strictly regulated. A religious man must not look a woman directly in the face, and, according to tradition, the religious woman, once married, must cut her hair and cover her head with a wig or scarf. In the interest of procreation, marital sexual relations are encouraged, however. Their regularity is even specified in the Shulkhan Arukh (the sixteenth-century Talmudic code compiled by Joseph Caro, still used today), varying in accordance with the man's profession. Men had a rather extensive right to divorce, but from the Middle Ages on, women were also granted the theoretical right to ask for a divorce, on grounds of sexual dissatisfaction among others. Rachel Biale suggests, however, that the Halakhic (Jewish law) trend toward women's rights in many areas was perhaps, with regard to sexuality, "more permissive and more generous to women than life itself."[2]

The sexual separation of men and women has important consequences for education. The high value Jews place on learning is legendary, but it is theoretically reserved for men only. Men are indeed obliged by religious law to study the Torah, but women are exempt. This exemption is somewhat contradictory, for women are after all the main practitioners of the laws regulating daily life. However, it is for men to reflect upon the theoretical underpinnings of the law, and for women to implement them, as keepers of the ritual and of the kosher home. Although some religious commentators argued that "exemption" did not necessarily mean exclusion, for the most part, in traditional society, Torah study was prohibited to women and even considered a sin by many religious authorities. The main character in Isaac Bashevis Singer's story "Yentl the Yeshiva Boy" was so determined to study Torah that she disguised her identity, thus doubly breaking the law: by studying at the yeshiva and wearing men's clothes.

The religious model must be nuanced in at least two ways. Although Jewish law exempts women from formal study and most public religious duties, religion is not absent from their private sphere. Rather it takes another form, which Barbara Myerhoff called "domestic religion."[3] Jewish women, as women in most societies, are the important bearers and transmitters of informal knowledge and emotional piety, which children often later describe as more important than the formal learning of the Hebrew school.

Second, not all men became full-time Talmudic scholars, of course, even when such was the ideal. However, to the extent that male religious study was encouraged, it meant a reversal of gender roles with regard to socioeconomic life. Men's public role in the sacred world was only possible thanks to the Jewish women's greater public role in the secular world. While men went to the synagogue during the week, women went to the marketplace. Women's greater access to the secular public sphere would have important consequences as Judaism confronted the Reform movement and migration.

The Salon Jewish Women of Berlin

Nothing could be further from the conduct of the ideal type of the religious Jewish woman than the way of life of the salon Jewesses in late eighteenth and early nineteenth-century Berlin. They have been praised as the avant-garde of female emancipation, damned as examples of how the Jewish Reform movement led to assimilation, and blamed as models for the conversion "mania" of German Jews in this period. Deborah Hertz has shown how these salons functioned at a particular historical moment in German history:[4] between the Enlightenment and the defeat of Prussia by Napoleon at Jena in 1806, in an era in which royal patronage of the arts had declined and the publishing industry had not yet come into its own. As Hannah Arendt put it, the Jews became "stopgaps" in an as yet unstabilized social situation.[5] In this period of early Romanticism (before it took on nationalist and anti-Semitic overtones), cash-poor nobles, commoner intellectuals, and wealthy Jews could come together in what Jacob Katz has called a "semineutral society."[6]

But were relations between Jewish women and Prussian noblemen and writers a real sign of Jewish integration or an exception? Hannah Arendt argued that it was rather their very marginality which made the Jewish salons "neutral territory." Marion Kaplan has more recently emphasized that the elite-centered, Berlin-centered histories of assimilated German Jewry and of the salon Jewesses may have been dramatic, but were not the norm.[7]

In the end, these Jewish women converted; what made them do it? Dorothea von Schlegel, née Brendel Mendelssohn (daughter of Moses), even converted twice, first to Protestantism and then to Catholicism with her husband, Friedrich. Rahel Varnhagen (née Levin) was explicit about her attitude to Judaism, which she called her "infamous birth," a handicap from which she sought to escape until the very last days of her life.[8]

The disaffection of these women for Judaism has been attributed to their education. They benefited from the best that an upper-class family could offer a girl: study of languages (French, English, Latin, Hebrew) and music, private tutors, guided reading by enlightened fathers. However, their education was too "decorative," complain some historians (and some of their contemporaries, contemptuous of female intellectual pretensions); it was ominously too secular for most Jewish historians. Deborah Hertz argues quite convincingly, though, that it was social opportunity in a specific historical environment, rather than early education, which led to these "misalliances."

The model of the salon Jewess, however extreme, brings into question the challenge of reform within Judaism. Indeed, one of the major issues of the Reform movement, to which not enough attention has been given thus far, is the implications it carries for gender relations. The forerunner of this movement, Moses Mendelssohn, writing in late-eighteenth-century Berlin, sought to integrate Enlightenment thought with Jewish principles and reinterpret Judaism as a religion of reason. Although Mendelssohn himself maintained a traditional home all his life, the implication of many of his ideas for subsequent reformers was the acceptance of ritualistic reform if not the abandonment of most Jewish observance altogether, in yet another historical adaptation of Judaism to its surroundings.

Education would be particularly affected by the new ideological currents within Judaism, with two questions central to educational reform. To what extent should secular subjects be introduced into Jewish education? And to what extent should women be admitted to study? One of Mendelssohn's followers, Naphtali H. Wessely, argued that general academic studies were necessary, and David Friedländer set up a Jüdische Freischule (Jewish Free School) along these lines in 1778. However, it would take another half century before coeducation was implemented and, ironically, it was Samson Raphael Hirsch, leader of the neo-Orthodox movement, who first offered formal religious education to girls along with boys in 1855. Worried that Jewish children were entering public schools in increasing numbers and that even the modern Jewish schools offered too little Jewish education, Hirsch sought to counter Reform through a modified traditional education, even if Talmudic studies were still off-limits to girls.

The Haskalah (Jewish Enlightenment) and neo-Orthodox thinkers alike realized that the growing disparity between male/religious and female/secular education was perhaps ultimately a threat to what the separateness of public and private spheres aimed to preserve: Jewish family purity and Judaism in general. While the Orthodox compromise was to increase women's access to religious study, the Reform solution was greater secular education for men and women alike. The Reform model of Judaism, in which religious education and identity were relegated to the private sphere, where greater public contact between the sexes was allowed, and where women would eventually participate in auxiliary synagogue functions, would be transplanted with the German Jews to the United States in mid-century.

Women's Education in the Shtetl: Exclusion, Integration, Emigration

The tea sipped in the Berlin salons could not have been physically or metaphysically farther from that served from the samovars in Eastern Europe. Of another class as well as of another country, the women of the almost mythicized shtetl bring us back to more traditional gender relations within the Jewish community, where the Talmudic scholar and the pious wife remained the idealized, if not always real, type.

Jewish education in early-nineteenth-century Russia was, of course, for boys and men only. And although highest praise and status was reserved for the scholar, the conditions of his study were far from ideal. From age five to thirteen, boys were sent either to the private *heder* or the communal *talmud torah* (for the poor), where the usually despotic, dirty, and poorly paid teacher would try to inculcate by rote the basics of Hebrew and Torah into the recalcitrant children. Conditions in the secondary schools, the *yeshiva,* and the local house of study *(beit midrash)* for adults were less chaotic, but the regime was nonetheless mentally rigorous and often materially difficult for the poor *yeshiva bokher* (yeshiva boy). If he came from another town, he usually slept at the synagogue and took meals every night at a different home, where families thus not only did a religious good deed, but often hoped to recruit a prestigious scholar as a son-in-law.

Occasionally young girls would be allowed to attend the heder, most likely in a separate room, instructed by the teacher's wife. But most never had more than one or two years of such training, just enough maybe to learn to read and perhaps write Yiddish (the spoken language), and memorize the necessary Hebrew prayers (Hebrew was used for religious purposes only). For the most part, especially throughout the first two-thirds of the nineteenth century, women's education remained as it had always been, largely informal. Some girls had brothers who would teach them their lessons at night. Girls from wealthier families might have private tutors. However, most girls did not go beyond the immensely popular Yiddish *Tseenah Ureenah,* the vernacular version of the Bible with commentary written in simple style.

The ideas of the Jewish Enlightenment began to reach the more urban areas of Eastern Europe by the middle of the nineteenth century and the villages by the 1870s and 1880s. Educational reform was once again a crucial issue, leading to vociferous debates concerning what subjects should be taught (secular as well as religious?), in what language (Hebrew, Russian, or Yiddish), according to what political tendency (Bundist or Zionist) but also, to whom: girls as well as boys? However, it was the tsar himself, in his efforts to "Russify" this minority population, who encouraged new educational models.

Until mid-century the Russian educational system had simply excluded the Jews. But in 1844 an edict promulgated by Uvarov, minister of education under Nicholas I, set up government elementary schools for Jewish children, along with two rabbinical seminaries. The tsar's efforts (aimed, among other things, at "the eradication of the superstitions and harmful prejudices instilled by the study of the Talmud") were never totally successful. Approximately 3,000 Jewish children attended seventy crown schools in 1854 and about 4,000 went to ninety-eight such schools in 1863. The number of children in the traditional hadarim was always much larger, however, and continued to grow, from 70,000 in 1844 to 76,000 in 1847. Nevertheless, as Michael Stanislawski has convincingly argued, the new school system did ultimately help institutionalize and consolidate the Reform movement among Russian Jewry.[9]

Under the more liberal measures of Alexander II, the doors to higher Russian education for the Jews opened wider. In 1870 the 2,045 Jewish students attending the gymnasia constituted 5.6 percent of the total number of students; ten years later they were 12 percent (7,004 students), well above their portion of the population. Nevertheless, 50,000 Jewish children still attended hadarim in 1879, and over fifty percent of Jewish families continued to choose this traditional mode of elementary education for their children at the end of the century.[10]

Girls, in contrast, entered government schools in appreciable numbers. One report states that by 1910 twice as many girls as boys were enrolled in the official state schools in nearby Galicia

(Austria-Hungary; almost 44,000 girls to 23,000 boys).[11] Like their counterparts in Germany, the Orthodox Jews became worried. Some attempts were made to set up separate religious schools for girls before World War I. But it was not until 1917 that the first Orthodox Bais Ya'akov schools for girls were founded in Poland.

By the end of the nineteenth century, the majority of Russian Jewish women were still illiterate. According to the Russian census of 1897, only 33 percent of them could read and write, compared to 67 percent of Jewish men.[12] However, girls were increasingly attending the modern, "improved" hadarim, and many young women from the enlightened bourgeoisie were, like their brothers, going directly into the Russian gymnasium and university. Family disputes often mirrored the intellectual debates over the value of education for women and of secular education in general, but an important minority of Jewish women was in the process of investigating new models of behavior.

The assassination of Alexander II in 1881 put a halt to Jewish access to Russian education, for men as for women. Elizabeth Hasanovitz remembers that it became practically illegal (although tolerated with a bribe) to teach Russian to Jewish children. Her father's little schoolroom was regularly disrupted by guards and papers quickly thrown down into the cellar, "that splendid hiding-place for the crime of stealing a Russian education."[13] The *numerus clausus* of 1887, which drastically limited the number of Jewish students allowed into the university, was an important factor spurring emigration to the West. Women, like their brothers, sometimes emigrated *for* education, and matriculated in striking numbers at the western universities. At the University of Paris, from 1905 to 1913, Russian and Romanian (Jewish) women constituted over a third of the total female students and approximately two-thirds of the total foreign female students. In certain disciplines, medicine and law, there were from one-and-a-half to twice as many Eastern European women enrolled as French women.[14]

Finally, a minority of Jewish women took two radical paths away from community gender norms. Prostitution and revolution each threatened Jewish society in very different ways. The great "white slavery" outcry of the turn of the century, in which Jews were involved both as prostitutes and as pimps, from Galicia to Buenos Aires, turned in part on a criticism of secular education for women. The Orthodox blamed the transgressions from norms of purity, chastity, and separation on the lack of religious and moral education in the younger generations in general and on the state schools in Galicia in particular. However, Bertha Pappenheim and Dr. Sarah Rabinowitch, after investigating Jewish prostitution in Galicia in 1903, suggested that ultra-Orthodox girls were also vulnerable because of their ignorance of sex and the disparity in girls' and boys' education. The strong prohibition against extramarital sex even within nontraditional Jewish homes could mean that once "fallen," a girl could feel, like Polly Adler, famous turn-of-the-century New York brothel owner, that there was no more place for her within the community fold.[15]

While Jewish prostitutes have since fallen by the wayside of Jewish memory, the Eastern European Jewish revolutionary women have not. From "Rosa" (Luxemburg) to "Red Emma" (Goldman), these radical women from Poland, Western Europe, and America were objects of the attention of journalists and police informers alike. Like Henriette Herz or Rahel Varnhagen a century before, the Jewish revolutionary women, if few in absolute number, nevertheless struck the imagination as yet another radical model of female emancipation, turning traditional gender roles around, demanding equality in the public sphere, rejecting separation, flaunting free love. Young working women made up approximately one-third of the Bund's (Jewish labor movement) membership from its inception in 1897,[16] and women were also prominent in the rival Zionist groups. Perhaps the most important aspect of this new role for women was a heightened visibility of their role in public, and even political, life. As Paula Hyman has thoughtfully argued, the "new Jewish woman" was already taking form in Eastern Europe.[17]

For many women, like many men, the biggest change in their lives, and one that would affect gender relations as well, was emigration. Chased from Russia by tsarist and popular anti-Semitism and by economic necessity, pulled by idyllic images of opportunities to the New World, over 1.5 million Jews emigrated to the United States alone between 1881 and 1924. Some went to carry on political activities abroad, others went to study. Most went in search of better economic conditions and greater freedom—escaping from the tsar or perhaps a despotic father. For women emigration could mean subjection or simply following fathers, mothers, sisters, or husbands, or it could mean emancipation. Men and women now faced each other on a new terrain, where the traditional model had long since been abandoned.

Emigration and the American Model

The samovars came too. As the mass migration to America got under way, the men most often went first, leaving wives and children behind, to carry on the business for perhaps several years while awaiting the (sometimes never forthcoming) ship tickets, and then to carry the bedding, the samovar, and other indispensable household items across the sea. Many women went reluctantly and fearfully. The land paved with gold was also seen as an unholy, unkosher land, where men shaved off their beards. But other women made the trip with determination, casting off their religious wigs en route.

Among its opportunities the new land offered free and compulsory education for girls as well as boys. Greater access to formal training for women was one of the hallmarks of the New World, and education for girls would slowly be accepted, even among the Orthodox. However, it would still take time to eliminate the educational discrepancies between the two sexes.

The Russian Jewish women who came to the United States in the 1908–1912 period were twice as literate as those counted in the 1897 Russian census (owing to expanded education in the interval, or self-selection through migration?): 63 percent compared to 33 percent. They were also more literate than most other immigrant groups arriving at the time. Nevertheless, arriving Russian Jewish women still had considerably lower literacy rates than Russian Jewish men (80 percent).[18]

The very first task of the immigrant, literate or not, was to transfer his or her language skills into English. Men did so almost to a man, and by one estimate 90 percent of Jewish immigrant women over fourteen also learned English, compared to only 35 percent of other immigrant women.[19] For workers, men or women, formal education meant night school: evening English classes, elementary or high school-level courses for credit, or vocational courses.

Children, however, entered the great American melting-pot: elementary school. It brought boys and girls together, American and immigrant children. Undoubtedly, not all students were as lyrical as Mary Antin in their vision of the benefits of public education. For her, America was the new Zion, the schoolteacher its female Moses. "Never had I prayed, never had I chanted the songs of David, never had I called upon the Most Holy, in such utter reverence and worship as I repeated the simple sentences of my child's story of the patriot [George Washington]."[20] Social workers commented on the good results of the Jewish immigrants and on their manifest desire for education.

This did not mean that there were no Jewish dropouts, and high enrollments did not necessarily mean sterling attendance rates, even if Jewish immigrants and their children tended to persevere longer than other groups. Poverty and exhaustion interfered. In evening schools, it was often difficult to concentrate after long days in the sweatshop; in elementary schools, classes of sometimes 60 to 100 students surely discouraged more than one budding scholar. It was largely a struggle between economics and education. Many children had to quit school early in order to contribute to the family income. And it was often the girls who were sacrificed, ultimately subsidizing their brothers' education. One historian notes, however, that age could be a more important consideration than gender in determining the amount of a child's education; older immigrant children helped put their younger siblings through school.[21]

Indeed, some recent research has sought to balance the somewhat overenthusiastic popular imagery linking Jews and education, and higher education in particular. As Selma Berrol and Sherry Gorelick have both pointed out, education indeed continued to be honored in the New World, but it was business that brought mobility. Particularly for the earlier generations, education was a result not a cause of upward mobility.[22]

Religious education was not entirely forsaken in America, but it was transformed into an after-school option. The immigrant Orthodox set up after-school hadarim, based on the East European model and for boys only. Approximately 500 such schools were serving the roughly 1.5 million Jews in New York City by 1917–18. Yiddish groups that were more cultural than religious, such as the Workmen's Circle, also offered after-school classes, where girls made up some 37 percent of the students.[23]

A more secular (and less "ethnic") Jewish education was offered in the German Jewish Sunday schools, where over half of the students were girls and most of the staff women. Rebecca Gratz had set up America's first Jewish Sunday School in 1838, along the Protestant model (in fact she used Protestant scripture lessons and pasted over the unsuitable answers).[24] The German Jews, who had been in the United States since mid-century and had brought Reform ideas with them, were by now largely middle-class and looked with suspicion and fear on the late-nineteenth-century influx of the East European immigrant poor. In New York they made various attempts to set up new forms of Jewish education to compete with the hadarim, "considered from hygienic, moral and Americanizing standpoints . . . of the very type which it is the chief aim of the [Educational] Alliance to extirpate."[25] First the more secular-style Hebrew Free School and the Educational Alliance into which it merged in 1899, then the Kehillah movement (including the immigrant bourgeoisie), begun in 1910 and stressing more religious training (three experimental girls' schools were started), tried to provide alternate models for the Eastern European immigrants. But the right balance between secular and religious Jewish education, between opportunities for girls and for boys, was difficult to attain, and both of these efforts came under sharp attack from the Orthodox on the one hand, the socialists on the other.

Public education meant Americanization, and religious education too had to come to grips with changing forms of religious observance within American life. In truth the real educational models, when formal training had to be forsaken for work, were to be found in the informal classroom: at home, in the workshop, on the street.

The home, the woman's sphere, has often been idealized. Indeed it functioned as the locus of cultural continuity. But the immigration experience interfered with the smooth passage of information from mother to daughter. "I am an American—you are only a greenhorn," cried one frustrated daughter; "You don't even understand what I say."[26] Migration caused a reversal of educational roles. Children now taught parents and took over certain adult roles because of their better grasp of English. Generational conflicts erupted over questions of gender separation and educational opportunities. There were also intrusions into the home through Americanizing middle-class (German Jewish) social workers, who tried to inculcate thrift and cleanliness in the newcomers through mothers' meetings and home visits. The famous

Settlement Cookbook was begun as a medium of acculturation: its kosher recipes were accompanied by explicit instructions for the immigrant housewife about how to clear the table, wash the dishes, and so on. The Yiddish press also got into the act, discussing changing relations between the sexes, advising and encouraging education for girls and night classes for married women. The compounded image of the immigrant mother is a double one. Resented for her old-world habits, she was also admired for her strength and tremendous resourcefulness, or what Ellen Schiff calls the "talent for creative survival."[27]

In the workshop young women learned to run their sewing machines up to sixteen hours a day; learned that they were at the managerial and often sexual mercy of their bosses; and many learned about socialism. The image of the "Uprising of the 20,000," the three-month garment strike of 1909–10, has left one of the most vibrant memories of immigrant Jewish women's participation in the labor movement. As Alice Kessler-Harris has shown, the Jewish women activists were caught between multiple class, gender, and ethnic identities. Yet they entered the public sphere in noticeably larger numbers than their Italian coworkers, and surprised their male compatriots with their strident demands.[28]

Girls and boys, together and separately, also learned about America in the streets, on the tenement rooftops, and at the dance halls, while their mothers exchanged information in their kitchens. Neighborhood networks among women were an important part of the learning and doing process and were at times put to forceful use. In the New York City Kosher Meat Boycott of 1902 and later in food riots (1907, 1917) and rent strikes (1904, 1908), the women canvassed for support from house to house and synagogue to synagogue, putting gender and class ties to the test against male (German Jewish) wholesalers and landlords.[29]

From another viewpoint, however, immigration also meant a certain loss of knowledge, felt keenly by those who crossed the ocean. Some experienced a loss of know-how: "When I came here, I knew more than I know now. I knew how to make a whole dress," said a sewing-machine operator.[30] All experienced the loss of language: "I came from the Ukraine where I was an educated girl, a teacher myself, and to come here and not know the language, not be able to go to college—it was terrible!"[31] Migration offered new roles, new formal and informal educational opportunities, but not without a price.

If there is no one model for Jewish women, given the variations of the Diaspora, there was not even one sole American model at the turn of the century. The German Jewish woman was much closer to her non-Jewish middle-class counterparts than to the Russian immigrant women. One of her short-lived magazines, the *American Jewess* (1895–1899), was concerned with educating women for marriage and motherhood and dealt with issues such as solving the servant problem, for example. By the end of the nineteenth century, German Jewish women were already entering higher education and becoming educators themselves, while Russian Jewish women were lucky if they could keep awake at night school.

The German Jews and the Russian Jews, separated by class, language, and attitudes toward religion, regarded each other with mutual suspicion. However, it is through the women more than the men that contact between the two groups occurred. German Jewish social workers such as Lillian Wald organized settlement houses, where nursing services, public lectures, and dressmaking classes were available to the immigrant women. The National Council for Jewish Women, set up during the Chicago World Fair of 1893, aimed, as one of its founders explained, at bringing women's nurturing work to the public sphere through philanthropy, religion, and education. Although the German Jewish woman may have intruded into the Russian woman's private sphere, nonetheless, as Baum, Hyman, and Michel suggest, she was probably the immigrant's closest real model of Americana.[32]

Like Gitl in the movie *Hester Street,* many immigrant women clung to old world traits longer than men in an effort to keep control over their own private sphere. Others combined old world practices and New World opportunities in claiming a vociferous part in public affairs. For younger women in particular, emigration could be a form of personal emancipation.

Variety and Transformation

In 1934, Bertha Pappenheim criticized the historical role of women in Judaism, calling it a "sin committed against the Jewish woman's soul and thus against all Judaism," and argued for their better education.[33] Unequal education for men and women resulted from and reinforced asymmetric gender roles. Boundaries only gradually broke down in the course of the nineteenth century under the combined and related impact of secularization (within the larger society), emancipation (of the Jewish communities), and Reform (within Judaism). Yet gender relations continued to differ by country, by attitude toward religion (Orthodox, Reform), and by class.

Although there is thus no one model for the "making of the Jewish woman," we can identify several constants in nineteenth-century Jewish attitudes concerning gender relations and women's education. First, access to education for women remained bound everywhere by two fears: conversion and spinsterhood. While German parents feared that secular education could lead to apostasy, Russian mothers and fathers often foresaw higher education as the road to socialism. In all classes and all countries common belief among anxious parents was that too much education made women unmarriageable.

Second, educational opportunities, for girls even more so than for boys, were conditioned on economic resources. The wealthy elite of Berlin's "protected" Jews and the Russian enlightened bourgeoisie paid for private tutors for their daughters as a parallel, and secular, substitute for the religious training provided their sons. By the end of the century, particularly in Russia, private lessons for men and women were the only way to hope to have access to the Russian university. But even in the United States, where education was free, money and knowledge were linked. Poverty made children go to work early, and boys' education was often given priority over girls'. As a general rule, the better-off the family, in Berlin, St. Petersburg, or New York, the better the chances of more equal access to education among men and women.

Finally, for most of the nineteenth century, the *shadkhen* (matchmaker), that symbol of traditional gender relations, still did a brisk business. Outside the charmed circle of the Berlin salons, romantic love did not triumph over arranged marriages for at least another century, and marriages remained the object of serious gossip and internal strategies within the community. In the ensuing struggle over the right to marital choice, there was plenty of *tsores* (Yiddish for heartache) for either thwarted couples or disappointed families. One could suggest that it was women's greater access to equal education, which in turn opened up new forms of sociability, that would ultimately help challenge the matchmaker's monopoly.

10

The Secular Model of Girls' Education

Françoise Mayeur

DURING MOST OF THE nineteenth century European women continued to be educated in accordance with models long established by custom. The educational establishment largely shunned the reforms that Talleyrand and Condorcet proposed first to the Constituent and then to the Legislative Assembly in the early years of the French Revolution. This failure compounded what one recent observer termed "a missed opportunity," the Enlightenment's failure to achieve lasting reform in the education of women.[1] In the wake of the Revolution former educational arrangements were continued or restored. A distinction must be made, however, between models and actual practices: secular aspects of the curriculum were developed in practice before there was a system of secular education as such. That system, in France at any rate, would have to await the passage of new laws and the establishment of new institutions at the end of the nineteenth century. In any case, education in the broader sense invariably means more than just instruction as dispensed by schools. The prevalent notion that men and women had different responsibilities in life made it necessary for girls to receive a part of their education in the home. But formal instruction, which might include subjects of interest specifically to women, played an increasingly important role. In France, especially in the public sector,[2] in Belgium, primarily through private or municipal initiative, and in a few schools in Germany and Switzerland secular instruction came into its own in the 1880s; it was secular in the sense that the curriculum either excluded religious subjects or drastically reduced the time devoted to them. After primary school, the same for both sexes, girls were to receive a new type of secular instruction, as distinct as possible from that offered to boys.

The gap between the polished arguments prepared for the revolutionary assemblies and the realities of girls' education is therefore an interesting area of study, as is the fate that the ultimately triumphant Republic reserved for the ambitious plans of the reformers. It turned out that for a variety of reasons the expansion of girls' education did not coincide with that of education in general, much less with progress in secular schooling.

In theory, the Revolution should have led to the adoption of a secular model of girls' education, because it closed down the convents that had served as girls' schools and dispersed the teaching orders. In fact, however, the education of young women continued much as it had always done, since much of the education girls received came outside the schoolroom. As the educational system expanded, however, secular subjects slowly made their way into the curriculum, although nearly a century elapsed before a purely secular system of education was made mandatory under French law. Spain and Italy continued to adhere to the traditional form of girls' schooling outside the home, with its emphasis on religious subjects and use of religious teaching personnel. In Germany and Great Britain, where the historical traditions were different, religious pluralism made it necessary to seek other solutions. Each religious community had its own school system, but as the importance of government subsidies increased, it became increasingly common, especially in Britain, to use interdenominational texts and prayerbooks that everyone could accept.

Such contrasts draw attention to the importance of the school's status. Secular education had no chance of getting established unless local or national governments asserted their right to oversee the educational system. Thus "secular" education and "public" education (that is, education outside the home) were linked. The secular idea gained importance in connection with girls' schooling when that issue began to attract the attention of public authorities.

When governments adopted educational regulations and provided subsidies (subject to control over how they were used), they inevitably had to face the question of what subjects of study were acceptable to all. In France the government's interest in the education of young women was expanded in the mid-nineteenth century to include secondary education, whose content had yet to be defined. It would be thirty years before the Third Republic finally adopted legislation defining in purely secular terms the standards of secondary education for all French women. The government's aim was not to offend public attitudes and at the same time to demonstrate that its new standards were rooted in a long philosophical, political, and pedagogical tradition. Revolutionary references were therefore common to many of the educators and legislators who founded the nation's system of girls' secondary education. They claimed a continuity transcending the vicissitudes of history: the new institution thus enjoyed a venerable republican legitimacy and could even lay claim to the great classics of French literature, although the canon and its lessons were revised and reinterpreted. The way the system unfolded indicates the influence of politics in the development of a secular model of women's education.

Foundations and Principles

The heir in this respect of Rousseau, the French Revolution yielded little in the way of new thinking about women's education and still less in the way of legislation. One school of thought did hold that boys and girls are intellectually equal, from which it might appear to follow that they ought to study the same subjects in school—but that would be to forget the indubitable principle that men and women have different responsibilities in life. Boys are destined for public life, for the army and legislature. Girls are raised for the home and marriage. Since political concerns always underlie plans of education, women, "naturally" excluded from political debate, were neglected in matters of education. Their indirect influence was not ignored, however. That is why the members of the Constituent Assembly closed convents as well as monasteries, knowing that the convents provided all or part of the education of the daughters of the nobility and of the privileged classes. The revolutionaries' hostility to the convents was due in part to a genuine aversion to the boarding-school model, the most prevalent type of schooling prior to 1789, but even more to a desire to strip education of its "religious" orientation. Girls, it was argued at the time, could learn true piety as well as the duties of their sex from their mothers. The principle of "maternal education" emerged as paramount, and paramount it would remain for more than two-thirds of the century that was about to begin. The secularism resulting from the closing of the convents was ambiguous, however. "Secular" was opposed to "clerical." But was there not a danger that rejection of one clerical form would ultimately lead to rejection of religiosity in general?

Mirabeau's essays on girls' education are illustrative of principles widely accepted at the time. Women, he wrote, are made for "indoor life," that is, in the home. Existing girls' schools that taught reading, writing, and arithmetic should be maintained, according to Mirabeau, and new ones should be created in any town without one; these were to be modeled on boys' schools. The classroom portion of a girl's education was thus to be limited to the basics; practical, not to say utilitarian, matters were to be left to private "industry" (by which Mirabeau meant initiative).

Talleyrand's truly comprehensive proposal to the Constituent Assembly was quite different. Instruction should be available to everyone, he insisted, and by the same token everyone was called upon to teach. Education was a common good and should be offered to both sexes. Thus it was essential to create schools "in every part of the Empire." And no guild or corporation should monopolize public instruction, since everyone is capable of teaching. It was up to society to develop, facilitate, and encourage all kinds of instruction. Schools should be established promptly for both boys and girls, and educational principles, the "true propagators of instruction" in the words of the bishop of Autun, should be laid down. But principles were one thing, practice was another. Of course the instruction to which everyone was entitled would be offered in public schools, these being the tangible sign of the state's interest in all its citizens. Under Talleyrand's plan, however, girls, unlike boys, were to leave school at age eight and thereafter were to be educated at home by their parents. Public educational and occupational training institutions were to be provided only for those children whose parents were unable to raise them. The goal was in fact to prepare girls for domestic life and to equip them with talents useful for raising a family.

Thus according to Talleyrand the purpose of girls' education was to meet the needs of society and the state as well as the family. Girls and boys were treated differently, in the name of the common good: "The purpose of every institution must be the happiness of the greatest number. . . . If the exclusion of women from public employment is a way of increasing the sum of the mutual happiness of men and women, then it is a law that all societies have had to recognize and honor." In support of this contention he further invoked "the will of nature." Later, during the Convention, others went even further, insisting that girls should be educated exclusively at home. Like Mirabeau, they saw the difference in male and female aptitudes and responsibilities as grounds for confining women wholly within the family. The exclusion of women from political debate, the sexual division of labor, and the need to maintain distinctions between social classes led these thinkers to design, as Rousseau had done before them, gender-specific curricula. After learning the basics, girls were to be taught spinning, sewing, and cooking, while boys would begin the study of mathematics and geography. The women of the future, Deleyre wrote in 1793, should study not only "household science" but also those decorative arts so essential to keeping their husbands at home.

Thus the catalogue of secular subjects to be taught to female students was set forth by an admittedly small number of authorities. That the education of girls was also religious was so obvious that it was not always explicitly discussed. Condorcet, however, took a totally different approach. He advocated equal education for boys and girls on the grounds that men and women enjoy the same rights. He was also the only contemporary proponent of coeducational schools, which he saw as a bulwark against the influence of priests and the prejudices that prevented people of different social classes from marrying. Although in other respects Condorcet continued to think of women in terms of their function as wives and mothers, his vision of an entirely secularized education was not lost on his successors in the Convention, and the legislators of the Third Republic would hark back to it in justification of their own innovations.

A few wild, fantastic proposals came up as well, such as that of Le Peletier de Saint-Fargeau, whose plan would have been more appropriate to ancient Sparta than to the France of the Revolution. But once these were disposed of, the First Republic did indeed, for a few years, provide public elementary education to girls as well as boys. The curriculum was a purely republican one, in which civic spirit was the only religion. Given the customs of the day and the widespread hostility to coeducational classes, boys and girls were taught separately wherever there were enough pupils and qualified teachers. But public education soon fell victim to desertion by its students: parents did not approve of the schools' indoctrination, and many were nostalgic for the old system. Meanwhile, the government, strapped for funds by the necessities of war, failed to pay its teachers, who soon disappeared.

Compulsory, universal, secular public education thus remained scarcely more than a principle. The material reasons for the system's failure are clear. Other factors included popular attitudes and deeply rooted habits. Girls were supposed to remain at home with their mothers, and religious instruction was intended especially for them. Nonjuring priests, monks, and nuns returned, clandestinely at first but later openly, and many found in teaching the livelihood of which the Revolution had deprived them. Some parish priests also served as teachers. Evaluation of secular education was thus sharply divided: the vast majority of the French, those who remained firmly attached to their religion, saw it as an obligation imposed from above; a smaller number, in certain towns and rural communities, saw it as a step toward emancipation from superstition. There were enormous inequalities in literacy, moreover, with women lagging far behind men in the southwestern half of the country.

A Competitor to the Religious Model

European countries did not all introduce the secular model of girls' education in the same way. In France the centralized public system coexisted with the private sector. In Belgium, by contrast, Catholics and secularists clashed so intensely after 1860 that it became impossible to pass a liberal law. Private groups, *sociétés de pensée,* and local governments therefore had to assume the burden of bringing secular education to young women.

In England, once the Anglican Church lost its legal control over the educational system, and given the custom (more prevalent there than in other countries, even among the middle classes) of entrusting private education to governesses and tutors, the central issue was not how to secularize education but how to offer religious instruction acceptable to all denominations as well as to secularizers.[3] The Forster Act (1870) established an "English-style compromise" among various shades of opinion.[4] Educational committees set up by local governments were supposed to determine what sort of religious instruction was to be offered. At the same time freedom of religion was ensured by requiring religious courses to be given in the first or last hour of the day; any pupil who did not wish to attend could skip this class without missing any other courses. In the public schools, religious instruction was of such a general nature that it was acceptable to all, even agnostics. This created a rivalry between the public schools, which in 1894 were attended by two-thirds of all pupils, and the Anglican schools. In the late nineteenth century many schools were built according to architectural designs that separated boys from girls. In 1893 school attendance was made compulsory until age eleven, and in 1899 the school-leaving age was increased to twelve.

In the same period coeducational teacher training colleges were established to train teachers for primary and secondary schools (although the legal distinction between primary and secondary education was not instituted until 1902). This system avoided not only the contentious issue of secular versus religious schooling but also the equally controversial question of the role of women in teaching. Women, in fact, accounted for the majority of teachers: their number increased from 70,000 in 1851 to 172,000, or 74.5 percent of the teacher corps, in 1901.[5] In 1865 Cambridge opened its so-called local examinations to young women, but they were still not allowed to take degrees. To avoid any hint of scandal the women's college was located at some distance from Cambridge. In 1875 a new law authorized the universities to grant degrees to women. Nevertheless, few women pursued a higher education before 1914, owing in part to powerful resistance from certain professions, especially medicine, but perhaps also to lack of ambition or to a diversion of women's energies into the suffragist movement.

Nonreligious schools existed in France as well as in England, but local governments in the two countries did not enjoy the same freedom. In postrevolutionary France the law governed relations between the public schools and officially recognized religious denominations. There had been no secular model of public primary education before passage of a law requiring secular subject matter in 1882 and a second law requiring secular teaching personnel in 1886. But except for schools run by nuns, educational associations developed and made available to teachers curricula in which the proportion of religious subject matter was gradually reduced. The formula for religious teaching was the same in both the 1833 and 1850 laws: "moral and religious instruction." Girls were more subject to it than boys, since a greater proportion of female pupils were taught by congregants. The Church's grip on the education of young women was a major issue in the battle for secular schools waged by republicans and *sociétés de pensée.* When Jules Ferry declared on April 10, 1870, that "woman must either belong to science or belong to the Church," his words were reminiscent of those spoken some six years earlier by the Antwerp journalist Arnould in an 1864 speech to the Friends of Commerce and Perseverance: "The education of women must be reformed. This must be done through science. . . . [Women] would then immediately reject the arbitrary assumptions and fantasies of religion, which contradict any positivist view of the world."

Secular education for girls developed on the fringes of a system of girls' education still strongly influenced by religion, change having been made to seem ridiculous by the dreams of the Saint-Simonians, the speculations of the Fourierists, and the raucous demonstrations of 1848. A Protestant woman with the same Saint-Simonian background as her husband, Elisa Lemonnier became aware of the misery and ignorance of women workers during the Revolution of 1848, and the discovery made a lasting impression. In 1862 she founded an occupational training school for poor girls. In 1864 she opened a second school, which was run by Clarisse Sauvestre, the wife of the anticlerical Bonapartist journalist Charles Sauvestre. In practice both schools also served daughters of the middle class who for one reason or another were obliged to seek occupational training outside the home. The schools were prototypes of secular institutions, for religious education was left entirely up to the pupils' families. There were three "orders" of instruction: general courses, special courses in business or industrial design, and practical work in the shop. The girls also received moral instruction: Elisa Lemonnier hoped that they would become "good mothers" and to that end tried to instill a sense of personal dignity and self-esteem. The principal of the first school, Melle Marchef-Girard, later became the first head of the Collège

Sévigné. She thus established a symbolic link between Elisa Lemonnier's work and the first secular secondary school for young women in Paris.

Also in 1864, this time in Belgium, the Association for the Professional Education of Women was founded at the behest of Senator Bischoffsheim. The first professional school, private and nondenominational, opened its doors in April 1865. It was adopted by the city of Brussels in 1868. Within ten years two similar schools were founded. The purpose of these institutions was to go beyond the homemakers' education to which the nuns were obliged to limit their teaching and provide theoretical instruction as well. But the model remained the same: the domestic activities of women were intended to contribute to the "happiness of the home."[6]

The ambiguities of the new model for girls of all classes are perhaps most evident in the curricula that secular reformers proposed to replace the courses offered by the teaching orders. Women were not exactly pushed into "science," and instruction beyond the primary level remained limited. French republicans and Belgian liberals had not given up on the ideal of the woman as homemaker. Like their opponents and predecessors, they were afraid that too much book-learning might divert women from their mission as wives and mothers. In fact, the secularization of girls' education was usually based on earlier models that allowed for the "weakness of the sex" and the force of custom. The most resolute reformers in France and Belgium may have wanted to hand women over to "science," but they did so in the interest of men, of sons and husbands. Jules Ferry, for instance, wanted to provide "republican helpmates for republican men." This, he believed, was the only way to avoid a spiritual divorce between religious wives and free-thinking husbands. The importance that he attached to this "conversion of education" shows that he considered women to have at least an indirect influence, but he still did not wish to give them access to a long course of study. The republican primary school was the same for boys and girls, except that instruction in needlework was deemed essential for the latter. But secondary schooling for young women was neither as lengthy nor as broad as that for young men; Latin, philosophy, and advanced science were all for boys only. In France this state of affairs led to a lengthy series of struggles (1905–1914) to win the right for young women to earn the baccalaureate, the ticket to a higher education.

The Introduction of Secular Curricula

The issue of secular primary schools did not arise in other major European countries in quite the same way as in France and Belgium, for reasons having to do with particular civilizations and histories, traditions of state intervention or nonintervention, and the religious situation. England is a case in point. In Belgium, Catholic resistance prevented a Ferry-style school reform from taking hold.[7] The passions aroused by the debate over education and the small number of citizens who wanted their daughters to attend universities account for the insults hurled at the free-thinking women who took the first steps toward providing girls with a secular education, as well as for the vehemence of the ecclesiastical authorities. The battle began with the *salles d'asile,* intended for very young children. A Société pour le Soutien des Ecoles Gardiennes (Protective Schools Support Society) opened one school (something of a cross between a charitable institution and an educational one, as the name implies) in Brussels in 1846 with help from the Philanthropic Friends' Lodge. Similar schools were established in other major cities. At this point a conflict erupted with the teaching congregations, which had previously enjoyed a monopoly of classes for very young children. The secular camp again scored a victory: the first inspector of these schools, appointed in 1847, was Zoé de Gamond, the daughter of a Brussels lawyer and a Fourierist. In 1851 she wrote a *Manual on Nursery and Primary Schools.* Many of these schools soon took up the so-called Froebel method, a program of active teaching: the first kindergarten in Belgium opened in Ixelles in 1857 with a government subsidy. But the collusion between Froebel's disciples and Isabelle Gatti de Gamond, Zoé's daughter, led to charges of atheism.[8] A few daughters of liberals and socialists, including Proudhon's girls, attended a "fathers' school" founded in 1857, also in Ixelles, and which charged tuition.

Socialists and Fourierists wanted free or at any rate low-cost education for the masses. They therefore investigated methods reputed to be both effective and relatively inexpensive, thus contributing to the success of the Froebel method and even more so of the Lancaster method advocated by the French Left under the July Monarchy. The Lancaster method used older children as monitors for younger children. More than just economical, it forced teachers to group students according to their level of achievement and made it possible to teach reading and writing simultaneously.

By the 1860s peer teaching systems such as the Lancaster method had matured, and liberals in both France and Belgium, ardent believers in free primary education for all, made them the centerpiece of their program. December 1864 saw the founding of the Ligue de l'Enseignement (League for Learning) in Belgium. By 1878 the league in conjunction with affiliated groups had collected enough money to fund a model school along with six primary and middle schools for boys and seven for girls.[9] Often these institutions were taken over after a few years by local authorities. Yet an attempt to establish a system of girls' primary education in Belgium in 1878 did not succeed, because the conservatives returned to power in 1884.

In Belgium secondary education for young women emerged after much heated controversy between local governments and educational associations on the one hand and combative bishops on the other, especially in Liège and Tournai. The middle-of-the-road curriculum included handiwork, home economics, and bookkeeping, along with such educational innovations as interdisciplinary coordination, teaching spoken foreign languages, and conducting practical scientific experiments—innovations harshly criticized as harboring the germs of naturalism and materialism. It may be useful to compare these efforts with parallel initiatives to create schools for midwives and nurses. The first secular school of nursing (for men and women) was opened in 1888 by a socialist physician, but it failed to inspire confidence. In 1907 Edith Cavell, a pastor's daughter, established the first graduate school of nursing. It, too, met with fierce opposition but slowly flourished. Royal athenaeums (classical high schools) for girls received no attention from the government prior to 1914. The first one was located in Ghent and was founded by private initiative.

Thus an explicit, legally sanctioned, strictly secular system of girls' secondary education remained solely a French specialty in 1880. A reflection of the century's boldness as well as of its doubts and timidity, the new schools gradually brought about changes in the condition of women, particularly in the middle class. The so-called Camille Sée Law responsible for the system was in large part the work of an isolated individual. But the Sée Law cannot be separated from the rest of Jules Ferry's legislative package, which marked a new stage in the struggle for secular education.

Ferry's work stemmed from two contradictory sources. First, in all European countries the trend was gradually to provide all children with an education aimed at achieving a level of competence somewhat beyond mere literacy, which at this point was quite widespread. Originally intended for daughters of the bourgeoisie, this education was also to provide a basis for cultural distinction, a cut above the elementary education that was all the lower classes were allowed. At the same time the new law, which pleased republicans because it promised to "snatch young girls from the clutches of the Church," made no pretense about having them participate in the traditional secondary culture, which was still reserved for boys. Once again it was argued that girls must not be diverted from their proper mission: making a home. And homemaking was incompatible with any outside occupation. Thus the Sée Law represented a departure from the custom, even among the nonreligious, of sending one's daughter to the convent school, yet it was in conformity with a society whose equilibrium was based on a division of responsibility between men and women, at least in the privileged classes (the labor of working women being seen as a necessity).

Introduced in October 1878 by a republican deputy of Jewish descent, the law was approved in the Senate by a small majority. It was an occasion for a fundamental debate between proponents of secular education and Catholics outraged by this sudden outburst of "irreligion" in a domain previously reserved almost exclusively to the Church. Camille Sée invoked two precedents in proposing girls' schools similar in structure to the existing schools for boys, with the possibility of accepting boarding students. One, a rival bill, drafted by Paul Bert, proposed simple day schools, or "courses," as Bert called them. He was following an older formula first developed by Victor Duruy in 1867: courses for girls given by local lycée teachers in facilities made available by municipalities. But only 2,000 girls had availed themselves of such courses, whose defects were numerous: many of the teachers were not prepared for their new assignment, for example, and the course schedules and teaching facilities often were not conducive to an orderly educational program. There was no plan of study extending over several years and integrating a variety of subjects in a harmonious manner. Nevertheless, these "Duruy courses," generally limited to a duration of two years and available only in a few cities, represented the first government initiative in an area previously considered to be a private preserve, and the curriculum they introduced was totally exempt from religious control. As the republicans gained strength in municipal governments in the late 1870s, the most resolutely "secular" of them seized on the idea of "courses" for young women. The advantage of such courses was that they were much more flexible than a full-blown system of secondary education and, for local governments more interested in symbolic gestures than in expenditures deemed to be excessive, also more economical. The courses remained, moreover, subject to strict control by the municipal governments that sponsored them.

The committee that considered the Sée and Bert bills made certain amendments that were incorporated in the ensuing legislation. Because the proposals concerned the education of girls, only certain "useful" subjects could be considered, but the grounds on which usefulness was decided were not stated. The fear of producing "overeducated" women was so great that philosophy was not to be offered. Literature, traditionally considered the best basis for the education of women, was to be paramount: as in the better boarding schools under the July Monarchy, female students were to study French and at least one other modern language, French literature, classical literature in translation, and "modern," that is, foreign literatures. In addition there were to be classes in history, geography, arithmetic, basic geometry, natural history, and physics, along with drawing, a little gymnastics, and needlework. On the matter of religious instruction two theories clashed. Camille Sée thought it better for "a priest to come [to the school], under the supervision of the academic administration." Paul Bert feared the possibility of an "invasion." Despite the practical advantages of Sée's proposal concerning what was obviously an elective subject, republican suspicion of the Church prevailed in the ensuing debate.

The republicans were able to draw inspiration for their work not only from the Duruy courses but also from studies of educational issues ranging from the establishment of an examination for *maîtresses de pension* in 1836 to a recent plan put forward by the Society for the Examination of Questions of Secondary Education, founded in November 1879 and headed by Michel Bréal. A special commission of the society issued a report which was adopted in 1881, in the period between passage of the law (December 1880) and the issuance of various implementation orders, on which it exerted a considerable influence. The subjects included in the curriculum were perhaps less important than the pedagogical principles put forward by the principal author of the report, Maurice Vernes:

- There should be no divorce between "education" in the broad sense and "instruction" in the narrow sense. Education should be construed liberally, and teachers should rely above all on their students' sense of solidarity, dignity, and personal responsibility.
- Instead of relying on the method that ascribed the principal role in the acquisition of knowledge to memory, preference should be given in all branches of teaching to methods calling upon intelligence and reflection.

These principles, which do not apply solely to the education of one sex, reflect Jacotot's theory of "self-education" with its consistent emphasis on intelligence. They also supply an excellent definition of the concept of "education of conscience" that flourished in the best secondary schools for women and at Fontenay under Félix Pécaut.

Because the teaching was secular, the Society considered questions of moral education at some length. In this it was greatly indebted to Clarisse Coignet, the author of *La Morale dans son principe et dans son objet* (Morality in Principle and Purpose, 1869) as well as of an 1880 textbook on ethics for use in secular schools. The author's intention was not to challenge "metaphysical and religious doctrines" but to save morality from their possible collapse. Morality, according to Mme Coignet, is not taught but communicated. Similarly, according to the Society, morality, or rather the teaching of morality, was aimed at "the formation of character." Each girl would be treated as an individual so long as she remained in school. Women should be in charge of female secondary education. There should not be too many teachers in any one grade: "Two will suffice in the lower division," according to the report, "and three in the upper division." To that end, foreign language teachers could also teach another subject. Eager to achieve "unity of teaching," the Society even envisioned "a class director," the forerunner of today's "lead teacher."

This desire to make "moral upbringing" a part of education through instruction in morality, which of course far transcended the boundaries of any one subject, led to a sort of educational revolution expressed in the changed views on discipline. "Everything comes from opinion," wrote Maurice Vernes, citing Clarisse Coignet. "To make young people sensitive to opinion is to develop their sense of honor, which is also an element of conscience." Given such principles, discipline could no longer be mechanical. It was to be based on a number of "strictly applied" rules, and punishment was to be "sober and impersonal." There was no reason for extra work or after-school detention. These punishments were to be replaced by bad grades for conduct, which counted in the ranking of students, as well as by reprimands and temporary or permanent expulsion. This system, for which the groundwork was no doubt laid by a tradition of female education lacking the severity of the Napoleonic lycée, was adopted in lycées for young women with widespread success.

Dogmatic teaching methods were dropped. "Reflection and comparison should be called upon constantly," according to Vernes, "efforts at understanding being in every way preferable to purely rote acquisition." Students, at the beginning at least, should proceed "from the known to the unknown." These general principles of republican pedagogy admitted certain exceptions, however, when it came to female pupils. For example, they would be taught the exact sciences in a new way: it would be unfortunate if by chance girls were led to develop faculties of abstraction or applied mathematical skills for which they would have no use, since they were not about to become engineers. Clearly, it was not by means of a solid foundation in philosophy or a thorough grounding in science that the Society's members hoped to free women from religious prejudice. And the classical languages were only barely tolerated: girls would learn to read Greek, "not for themselves but for their children." Thus the theme of the "mother as educator" endured from the beginning of the century to the end. And the Society's innovative ideas about girls' education themselves turned out to contain certain ambiguities. In fact, the key was not to teach a particular subject in some depth but to seize control of the pupils' thinking. It was therefore important not to frighten their families by changing the usual content of the curriculum or assigning homework that might deter girls from their family obligations.

The Collège Sévigné, a school for girls newly established in Paris, may have served as an example. A secular private school, it, too, had been founded under the auspices of Michel Bréal, the head of the Society. After a difficult start, the collège began to assert its personality under the leadership of Mathilde Salomon, its guiding spirit. Salomon exerted an indirect influence on state secondary schools not only by her example but also by training future teachers for the competitive hiring examinations.

The debates on the Sée Law in the Chamber of Deputies and later the Senate thus had plenty of background material to draw on, but educational issues were not at the heart of the controversy. The opposition attacked the republican party on the themes of moral and religious instruction. The Senate debate on secondary education for women coincided with discussions in the Chamber of bills on the issue of free and secular primary schooling, which of course lent particular resonance to the occasion. The debate soon ranged beyond the old fears about the place of women in society and the "danger" of overeducated females. Conservatives in fact envisioned the law as "the continuation of enterprises against God and religion," language reminiscent of the vehement Catholic assault on the Duruy courses led by Monsignor Dupanloup in 1867. The compromises envisioned by centrists and even Ferry himself in the hope of wooing undecided senators were wrecked by this interpretation. The two principal charges of the opposition were that the law was intended to bring about the "complete elimination of religious instruction" and to create a "feminine wing of the university."

For conservatives, the proposed law was pointless, since girls were already more than adequately educated in religious schools. It would also cost a great deal of money. And the Catholics, who twelve years earlier had been fierce opponents of Duruy's proposals, now sang the praises of secondary courses for women, which they portrayed as bulwarks of freedom against the encroachments of the state.

In the eyes of Catholic legislators, the proposed law also represented a moral danger. In the new system, in contrast to the religious schools, "education" would be subordinate to "instruction." In time this theme became a cliché. The new schools would, it was alleged, facilitate promiscuity between male and female teachers and, even worse, bring students of different social backgrounds together in the same classroom. For want of the hoped-for clientèle (the law allegedly having been designed for the daughters of the well-to-do), it would become necessary to draw students from the "new strata of society." These students would be encouraged in hopes that could not be satisfied, and the result would be "an enormous group of individuals without a class." And this might lead to nihilism: the Russian gymnasia from which emerged a "literate and long-haired proletariat" served as an ominous example.

But the crucial issue was secularization. "Respectful of the freedom of conscience," Camille Sée wrote in the report on his own bill, "your committee is of the opinion that religious instruction should have no place in the classroom. Instruction in this subject should be carried out at home by the parents." The problem was with boarding students. Chaplains were allowed to visit the schools to give lessons in religion. Was this proof of a conciliatory attitude or a sign of distrust? The last straw for Catholic deputies was the issue of moral instruction, which figured at the head of the curriculum in isolation from religion. In the Chamber the notion of an independent morality, inherited from the *Encyclopedia,* was defended as "the universal morality." Broca, who reported on the bill to the Senate, emphasized the ways in which the moral instruction to be offered to girls differed from the method used for boys. The moral course for girls was what was left of the philosophy course given in the boys' lycées. It was impossible to add religious instruction owing to "the many denominations recognized by the state" and the legal guarantee of freedom of worship. Furthermore, the only available teachers would be laymen and -women, and lay teachers had "neither the competence nor the authority to teach their own religion."

The principal argument of those who opposed religious instruction in girls' day schools was summed up by one deputy's question: "Does religious instruction figure in the curricula of boys' lycées?" The conservatives retorted that it did not, but that was hardly grounds for congratulation. The leading orators waited for the bill's second reading, the prelude to the final vote. In the Senate the Duc de Broglie emphasized the consequences of an "independent morality." To attempt to teach such a thing, he argued, was an experiment. No doubt there was but one morality "if one takes the word in the most superficial, the most vulgar of its senses." But an advanced course in morality would always encounter religious questions: they could either be avoided, in which case the course would be insignificant, or they could be incorporated into the curriculum. This was the case with philosophy classes for boys: their curriculum abounded "with questions that can be resolved only by religion or philosophy"—to begin with, the most fundamental point of all, the foundation of morality and the problem of moral freedom. Last but not least, there could be no morality without sanctions. One of the last items in the curriculum mentioned duties toward God. The orator, who in passing recalled the "accolade to positivism" that Jules Ferry, the head of the government, had given five years earlier in a speech accepting membership in the Freemasons, concluded that there was no escaping the issue: "Some omissions are as good as outright negations." It was best, therefore, to revert to "the old morality, that of the catechism," for otherwise "you may risk exposing young minds to detestable negations and inextricable controversies."

The law was passed on December 21, 1880, in the form favored by the republicans, but not without division on the republican side. Although all the republicans were anticlerical, many were more than willing to allow the women in their own families to assume the burden of religion. Others, the eldest of the group, those who had witnessed 1848, remained deists. Thus it was not surprising that the Conseil Supérieur de l'Instruction Publique, which was dominated by moderate academics, saw to it that the detailed curriculum mentioned the need to teach girls their "duties toward God," a provision that remained until 1923, and then was rescinded only briefly.

The "secular model" of girls' education was thus created in France, but it was a long way from achieving dominance. The lycées and collèges that came into being as a result of the new law grew slowly but steadily during the first twenty years of their existence. Ultimately they became an accepted element of the French educational system precisely because they strove not to offend public attitudes nor to appear as "Trojan horses of irreligion." Some Catholic families interested in obtaining the most comprehensive education available for their daughters even preferred these secular schools to religious ones. By the eve of World War I, the problems that the 33,000 young women in secondary schools faced along with their teachers were no longer of a religious nature. More prosaic, they concerned opportunities in the workplace, which republican lawmakers, secular but conservative, had thus far denied them.

Translated from the French by Arthur Goldhammer

11

Images—Appearances, Leisure, and Subsistence

Anne Higonnet

FEMININITY IS PARTLY a question of appearances.

Nineteenth-century visual culture produced countless images of women, many of them consistent with one another, some of them contradictory, all of them powerful elements in the ever-changing definition of what it meant to be a woman. Images continued to give form to social and economic flux. But for the first time in history, women as well as men were able to represent their perception of experience.

Archetypes

Madonna, seductress, muse—these three feminine archetypes retained their hold on the nineteenth-century imagination (figs. 1, 2, 3; all illustrations appear between page 262 and page 305). They recur in all registers of visual culture, low and high: in prints, advertisements, photographs, book illustrations, and crafts, as well as in sculpture and in both casual and official painting. While in most European countries and in the United States feminine archetypes drifted during the course of the century from the religious toward the secular (figs. 1, 3), their references and purposes remained remarkably constant and were closely related to similar tendencies in literature.

Times of crisis brought new vigor to feminine archetypes, either through formal and thematic innovation or through sheer repetition. Such critical moments occurred around the 1860s and again around the turn of the century. Bourgeois challenges to artistic establishments in the 1860s encouraged new images of contemporary domestic subjects that insisted on women's roles as chaste daughters, wives, and mothers (figs. 6, 7, 8, 14, 15). By the end of the century, alienated bourgeois aesthetes reacted against those values with a spate of images aptly called "idols of perversity" (figs. 2, 38, 40). Feminine archetypes did much more than reflect ideals of beauty; they constituted models of behavior. Their means of persuasion, though particular to the visual arts, were activated by their cultural context.

Visual archetypes precluded individuality and fostered rigid distinctions between limited behavioral possibilities. The muse remained as she had been, an allegorical figure or the embodiment of an idea rather than a specific person. Obviously, she represented ideals: the ideal of Liberty, for instance, incarnated by Frédéric-Auguste Bartholdi in his colossal 1884 *Statue of Liberty* that still welcomes travelers into the port of New York City. Images of madonnas and temptresses were no less abstract. They organized femininity around two poles: one normal, orderly, and reassuring, the other deviant, dangerous, and seductive; one realm showed figures of dutiful domesticity (figs. 1, 6, 7, 8, 14, 15, 26, 27, 28, 29, 35); another displayed prostitutes, professionals, activists, and most working-class women as well as women of color (figs. 2, 9, 10, 11, 13, 18, 31, 34, 36, 37, 38, 45). Normally feminine women were depicted as admirable, virtuous, happy, or rewarded, while deviant women were represented as ludicrous, depraved, miserable, or punished.

Images endowed definitions of femininity with an aura of truth by depicting abstract concepts as portraits of people and places. In one way or another most visual arts claimed to be realistic, that is, to have observed actual physical phenomena and to have reflected them objectively; the farther the century advanced the more currency this doctrine gained. Akin to positivism in philosophy, field investigation in journalism or sociology, and empirical experimentation in the natural sciences, realism in art guaranteed the universal validity of its opinions. For a bourgeoisie in search of legitimation, the consumption of art through collecting, exhibitions, art criticism, or reproductions provided a unifying activity that confirmed and gave value to its vision of itself.

It was also characteristic of the period, however, for all established positions to generate opposition. In art as in other domains, individualism motivated unexpected self-affirmation on the part of marginal social groups. Moreover, high art began to renew itself in accelerating cycles of repudiation and cooptation, each successive generation winning its credentials by rebelling against the one before. Even within generations, critics, artists, and administrators proposed competing criteria of artistic value. This instability provided women with unprecedented opportunities to enter the art world and thus to gain the means of self-representation.

The social values women experienced as their reality nonetheless discouraged pictorial experimentation. Femininity included security and pleasures that would be forfeited by challenging more oppressive or restrictive aspects of the same identity. Most of the women who entered elite artistic careers in the nineteenth century were from the middle class; they belonged to the group of women whose class privileges depended on a social stability feminism threatened. Caught between these contradictory impulses, women did not generally produce images of themselves that were fundamentally different in style or content from men's images of them.

But women advanced their condition by the mere fact of their participation in the arts. In increasing numbers and on an increasingly professional basis, women altered their conceptions of their place in visual culture by becoming its active producers rather than its passive objects. Many women negotiated extremely successful careers on the edges of high art. Some, like Beatrix Potter (English, 1866–1943) in children's book illustration, and Gertrude Jekyll (English, 1843–1932) in landscape gardening, set the standards of excellence for their fields (figs. 21, 41). Entry into the more prestigious professions of painting and sculpture demanded a stiff price, paid with either conformity to artistic conventions or personal sacrifices or both. Yet women like Rosa Bonheur (French, 1822–1899) and Mary Cassatt (American, 1844–1926) did win places in the history of art and thereby gave future generations role models to believe in (figs. 1, 20).

Genius

Other essays in this volume explain many of the factors that prevented women from choosing any careers or even wanting to. The most pervasive and persuasive factor specific to the arts was the exclusively masculine concept of genius. A concept that developed slowly since the Renaissance in tandem with a hierarchy of art forms, genius was thought to explain art's creation and its quality. A great artist was supposed to be born with genius, which would triumph over any circumstantial obstacle and manifest itself in transcendentally beautiful masterpieces. All art forms were classified according to the degree of genius they could accommodate. Historical, mythological, or religious painting ranked highest among the visual arts, manual crafts ranked lowest, and everything else fell somewhere in between. Imagination took precedence over imitation, design over execution.

Women in whose work genius thus defined could be perceived were pronounced abnormal or at best asexual. The attributes of femininity were diametrically opposed to those of genius; to the extent that a woman aspired to artistic greatness she was supposed to betray her domestic destiny. The assumptions underlying genius are most clearly exposed in novels featuring heroes or heroines in the arts, such as Honoré de Balzac's 1837 *Le Chef d'oeuvre inconnu,* Nathaniel Hawthorne's 1860 *The Marble Faun,* or Kate Chopin's 1899 *The Awakening.* Whereas artists and art critics simply bestowed or withheld the label of genius, narratives which develop genius through characters and social situations reveal how the idea of genius gendered creativity. Against the conflated values of activity, imagination, production, and masculine sexuality are pitted the similarly indivisible values of passivity, imitation, reproduction, and feminine sexuality. Men create original works of art; women recreate themselves in their children. Genius helped differentiate femininity from masculinity by establishing binary cultural identities anchored to sexualities founded on biological difference.

Germaine de Staël (Swiss, 1766–1817) and George Sand (French, 1804–1876) retorted. Both Staël in her 1807 *Corinne* and Sand in her 1844 *Consuelo* dared to imagine heroic women geniuses, neither of whom fit into conventional artistic categories. Corinne is at once a poet, an actress, a rhetorician, and an improvisational performer; Consuelo goes from diva to composer to ambulant singer. Both heroines are threatened by patriarchal law embodied in father-figures as well as in political authority. Corinne succumbs, but Consuelo is saved by a mother-figure who awakens her political conscience and reconciles her sexuality with her intellectual ideals. Consuelo rejects all the distinctions so tenaciously maintained elsewhere; her maternity empowers an art that merges composition with performance, invents on the basis of repetition, and can only flourish outside ordinary society. Sand suggested that while talent might be innate, its manifestation and its reception depended entirely on the artist's sex, wealth, and class. Paradoxically, this most utopian and fantastic of Sand's writings argued for an understanding of women's art in more materialistic terms than any proposed by realist novels or by art criticism.

Accepted Forms of Self-Expression

Articulated as fictions or theories, aesthetic positions eventually translated into actual occupations and livelihoods. Artistically inclined women overwhelmingly chose to enter fields low in status, fields in which they would encounter as few obstacles as possible and feel confident both artistically and socially. In the first half of the century wealthy women tended to practice amateur painting, while women who had to earn their living moved into crafts, decorative arts, or design. In the related fields of music, dance, and theater, women could and did lead acclaimed performance careers. Yet the ultimate accolades went not to those who executed works but to those who composed the music, choreographed the ballets, or wrote the plays, and they were almost always men.

Throughout Europe and the United States, middle- and upper-class women pursued amateur painting and music. Few bourgeois girls did not learn to play the piano or violin (figs. 6, 25) and to sing, draw, or sketch with watercolors. Such artistic skills were considered accomplishments that cultivated a girl's sensibilities and made her socially attractive. Many women—perhaps as many as one in every extended family—assiduously practiced painting or music for several years, sometimes all their lives, usually in the company of other women friends or family members. While Jane Austen (1775–1817) wrote, for instance, her sister Cassandra (1773–1845) sketched. Paintings were displayed in family living-rooms; music was performed for family guests (fig. 6), often quite discriminating ones. Thus Suzanne Leenhoff (Dutch, 1830–1906), wife of Edouard Manet, was renowned among their friends and colleagues for her renditions of Chopin.

In their pictures women represented a domestic identity with images of family members and companions, home, local walks, vacation sites, or scenes of family trips. Their portraits focused on themselves and other women, their images of the home centered around the women's parlor. Sophie DuPont (American, 1810–1888), for example, made more than 200 sprightly caricatures of home life in Delaware between 1823 and 1833. Victor Hugo and Adèle Hugo (French, 1806–1868) both drew; he imagined Gothic castles and fantastic landscapes; she made portraits of their children. Aristocratic women followed this bourgeois pattern. Queen Victoria (English, 1819–1901) almost always sketched images of her private life, and even when she represented state occasions she concentrated on their emotional moments or personal interactions; among her thousands of pictures she made barely a half-dozen of her beloved husband.

Amateur painting and music spread their own kind of basic literacy among women, much as novels did. In the case of visual art, however, amateur work and academic painting functioned according to a fundamentally different logic. While this would be of some help to women entering the avant-garde art world later in the century, at the time it impeded rather than accelerated women's passage toward professional status.

Small and fragile, typically made on sheets of paper, women's amateur pictures carried fleetingly contextual meanings. Women often mounted their pictures in albums, sometimes together with miscellaneous objects and pictures both made and found, often with explanatory captions. Amateur images were meant to be understood in groups and as parts of family history. None claimed autonomy; each depended on its relationship to other images and to knowledge brought to it by a private audience. These amateurs were picture-makers rather than authors; they did not strive for recognizable styles or didactic subject matter, nor did they work for a market. Amateur pictures therefore had almost no formal, intellectual, or economic value as those values were then defined by high art, and consequently have all but disappeared.

Meanwhile women in the working and lower-middle classes needed wages. Yet very few careers were open to them and fewer that did not entail loss of caste. These rare professions were distinguished from other kinds of artisanal labor by an aesthetic dimension associated with a feminine temperament. Contemporary commentators in Europe and America reported that trades such as miniature, wallpaper, and porcelain painting, artificial flower-making, enameling (fig. 19), hand-coloring, and textile pattern design were staffed largely by women and offered them continuing employment possibilities. By 1894 a writer estimated that 10,000 women were so employed in America, about 2,000 of them in New York City alone,[1] where the Cooper Union School, founded in 1859 and directed in its early decades by a Ladies Advisory Council, had initiated a model training program for young women of limited means.

While design trades could be as fastidious, as tedious, and as badly paid as any other, their artistic reputation elevated them to a status of "gentility" or "respectability." They demanded patience and dexterity but required little physical strength. Most were carried out in all-female workshops and some even in the home. Design careers therefore reconciled gender, class, and subsistence imperatives.

"Taste" had become a financial asset for women, a marketable commodity, especially in the dress and millinery trades. Guides to Paris called gifted milliners "artists" and elite shops competed with each other on the intangible basis of style and fashionable novelty more than on the material criteria of price or durability. Margaret Oliphant voiced a dream of success at once commercial and artistic in her 1895 novel *Kirsteen;* Kirsteen, a Scot, rises through the workshop ranks by dint of her industry but also her flair to build a highly profitable business of her own. She had been inspired by the fashion plates on the walls of her first workshop; the pictures themselves as well as the products were made largely by women and designed for female audiences (figs. 16, 17).

An association of femininity with beauty encouraged women to invest their work with aesthetic value. Whether striving to design more profitable products or enhancing the pleasure of a leisure activity, women exercised their right to taste. Embroidery's decorative scope, for instance, distinguished it from more functional needlework and made it middle-class women's preferred pastime. Originally intended to salvage tiny fabric remnants, pieced quilt tops became an indigenous American and almost completely female art form practiced by women of all social classes (fig. 22). Some quilts were reserved for ceremonial occasions, others used every day, some were made with expensive silks, others with simple cottons, but each quilt's beauty depended on its maker's sense of color and composition; which ones were works of art and which were household furniture? Some slave women on big plantations were recognized for their quilting talents and obliged to quilt full-time for their masters; were they professionals?

Women not only transformed the ordinary into the exceptional and occupations into vocations; they also took professions in new directions. Elizabeth Keckley (1840–1900) began life as a slave sewing in the American South. She harnessed her art and energies to her political convictions and used her work to buy back her own freedom and also her son's. During the American Civil War she became the seamstress and confidante of Mary Todd Lincoln. She continued to put her gifts in the service of civil rights by creating works like her Liberty quilt, made out of scraps from Mary Todd Lincoln's gowns. Three French sisters, Heloïse Leloir (1820–1873), Anaïs Toudouze (1822–1899), and Laure Noël (1827–1878), all born Colin, were among the artists who set the style and themes of industrial fashion illustration in the 1840s. The Colin sisters and other artists produced the drawings and watercolors from which engravings were made and then hand-colored after printing. The Colins' work appeared constantly in leading women's magazines for close to half a century (fig. 16).

Institutional Reform

What was new about women in crafts was perhaps more the evolution of crafts into professions than women's involvement in them. We know that women in the artisan classes had worked for centuries in family workshops. Keckley exploited the needle skills all women passed on to each other at home. The Colin sisters learned to draw and paint from their father in his studio while they were children, and began to earn money from their art in early adolescence. With the onset of capitalism women suddenly had to enter a public labor market and apply for jobs their mothers and grandmothers had inconspicuously inherited.

By the second half of the century, the decline of family labor organization meant that younger generations were no longer being trained as Keckley and the Colins had been. In order to compete for jobs in crafts, or for jobs in industrial design supplanting some crafts, women had to demand public training. Moreover, some women began to aspire to positions in the high arts, and to feel they could not attain them without official educations and affiliations. We can recognize Jennie Louise Bethune (née Blanchard, American, 1865–1913) as one of the earliest professional women architects, for instance, because in 1888 she became the first woman accepted into the American Institute of Architects, still today America's most important architectural professional organization. Converging economic and artistic factors provoked debates over institutional reform throughout Europe and the United States in the last third of the century.

In each country the issues were more or less the same. Opponents of women's professionalization claimed women should remain in the home, while supporters argued that not all women could afford to do so (especially single women) and that of all types of education, an artistic one would enhance rather than damage a young woman's femininity. In each country, however, the chronology of protests and concessions varied according to the greater or lesser mobilization of women artists and the proclivities of national or municipal art establishments. Because in the nineteenth century Paris was the center of the art world, the French case is at once the most unusual and the most important.[2] By the end of the century women from Belgium, Britain, Finland, Germany, Holland, Italy, Norway, Russia, Switzerland, and the United States who would become their respective countries' leading women painters had all gone to study in Paris.

France had one of the earliest publicly funded art schools for women. Founded in Paris in 1803 by two women, the Ecole Gratuite de Dessin pour les Jeunes Filles served as the model for similar schools in other countries. It provided a basic design training which oriented most of its students toward crafts. By the 1860s analogous schools had been founded in many provincial towns and by 1869 there were as many as twenty in Paris alone, compared with only seven comparable schools for men. Art became an integral part of public school curricula for girls, which in turn created new teaching positions for women artists. By the end of the century the national Union Centrale des Arts Décoratifs had instituted a "section féminine" to promote higher standards of quantity and quality among craftswomen.

Women whose painting or sculpture passed jury judgment

could exhibit in the hallowed Salon under the aegis of the state and its artistic organ, the Académie des Beaux-Arts. In 1800 women exhibited 66 works, 12.2 percent of all entries. By 1900 the figures had risen steeply; that year women showed 609 works, or 21.2 percent of the total. Women exhibited sculpture least and watercolors most, with oil painting slowly gaining currency over time. To confront the Salon, however, which was tantamount to braving not only critical reaction but also the market, was not possible for women, because they did not benefit from the same preparation as men. Beginning in the 1860s, the fashionable painter Charles Chaplin ran a professional teaching studio for women. Others followed his lead, notably Tony Robert-Fleury at the Académie Julian from the 1870s onward. But even in these serious studios women received a diluted program; the hours were different, the teachers fewer, work from the nude not allowed, or anatomy not offered.

Finally women realized they would have to take matters into their own hands. In 1881 the sculptor and educator Mme Léon Bertaux (born Hélène Pilate, French, 1825–1909) founded the Union des Femmes Peintres et Sculpteurs, an organization with counterparts elsewhere in Europe. The Union began to hold an annual art exhibition of its own starting in 1882: from 38 exhibitors that year it grew to 942 exhibitors in 1897. By 1890, the year it started to publish its *Journal des Femmes Artistes,* the Union counted 500 members. Through its magazine and through the efforts of the indefatigable Mme Bertaux, the Union campaigned for women's admission into the most prestigious of all European art schools, the state-run and state-funded Ecole des Beaux-Arts. Success came at last in 1896, long after comparable Danish, German, Russian, and English schools had capitulated, notably England's famous South Kensington School. Nonetheless women were still excluded from mixed life-study classes, as well as from competition for the school's highest prize, the Prix de Rome.

Victories like the Union's unfortunately won for women the right to outdated privileges. Leaders and members of the Union had understood that successful careers required institutional foundations, and justly insisted on the principle of equal access for women; but they did not understand which privileges were the crucial modern ones. By the time women could attend the Ecole des Beaux-Arts, art history moved away from the state toward independent exhibitions, avant-garde movements, and private dealers. In the Modernist art world, so much more volatile, self-motivated, and individualistic than its predecessor, women were as unprotected as they had ever been.

Spectacle and Sexuality

Images continued to reflect the attitudes men brought to their perceptions of women: attitudes about sexuality, class, race, work, and art. Male artists controlled their female subjects. Not only did men represent women as the objects of a sexually authoritative gaze, but in many cases class difference exacerbated gender inequities. Painters and sculptors at least aspired to middle-class status, while the models they hired belonged to the working classes. Similarly, print-makers and photographers looked at their female working-class subjects with middle-class eyes both condescending and covetous.

Nowhere was this power relationship between the artist and the model more evident than in images of the naked body. More than ever before, the nude in art meant the female nude. But did the nude expose women's bodies, or masculine erotic fantasies? Sexualized female bodies were usually pictured as both submissive and foreign in some way: women from other times, other places, other cultures, other worlds: primitively lustful working girls, alluring odalisques, recumbent goddesses. Myth surrounded both the subject of nude and the women who posed in the nude. It was widely believed that models willingly engaged in sexual relationships with the artists they worked for. Regardless of its actual truth or untruth, the myth of the artist's model accurately expressed the imaginary relationship between the masculine viewer and the high-art nude.

Pornographic images provided more direct access to women's bodies for the possessive sexual gaze. Mass-reproduced lithographs, wood engravings, and later photographs did away with high art's idealizations and provided a burgeoning market with explicit visual displays of sexuality. In one raid on one London shop alone in 1874 police seized 135,248 photographs termed obscene.[3] Within such proliferation many degrees of aesthetic intention could coexist; among early daguerreotypes, particularly, careful composition and the exploitation of the camera's foreshortening could enhance an image's eroticism (fig. 38).

Visual culture virtually ignored women's bodies that did not provide visual pleasure to men. Older women rarely appear in nineteenth-century imagery except as caricatures or saccharine stereotypes. Women's physical labor became almost invisible. Just as the myth of the artist's model avoided the material conditions of her employment and instead emphasized her sexual services, so other working women were either passed over or eroticized. Even traditional agricultural work by women shocked the middle class at first, when Millet represented peasants painfully bent over repetitive tasks on the grand scale of painting (fig. 32). Popular imagery preferred to dwell on relatively privileged trades like millinery associated with feminine pleasures, and on trades believed to be plied by women sexually available to middle-class men (figs. 30, 31). Later such crafts were joined by new but similarly gendered industrial jobs like clerical work or operating a telephone switchboard (fig. 33).

Women in theatrical professions, however, thrived on a vastly increased visibility. Singers like La Malibran (Spanish, 1808–1836), actresses like Sarah Bernhardt (French, 1844–1923), dancers like Carlotta Grisi (Italian, 1819–1899) and Marie Taglioni (Italian, 1804–1884) mesmerized male and female audiences all over Europe and the United States. In their wake came a popular imagery that did as much as actual stage appearances to propagate their fame (fig. 13). By mid-century photographic firms did more than a third of their business in portraits of entertainers.[4] Celebrity pictures also created myths about women's bodies, but these valorized the women depicted and celebrated their ability to transform their own bodies into technically brilliant performances.

Still the Virgin Mary remained the greatest celebrity of all. Despite a general decline in religious imagery both popular and academic, nineteenth-century cults gave Mary's image topical relevance (fig. 14). Pope Pius IX's proclamation of the doctrine of the Immaculate Conception in 1854 and the success of the schools for girls run by the female Society of the Sacred Heart signaled the importance to nineteenth-century Catholicism of feminine religious role models. From the Pre-Raphaelite painters to the anonymous engravers of religious cards (fig. 14)—the religious equivalent of the *carte-de-visite* photograph—artists cast Mary as a middle-class mother whom even Protestants could emulate. Anna Jameson (English, 1794–1860), the first professional English art historian, reserved the culminating volume of her immensely popular *Legendary and Sacred Art* for "Legends of the Madonna." Above all she praised paintings of the Madonna and Child: "the glorified type of what is purest, loftiest, holiest in womanhood."[5]

Production and Consumption

Together with prints, photographs exponentially expanded the scope of visual culture. The media explosion that began in the 1830s and accelerated throughout the century popularized contemporary feminine subject matter, elicited specifically female audiences, and induced new visual identities. Women were able to make and acquire pictures more easily than ever before, but their deeper involvement in visual culture also rendered them more susceptible to its suggestions.

Mechanical devices relaxed definitions of authorship. Women with no professional training like Julia Margaret Cameron (English, 1815–1879, fig. 7) could pick up a camera and negotiate an eminent place in a field that did not yet rigidly distinguish art from science or amateur from professional. In the photographer's studio the relationship between artist and model could almost be reversed; the photographer might be passive while his subject staged herself, fashioning an identity for the camera's machinery to record.

Virginia Verasis, Countess de Castiglione (Italian, née Oldoini, d. 1899), several of Jean-Martin Charcot's patients in his Salpêtrière hospital for insane women, and Hannah Cullwick (English, 1833–1909) all used photography to produce anomalous but evocative serial images of themselves. The Countess de Castiglione had herself pictured as an outrageous courtesan, spectacle of sexuality and object of desire (fig. 18); Blanche Wittman (French, 1859–d. after 1905) and "Augustine" (dates unknown) performed the phases of hysteria for the pictures Charcot used as clinical evidence (fig. 37); Hannah Cullwick, a scullery maid, posed in roles ranging from slave to lady in order to please Arthur Munby, the eccentric photograph collector who eventually married her. Were these women expressing or exploiting themselves? Were they asserting the validity of marginal identities or were they trapped by roles their images sealed? The contradictions of their self-representations clarify by exaggeration the tensions inherent in all women's identities in a modern industrial consumer culture.

Women controlled images by purchasing them but were in turn

controlled by the urge to purchase. Industrialization converted the amateur feminine tradition into mass-reproduced images. Women gradually ceased producing their albums with hand-made pictures and began assembling them with photographs of similar subjects. Women had imagined themselves from within a domestic world in their amateur art; now prints and photographs, and above all fashion plates, recycled amateur imagery to represent women commercially (fig. 16). Fashion plates, as well as their vehicle the women's magazine, had been in existence since the late seventeenth century, but became a cultural force in the 1840s. In America, *Godey's Lady's Book,* edited by Sarah Josepha Hale, had 40,000 subscribers by 1849, while in France several women's magazines like *Le Petit Echo de la Mode* had circulations of 200,000 by 1890; moreover, several readers shared each magazine copy. Women had been identified as a market and targeted by the clothing and publishing industries. The fashion plate introduced women to advertisement (figs. 17, 28) with its paradigmatic alliance of image and shopping information that sold its products as a gender and class ideal.

Advertisements redefined femininity in terms of surfaces and objects: clothing, cosmetics, and accessories. Other essays in this volume explain more fully how women evolved during the nineteenth century from producers working within the home to consumers spending outside it. Advertisements played their visual part in this process by reworking women's traditional self-images. These new self-images were commodities, available to all women for a price, and perhaps the women who adopted their values themselves became commodities.

"Men act, women appear," said the critic John Berger. As appearances became increasingly important to feminine identity, images played a correspondingly greater role in women's sense of self. The unprecedented numbers of women entering artistic professions were responding to an association between women and images. By entering into artistic fields women perpetuated gender stereotypes, yet their accomplishments began to make women appear different.

Strategies

Ambiguity and compromise characterized women's cultural production both negatively and positively. The most successful women's careers in the arts—whether success is measured in terms of social approval, fame, wealth, or influence—owed less to equal access to masculine institutions and official privileges than to the ability to function at the edges of institutions while maintaining contact with either the amateur tradition or a craft profession.

One of the principal resources for women with artistic aspirations remained men artists, although association with male colleagues carried not only the peril of a damaged personal reputation (the myth of the artist's model) but also the danger that work would be attributed to men's inspiration or even execution. Nonetheless, a majority of the women who achieved artistic prominence in the nineteenth century went through at least a phase as models or companions or pupils of recognized male figures in the art world. May Morris the embroiderer (English, 1862–1938) was both the daughter and the student of the designer William Morris; the Schumann composers Clara (German, 1819–1896) and Robert were a married couple; Carlotta Grisi was the lover of the choreographer Jules Perrot; Berthe Morisot (French, 1841–1895) posed for fellow-painter Edouard Manet (fig. 24). The prevalence of the phenomenon suggests both the continuing practical dependence on men for an introduction into the art world, and women's psychological need for masculine valorization.

Liminal careers provided women with uncharted terrain to claim as their own. By choosing to illustrate books, as did Potter and Kate Greenaway (English, 1846–1901), to specialize in unusual and marginal painting genres, such as Bonheur's animals or Lady Elizabeth Butler's (English, 1846–1933) military scenes, to work in new fields as did the Colin sisters in fashion illustration or Cameron in photography, or even to write about art as Anna Jameson did professionally and Marie Bashkirtseff (Russian, 1859–1884) did in her best-selling diary, women could go far without seeming to break any rules.

Another strategy of female artists incorporated high art by men into projects with domestic origins. Women could extend outward from their identification with the home to reorganize crafts, paintings, architecture, or nature itself into composite works of art in their own right. Edith Wharton (American, 1862–1937) coauthored with Ogden Codman the first book professionally dedicated to interior decoration, their 1897 *The Decoration of Houses*. Gertrude Jekyll planned and planted gardens around homes (fig. 41). Isabella Stewart Gardner (American, 1840–1922) modeled a public institution on a private home in the house-museum she founded, designed, and installed (figs. 42, 43).

Women could not separate their professional from their personal lives the way men could. Some women used this to their advantage, others were defeated by it. Radical careers could be compensated for by traditional subject matter. Mary Cassatt and Berthe Morisot, the most stylistically adventurous women painters of the late nineteenth century, worked exclusively on the conventionally feminine subjects of the amateur tradition (figs. 1, 25). Both women also led staid middle-class private lives. Audacity in medium, career, and personal behavior all at once added up to disaster. Camille Claudel (French, 1864–1943) has become the mythic archetype of the cursed woman genius. She dared to work in sculpture, the most masculine of all mediums, to model for and work with a dominant male artist, Auguste Rodin, to take him openly as her lover, and to represent women's erotic desire (fig. 40). Her family and Rodin abandoned her, she lost her reason, and art history forgot her for three-quarters of a century.

Women faced complex and evolving configurations of aesthetic, economic, sexual, technological, and political values that materialized as art forms, art institutions, or art industries and together constituted visual culture. Some of these values were compatible with the values of femininity, many were not. Women had to reconcile conflicting values and devise new configurations of meaning to make a place for themselves where before they had had none. They had to invent careers, art forms, and femininities. To appreciate what they accomplished we need to step back from the very partial view of cultural history afforded us by paintings and sculpture and look at the entire field of visual culture in its historical context. It will then become apparent how courageous women's work was, how astute, lucrative, diverse, creative, and for those reasons, how beautiful.

1. Mary Cassatt, *The Bath,* (1891–92), oil on canvas. Chicago, Art Institute of Chicago.

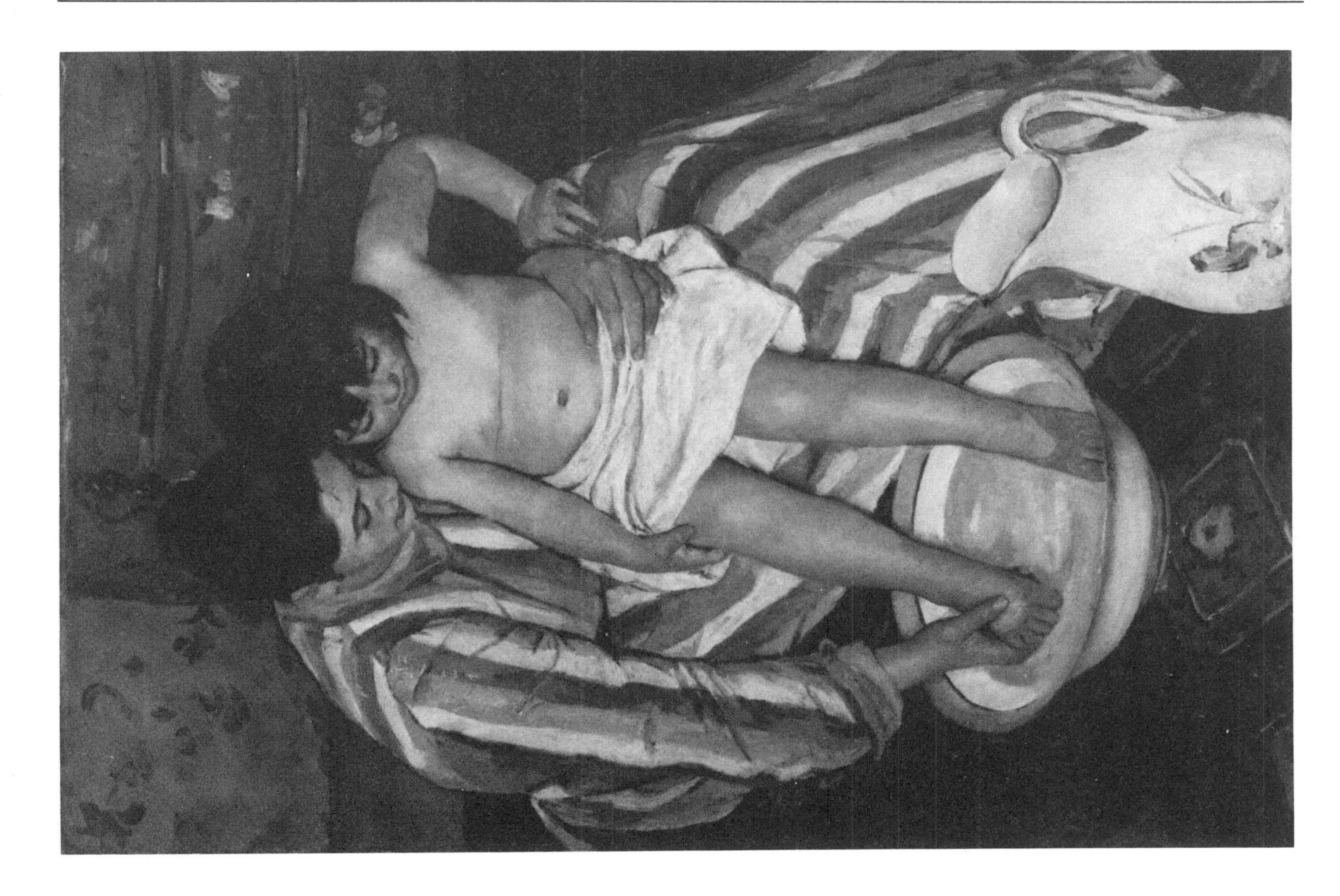

JVDiTH VND
HOLOFERNES

3. Eugène Delacroix, *Liberty Guiding the People* (1830), oil on canvas. Paris, Louvre. Photograph Réunion des Musées Nationaux.

2. Gustav Klimt, *Judith* (1901), oil on canvas. Berlin, Archiv für Kunst und Geschichte.

4. Jacques-Louis David, *The Oath of the Horatii* (1784–85), oil on canvas. Paris, Louvre. Photograph Réunion des Musées Nationaux.

5. *Mountain Built on the Field of Mars for the Feast of the Supreme Being, June 8, 1784*. Engraving of a commemorative design by Jacques-Louis David. Paris, Bibliothèque Nationale.

8. George Elgar Hicks, *Companion to Manhood* (1863), oil on canvas. London, Tate Gallery.

6. Diana Sperling, *Newport Pagnell. Mrs. Hurst Dancing. September 17, 1816.* Page from an album (1816). Watercolor. © Neville Ollerenshaw c/o Victor Gollancz, London.

7. Mary Ellen Best, *Anthony and the Three Children.* Page from an album (1847). Watercolor and gouache. Chatto and Windus Photographers, London.

9. Maleuvre, *Young Saint-Simonienne.* Engraving, 1832. Paris, Bibliothèque Nationale.

10. Alcide Lorentz, *George Sand.* Lithograph, 1842. Paris, Bibliothèque Nationale.

Une femme comme moi . . . remettre un bouton ? . . . vous êtes fou ! . . . .
Allons bon ! . . voila qu'elle ne se contente plus de porter les culottes . . . . il faut encore qu'elle me les jette à la tête ! . . . .

12. Joseph Danhauser, *Franz Liszt at the Piano* (1840), oil on canvas. From the left: Paganini, Berlioz, Dumas (standing), Rossini, Sand, Liszt, d'Agoult. Berlin, Archiv für Kunst und Geschichte.

11. Honoré Daumier, *The Bluestockings.* "A woman like me—replace a button? Are you crazy?" "That's a good one! She is no longer content with wearing the pants—now she throws them in my face!" Lithograph. *Le Charivari,* May 23, 1844, Plate 28. Paris, Bibliothèque Nationale.

Marie Taglioni
(Sylphide)

14. *The Virgin Mary.* Holy card. Colored engraving (before 1860). Private collection.

13. Achille Devéria, *Marie Taglioni.* Lithograph (1840). Cambridge (Massachusetts), Harvard University Theater Collection.

15. Kronheim firm, *Woman and Children in a Garden.* Colored engraving (1850–1860). Private collection.

16. Laure Noël, Plate n. 427 of *Le Papillon.* Colored wood engraving (ca. 1860). Private collection.

1er OCTOBRE 1881. L'ILLUSTRATION N° [illegible] — 227.

GRANDS MAGASINS
DU LOUVRE

PARIS. — Les plus vastes du Monde. — PARIS

LUNDI PROCHAIN 3 OCTOBRE

ET JOURS SUIVANTS

INAUGURATION DE

L'EXPOSITION GÉNÉRALE DES NOUVEAUTÉS D'AUTOMNE ET D'HIVER

GRANDE MISE EN VENTE DES TOILETTES NOUVELLES

MANTEAUX, COSTUMES, ROBES, JUPES, PEIGNOIRS, MODES, VÊTEMENTS D'ENFANTS, LINGERIE FINE

Conformément à l'usage adopté par les GRANDS MAGASINS DU LOUVRE, le programme de cette Exposition sera publié à la dernière page dans les grands journaux de Paris, à la date du 3 octobre.

Les préparatifs faits en vue de cette Exposition ont pris des proportions colossales : le Grand Hall du Palais-Royal et les Galeries qui l'entourent contiendront de véritables merveilles en SOIERIES, SATINS, MOIRES et PELUCHES ; en un mot, toutes les Etoffes Nouvelles que la mode favorise le plus.

18. Mayer and Pierson, *Countess of Castiglione.* Photograph (ca. 1850–1860). Colmar, Unterlinden Museum.

17. *Grands Magasins du Louvre.* Advertisement for the unveiling of the fall-winter fashions in *L'Illustration,* October, 1881. Cambridge (Massachusetts), Harvard University, Widener Library.

19. Marthe Leclerc, *Self Portrait in Her Studio.* Miniature on enamel (1917). Geneva, Musée de l'Horlogerie et de l'Emaillerie.

20. Rosa Bonheur, *Horse Market* (1853), oil on canvas. New York, The Metropolitan Museum of Art.

21. Beatrix Potter, cover illustration for the first edition of *The Tale of Peter Rabbit.* Published by Frederick Warne and Company, 1902. London, Penguin Books.

22. Harriet Powers, *The Creation of the Animals* (ca. 1886). Quilt. Boston, Museum of Fine Arts.

23. Edgar Degas, *Mary Cassat and Her Sister at the Louvre* (ca. 1885), etching. Chicago, Art Institute of Chicago.

24. Edouard Manet, *Berthe Morisot Reclining* (1873), oil on canvas. Private collection. Photograph by André Held, Ecubens, Switzerland.

25. Berthe Morisot, *Julie Playing the Violin* (1893), oil on canvas. Private collection. Photograph by the Mount Holyoke College Art Museum, South Hadley (Massachusetts).

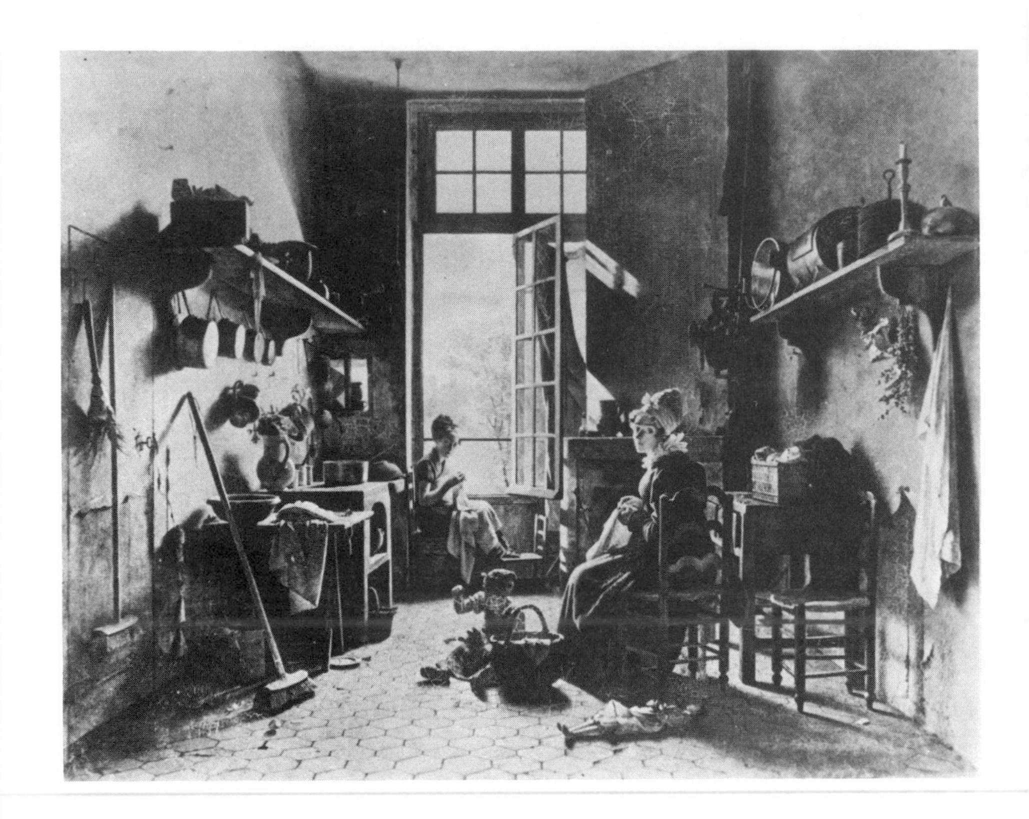

26. Martin Drölling, *Kitchen Interior,* oil on canvas. Berlin, Archiv für Kunst und Geschichte.

27. *City Kitchen.* Chromolithograph from a children's book with "illustrations for the first visual lesson," 1889. Berlin, Archiv für Kunst und Geschichte.

MOST WELCOME
WEDDING GIFT.
SIMPLE
STRONG
SINGER
SEWING
MACHINES
THE SINGER MANFG. CO.
TRADE MARK.
SINGER
SILENT
SPEEDY
"Mother's Machine"
With Latest Improvements. Lightest
Running, Easiest Managed.
Greatly aids domestic bliss.
The SINGER MANUFACTURING CO.

29. *At Night a Bedroom, During the Day a Workroom for the Manufacture of Fur Articles.* Photograph from a study by the Berlin Ortskrankenkasse (1910). Berlin, Archiv für Kunst und Geschichte.

28. *Advertisement for the Singer Sewing Machine,* in *McLure's Magazine,* VII, 5 (October, 1896).

30. Larylumé, *Look! He's Following Me.* Lithograph (ca. 1810). Paris, Musée Carnavalet photograph.

31. M. de Charly, *At the Dressmakers . . . Fine Work for an Elaborate Toilette.* Photograph (1862). Rochester, (New York), International Museum of Photography. George Eastman House photographer.

34. *Woman Coal Miner at Wigan,* between 1867 and 1878. Photograph from the collection of Arthur Munby. Cambridge, Trinity College.

32. Jean-François Millet, *The Gleaners,* oil on canvas. Paris, Musée D'Orsay. Photograph Réunion des Musées Nationaux.

33. Anonymous, *Telephone Operators.* SIP Photographers.

35. Paul Poncet, *Let Us Shorten the Work Day* (1912). Poster for the C.G.T. "Eight-Hour" campaign. Paris, private collection.

36. Jacob Riis, *Italian Mother and Baby, Jersey Street* (ca. 1889). Photograph from his *How the Other Half Lives* (1892). Museum of the City of New York.

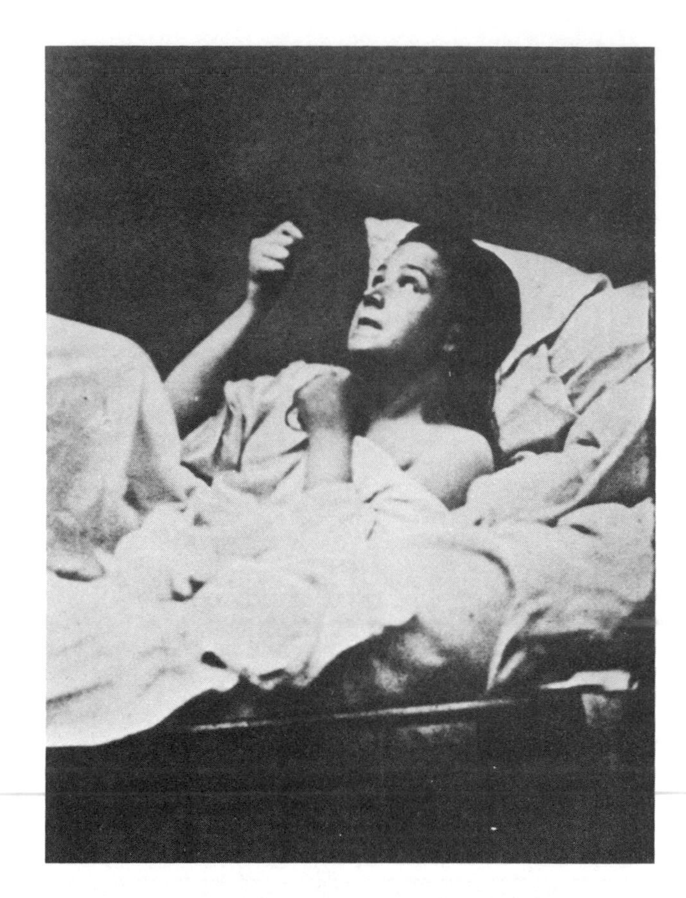

37. *Expressions of Passion: Menace.* From Bourneville and Régnard, *Photographic Collection for the Salpêtrière* (Paris: Delahaye and Lecrosnier, 1878), Plate XXVII. Paris, Bibliothéque Charcot of the Salpêtrière photograph.

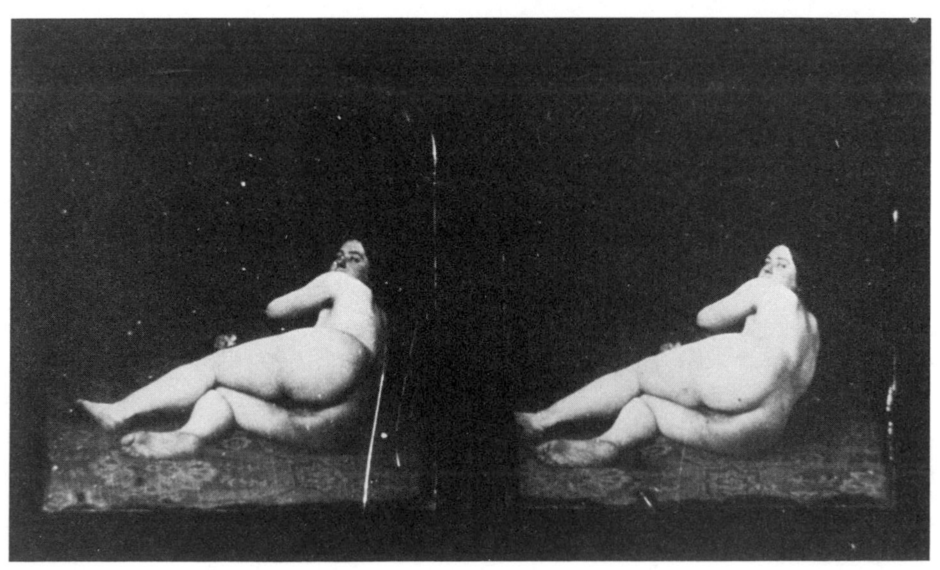

38. *Erotic Photograph.* Anonymous hand-colored stereoscopic photograph. Paris, Gérard Lévy Collection.

39. Auguste Rodin, *The Kiss* (1886), marble. Paris, Musée Rodin.

40. Camille Claudel, *Abandon* (ca. 1888–1905), marble. Paris, Musée Rodin.

41. Gertrude Jekyll, *Wild Aster Borders Seen through a Laburnum Arch.* Photograph of Munstead Wood's garden, published in 1908. Documents Collection, College of Environmental Design, University of California, Berkeley.

42. ***Inner Courtyard of the Isabella Stewart Gardner Museum,*** **Designed (1898–1903) by Isabella Stewart Gardner. Boston, Isabella Stewart Gardner Museum.**

43. *The Titian Room of the Isabella Stewart Gardner Museum.* Designed (1898–1903) by Isabella Stewart Gardner. Boston, Isabella Stewart Gardner Museum.

44. *Graduates of Wellesley College in Academic Regalia.* Photograph by Wilma Slaight, Clapp Library Archives, Wellesley College, Wellesley (Massachusetts).

45. *Suffragettes Demonstrating for the Vote in 1905.* Anonymous photograph. Berlin, Archiv für Kunst und Geschichte.

46. *Banner of Graduates of Cambridge for the NUWSS March of June 13, 1908.* Designed by Mary Lowndes and sewn by Girton and Newnham College students. Newnham College Photograph, Cambridge University.

47. Julia Margaret Cameron, *Mrs. Herbert Duckworth.* Silver plate photograph (1867). Gernsheim Collection, University of Texas, Austin.

12

Representations of Women

Anne Higonnet

IMAGES CAN BE INTERPRETED in many ways. The illustrations I have used could be understood with only the minimal technical information provided by their captions. Or they could be understood in a much broader way in the context of this volume as a whole as the visual analogues, complements, or clarifications of the issues of revolution, subversion, sexuality, family, work, feminism, identity, and representation raised in various essays. "Images—Appearances, Leisure, and Subsistence" refers to the illustrations as examples for a history of woman's place in nineteenth-century visual culture. The following notes are organized around those examples to amplify their specific meanings and draw attention to their visual tactics.

Madonna, Seductress, Muse

Mary Cassatt's 1891–92 *The Bath* (fig. 1), Gustav Klimt's 1901 *Judith* (fig. 2), and Eugène Delacroix's 1830 *Liberty Leading the People* (fig. 3) repeat high art's three feminine stereotypes: the madonna, the seductress, the muse. But each of these paintings updates its stereotype in characteristically nineteenth-century ways.

Cassatt's madonna, the bourgeois mother of a daughter, signals the decline of religious subjects in art, especially in Protestant countries but also in France, as well as the growing interest in pictures of little girls and the mother-daughter relationship. Cassatt's maternal figure bathes her child, an ordinary occurrence with which any middle-class viewer can identify. Cassatt maintains traditions by emphasizing maternity's physical bond; the places where flesh touches flesh define the central axis of her image. As a fin-de-siècle aestheticism luxuriated in sexuality, it also brought to the surface latent fears of women's sexual power. Klimt's image of the female body plays lushly represented flesh against precious patterned gold. Judith's palpable sensuality both seduces and repels. She approaches the viewer, invites him with her glistening opened mouth and revealed breast. But her name reminds him that she is a dangerous woman, one who lures in order to destroy. Delacroix's Liberty leads men into revolution with the promise of democracy. Delacroix imagined her unabashedly as a woman of the people, brown and muscled, striding toward us across the barricade. She remains the unrivaled embodiment of Marianne, emblem of the French Republic.

Woman's Place in the Revolution

David summarized women's place in French revolutionary ideology with his 1784–85 *Oath of the Horatii* (fig. 4). The three Horatii brothers vow to defeat the corrupt Curatii or die in the attempt. On one side are the men: tautly united, striving toward a common goal, exhorted by their father to become instruments of justice as remorseless as the swords he clasps in his hand. On the other side are the women: gently wilting with personal emotion, gracefully joined by a sinuous rhythm of gestures and drapery. Each side makes the other's meaning clear—masculinity and femininity are the opposites of each other. The only connection between them is the small boy who gazes out from the women's unconscious group to learn from the men's example.

David put his concepts into practice with his designs for the festivals of the Revolution. Though they celebrated dramatically new political ideals, women found themselves relegated to traditional roles within revolutionary parameters. In the 1794 *Fête de l'Etre Suprême* (fig. 5) women were grouped collectively as white-clad virgins, or represented allegorically as Abundance riding the chariot of plenty or as Wisdom revealed by the burning away of an outer façade representing Atheism. Women were virtually never represented as active individual participants in the Revolution, but rather as members of collective political action motivated by immediate material needs, and more usually as symbols of the domestic and chaste virtues which guaranteed the purity of the Revolution's intentions.

Focus on the Home

Bourgeois ideology in the early decades of the nineteenth century firmly situated virtuous women in the home. In the amateur art so prevalent throughout Europe in the first half of the century, women represented themselves in domestic roles, but sometimes with a humorous or reflective twist. Diana Sperling's spry 1816 watercolor depicts after-dinner family dancing (fig. 6). Women outnumber men; one woman happily dances alone; a little girl looks out at us from her seat on the edge of the picture. Accompaniment on the piano is provided by another amateur woman artist, Sperling's musical counterpart.

Best's 1847 gouache (fig. 7) shows her husband playing the piano and their three children entering the music and dining room in which a table is set for an intimate meal. Best pays detailed attention to the furnishings of her home, meticulous enough for us to perceive her self-consciousness as an artist. The lower of the represented paintings on the left of the image is Best's wedding portrait of her husband. Her portrait of him looks out at us on the left, their son looks out at us on the right. Best has composed her intellectual and physical creations symmetrically; she and her husband are also imagined symmetrically—he plays opposite her while she paints.

Women's amateur art remained within the home; men made pictures of private life destined for the public sphere. Part of a triptych called Women's Mission, George Elgar Hicks' *Companion to Manhood* (fig. 8) is one of many mid-century domestic genre scenes produced by and for the middle class. Amid the signs of respectable domesticity—hearth, rug, cozy breakfast table and polished silver—a wife consoles her husband who has just learned of a death. She is his tender comfort but he is her upright strength. Sperling's and Best's images were painted on sheets of paper, mounted in albums, and handed down to their families. Hicks' image was painted with realistic virtuosity in the prestigious medium of oil on canvas, was publicly exhibited as soon as it was made, and now belongs to England's national museum, the Tate Gallery.

Dress as Statement

Nothing more superficially but more tenaciously conveyed gender than dress. In no century were masculine and feminine costumes so differentiated, and in none were clothing transgressions so carefully monitored and so readily used in images of conformity and subversion. Maleuvre's 1832 picture of a young Saint-Simonienne (fig. 9) seems dainty by twentieth-century standards, but to nineteenth-century eyes her costume suited her revolutionary doctrine. Her dress was ostentatiously simple, and reached to just below her knees—short enough to make what she wore beneath look like pants. Pants symbolized masculinity. To wear them was to claim masculine rights.

George Sand's completely masculine attire conveyed her radical stance more plainly than her male pseudonym or even the radical content of her writing. Her appearance had the power to stand for the substance of her endeavors. Lorentz's 1842 image of Sand (fig. 10), for instance, mocks her political positions, represented as slogans written on floating sheets of paper, by ridiculing the way she looks. The point Sand is making, his caption tells us, is that "Genius has no sex." The point is mocked, but at least it has been clearly understood and stated.

"Je me fiche bien de votre madame Sand qui empêche les femmes de raccomoder les pantalons!" (I couldn't care less about your madame Sand who keeps women from mending pants) exclaimed an injured husband to his independent wife in the caption to one of Honoré Daumier's lithographic prints. Daumier, otherwise a committed radical, reserved his conservative ire for feminists with literary aspirations. In another print from his "Bas-Bleus" (Bluestocking) series (fig. 11), a wife angrily refuses to sew a button back on her husband's pants. He, standing woefully with hands held limply in front of his phallus, comments that not only does his wife "wear the pants" but now she throws them back at him.

Maleuvre's, Lorentz's and Daumier's prints all address a gender issue unimaginable in high art. Improvements in the lithographic and wood engraving techniques during the first decades of the century made possible a widespread distribution of inexpensive images that undertook topical commentary by means of interactions between pictures and captions. Proper femininity acquired a popular image against which any deviancy could be equally easily visualized. Images of women became powerful tools in debates over their place in society, with references to representations as ineluctable facts.

At the same time Romanticism created new images of femininity. George Sand could be caricatured, but she could also be pictured as the exalted auditor of Franz Liszt's music (fig. 12). If, as the Romantics proposed, artistic inspiration came from the universal forces of nature, then all the arts had a common basis, and if all human beings were equal before nature then all artists could be equal before genius. Danhauser depicts Sand among an egalitarian group of musicians and writers. Sand on the left is both compared and contrasted with Daniel Stern (pseudonym of Marie d'Agoult) on the right; Sand dons masculine garb, complete with cigarette, while Stern wears an elegant, feminine dress. Sand belongs to the group of male geniuses on the left from whom she is virtually indistinguishable.

Wreathed in gossamer white, the Romantic ballerina brought to perfection a feminine ideal of disincarnation. Both quintessential Romantic ballets: *La Sylphide*—first produced in 1832 with Marie Taglioni dancing the lead—and *Giselle*—which opened in 1841 with Carlotta Grisi dancing the title role—cast female heroines as sprites. The fragility of their appearance made the strength of their self-sacrificing and tragic love all the more poignant. Taglioni was the first ballerina to dance on the tips of her toes, a grueling technique that created illusions of weightlessness. When Devéria represented Taglioni in one of her many popular images (fig. 13), he dispensed altogether with the conditions of her illusions—her pointe shoes—and showed her floating barefoot above the ground.

Mass-Produced Images

Some traditional images of femininity retained their hold on the female imagination, but in newly industrialized and middle-class variants. Religious images (fig. 14) had always been a staple of popular print repertoires, and with the advent of mass production technologies they could be distributed and collected even more widely. In their new very small format, sometimes hand-colored after printing and surrounded with lacy cut-outs, "holy cards" were often tucked casually into missals. No longer implacably majestic arbiters, the placidly benign and almost androgynously adolescent religious figures of nineteenth-century holy cards contributed to the feminization of religion. Many cards seem to have been specifically designed to encourage girls to emulate Catholic role models, above all the Virgin Mary (fig. 14).

The expansion and diversification of the print market led to its specialization. A genre of print representing bourgeois femininity and aimed at a middle-class women's market proliferated in the early decades of the century onward (fig. 15). This type of print occupied an intermediate position between the amateur pictures women had been making since the late eighteenth century (figs. 6, 7) and the fashion illustrations made of them which became increasingly current after the 1840s (fig. 16). Fashion illustrations themselves furnished visual transitions from ostensibly neutral images to those which, beginning in the last third of the century, deployed representations of women for avowedly commercial purposes. Advertisements (fig. 17), fashion illustrations, and feminine genre prints all depicted women as static and uncommunicative mannequins elaborately dressed in minutely detailed costumes, placed in emblematically feminine settings. To the domestic interior, the garden, the family vacation spot, the church, and the ballroom were gradually added urban places like the museum, the store, and the train station. The identification invoked was not with a particular individual but with a spectacle of femininity constituted by place and by costume. The Countess de Castiglione flaunted this commodified identity in the over 400 photographs she had taken of herself between about 1856 and 1865, and then around 1895–1898. Several photographs also make explicit references to herself as an object of vision, using picture frames and mirrors (fig. 18) to remind us of her artifice. Her self-presentation emphasizes the extravagant surfaces that substitute for an interior being.

Art out of the Mainstream

Avoiding the contested arenas of high art and sexuality restricted women artists' prestige but expanded their economic and expressive opportunities. Crafts or minor genres of painting not only earned women incomes outside the home, they offered an escape from the dilemmas posed by the female subject. Although dating from 1917, Marthe Leclerc's miniature self-portrait on enamel (fig.

19) captures the security felt in a nineteenth-century crafts career. The tools of her trade barricade her within a safe space. She includes as many references to artifice and sight in her self-image as Castiglione did in hers (a plaster cast, pictures, an empty candlestick, an open window reflecting the outside), but Leclerc imagines herself absorbed in her own work rather than displayed to the viewer.

Women designed worlds which mitigated gender difference. Each in very different ways, Rosa Bonheur (French, 1822–1899) and Beatrix Potter made supremely rewarding careers out of animal pictures. Bonheur—like Sand, famous for wearing men's clothes—received a gold medal at the official Salon painting exhibition in 1848, France's Légion d'Honneur medal in 1865, and became Officer of the Légion d'Honneur in 1894. Her paintings and the rights to have them reproduced commanded huge sums. The 1853 *Marché aux chevaux* (Horse Market) (fig. 20) was sold for 40,000 francs to a London dealer, and later to an American collector for 55,000 dollars.

Potter's watercolors were as tiny and imaginative as Bonheur's oil paintings were enormous and realistic, but over time her success has eclipsed even Bonheur's. Potter had no professional training and her early children's books grew out of illustrated letters she sent young friends. She titled her first book *Peter Rabbit* (fig. 21). Initially printed in October 1902 in an edition of 8,000, by the end of the year it had gone through two more printings and 28,000 copies were in circulation. Potter's popularity continues unabated; her work is reproduced and imitated in countless products and her books are still being published; her original drawings are collected by museums and recently received the accolade of a museum exhibition.

Like Potter's work, American quilts are being rescued from marginality. Once dismissed as anonymous crafts, quilts are now appreciated both for the individual authorship of their tops and for women's collective production of the final assembled work. American quilters usually chose abstract or extremely stylized motifs. Yet their images dealt not only with facets of private life like friendship, death, and marriage, but also with public issues like religious beliefs, the abolition of slavery, and the prohibition of alcohol. Harriet Powers pieced fifteen scenes together to depict God's apocalyptic punishment of the unjust and redemption of the innocent in her c. 1886 *Bible Quilt* (fig. 22). This quilt is one of the few surviving art works that trace black Americans' African visual heritage. Powers deftly synthesized a Fon Dahomey appliqué technique and style with American quilt forms and techniques to create a vibrant and sophisticated image of humanity, animals, God, and the heavens. At the center of the bottom edge is a female hog, a symbol of independence and a reference to the route traveled by slaves to freedom.

The Woman Artist's Identity

Women's conception of themselves in the high arts and men's attitudes toward them evolved gradually. Edgar Degas was interested enough in an image of his colleague Mary Cassatt at the Louvre museum to rework it twenty-four times (fig. 23). He represents her turned away from us toward the paintings, her attention conveyed by the alignment of her head and shoulders along the axes of picture frames. Yet in his images she is not a maker of paintings but a viewer of them. Edouard Manet painted eleven portraits of his colleague Berthe Morisot (fig. 24), and though he paid tribute to her intellect as well as to her beauty he did not show her once as a painter.

Nonetheless, the Impressionist movement nurtured Cassatt's and Morisot's confidence in themselves to an unprecedented degree. In 1893 Morisot painted a picture (fig. 25) which, like Best's (fig. 7), insists on the multiplicity of her identity. In the background of the image of her daughter Morisot reproduced two portraits: on the right a narrow slice of Degas's portrait of her husband; on the left Manet's portrait of herself (fig. 24). Morisot has paired herself with her husband and given her child a lineage decidedly weighted in favor of the maternal side. Moreover, Morisot gives the mother-child relationship a new dimension, for by depicting herself and her daughter in the same image but in different representational registers she makes the bond between them more intellectual than physical. Mother and child each have artistic preoccupations, in painting and music, which simultaneously connect and separate them. While acknowledging that her artistic identity includes being Manet's model, Morisot appropriates his image of her for her own purposes.

Women at Work

Rather than ponder issues of identity, it seemed much simpler to represent women doing what they were supposed to do in the places they were already thought to belong. Sewing appealed to the nineteenth-century visual imagination more often than any other female task (figs. 26, 28, 29), even more than traditional peasant labor (fig. 32). More closely identified with gender than with class, sewing provided a way of representing women's work that avoided controversial questions of social or economic difference and of industrial labor by diverting attention to consensus about femininity. Manifestly working-class women tended to be represented in the kitchen, engaged in the reassuringly domestic tasks of sewing or cooking (figs. 26, 27). Advertisements for sewing machines exploited the identification of sewing with femininity and promised an improved performance of traditional roles. One 1896 Singer advertisement called its product a "mother's machine" and a "most welcome wedding gift" that "greatly aids domestic bliss"; a giant letter "S" winds around the plump figure of a confident matron (fig. 28). Thus gender difference persisted despite the Industrial Revolution, in sweatshop labor as women worked sewing machines either at home (fig. 29) or in the factory.

Even the newest media restrained women's emergence into the public industrial workforce with conservative imagery. An early popular lithograph by Larylumé (fig. 30) depicts two millinery assistants delivering their wares. Although it was an intrinsic part of their job, their presence out on a Parisian street has been transformed into an amorous encounter. One woman whispers to the other: "Look! He's following me." Larylumé interprets the sexual freedom working women may in fact have enjoyed as evidence of their availability that encourages a male predator. Working women themselves perpetuated pictorial stereotypes by electing middle-class guises that lent them dignity when they went on display. Two seamstresses chose to wear clothing as elegant as anything they sold for their portrait by a M. de Charly in 1862 (fig. 31). Around them have been arranged the materials and the products of their trade, including, on the wall just behind their heads, one of the fashion plates that both inspired them and promoted their skills.

Labor reformers who could be quite radical in some respects used conservative images of gender to further their causes. The campaign for a shorter working day enlisted a middle-class gender ideal on its behalf (fig. 35). Long days "make the family unhappy": a man enters a bar despite the pleas of his scrawny child while his wife stands forlorn in the street. Shorter days "make the family happy": a man plays with a chubby toddler on the threshold of a domestic interior presided over by a tidy wife.

Arthur Munby provides the exception that proves the rule. Munby collected photographs of women who did jobs like scullery scrubbing, fishing, and mining (fig. 34). The dirtier the work and the more unfeminine the physique or the costume, the more eagerly he sought the photograph. Munby's diaries explain how he had to commission many of his documents or take them himself because the kinds of images he wanted so rarely existed.

The Intimate Eye of the Camera

Photography responded to the new. Attentive to consequences of industrial inventions such as telephone switchboard operation (fig. 33), photographers also sought to capture previously invisible aspects of women's lives. Social reformers like Jacob Riis took cameras into urban slums to reveal a poverty and degradation many members of the middle class had never visualized. His images shocked because of the conditions of immigrant life they recorded, but also because of the abject pathos Riis concentrated on. In his 1889 photograph *Italian Mother and Baby, Jersey Street* Riis sought to enhance the appeal of his subject by casting her as a mother and a victim (fig. 36).

Doctors enlisted photography to replace or supplement verbal or printed descriptions of disease, none more extensively than Jean-Martin Charcot, who used it to document his analysis of female hysteria. A photographic image of the body, he believed, could reveal an inner state of mind. He chose as models patients who displayed the most legible somatic symptoms of their mental disorder and could reenact them for the camera. Charcot classified and labeled each image as a stage of hysteria—"Expressions of Passions—Menace," for example (fig. 37)—so that it could serve in the future as a teaching and diagnostic tool.

As soon as photography was invented it spawned its own brand of eroticism and pornography. Poses and themes used in older types of pornographic prints were recycled, but the new medium also suggested less emphasis on implied movement or evocative setting in favor of detailed genital exposure (fig. 38). Hand-colored stereoscopic photographs viewed through devices held to the face that gave the illusion of three-dimensionality produced a particularly strong effect of intimate proximity (fig. 38). Social reformers, scientists, and pornographers all founded the truth value of their photographs on the medium's mechanical optical accuracy. But what the camera faithfully recorded was the choices brought before its lens, choices of setting, pose, framing, lighting, model, and moment that continued to be as affected by cultural assumptions about women's poverty, health, and sexuality as hand-made images.

Female Sexual Desire

Erotic images in all media were almost always made by men. Women were rarely allowed even to attend anatomy classes or work from the nude in art schools. Middle-class mores placed an absolute taboo on women's representation of the male nude and consigned feminine sexual desire to abnormality, taboos which Camille Claudel flagrantly violated. Auguste Rodin's sculptures of heterosexual love like his 1886 *Le Baiser* (fig. 39) were hailed as classic representations of a universal life force, but Claudel's analogous 1888–1905 *L'Abandon* (fig. 40) contributed to her marginalization. If, as it has usually been alleged, Claudel had merely imitated Rodin, her gesture would already have been a remarkable assertion that women could represent erotic subjects as well as men. But *L'Abandon* is just different enough from *Le Baiser* to suggest an alternative image of women's sexual desire utterly exceptional in the history of nineteenth-century art. Claudel imagined desire not as a relationship of force in which a woman clings from below to a dominant man, but as the mutual surrender of two reciprocal bodies. He, sensuously slender, kneels ardently before her; she, strong and muscled, gives herself to him. Claudel's command of modeling and carving techniques gave her conception of sexuality physical presence. No other artist, not even Suzanne Valadon, a working-class former model who painted bold images of the female nude, broke so many cultural rules.

Artistic Detours

Women found diverse and multiple detours around the artistic domains forbidden to them. Gertrude Jekyll was only the most successful among many women landscape artists who transformed nature itself into spatial and temporal art works that often subsumed architecture. Jekyll not only designed famous gardens like

Munstead Wood as settings for buildings by the eminent architect Edwin Lutyens; she also took her own photographs of her work to use in the fourteen books on gardening she published between 1899 and 1925 (fig. 41).

Some women, notably Isabella Stewart Gardner and Nélie Jacquemart, collected art with their husbands and founded museums to institutionalize their achievements. After her husband's death Gardner designed a museum she named after herself, orchestrating architecture, paintings, decorative arts, and plants into a complex whole. The museum is turned inward onto a central court (fig. 42) and included a domestic apartment for its director. Like all house-museums, its galleries resemble the rooms of a home, but Gardner went further than other museum founders in her consistent subordination of masterpiece paintings to installations of her own design (fig. 43), which she protected with a will.

The Public Sphere

By the turn of the century women were demanding the means to enter the public sphere in more direct ways. The first women's colleges were founded in America and in England at mid-century. Women's college albums and later their yearbooks trace their adjustment to an academic persona. Wellesley College students first petitioned their faculty in 1885: "We recognize that the change will cause talk, and that many will regard it as too radical, but we feel that we are prepared to meet that talk with such good and sufficient defense of our position, as shall justify us in the eyes of the world."[1] At first women presented themselves to the camera in academic gowns only in the context of masquerades. Caps and gowns appear with increasing frequency, especially in college rituals, until finally in the 1880s women posed for their group portraits at graduation in academic regalia, affirming an image of themselves as members of an intellectual community and tradition (fig. 44).

Spectacle brought the suffrage campaign to international attention (fig. 45). Particularly in England, women deployed banners, badges, posters, color-coded ribbons, pageantry, and above all themselves to make their cause visible. The Artists' Suffrage League and the Suffrage Atelier marshaled the efforts of dozens and sometimes hundreds of stitchers to create more than 150 new banners emblazoned with mottos like "Better Wisdom Than

Weapons of War" (fig. 46).[2] Wielding these emblems, women marched through the streets of London: 3,000 in 1907, between 10,000 and 15,000 in 1908, 30,000 again in 1908, 40,000 in 1911.[3] For the first time organized groups of women took control of images to create a public political identity for themselves.

Julia Margaret Cameron's 1867 photograph of Mrs. Herbert Duckworth (fig. 47) sums up the artistic legacy left to us by the women of the nineteenth century. Cameron, like so many aspiring women in the arts, had enormous talent and virtually no professional training; she forged a short but energetic career in a marginal field that allowed her to reconcile family obligations with aesthetic ambitions, to work at home and use for her subjects local inhabitants, friends, and family members like her niece Julia (Prinsep) Duckworth. To Julia's daughter Virginia Woolf, Cameron seemed both an eccentric and a role model. Woolf drafted a comedy about her great-aunt, but she also re-edited Cameron's photographs for the first time since her death. *Victorian Photographs of Famous Men and Fair Women* appeared in 1926 with an introduction by Woolf. So many introductions to women's art still wait to be written.

three

The Civil Woman, Public and Private

Family Is Women's Work

The redefinition of the political in the nineteenth century had as its corollary a particularly thorough redefinition of civil society. Theorists (mainly English-speaking) and organizers distinguished between "public" and "private" and attempted to equate each "sphere" with each sex. Despite their efforts, however, spheres and sexes intersected and overlapped, their boundaries vague and fluctuating. The public sphere was not entirely masculine; the private was not entirely feminine. Women went about in public, and thanks to the salon homes remained open to the outside world. Nor were men absent from the private sphere: the powers of the father weighed on the family. The "civil woman" was at once public and private, at home in the city, in the family, and in society. One must therefore be careful to avoid the pitfalls of discourse and deconstruct the traditional stereotypes.

Body, heart, sexuality, work, solitude—these terms denote cross-sections of the social tissue. A woman's body is at once public and private. Images being important, appearances—beauty, carriage, clothing—were an issue. The women of what Veblen called the "leisure class," whether aristocratic or bourgeois, were dedicated to society's theater, a substitute for the courts of a bygone era and governed, as they were themselves, by a confining etiquette, that of fashion. The apparel industry was feminine through and through, from production to consumption, and no doubt served as a vehicle for raising women's economic consciousness.

Because women bear children, their bodies are central to society's functioning. Birth became the business of the state. Physicians supplanted midwives at the bedsides of women in labor, while demographers peering into bedrooms suspected an insidious form of birth control in the practice of abortion by women who had already given birth to several children. Although the neo-Malthusians' call for "free maternity" still was not widely heeded, women seemed to want smaller and smaller families, and the demographic consequences of this desire now had to be reckoned with.

Of course the term "public woman" had a more sinister connotation as well. Indeed, prostitution was increasingly regulated in the name of hygiene and "purity of the race." Although men tried to build an unbreachable barrier between the marriage chamber and the bordello or "love nest," complete separation was impossible. Contraceptive techniques were learned in whorehouses. Sexually transmitted diseases were carried from the bawdy house to the home—by men. Prostitutes themselves were only temporary visitors in that domain, and many eagerly moved into normal family life if an opportunity arose. Yet the fortifications along the borders of respectability were strengthened toward the end of the nineteenth century, as "decent" women were increasingly segregated from those who were not.

Prostitutes were ambiguous figures even in the eyes of women, objects of fear and scorn but also of compassion and solidarity, symbols of a fancied freedom but also of a still greater oppression. "Purity" was the issue at one of the nineteenth century's biggest women's meetings, held in London in 1885 as women took to the streets to protest the contemptuous treatment of their sex. Thus it was through one of the most intimate aspects of their being that women acquired a public role.

Sex, their sex: women claimed something of sexuality for themselves, driven by a "will to know" yet hindered by age-old taboos. This was not to be the century of women's sexual "liberation." Lesbians lived inconspicuously, their sexual preference tolerated because it was little understood and scarcely even recognized (some called it "pseudo-homosexuality"). In any case it was considered much less scandalous than male homosexuality. Lesbians were therefore able to avoid trouble with the authorities and protect their privacy.

As for women's work, there is no hope of understanding it in isolation from the family. The family was crucial to the condition of the working woman, because her marital status and the number and age of her children determined her access to the labor market. The nature of women's work was not dramatically transformed by industrialization, which invaded the home, or by urbanization, which increased the opportunities for domestic labor. It was not until the second half of the nineteenth century, moreover, that women became by far the predominant group in domestic service. Political economists tried to define the characteristics of female labor and to find a basis in nature for the notions of "women's work" and "women's occupations." The sexual division of labor was, as we shall discover, a product of language as construed by economists, employers, and trade unions, and analysis of that language is therefore of the utmost importance. Sexual difference is frequently a social artifice.

The solitude of women is just as difficult to appreciate, given the many negative stereotypes that veiled the reality. Solitude is not a static condition but a constantly changing relation—to time, to others, to oneself. It can be a transitory experience, one that every woman knows at one time or another. The growing differential between the life expectancies of men and women meant more widows in an ever wider variety of situations, a subject worthy of study in its own right, along with the (gender-conscious) history of old age. Some forms of solitude are more extreme than others, however. The solitude of women who failed to realize their dreams was a far cry from that of women who chose independence, who preferred to pay the price of celibacy for the rewards of greater freedom (in French law, *la fille majeure,* literally, the "adult girl," a misnomer for a woman above the age of majority, was considered a man's equal).

Many other areas could be explored as well: money, social relations, or violence, for example. There is a need for comparative study of changes in marriage contracts and dowries, women's legal rights to manage businesses and household finances, and the part played by women in family businesses and strategies of inheritance.

Similarly, there is a need for a comprehensive survey of public spaces, especially in cities, for observations (like those made by nineteenth-century travelers such as Tocqueville, Flora Tristan, and Jules Vallès) of how men and women behaved together in public and how the desire to keep women segregated was constantly thwarted by their spontaneous movements. Were "feminized" salons still centers of female power? Were cafés as "masculine" as has been said?

Violence, whether endured or perpetrated by women in the family or in society, is an especially sensitive indicator of the persistence (or decline) of patriarchy. Incest, rape, sexual harassment in the workplace, "seduction by deception," the deliberate withholding of food, battering—all are signs of a physical oppression of women whose scope is difficult to measure.[1] Conversely, the constant talk of "criminal women," despite statistical evidence proving that fewer than 20 percent of all people accused of crimes were women, shows what fantasies fed fears of equality and rebellion. Alexandre Dumas associated *Women Who Kill and Women Who Vote* (1880), while urging needed reforms. Give them their rights, he hinted, or they will kill us![2] Even the extreme formulations of criminological discourse (yet another language to analyze) are revealing of sexual tension.

G.F.–M.P.

13

Bodies and Hearts

Yvonne Knibiehler

IN 1800 THE NEWLY fashionable item of furniture was a kind of mirror known as a "psyche," or cheval glass, which tilted so that one could examine oneself from head to toe. Now, *psyche* of course means "soul." Does the word hint at a new concept of female identity, one that incorporated the whole of a woman's body? Not yet. The women of the nineteenth century, most of whom were believers if not actually religious, were taught that the body is the enemy of the soul, the major impediment on the road to salvation. And in any case the female body, so often incapacitated by pregnancy, childbirth, and breastfeeding, was literally the incarnation of woman's alienated existence as servant to the species. How could women identify with *that?*

By contrast, the heart was central to female identity. On this point secular society and religion agreed. Anthropologists and physicians taught that the sensibility, the emotions, and the instincts with which women were richly endowed were the source of qualities indispensable to the proper functioning of society. Veneration of the Sacred Heart of Jesus became remarkably widespread in Catholic countries. The iconography of this cult featured Christ with an open chest, inside which lay a heart also rent by a deep gash: these were symbols of a direct and intense communication or communion that involved not reason or science but the miracle of love.[1]

In the meantime progress in hygiene was beginning to firm up the contours of a previously vague and fragmented body image. There were new ways to take care of the body, whose functional priorities were altered by a declining birth rate. High culture influenced the education of women and tended to supplant more personal forms of learning. Slowly but steadily—and ever so discreetly—women's consciousness began to drift away from its traditional moorings.

Body

While the body inspired little discourse, beauty regained its prestige in the aftermath of the revolutionary crisis.[2] Whereas Christian moralists had been suspicious of beauty, Enlightenment naturalism had rehabilitated it. Not only was beauty a useful inducement to the procreative act, it was also the intrinsic, and legitimate, weapon of the weaker sex, with which it might hope to tame the stronger. To do this, however, it was obliged to assert its difference. Sexual dimorphism thus asserted itself as a dogma, to the detriment of individual morphologies. Positive value was ascribed to anything that signified sensibility and delicacy: skin so fine that it revealed the ramifications of the nerves, soft flesh to cradle an infant or a sufferer, a slight frame, tiny hands, small feet. But value was also ascribed to signs of the natural reproductive functions: round hips, ample breasts, well-fed flesh.

The Social Definition: Beauty's New Functions

For a woman to look mannish was to look freakish. This accounts for the durable success of the corset, which made a comeback in 1810. The new corset was not as high or as stiff as the old whalebone model, and its mission was now aesthetic: to make the waist slender and push out the backside and bosom. Furthermore, the corset enabled the "proper" woman to be at all times in control of her shape and posture. It served as tutor to her dignity, physical as well as moral. Yet durability did not mean constancy of form, as evidenced by two stars of international renown: on the threshold of the nineteenth century stood the resplendent figure of the fine, white, and chaste Juliette Récamier, while that continuing spectacle of opulent sensuality, the Comtesse de Castiglione, enjoyed a long run in later decades.

The Romantics dreamed of an ethereal woman, and the opera's talented ballerinas aptly filled the bill. Dancing on "points," a newly invented technique, thinned the silhouette and permitted flights of aerial weightlessness. Ballets such as *La Sylphide* (1832) and *Giselle* (1841) temporarily divested women of the burden of flesh. The heroines of novels were slender and delicate. Their faces, mirroring their souls, expressed inner tempests. A languid pallor, if possible accentuated by black hair, dark circles around the eyes, and clouds of rice powder, symbolized the sufferings of the romantic self.

By mid-century good health was back in vogue. Décolleté evening gowns displayed full figures in all their milky voluptuousness. Women threw out their chests and straightened their backbones so as to delight male eyes with the spectacle of a full bust or a breathtaking small-of-the-back: curvature of the spine became endemic in the weaker sex. Even after pallor went out of fashion, a clear complexion remained an unquestionable criterion of beauty. Ladies sought to preserve a nacreous, pearly-white flesh tone, proof that they did not go out much and loved the indoors. Along with roundness of form and whiteness of skin, abundant and lustrous hair connoted beauty. Long "English" curls into which one could slip a finger were fashionable, as were bouffant loops, thick hairbands, and heavy buns—prosthetics were permitted in the quest for an abundant coif. Poor peasant women could thus earn a bit of money by selling their hair, a cruel sacrifice and inevitably a hard blow to bear, especially for husbands. Hair was not washed for fear of colds, but it was lavishly brushed. Its scent was supposed to drive men wild. But olfactory sensibilities grew more squeamish. The emanations of the female body, long considered aphrodisiac (according to Michelet), now began to inspire repugnance, perhaps because of urban crowding, perhaps because of ever greater sophistication in amorous relations. The popularity of eau de cologne increased steadily.

The collapse of privilege after the Revolution enforced austere sobriety in men's dress. Ambitious men demonstrated their success or their pretensions on the bodies of wives and mistresses, whose looks and finery were meant to impress. Perhaps never before in history had women wrapped themselves in such quantities of fabric. Gowns, still tight and tubular during the First Empire, grew ever more ample down to the Age of Crinoline (1854–1868): in those days a skirt might measure ten feet in diameter and require more than thirty yards of fabric. An imposing idol, madame kept her entire entourage at a distance. It was difficult for her to move or sit. Going to the ladies' room required the assistance of a maidservant. Later, these vestimentary monuments were supplanted by tournures, trains, and bustles, which called attention to the figure with humor and elegance. Waistline heights, sleeve shapes, and necklines now varied from one season to the next. Fashion accelerated the production of the ephemeral in order to forestall any possibility of democratization. In this game great ladies allowed themselves to be outdone by demimondaines: of course restraint then became the sign of true elegance and authentic distinction.

An important innovation occurred when men moved into the fashion industry. Leroy had managed to make his mark during the First Empire, but the true father of *haute couture* was Worth. It was he who first thought of using live models and having them march past onlookers in a parade of elegance. And it was he who encouraged the manufacture of iridescent fabrics and gracious ornaments to add that personal touch to a woman's toilette. His enchanting creations and staggering bills were as celebrated as his arrogance: in his establishment even the greatest ladies cooled their heels in the waiting room.

Despite the new design establishments, independent seamstresses still had some fine days ahead of them, and their numbers grew beyond counting. Their livelihood was threatened from another quarter, however: the ready-to-wear industry, which transformed the way women dressed. At the beginning of the century many items of clothing and trinkets passed from one class to another: that redoubtable temptress and occasional go-between, the *marchande à la toilette,* purchased used dresses, capes, bonnets, and nightgowns and then sold them to young coquettes. Later, however, department stores—an innovation—began to sell the same items new and ready to wear. Spacious, well lit, with racks of clothes that one could see, feel, and try on, these stores offered women a veritable feast for the eyes, as well as for the fingers and the imagination—a new source of happiness. Shopping, now full of surprises and temptations, became even more exciting as prices fell. Modest middle- and even working-class women experienced the euphoria of a hitherto unimaginable range of choice. A woman who used to wear the same blue or gray dress for ten years could now afford to buy several calico dresses in a variety of colors every year.

The new vogue met with some resistance, however. The countryside had long remained untouched by urban fashions. To be sure, the prosperity that rural areas enjoyed after 1850 found expression in handsome finery, but vernacular costumes were the first to benefit. The most picturesque of these flourished in Holland, Bavaria, Alsace, Britanny, and the area around Arles. Conventions and traditions were represented by a complex code: forms, colors, dimensions, hair ornaments, scarves, aprons, skirts—all were signs. Suddenly, after 1880, within the space of a few years, the regional costumes vanished or suffered the indignity of being turned into "folklore."

Religious costumes survived longer.[3] People were amazed by the innovative attire of the new orders, of which there were many. Incredible attention was paid to such details as cornets, veils, hairbands, collars, scapulars, sleeves and cuffs, colors and fabrics. Here, clothing was a mystical symbol, each item expressing the spirit of penitence. In an age when many women still did not know how to read, a nun's habit conveyed a lesson more powerful than mere words: it expressed the body, its duties, its destiny.

Clothing also expressed innocence. Brides now dressed in white, at least in the city. The first communion dress was white. And so was the transparent muslin of the first ball gown, which veiled a still intact chastity. A maiden was a lily, a dove: her fresh innocence was like the spring. She had no right to luxury: modesty was her lot. But her mother's sumptuous display made marriage seem like a blossoming to come, a flourishing of beauty as well as attire.[4] Dress also emphasized the stages of growth, the formation of the personality. A young lady's skirt scraped the ground, and she wore her hair elaborately done up. A slightly younger girl, in the throes of puberty, might braid her hair or wear it in a net, while her hemline descended no further than her ankles. A very young girl, under the "age of reason," wore her hair loose. Her dress might allow a glimpse of her boots and even her drawers. In the works of writers like the Comtesse de Ségur and Lewis Carroll little girls appeared as powerful figures. Sophie at age four was already a rebel, and Alice passed through the looking glass to discover Wonderland on her own.[5]

The strange fate of women's trousers is worth pondering: what was taboo at the beginning of the century had by the end mutated into an unmentionable undergarment (pants into panties, to put it slightly anachronistically). True, the taboo never did stop some women from dressing as men, whether for convenience (Mme Marbouty was delighted to disguise herself as a man in order to accompany Balzac to Turin in 1836) or in a spirit of emancipation (as in the case of George Sand, separated from her husband, or the Vésuviennes in 1848). But these were exceptions that prove the rule. Meanwhile, the foundational knicker gained favor. Opera dancers were required to wear bloomers for decency's sake (this was the origin of the "tutu"), and so, later on, did active little girls. Prostitutes first took to them in a big way in the 1820s. Matrons began wearing drawers when the crinoline frame pushed skirts and petticoats away from the body, allowing too much air to reach the area between corset and garters. But was it necessary, in covering this area, to part the thighs and block off the vagina? If panties triumphed, it was primarily as a symbol: the battle over who would "wear the pants," an enduring theme of popular imagery, suggests the importance of what was at stake. The female undergarment became at once "indispensable" and "unmentionable": it could not be named because of what it suggested. At this time the thighs and indeed even the legs were considered indecent. Victorian prudery went so far as to clothe the legs of tables. Was it an accident that the famous "French cancan" of the Belle Epoque, that impertinent expression of a counter-culture, exhibited a profusion of legs, legs, legs, kicking wildly?

Bloomers, slips, under-bodices, lace *canezous,* petticoats, camisoles, tuckers, chemisettes, and other dainties: the period witnessed an extraordinary proliferation of female undergarments. The mechanization of the textile industry and the fall in the price of cotton goods can only partially account for this phenomenon. The almost neurotic need to cover up, wrap, and hide may suggest a search for new rules of amorous exchange, a desire to honor both modesty and eroticism in the context of a slower, gentler, more tender coming together of male and female. Is it necessary to add that such *froufrous* were luxuries inaccessible to the majority of women, who made do with slips and petticoats cut from old dresses and did not wear bloomers until the First World War? The orphans of the Bon Pasteur had no linen at all in 1903: they were given one plain-woven skirt, which was washed only once every three months even if soiled by "accidents of the female organs."

A pillow dolled up with lace, sheets artfully embroidered: these, too, were articles that enhanced a lady's beauty. On them she would experience the excitement of the wedding night and the birth of her children. Along with a woman's body linen, her household linen accompanied her and served her in her feminine duties, in bed, at the dressing table, and while dining. This was why the bride's trousseau was such a valuable possession, a personal treasure, an inalienable fortune. Assembling the trousseau marked an important stage in a girl's upbringing: she learned not just the skills of needlework but how to sit still and toil patiently, and as she did she meditated at length on the body and its various parts and functions. Between puberty and marriage a girl "marked" her linen by embroidering it with her initials, surrounded by ever more elaborate motifs. Lovingly kept but little used, the set retained memories of a woman's virginal years, almost a symbol of autonomy. The trousseau was particularly important in southern Europe (the south of France, Spain, and Italy), where women were kept on the tightest rein. Was it perhaps a naïve, stubborn expression of an inexpugnable narcissism?[6]

The linen maker, the corset maker, and the laundress understood, shared, and flattered this love of fine, immaculate linen. Because of their professions these women enjoyed the right to see their clients' bodies and share their intimacy. Aware of many secrets, they established a discreet complicity with the women they served that transcended social differences. Countless women practiced these trades; many earned a good living and were proud of it, like Gervaise in Zola's *L'Assommoir.*

At the turn of the twentieth century the appearance of the female body was again radically transformed. One couturier, Poiret, dared to get rid of the corset in 1905. His discreetly elegant gowns were smooth and fluid and tailored to reveal slim figures to good advantage. Meanwhile, the American dancer Isadora Duncan relegated the tutu and the ballet slipper to the scrap heap by dancing barefoot and wearing tunics reminiscent of ancient Greece. Her quick success and enormous prestige suggest that many women secretly craved emancipation.

When the volumes of textile that had swollen the female body collapsed, the result was not merely a change of fashion but a cultural revolution. Some saw it as "the collapse of beauty." In a more lucid vein Zola wrote: "The idea of beauty is changing. You are vesting it in sterility, in long, slender figures with shrunken flanks."[7] The whole century had been moving unwittingly toward this change. But as the fertility of the reproductive agent diminished, she became the focus of ever more attentive gazes.

The Biological Definition: Medicalization

"Pregnant woman must become an object of active concern, religious respect, and a kind of veneration," Dr. Marc wrote in 1816.[8] This concern focused primarily on the fetus, but it also benefited the woman who carried it. Marc proposed measures that tell us a great deal about the lives of women in need of protection. He hoped to curtail the violence so prevalent in the lower classes. Many abortions stemmed from the brutal behavior of drunken husbands. The doctor also proposed exempting women from hard physical labor, of which he provided a horrifying description. These ideas began to catch on, yet the consequences for the intended beneficiaries were not all positive: Marc and others like him sought to protect women from themselves by strictly supervising all their activities and limiting their amusements: swings and waltzes were to be avoided, for example. Paternalistic physicians dreamed of transforming pregnancy into a kind of supervised asceticism. Despite these early initiatives, protection for future mothers was not formally codified until the end of the century, when new labor laws were adopted.[9]

Meanwhile, in response to Victorian prudishness, pregnancy became taboo: a woman who found herself in this "interesting condition" stayed home so as to be seen as little as possible. An analogous taboo applied to childbirth: in Alsace the newborn was said to be brought by the stork, elsewhere to be found under a cabbage or delivered by the midwife. The point was of course to deny or at any rate to mask the animality of the human species. Meanwhile, pregnant prostitutes were particularly sought after by the customers of brothels.

The medicalization of childbirth, which began in the eighteenth century, became widespread in the nineteenth. Since doctors were paid three or four times as much as midwives, employing the services of a physician was a sign of wealth. Mothers of humbler background continued to rely on midwives, while the very poorest went to hospitals. Geographical differences in childbearing customs often reflect economic differences. In London in 1892, half the women who gave birth in the poor East End used midwives, but only 2 percent of those in the West End did so. In Boston practically all obstetrical practice was in the hands of men by 1820.[10]

It is by no means certain that the involvement of doctors reduced mortality (prior to 1870). In Rouen, where the degree of medicalization was high but the poor lived in crowded slums, the maternal mortality rate remained steady at around 11 percent. In Utah, where midwives still went by the old rules of thumb, the losses were about 6 percent, but the setting was one of wide-open spaces surrounded by lofty mountain peaks, the ideal anti-epidemic environment.[11]

Nor is it clear that doctors reduced suffering. Anesthesia with ether or chloroform, first tried in the late 1840s, was soon much sought after despite the Christian belief that Eve's daughters ought to accept their suffering and treat it as an offering. Queen Victoria asked for chloroform in giving birth to her eighth child in 1853. But physicians were reluctant to use anesthesia owing to the possible adverse consequences. When Empress Eugénie went through a very difficult delivery in 1856, she refused the solace of ether—but she never had another child. Midwives charged that doctors lacked patience and were too quick to resort to forceps.

Major progress in obstetrics came not in the homes of birth mothers but in hospitals, which were used only by women in the most wretched circumstances. Everyone agreed that it was indecent, almost inconceivable, for a child to be born anywhere but in the home of its parents. Nevertheless, steps were taken early in the century to provide services for these impoverished mothers. In the best of cases, new facilities were created, such as the Port-Royal maternity hospital in Paris, opened in 1794. At a minimum, hospitals set aside one or more special wards for maternity cases. Statistics compiled with some regularity after 1850 indicate that mortality rates in these institutions remained very high, between 10 and 20 percent. Part of the reason for the high death rate was that many mothers who sought hospital deliveries suffered from rickets or tuberculosis and were very frightened. But the primary cause of death was puerperal fever transmitted by attending physicians and their students, who moved from autopsies right on to vaginal examinations without precautions of any kind. The Austrian physician Semmelweiss, who in the 1840s suspected the cause of the infection, reduced the mortality rate in his clinic by insisting that his subordinates wash their hands. In France, Tarnier was one of the first to improve the practice of obstetrics. But real progress came only after hospitals throughout western Europe and America instituted antiseptic practices between 1870 and 1900. By the end of that period maternal mortality had dropped to around two percent. Then and only then did it become safer to give birth in a hospital than at home. Progress in suturing, moreover, opened the way to an audacious new surgical operation: the cesarean section became common after the turn of the century.

In the meantime, midwives saw their practices dwindle. As private midwifery became financially unfeasible, midwives took jobs as salaried employees of hospitals and private clinics. There they found themselves in subordinate positions, taking orders from now all-powerful doctors and no longer free to respond to women's needs. A traditional form of female solidarity thus collapsed, and women forfeited all autonomy in the area of reproduction. The fact that the barriers of modesty folded so quickly is perhaps the best proof that their origin was cultural rather than "natural." Henceforth the woman who wanted a child turned not to her husband but to her doctor, the new "natural" protector.

Midwives were not the only victims of medical progress. Other traditional caretakers saw their knowledge and skills discredited. In the post-Pasteurian age nuns, visiting nurses, and healers became doctors' subordinates and even servants, though in England and America nurses still managed to retain some autonomy thanks to the energetic efforts of women such as Florence Nightingale. True, women themselves eventually also became physicians and thus returned to medical practice in positions of authority, but their access to the profession was a long time coming. Viewed with suspicion by their male colleagues, women students traded docility for acceptance and eschewed posts of initiative and responsibility. Hence they were, with few exceptions, unable to influence the evolution of women's medicine.[12]

Nineteenth-century women were perpetual patients. Enlightenment medicine had presented the stages of a woman's life as a series of terrible crises, even in the absence of any pathology. Along with pregnancy and childbirth, puberty and menopause had come to be seen as more or less dangerous ordeals, and the menstrual flow that emanated from a "wound" in the ovaries was said to pose a threat to a woman's nervous equilibrium. All available statistics concur that women in the nineteenth century suffered much higher rates of morbidity and mortality than did men.[13] Popular opinion as well as medical experts blamed the "weakness" of "feminine nature." This, the allegedly universal and eternal biological "cause" of women's suffering, was apt to encourage abject fatalism. Yet the fact was that girls and women became ill because of the wretched conditions in which they were forced to live. Few physicians at the time knew how to take social factors into account, however.

"Girls are the most delicate and sickly element of the human race," Dr. Virey declared in 1817.[14] Excessively high female mortality from the age of five on was in fact a glaring problem in all Western countries. Already evident in the eighteenth century, the problem grew worse between 1840 and 1860, particularly, it seems, in France and Belgium.[15]

"Phthisis" (a term that encompassed wasting consumption of all kinds, primarily pulmonary tuberculosis) was the most deadly of diseases. In Belgium it accounted for 20 percent of all deaths among girls between the ages of seven and fifteen and 40 percent of deaths of those between fifteen and twenty-one. Girls were twice as likely to succumb as boys. Doctors who treated wealthy families found it hard to understand why pampered and coddled young women were so vulnerable to the disease. True, urbanization abetted contagion. But the best physicians, including the great Laennec, were equally suspicious of emotional suffering, disappointment, and heartache. The case of the Brontë sisters argued in favor of this theory. Was it an accident that tuberculosis was the romantic malady *par excellence?* Sorrow and disappointment, depression, and disgust with life were themselves consequences of more general conditions: from birth daughters were less welcome than sons. Consciously or not, parents neglected them. A tenacious prejudice, shared by Michelet, excluded meat, particularly red meat, from girls' diets. The principles of proper upbringing required young women to be confined inside dark apartments, deprived of fresh air, sunshine, and exercise, and required to devote long hours to needlework. In more modest homes even very young girls were required to do domestic chores, often quite draining ones. Some spent long days in the fields, factory, or workshop.

Tuberculosis also numbered among the factors contributing to maternal mortality, and it was frequently a consequence of the way the mothers were raised as girls. Rickets, another contributor, was also a common consequence of an impoverished background. Poor women tended to have very narrow pelvic girdles, which complicated delivery. But even young girls suffered from disorders affecting the spinal column: words such as scoliosis, kyphosis, and lordosis entered the medical vocabulary at this time. When girls with such deformities matured and married, these conditions complicated their pregnancies.

Diseases of the genital organs were also significant. Physicians knew little about them, because they did not dare require prudish patients to submit to vaginal examinations. In any case many doctors believed that metritis (inflammation of the uterus) was an inevitable, universal condition. Doctors, though not unaware of venereal disease, showed little interest in the subject: "Husbands and wives share the pox as they share their daily bread."[16] The chaste wife, the usual victim of this "sharing," was often kept in ignorance of her disease for the sake of family harmony. Doctors would not treat the condition without authorization from the husband, because to treat it would be to reveal the secret cause of the disease. We will never know how many young wives, married to safeguard their well-being, were sacrificed in this way to male collusion. But regardless of background not all women were dupes or resigned to their fate. Two examples will suffice: Cristina Trivulzio, Princess Belgiojoso, a wealthy Lombard aristocrat, and Suzanne Voilquin, a Parisian embroiderer, whose lives were dramatically transformed when they were forced to confront the ordeal of venereal disease. Both women obtained amicable separations from their polluting husbands, and both became experts on the subject. Cristina, who suffered from horrible neuralgia, gained an extensive knowledge of contemporary medications with which she was then able to treat relatives and friends. During the siege of Rome in 1849 she organized and directed the city's hospitals and clinics with an efficiency that compelled the admiration of all. Suzanne trained in homeopathic medicine with Dr. Hahnemann. Later, in Cairo, where she had gone to join Saint-Simonian friends, she dressed as a man in order to take courses in a hospital. After earning certification as a midwife, she practiced in France and Russia. Toward the end of the century, when the specter of syphilis haunted all Europe, doctors at last obtained the right to treat even the most respectable matrons.

It was also generally accepted that all women had been, were, or someday would be subject to "nervous disorders." At a time when rural quiet still inspired an anxious nostalgia, doctors were quick to blame urban life, which did indeed affect the status, functions, and living conditions of the wife and mother. Some were irritated by the "dolls with migraines" who defied all attempts at therapy. The malady belonged to that mysterious class of incapacitating afflictions that could be simulated or cultivated. To what extent did migraines serve as a refuge or pretext for disappointed or overwrought women? To what extent did they point to painful crises of identity or conscience? During menopause the Comtesse de Ségur experienced a debilitating series of headaches followed by lethargy. Her cure coincided with her début as a writer.[17] But in the north of France migraines forced Mme Vrau-Aubineau to abandon her work in industry, and she would suffer from terrible headaches for the rest of her life.[18]

Far more than migraine, however, hysteria was the quintessential malady of the weaker sex. Some looked upon it as inherent in the "female nature." Indeed, this pathology was disturbing not only to families but also to society and even medical science. Everyone suffered, everyone endured this terrible affliction in one way or another. Afraid of provoking a crisis, relatives treated the patient with the utmost care; victims thereby obtained gratifying attention and, in some cases, discretionary authority. Hysteria at times seemed contagious: there were impressive collective breakdowns, for example in Morzine between 1857 and 1873. Girls and women screamed, writhed, shouted insults, battered fathers and husbands, drank alcohol, and refused to work. Alarmed, the authorities launched a veritable crusade to rescue an entire rural population from isolation and misery: they built roads, installed a garrison, and organized dances. The theatrical displays of hysterical patients at the Salpêtrière from 1863–1893 provoked, exhibited, and intensified the victims' anguish and suffering. They also revealed the medical profession's fascination with the disease. Freud was the first who really tried to listen to what these unfortunate women were saying—and to let them talk about themselves indefinitely.

Doctors enjoyed a growing audience throughout the century, especially after Pasteur, and the values they championed gained ground. The naturalist Enlightenment had already held that hygiene is the true morality, the one that protects the body from disease and the soul from vice. But progress in hygiene was impeded by two obstacles. Modesty was one: excessive enjoyment in washing one's body, particularly its most intimate parts, was regarded as dangerously libertine; better to change one's linen. The absence of running water and sewers was the other. The face and hands could be washed (nearly) every day in a basin, the rest of the body at most once a week. Showers and baths were for a long time limited to the sick (hydrotherapy). Women fortunate enough to have a bathtub bathed once a month, after their period. Invented in England, the tub gained popularity on the Continent toward the end of the century. In the work of Degas and others we see how the custom of washing the body in copious quantities of water transformed the representation of the female nude: the woman at her toilette became almost a cliché subject.

Good hygiene also called for exercise and fresh air. Such a prescription was a terrible problem for women, whose skin was supposed to remain immaculate. Nevertheless, as early as the 1820s, Marie de Flavigny (the future Comtesse d'Agoult) employed the services of a "master of graces" (that is, a dance instructor with a rather inflated sense of his importance) and a (female) fencing teacher who taught her to use the foil. She often rode horseback. The curricula of girls' boarding schools changed. The "posture classes" that taught girls to carry themselves correctly at all hours of the day and in all phases of life gradually gave way in the early 1880s to training in gymnastics, which was practiced without a corset and with the aid of various kinds of equipment. The intention now was not so much to promote women's freedom as to make them more vigorous and energetic, often in a nationalist, not to say racist, spirit.

The crusade for girls' gymnastics began in Germany and England and conquered Latin Europe at the end of the century. It sparked fanatic enthusiasm in certain quarters—witness a wicked and sensual novel by Edmondo de Amicis.[19] Women's sports, especially competitive sports, aroused greater resistance and in some cases violent hostility. Observers were critical of women who, they said, made themselves ugly through exertion. They claimed to miss the grace that went along with feebleness and expressed fears that muscular overdevelopment might prove harmful in later childbearing. Nevertheless, swimming and tennis soon caught on with upper-class women.[20] Various associations promoted cycling and track and field at the other end of the social spectrum. And despite the objections of Pierre de Coubertin, women participated in the 1912 Olympics.

In the meantime, doctors, invoking the battle against syphilis, vehemently urged that the sexual education of young women be entrusted to them. Properly instructed, young women would be better equipped to resist seduction and could ask prospective husbands for evidence of sound health. Instruction manuals were published. But it was already something of a revolution that women had acquired the right to protect their own bodies. Gaining the right to scrutinize the bodies of men would have to wait.

Bodies or Hearts?

The "relation between man's physical and moral condition" had been of great concern to Enlightenment physicians.[21] Were conjugal and maternal love, on which society depended for its very existence, noble sentiments inscribed for all eternity in the female soul? Or were they merely uncertain, perhaps deficient, products of a womb keen to fill a void with sperm and a fetus? Between bodies and hearts the relation remained mysterious. Did the changes that transformed the social and familial roles of the weaker sex over the course of the century help clarify or modify that relation? How did relations between woman and man and between woman and man's offspring evolve?

The Sex of Angels

During the 1840s the word "frigidity" began to be used to refer to lack of sexual appetite in women. In fact, the Victorian era witnessed the birth of a literature that denied the very existence of such an appetite. We know, for example, that Michelet never managed to elicit a "shudder" from Athenaïs, who was content to be an object of desire and to eat and sleep well—that was the extent of her sensuality. Now that arousing one's wife had become a problem, Dr. Debay, an army doctor and unblinking realist, wrote a book detailing various ways of stimulating a woman; it went through a hundred editions between 1848 and 1888.[22] But another doctor, William Acton, whose works were widely read in England and America, argued that women's sexual needs were fully satisfied by childbearing and domestic life.[23] He contributed greatly to the definition of "true womanhood" and the separation of the "two spheres."

Victorian moralism, it is well to remember, disapproved of sex in general. The same Acton urged gentlemen to limit their sexual activity. Intercourse once every seven to ten days was enough.

Some French physicians shared this view. Most doctors recommended rapid coitus so as to save the man's energy, advice that could hardly have been conducive to simultaneous orgasm. Furthermore, the science of ovology, which flourished from 1840 to 1860, established that the female orgasm was not necessary to fertilization. This discovery confirmed woman's maternal vocation, justified male selfishness, and provided grounds for hostility to the useless clitoris.[24] In short, a number of factors conspired to promote a new conception of sexual relations. Its principles are quickly stated: men must conserve their energy for productive labor; women must devote themselves to maternal and domestic chores; small families are best. For women, the determining factor was not sexual desire but the constraints they lived under.

Elizabeth Blackwell, who in 1845 became the first female physician in the United States, held that frigidity was in the first place a product of upbringing: girls were taught that thinking about sex was sinful in order to keep them virginal until marriage.[25] Indeed, a girl was not a "natural" creature: although most attained puberty between the ages of twelve and fifteen, few married before they were twenty. This socially imposed postponement of childbearing was contrary to nature. To keep young girls waiting without resorting to coercive measures, the best course was to postpone the awakening of desire by concealing the carnal realities of sex. A "pure" girl knew nothing and suspected nothing. In this respect, virginity was not primarily a Christian virtue, and in any case freethinking fathers and husbands were as keen on purity as the most pious of men: it was a label, a guarantee with which to entice a future husband.

Strict principles therefore governed the upbringing of young girls, for which mothers assumed responsibility. Handbooks recommended the proper dietary regimen (bland dishes, milk at night) and sleep hygiene (bed not too soft, early rising). Masturbation was difficult to prevent. Doctors claimed that it was more widespread among girls than among boys. One militant for Social Purity, an ardent champion of chastity, was horrified to discover, upon reading a pamphlet denouncing the "solitary vice," that she had been practicing it for years in all innocence.[26] A well-bred young lady wore a chemise while grooming and even while bathing; when changing she closed her eyes.

At the approach of menstruation a girl's mother was supposed to warn her what was about to happen. Even priests urged this course of action: the *Hail Mary* ("Jesus, fruit of your womb") could be used to stimulate the child's interest, and mothers could then explain that the monthly period served as a reminder of a woman's true destiny. How many mothers dared to speak? Madeleine Pelletier, who was born into a family of modest background, recounts that one day when she was twelve (the year was 1886), she arrived at school in a state of anxiety with a bloodstained skirt. After being reprimanded by a nun, she returned home, where her mother, an unbending prig, refused to answer her questions. In the end, it was her invalid father who in a few brusque sentences imparted what little sexual education she received.[27] Madeleine grew up to be a doctor but could never suffer a man to come near her. Similar circumstances no doubt account for certain religious vocations. Should we be surprised? Mothers brought up to despise their bodies and to be ashamed of their sexuality could hardly be expected to teach anything other than blind, rote passivity. Many girls had no idea what awaited them on the wedding night. Mothers were silent on this score as well. Perhaps they were afraid of inspiring distaste for the sexual act by describing it in words, divorced from the sensations and caresses that made it bearable. Such fears were not idle: Zélie Guérin, the mother of the future Saint Teresa of Lisieux, wanted many children but was shocked to learn what she would have to go through. Her husband, an understanding man, waited several months before consummating the marriage.

An effort was made nonetheless to awaken the "maternal instinct." Joséphine de Gaulle, the general's grandmother and the author of many children's books, suggested allowing adolescent girls to raise a kitten or puppy. Older girls could become godmothers ("spiritual mothers," they were told) and participate in the moral upbringing of their godchild. But the doll became the instrument of choice for teaching mothering. Dolls quickly caught on, even as their nature changed radically. At the beginning of the century dolls represented elegant ladies, as if to inspire the girls who played with them to turn into beautiful women when they grew up. Around 1850 manufacturers began turning out infant dolls, which met with instant success. These babies, with which little girls "played mama," had no sexual organs (and did not acquire any until after World War II).

For "innocent" girls modesty became second nature, something of which the "silly little geese" were not even aware. Emphasis on this angelic ideal was heightened around mid-century, but not everyone accepted it totally. In the countryside, where anyone could see animals coupling and giving birth, it was difficult to preserve a girl's innocence. Rites and festivals of pagan origin contributed to the awakening of sexuality. In Provence at carnival time boys chased girls and smeared mud on their breasts and thighs.[28] In central and western France there were so-called girl fairs *(foires aux filles)*.[29] And even if rural society exercised its own forms of control on young people, fraternization between the sexes was fairly free. In the Vendean marshes lovers nestled together beneath huge umbrellas and their families put up with it. They exchanged long kisses and indulged in mutual masturbation. Some girls were curious enough to try several swains. When the Church attempted to impose its idea of virtue late in the century, it met with considerable resistance. Among the urban lower classes premarital relations appear to have been common.[30]

In the United States at the height of the Victorian era flirting was freely practiced. Such liberated ways surprised European visitors, from Tocqueville (in the 1830s) to Mlle Marie Dugard (who represented French secondary school teachers at the Chicago World's Fair in 1893).[31] Girls went out without chaperones with boys of their own choosing and returned home late at night. Private diaries and letters reveal what pleasure they took in being kissed and caressed, and they were by no means bashful about returning the favor.[32] Flirting with twenty boys would not stand in the way of a girl's later marrying and making an excellent wife.

Even in the most priggish segments of old-world society, well-bred young ladies were not required to avoid all contact with men. There were balls, for instance. *Quadrilles* and *contredanses* mimicked the stages of love: meeting, separation, return. Only the hands or fingertips touched. But the waltz opened up a new world of emotions and sensations. Wrapped in each other's arms, the partners whirled about, their bodies touching, in a swirl of rhythm, vertiginous intimacy, celebration, and sensual excitement. Some young ladies also enjoyed the benefit of an improvised education acquired with the help of servants or gleaned from forbidden books.[33] Louise Weiss went down every night to her father's library to educate herself from dictionaries.[34] Even flirting is attested in France at the turn of the twentieth century.[35]

Silly goose or immaculate virgin, the young girl one day became a wife. Even if her wedding night went well, she soon met with new obstacles on the way to sexual fulfillment. Childbearing was by far the heaviest burden. Many women still believed that sexual relations during pregnancy and breastfeeding (a period of nearly two years) could harm the child. But more and more wives were determined to have fewer children. Fear of becoming pregnant inhibited desire at a time when people still believed that orgasm contributed to conception. For their part, some men, many of them English, called for contraception: for example, Thomas Malthus, Francis Place, Richard Carlyle, Charles Knowlton. Women, even feminists, were hesitant to express their views. In confidence, however, in letters and private diaries, they owned up to weariness and disgust with endless pregnancies. Queen Victoria was no champion of motherhood. Pregnant nine times, she endured each delivery as a cross to bear; it ruined her married life and consumed her freedom. Her horror of large families was widely shared in the upper classes of British society, prolific though they were.

Nevertheless, progress in contraception was slow, and differences between countries are hard to explain. The two leading countries were France, where there was a sharp decline in the birth rate as early as the 1790s, and the United States, where a similar decline occurred after 1800. Both were of course countries that had made revolutions and proclaimed their belief in the rights of man and individual liberty. It would be difficult to prove, however, that this was a decisive factor. The countries of northern Europe did not reduce their birth rates until after 1870, and those of southern Europe still later. One cannot argue that the decline was linked to industrialization, because it preceded industrialization in France and the United States. It cannot be said to correspond to a decline in infant mortality either, since this did not really go down significantly until after the Pasteurian revolution. Nor can it be associated with Protestant concern for freedom of conscience, since in France Catholics were in the majority. The behavior of the various social groups is just as puzzling. It was not the wealthy and cultivated upper classes that took the lead. In France the ladies of the aristocracy and grande bourgeoisie remained the most prolific mothers. Peasant women, reputed to be conservative, in some cases learned to control births very early (in the Aquitaine Basin, for example), whereas working-class women everywhere continued to give birth in large numbers, at least until child labor was outlawed. In the United States it was observed that women born in America had fewer children than did immigrants. Fertility rates in some groups increased after immigration: this was the case with women who emigrated from Brabant to Wisconsin between 1852 and 1856.[36] The decline in the birth rate is a complex phenomenon, involving a combination of economic, cultural, and psychological factors. Each case is special. One scarcely even dares to venture the tentative proposition that it was the middle classes that set the example.[37]

Not all birth control techniques were equivalent. The issue is not so much effectiveness as significance: how much initiative, responsibility, and freedom did a particular technique allow the woman? What power did women have over their own bodies? How much opportunity did they have for sexual pleasure?

The ancient method, based on late marriage, prolonged breast-feeding, and a high rate of celibacy, persisted in many rural areas (such as Ireland, the Iberian peninsula, and mountainous regions of France and Italy). But with the decline in the death rate it proved inadequate: to prevent overpopulation in the late nineteenth century, women would have had to wait until they were thirty-five to marry, or else 40 percent of them would have had to choose celibacy. In fact, in rural France in 1850, women married at around age twenty-five and only 13 percent remained celibate.

Some couples slept in separate bedrooms. Of course one had to be wealthy enough to afford the extra space. The effectiveness of this technique was beyond doubt, but the separation could prove frustrating. For whom? The man who "respected" his wife rarely hesitated to deceive her with a kept woman or (if tightfisted) with a servant. But what about the woman?

Middle-class husbands were more likely to try to avoid conception. Methods long known to libertines now made their way into respectable households. The various contraceptive devices enjoyed only late and limited success: condoms, diaphragms, and syringes would remain costly and inconvenient for some time to come. Sodomy and fellatio were invoked as grounds for separation, but the real extent of such practices is unknown. All signs are that the favored method almost everywhere was *coitus interruptus,* which was simple and cost nothing. The method, which required the man to maintain a difficult discipline, therefore depended primarily on his initiative. The logic was still that of patriarchy: the woman submitted passively to her "conjugal duty." Yet everything was somehow different: the man was seeking only his own pleasure, and in so doing he set an example for his companion that at least made her aware of the possibility. Furthermore, even if his only intention was to avoid the burden of supporting a large family, the husband who practiced *coitus interruptus* spared his wife's health and energy and preserved her freedom. He offered her a chance to live a different kind of life, free of maternal worries.

The Catholic clergy was slow to react, by which time the practice was regular and widespread. Why did the Church wait so long? Because after the Revolution it was primarily women who went to confession, and women did not spontaneously raise the issue and did not like to be questioned about it. Most women felt that they bore no responsibility in the matter, since they were simply acceding to their husband's wishes. Some confessed that they went along but claimed that they felt they were not sinning but only acting prudently. Priests did not insist: procreation was a man's affair. Physicians were quicker to protest and spoke more straightforwardly. Some worried about wives' frustrations, suggesting that women were not as frigid as many people believed. Dr. Bergeret, whose book, translated into English, was widely read, threatened "cheaters" with the gravest of diseases but did not manage to intimidate them.[38]

The use of contraceptive techniques resulted not in more widely spaced births but in an early halt to childbearing.[39] Women apparently did not wish to delay having children. They preferred to get this burdensome chore out of the way as soon as possible so as to enjoy more free time in a later, more personal phase of their lives.

Abortion is often portrayed as a practice employed mainly by women of the lower classes, but this picture is misleading. Although common in the lower classes, abortion was also sought by women from other segments of society. Lady Henrietta Stanley, for example, finding herself pregnant for the tenth time, induced a miscarriage by means of a purge, a very hot bath, and a long walk, whereupon she informed her husband, Lord Edward. And abortion was indeed practiced by women: women had always aborted themselves or helped one another when necessary and with no sense of guilt, since they were convinced that the fetus was not alive until it moved, that is, in the fourth month (as English and American laws appeared to concede).[40] Though ancient, however, abortion changed in character and significance owing to technical advances and the degree to which men became involved. Fuller knowledge of female anatomy and physiology made it possible to use methods less traumatic than the drugs and deliberate falls of an earlier period. Knitting needles were used to pierce the bag of waters. Later it became increasingly common to inject soapy water into the uterus. If precautions were taken to avoid infection, the risks were much smaller.[41] By 1910 the injection method was widespread: doctors and midwives offered their services almost openly. Whatever method was used, the number of abortions increased everywhere in the second half of the nineteenth century. Abortion was no longer the last resort of desperate victims of seduction or mothers of large families; it had become a method of birth control. A practice once private, discreet, and hidden within the world of women now became a commercial commodity in the world of men. In London the Chrimes brothers had no fewer than 10,000 clients in 1898.

The reaction that erupted late in the century is astonishing for its scope and vigor: it raised abortion to the rank of a major political issue. In the United States this followed the Civil War; in England it was not unrelated to the hardships of the Boer War; in France the desire for revenge against the Prussians after the defeat of 1870–71 was an indirect cause. After any war life is sacred. There is a tendency at such times to identify abortion with infanticide: the fetus, and even the embryo, become full-fledged human beings. This was indeed what Christian doctrine had always taught. But it was as if society now secularized this revelation, as if for the first time it had decided to confront its full consequences.

To return to the subject of female sexuality, abortion, which at the time was painful and on occasion mutilating, surely was not the best way to promote it. Police archives revealed that many women of the lower classes refused to do their "duty" when ordered to do so by their husbands, even at the risk of being beaten. Yet one woman masturbated while lying alongside the man she had just rejected.[42] These women explained that they wanted to avoid pregnancy or, in a few cases, venereal disease. As long as such impediments existed, how could eroticism find its way into the marriage bed?

American women, more determined than their European counterparts, launched a vigorous offensive in the 1880s and 90s.[43] In the hope perhaps of reducing the number of pregnancies, they called upon religion to mount an explicit challenge to sex roles and husbands' rights. The militants of Social Purity insisted that it was up to the woman to determine how often and when sexual relations would take place, since the doctrine of "two spheres" gave women all power in the private domain. Women, they claimed, did not experience less desire than men, but they knew how to control themselves, whereas men gave in too easily to their lust. What was the impact of this puritanical (not feminist) crusade? A study carried out by Dr. Clelia Mosher in 1892 suggests that a sort of compromise was reached: couples had intercourse on average twice a week, whereas men wanted it three times and women once.

Meanwhile, the decline in the birth rate began to transform the female sensibility. Although the angelic ideal of feminine behavior survived until the end of the century, sex was no longer considered shameful nor was marital love seen solely as a duty. Available for pleasure, the wife became not only a more responsive and active partner but also a more demanding one. This gave rise to a desire for intimacy in couples: despite protests from doctors, honeymoon travel quickly became fashionable because it allowed newlyweds to avoid indiscreet questions, broad allusions, and knowing smirks. The marriage chamber became an inviolable refuge. At the same time affection was now openly displayed: wives called husbands "dear" and kissed them in public. As marital relations became more refined, they yielded more intense pleasure, but fatigue and disappointment could also set in. No matter what the law said, the husband was no longer the lord and master and never would be again. He might become a lover—for better or for worse. There was also a marked change in maternal feelings. Childrearing now took precedence over childbearing: with fewer children mothers could pay more attention and show greater affection to each one. Mother and child lived in idyllic leisure.

Mother and Infant

Was the woman who breastfed a "female" or a mother? What role did animal instinct play, and what role human feeling? Western societies have never been sure of the answers to these questions. Two rather forlorn figures have paid the price of that uncertainty: the wet nurse and the unwed mother.

Rousseau notwithstanding, the wet-nursing industry prospered throughout the West, with certain regional variations. In the southern United States the black "mammy" was common. The English employed unwed mothers. The French preferred married peasants. Custom honored the persistent taboo against sexual relations during breastfeeding. When Eve gave birth, "Adam bade farewell to paradise," moaned Michelet.[44] "Conjugal pleasures should be moderated if not eliminated," Dr. Garnier reaffirmed in 1879.[45] Not that the decision, in theory, was always up to the father.

The major nineteenth-century innovation in this area was the live-in wet nurse, who came to the child's parents' home. Indeed, parents aware of the high mortality rate among children put out to nurse with ignorant women preferred to keep an eye on their newborn. But the often strained relations between the mother and her "replacement" were a problem. Young mothers became jealous of their prerogatives. By the time the baby arrived they had spent a fortune on outfits, a crib, and decorating the nursery, and they wanted to show off the baby and enjoy its first smiles. But they did not dare go against the nurse, whose milk might "go bad" if they did. Seizing the advantage, some nurses proved demanding and capricious.

The wet nurse was above all a domesticated body—though a well-treated one. Since she was a tangible sign of her employers' wealth, she was always nicely dressed. In their home she was pampered. Her wages were high, and she received many gifts. She slept in the child's room, not in an attic loft with the other servants. She was required to keep scrupulously clean but could eat what she liked and did not work much: a little washing, perhaps, and some sewing. In the harsh life of a poor woman, a stint as a wet nurse could prove a strange interlude indeed—and one likely to leave indelible traces.

But the experience was not without harsh sacrifices: the wet nurse had to leave her own family and entrust her own child to the care of another woman. Before being hired she had to submit to examination by a doctor, who felt her breasts, tasted her milk, and sniffed her breath. Sexual relations, while not exactly forbidden (it was impossible to cut her off from her husband entirely), were strongly discouraged. One doctor put it bluntly: "A wet nurse is to be regarded solely as a milch cow. The moment she loses that capacity, she should be dismissed at once."[46] As democratic sentiments gained ground in France during the Third Republic, the condition of the wet nurse was denounced as scandalous and compared to that of a prostitute.

Yet the wet-nursing industry was not simply a product of the selfishness of the rich. Paid nurses were needed for abandoned children and children whose mothers were obliged to work. There were many in Catholic countries, especially France.[47] Peasant women who agreed to raise pauper infants went to fetch them from hospitals or orphanages in the cities. It was primarily among these women that two revolutions in childrearing took place toward the end of the century: the advent of bottle feeding and the triumph of medicalization.

The children these women brought home often were sickly and brought in little money. Overwhelmed by a variety of chores, the women devoted little time to their charges and watched them die without great emotion. In 1870 in the Morvan, where foster parenting was common, death claimed 65 to 70 percent of the orphans brought into the region from Paris, 33 percent of orphans of local origin, and 16 percent of children raised by their own mothers. Physicians and philanthropists had long wrung their hands over these appalling figures, but to no avail. The defeat of 1870–71 sounded an alarm, however: if France hoped someday to take revenge, if the nation hoped to increase the number of its future conscripts, then something would have to be done about infant mortality. And for a model French reformers looked to the victor in the Franco-Prussian War: Bismarck's Prussia had implemented an effective social welfare program.

The Roussel Law (1874) placed wet nurses under the supervision of medical inspectors. These inspectors visited the homes of nurses to evaluate the "breeding conditions" (the word used was *élevage,* and its clear connotation of animal breeding shocked and offended no one). Just as in Rousseau's day, the doctors attacked the prejudices of the peasants, particularly elderly women. But they also discovered the wretchedness of rural housing, a veritable challenge to public health, and called for the promulgation of standards in regard to the recruitment of wet nurses. The resulting regulations improved conditions dramatically: reports from the 1900s describe better houses with several bedrooms, windows, and furniture. Wet nurses themselves were subject to regular medical examination.

The inspectors also noted the rapid acceptance of bottle feeding. Nurses saved their milk for their own children. Since Pasteurian principles now made it possible to eliminate microbes and guard against infection, doctors at first tolerated, then actively encouraged the change. If we look at how things stood in 1900, the northern half of France—more industrial, wealthier, better educated than the south—had for the most part switched over to bottle feeding; the southern half would continue to rely on the breast for another twenty years.[48]

The triumph of the bottle transformed the relation between women and infants symbolically as well as practically.[49] A wet nurse's livelihood depended on her fertility. The danger was that women would get pregnant and abandon their babies in order to profit from the milk. Hiring had been based largely on the nurse's physical endowments. Bottle feeding put an end to this emphasis on the body. Although the term "nurse" continued to be used, she was in fact more a "breeder" or caretaker, whose age and fertility no longer mattered. At the same time breastfeeding returned as an exclusive right of the mother. Rather than suckle the infant at another woman's breast, the mother could give it breast milk in a bottle if necessary. From this point on breastfeeding acquired a positive emotional connotation: a breastfeeding woman was no longer a "milch cow" but a tender mama.

Another consequence of the triumph of the bottle was to encourage physicians to intrude upon the relation between nurse and nurseling that had long eluded their grasp. At last they could study the quantity of milk that an infant needs at different ages, as well as the best schedule for feedings. Doctors soon knew enough to advise mothers and nurses. But there was also another motive for their intervention: the distress of the unwed mother.

The French term for unwed mother, *fille mère,* first entered the language during the Revolution and is only now disappearing. For two centuries it connoted an affront to the very logic of patriarchy. To allow unwed mothers a place in discourse and society was to admit, consciously or not, that women are alone responsible for their children and that mother and child can exist without knowing who the father is and without his assistance. This was to shake the central pillar on which the family and the social order rested.

To be sure, illegitimate births were not unknown in previous centuries. But between 1750 and 1850 their status changed, as it were. There were a variety of reasons for this: the number of illegitimate births increased, "seducers" were denounced as irresponsible, and the authorities became increasingly concerned about the problem. The number of unwed mothers increased everywhere, although not always at the same pace.[50] In France the illegitimacy rate rose from 3.3 percent of all births in 1790 to 7.4

percent in 1840, stabilizing at somewhere between 7 and 8 percent by the turn of the twentieth century. In Paris, however, a destination to which girls in trouble flocked, the rate rose as high as 30 percent in the period 1830–1840. In England, the increase began earlier, around 1750, but it was less severe: the illegitimacy rate in London in 1859 was only 4 percent.[51] By contrast, in Vienna it seems that the number of illegitimate births surpassed the number of legitimate ones. Some women lived as concubines of their children's father, regardless of whether or not he accepted paternity. But the true "unwed mothers" were those deprived of all male support. Nearly all had given in to force, intimidation, or promises of marriage. Ill-protected by the law, defenseless young women remained vulnerable in the countryside as well as in the cities. In fact, public opinion made no exception for rape.[52] Any girl who gave in, even if forced to do so, was "ruined," "fallen," unworthy of respect or help. When pregnant, she was thrown back on her own resources, except in unusual circumstances.[53]

Infanticide did not disappear, but its frequency rose and fell in inverse proportion to that of abortion. An unwed mother who allowed her child to live had to choose between two equally distressing solutions: either give the child up or try to raise it singlehanded. This is where the authorities took a hand in the matter. The various steps they took speak volumes. In Latin Catholic countries, municipalities had long encouraged unwed mothers to give up their children. Hospital orphanages closed during the Revolution were reopened in 1811. The possibility of giving up one's child anonymously reduced the danger of infanticide and restored the guilty mother's freedom, though she had, of course, lost her "honor." Even relieved of the burden of the child, she could look forward to nothing but contempt and scorn. Morally, few emerged unscathed by anguish or remorse. Abandoned children often were left with recognition tokens and notes expressing regret and asking the finder to care for the child. Yet many officials believed that no woman could love the living proof of her sin, and no child could help feeling contempt for the woman who had inflicted such a life on him or her. The unwed mother was not fit to be called a mother at all.

But orphanages were costly to maintain. They encouraged abandonment by making it easy. Even married couples, in financial distress, sometimes rid themselves of a burdensome child this way. Overwhelmed city governments closed their orphanages. In France the last one closed its doors in 1860; in Italy it was in 1880. They were replaced by orphan agencies, where children could still be given up for adoption, but no longer anonymously. It was not until 1904 that France once again legalized anonymous childbirth and abandonment.

In the meantime, the Anglo-American model gained popularity in Latin Europe. The key was to offer assistance in the form of a subsidy to unwed mothers. In England this was done by private charities. The very idea at first scandalized strict Catholics in France and Italy, who were afraid of encouraging vice. But time worked in the subvention's favor. In France economists worried about the declining birth rate. In their eyes, an illegitimate child was worth just as much as a legitimate one, and the least expensive and most reliable way to bring the child up was to leave it with its mother. Christians, meanwhile, gradually conceded that by caring for the child the mother accomplished an act of penance and thereby became worthy of redemption: she covertly attained the dignity of motherhood. The Revolution of 1848 accelerated the change. Regular subsidies were awarded by a committee, which kept a close eye on the morals of women receiving assistance. The state, by providing funds, took the place of the father and husband and arrogated to itself a portion of their power. With all its drawbacks, the subsidy still amounted to a modest income, enough to make the condition of the unwed mother attractive to some. The question then arose: did the mother keep her child for love or for money? And welfare fraud came into being: women who lived with their lovers hid the relationship and delayed a possible marriage in order to receive the subsidy.

Unwed mothers who gave birth in hospitals were reasonably well treated. In Bismarck's Prussia homes were built for prospective mothers to live in reasonably decent conditions before century's end. French and Italian institutions were more primitive. Patients became specimens for medical students who showed little concern for their modesty, and after giving birth a new mother might be given two or three babies to breastfeed, but not her own, which was taken away lest she show it any special favor. Dr. Fodéré, who observed such practices at the Hôtel-Dieu in Marseilles, condemned them strongly but to no avail.[54] It was the same in Milan, where in July 1899 thirty-two nursing mothers fed seventy-four infants, and Mantua, where one young mother who gave birth in January 1900 gave suck to eighteen different newborns between March and November. There was a danger that babies infected with syphilis would transmit the disease to the nurse and through her to other children, who would in turn infect still other nurses, and so on. But the doctors blamed everything on the wet nurses, denouncing promiscuous breastfeeding and frequent exchange of infants between nursing mothers out of friendship or for money.

Hospitals were crawling with microbes as well as patients, and it is no wonder that Pasteurian hygiene took them by storm. The "breeding" of human beings became more humane, but at the same time it fell into the hands of the doctors, who set out patiently and methodically to educate mothers and wet nurses.

They began by devaluing the "maternal instinct," that symbol of the difference between the world of women—empirical, emotional, traditional—and that of men—innovative, rational, and scientific. From now on, doctors insisted, even the most physical aspects of motherhood required training based on science. Family physicians addressed their wealthier patients in a tone of friendly condescension. With patients of more modest background the tone grew more imperious. Everything was rigorously spelled out: the number and schedule of feedings, the sterilization of bottles and nipples, how to change and bathe the child, when to put it to bed, how to use a thermometer. To educate working-class mothers doctors added well-baby consultations to their obstetrical clinics. Private charities such as the *Gouttes de lait* (Drops of Milk) in France also offered their services. Mothers eagerly consulted these "experts" and apparently heeded their advice. Each child was issued a medical record book. The original model, designed by Dr. Fonssagrives in 1869, made its way across the Atlantic thanks to Dr. M. W. Garrisson. It was used to record the child's weight, height, diet, vaccinations, and illnesses. Charity ladies helped doctors by getting to know mothers and visiting their homes to make sure that they had properly understood the doctor's prescriptions. Thus a new form of mutual aid developed among women, but this time entirely under medical supervision, devoid of autonomy.

Some people wanted courses on childrearing to be included in the girls' primary and secondary curriculum. The goal was to prepare young women for motherhood, which everyone still regarded as woman's quintessential social role. But no such courses were approved. The curriculum for girls gradually came to look more and more like that for boys, and ultimately this convergence helped diminish the sexual division of labor in the family as well as in public life.

Hearts

Cultural and economic development led to revision of the sexual division of roles and functions. In theory as well as practice, however, everyone recognized the distinction between public life, which was man's domain, and private life, which was woman's—the so-called two spheres. Thus there was a woman's world, a place where a culture peculiar to women, still essentially physical and emotional, was elaborated and passed on from generation to generation. What was the role of personal relations among women who lived together? Between women and the men who lived with them? Education was beginning to produce women with increasingly forceful and independent personalities. How did such women reconcile their own objectives with what they owed to the people around them?

Among Women

When Victor Hugo described Cosette's bedroom or Balzac furnished that of Césarine Birotteau, they drew on their own fantasies. Real girls quite simply liked to have rooms of their own. None expressed regret for the bedrooms they had once shared with sisters and brothers. The place where a girl kept her old dolls, hid her souvenirs, and locked herself away when she wished to be alone to dream or to cry was a refuge, a space where inchoate autonomy could flourish, where a personality could struggle to express itself. Private diaries were one form of self-expression.[55] Keeping such diaries was nothing new, but as the practice gained in popularity it took on new meaning. At the beginning of the century diaries were still a device for scrutinizing one's conscience, a tool of Christian penitence in which little girls recorded sins and temptations and resolved to be good. Before long, however, diarists were gazing inward, seeking to understand themselves and practicing what psychologists were already beginning to call introspection. Girls like Marie Bashkirtseff expressed their anxieties about the future or their rebelliousness or their desire for independence. Women like Eugénie de Guérin and Alix de Lamartine, who continued to keep diaries into adulthood, often did so to fill a kind of inner void, to hold on to days that otherwise might vanish without a trace.[56]

For little girls and even young ladies a mother's guidance was thought best, because mothers knew how to prepare daughters for private life. Letters and diaries show that upbringing to have been gentle and tender, part coaxing and part sharing. Hugs were commonplace, as was intimate conversation, while physical punishment disappeared, at least in the middle classes; aristocratic and peasant mothers remained more aloof and preserved traditions somewhat longer than did middle-class mothers.[57] Mothers willingly served as teachers and tutors, and moral guidance especially was their exclusive province. Many mothers explored the educational literature. Mothers and daughters achieved greater intimacy perhaps than ever before, because male and female roles had never been so completely differentiated. In addition, the lower birth rate left more time for sustained, personal relations. But ambivalence remained. Mothers often felt disappointment at giving birth to a daughter, "so deeply rooted was the idea of man's superiority in happiness and dignity." Mothers sometimes expressed contempt for their own sex by neglecting their daughters: there is no shortage of examples. Or, going to the other extreme, they might give in to "feelings of identification" and attempt to create an idealized copy of themselves, a "more perfect" woman.[58] This could make them overbearing, veritable inquisitors. Yet the death of a mother was often the hardest blow for a young girl to bear. Though surrounded by relatives and friends, motherless Caroline Brame[59] and Stéphanie Julien[60] felt horribly alone, especially when it came time for major decisions like choosing a husband.

By the end of the century the quiet intimacy of mother and daughter began to be endangered. Mothers no longer had a clear sense of what they were expected to pass on. Clémence Royer, a woman of science, saw herself as a hybrid. All that she asked of her daughter was to "replace [her] on the field of battle."[61] Meanwhile, what Louise Weiss called "moral puberty" could lead an adolescent to judge her mother, sometimes harshly. Educated, equipped with a degree, and eager for independence, a young lady might reject the maternal model yet still want to please men, find a husband, and have children. These contradictory desires gave rise to tensions that were hard to live with. Were such tensions a factor in the strange disease that Dr. Lasèque dubbed "anorexia" in 1873?[62]

In practice, few girls were brought up entirely at home. Thanks to boarding schools, mothers gladly relieved themselves of the burden of "the difficult years." Boarding school kept the crisis out of sight and moderated its severity: the young woman found other confidantes. A proper distance was established between mother and daughter. After entering the Sacré-Coeur school, for example, Marie de Flavigny developed a warm attachment to Mme Antonia, a nun of distinguished background and full of charm. At the other end of the social scale, little Marie-Claire, brought up in an orphanage, came under the protective affection of Sister Marie-Aimée. Lay teachers enjoyed less of a reputation in this regard.

Many adolescents discovered the joys of friendship while in boarding school. It was not unusual for two girls to form a passionate friendship, become inseparable, and exchange oaths and pictures and such symbols of undying affection as braids or locks of hair or rings or bracelets. In Catholic convents a vigilant surveillance guarded against "guilty practices" but did not inhibit sentimental outpourings. English and American girls appear to have enjoyed unlimited freedom: letters reveal that boarding-school students could live in complete intimacy, exchanging items of clothing, sleeping in the same bed, cooking for each other, and even retiring to a "snug little room" to make music.[63]

In Europe marriage placed a strain on such friendships. But in America these mutual passions sometimes survived separation. To cite just one example, Mary Hallock Foote and Helena Dekay Gilder exchanged tender letters that spoke of ardent physical desire: they longed to see each other, to embrace, to lie down together and trade caresses. Must we see homosexuality in such expressions? The girls themselves saw no such thing: their culture gave them neither the concept nor the word.[64] In any case, they came from respectable, conservative families, which accepted their relationship without anxiety and apparently deemed it compatible with marriage. Even the pair's husbands were not offended: they knew women to be emotional and expressive. Indeed, men knew that women shared a peculiar sensuality of their own, but it was too inconsequential to bother repressing. The Victorian ethic, often denounced as rigid and repressive, was in this respect flexible enough to adapt to women's needs.

Sisters and female cousins formed a sort of clan within the family. In Catholic countries it was not unusual for several of them to take holy orders. The Martin sisters (sisters of Thérèse de l'Enfant-Jésus) were no exception. The desire to live among women was probably one element of a religious vocation: holy daughters not only escaped the discipline of father and husband and avoided the perils and cares of motherhood but also made sure that they would always have a mother and sisters. If occasionally jealousy and rancor erupted within the closed confines of the convent, weekly public confession helped to minimize conflict.[65] Sisters in the religious orders played an important social role. Wherever dispensaries and schools were established, they soon became focal points of women's solidarity.[66] Some nuns gained real power: in the 1840s Sister Rosalie, the guardian angel of Paris's "dangerous classes," was allegedly able to influence the selection of government ministers. And Mother Javouhey, although not eligible for office, was elected to a seat in the Chamber of Deputies in 1848 by the black French citizens of Guiana, former slaves whom she had emancipated.

Apart from these institutionalized "sororities," relations among women were determined by family structures and economic conditions. They were not always idyllic. In some poor rural areas still under the sway of tradition, women lived in mutual hostility and suspicion—for instance, in the Italian province of Friuli as recently as the turn of the century.[67] Several generations lived together under one roof. A mother's power stemmed from her reproductive role: her sons protected her from her husband's tyranny. When a son married, his mother looked upon the new daughter-in-law as a rival and was apt to humiliate and exploit her. The only way for the wife to improve her status was to give birth to a son of her own, so mothers-in-law hated it when their daughters-in-law became pregnant. And despite pregnancy there was no easing of the burden. On the contrary, the daughter-in-law was forced to work up to the onset of labor, and no one bothered to notify her mother or sisters that her time had come. A neighbor might perhaps offer assistance. But later the victim would treat her own daughter-in-law the same way. These divisions within the family, which precluded any solidarity among women, are one sign of the barbarous nature of traditional male-dominated rural Mediterranean society.

Economic change caused the old family structures to break up in a bewildering variety of ways, however. Even in rural areas relations among women were complex and not always limited to the private sphere; they were never static, moreover, but constantly changing. In Minot, for example, the women of the village formed a subculture rich enough to compensate for the constricted and occasionally nasty character of family life.

In town, "proper" ladies learned to tailor society to their own taste. The *bourgeoises* of northern France in the 1850s and 1860s provide an excellent example of this.[68] At the beginning of the century they were still participating in their fathers' and husbands' businesses. Their feminine roles were at that time secondary. They entrusted their children to servants, gave little thought to interior decoration, and were not particularly religious. But industrial growth in the second half of the century cut the factories off from family residences, a concrete, physical manifestation of the divorce between public and private. Wives and mothers were relegated to the domestic sphere, where they asserted their authority and defined their own values—values that contrasted almost point by point with those of their men.

Instead of extolling the production of goods and wealth, these women emphasized the family and reproduction. At a time when the birth rate was declining everywhere, they had more children than their mothers had had. Bearing children became their way of asserting their difference and making it count. They took care of their offspring themselves. For sisters and cousins, neighbors and friends, life was an endless round of pregnancies, births, feedings, weanings, and resumptions of menstruation from puberty until the change of life. Biology was at once these women's strength and their weakness, the basis of their solidarity and identity. They scrupulously supervised their children's studies and moral upbringing. Having households full of children complicated their chores, but they took pleasure in the complications: their cuisine became ever more elaborate, their menus ever more sumptuous, and their bibelots ever more numerous. They spent considerable amounts of money, and husbands complained that their wives had no idea of money's value. The women kept scrupulous accounts, however; it was just that there was no economic purpose to what they were doing. To round out ever larger household staffs they hired women in preference to men. The relation between the mistress of the house and her maids was a personal bond of quasi-feudal dependency. The maid was part of the family and had no existence in her own right: in theory she could not marry or have children. She had no freedom, and her life was governed by the daily rhythms of a job that had no tangible product or purpose.

The *bourgeoises* of the Nord made religion the center of their world, and every minute of their day was suffused with the aura of the sacred. In their piety they rejected science and denied any rational basis for causality: sickness, death, misery—all were expressions of God's will, accepted with resignation. Mary, Queen of the Heavens, symbolized all feminine values: at once virgin and mother, she defied nature and science. She expressed the dream of disincarnate reproduction, dissociated from carnal union and bloody birth. Out of Christian charity these women founded crèches, kindergartens, church groups, and charitable organizations, but the objects of charity had to be legitimate and baptized. Confident of their values, they sought to ensure the triumph of those values in the public arena, forming "leagues of mothers and patriots" to combat the atheistic press.

The two spheres did not then always complement each other; they sometimes moved apart or even clashed. Similar phenomena can be observed during the great religious awakenings in the Protestant countries. Were emotional and personal bonds sufficient to bring the two sexes together within the family?

Women and Men

Relations between fathers and daughters may have known an idyll of sorts in the eighteenth and early nineteenth centuries. Men were touched by their daughters' fragile delicacy and docility and open, disarming affection. Little girls, for their part, had every reason to seek the esteem and favor of the master of the household: this, according to educators, was the best possible preparation for marriage. Some adolescent girls, though, were strongly attracted to their fathers' intelligence. Germaine de Staël's attachment to her father, Jacques Necker, was based on an admiration of this kind. Similarly, the Comte de Flavigny, adored father of Marie, was a man of the Enlightenment, a creative thinker and fountain of knowledge. And one could easily cite many similar examples from the early nineteenth century: so long as men had free time on their hands, they conversed with their daughters, guided their reading, and cultivated any gift they might have for literature or the arts. But as the century progressed and men became ever more caught up in business, they had less and less time to devote to raising their children and engaging with them personally. They were more likely now to use daughters, generally more docile than sons, for their own ends. There could be benefits to assisting an active father: Mlle Dubois, who learned all about the textile trade early on by working with her father, remained in this lucrative business all her life, despite an excellent marriage.[69] But all too often collaboration between father and daughter looked more like pure exploitation: the girl served as an unpaid secretary or copyist with no hope of promotion. Many peasant girls were obliged to "help" their fathers until the strength was drained from their bodies. And girls at all levels of society were expected to care for the author of their days when he became old.

Conflict began the moment a young woman showed signs of hankering after freedom. The choice of a husband was a crucial issue, and even the most politically liberal fathers found it difficult not to interfere. Victor Hugo and Karl Marx, both revered if despotic fathers, persecuted their daughters with the best of intentions.[70] Elizabeth Barrett was nearly forty when she was forced to elope with the respectable Robert Browning because of an abusive father. Another occasion for conflict was a daughter's decision to pursue a higher education rather than devote herself to domestic life. Louise Weiss was not allowed to enroll in the Sorbonne until she had spent a year at a German institute of home economics.[71] Yet fathers soon learned to take pride in their daughters' scholastic successes and even to prize such achievements, especially if they had no sons. When daughters became politically aware, they often followed their father's lead.[72] In short, beyond conflict, beyond even mutual affection, fathers and daughters discovered new common ground.

In the absence of a father, some girls sought support and affection from their brothers. Brother-sister relationships were particularly common and rewarding in the Romantic period. One could cite numerous examples from many countries.[73] Parents looked favorably upon such relationships. They relied on the sister for the brother's moral education. An older sister became a second mother. A younger sister, being weak, taught a boy to be protective. In any case her innocence made an impression on the young male. But other factors were also involved: a brother was one of the few young men a girl could get close to and talk to in a free and familiar manner. The reverse was also true. Boys, moreover, often wanted a mirror, a reflection, a double, and some were tempted to play Pygmalion. Girls saw their brothers as intermediaries: through them they heard echoes of the public life to which they were denied access. Some girls willingly sacrificed their dowries and therefore their futures so that their brothers could continue their studies and make their mark in the world. A sister who felt that her brother might be about to lapse from religion might pray for him, make an offering, or perform some other act of piety: witness the examples of Eugénie de Guérin and Caroline de Gobineau.

Incest fantasies were common in literature: Emily Brontë's *Wuthering Heights,* for example, or Robert Musil's *Man Without Qualities.*[74] Some male writers dreamed of incest with their mothers. This was true of Freud, as is well known, and also of Jules Renard. Magistrates, forensic physicians, and social commentators all noted the frequency of incest, especially father-daughter incest, in the countryside as well as the city. They tended to see it, however, as a problem limited to families on the fringes of society. The criminal law and the courts essentially ignored the problem.[75] It was essential that the family remain above suspicion and that the victims remain silent.[76]

Michelet says somewhere that every man is his mother's son. He was not the only one to note the immense influence, the unlimited power of mothers over small children, especially only children. But maternal love was so highly regarded at the time that no one feared this power, even when the child was a boy. Indeed, the role of mothers in raising their sons steadily expanded as fathers increasingly worked outside the home.[77] Early in the century boys as young as seven were sent away to boarding school; by the end of the century a boy was not likely to be sent away before he turned twelve. The popularity of boarding schools declined, moreover. A mother, with the approval of her husband, preferred to keep an eye on their son's health and studies, to help him with his homework, to review his lessons. Above all she was determined to monitor his religious and moral upbringing. Often it was in this area that mothers sought and found deep and lasting communion with their children. Edgar Quinet referred to his mother as "my oracle" and compared her to a spiritual master; later he would accuse himself of having worshiped her more than he should have done.[78] For mothers it was often a problem to find the right place between father and son. Women generally decried male strictness and protested against physical punishment, but they also were afraid that any display of weakness might spoil the child. Some mothers tried to keep sons at home, while others wished to influence the choice of a profession and a wife. Such practices were especially common in the middle class, where the desire to rise in society was acute and family relations were often limited and unrewarding. The complexity of mother-son relations has left an indelible mark on literature. Writers like Baudelaire and Proust never quite separated from their mothers. On the other hand, Jules Vallès, Arthur Rimbaud, and Jules Renard learned rebellion through conflicts with theirs. It should come as no surprise, then, that Freud conceptualized the Oedipal complex at the end of the nineteenth century. The unique historical conditions of the time favored certain pathologies in the mother-child, and particularly the mother-son, relationship.

Did women cling to their sons because of difficulties in husband-wife relations? An examination of the couple may shed light on the question.

Households and Couples

A married woman was said to be "making a home" and "starting a family." But was she also forming a couple? Did she want to? Could she succeed if she did? The household and family were traditional institutions, whose values were formalized and understood. The couple was something new, still in the process of being invented. Daughters were no longer forced to marry men chosen by their parents and usually were free to choose among several suitors. Now, to choose was to indicate a preference, an inclination, a desire for love: the hope was for a more intimate and more perfect union. Under what conditions could this desire, this hope, be satisfied?

The importance attached to the dowry varied from country to country. In England and America, where dowries were frowned upon, young people enjoyed greater freedom (yet "homogamy" was hardly threatened: they continued to choose mates within their own social group). In Latin countries, and especially France, no girl, no matter how modest the family fortune, married without a dowry. This resulted in elaborate matrimonial strategies, particularly in the families of well-to-do farmers, industrialists, and businessmen. Daughters, aware of the stakes, went along with such plans without feeling "sacrificed," so long as the husbands chosen for them were of their own rank and deemed worthy of them. In any case, they were told that love came *after* marriage. If it did not come, they made do without it: marriage gave these women a social identity, and that was more important than happiness. But the idea of the dowry began to change: people increasingly came to value a woman's talent, knowledge, and tact, qualities that a wife needed in order to be useful to her husband. A tailor was apt to court a seamstress. A small merchant was apt to want a wife educated well enough to keep his books. Toward the end of the century some economists, such as Paul Leroy-Beaulieu, suggested that homemaking ability be assessed and included as part of a working-class woman's dowry.

The age of bride and groom at the time of marriage was also likely to affect the couple's relations. In Amsterdam at the beginning of the nineteenth century the bride was older than the groom in 29 percent of all marriages.[79] By contrast, in America, a shortage of women led to early marriage for girls.[80] The effects of such differences are difficult to spell out.

America offered the curious example of Mormon women who rejected the idea of the couple.[81] They accepted male polygamy and sought to take advantage of the concomitant double standard. Arguing that the male is "naturally" more insatiable than the female, these women held that it was good for men to have more than one wife. One thereby avoided adultery, illegitimacy, infanticide, and prostitution. Every man was responsible for raising *all* his children. For a chaste woman, it was better to marry a respectable man, even if he was already married, than to live alone or with a depraved husband. A pregnant or nursing woman could reduce the frequency of her sexual relations for her child's sake without feeling any guilt. She could also exercise more control over the number of her pregnancies. For her, motherhood was paramount. To be sure, there were sometimes difficulties over sharing a husband. Janet Snyder held out for three years after her husband told her he wanted to take a second wife, but in the end she had a vision that persuaded her to consent. Later she explained to a friend that a woman had to steel herself and not think too much about her husband. She forgot her own so effectively that one day she called her children to the dinner table without thinking to include him. This comparative solitude left a woman considerable independence. Sometimes a man's wives got on so well together that they formed a happy community. Polygamy was outlawed, however, in 1890.

Growing numbers of young women dreamed of finding idyllic love in married life. Consider two cases: Bessie Lacy, the daughter of a South Carolina planter, and Fanny Arnaud, the daughter of a physician from Aix-en-Provence, anxious fiancées both. In 1851 Bessie (then nineteen) accepted the marriage proposal of Thomas W. Dewey, the brother of a friend of hers from boarding school.[82] For a year their only relationship was an active correspondence. Their first letters were conventional, but Bessie soon aspired to greater intimacy. She wanted to express her feelings, to talk about love, and to be "molded" by and for Thomas: "Mold me as you please." She asked him to address her as "dearest." But Thomas kept his emotional distance: he was preparing a home for her. So, little by little, Bessie withdrew: in her final letters she spelled out her rights and duties along with Tom's. She restored the formality between them that she had once hoped to abolish: by marking out her territory, she protected herself from passion and disappointment.

Fanny, a highly talented and very pretty young woman, chose from among her various suitors Charles Reybaud, the son of a Marseilles industrialist.[83] It was 1822, and Fanny was twenty years old. She hoped to give totally of herself, to make herself transparent, but was afraid that Charles would not reciprocate. "I dare not trust too much in the future," she wrote a friend. "It smiles on me, I think, only in order to deceive me." And indeed it was difficult to think of the couple as an ideal in a world where the segregation of the sexes, the sovereignty of the husband, and the double standard still existed. What likelihood of success did Bessie and Fanny have?

America, it appears, offered the greatest opportunities. The universal acceptance there of the "two spheres" meant that the female functions were truly valued. As wife, mother, and educator, a woman deserved as much attention and respect as the man who provided for her. And her domain was vast: in the name of moral responsibility she watched over her family and intervened whenever the virtue of one of its members was threatened. Husbands accepted their wives' observations, even about their own conduct. Harriet Beecher Stowe lambasted her husband, Calvin, a minister of the Gospel, because, among other things, he read too many secular books, worried too much about Luther and not enough about Christ, and failed to control his sexual impulses adequately.[84] All European travelers to the New World, Tocqueville foremost among them, agreed that women in America were considered important and that their opinions and demands were taken seriously. Emotional harmony was also underscored: married men rarely had mistresses. Couples made all important decisions together. Bessie and Tom had a happy home (but were they also happy as a couple?). Tom was a busy banker, and Bessie was active in various organizations. They had several children.

By contrast, Fanny's marriage turned sour. Charles proved to be not only jealous but also dissolute. His wife's success annoyed him, yet he refused to "put his bachelor life behind him." He had a number of affairs, most flagrantly while Fanny was pregnant. Disillusioned, the young wife demanded a separation after only three years of marriage, and despite the birth of a son. She soon became one of the most widely read novelists of her generation. Her case was fairly typical: adultery by men was tolerated by law and public opinion, and wives either resigned themselves to their husbands' escapades or sought refuge in a separation (official or unofficial), which restored neither their freedom nor their dowry. When divorce became possible (in France as of 1884), it was mostly women who filed, but adultery by the husband was not the principal grounds: petitioners were more inclined to cite assault or bankruptcy, charges more likely to impress the judge. In the meantime, adultery by a wife was reduced to the status of a misdemeanor, but husbands no longer dared to file complaints for fear of looking ridiculous.

Lower down the social scale wives were more fearful of their husbands' brutality and greed. Although peasants' and artisans' wives shared their work, the husband remained in charge, as countless proverbs recalled. In some poor provinces this power took the form of brutal oppression: peasant women in the Gévaudan were not allowed to keep the keys to the pantry. Deprived of the barest necessities, they were obliged to steal in order to survive. In the fields or the family workshop, the woman was seen as the man's assistant, but she never received any help with her own chores in return. Women therefore often worked beyond their capacities, aged quickly, and died young. Peasant women did not really see themselves as housewives.

In working-class households, however, the "housewife" became the axis around which the family revolved. Husbands appreciated the value of the services their wives performed: raising the young, preparing meals, washing and mending linen and clothing, caring for the sick. But relations frequently were poisoned by two sources of conflict: religion and the family budget. Many working-class women kept faith with the religion of their childhood, whose holidays, pomp, and ceremonies they liked. They heeded the priest and sisters and willingly gave what little money they could to purchase a share of paradise, something that no one could take from them. In this way they hoped to attract God's protection to their loved ones. Although their husbands were apt to be freethinkers if not downright anticlerical (especially in Catholic countries), men did not dare interfere with their wives' religion, for piety was also a guarantee of virtue. Yet they might berate the old "church hen," insult her, even slap her around. As for money, the man was the breadwinner and was sometimes reluctant to part with his earnings. Around mid-century Le Play noted that in France (though not in England) many workers turned their pay over to their wives, although not without sometimes violent disputes. Court archives throw a harsh light on these rows as well as on the energy of the women involved. When separation cases went to court, women often accused their spouses of laziness and hard drinking.[85] They complained about being left penniless with the children while the man "ran around" Lord knows where. They told of wanting to move out of furnished rooms into homes of their own with furniture of their own choosing. When beaten, some of them got in a few good licks of their own before fleeing.

One thing is perfectly clear: the couple became one of the central problems of Western society in the nineteenth century, a problem that affected all classes of society and spilled beyond the boundaries of private life. The subject deserves much lengthier treatment.

In the eyes of contemporaries, the happy wife was the one who identified with her husband. Travelers to France were surprised to find shops in which mama worked the cash box while papa made the goods: such economic solidarity strengthened the bond between husband and wife. Michelet admired Mme Pouchet, who assisted her physician husband in his research and kept up his scientific correspondence, yet delighted as well in marriage's other pleasures.[86] The wives of some writers and artists, such as Julia Daudet and Alma Mahler, ably assisted their husbands' careers to the detriment of their own. Collaboration with a politician was more difficult. Mary Waddington, a sharp-tongued ambassador's wife, found the wives of French deputies incapable of discussing anything other than their children and a bit too homespun for her taste. By contrast, the wives of politicians in Italy, England, and the United States were at home on any subject.[87]

A Certain Age

The onset of old age, imperceptible in men, is identifiable in women because of menopause. Doctors took an increasing interest in this condition, which some saw as the "Indian summer" of a woman's life.[88] But most continued to issue the traditional prescriptions: renunciation and moderation. Women themselves expressed ambivalent feelings about the "change of life."

It was a time for taking on new roles: mother-in-law, grandmother, widow. Mothers-in-law were, typically, widely denounced: in centuries past some had tormented their daughters-in-law, and now sons-in-law too found them intrusive. It was of course hard, even when children married, to let them go after devoting one's life to them. But a mother-in-law was one thing, a grandmother another: grandmothers were easier to accept. If a woman without means was forced to ask her children to take her in, things were more bearable if she could help out around the house. One stereotypical image of the time was that of the old woman knitting while tending her grandchildren. The grandmother who passed on family traditions and ancient wisdom, a nursery rhyme or a lullaby, a favorite recipe for preserves or a ghost story or a fairy tale, was universally appreciated. Only doctors were wary of her old-fashioned ways. When the elderly ceased to be useful, they might be cast out of the household. There were of course charitable institutions for taking care of them, but by the end of the century the authorities had begun to become concerned about the burden they represented.[89]

In wealthy families aging mothers and grandmothers achieved a certain power. Often widows, they managed their considerable wealth with conservative caution.[90] They reigned as "matriarchs" over fussily attentive offspring.

Writers and poets remained as cruel as ever to women who had lost their youth and beauty. "Shriveled shadows," Baudelaire called them, "human flotsam." But sarcasm could not halt a now irreversible demographic process. The health of women was improving and their lives were lengthening (the life expectancy of a French woman increased from thirty-four to fifty-two years over the course of the century). Thus old age began later, while the age of maternity ended earlier. In between, middle age came into its own: in the best of circumstances it offered women an enticing prospect of freedom.

TRANSLATED FROM THE FRENCH BY ARTHUR GOLDHAMMER

14

Dangerous Sexualities

Judith R. Walkowitz

THERE IS NOTHING NATURAL, inevitable, or stable about sexuality. To quote historians Kathy Peiss and Christina Simmons, sexuality is not "an unchanging biological reality or a universal natural force," but rather "a product of political, social, economic, and cultural process." Sexuality, that is, has a "history."[1] While certain patterns of behavior and meaning have prevailed over a long time—for example, transvestism or the image of the procuress as mother—other practices manifest considerable variability. Even incest prohibitions, that supposed bedrock of social taboos, have variously expanded and contracted, shifting the boundaries of permissible sexual relations over the course of European history.

Sexual cultures in the nineteenth century exemplify the socially constructed character of sexuality. Nineteenth-century sexuality was a highly contested arena, in which conflicts over class, race, and gender were played out in private and public. Through moral panics, sexual scandals, and legislative enactments diverse social groups and professional interests tried to extend their cultural and political authority. At the most public level, men and women participated in struggles that would also redefine their most private identity and subjectivity.

When Victorians talked sex, they mostly focused on sexual danger, on the proliferation of sexual practices outside the sanctity of the home, disengaged from the procreative act. These subjects, however, were also linked to tensions over a changing middle-class marital norm; plummeting birthrates made it increasingly apparent that the marital bed had also become a place for non-procreative sex, for personal intimacy, and individual growth. Because of its implications for normative femininity, nonprocreative sex within marriage proved as troubling to Victorians as the expansion of commercial sex and same-sex relationships outside heterosexual domesticity. Accompanying the rise of the middle-class cult of domesticity was a celebration of the "true" bourgeois woman as mother and an insistent denial of nonreproductive female sexuality. Over the course of the nineteenth century, this class-based model of female asexuality became increasingly somatized, supported by the opinion of medical authorities who were anxious to extend their cultural authority over the female body. Although doctors disputed the degree of female passionlessness, they tended to accord respectable women at most a secondary, second-hand sexuality, subservient to male pleasure, lacking its own autonomy, a pale imitation of male erotic desire.

Female passionlessness emerged in juxtaposition to an active male sexuality and to transgressive female practices that tended to be coded as male or déclassé. In the nineteenth century, four female practices—prostitution, abortion, cross-dressing, and romantic friendships—acquired notoriety as sexual transgressions involving female agency and choice. These practices all predate the nineteenth century, but they occupied a new position in the modern urban landscape—either because they were associated with a different social class of women or because they assumed new weight and meaning as a social problem and identity. At different points in the century, these four practices became encoded in official definitions of illicit activities of sexually disorderly women. Yet these categories encompassed much more than disorderly sexual conduct: they had as much, if not more, to do with women's work, life-style, reproductive strategies, fashion and self-display, and nonfamilial attachments, as with nonprocreative sexual activity.

The history of dangerous sexualities in the nineteenth century illustrates the complicated process of cultural negotiation and debate in the formation of Victorian sexuality. Debates and cultural exchanges around dangerous female sexualities were conducted across the social spectrum and in numerous urban spaces: in the brothel and the street, in the music hall and the clinic, in the back alleys of slums and in the comfort of middle-class salons. Diverse men and women employed a variety of competing social languages to interpret sexual experience, from the language of sexual bartering and melodramatic newspaper accounts to the authoritative language of the law and medicine. In these discussions, gender transgression and sexual transgression continually overlapped, and any sexual identity constructed in relation to those practices was inherently unstable and contradictory.

The nineteenth century produced the historic moment when middle-class women gained access to public space to speak about sexual matters, thanks to the new mass media and political networks available in a redefined public domain. However innovative, these women were still bound imaginatively by a limited cultural repertoire, forced to reshape cultural meanings within certain parameters. They did not simply experience sexual passion and naturally find the words to express those feelings, nor did they experience sexual danger and naturally find the words to express sexual danger. They had to rely on culturally available constructs to speak their "truth."

Prostitution

The extent, visibility, and protean nature of prostitution was a distinguishing feature of nineteenth-century cities. Observers were affronted by the "painted creatures" sauntering down the thoroughfares and byways of the city with their "gaudy dress" and aggressive gaze; in the major cities prostitutes allegedly counted in the tens of thousands (these official numbers, however, were notoriously unreliable). The social hierarchy of prostitutes mirrored the class structure and social distribution of urban centers. The New York sexual underground ranged from fashionable Fifth Avenue mansions, where wealthy men kept their mistresses, to Canal Street cigar stores catering to workingmen and sailors. In London, the social geography of vice extended from the courtesans of St. John's Wood to the elegantly attired streetwalkers who perambulated around the fashionable shopping districts of Regent Street, mingling with respectable ladies, to the impoverished women—the "kneetremblers" and "round the corner Sallies"—committing "acts of indecency" in the ill-lit back alleys and courts of the city's slums to earn money for their night's lodgings. In the United States, racial segregation also structured the prostitution market: in New Orleans, segregated black and white brothels stood side by side; in the multilevel "cribs" of San Francisco, European and American women occupied the top floors, while Mexican, Japanese, and Chinese women were relegated to the lower levels. In these urban centers, the geography of prostitution constantly shifted in response to changes in the physical and social environment. In Berlin, Paris, and London, poor streetwalkers often plied their trade in traditional centers of prostitution, usually the old, narrow streets of popular districts, but a new entertainment center or railroad terminus could also prove a strong magnet for public women.

Compared to male prostitution, female prostitution could be a highly visible and capitalized business, with an elaborate infrastructure and organization of work. This is certainly the case for the most organized prostitutes, who worked in brothels where they often received wages, clothing, room, and board. Alternatively, prostitution could be a form of self-employment, particularly for the large number of women who walked the city streets and frequented its taverns and theaters. Over the course of the nineteenth century the sites of commercialized sex expanded to massage parlors, baths, dance halls, *tableaux vivants, cafés chantants,* and music halls. To familiarize himself with the local vice emporia, a male visitor to the city often felt obliged to purchase a pocket book or "gentleman's guide" that would detail the price, location, and services of various establishments.

Whether stationary or perambulating, highly organized or casual and impromptu, prostitutes were the "unskilled daughters of the unskilled classes."[2] Their lives were of a piece with the lives of the large body of laboring women—those who resided away from their families and had to eke out a precarious living in the urban job market. Social investigations of prostitution in different locales consistently identified women on the town as recent migrants from the local countryside or as daughters of urban artisans in declining trades. These women had previously worked at jobs paying subsistence wages or less, such as the low grades of domestic service, laundering, needlework, and certain forms of factory labor. A slightly altered recruitment pattern developed in the last decades of the nineteenth century: shopgirls, waitresses, and barmaids entered the ranks of prostitutes, reflecting the new but equally low-grade and unskilled female occupations in the tertiary sector of the economy. The pattern also reflected the movement of prostitution from the street into new spaces of commercialized sex. The fluid and noninstitutionalized character of streetwalking permitted a considerable number of working women to supplement their insufficient wages with money gained from sexual favors traded on the streets. Even for those who earned their living principally from prostitution, the "gay life" represented only a temporary "refuge from uneasy circumstances";[3] young women mostly left the trade by their late twenties.

While in prostitution, women participated in a distinctive collective life. On entering a brothel, a woman frequently acquired a new name and learned new rituals and an elaborate argot related to the sex trade. Despite the economic exploitation of brothel inmates, the constraints on their freedom, and the tensions arising among inmates and between prostitutes and the madam, the brothel often functioned as a surrogate family and support system for women. Middle-class observers condemned life in the bordello as tedious, claustrophobic, and as we shall discuss below, perverse, but it is not clear that working women resented it on these grounds (although they had other complaints). Life in the bordello allowed for free time and leisure activity—playing the piano, talking, singing, reading light romances—that may have constituted a real pleasure for working-class women whose alternative employments had been as seamstresses and domestic servants.

Prostitutes who walked the streets and lived in lodgings also participated in a subculture that both defied codes of female respectability and was conditioned by the precariousness and predatory danger of the "life." Middle-class commentators repeatedly complained of the physical and visual aggressiveness of the "painted dressy women flaunting along the streets" in "dirty white muslin and greasy cheap blue silk."[4] Bonnetless, without shawls, casting "wicked glances," these women exposed themselves "in their figure" to passersby. The dress code of prostitutes served as a way of advertising themselves and attracting male customers. Sometimes prostitutes would go even further to demonstrate their wares, baring their ankles, legs, and bosoms, or visibly sucking their thumb to indicate the kind of sexual service offered.

Male clients frequently found themselves disappointed by these sexual services. In the 50-cent "cribs" of San Francisco, men sat on wooden benches, waiting for an encounter so quick that they barely had time to pull down their pants. Even in more expensive parlor houses the emphasis was on speedy orgasm, lack of emotional connection, absence of mutuality. One young man, brought by his father to a fancy parlor house in New Orleans for his sexual initiation, later described the experience as a "mechanical procedure that . . . endured for perhaps a minute."[5] Clients may well have preferred the voyeuristic entertainments provided by large brothels of the late nineteenth century, featuring *tableaux vivants*, stripteases, and lesbian scenarios.

Clients were especially aggrieved when they contracted venereal disease from commercial sexual encounters or when prostitutes turned to theft as a more lucrative activity than sexual labor. Streetwalkers routinely worked together in pairs, both to protect themselves from abusive men and to overpower and rob tipsy customers. The police columns of local newspapers were filled with accounts of drunken brawls and acts of petty theft between prostitutes and their clients. Such violent, predatory behavior was not unique to the world of prostitutes and their clients. Physical violence was a common feature of heterosexual relations throughout rough working-class neighborhoods. When social investigators tried to grasp the nature of gender relations among the unskilled poor in London and Paris, they often found themselves in an "incomprehensible region," to quote historian Ellen Ross, "where women were neither ladylike nor deferential, where men struggled to hold on to their authority over them, where 'sexual antagonism' was openly acknowledged."[6]

In a number of ways, however, prostitutes were distinct from the people in the working-class neighborhoods where they frequently resided. First, their standard of living was often higher. Despite the instability of their income and the dangers and occupational hazards attached to sexual labor, prostitutes usually dressed better than other women in the neighborhood and had spending money comparable to male neighbors. Prostitutes who lived in lodgings or brothels were strikingly cut off from the family system that was the social and economic organizing principle of working-class communities.

Nonetheless, among the casual laboring poor who were accustomed to hard times and who also had to make difficult, temporary accommodations to pressing social necessities, prostitutes could enjoy a certain social integration. In his 1836 study of Parisian prostitutes, Parent-Duchâtelet found evidence of working-class complicity and tolerance of prostitutes: about half of the women who married had chosen men who lived on the same street, often in the same building, while about half of the women whose parents had reclaimed them from prostitution had been living at home.[7] Certain institutions of the working-class neighborhood encouraged this integration, particularly the pub and music hall, where middle-class observers were shocked at the "elbowing of vice and virtue."[8] The camaraderie of the pub was demonstrated at the funeral of one of Jack the Ripper's murder victims in 1888. The casket of Marie Jean Kelly was covered with wreaths from friends "using certain public houses in common with the murdered woman."[9]

Outside the pub, not all respectable women responded as kindly. Community toleration of prostitutes depended on the specific character of the working-class neighborhood: its ethnicity and race, its level of respectability and prosperity. It also depended on the amount of external pressure placed upon the poor to adhere to a more stringent standard of sexual respectability. This external intervention would directly affect the structure of the market for prostitution as well as the character of the women's social relationship with the laboring poor community.

The highly visible, disorderly activity of prostitutes deeply upset middle-class reformers in the middle decades of the nineteenth century. In the wake of the popular revolutions and devastating cholera epidemics of the 1830s and 1840s, sanitary reformers and writers on "moral statistics" became obsessed with the immorality, city waste, contagion, and social disorder emanating from the Great Unwashed. They identified the prostitute, literally and figuratively, as the conduit of infection to respectable society—a "plague spot," a pestilence, a sore. Like the slums from which she emanated, she was thought to carry with her, writes Alain Corbin, the "heavy scents of the masses," with their "disturbing messages of intimate life." She evoked a sensory memory of all the "resigned female bodies" who serviced the physical needs of upper-class men in respectable quarters: the nurse, the old servant maid, the "lower-class woman at the heart of the bourgeois household who manages the bodily needs"—who is at the "beck and call of the bourgeois body."[10]

Official concern over prostitution as a dangerous form of sexual activity, whose boundaries had to be controlled and defined by the state, led to the passage of an array of regulations in almost every country in Europe by the 1860s. Based loosely on the Napoleonic model, regulation systems required prostitutes to register with a "morals police" and to submit themselves to medical inspection for sexually transmitted diseases. Some regulation systems also required prostitutes to reside in registered brothels. With the exception of Great Britain and Belgium, the police regulation of prostitution was developed through administrative procedures, rather than by statutory enactment.

Regulationists praised the supervision and inspection of prostitutes as a defense of public health, public decency, and public order. By treating prostitution as a "necessary evil," they upheld a double standard of sexuality which justified male sexual access to a class of fallen women. They were confident of the physiological imperative of sexual desire for men, but often hedged their bets on a female counterpart. On the one hand, regulationists condemned prostitutes as flagrant sexual transgressors, so "unsexed" that they exhibited "male" lust; on the other hand, they insisted that sexual desire on the part of prostitutes did not enter into the picture at all. A British parliamentary report insisted in 1871 that there was "no comparison to be made between prostitutes and the men who consort with them. With the one sex the offense is committed as a matter of gain; with the other it is an irregular indulgence of a natural impulse."[11]

Defenders of regulation asserted that the sanitary inspection of prostitutes would control the spread of venereal disease. They based this claim on the assumption that syphilis, which was endemic in certain populations, was spread through promiscuous sexual contact with diseased prostitutes and also that available diagnostic and therapeutic methods were adequate to carry out the inspection and treatment of diseased prostitutes. In response to critics who maintained that "contagion" affected males and females alike, and that to examine and confine one sex alone would be analogous to vaccinating only one sex, regulationists retorted that only women "generated contagion," "plied a trade," and "could hide the disease" so well.[12] Class and sex prejudice permeated the entire procedure for inspecting prostitutes for disease. Doctors were surprised at the hostility toward the speculum examination on the part of registered women, who referred to the doctors' speculum as the "government's penis."[13] Prostitutes clearly interpreted the speculum exam as a voyeuristic and degrading act, one that inflicted mental and physical pain on the female sufferer.

A system of *police de moeurs,* regulationists claimed, would also contribute to public decency by checking the public spectacle of vice. This became a particularly important police objective in the second half of the nineteenth century, as police found themselves under increasing pressure to clear public thoroughfares and theaters of streetwalkers to make room for respectable women. In Paris, prostitutes were prohibited from appearing in public in any manner that drew attention to themselves before the street lights were lit; they had to be dressed decently. In Hamburg, the municipal code regulated in detail the costume of women of ill-fame and the districts where they were allowed to circulate. The intention everywhere was to control the perambulating clandestines, those unregistered women whose "glaring colors," "provoking deportment," and shameful looks endeavored to arrest the attention of passersby.[14]

Also crucial to the preservation of public order was the segregation of prostitutes from a working-class community. With this end in mind, regulationists exhibited considerable enthusiasm for state intervention into the lives of the poor. The police in Danzig insisted that unsupervised brothels turned into havens of criminality and social disorder. The removal of prostitutes from registered brothels into private rooms or lodgings, they warned, would result in the general demoralization of poor families, who would be encouraged to take up procuring and other parasitic relationships in connection with commercialized sex. Through publicly stigmatizing procedures—such as police domiciliary visits, notification of employers and family members about women who were "on the town," requirements that prostitutes visit a publicly situated examination house—regulation officials endeavored to clarify the relationship between the unrespectable and respectable poor, and specifically to force prostitutes to accept their status as public women by destroying their private associations with the poor working-class community.

Regulation provoked opposition, however, and not just from its victims. Political opposition to regulation first mounted in Great Britain in 1869, when a coalition of middle-class moral reformers, feminists, and radical workingmen demanded the repeal of the Contagious Diseases Acts, which established a system of police and medical inspection of prostitutes in garrison towns and ports in Southern England. Under the charismatic leadership of Josephine Butler, the repeal campaign drew thousands of women into the political arena for the first time, by encouraging them to challenge male centers of power such as the police, Parliament, and the medical and the military establishments that were implicated in the administration of the acts. The participation of middle-class women in these repeal efforts shocked many contemporary observers, who looked on with horror as ladies mounted public platforms across the country to denounce the acts as a "sacrifice of female liberties" to the "slavery of men's lust" and to describe in minute detail the "instrumental rape" of the gynecological exam.[15]

Mid-Victorian feminists denounced regulation as a bodily invasion and violation of the constitutional rights of working-class women. They interpreted prostitution both as sexual slavery and as the result of the artificial constraints placed on women's social and economic activity: inadequate wages and restrictions on women's industrial employment forced some women onto the streets, where they took up the "best paid industry"—prostitution. At certain moments, feminists articulated a subtle understanding of prostitution's relation to the mores of the laboring poor. "Among the poor," declared Josephine Butler, the "boundary lines between the virtuous and the vicious" were "gradually and imperceptibly shaded off" so that it was "impossible to affix a distinct name and infallibly assign" prostitutes to an outcast category.[16] It was the regulation system, feminists argued, not prostitution as such, that doomed inscribed women to a life of sin by stigmatizing them and preventing them from finding alternative and respectable employment.

Feminists also denounced regulation because it sanctioned and sanitized male "vice." To men and women alike they upheld a single standard of sexuality based on the ideal of female chastity. They not only articulated a criticism of aggressive male sexuality, but also voiced deep ambivalence and repugnance toward prostitutes, particularly those who did not want to be reformed and who manipulated their sexuality as a commodity. "She had travelled through many towns," declared Butler, "and she never found one unfortunate woman" "without [modesty] left in her." But when she arrived at the towns where regulation was in force, she encountered unrepentant prostitutes who "did not meet her frankly. They looked cold and hard, and they told her callously that they were registered, that they were doing no ill, no harm, because they went regularly to their examination."[17] Nonetheless, as an antistatist libertarian, Butler advocated self-restraint and rescue work among prostitutes, instead of state regulation or repression. If prostitutes chose to sell their bodies on the street, they had the right to do so unmolested by the police.

Butler's example inspired women in almost every European country to take up the issue of prostitution. The opposition of American feminists successfully forestalled the introduction of regulation into the United States, except in St. Louis, in 1874, but even there it was soon repealed, in the face of massive religious and feminist opposition. Butler's libertarian views were not shared by many of her followers, however. Challenges to Butler's leadership and her policies developed quickly, both in Britain and abroad. Many women in the German Moral Associations, for example, condemned prostitution as a crime and accused the government, with its system of *police de moeurs,* of complicity; alternatively, a more liberal position was taken up by German abolitionists, who focused their energies on the repeal of state license.

In the name of social purity and the single standard of sexual chastity, many British abolitionists helped to launch a massive assault on nonmarital, nonprocreative sexuality. After the regulation system was suspended in 1883, Butler and her female allies shifted their attention to the foreign traffic in women and the entrapment of children into prostitution in London. They persuaded the journalist W. T. Stead to publish a sensational exposé of child prostitution, the "Maiden Tribute of Modern Babylon," in the *Pall Mall Gazette* in 1885. "Maiden Tribute" had an electrifying effect on public opinion and forced the British Parliament to pass the Criminal Law Amendment Act of 1885, raising the age of consent for girls to sixteen and also giving police greater summary power to repress brothelkeepers and streetwalkers. An additional clause of the bill made indecent acts between consenting male adults illegal. Throughout Britain, grass-roots social purity groups were formed to oversee the local enforcement of this act. Purity groups soon turned their attention to obscene books, birth control literature and advertisements for abortifacients, music hall entertainment, and nude statuary. To these crusaders, pornographic culture thus broadly defined was a vile expression of the "undifferentiated male lust"[18] that ultimately led to homosexuality and prostitution.

These mobilizations had a complex effect on the organization of prostitution. Legal repression remapped the social geography of vice, particularly in Great Britain and the United States, where social purity groups had forced the police to crack down on streetwalking and brothels. As a result of police repression, prostitutes were uprooted from their neighborhoods and forced to find lodgings in other areas in the city. Cut off from any other sustaining relationship, they had to rely increasingly on pimps for emotional security as well as protection against legal authorities. In these and other respects, a heightened policy of repression drove a wedge between prostitutes and the poor working-class community. It had the effect of dispersing prostitution, rendering it more furtive and more tied to a criminal underground. In the United States, repression of prostitution also reinforced patterns of racial prejudice. The closing of red-light districts coincided with the migration of southern blacks to northern cities in large numbers. While white prostitution became largely invisible, black women who went on the streets were much more liable to arrest.

On the Continent, even without changes in police administration, regulated brothels were already in decline and the proportion of "surreptitious" prostitutes who escaped the police net seemed to grow. The whole bordello system had fallen victim to changing consumer taste. "The public has lost its appetite for officially designated resorts," explained one French observer: "the trade inclines rather to houses of rendezvous, where greater discretion is practised and where, with a little imagination, one is conscious of an air of adventure."[19] "The women, too," added the abolitionist Abraham Flexner, "are filled with the desire to enjoy their own freedom. They prefer the reckless abandon of the streets, the cafés, and the theaters."[20] In London and Paris "every imaginable subterfuge" was employed in the effort to carry out "surreptitious" prostitution: chambers were advertised, foreign language lessons announced, dressmaking and massages "employed as baits for the curious."[21] Abolitionists insisted that the large brothels that remained were only able to survive by offering "exotic" sexual services and fantastic displays.

For women as well as for men, the prostitute occupied a deeply symbolic and equivocal position in an imaginary urban landscape. Middle-class women organized their own identity around the figure of the "fallen woman," a fantasy they reshaped and manipulated to explore their own subjectivity. Most women accepted the prostitute as a degraded Other, the debased sexualized alternative to domestic maternal femininity. When Margaret Boveri, aged twenty, asked her mother what "prostitute" meant, the answer she received was: "Prostitutes are fallen girls, for sale, who do it for money—who even enjoy it."[22] Even female reformers, who were sympathetic to the plight of prostitutes as economically pressed women, still hated their "sin" and upheld an opposition between good and bad women, Madonnas and Magdalens. Josephine Butler tried to surmount that division by transforming prostitutes into Magdalen Mothers and innocent female victims of male vice. In her repeal propaganda she used the traditions of female literary melodrama to tell the story of registered women, allowing her fallen Magdalens to speak out and "curse" men for their iniquity.

Butler's identification with "suffering womanhood" was still fraught with contradictions and difficulties. While championing the cause of fallen women and "endangered" girls, female reformers established a hierarchical and custodial relation to the "daughters" they had set out to protect. Their melodramatic language of female victimization deprived prostitutes of any agency and complex subjectivity: they were innocent victims entrapped into a life of vice—involuntary actors in their own history, without sexual passion, not yet "dead to shame," with cherished remnants of womanly "modesty."

A feminist politics of prostitution may have had an ambiguous impact on prostitution, but it certainly gave middle-class women access to public space and new license to speak publicly on sexual matters. These campaigns brought into the open the "ominous shadows," "specters," and "haunting fears" that darkened women's views of heterosexual relations. The exposé of the "Maiden Tribute," declared one London feminist, opened up "new possibilities."[23] Stead's revelations, declared another woman, "broke down a barrier for women . . . After them, no one was of necessity to be ignorant."[24] Driven by "fear" into "speech,"[25] some progressive New Women at the end of the century—notably the writer Olive Schreiner—transgressed the boundaries of social purity and passionlessness to contemplate mutual heterosexual desire. Their explorations, however pioneering, continued to be darkened by a sense of sexual vulnerability and by reservations about men. For them, as well as for more conventional women, the prostitute remained a troubling and threatening symbol, an example of women's sexual nonfreedom because her sexuality was linked to economic need.

For working-class women the prostitute was also a central spectacle in a set of urban encounters and fantasies. In public a poor woman continually risked the danger of being mistaken for a prostitute; she had to demonstrate unceasingly in her dress, gestures, and movements that she was not a "low" woman. Like their middle-class counterparts, working-class women demonstrated their respectability through their public self-presentation and their private identity as wives and mothers. As a "hardworking wife," "anxious mother," and "poor widow," working-class women petitioned city officials in Great Britain and the United States to close down "bad" houses where husbands and sons contracted venereal diseases and spent sorely needed household money or where a "daughter, a Sunday school girl," met her "ruin."[26] Local matriarchs were particularly distressed over the invidious comparisons their impressionable offspring drew from the comparative affluence of prostitutes.

Yet respectable working women also looked on prostitutes as "rebel girls," outside the pale, but powerful and dangerous. They were women who got paid for what they "did," insisted one dock laborer's wife, as opposed to a married woman like herself who had to perform sexual services "for nothing. She didn't get paid for it."[27] At times prostitutes were objects of fascination: "fierce" and independent, not to be interfered with, but occasionally "the loveliest woman in the East End" who "could have had any woman's husband."[28]

Prostitutes spoke about their own situation. They were by no means cut off from the controversies that surrounded them. During the repeal campaign in Great Britain, registered prostitutes used the language of rights to defend their bodily integrity against invasive medical and political surveillance. Through their agitation, feminist repealers had established a political arena that made it possible for prostitutes to resist the intrusive rules of regulation, "to show the officers," in the words of one registered woman, "that we have some respect for our own person."[29]

Facing a judge or charity official, a prostitute would often tell her "tale of woe," using the same melodramatic conventions—about seduction of female innocents by evil upper-class rakes—that middle-class women utilized to explain prostitution. They borrowed this rhetorical strategy from the theater and popular literature: the light romances, the "low trashy wishy-washy cheap publications"[30] that middle-class observers condemned as the first step in the "ruin" of many girls. Alternatively, they made sense of their lives through the language of sexual bartering. "I went into the sporting life for business reasons and for no other," explained one Denver madam. "It was a way for a woman in those days to make money and I made it."[31] Two girls from Crosse and Blackwell's jam factory who walked the streets at night were less upbeat about sex work: they told W. T. Stead that they liked "the work in the factory better than the work in the streets. But the difference in pay was very great. Times they said was hard; and beggars could not be choosers."[32]

Abortion

Despite its illegal status throughout the nineteenth century, abortion, like prostitution, was a highly visible practice, a "booming business" in urban centers throughout Europe and the United States. Like prostitution, it provoked medical outcry and lobbying efforts to suppress women's ready access to abortion and to reserve for doctors the sole right to perform therapeutic abortions. Similarly, the definitions of abortion were many and contested. The disorderly woman who aborted, however, was no longer principally depicted as the single, proletarian prostitute but as an upper-class, married woman of leisure bent on denying her maternal destiny. This image of the aborting privileged lady also shifted the social site where the transgression allegedly took place. Public discussions of abortion often focused as much on the private performances of middle-class marriage and family life as on the back alleys where both the abortionist and the prostitute plied their trade.

Abortion was linked to a general strategy to control reproduction, at a time when middle-class birthrates plummeted yet available contraceptives were unreliable and often ineffective. Falling birthrates in Western Europe and the United States stand testimony to the efforts of middle-class and working-class couples to limit offspring. In the vanguard of this trend was France, with its "precocious" decline in birthrates as early as the eighteenth century: by 1854 more deaths were registered than births. In the United States the fertility rate of native-born whites decreased by half between 1800 and 1900, while working-class immigrant families still produced large families. In the 1870s, observers in Germany and Great Britain began to note a significant decline in fertility; within two generations, the German birthrate would decline by 60 percent, while the average family in England had declined from 6.6 live births to slightly more than two in the 1920s.

Contraceptive techniques, historians argue, made the practice of abortion within marriage "thinkable." To begin with, use of contraceptives forced couples to become more self-conscious about their sexuality, to think of sexual intercourse as something separate from the reproductive act. But abortion, as a specifically female practice, added a further dimension to sexual self-consciousness: it made women particularly active agents in the sexual drama, directly communicating the fact that "women who utilize it are engaging in sex without the intention to procreate, are having sex for its 'own sake' (to satisfy 'male lust' if not their own)."[33]

A range of contraceptive techniques were available to men and women in the nineteenth century, including abstention, *coitus interruptus,* the rhythm method based on an erroneous notion of the "safe period," syringes for postcoital douches, and the condom. All of these procedures required time, money, space, perseverance: they were often unreliable and highly dependent on male cooperation. Abortion remained a woman's back-up for contraceptive failure. Although dangerous and illegal, it had the advantage, particularly for a working-class woman, of giving her some control over her own person, especially if her partner refused to use contraception. It was cheap and did not require previous planning, organization, or forethought.

If a woman desired to abort, her first strategy would be self-induction. This usually required the complicity of others, in contrast to infanticide, the secret act of a lone individual. Support networks of working-class women frequently disseminated abortion information to other neighbors and coworkers. "Women . . . do not make a mystery of these [abortive] practices," explained the French feminist Madeleine Pelletier. "On the landings of the working-class tenements, at the baker's, the butcher's, the grocer's, the housewives advise neighbors whose husbands, as brutal as they are shortsighted, inflict unwanted pregnancies on them."[34]

French neighbors would most likely recommend an infusion of one of the traditional abortifacients, such as rue, savine, or ergot of rye. Doctors believed that some of these traditional remedies worked as poisons or because they produced sufficient irritation to the bowel to induce expulsion. In the United States, different ethnic and racial groups also passed on their traditional knowledge of abortion. Native American healers and midwives regularly prescribed roots and herbs; at mid-century, black women in Texas employed indigo or a mixture of calomel and turpentine to "unfix" or miscarry. By the 1890s, working-class women in the north of England had begun to consume lead pills, after it was observed that women workers in white lead factories often had miscarriages. If drugs did not work, women would try bleeding, hot baths, violent exercises.

If they still had no success, they would resort to an abortionist to induce miscarriage by mechanical means or answer commercial advertisements for "female remedies" appearing in the same newspapers and popular magazines that advertised "Gentlemen's Guides" to vice emporia and "French lessons." By mid-nineteenth century commercialized abortion had become an "industry," a source of considerable profit for doctors, pharmacists, herbalists, veterinarians, masseurs, and quacks, as well as the drug industry. Abortionists became notorious figures, like Madame Restell of New York or her French counterpart "La Cacheuse." One French authority reported that fifty abortionists were advertising in Paris newspapers at the end of the century. Abortionists often clustered near the train stations and the *grand magasins* to provide service for women up from the country, but they also operated out of poor and disreputable neighborhoods.

A pattern of ineffective legislation helped to shape this illegal market but did very little to suppress abortion altogether. Britain was one of the first nations to introduce new criminal legislation in 1803, revised it in 1837, and again in 1861. France and Belgium had laws dating from 1810, founded on Napoleon's Civil Code. New anti-abortion statutes appeared in the various states of the United States in the 1820s; they were significantly amended between 1860 and 1880. By the second half of the nineteenth century similar criminal statutes appeared in Scandinavia, Germany, and Italy. Most of these statutes stipulated punishments for the woman as well as for the abortionist: from five to ten years penal servitude for the woman and up to life imprisonment or death for the "operator"; but usually prosecutions of abortionists only took place if women died or became seriously ill.

Overall, these statutes signaled the intention of legal and medical authorities to intervene in the reproductive strategies of women. In the early nineteenth century lawmakers tended to justify new criminal statutes as "tidying up" measures, part of legal reform of infanticide statutes. In Great Britain and the United States, these early laws only prohibited abortion after "quickening" (the moment when women felt life stirring in them, about three to four months into the pregnancy) and principally focused on the danger to maternal health posed by abortifacients. The 1803 statute did not satisfy the medical lobby in Great Britain, which objected to the concept of "quickening" as imprecise and based on female knowledge; in deference to medical opinion, the 1837 statute prohibited abortion at any stage in the pregnancy, without reference to quickening. By the mid-century doctors in France and the United States had changed their perception of abortion: from being the last resort of the unwed mother it turned into the married woman's back-up method of birth control. One consequence of this modified image was the intensification of public propaganda and the expansion of legal measures against aborting women.

In the United States, opponents of abortion waged a state-by-state campaign to toughen legislation, with medical doctors taking the lead. Between 1860 and 1880, the American Medical Association campaigned heavily to suppress abortion, pitching its appeal to state medical associations, state legislatures, professional journals, and the popular press. Its goal was to secure the criminalization of abortion at any point in a pregnancy, unless it was necessary to save a woman's life.

American doctors may have been more active than their European counterparts in fighting illegal abortions, but doctors in France, Great Britain, and Russia voiced similar concerns over professional competition from abortionists, female misconduct, and threats to the social order posed by abortion. Everywhere medical concern over abortion and contraception signaled that "the doctor is replacing the priest"—that is, he was taking over the role previously held by religious authority in the arena of sex and the family.

Although doctors were the principal ideological actors in these campaigns, they undoubtedly crystallized a set of class, race, and gender fears widespread in the population. Doctors were particularly alarmed over the adoption of abortion, a "degraded" activity, by privileged matrons. "Now we have ladies," exclaimed the Medical Society of Buffalo in 1859, "yes, *educated and refined ladies*,"[35] undergoing abortions. In the image of the self-indulgent "upper-class lady" who had abandoned maternal and child care duties to "selfish and personal ends," doctors saw the apparent seduction of women by the market values of pleasure and consumption, as well as by feminism. Rebelliously pursuing their selfish interests against the self-sacrifice of traditional reproductive womanhood, these women had become disloyal to their husbands by placing themselves at the disposal of "unscrupulous and wicked" male abortionists. As the American Medical Association's Committee on Criminal Abortion summed it up: "She becomes unmindful of the course marked out for her by Providence, she overlooks the duties imposed on her by the marriage contract. She yields to the pleasures—but shrinks from the pains and responsibilities of maternity; and destitute of all delicacy and refinements, resigns herself, body and soul, into the hands of unscrupulous and wicked men."[36]

Women's flight from maternity, insisted French, British, and American doctors, would lead to "race suicide." Along with eugenists, doctors applied certain elements of Darwinian thought to the population problem of their own nations: a superior "racial stock" was crucial to the survival of the fittest in class and nationalist struggles for existence. In the United States, alarmists worried that women of "good stock"—prosperous, white, and Protestant—were not bearing enough children to maintain the political and social dominance of their group. In Great Britain, eugenists fretted over the failure of middle- and upper-class women to reproduce at the same rate as the lower orders. In the late nineteenth century French demographers blamed France's population problem on the general decadence of society and on selfish, independent-minded women's shirking of their civil duty to provide children for the defense of the Republic.

Finally, medical opponents of abortion attacked "irregular" doctors and other health practitioners for providing illegal abortion services. In all countries, allopathic doctors had to contend for recognition and patients with a panoply of popular health practitioners, including chemists, herbalists, hydropathists, and midwives. "Regular" doctors became increasingly alarmed as their competition began to advertise abortion services openly, especially after the 1840s. Competition between "regular" and "irregular" doctors was particularly fierce in the United States, which partially explains the concerted efforts of the American Medical Association to criminalize abortion. But doctors in European countries manifested similar anxiety over professional status. Although many of their professional colleagues performed abortions, particularly for well-to-do patients, French and British doctors focused their criticism on midwives. It was a commonplace in the 1890s that *sage-femmes* made more profit from abortions than births.

By the end of the century a few voices for abortion reform could be heard, although the movement ran more than a generation behind that for contraceptive availability. By the 1880s and 1890s obstetricians felt considerable pressure from their patients to define conditions that would justify abortions. On the whole, their professional associations ignored this pressure. Some French doctors began to challenge the abortion statutes as too rigid, class-biased, and perilous to public health, in that they forced women to resort to dangerous illegal abortions. Sweden modified its legislation in 1890, to permit termination of pregnancy on genuine medical grounds. In 1910, a gynecological congress in Russia voted to decriminalize abortion, provided it was carried out under medical supervision. With the exception of women like Madeleine Pelletier, few voices defended women's right to make personal choices in the area of reproduction, independent of medical supervision.

Although doctors often blamed "strong-minded women" and the influence of feminism for encouraging women's flight from maternity, leaders of the women's movement by no means condoned women's choice of abortion. On the contrary, American feminists responded favorably to the physician-led campaign to outlaw abortion in the late nineteenth century. They condemned abortion as part of the sexual degradation and exploitation of women, but they tended to focus on the causes of abortion—the exploitative sexual relations that made abortion necessary—rather than its consequences.

Feminist opposition to both abortion and contraception reflected a complicated position toward sexuality and reproduction. Struggles over state regulation of prostitution had made feminists wary of doctors as illegitimate authorities of women's biological destiny and as upholders of the double standard. In the same period, feminists also locked horns with doctors as prominent opponents of women's rights and higher education. Yet feminists, like doctors, opposed the separation of female sexuality from reproduction. They too believed that access to contraception and abortion made women "impure," too much like prostitutes, sullied by sexual desire, and vulnerable to male sexual demands. Instead, British and American feminists celebrated motherhood as woman's highest duty, yet advocated a sexual strategy of "voluntary motherhood" that allowed women control over their reproduction through abstinence. In this way the exaltation of maternity in France, Great Britain, and the United States could end in a call for its conscious restriction, with important class and racial overtones. When feminists linked "voluntary motherhood" to a concern that women "improve the race" and produce "fewer and better children,"[37] they voiced some of the same anxieties over class and race that informed medical campaigns against abortion. Moreover, even the minority of feminists who joined with neo-Malthusians at the turn of the century to promote birth control were adamant in distinguishing contraception from abortion: the former was a prudential and dignified practice, the latter, a "high risk" and back-alley affair.

Yet many middle-class women resorted to abortion precisely to fulfill their class/gender role as bourgeois matrons. The "cult of true womanhood," feminist scholars have explained, incited both antinatal and pronatal strategies. It exalted motherhood as a sacred profession, but it also called upon a woman to apply the values of thrift and planning to ensure the class status of her household. By the early nineteenth century smaller families had become a "signifier" of bourgeois class identity. Family planning was part of the bourgeois family ethic, integral to women's maternal duty to produce "fewer and better children." Far from being a flight from maternity, abortion as the back-up to contraception fulfilled a bourgeois woman's duty to children, to class, to race.

Working-class women openly endorsed abortion on similar and different grounds. French and British doctors were disturbed by the casual attitudes of working-class women toward abortion, as a perfectly legitimate measure and not a question of killing. Until quickening, women did not perceive themselves as pregnant but "irregular." Commercial abortifacients responded to this understanding in their advertisements by promising to cure irregularity and bring on the "menses."

Although working-class women clung to the traditional view that there was "no baby" prior to quickening, by the late nineteenth century they could also assert a more "modern" defense of abortion. Like prostitutes, married working-class women were by no means immune to the controversies surrounding this issue. They too began to articulate notions of bodily integrity and to participate in public debates over fertility and "race suicide." When the Women's Cooperative Guild of Great Britain asked its members, mostly wives of skilled workers, to describe their childbearing experiences, many respondents invoked a concept of responsible motherhood involving rational planning and budgeting. Like their middle-class counterparts, they too defended a maternal duty to produce "fewer and better children": "I have not had children as fast as some . . . not because I do not love them, but because if I had more I do not think I could have done *my duty to them* under the circumstances."[38] French women went even further in their defense of abortion as a right: doctors were shocked to find how "freely they related their adventures, without the shadow of shame or remorse, because they say, 'the woman must have the freedom of her body.'"[39] As Rosalind Petchesky observes, this was not a statement of a positive freedom of sexual fulfillment, but, like the middle-class doctrine of "voluntary motherhood," an assertion of a negative freedom from "unwanted sex" and "unwanted childbearing."[40]

Same-Sex Attachments: Transvestism and Romantic Friendships

In the nineteenth century transvestism and romantic friendships were two possible ways for women to explore same-sex attachments. Although transvestism was generally associated with proletarian behavior, it made some inroads also among middle-class women as they emulated the prerogatives of gentlemen and sometimes even made aggressive sexual advances toward other women. Romantic friendships between women were a notable, publicly sanctioned feature of middle-class women's culture; here, too, historical evidence indicates some cultural crossover, particularly among literate factory girls in the United States who pledged their undying love in ornate, sentimental letters to female friends.

Female transvestism, adopting the clothes and/or the life-style, work, and manner of the opposite sex, was a popular tradition at least four hundred years old, told in songs, on the stage, in written works, and by word of mouth. Some historians identify its heyday in the seventeenth and eighteenth centuries, particularly for Holland and England. American historians, however, note the increase in newspaper accounts of "passing" women after 1850. In any case, women took to cross-dressing with the knowledge that other women had preceded them. Old stories of female swashbucklers and "female husbands" still gripped readers in the nineteenth century. When Emma Edwards read the pulp novel tale of *Fanny Campbell or the Female Pirate Captain* (1815), it occurred to her that like Campbell she too might achieve "the freedom and glorious independence of masculinity"[41] simply by cutting her hair and donning men's clothes. She did just that, ran away from home, "came near" to marrying a pretty girl in Nova Scotia, and ultimately enlisted in the Union Army during the Civil War.

Edwards explained her decision to cross-dress in terms of a desire to gain the freedom and privileges of men. For cross-dressing women, these privileges could entail male wages, job opportunities, mobility, and an adventurous life. It could extend to carousing with prostitutes and marrying a woman. Building up a masculine identity might involve performing skillful or heavy labor or being the bravest sailor on the ship; for Eliza Ogden, the female porter of Shoreditch, it also meant smoking and drinking with her brother's shopmates and courting "every pretty wench that came her way." Ogden, in short, was a "computed Rake, and real Romancer." Mary Chapman, reported the London *Times* in 1835, also effected a superior degree of "manliness": she boxed, swore, and supported a mistress as well as her wife.[42]

Some women cross-dressed for special occasions or without trying to pass fully as a man: writer George Sand and artist Rosa Bonheur were two famous examples of middle-class and upper-class women bent on freeing themselves from the constraints of their sex. Some women who did pass were able to achieve a degree of social respectability; others mingled with a sexual underworld. In the 1850s Lucy Ann Lobdell left her husband in upstate New York and passed as a man to support herself. "I made up my mind to wear men's attire and to seek labor," she explained, "and to earn men's wages." She later became the Reverend Joseph Lobdell and settled down with Maria Perry.[43] In the 1870s a French immigrant, Jeanne Bonnet, frequently arrested by the police for wearing men's clothing, visited a brothel as a male customer and fell in love with prostitute Blanche Buneau, whom she persuaded to leave the trade. In 1876 an angry pimp shot her while she was in bed with Buneau. In both cases conventional gender roles were strictly observed, with the "passing" woman playing the dominant masculine part and the other female playing the conventional passive role of wife or mistress.

Like abortion and prostitution, cross-dressing frequently involved the complicity of others. Some ministers agreed to marry female couples; workmates and families kept their secrets; some friends simply chose to believe that their old friend had turned into a man. At her husband's death, a London wife purported to be surprised at the discovery that her mate of twenty-one years was a woman. Yet this community sanction was provisional; when the cross-dresser was subject to prosecution (for "fraud" or disorderly conduct), both the law and the local community tended to blame the "husband" and leave the wife alone.

Indeed, throughout the nineteenth century cross-dressing remained a suspect practice: an unlicensed form of gender transgression, smacking of hypersexuality or sodomy. Legal statutes prohibited cross-dressing as disorderly behavior; culturally, it remained a common trope of female disorder and infringement of male prerogatives. Caricatures featured nagging wives and aggressive women as masculine-featured viragos trying to wear the breeches; the pejorative noun "George Sandism" appeared in English, French, German, and Russian to denounce women who dared to emulate her life and behavior. In response, rebellious women often took up the cross-dressing role: Saint-Simonian women dressed in breeches, while the mid-century Bloomer movement tried to persuade women to don bifurcated garments, discreetly orientalized into Turkish trousers, so as not to appear to be passing as men. Instead of reviling her, late-Victorian feminists embraced George Sand as the embodiment of woman's genius and her dangerous side, even if they did not take to wearing trousers themselves.

At the level of fantasy, cross-dressing enjoyed a far greater purchase on the female imagination: dressing up like a man and running away to sea or to the army was the most persistent adolescent fantasy of British female diarists throughout the century. The transvestite fantasy also found powerful expression during the spiritualist fad: when young female mediums called up spirits to commune with the dead, their spirit guides frequently turned out to be hypermasculine sailors or soldiers. When male impersonators of the music halls decked themselves out in evening wear to masquerade as gentlemen out on the town, they often poked fun at the "magnificent cheek" of the class-marginal clerks in the audience who were themselves aspiring to be "swells."

Unlike female prostitution and male homosexuality, there is little evidence of a transvestite or lesbian subculture in the nineteenth century. Paris was a notable exception: by the 1890s, observers had identified a network of cafés, restaurants, and meeting places for transvestites, lesbian prostitutes, and the bohemian set. The association of lesbianism and prostitution also had some resonance in other urban centers. In 1900, the term "bulldyke" came into use in the "red light" prostitute district of Philadelphia to mean lesbian lover. By the 1920s, black neighborhoods and furnished room districts provided accommodations and leisure spots for working-class lesbians. The blues singer Bessie Jackson would immortalize the rebellious spirit of the "Bulldagger Woman" as a lesbian who adopted a masculine style. A nascent lesbian subculture of middle-class female writers and artists also emerged in the early years of the twentieth century in Paris and New York, a subculture of salons, bars, and shared apartments celebrated in poems, novels, and plays that synthesized the traditions of cross-dressing and romantic friendships.

Within the Victorian middle-classes, women formed same-sex relationships around the practice of romantic friendships. These friendships were, in part, a consequence of the sharp segregation between the sexes in bourgeois life. Female socialization encouraged bonds between women that often developed into lifetime friendships formed during school years. Although romantic friendships were socially condoned, there always existed some tension between close female attachments and family duties.

Women enjoyed a cultural license to express passionate longings for emotional, spiritual, and physical love in a same-sex relationship because it was seen as distinct from heterosexual associations of sexuality and reproduction. "I wanted so to put my arms round my girl of all the girls in the world and tell her . . . I love her as wives do love their husbands, as *friends* who have taken each other for life—and I believe in her as I believe in my God."[44] Letters of this sort adhered to the conventions of literary sentimentalism; to the "sentimental language of blushes, moral uplift, and the pleasures of the heart" that trained Victorian women to "reject sexual passion, anger, worldly ambition."[45]

A set of corporate rituals also managed the crushes, "smashes," and raves that characterized nineteenth-century boarding school life. Through school crushes on an older, publicly successful woman or a more experienced schoolmate, girls learned to channel erotic desire into bodily denial and a "higher" cause. Such unfulfilled crushes also taught girls lessons in self-control and self-denial, what historian Christine Stansell calls "a coyness about the legitimacy of one's appetite."[46]

Whereas earlier in the century a woman could not expect to live with her beloved friend after school years, by the last decades of the century new possibilities for an independent life outside heterosexual domesticity permitted some women to realize that goal. Among the Glorified Spinsters and New Women of the *fin de siècle,* "female marriages" or "Boston marriages" became more common. New occupations in the "helping" professions, new social spaces—the college and the settlement house, as well as the availability of flats and ladies' residences in Britain and the United States—encouraged some women to choose celibacy and the company of a long-time female friend. An extraordinarily high proportion of American female college graduates never married: between 1889 and 1908, 53 percent of Bryn Mawr graduates remained single. According to a 1909 report, only 22 percent of the 3,000 women who had entered Cambridge University had married. Institutions of higher education had become, according to one observer, "hotbeds of special sentimental friendships"[47] where couples were an established tradition on the faculty and crushes and raves powerful rituals among the undergraduates.

Unlike the hidden world of working-class female couples, Boston marriages were publicly visible and accepted by elite circles of society. Women lived together, owned property, traveled together, celebrated family gatherings, and slept in the same bed. In her 1889 autobiography, Emma Willard, the American temperance leader, extolled the virtues of female "companionships," openly detailing her own history of "heart affairs" and observing that "the loves of women for each other grow more numerous each day."[48]

Before the late nineteenth century few commentators associated respectable women's physical closeness with illicit sexuality, believing that such women did not experience autonomous erotic desire outside of reproductive sexuality. However, the flight from maternity, expressed both through voluntary spinsterhood and contraceptive strategies of married women, provoked doctors to scrutinize the sexual drives and objects of women. By the 1880s medical theorists had begun to collapse the transvestite and the romantic friend into the category of the female sexual invert or lesbian.

Sexology, the scientific study of sexuality, emerged on the Continent as a subspecialty of forensic medicine. One of its founders was Richard von Krafft-Ebing, Professor of Psychiatry at the University of Vienna, whose professional duties included finding proof of morbidity or "degeneracy" for sexual offenders dragged before the court to determine whether they could be held responsible for their actions. He collected his case-histories and published them in *Psychopathia Sexualis* (1886), a "medico-forensic study" of the "abnormal." Although the most graphic sexual descriptions were in Latin, to thwart the merely prurient, the book still provoked an enormous popular as well as professional response. Krafft-Ebing found himself deluged with confessional letters from sufferers of sexual misery and victims of sexual oppression. *Psychopathia Sexualis* grew from 45 case-histories and 110 pages in 1886 to 238 histories and 437 pages by the twelfth edition of 1903. The appearance of *Psychopathia Sexualis,* observes Jeffrey Weeks, marked the "eruption into print of the speaking pervert, the individual marked or marred by his (or her) sexual impulse."[49]

In their taxonomies of sex, late nineteenth-century sexologists highlighted the "contrary sexual impulse" or "sexual inversion." They did not autonomously invent the category of the sexual invert: they were reproducing categories and prejudices of nineteenth-century culture, both proletarian and elite. As we have seen, proletarian communities had their own understanding of the "female husband." The lesbian prostitute was already a literary cliché among writers like Baudelaire and Gautier, themselves indebted to the prostitution studies of Parent-Duchâtelet. Nor did sexologists produce in the end a coherent interpretation of sexual inversion: to organize the myriad varieties of sexual experience they uncovered, they resorted to overlapping, confused, and contradictory explanations. Nonetheless, they offered a new vocabulary that would problematize female same-sex practices as well as provide some practitioners with a form to speak "the truth" about themselves.

In the 1860s Karl Ulrichs pioneered congenital theories of sexual inversion for men, arguing that the "urning" (male homosexual) was the product of anomalous embryo development, a female mind in a male body. In 1869 Dr. Carl Westphal, a German psychiatrist, extended the concept of "urning" to women. He published a case study of a young woman, Miss N, who from childhood preferred to dress as a boy, became attracted to women, and in her "voluptuous" dreams appeared to herself as a man. Hers, Westphal concluded, was a case of "an inverted sexual temperament," a congenital defect quite analogous to the male cases.[50]

Miss N eventually found a place in Krafft-Ebing's pantheon of sexual perverts. Krafft-Ebing constructed an ascending scale of female sexual inversion, from the woman who does not portray her "anomaly by external appearance," to the woman who has "strong preference for male garments," to those who play a masculine role, to the most degenerative form of homosexuality: the woman who is female in genital organs only, but whose thought, sentiment, action, even external appearance are those of a man.

Krafft-Ebing and his fellow sexologists could only imagine a lesbian erotic as a version of male desire: a woman's expression of male lust for another woman. Yet they also acknowledged that sexuality was more than a genital act: it encompassed feelings, impulses, emotions, as well as clothes, walk, facial appearance, and life-style. The early sexologists imagined the congenital female pervert as a complete transvestite in both thought and action, at the same time largely ignoring the "feminine" member of the female couple. In 1883, for example, Dr. Kiernan of the United States distinguished the congenital "sexual pervert" from the "young girl she married."[51]

In his study of *Sexual Inversion* (1897) Havelock Ellis collapsed Krafft-Ebing's four categories of female sexual inversion into two: congenital sexual inversion and acquired sexual vice. The congenital female invert was the aggressive masculine woman epitomized by the proletarian cross-dresser. Ellis also turned his attention to the woman who played the passive female role. Referring to the "spurious imitation" of "sexual perversion" that existed when "normal" women copied the congenital invert, he delineated the social environments that would encourage this acquired behavior, mostly the milieu of the educated New Woman. He fixed his gaze on the "passionate friendships" of females, which, he claimed, were of "a more or less unconscious sexual character."[52] Thanks to the modern movement of emancipation, Ellis argued, homosexuality was increasing among women in America, France, Germany, and England.

By "tearing away the New Woman's cloak of respectability," argues Carroll Smith-Rosenberg, Ellis presented "genteel, educated women, thoroughly feminine in appearance, thought, and behavior" as potential lesbians.[53] Historians, however, disagree over the effects of this scholarly exposé: whether it in fact "blew women's protective cover" or instead provided homosexual women with a new sexual discourse. Furthermore, it remains unclear how pervasive and influential was the "medical model." A brief survey of female discourse and practice after the 1890s reveals continuities and discontinuities of female homoerotic expression.

Some women seized the opportunity presented by the new sexological studies to tell their story. Writing to Magnus Hirschfeld, another prominent sexologist who had insisted that homosexuals constituted an "intermediate sexual type," a German woman claimed that the works of Krafft-Ebing "opened" her eyes. "I felt so free and clear-sighted after reading these works." Characterizing herself as one of the "exceptions from the usual mold and the ancient, eternal law of nature," she recounted her life history, ending with a domestic idyll: "My lovely confident little wife directs and guides our happy home like a genuine German housewife and I work and provide for us like an energetic light-hearted man."[54] Radclyffe Hall would immortalize the sexologists' model of female sexual inversion in her pathbreaking lesbian novel, *The Well of Loneliness* (1928), featuring an upper-class mannish lesbian of the "congenital" type in love with a "normal" woman.

Alternatively, women felt deeply threatened by the sexualization and morbidification of female friendships. Some women took the sexologists' warnings to heart: in 1908 Jeanette Marks (herself a partner in a Boston marriage) wrote an unpublished essay, "Unwise College Friendships," warning against sentimental friendships as "abnormal" and "unwholesome."[55] In contrast, Johanna Elberskirchen, author and women's rights advocate, vehemently protested the interpretation of woman loving a woman as a "masculine propensity."[56] In the 1920s a group of lesbians in Salt Lake City privately condemned *The Well of Loneliness* for publicizing their existence, depriving them of the protective cover of an earlier, more reticent age.[57]

These older forms of same-sex attachments continued into the twentieth century. We have already seen in the case of the Bulldagger how certain meanings about the cross-dressing woman endured among working-class lesbians of color. Among middle-class women, Boston marriages and romantic friendships also endured. Although lesbian subcultures had become features of urban life and labels of lesbianism were widespread in the culture, these women rarely identified themselves as lesbians. Yet, as Leila Rupp has observed, once the category of the lesbian was culturally available, "the choice to reject that identification has a meaning of its own."[58]

Over the course of the nineteenth century, middle-class reformers mobilized a medico-moral politics to stigmatize the prostitute, the aborting mother, the transvestite, and passionate female friends as illicit and dangerous. Their mobilizations served not only to mark off deviant females from the feminine norm, but also to specify that norm, to shore it up, to assuage a mounting anxiety that the erotic had lost its moorings and fixed identity in reproductive sexuality. Despite their efforts, these female Others did not remain safely bounded and detached from respectable society. They incorporated and overlapped with bourgeois femininity, in the shopping streets of London's West End where prostitutes mingled with fashionable ladies, in the Malthusian logic of an aborting matron, in the moral superiority of female reformers who took to the streets to save prostitutes, in the preference of high-minded spinsters for the company of members of their own sex, and even in the acceptance by female cross-dressers of distinct male and female identities.

Although the institutional power of the law and medicine was frequently mobilized to control, define, and repress female disorderly conduct, law and medicine were not the only forces at work. Particularly in the case of prostitution, state efforts to regulate provoked public opposition and female resistance. Middle-class women seized the opportunity to tell the story of prostitution as a story of sexual victimization and seduction. In this way they articulated their own grievances against men and established authority over other women. The ability to talk about sex opened up a world of new possibilities for them, but fewer possibilities for the objects of their solicitude, the "daughters of the people." Meanwhile, working women's sexual lives and subjectivities also changed, in response to official controls and regulation and to new opportunities for sexual self-expression within urban commercial culture. Improvisational spaces, anonymity, and specialized services enabled the cross-dresser, the prostitute, the aborting woman, and the female couple to obscure their illicit acts or to create social networks in a modern urban landscape.

15

The Woman Worker

Joan W. Scott

THE WOMAN WORKER CAME into extraordinary prominence during the nineteenth century. She, of course, existed long before the advent of industrial capitalism, earning her keep as spinner, dressmaker, goldsmith, brewer, metal polisher, buttonmaker, lacemaker, nursemaid, dairymaid, or houseservant in the towns and countryside of Europe and America. But in the nineteenth century she was observed, described, and documented with unprecedented attention as contemporaries debated the suitability, morality, and even the legality of her wage-earning activities. The woman worker was a product of the industrial revolution, not so much because mechanization created jobs for her where none had existed before (although that surely was the case in some areas), but because she became a troubling and visible figure in the course of it.

The working woman's visibility followed from the perception of her existence as a problem, one which was described as having been recently created and needing urgent resolution. This problem involved the very meaning of womanhood itself and the compatibility between womanhood and wage-earning; it was posed and debated in moral and categorical terms. Whether the object of attention was a promiscuous factory operative, an impoverished seamstress, or an emancipated compositor; whether she was described as a young, single girl, as a mother, as an aging widow, or as the wife of an unemployed laborer or skilled artisan; whether she was taken as the ultimate example of capitalism's destructive tendencies or as proof of its progressive potentialities, the questions raised about her were the same: Ought a woman to work for pay? What was the impact of wage-earning labor on woman's body and on her ability to fulfill maternal and familial roles? What kind of work was suitable for a woman? Not everyone agreed with the French legislator Jules Simon, who asserted in 1860 that "a woman who becomes a worker is no longer a woman," but most parties to the debates about women workers framed their arguments in terms of an assumed opposition between home and work, maternity and wage-earning, femininity and productivity.[1]

The nineteenth-century debates usually rested on an implicit causal story about the industrial revolution which was taken for granted in most subsequent histories of women workers. (By using the term "story" I mean to emphasize the constructed rather than objective nature of narratives about the past. There is no way simply to recount what happened; rather any story—this one included—offers an interpretation by assembling information to promote a particular and contestable meaning.) This story about the industrial revolution located the source of the problem of women workers in the transfer of production from the household to the factory during the course of industrialization. While in the preindustrial period women were thought to have successfully combined productive activity and childcare, work and domesticity, the presumed change in the location of work was said to have made this combination difficult, if not impossible. As a result, it was said, women could work for only short periods of their lives, withdrawing from paid employment after they married or had children, returning to work later only if their husbands could not support the family. From this followed their clustering in certain low-paying, unskilled jobs, a reflection of the priority of their maternal and domestic commitments over any long-term occupational identification. The "problem" of the woman worker, then, was that she was an anomaly in a world where wage labor and family responsibilities had each become full-time and spatially distinct jobs. The "cause" of the problem was inevitable, a process of industrial capitalist development with a logic of its own.

My argument is that rather than reflecting an objective process of historical development, the story of the separation of home and work contributed to that development. It provided the legitimating terms and explanations which constructed the "problem" of the woman worker by minimizing continuities with the past, assuming the sameness of all women's experience, and stressing differences between women and men. By taking the textile industry as emblematic of industrial development, this account obscured other areas of employment (domestic service and garment making are two examples), in which far larger numbers of women were hired throughout the century and which represented greater continuity with women's occupational history in previous centuries. By not differentiating "women" according to age, marital status, race, or social position, the story of home versus work made married women stand for all women even though most working women, in the nineteenth as in previous centuries, were young and single. And it took marriage and childbearing to be the primary and ultimate destiny of women. Moreover, it assumed that domestic and childrearing responsibilities were fixed and unchanging, that previous generations shared the new standards of the bourgeoisie. As a result, attention was drawn and policy directed to the work side of the working woman's dilemma, the side that was presumed to have changed and so to have created the dilemma for contemporaries. By representing the skilled male craftsman as the exemplary "worker," the account repressed differences of training, job stability, and tenure among male workers and thus also similar patterns of irregular and changing employment for male and female workers. The association of male workers with lifetime commitments to a single occupation and of females with interrupted careers imposed a specific kind of order on a far more diverse situation (one in which some women held permanent craft positions and many men moved from job to job, trade to trade, enduring periods of chronic unemployment). As a result gender was offered as the sole reason for differences between men and women in the labor market, when these differences might otherwise have been understood in terms of labor markets, economic fluctuations, and the changing relationships of supply and demand.

The way the story of the separation of home and work selects and organizes information achieves a certain effect, one that sharply underscores functional and biological differences between women and men and so legitimizes and institutionalizes these differences as a basis for social organization. This interpretation of the history of women's work drew on and contributed to the medical, scientific, political, and moral opinion that has variously been called the "ideology of domesticity" or the "doctrine of separate spheres." It might better be referred to as the discourse that conceptualized gender as a "natural" sexual division of labor in the nineteenth century. Indeed, I would argue that attention to gender as a division of labor in the nineteenth century has to be read in the context of the rhetoric of industrial capitalism about divisions of labor more generally. Divisions of labor were touted as the most efficient, rational, and productive way of organizing work, business affairs, and social life; the line between the useful and the "natural" was blurred when gender was the object of concern.

My interest in this essay is in the discourse of gender which produced the woman worker as an object of investigation and as a subject of history. I want to examine how the dilemma of home versus work emerged as the predominant analysis of working women; how this related to the creation of a female workforce defined as a source of cheap labor and fitted only for certain kinds of work. In order to do this I will retell the story of woman workers in the nineteenth century, attributing change not to objective processes of industrialization, but to the discourse of gender which elaborated, systematized, and institutionalized a sexual division of labor. This division of labor, then, was taken as an objective social fact originating in nature. I attribute its existence not to inevitable historical developments, nor to "nature," but to discursive processes. I do not mean to suggest that distinctions according to sex were new in the nineteenth century; they were, however, articulated in new ways with new social, economic, and political effects.

The standard story of woman's work that stresses the causal importance of the move from household to workplace relies on a schematic model of the transfer of production from farm to factory, from cottage industry to factory, from small-scale craft and commercial activities to large-scale capitalized enterprises. Many historians have complicated this linear picture, arguing, for example, that domestic outwork persisted alongside mechanized manufacture well into the twentieth century, even in textiles. But the image of a cooperative home-based workforce in earlier periods endures—father weaving, mother and daughters spinning while the small children prepare yarn. The image works to construct a sharp contrast between a preindustrial world in which women's work was informal, often unremunerated, and in which priority could always be given to a family, and the industrialized world of the factory, which demanded full-time wage-earning away from home. In the early period production and reproduction are described as complementary activities; in the later period they are presented as structurally irreconcilable, the source of insoluble problems for women who wanted or needed to work.

Although the household model of work surely describes an aspect of seventeenth- and eighteenth-century working life, it is also oversimplified. In the period before industrialization women already worked regularly outside their homes. Married and single women sold goods at markets; earned cash as petty traders and itinerant peddlers; hired themselves out as casual laborers, nurses or laundresses; made pottery, silk, lace, clothing, metal goods, and hardware; wove cloth and printed calico in workshops. If work conflicted with childcare, mothers sent their babies to wet nurses or other caretakers rather than give up employment. In pursuit of wages, women entered a wide range of trades and also moved from one kind of job to another. Maurice Garden comments in his book on Lyon that "the extent of women's work is one of the outstanding features of social life in eighteenth-century Lyon."[2] Dominique Godineau's study of women in revolutionary Paris describes for the woman worker "a ceaseless movement from one sort of activity to another," which was accelerated but not created by the economic crisis that accompanied the Revolution. "The same worker can be found in a workshop making buttons, selling her wares at a stall in the market, or in her room, hunched over her sewing."[3] And in Paris, it has been estimated that at least one-fifth of the adult female population earned wages in the early nineteenth century. Even when work was located in a household, many wage-earners, especially young single women, were not working in their own homes. Domestic servants, farm hands of all kinds, apprentices, and assistants constituted a sizable female labor force which did not work at home. In Ealing (England), for example, in 1599, three-quarters of females aged 15 to 19 were living away from their parents working as servants. In seventeenth-century New England cities girls received their education bound out as apprentices or servants. Young girls journeyed alone to America (particularly to the Chesapeake tobacco region) from England as indentured servants, and others were brought from Africa as slaves.

In the preindustrial period, then, most women workers were young and single, and they typically worked away from their own homes, whatever the type of workplace they went to. Married women were also active members of the labor force; for them, too, the location of work—a farm, shop, workshop, street, or their own homes—varied and the time spent pursuing domestic tasks depended on the pressures of work and the economic circumstances of the household.

This description also characterizes the industrializing period of the nineteenth century. Then, as in the past, the female labor force was overwhelmingly young and single, whether in the more "traditional" field of domestic service or the emerging area of textile manufacturing. In most of the industrializing countries of the West, domestic service surpassed textiles as an employer of women. In England, the first industrial nation, 40 percent of all women workers were servants in 1851 while only 22 percent were textile factory operatives; in France the comparable figures in 1866 were 22 percent in domestic service and 10 percent in textiles; in Prussia in 1882 servants accounted for 18 percent of the female labor force while factory workers were about 12 percent. But whether one looks at servants or factory operatives, one finds girls of similar age. In fact, in regions where manufacturing drew large numbers of young women, there were likely to be complaints about servant shortages. In the French textile town of Roubaix, 82 percent of female employees were under 30; in Stockport, England, the average age of women weavers in 1841 was 20, in 1861, 24. In the mills of Lowell, Massachusetts, in the 1830s and 1840s, 80 percent of female workers were between the ages of 15 and 30 years; in the 1860s, when immigrants replaced native farm women, the female labor force was even younger, with a mean age of 20 years. Married women were also, of course, employed in textile factories since the demand for female labor was so high, and since jobs for men were scarce in textile towns. But these women would have engaged in some kind of wage work wherever they lived, and not necessarily in their own homes. For the bulk of the female wage-earning population, then, the movement was not from work at home to work away from home, but from one kind of workplace to another. If there were problems associated with this move—a new time discipline, noisy machinery, wages dependent on market conditions and economic cycles, profit-driven employers—they nonetheless were not caused by the removal of women from their own home and family settings. (In fact, factory work often enabled girls who might have previously boarded with their employers to reside with their families instead.)

The focus by contemporaries and historians on the textile industry's impact on women's work drew enormous attention to this sector, but it was never, in the course of the nineteenth century, the primary employer of women. More women worked in "traditional" areas of the economy than in industrial factories. In small-scale manufacturing, commerce, and service, married and single women continued patterns of the past, working in markets, shops, or at home, hawking food, carting merchandise, doing laundry, keeping boarding houses, making matches and matchbooks, paper boxes, artificial flowers, jewelry, and articles of clothing. The location of work varied, even for the same woman. The English straw-plaiter Lucy Luck remembered that she "was in the workroom part of the time and had work at home the other part." In the slow season she supplemented her wages by "charring or washing, and I have looked after a gentleman's house a few times, and I have taken in needlework."[4] For Lucy Luck it would be wrong to say there was ever a dramatic break between home and work.

As needlework was synonymous with women in the eighteenth century, so it continued to be in the nineteenth century. The predominance of needlework as woman's work makes it difficult to sustain the argument that there was a dramatic separation between home and work and so a decline in acceptable opportunities for women to earn wages. Indeed, needlework expanded as the clothing, footwear, and leather trades grew, providing steady employment to some women and a last resort for others. The garment trades provided employment for women at various levels of skill and wages, although the vast numbers of jobs were irregular and poorly paid. In the 1830s and 1840s in France and England, outwork for seamstresses (based either at home or in sweatshops) burgeoned with the growth of the ready-made clothing industry. Although some factory-based garment production appeared during the course of the century (in the 1850s in England, the 1880s in France), sweatshop labor prevailed. The passage of protective legislation for women in the 1890s, with exemptions for domestic production, increased employer interest in a cheap, unregulated labor supply. Outwork reached its peak only in 1901 in Britain and in 1906 in France, but this was not the beginning of a permanent decline. Many twentieth-century cities even today are centers of subcontracting; like the domestic industry of the eighteenth century and the sweated homework of the nineteenth century, this practice employs women for piece rates in the clothing trades. In the garment trades continuity is a more obvious characterization than change for the location and structure of women's work.

The case of the garment trades also questions the idealized picture of work at home as suitable for women, because it allows them to combine domesticity and wage-earning. When wage levels are taken into account the picture becomes more complex. Garment workers were usually paid by the piece, and their wages were often so low that the women could barely subsist on their earnings; the pace and timing of work were intense. Whether working alone in her rented room or in the middle of a bustling household, the typical seamstress had little time for domestic responsibilities. One London shirtmaker told Henry Mayhew in 1849 that she could barely get by on what she earned, although she often worked "in the summer time from four in the morning to nine or ten at night—as long as I can see. My usual time of work is from five in the morning till nine at night—winter and summer."[5] Indeed, the location of work at home could be as disruptive of family life as when a mother left for the day, but it was the impossibly low wages and not work itself that caused the disruptions. (Of course, if a woman's economic need were not great, she could moderate the pace of work and combine household chores with wage-earning. These women, a small minority of seamstresses, perhaps provided confirmation of an idealized past when domesticity and productive activity were not in conflict.)

While the garment trades provide an obvious example of continuity with past practices, "white-collar" jobs, too, preserved certain crucial features of women's work. These were jobs that became available towards the end of the nineteenth century in the expanding commercial and service sectors. They, of course, involved new kinds of tasks and developed skills different from those learned either in domestic service or needlework, but these jobs recruited the same kinds of women who had typically constituted the female workforce: young, single girls. Government offices, businesses, and insurance companies hired secretaries, typists, and file clerks, post offices got women to sell stamps, telephone and telegraph companies employed female operators, shops and department stores recruited salesgirls, newly organized hospitals took on nursing staffs, and state-funded school systems sought teachers. The employers usually specified an age limit for their workers and sometimes enforced a marriage bar, thus maintaining a fairly homogenous labor force, under 25 and unmarried. The type of workplace may have changed, but that ought not to be confused with a change in the relationship between home and work for the workers themselves; for the vast majority of those affected, work had typically taken them away from home.

A massive shift thus occurred over the course of the nineteenth century from domestic service (urban and rural, household, craft, and agricultural) to white-collar jobs. In the United States, for example, 50 percent of women wage-earners were servants in 1870; by 1920 close to 40 percent of women workers were office workers, teachers, or shop girls. In France, by 1906, women were more than 40 percent of the white-collar workforce. This transformation of the service sector provided new occupations, to be sure, but it also represented another continuity: the continued association of most women wage-earners with service rather than productive jobs.

To point out continuity is, of course, not to deny change. In addition to the large shift from domestic service to white-collar work, professional opportunities opened for middle-class women, a group relatively new to the labor force. It might well be that much of the attention drawn to the problem of women's work in general stemmed from a growing concern about the marriageability of middle-class girls who became teachers, nurses, factory inspectors, social workers, and the like. These were women who, in the past, would have assisted on a family farm or in a family business, but not actively earned wages on their own. It is perhaps they—a minority of wage-earning women in the nineteenth century—who provided the basis for the claim that the loss of household-based work compromised woman's domestic abilities and her reproductive responsibilities. When reformers talked about "woman workers" as a single category and made their case primarily about factory employment, they may have been generalizing from their anxiety about the position of women in the middle class.

There is not, then, a strong case to be made for the argument that industrialization caused a separation between home and work, forcing women to choose between domesticity and wage-earning. Neither does it follow that this separation caused women's problems by restricting them to marginal, low-paying jobs. Rather, a set of assumptions about the value of women's labor seems to have informed employer hiring decisions (whether in the eighteenth or the nineteenth centuries) quite apart from the location of work. Where women worked and what they did was not the fruit of some inexorable industrial process, but the result, at least in part, of calculations about labor costs. Whether in textiles, bootmaking, tailoring, or printing, whether associated with mechanization, the dispersion of production, or the rationalization of labor processes, the introduction of women meant that employers had decided to save on labor costs. "In proportion as manual labor needs less skill and strength, that is to say in proportion as modern industry develops," wrote Marx and Engels in the *Communist Manifesto,* "so the work of women and children tends to replace the work of men."[6] London tailors explained their precarious situation in the 1840s as a result of the masters' desire to undersell competitors by hiring women and children. American printers saw the employment of women compositors in the 1860s as the "last stratagem of capitalists" who lured woman "from her appropriate sphere" to make her "the instrument of striking down wages, and thus sink both sexes to the level of her present unrequited servitude."[7] Male unions often barred female members, or insisted that they be earning wages equal to men's before they could join. Delegates to the London Trades' Council in 1874 hesitated to admit a representative of the women bookbinders' union to its ranks because "women's labour was cheap labour and many of the delegates . . . could not get beyond that fact."[8]

Women were associated with cheap labor, but not all such labor was considered appropriate for women. If they were deemed suitable for work in textiles, clothing, footwear, tobacco, food, and leather, they were rarely to be found in mining, construction, machine manufacture, or shipbuilding, even when there was a need for so-called unskilled labor. A French delegate to the Exposition of 1867 described clearly the distinctions according to gender, materials, and techniques: "For man, wood and metal. For woman, family and fabrics."[9] Although opinions varied about what was or was not appropriate work for women, and they were put into effect differently in different times and contexts, gender nonetheless regularly entered into considerations of employment. The work women were hired for was defined as "woman's work," somehow suited to their physical capabilities and their innate levels of productivity. This discourse produced sexual division in the labor market, clustering women in some jobs and not others, placing them always at the bottom of any occupational hierarchy, and establishing their wages at less than subsistence rates. The "problem" of the woman worker emerged as various constituencies debated the social and moral effects, as well as the economic feasibility, of such practices.

If the story of the objective separation of home and work does not account for the "problem" of woman workers in the nineteenth century, what does? Rather than searching for specific technical or structural causes, we must use a strategy that examines the discursive processes by which sexual divisions of labor were constituted. This will yield a more complex and critical analysis of prevailing historical interpretations.

The identification of woman's labor with certain kinds of jobs and its description as cheap labor were formalized and institutionalized in a number of ways during the nineteenth century, so much so that they became axiomatic, a matter of common sense. Even those who sought to change the status of woman's work found themselves having to argue against what were taken as observable "facts." These "facts" did not exist objectively, but were produced by histories that stressed the causal effects of the separation of home and work, by theories of political economists, and by employer hiring preferences that created a labor force clearly segregated by sex. The policies of most male trade unions effectively naturalized the "facts" by taking for granted woman workers' lower value as producers. So did the studies of reformers, doctors, legislators, and statisticians, whose outcry led to the passage of protective legislation for women. From the early factory acts to the international movement of the late nineteenth century, this legislation assumed (and so assured) the representation of all women as inevitably dependent and of women wage-earners as an unusual and vulnerable group necessarily restricted to certain kinds of jobs. In this vast chorus of agreement, the dissenting voices of some feminists, labor leaders, and socialists had difficulty making themselves heard.

Political Economy

Political economy produced one of the discourses of the sexual division of labor. Nineteenth-century political economists developed and popularized the theories of their eighteenth-century predecessors. And although there were important national differences (between, for example, British and French theorists) as well as different schools of political economy within the same country, certain basic tenets were held in common. Among these was the notion that men's wages had to be sufficient not only for their own maintenance, but for the support of a family; otherwise, noted Adam Smith, "the race of such workmen could not last beyond the first generation." A wife's wages, on the contrary, "on account of her necessary attendance on the children, [were] supposed no more than sufficient to provide for herself."[10]

Other political economists extended this supposition about the wife's wages to all women, whom they characterized, whatever their marital status, as naturally dependent on men for support. Although some theorists suggested that women's wages should cover their subsistence costs, others maintained that this could not be the case. The French political economist Jean-Baptiste Say, for example, argued that women's wages would always be driven down below subsistence because of the availability of some women who could rely on family support (those in the "natural" state) and thus did not need to live off their wages. As a result, those single women who were outside family contexts and those who were the sole support of their households would inevitably be poor. According to his calculus men's wages were primary for families, covering the costs of reproduction; women's wages were supplementary, either compensating for shortages or providing money over and above what was needed for basic survival.[11]

The asymmetry of the wage calculation was striking: men's wages included subsistence and reproductive costs, women's wages required family supplements even for individual subsistence. Moreover, men's wages were supposed to provide the economic support that maintained a family, that enabled babies to be fed and turned into working adults. Men were, in other words, responsible for reproduction.

Reproduction in this discourse did not have biological significance. Rather, according to Say, reproduction and production were synonymous, each referring to the activity that gave value to things, that transformed natural matter into products with socially recognized (and thus exchangeable) value. Childbirth and childrearing, activities performed by women, were raw materials. The transformation of children into adults capable of earning a living was effected by the father's wage; it was he who gave his children their economic and social value because his wage included their subsistence.

The wage of the worker had a double meaning in this theory. It reimbursed him for his labor and, at the same time, gave him the status of value-creator in the household. Since the measure of value was money and since the father's wage included family subsistence, only the father's wage mattered. Neither the domestic activity nor the wage-earning of the mother was visible or relevant. It followed that women did not produce economic value of significance. Their household labor was not taken into account in discussions of the reproduction of the next generation and their wage work was described as always insufficient even for their own subsistence. Political economy's description of the "laws" of women's wages created a kind of circular logic in which low wages both caused and demonstrated the "fact" that women were less productive than men. On the one hand, women's wages were set low assuming their lower productivity; on the other hand, women's low wages were taken as proof that they could not work as hard as men. "From the point of view of industry, woman is an imperfect worker," wrote Eugène Buret in 1840.[12] And the workers' paper *L'Atelier* began a discussion of women's poverty with, what for them was a truism, "Since women are less productive than men . . ."[13] In the 1890s, the Fabian socialist Sidney Webb concluded a long study on the differences between women's and men's wages this way: "The women earn less than men not only because they produce less, but also because what they produce is usually valued in the market at a lower rate." He observed that these values were not arrived at in an entirely rational manner: "Where the inferiority of earnings exists, it is almost always coexistent with an inferiority of work. And the general inferiority of women's work seems to influence their wages in industries in which no such inferiority exists."[14]

The idea that men's and women's work had different values, that men were more productive than women, did not entirely exclude women from the labor forces of industrializing countries, nor did it confine them to the domestic hearth. When they or their families needed money women went out to earn it. But what they could earn and how they could earn it was shaped in large part by the theories that defined women's work as cheaper than men's. No matter what their circumstances—whether they were single, married, heads of households, or the sole support of dependent parents or siblings—their wages were set as if they were auxiliary to the earnings of other members of a family. Even in situations where mechanization enhanced their productivity (as it did in the Leicester [England] hosiery industry in the 1870s), women's wages remained at the same low levels (in relation to men's) as what they were in domestic work. In the United States in 1900 women in both semi-skilled and unskilled manufacturing jobs earned only 76 percent of the hourly wage of unskilled men—the lowest paid of male workers.

There were other effects of political economy as well. In proposing two different "laws" of wages, two different systems for arriving at the price of labor, economists separated the workforce by sex, explaining their procedure as a reflection of a functional sexual division of labor. Furthermore, by appealing to two sets of "natural" laws—those of the market and of biology—to explain the different situations of men and women, they offered powerful legitimation for prevailing practices. Most critics of capitalism and of woman worker's situation accepted the inevitability of the economists' laws and proposed reforms that retained their premises. Although some feminists (male and female) demanded that women have access to all jobs and be paid wages equal to men's, most reformers urged that women not be required to work. By the end of the nineteenth century in England, France, and the United States, this meant demanding that employers implement the ideal of the "family wage," the wage sufficient to maintain wife and children at home. The demand for the "family wage" accepted as inevitable the greater productivity and independence of men, and the lesser productivity and necessary dependence of women on men. The association between women and cheap labor was, if anything, more firmly in place at the end of the nineteenth century.

One of the premises of political economy, it had become, through the practices of a diverse group of actors, an ever more visible social phenomenon.

The Sex-Typing of Jobs

Employer practices likewise constituted the discourse of the sexual division of labor. When employers had jobs to fill they usually specified not only the age and skill level required, but the sex (and, in the United States, race and ethnicity) of workers as well. The characteristics of jobs and workers were often described in gendered (as well as racial and ethnic) terms. In American cities in the 1850s and 1860s newspaper advertisements for jobs often ended with "No Irish need apply." British textile manufacturers recruited "strong healthy girls" or "families consisting of girls" for mill work.[15] In the American South they specified that these girls and their families be white. (In contrast, the southern tobacco industry hired black workers almost exclusively.) Some Scottish factory owners refused to hire any married women; others made more careful distinctions, as did this manager of the Cowan's paper mill (in Penicnik) when he explained his policy in 1865: "With a view to prevent the neglect of children in their homes, we do not employ mothers of young children in our works, unless in the case of widows or women deserted by their husbands, or having husbands unable to earn a living."[16]

Often employers described their jobs as having inherently gendered qualities. Tasks requiring delicate, nimble fingers, patience, and endurance were marked as feminine, while muscular strength, speed, and skill signified masculinity, although none of these descriptions was used consistently across the range and variety of jobs offered and, in fact, they were the subject of intense disagreement and debate. Still, the effect of these descriptions and of decisions to hire women in some positions and not others was to create a category of "woman's work." Wages, too, were set with the gender of workers in mind. Indeed, as calculations of profit and loss and the search for competitive advantage in the market intensified, saving on labor costs became an increasingly important factor for employers.

Employers developed a variety of strategies for cutting labor costs. They installed machinery, they divided and simplified tasks in the manufacturing process, they lowered the skill (and/or education and training) requirements for their work, they speeded up the pace of production, and they reduced wages. This did not always mean bringing in women, for there were many jobs considered unsuitable for women, and others in which the resistance of male workers made hiring females unthinkable. But if the drive to cut labor costs did not always lead to feminization, hiring women usually meant that employers were trying to save money.

The Scottish economist Andrew Ure described the principles of the new factory system in 1835 in terms familiar to manufacturers:

> It is, in fact, the constant aim and tendency of every improvement in machinery to supersede human labour altogether or to diminish its cost, by substituting the industry of women and children for that of men, or that of ordinary labourers for trained artisans. In most of the water-twist, or throstle cotton mills, the spinning is entirely managed by females of sixteen years and upwards. The effect of substituting the self-acting mule for the common mule, is to discharge the greater part of the men spinners, and to retain adolescents and children. The proprietor of a factory near Stockport states . . . that by such substitution, he would save £50 a week in wages.[17]

In the Massachusetts shoe industry in the 1870s manufacturers experimented with a variety of changes in the sexual division of labor in their factories. They lasted shoes with thread instead of tacks, thereby transferring work from men to women, and they introduced cutting machines run by women. In both instances women's wages were lower than those of the men they replaced. Women began to be hired in the printing industry, also as a way of cutting labor costs, in the mid-nineteenth century when newspaper publishing expanded in urban centers. Publishers attempted to meet the need for more compositors for morning and evening editions of daily newspapers by training and hiring women for the jobs. The opposition of unionized male printers kept these practices to a minimum and effectively prevented the feminization of the printing trades. Still, in many small towns large numbers of women continued to be employed (at lower wages than men) in book printing and book binding.

In the expanding areas of professional and white-collar work, women were designated suitable employees for many reasons. In teaching and nursing they were said to be nurturing; typing was likened to piano playing; and clerical tasks supposedly drew on feminine submissiveness, toleration of repetition, and fondness for detail. These traits were deemed "natural," as was the "fact" that the cost of women's labor was necessarily lower than men's. In the United States in the 1830s and 1840s the great debates on public education involved questions of cost as well as of wide public access to tax-supported common schools. Federalists and Jacksonians alike were concerned that if such schools were established, their costs be minimal. Jill Conway explains the turn to women teachers and the lower status of teaching in the United States, as compared to most countries in Western Europe, as the result of the emphasis on low costs. "The goal of cost containment made the recruitment of women completely logical because all parties to the educational debate agreed that women lacked acquisitive drives and would serve at subsistence salaries."[18] A similar reasoning informed decisions to bring women into clerical work in government service and private commercial firms. In Great Britain, according to Samuel Cohn, women were hired where work was labor-intensive and because there was a growing scarcity of boys for clerical jobs. Hiring women often meant a change in strategy; a desire to increase economic efficiency and cut labor costs, while at the same time recruiting better educated workers.[19] The director of the British telegraph services noted in 1871 that "the wages which will draw male operators from but an inferior class of the community will draw female operators from a superior class."[20] His French counterpart, who had carefully studied the British experience with female personnel, commented in 1882 that "the recruitment of women is carried out under conditions of education generally superior to that demanded of new clerks."[21] For similar reasons, but with more reluctance, the German telegraph administration hired women as "assistants" (a position that distinguished their grade and salary from men's) beginning in the late 1880s.

In the French telegraph service women and men worked in different rooms and on different shifts in the 1880s, presumably to prevent contact between the sexes and the immoral behavior that might follow it. In addition, the sharply differentiated workspaces underscored the different statuses of male and female workers, statuses reflected in the different wage scales paid to each group. The organization of work in the telegraph service in Paris was at once a visible demonstration and an implementation of the sexual division of labor.

The French postal service began hiring women in urban centers in the 1890s; this was considered a major departure, although women had managed provincial post offices for decades. The postal administration opened applications to women when, in a period of expanding volume of mail and of pressure to make the service more financially efficient, men failed to apply for positions at the salaries offered. Eventually a special category for women workers was created, the *dames employées,* a clerical position with a fixed wage and no opportunity for advancement. High turnover in the female labor force followed from these conditions of employment. (It also resulted from requirements of age and marital status—some sales and clerical jobs took women only between the ages of 16 and 25 and specified that they must be single. In England and Germany a marriage bar was enforced for clerical workers, increasing turnover and making it impossible for women to combine marriage and clerical work.) The result was a sharp distinction between male and female careers in the postal service, a distinction that reflected management strategy. A personnel manager described it this way:

> Today there exists a category of employees who resemble in some ways the auxiliary clerks of old. These are the *dames employées.* They have the same duties as clerks, but they cannot aspire to chief clerk positions. . . . Feminization is a convenient means of giving male clerks greater chances of advancement. The number of men employees is less numerous and the number of supervisory positions tends to increase; it is clear, therefore, that men clerks can more easily attain the position of chief clerk.[22]

The spatial organization of work, hierarchies of wages, promotion, and status, and the concentration of women in certain kinds of jobs as well as certain sectors of the job market constituted a sex-segregated labor force. The assumptions that structured sex-segregation in the first place—that women were cheaper and less productive than men, that they were fit to work only at certain periods of their lives (when young and single), that they were capable of only certain kinds of work (unskilled, casual, and service jobs)—seemed to be borne out by the patterns of women's employment they had constructed. Low wages, for example, were attributed to the inevitable "crowding" of women into the occupations suitable for them. The existence of a sex-segregated labor market was then taken as proof of the prior existence of a "natural" sexual division of labor. I have been arguing instead that there is no such thing as a "natural" sexual division of labor. Instead, such divisions come into being through practices that naturalize them; of these, the segregation of the labor market by sex is an example.

Trade Unions

Another example of the way the sexual division of labor is discursively constituted can be found in the policy and practices of trade unions. For the most part, male trade unionists sought to protect their jobs and wages by keeping women out of their trades and, in the long term, out of the labor market. They accepted the inevitability of women's wages being lower than men's, and so treated women workers as a threat rather than as potential allies. They justified their attempts to exclude women from their particular trades by arguing in general terms that women's physical structure determined her social destiny as mother and homemaker and that, as a result, she could be neither a productive worker nor a good trade unionist. The solution, widely endorsed by the end of the nineteenth century, was to enforce what was taken to be a "natural" sexual division of labor. Henry Broadhurst told the British Trades Union Congress in 1877 that union members had a duty "as men and husbands to use their utmost efforts to bring about a condition of things, where their wives should be in their proper sphere at home, instead of being dragged into competition for livelihood against the great and strong men of the world."[23] With few exceptions, French delegates to the workers' Congress of Marseille in 1879 endorsed a position that Michelle Perrot has called "praise for the homemaker": "We believe that a woman's true place is not in the workshop or the factory but in the home, within the family."[24] At the Gotha Congress in 1875, the founding meeting of the German Social Democratic Party, delegates debated the question of women's work and finally called for a ban on "female labor where it might be deleterious to health and morality."[25]

Like employers (but not always for the same reasons) union spokesmen invoked medical and scientific studies to argue that women were not physically capable of performing "men's work," and they predicted dangers to women's morality as well. Women might become "socially unsexed" by doing men's work and they might emasculate their husbands if they spent too much time earning wages away from home. American typographers countered their bosses' arguments that typesetting was a feminine task by insisting that the combination of muscle and intellect required for the job was quintessentially masculine. They further warned in 1850 that an influx of women into the trade and into the union would make men "impotent" in their struggle against capitalism.[26]

There were, of course, unions that accepted women as members, and unions formed by women workers themselves. These tended to be in the textile, garment, tobacco, and shoe trades, where women formed a significant portion of the labor force. In some areas women were active in local union and strike efforts, even when national unions discouraged or prohibited their participation. In others, they formed national women's trade union organizations and recruited women workers from a broad spectrum of occupations. (The British Women's Trade Union League established in 1889, for example, founded the National Federation of Women Workers in 1906 and, on the eve of the First World War in 1914, had some 20,000 members.) But whatever form it took, their activity was most often defined as women's activity; they were a special category of worker no matter what specific job they performed, and they were usually organized into separate groups or (in the case of the American Knights of Labor) "female assemblies." In mixed unions, furthermore, women were given a decidedly subordinate role. Not all such organizations followed the example of the Associations Ouvrières du Nord de la France, which required in the period 1870–1880 that women who wished to speak at meetings have written authorization from their husbands or fathers, but many defined woman's role as that of following the male lead. There were successful challenges to this definition that brought women into prominence for a while, as happened in the Knights of Labor from 1878 to 1887, but instead of being evolutionary steps forward, these victories tended to be brief and did not permanently alter the subordinate status of women in the labor movement. However dramatic their strike efforts or convincing their commitment to union organization, women workers did not dislodge the prevailing belief that they were not fully workers—not, that is, men with a lifetime commitment to wage-earning.

When they argued for representation, women justified their claims by appealing to contradictions in union ideology which called for equality for all workers, on the one hand, and the protection of working-class family life and domesticity against the ravages of capitalism, on the other. Framed as it was by this opposition between work and family and men and women, the argument for women's equal status as workers was as difficult to make as it was to put into effect. Paradoxically, it was made more difficult when union strategies sought to exclude women by endorsing the principle of equal pay for equal work. Printers' unions in England, France, and the United States, for example, admitted women to their ranks only if the women earned the same wages as their male counterparts. Instead of making equal pay the union's goal for women, it became a prerequisite for membership. This policy assumed not only that employers hired women because they could pay them lower wages than they did men, but also that women's work was not worth as much as men's and therefore could never be equally reimbursed. It subscribed implicitly to political economy's theory of women's wages, and so endorsed the idea that there was a "natural" explanation for wage differentials between women and men. In view of this belief, the printers' solution was to bar women from wage-earning and call for the fulfillment in practice of political economy's postulate that a man's wage ought to provide a comfortable subsistence for his entire family.

The demand for a family wage became increasingly central to trade union politics during the nineteenth century. Even though it was never fully implemented and married women continued to seek employment, the nonworking wife became the ideal of working-class respectability. Daughters were expected to work and contribute to household expenses, but only until marriage. Their status as workers was seen as a short-term expediency, not an enduring identity, even if, as was the case for many women, they did spend most of their lives earning wages. The woman worker was represented as definably different from the male worker. If for men work was supposed to create the possibility of independence and individual identity, for women it was undertaken as a duty to others. When young and single, a woman's work fulfilled family obligations; when married and a mother, it was taken as a sign of economic trouble in the household. The discussions of the unsuitability of paid employment for married women were framed in terms of generalizations about female physiology and psychology and so conflated married women with all women. As a result, maternity and domesticity were equated with womanhood, and these tasks were taken to be exclusive and primary identities, explaining (rather than following from) women's opportunities and wages in the labor market. The "woman worker" became a separate category, a problem to address more often than a constituency to organize. Clustered in women's jobs, grouped separately in women's unions, women's situation became further demonstration of the need to recognize and restore "natural" differences between the sexes. In this way an understanding of the sexual division of labor that counterposed production and reproduction, men and women, was institutionalized through the rhetoric, policies, and practices of trade unions.

Protective Legislation

What happened in trade unions for one reason, happened under state auspices for other reasons; the resulting construction of the sexual division of labor, however, was similar. Over the course of the nineteenth century the United States and the countries of Western Europe increasingly intervened to regulate the employment practices of manufacturers. Legislators responded to pressure from various constituencies which, for different (sometimes antithetical) reasons, sought to reform conditions of work. Most attention was directed to women and children. Although both groups had worked long hours in the past, concern about their exploitation seems to have been connected to the rise of the factory system. Reformers who were reluctant to interfere with "the individual liberty of [male] citizens" had no such difficulty with women and children.[27] Since they were not citizens and had no direct access to political power, they were considered vulnerable and dependent and therefore in need of protection.

Women's vulnerability was described in many ways: their bodies were weaker than men's and they therefore ought not to have to work as many hours; work "perverted" the reproductive organs, rendering women unfit to bear and nurse healthy babies; employment distracted them from domestic tasks; night jobs exposed them to sexual danger in the shop and on the way to and from the workplace; working alongside men or under male supervision carried the possibility of moral corruption. To those feminists who argued that women did not need the protection of others but collective action of their own, legislators as well as representatives of working men and women replied that since women were excluded from most male unions and seemed unable to form unions themselves, they needed a powerful force to intervene on their behalf. Jules Simon argued at the International Conference on Labor Legislation in Berlin in 1890 that maternity leaves for working women ought to be mandated "in the name of the evident and superior interest of the human race." It was, he said, protection due "persons whose health and safety can only be safeguarded by the State."[28] These justifications, whether physical, moral, practical, or political, construed women workers as a special group whose wage work created problems of a different order from those typically associated with (male) labor. From its first appearance in the various factory acts in England in the 1830s and 1840s through the organization of international conferences designed to propagate and coordinate national laws in the 1890s, protective legislation was enacted not to remedy industrial working conditions generally, but as a specific solution to the problem of the woman (and child) worker.

Although its proponents talked in general terms about women (and children), the legislation that was passed was narrowly circumscribed. Laws that limited the hours of women's work and prohibited night work entirely usually applied only to factory work and to those trades where men predominated. Many areas of work were entirely excluded, among them agriculture, domestic service, retail establishments, family-run shops, and domestic workshops. These usually constituted the major employers of women in the first place. In France some three-quarters of all working women were not covered by the legislation. In Germany, France, England, Holland, and the United States, homework for women proliferated after the passage of protective laws. Mary Lynn Stewart sums up the impact of the legislation, whose most characteristic feature was a long list of exemptions from regulation:

> Exemptions accommodated industries accustomed to cheap female labour, accelerated women's movement into unregulated sectors and thereby accentuated female crowding in the

backward industries. Administration of the law reinforced these effects. Inspectors implemented the letter of the law in masculine trades yet overlooked infractions in feminine occupations. In short, sex-specific labour legislation sanctioned and enforced the assignment of women to lower paying secondary labour markets.[29]

Even in industrial employment the laws had the effect of intensifying the segregation of male and female workers, whether to accommodate the need for different shift lengths or to separate day and night work. These distinctions further justified pay differentials and the attribution of different characteristics, qualities, and statuses to men and women. Stewart's conclusion is apt: "Overall the most striking outcome of sex-specific hours standards was an entrenched and exaggerated sexual division of labour."[30] The premise of the law thus became its effect and the breach between male and female work was widened. Having defined woman's reproductive role as primary, the state enforced the secondary status of her productive activity.

The "Problem" of the Woman Worker

Debates about hiring, union policy, and protective legislation generated a great deal of information about women workers and the social facts of their existence. The documentation provided in parliamentary reports, private investigations, and personal testimony can be read to show that women worked for a variety of reasons: to support families or themselves, as part of a long tradition of skilled female crafts (in dressmaking or millinery, for example), or because they were recruited to new kinds of jobs. The information can be used to argue that work had the effect of depressing and exploiting women or of providing a way to achieve a sense of autonomy, a place in the world. Wage-earning can be portrayed as an impossible exaction, a necessary evil, or a positive experience, depending on the context and the framework within which it is analyzed. Indeed, it was depicted in all these terms during the nineteenth century, sometimes for the same person at different points in her life. The French woman Jeanne Bouvier (born in 1856) had a succession of terrible jobs as a child, first in domestic service and then in a factory. Later she worked as a seamstress in Paris and ultimately became a skilled dressmaker. She then pursued a satisfying career (as she recounts it) as a writer and union organizer.[31] Similarly, the women (born in the 1850s and 1860s) who recalled their working lives in memoirs written for the Women's Cooperative Guild in England tell of diverse wage-earning situations, some of which left them exhausted and penniless, others of which gave them a sense of purpose and strength and exposed them to political movements that developed a collective identity among them.[32] Some needlewomen told Henry Mayhew that low wages and not the work itself drove them to prostitution, others dreamed of marriage to a man whose earnings would be sufficient to support them and end their need to work forever. Even the most horrified of reformers often noted the pride and independence of some of the women workers they described as downtrodden and depraved. They argued that such attitudes were as dangerous to domestic stability as the physical and economic exploitation women workers endured. When female trade unionists called for equal wages for women, they assumed not only that women would have to continue to work but that they might want to; that in addition to economic necessity, a desire to have an occupation accounted for women's presence in the labor force.

These competing accounts and contradictory interpretations tended to be subsumed in the dominant discourse of the period, which conceptualized a standard woman and defined work as a violation of her nature. The definition of the "problem of the woman worker" made working women visible not as mistreated agents of production, but as social pathology. For the problem was usually framed in terms neither of the satisfactions or difficulties work offered to individual women, nor of their long and continuing history of workforce participation, nor of the inequity of their lower-than-subsistence wages, but rather in terms of the effects of physical exertion on their bodies' reproductive capacities and of the impact of their presumed absence from home on the discipline and cleanliness of their households. Even proposals which did not assume that work and womanhood were incompatible shaped their appeals to that notion, stressing the effects of exploitation on family life and maternity.

During the debates on the English factory acts in the 1830s and 1840s, William Gaskell argued that working women's breasts became unfit to nurse children in the course of factory work.

Others cited the incompatibility of women and machinery, counterposing soft and hard, natural and artificial, future and present, reproduction of the species and production of inanimate goods. Still others depicted the immorality that followed from women's engaging in hard work, from their exposure to coarse male language in mixed workplaces, from the predations of male overseers who required sexual favors, and from the pressure of poverty to engage in prostitution. Even as they took account of low wages and poor working conditions, these descriptions tended to blame work itself, especially "public" work outside the home, as the cause of women's ills. Paul Lafargue, deputy of the Parti Ouvrier Français, proposed in 1892 an innovative maternity leave policy for French working women that would pay them a daily stipend from the fourth month of pregnancy to the end of the first year after childbirth. He suggested that employers be taxed to support childbirth because it was women's "social function." He offered the measure, he said, as a corrective to capitalism's rapacious disruption of family life, which "pulls women and children out of the domestic sphere to transform them into instruments of production."[33] Here a progressive social program was justified by appealing to an ideal that assumed the secondary status of women's productive activity.

Similarly, many of the attempts to ease the effects of work on a mother and her family by providing day care and schooling for children took the form of emergency measures rather than long-term social policy. Some reformers sought to establish nurseries or other publicly supported institutions to relieve working women of their double burden, others were concerned about high levels of infant mortality and "the future of the race," but both groups dramatized the need for reform through exposés of child neglect by careless babysitters, "baby farmers," or wet nurses, those "unnatural" substitutes for full-time maternal care. The underlying assumption, even by those who concluded that women's work itself was not harmful, seemed to be that domesticity ought to be a full-time occupation.

But as an occupation, household activity was not considered productive work. Although the emphasis on domesticity seemed to heighten women's social status and brought with it eulogies to women's affective and moral influence, it was work devoid of economic value. In Britain, according to Jane Lewis, the census of 1881 was the first to exclude women's household chores from the category of work. "Once women engaged in domestic labour were classified as 'unoccupied,' the female activity rate was cut in half." Before then, women and men over age 20 had had similar levels of economic activity.[34] After 1881, domesticity and productivity were represented as antithetical. This reclassification (which occurred in other countries as well, though at different dates) did not so much reflect changed employment conditions as it did social understandings of gender. Women at home were not workers or not supposed to be workers; indeed, even if sometimes they earned wages by sewing or doing other tasks in the household, census takers did not consider this to be bona fide work since it neither took "full time," nor was it performed outside of the house. As a result, much of women's wage-earning work was ignored in official government statistics; invisible, it could not become the object of attention or improvement.

In the discourse of the sexual division of labor, the assumptions of what constitutes "woman's nature" made the woman worker herself a problem. This drew the discussion of solutions away from the conditions of her work, her low wages, or the lack of social support for childcare, all of which were taken as symptoms of the violation of the "natural" functional difference between men and women rather than as causes of female wage-earners' distress. The effect was to prescribe a single desirable goal: the removal, as much as possible, of women from permanent or full-time wage-earning. Although this policy was rarely achieved in practice, it made practical solutions for women workers difficult to formulate, for it accepted as natural and inevitable the fact that they would always be second-class employees whose bodies, productive capacities, and social responsibilities made them incapable of the kind of labor that would win economic and social recognition of them as full-fledged workers.

The prominence of women workers in the nineteenth century, then, came not so much from an increase in their numbers or a change in the location, quality, or quantity of their work, as from contemporaries' preoccupation with gender as a sexual division of labor. This preoccupation was not caused by objective conditions of industrial development; rather, it helped shape those conditions, giving relations of production their gendered form, women workers their secondary status, and home and work, reproduction and production, their oppositional meanings.

To write the history of women's work as the story of the discursive construction of a sexual division of labor is not to legitimize or naturalize what happened, but to question it. In this way we open the story to multiple explanations and interpretations, ask what might have occurred differently, and put ourselves in a position to think anew about how women's work today might be conceived and organized.

16

Single Women

Cécile Dauphin

"A SINGLE WOMAN! Is there not something plaintive in the two words standing together?"[1] This exclamation by a mid-nineteenth-century English journalist echoes many other articles and books of the time, which discovered the problem of "redundant women."[2] Victorian society was troubled by the

> enormous and increasing number of single women in the nation, a number quite disproportionate and quite abnormal; a number which, positively and relatively, is indicative of an unwholesome social state, and is both productive and prognostic of much wretchedness and wrong. There are hundreds of thousands of women—not to speak more largely still—scattered through all ranks, but proportionally most numerous in the middle and upper class, who have to earn their own living, instead of spending and husbanding the earnings of men; who, not having the natural duties and labours of wives and mothers, have to carve out artificial and painfully sought occupations for themselves; who, in place of completing, sweetening, and embellishing the existence of others, are compelled to lead an independent and incomplete existence of their own.[3]

The "single woman" was thus a contemporary category. Behind the endless laments and alarmist warnings lay questions of definition. Who were these single women? Why did they exist? What could be done about them? Their disproportionate numbers, a sign of economic and social turmoil, and their life situation, antithetical to the ideal of womanhood, thrust these single women before the public mind. Yet perception inevitably was haunted by the specter of the "spinster"; the single woman showed only the tragic mask of the "woman without a man." The tag has since become a commonplace, even if it has no precise masculine counterpart. Today it is applied indiscriminately to women without husbands, to widows, to the celibate, to mothers as well as to childless women.

A Feminine Fact

Two things are clear about the phenomenon of the single woman in the nineteenth century: it was widespread, and it was new. "In every census the [female] sex has been superior in numbers" to the male: Levasseur's remark sounds as though this reflected an anomaly of nature.[4] Indeed, while the ratio of 106 male births to every 100 female births appears to have remained more or less constant through the ages, Europe in the "age of statistics" discovered, and deplored, the fact that its population contained an excess of females. In part this was a consequence of the times. Because the wars and violence of the Revolution and Napoleonic period had claimed large numbers of males, it has been estimated that 14 percent of all females born in France between 1785 and 1789 were destined to remain celibate.[5]

Writers such as Balzac were quick to seize on this fact to explain the increase in the number of single women: "France knows that the political system favored by Napoleon left many widows. Under this regime, the number of heiresses far outstripped the number of marriageable bachelors."[6]

These losses, which affected all Europe in the nineteenth century, were never entirely evened out by the high mortality rate of women in childbirth and of girls dying at birth and from child labor.[7] Although advances in hygiene and medicine generally increased life expectancies after the end of the eighteenth century, the most spectacular gains were registered among women. Whether the causes of excess male mortality were economic, biological, or a combination of factors, the consequences for women in terms of celibacy, widowhood, and solitude were considerable.[8] Consider the French population over the age of fifty in 1851, for example: only 27 percent of the men were celibate or widowed, compared with 46 percent of the women (12 percent celibate, 34 percent widowed).

A European Model

Wartime slaughter was by no means limited to the nineteenth century or to Western Europe. What did distinguish Europe from other continents was the nonuniversality of marriage. Since Hajnal, various demographic researchers have examined the way in which the European model of late, monogamous marriage served to regulate the population, acting in a sense as a contraceptive device.[9] Strange as it may seem, the phenomenon of single women first appeared in history as a negative variable in studies of population growth. Experts have calculated that confirmed celibacy reduced the fertility rate by something on the order of 7 or 8 percent.

To be sure, anthropologists have noted other exceptions to the rule of universal marriage: in Tibet, for example, celibate women were numerous early in this century. In China and India widows (in the upper strata of society) were expected not to remarry—their lot was one of postconjugal celibacy, as it were.[10] Note, however, that in China in the 1930s only one woman in a thousand went through life without marrying (and only three men). In the West, by contrast, the rate of "permanent" celibacy (the percentage of women who lived beyond the age of fifty without ever marrying) rarely fell below 10 percent. Looking at the long-term situation, the greatest increase in this rate occurred in the late eighteenth century; after peaking in the first decade of the nineteenth century, it leveled off or declined slightly, coincident with a decrease in the age of marriage.[11]

Regional Contrasts

If celibacy was indeed a characteristic and more or less permanent feature of Western civilization (the reasons for which remain to be elucidated), its uneven distribution in different countries and social groups tended to distort contemporary perceptions. The celibacy rate, which stood below 5 percent in Russia in 1897 and around 8 percent in rural Prussia and Denmark in 1880, reached as high as 20 percent in certain parts of France and Portugal at mid-century, and 48 percent in the Swiss canton of Obwald in 1860.

There is as yet no comprehensive map or global study of celibacy in Europe, but all the monographs on the subject show a stark contrast between the northeastern part of the Continent, where marriage was nearly universal, and the southwestern part, where many women remained single. There were also regional differences within countries.[12] In France, for example, Brittany, Cotentin, the Pyrenees, and the area southeast of the Massif Central were areas of high celibacy and widowhood, whereas the Paris basin exhibited much lower rates. The states of northeastern Germany had celibacy rates below 10 percent, whereas Bavaria and Württemberg were above 15 percent. In England the highest proportions of single women were found in northern agricultural regions and Wales.[13]

Beyond such purely demographic parameters as sex ratio, mortality differentials, age structure, and age difference between spouses, these regional patterns suggest that celibacy and widowhood were governed by certain unwritten rules inscribed deeply in the social consciousness. Demographers invariably point out that in a given society celibacy frequently coincides with late marriage and absence of contraception. On the basis of these observations, they have formulated the so-called ascetic Malthusianism hypothesis: namely, that the religious authorities that preached continence and virtue thereby unwittingly promoted a reduction in the birth rate and inhibited the dispersion of family property. It turns out that regions that "produced large numbers of celibate individuals" share the following characteristics: family structures are patriarchal; marriage tends to be carefully controlled and delayed; and in each generation the one child chosen to inherit the family fortune marries, whereas the other children either remain celibate or go elsewhere to seek their fortunes. In the nineteenth century, however, urbanization and industrialization disrupted these traditional structures, whereupon families broke up, releasing workers needed for economic development into the labor market.

Urban Poles

Against this background of major upheaval, the cities, traditionally the reservoir into which the excess population of rural society was funneled, likewise attracted the celibate individuals. Of course cities created single women as much as they brought them in.

Already in the eighteenth century observers had been struck by the "legions of single women [living] in large cities, strangers to marriage and dedicated to an irregular existence."[14] In France the 1866 census revealed that three out of four cities exhibited a "female excess." In some places the imbalance was extreme: 61.4 percent of the population was female in Saint-Jean d'Angély, 60.2 percent in Avranches, and 59.9 percent in Clermont, to name a few. A comparative study of the effects of urbanization on celibacy (in Prussia, Saxony, Bavaria, Belgium, Denmark, England, Norway, Switzerland, western Russia, and Austria) shows that the celibacy rate was always higher in the urban than in the rural population (indeed, twice as high in Saxony, Denmark, and western Russia), and marriage among city dwellers generally came later; this was true for both women and men.[15]

Indeed, single women attained visibility when they moved to the city. They became visible, first of all, to observers, themselves urban, who were attempting to understand and write about social realities. More important, they became visible socially: single women (daughters, sisters, aunts) had always been part of the family production unit, but now they joined the labor market and were subject to its vicissitudes. In other words, the gradual destruction of rural industry and the general crisis of agricultural employment disrupted the traditional role of single women in the domestic economy and marginalized them.

At the same time women, particularly younger women, appear to have abandoned the old pattern of moving away for a while over short distances (to smaller towns and cities) in favor of moving away permanently to more remote destinations. In the end female migrants outnumbered males. Yet women were little tempted by the prospect of intercontinental migration, unless they were already married or else had become missionaries called to carry the gospel to far-off lands.[16] Some women remained where they were, but alone. In Norway, for example, massive emigration to America at mid-century left a shortage of men, resulting in an increased celibacy rate for women, as high as 21.8 percent in the 1880s, and a decreased probability of remarriage for widows.[17]

Adult and Active

The scandal unanimously denounced by the Victorian press and more or less accurately perceived throughout Europe had less to do with the number of single women than with their social identity. Because these women somehow inadvertently wound up outside their legitimate place in society, their numbers were seen as "excessive." "What shall we do with our old maids?" Frances P. Cobbe asked in *Fraser's Magazine.*[18] In retrospect, this displacement, at once geographic, social, and cultural, is a crucial phenomenon for the history of women and their conquest of economic autonomy. Outside marriage no salvation! Yet the Napoleonic Code, widely copied by France's European neighbors, offered single women a choice: outside marriage a woman became, in the eyes of the law, a responsible adult, competent to deal with her own affairs and property. Unlike a married woman, a *feme sole* enjoyed the same rights as a man, except that she was not considered a citizen. Although widows and separated and divorced women were generally helped out by their families or assisted by the state, adult, unmarried women (or at any rate those without the luxury of a private income) were obliged to leave their families and provide for their own needs.

The correlation between the entry of single women into the labor market, the growth of the female working population, and the development of the service sector suggests a signal evolution. Census data indicate the extent of the phenomenon in late-nineteenth-century France: "Although more than 80 percent of the men and women working in agriculture and of the men working in industry and services are married, and fewer than 20 percent are single (celibate or widowed), the women surveyed who are working outside of agriculture often seem compelled to do so by necessity, as a result of their being single: nearly one in two is celibate, widowed, or divorced."[19] In 1906, 8.5 percent of female farm workers between the ages of twenty-five and forty-four were unmarried, compared with 33 percent of women employed in the industrial and service sectors.

The involvement of single women in the working world followed the ups and downs of the economy. Education seems to have been the decisive factor in guiding unmarried women into new branches. To be sure, their choices were limited, but the end result was a profound transformation of traditional solidarities, an upheaval in male-female relations in the workplace (including competition and resistance), and a gradual recognition of the new reality that women were now part of the workforce.

Solitude Is Living with Strangers

The nineteenth century did not invent domestic service. But what had previously been limited to aristocratic milieus now became a necessity of bourgeois existence, the *sine qua non* of social distinction. As domestic service became more democratic, it also became less masculine and hierarchical, but feminization meant declining prestige. Cities and towns across Europe attracted country girls whose only qualifications were youth and vigor, some as young as thirteen or fourteen. In Munich, a city with a population of more than 70,000 in 1828, a census revealed 10,000 domestics, or nearly 14 percent of the population. In London of the 1860s one-third of the women between the ages of fifteen and twenty-four were domestics. The same was true of Prussia in 1882, where 96 percent of domestics were unmarried. Berlin, Leipzig, Frankfurt, Paris, Lyons, Prague—not a city in Europe was without its share of female domestics, poor, unmarried, and recently arrived from the country.

Many women worked as domestics only in preparation for an eventual marriage. Accumulating savings (which many domestics deposited in bank accounts), learning housekeeping skills, and acquiring a basic familiarity with elements of urban culture could lead to a better place in society. Servants' wages were in any case better than wages in the textile industry. For roughly a third of female domestics, the solitude of service ended in promotion through marriage.[20] Servants married at a relatively advanced age, much older in any case than the general average. Yet large numbers of unmarried women continued in service to age fifty and beyond, which suggests that domestic service could easily take on a permanent character that left thousands upon thousands of women in a celibate state.

A new hierarchy of domestic personnel developed over the course of the nineteenth century. Above the "maids" were the governesses, many of whom came from modest middle-class families: daughters of ministers or minor officials, orphans, daughters of large families. Contemporary observers focused their spotlights almost exclusively on this class of single women, immortalized by the Brontë sisters in *Jane Eyre* and *Agnes Grey*. The misery of female workers and domestics was seen as a grim social inevitability. But it was thought to be even more pitiful that a middle-class woman should be forced to work in harsh conditions or seek employment for the first time at the age of forty or fifty after the death of her parents. Although widespread in Russia, Germany, and France, this phenomenon took on particular importance in England, where the Victorians, seeking a third term to set against the stark contrast of "mother" versus "whore," sentimentalized the image of the "spinster" and invested it with qualities of purity, virginity, and sacrifice.

In 1851 there were 750,000 female domestics in England, compared with just 25,000 governesses. Despite these modest numbers, which made them economically insignificant and politically nonexistent, governesses came to symbolize the values, problems, and fears of the Victorian middle class. By definition, a governess was a woman who gave lessons in a home or lived with a family as a companion and teacher for the children. In fact, the governess was painfully aware of the contradiction between the values ascribed to her education as a "gentlewoman" and the functions she was obliged to perform. A symbol of the new power of the middle class (she was talked about and appeared in public) and proof that certain wives were now free to enjoy lives of leisure and play an ornamental role, the governess, even though still regarded as a "lady," in fact suffered a loss of status as a result of receiving wages. A victim of fate (the death of a father, perhaps, or the ruin of a family), she was a middle-class woman in need, whose work was tantamount to a "prostitution" of her education. Caught up in a triangular conflict with parents and children, the governess could expect little support from other servants. Dependent on her room and board and meager wages, the governess who became too ill or old to work or who lost her job had no choice but to seek some form of assistance, such as that offered by the Governesses' Benevolent Institution, founded in 1841.

"Solitude is living with strangers": domestics and governesses learned this lesson the hard way. They lived in close quarters with people with whom they shared no intimacy. Theirs was an exile without hope of return, a sheltered yet homeless existence. A similar confinement, which carried with it restrictions on one's movements and denial of one's identity, affected broad sectors of industry.

Industrial Cloisters

The industrial worker, at times celebrated, at other times condemned, symbolizes female toil in the nineteenth century. We usually picture her as a wife and mother. But mechanization and specialization, which proceeded at an accelerating pace over the course of the century, brought far-reaching changes in the organization of factories and workshops. Some new, experimental forms of work were particularly likely to create solitude. Thus the "silk convents" that sprang up around Lyons after 1830, modeled on the textile plants of Lowell, Massachusetts, recruited unskilled and docile young women who went to work with their parents' consent and the Church's blessings.[21] Factory managers supervised the morals of their young charges, for whom there was no shortage of opportunities to go astray and fall into prostitution. Reybaud commented: "These young country girls, abandoned by their parents to their fate in the whirlwind of the big city, at least found [in the factory] a refuge where their apprenticeships could proceed without peril, in calm and security, and safe from the perversion that few escaped and that was the all-but-inevitable consequence of inexperience in some cases, the goad of vanity in others, but most of all the counsel of misery. Here, they were protected from themselves as well as others."

These veritable "industrial cloisters" sprang up not only at Jujurieux, Tarare, La Seauve, and Bourg-Argental in France, but also in Switzerland, Germany, Great Britain, and Ireland. They marked the "collusion" of industrial interests and church authorities, as young women were subjected body and soul to the harsh virtues of labor and morality until they found a husband. It has been estimated that the number of young women "confined" in this way in the Lyons region was roughly 100,000 in 1880.

The Price

Company housing, which brought with it surveillance not only of the work of female employees but also of their everyday lives, their behavior and identity, was also tried in other sectors of the modernizing economy, most notably by the large department stores. Most salesgirls in large Parisian stores came from the provinces and had no choice but to accept the rooms offered by their employers. Subject to constant surveillance, they were required to remain single; marriage was invariably cause for dismissal. The situation was similar in other parts of Europe. In Bohemia, for example, schoolteachers and female government workers were forbidden to marry until 1919. In the private sector, switchboard operators, typists, salesgirls, and waitresses were obliged to quit their posts if they married. It is true that in certain German states and in Vienna marriage regulations forbade indigent males to marry. It is also true that certain bureaucracies imposed marriage quotas or required male employees to obtain administrative authorization before marrying. Nevertheless, the notion of incompatibility between marriage and work applied primarily to women. It gave rise, moreover, to the idea that professions embodying some sort of humanist ideal, including those of nurse, schoolteacher, and social welfare worker, should be approached as a kind of secular priesthood. In short, the choice or the need to work confronted women with the alternative of profession versus family, a choice which shaped their lives and social identities. And not all the barriers were legal: resistance to social change was also a potent factor.

The Western mode of female celibacy profoundly influenced the economic logic of the nineteenth century. It was possible to enforce female solitude through work "because [solitude] was deliberately utilized as an essential cog without which the economic machine could not have run smoothly."[22] Many white-collar women came from petty-bourgeois backgrounds and were keen to set themselves apart from blue-collar workers; better educated than the average woman, they sought to assert their intellectual and social superiority. But such aspirations, coupled with objective constraints and psychological investment in their work, prevented them from finding husbands. As single women they had to cope with the distrust and lack of prestige associated with their condition. Many of the growing number of shopgirls and postal workers, schoolteachers and welfare workers, found that their work lives limited their personal development: such was the price to be paid for climbing a few steps up the social ladder.[23]

The state, the leading employer of women in all European countries, was also the leading "promoter" of celibacy. This phenomenon has been particularly thoroughly studied in the case of postal workers in France, England, Germany, and Norway.[24] At the turn of this century, for example, 53.7 percent of the women employed by the French government were unmarried, compared with 18.9 percent of the men. Single women (celibate or widowed) were more numerous in the better-paid positions, whereas single men were found mainly in the lowest-paid jobs.[25] Female white-collar workers tended to marry later than their blue-collar counterparts and to have only half as many children. Clearly, there is good reason to suspect a relation between celibacy and level of qualification. In the United States 75 percent of women who graduated from college between 1870 and 1900 did not marry. In France, during the first twenty years of secondary education for women (instituted by the Camille Sée Law in December 1880), 62.5 percent of the female teachers and administrative personnel in the schools were unmarried. The proportion was just as high in primary teaching, and it exceeded 75 percent among teachers of sewing, gymnastics, and drawing.[26] This correlation of work and celibacy only intensified when large numbers of women moved into higher education and the upper levels of government in the twentieth century.

The Religious Imprint

In the past, a long line of male theorists, convinced that simultaneous development of the brain and the uterus was impossible, had confidently asserted that certain intellectual capacities were beyond the reach of women. But women who now exhibited precisely these capacities seem to have been dissuaded from marriage by their access to culture. Meanwhile, professions in the social sector proved attractive to independent women, thereby consecrating qualities of compassion and service that had traditionally been recognized as female.

Single women were charged with carrying domestic virtues outside the home into the wider world, there to raise the moral level of factories, hospitals, schools, and other public institutions. In the field of social work, it is tempting to draw a contrast between the Protestant model that flourished in the United States, England, and Germany (with its deaconesses, missionaries, and volunteer organizations) and the Catholic model of religious orders and patrons, prevalent primarily in France and Italy.[27] But it is more instructive, perhaps, to focus attention on the common points, which reveal how industrial society's response to the "social question"—a response that involved single women in a fundamental way—supplanted the traditional forms of charity. The religious revival, whether Pietist in Germany and the Netherlands, Methodist in England, or Marian in Catholic countries, channeled the energies of generations of "redundant" women into positions of responsibility where they were able to demonstrate energy and initiative. Women "called" to this kind of work discovered the freedom to inform themselves about socioeconomic and political issues, and that discovery provoked new ambitions.

The communities of women organized around social work were virtually the only places where women, particularly in the early stages of their careers, could learn a variety of jobs while satisfying both religious longings and practical ambitions. They brought boldness, power, and imagination to the job, along with meditation, prayer, and spirituality. This "women's Catholicism" reveals a distinctive form of religious practice; it is one based on introspection, an extremely refined form of mysticism, and a personal relationship with God.

The success of these various organizations proved that women could effectively organize to care for the sick, teach, and help the poor, yet it also helped spread the tenacious notion that certain "callings" are specifically feminine, most notably in the areas of education, health, and welfare. A great deal of the work was done by volunteers: we have no idea exactly how much. In any case, it came to be taken for granted that the practice of certain professions implied celibacy.

The "new professions" that opened to women at the end of the century would bear the double stamp of the religious model and the maternal metaphor: devotion-availability, humility-submission, abnegation-sacrifice. These same motifs were opportunely incorporated into papal pronouncements intended to restore the dignity of the spinster.[28] The ideal of religious virginity dates back to the origins of the Church. But in confronting the problem of "superfluous females" and the scourge of social misery, the ecclesiastical authorities now preached an alliance between Martha and Mary: the contemplative life need not exclude commitment in the world. Thus the young Christian woman who (regrettably) remained unmarried (and shouldn't this be seen as an act of Providence, after all?) was exhorted to become "the educator and guide of her own sisters. . . . She should apply herself primarily to matters requiring tact, delicacy, and the maternal instinct rather than bureaucratic rigidity."

Change and Protest

Religious pronouncements on demographic problems were not enough to save marriage, however. Victorian upbringing and Catholic morality, which taught resignation and chastity, apparently sowed seeds of protest. It was by no means a discovery of the nineteenth century that marriages were sometimes unhappy, but examination of possible remedies to the disorders of the family threw certain modern forms of the venerable institution into sharp relief. No sooner was divorce legalized than women besieged the courts with petitions to dissolve their marriages (80 percent of the filings were by women). Cruelty and violence that had once been tolerated were no longer acceptable. By the end of the century divorce was growing exponentially. Apparently, the legalization of divorce and separation gave legal sanction to longstanding practices of de facto abandonment. Women who filed for divorce were more often battered than betrayed, moreover. Although divorce laws and divorce rates varied widely from country to country, more and more women availed themselves of this instrument of liberation.[29] The increase in divorce was most rapid in Protestant countries (other than England, where it was very costly), in cities, and among the middle class. Regardless of whether divorce led to unwanted solitude or coveted freedom, it was also encouraged by the increased availability of secondary education for women and a rising standard of living.

While lawmakers directed all legislation concerning divorce—whether to legalize it, outlaw it, or restore it—toward the single purpose of saving the family and refurbishing the institution of marriage, critics of marriage were having a field day. In the face of attacks by misogynists, quick to stigmatize "the invasion of female pedants, as incapable as barbarians of sowing seed in the world," many women now took up their pens.[30] They did so in protest, in a cry of revolt against domestic confinement, as well as in the interest of self-affirmation and economic independence. Beyond the institution of marriage, the issue was male-female relations: the ideal of love seemed impossible to achieve in conditions of inequality, inferiority, and dependence of one sex on the other. Certain great literary figures had rendered harsh verdicts on marriage and even dared to practice what they preached. But who now remembers these tireless female columnists and topical writers who clung to the often disparaged popular press as to a life raft? Single, widowed, divorced, or separated, many of them had received a minimal education. To them, the new institution of author's royalties was a godsend, a source of revenue.

Not all of women's writing wound up being published. Much of it remained hidden or secret if it did not end in the fire or trash barrel. If one got hold of these private diaries, as V. Chambers-Schiller was able to do, they reveal some of the reasons why women chose to remain unmarried.[31] If circumstances were often to blame, a desire for independence forged by upbringing is even more frequently cited. In America between the Revolutionary War and the Civil War, many women, admittedly privileged culturally as well as economically, claimed to be choosing freedom rather than marriage: "For liberty is a better husband than love to many of us."[32] To remain celibate rather than lose one's soul in the marriage lottery: this principle was inherent in the individualist ethic that steadily invaded Western culture in the nineteenth century. It found its consecration, quite literally, in an alliance with Protestantism. Celibacy, idealized and justified after the fact, was in fact rooted in the Protestant idea of perfectionism: the primacy of the individual over human institutions in general and marriage in particular led to the idea of an individual salvation, "alone with God." In the Last Judgment a woman appeared alone, without husband or children, responsible for herself. In early nineteenth-century American texts the term "single blessedness" was widely used to denote celibacy, and this became the object of a veritable cult.[33] Its adepts gave of themselves in beatitude and sublimation, in a harmonious blend of goodness, utility, and happiness. It should come as no surprise that in 1840 as many as 40 percent of Quaker women were celibate.

A Preferred Choice

The various forms of protest that came out of the socioeconomic turmoil of the nineteenth century proved conducive to the formation of a veritable cultural and political movement devoted to achieving independence for women through celibacy. After "feminists" such as Pauline Roland publicly renounced marriage and Florence Nightingale declared that she did not wish to deny her own destiny for the sake of a husband's, Christabel Pankhurst stated that female celibacy was a political decision, a conscious response to conditions of sexual slavery.[34] The final decades of the century witnessed a series of campaigns, particularly vehement in England, against sexual violence and abuse. To protect themselves and publicize their struggle, some women made the radical choice of renouncing sexuality altogether. Christabel Pankhurst was not the only one to come to such a decision; in 1913, 63 percent of the members of the Women's Social and Political Union were celibate, and most of the rest were widows. Celibacy, along with refusal of sexual favors, was now seen as a temporary political gesture, necessary until such time as a new social consciousness emerged.

After 1870, a new kind of woman—the self-avowed celibate, generally the product of a comfortable urban background, cultivated, cosmopolitan, and ostentatiously disdainful of the role of the bourgeois wife—became a common enough figure in certain artistic and political circles, setting an example of new possibilities for others. In England and the United States, where the laws concerning property, divorce, education, and suffrage were most progressive, fascination with the new independent life-styles was greatest. Gradually the images of economic independence and free love merged to give rise to the myth of the "new woman."[35]

The assertion that women ought to have the same freedom as men in all walks of life looked like a challenge to men's hegemony. Scientists, physicians, and sexologists, lumping together the rejection of marriage, the demand for a career, and the repudiation of the sacred image of the mother-wife, hastened (in the wake of the Viennese psychiatrist Richard Krafft-Ebing) to dismiss the audacious progressives as marginals and brand them lesbians.[36] In so doing they were simply rephrasing the usual condemnation of "uterine deviance" first formulated in the eighteenth century and endlessly repeated in the learned discourse of the nineteenth.

The Power of Images

The struggle between the golden legend of marriage and that grotesque scarecrow, the spinster, is never-ending. No matter what the level of discourse, from dictionaries to scientific texts, from proverbs to novels, there is no escaping the fact that the words used to denote the husbandless woman invariably invoke a discriminatory representation of the female. But when it comes to the male counterpart of the spinster, the aging bachelor, the pejoratives disappear: here one finds "geniuses" and "writers."[37]

Virago, lesbian, amazon, whore, *grisette,* bluestocking—these pejoratives for single women have no real foundation and are ubiquitous in Western culture. But the literary figure of the spinster and the popularization of the stereotype were the work of the nineteenth century.[38] Never had there been as much discussion of the spinster's appearance, physiology, character, or social life. Wherever a single woman was portrayed, no matter what the nature of the text, the writer invariably described a deviation from a feminine ideal as defined by law, by a certain concept of love, by biological determinism, and by a code of female beauty.

It was as if single women somehow crystallized all the fears of women's autonomy—sexual, social, economic, and intellectual. The advent of physiology and the "discovery" of a "female nature" toward the end of the eighteenth century had inverted the values associated with virginity to the point where they became an obstacle to, and indeed the negation of, femininity itself; concurrently, the social role of celibate and widowed women could be ignored to the point of symbolizing uselessness, and female solitude could be suspected of posing a threat to the family.[39]

In the face of this veritable denial of identity, single women could only define themselves in relation to the triumphant image of the mother-wife through complex maneuvers of participation and challenges. At times they conformed to the model, at times they resisted it; there were experiments and there were utopian dreams, there was resignation and there was sublimation. But one thing is certain: the images of derision and pity that formed a leitmotif of contemporary discourse failed to capture the reality.

To sum up, the historical phenomenon that I have been attempting to trace, the emergence of the category of the "single woman," was intimately related to the major social and economic upheavals of the nineteenth century. It reveals in some sense the grammar of Western "modernity," which has been characterized by "a plurality of forms of individualism corresponding to a like plurality of forms of sociability."[40] As the exception that confirmed the rule, the single woman supplanted the "holistic" society of the Ancien Régime.[41] Anonymous and individual, selfish or sublimated, unfettered and critical, the single woman ultimately can be seen as the heir to revivalism and puritanism. She also offered a tentative, almost furtive response to the great issue of individual freedom raised by the Enlightenment and the French Revolution.

TRANSLATED FROM THE FRENCH BY ARTHUR GOLDHAMMER

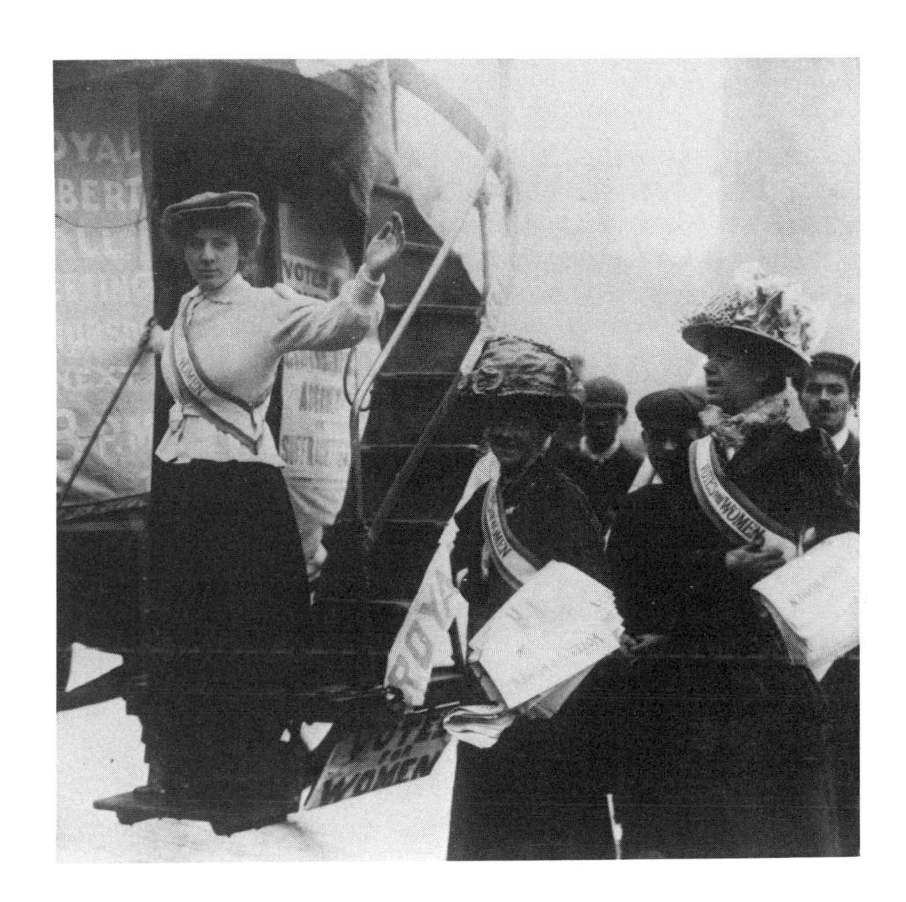

four

Modernities

The Great Enterprise of Feminism

> Je suis femme.
> Née ici je mourrai. Jamais l'heureux voyage
> Ne viendra de son aile ouvrir mon horizon.
> Je ne connaîtrai rien du monde de passage
> Au-delà de ce mur qui borne ma maison . . .
> Je suis femme.
> Je resterai dans mon enclos . . .
> Aux âges dont il reste un sillon de mémoire,
> Je ne pourrai jamais revivre par l'histoire.
> Pas un mot qui parle pour moi.
> Je suis femme.

Clémence Robert, *Paris silhouette,* poetry anthology, 1839.

> [I am a woman. Born here, I will die. No happy voyage will ever broaden my horizon with its wing. I shall know nothing of the transitory world beyond this wall, which bounds my house. . . . I am a woman. I shall remain within my cloister. . . . For the ages that turn over the past in memory, I will not live again through history. Not a single word speaks for me. I am a woman.]

In the nineteenth century the pendulum began to swing, however. No doubt this had something to do with modernity and its intrinsic insistence on change, and no doubt it had something to do with the actions of women themselves, with their desire to break out of the limits imposed on their sex.

In the next few chapters we evoke this multidimensional effort, individual as well as collective, to subvert customary conceptions of space, time, and memory so as to claim a historical existence for women. We focus on ventures outside the enclosure: journeys, social actions, union organizing, strikes. And we are particularly interested in feminism, which was surely the century's great new enterprise. Anne-Marie Käppeli describes the emergence of feminism: its key moments, its main forms of expression (associations and newspapers), its demands, its participants (a star-studded cast of characters and works that really requires its own "Dictionary"), its alliances (in particular, its uneasy relation to socialism, which thought "class" instead of "sex"), its diversities and debates. Indeed, as feminism began to spread, it became multifarious and contradictory. Already a debate had begun between one brand of feminism, whose goal was equality in assimilation, and another, which aimed at the exaltation of difference. Whatever the risks of a dualist conception of the masculine and the feminine, such a view is informed by a wealth of reflections on sexual difference, reflections that at times come close to certain discoveries of Freud. The participation of women in such movements as vegetarianism, animal protection, and homeopathy was important. Many women rejected war, while others, such as Olive Schreiner, asserted that "the personal is political." Taken together, these new ideas began to trace an alternative vision of the world and of existence. To be sure, there is a note of artificiality in bringing together scattered ideas produced by a variety of small groups. But these groups were no doubt more representative than their numbers suggest. While it may be true that isolated individuals attempted to speak for their sex, boldly proclaiming that "we women" wanted this or that, the positions of these self-appointed spokeswomen gradually gained coherence. It is striking to note how ideas circulated in Europe and across the Atlantic. The nineteenth century was, in a sense, a "golden age" of feminism in the West, one that drew upon and shared in the progress of democracy and individualism. This hastened the birth of the "new woman" at the turn of the century. At times celebrated, at other times denounced, in any case she obliged men to redefine themselves.

To be sure, it would not be difficult to show that the changes were limited and that there was powerful resistance to the rise of women at all levels of economic, professional, cultural, and above all political life. And one could easily concentrate on the rigidity of the law, the closing of such male bastions as the Church, the army, the government, and science, the constant redrawing of the boundaries of knowledge, and the smug or resigned passivity of the majority of women, so many of whom were hostile to the boldest representatives of their sex. To confuse matters still further, it should be noted that differences of opinion sometimes cut across sexual boundaries. Withal, if the omnipotent father of the Civil Code found his authority shaken, he still managed somehow to hold his own: the Old Adam stood up to the New Eve.

Nevertheless, changes were palpable, and we have seen evidence of them throughout this book. Women's insistence on control over their own bodies and access to sexual knowledge—the forbidden fruit of the Tree of Life—were perhaps signs, fleeting and elusive, of an emancipation whose effects the anxious male consciousness anticipated. From Vienna to London, from Stockholm to Boston, novels and plays took up this obsession. Romantic "idolatry" gave way to "black" naturalism. The Muse and the Madonna mutated into the shrewish wife, the castrating mother, the suffocating lover, the independent tomboy, the insolent, unsatisfied woman, the serpent-woman or Medusa of the Modern Style. And was not Art Nouveau, which attempted to enclose the serpentine sinuosities of the elusive female body in its curvaceous forms, an attempt to break the evil spell?[1]

Though magnified by the wild fantasies of a baroque imagination, the identity crisis was nevertheless real. Women, hesitating at the crossroads, found that they shared the experience with men. Divided among themselves, men too suffered, with greater or lesser intensity, a loss of confidence in their powers and certitudes. The exercise of freedom is a harsh apprenticeship. It is not easy to be an individual.

Whenever sexual differences are redefined, crisis ensues—and identifying such moments in history is an important task. The crisis that marked the turn of the twentieth century, moreover, was unusually intense, as we gather from such symptoms as the passionate debate over matriarchy,[2] the suicide of Otto Weininger shortly after writing *Geschlecht und Charakter* (Sex and Character, 1903),[3] and *The Futurist Manifesto* of Marinetti

(1909), who called upon his male readers to "combat moralism and feminism" and "glorify war, the world's only hygiene." War in a sense would mark a return to sexual hierarchy. Beyond a shadow of a doubt, the nineteenth century placed the historicity of male-female relations at the center of our attention.

G.F.—M.P.

17

Stepping Out

Michelle Perrot

"A WOMAN MUST NOT STEP outside the narrow circle traced around her," said Marie-Reine Guindorf, a Saint-Simonian worker. She had been determined to break out of this encirclement and committed suicide when she realized she had failed.[1] In the nineteenth century European men did indeed attempt to hold back the rising power of women, a power that had aroused bitter resentment during the Enlightenment and Revolution, for whose woes the female sex was readily blamed. Not only were women, as a result, confined to the home and excluded from certain fields such as literature and the arts, industry and commerce, politics and history, but their energy was funneled back into a newly revalued domestic sphere, or, more precisely, into a domesticated version of the social. The theory of the two "spheres," as interpreted by Ruskin in *Of Queen's Gardens* (1864), was a way of conceptualizing the sexual division of the world and rationally organizing, in a harmonious complementarity of roles, tasks and spaces reconciling "natural" vocation with social utility.

Women developed the knack of taking charge of areas abandoned or entrusted to them and from them exerting influence that extended to the very gates of power. Here they found the lineaments of a culture, the matrix of a "gender consciousness."[2] They also attempted to "break out" so as "at last to be at home everywhere." Breaking out could be as simple as physically stepping out: taking a walk outside the home, in the streets, traveling, entering a forbidden place such as a café or meeting hall. It could also mean breaking out morally, stepping outside one's assigned role, forming an opinion, abandoning subjugation in favor of independence—and this could be done in public or in private. Let us consider a few of these excursions.

In the City

Charity, that ancient Christian duty, had long taken women outside the home: visiting the poor, the imprisoned, and the sick was not only permitted but blessed. The magnitude of the nineteenth century's social problems transformed this custom into a necessity. Women enjoyed a preeminent position in philanthropy, meaning the private management of social needs. "The Angel in the house" was also "the good woman who rescues the fallen," and Ruskin looked upon this activity as an extension of domestic chores. Catholics and Protestants (the former more directive, the latter more tolerant of autonomy)[3] exhorted wealthier women to look to the material and moral needs of the underprivileged.

Organizations, leagues, and clubs of all sorts—for temperance, for hygiene, for morality—sometimes in competition with one another, solicited the participation of women, especially single women, whose idleness—and sterility—might otherwise, it was feared, turn bitter. Founded in 1836, the Rhenish Westphalian Association of Deaconesses trained Protestant nurses and volunteer workers for hospitals, crèches, asylums, and so on. More than 13,000 were at work in Germany by the end of the century. Women throughout the West mobilized to provide services of "social maternity." Growth of this broad-based movement was accelerated by epidemics (such as the cholera epidemic of 1832), war (which produced large numbers of wounded), and economic crises (which produced large numbers of unemployed) and exacerbated by the endemic urban problems such as alcoholism, tuberculosis, and prostitution.

Women were not supposed to expect compensation for this "labor of love": cleaning house for the city was no more to be remunerated than was ordinary housework. Great philanthropists were honored, decorated, and commemorated with statues, but most of the women who, for at least the first third of the century, organized no meetings and wrote no reports have been forgotten. Catherine Duprat had a hard time identifying the "mute participants" in the Société de Charité Maternelle of Paris, despite its active role during the Restoration and July Monarchy.[4] As Sylvain Maréchal wrote, "a woman's name was supposed to be engraved in the heart of her father, her husband, or her children, and none other"—except that of her other children, the poor.[5] The obscurity of anonymous volunteer work swallowed up vast amounts of female energy, whose social effects are difficult to gauge.

Philanthropy provided, nevertheless, substantial experience that altered women's perception of the world, their sense of themselves, and, to a certain extent, their public role. At first they joined integrated groups that were run by men; later they formed groups of women run by women. Examples include the Elisabethvereine, an early (1830) group of Catholic women in the Rhineland; the Weiblicher Verein für Armen- und Krankenpflege (Women's Union for Poor and Sick Relief), organized by the Protestant Amalie Sieveking in Hamburg in 1832;[6] the London Bible Women and Nurses Mission, organized by Ellen R. White in 1859; and Octavia Hill's Charity Organization Society (1869).[7] If the first charity women were in part spurred on to good works by their confessors or husbands whose names they made famous, a more independent breed followed in their footsteps, many of them unmarried or widowed, women outraged by physical and moral misery and animated by a missionary spirit. Octavia Hill, a shrewd businesswoman and indefatigable committee member, conceived of philanthropy as a science whose purpose was to promote individual responsibility. Her book, *Our Common Land* (1877), imbued with liberal ideology, expressed an optimistic faith in private initiative, which she preferred to state intervention. If charity groups at first relied on an aristocratic elite, later, as they grew in size, they drew increasingly on the middle class. These later recruits hoped through charity to promote middle-class precepts of home economics, as Josephine Butler observed in *Woman's Work and Woman's Culture* (London, 1869). Some groups made systematic use of working-class women, who were sometimes paid for their services. The Bible Women of the London Mission were converts whose down-to-earth language and familiarity (they were known by their first names) were greatly appreciated by the people they served.

Methods and objectives both changed. Initially the aim was to "do charity" through good works. Later, the goal became to teach good morals and hygiene. Fundraising methods ranged from local collections to huge charity sales or bazaars (of which there were more than a hundred annually in England between 1830 and 1900). These "ladies' sales" were run strictly by women, who were delighted to have a chance to handle money (many were denied this privilege) and deal in commodities they otherwise passively consumed. They learned the ways of business, for which some showed a real flair. Under cover of performing a ritual, they reversed roles and at times promoted a political message. There were anti-free-trade bazaars during the controversy over the Corn Laws and antislavery bazaars in some cities of the northeastern United States.

The distribution of relief funds also changed. Home visitors, whose purpose was to single out the "deserving poor" from the rest, began making new demands. They asked about individual and family histories, and their assembled reports contributed to a composite portrait of poverty. Women thereby acquired almost professional knowledge of social problems and familiarity with the terrain of poverty. The poor were increasingly monitored and disciplined. The hope was to change the habits at the root of their woes and restore broken families. The family—the heart of society, particularly its "mother-child" dyad—was the area of most concern to women, more even than hospitals, which were the fief of Florence Nightingale (1820–1910), and prisons, where Elizabeth Fry, Conception Arenal, Joséphine Mallet, and Mme d'Abbadie d'Arrast distinguished themselves.

Women worked above all on behalf of other women—their sisters in need of understanding, education, and protection. The London Bible Women's Mission held teas and mothers' meetings to teach home economics and child care and to instill a desire for a "clean and cozy" home, with a clean cloth on the table at dinner and curtains on the windows. It was hoped that through homemakers one could wage war on alcoholism among fathers and vagabondage among children. Indeed, housewives emerged as the new hope for winning an old battle, the linchpin of social peace.

But moral education did not exclude compassion for, or for that matter rebellion against, the conditions in which women were forced to live. Protest focused on two categories of women: home workers and prostitutes. To combat the depredations of the textile industry, at the time in the throes of expansion owing to the rise of the department store and the invention of the sewing machine, philanthropists financed studies and sought to influence the behavior of consumers. American women organized buyers' leagues, which Henriette Jean Bruhnes, a disciple of Le Play, introduced in France in the hope of making store customers more responsible. If women limited their demands and planned their purchases better, seamstresses employed by sweat shops and fashion houses would not have to work into the wee hours and risk exhaustion. Although these efforts were praised by Charles Gide, a Protestant proponent of workers' cooperatives, they were strongly criticized by liberal economists, who disliked seeing women interfering with the sacrosanct laws of the market and disapproved even more strongly of the idea that production, a man's province, might be subject to control by female consumers. Feminists and trade unionists such as Gabrielle Duchêne and Jeanne Bouvier set up an Office of Home Labor and were instigators of the law of July 10, 1915, which for the first time imposed controls on home labor and established a minimum wage, two measures that inaugurated a new chapter in social legislation.[8] Clearly, philanthropy had ventured onto new ground, and women had broken out of their narrow circle.

Prostitutes were pitied by everyone from charity ladies to radical feminists, from Flora Tristan to Josephine Butler. Saint-Lazare, a women's prison and hospital for venereal diseases, was a center of agitation, especially by Protestants (Emilie de Morsier, Isabelle Bogelot, and L'Oeuvre des Libérées de Saint-Lazare). While Josephine Butler launched a crusade for the abolition of regulated prostitution, philanthropic organizations staged the largest "anti-vice" rally of all time at Hyde Park in July 1885: 250,000 people gathered in the name of "purity" to combat the "white slave trade." Ambiguous as such watchwords may have been, they raised the crucial issue of the commercialization of the bodies of women.

The so-called settlement houses played a key role in the transformation of philanthropy into social work. Rather than visit the poor periodically, the volunteers established full-time outposts in impoverished zones: the suburbs, peripheral neighborhoods, and "east ends" of major cities. The movement, once again of Protestant inspiration, began in Britain with the Barnett house at Toynbee Hall. Octavia Hill founded the first women's settlement at Southwark in 1887. Other houses were run by unmarried or divorced women, in some cases pairs of sisters or academics (as at the Women's University Settlement). In this way communities begun at college retained continuity. Martha Vicinus has described both the conviviality of these groups and the difficulties they faced. Young women often could not decide between the austerity of a permanent social commitment and its emancipatory promise. Free in their movements and attire, these women—in other respects apostles of family and home—rejected traditional marriage and compared themselves to their brothers, soldiers of the empire. The slums were their Africa and India.[9]

In France similar experiments in popular education were carried out in the proletarian sections of Charonne (Marie Gahéry's Union Familiale) and Levallois-Perret, a neighborhood of ragpickers. There the rebellious Marie-Jeanne Bassot, a Social Catholic with ties to the Sillon movement and influenced by Jane Addams and the American settlement-house model, tried to make the Social Residence the seed of a new city. Her movement was hampered, however, by the stewardship of suspicious priests and by right-wing attempts to coopt it. After World War I groups such as the Redressement Français (Bardoux, Mercier) mobilized "volunteer armies" and female "charity workers" to "stem the tide of barbarism," meaning communism. The first Congress of Settlements in 1922 clearly revealed the effects of regimentation on these still hesitant attempts at social action.[10]

Philanthropy had a variety of effects on the social perception of sexuality. It revealed another world to women of the bourgeoisie, and for some this came as a shock. Women learned about administration, finance, communication, and above all research. Flora Tristan (*London Journal,* 1840) and Bettina Brentano *(The Book of the Poor)* were the first women to report on poverty.[11] "Put yourselves on a diet of incessant investigation," Henriette Jean Bruhnes recommended in 1906, thereby expanding—and routinizing—their work. Through this work women acquired enough knowledge and experience to become potential experts. As paid workers for the London Mission or the settlement houses, as guardians for French "children of either sex" (instituted under the law in 1912 and appointed by the children's courts),[12] as inspectors of women's prisons, schools, workshops, and factories, women gained positions of authority in a social work profession just coming into its own. Teaching, caring, helping: these three missions constituted the basis of the "women's professions," which for a long time to come would bear the imprint of their origins as voluntary callings.[13]

Through social work women acquired a competence that legitimated their desire for managerial autonomy. In 1834, the ladies of the Maternal Charity Society suggested that they be "granted what is necessary for this very special mission. Men would make better administrators of large establishments and significant sums of money. But it is the job of women who know how to dedicate themselves and bear up under harsh treatment without ceasing to love to persuade the lower classes to resign themselves to a hard life."[14] With Octavia Hill and Florence Nightingale this modesty of tone vanished in favor of radical critique and unyielding demands. On the strength of her experience in the Crimean War Nightingale undertook to reform not only the hospitals but the army, "the first place where the initial investment of many women enables them to gain access to science and knowledge."[15]

Charity ladies, confident in their aptitude for "social housekeeping," turned their attention to housing and neighborhoods of which they had concrete knowledge. They challenged male administration. The bourgeois matrons of northern France came into conflict with municipal councillors who refused to give them the subsidies they asked for.[16] English ladies such as Louise Twining waged campaigns against the administrators of workhouses—places they denounced as anonymous and inhumane—and worked for reform of the poor laws.

As ministers to the poor, over whom they exercised a power that was not without certain ambiguities and overtones of class conflict, charity women thought of themselves as mediators for people who, as they saw it, had neither voice nor vote. There was a symbolic, not to say organic, link between women and proletarians, as the Saint-Simonians demonstrated. "I like to act upon the masses," Eugénie Niboyet confessed, "because that is where I feel my full power. I am an apostle."[17] In the name of the excluded, the weak, the children, and most of all of other women, they claimed a right of national, not just local, representation. But in fact they operated mainly locally, for that is where their formal and informal networks were most effective, especially in the first half of the century. In Utica, New York, a small Presbyterian town shaken by fiery revivals, there were some forty women's organizations in 1832, dedicated mainly to the protection of young women in danger of rape and prostitution. Groups like the Maternal Association and the Daughters of Temperance acted as nothing less than sexual police.[18] Suffragettes in Great Britain and the United States availed themselves of this kind of community power to demand the right to vote, initially at the municipal level. To a lesser extent women intervened at the legislative level as well, by lobbying, organizing, and filing petitions (in favor of divorce, workplace protection, and so on). Through such channels women became participants in local and national government.

As a result, they attracted renewed interest on the part of men, who were quick to make use of these politically active women but anxious to protect their own prerogatives. As pauperism became the "social question," men intervened with greater urgency. Generosity—the "father's" largesse—could not be left exclusively to the benevolence of women. Already de Gérando in *Le Visiteur du pauvre* (The Poor Visitor, 1820) had voiced his desire that more poor visitors should be men involved in business and capable of finding work for the paupers they visited. By the end of the century the leading philanthropists were men: Barnett, Booth, founder of the Salvation Army, Henri Dunand, founder of the Red Cross, and Max Lazard, organizer of the first international conference on unemployment in 1910, to name a few. The administration of social welfare passed into the hands of politicians and professionals: doctors, jurists, and psychologists quick to treat women as auxiliaries fit only for subordinate roles as nurses and social workers. A different kind of battle, this time for professional training and recognized credentials, now began, and so the issues changed.

Philanthropy had other effects as well. It established contacts among middle-class women and helped sow the seeds of "gender consciousness" from New England to Athens. In many cases these seeds later developed into a full-blown feminist consciousness. According to Carroll Smith-Rosenberg, the New Women of the 1880s and 1890s were the daughters of the New Bourgeois Matrons of 1850–1880.[19] Straddling the divide between the political and the social, the public and the private, the religious and the moral, this crucible of identity served as an experimental laboratory.

Working Women

Working women endured a twofold attack: as women because they were the antithesis of femininity (Michelet said that *ouvrière,* working woman, was an "impious word"), and as workers because their wages, which the law stipulated had to be lower than men's wages, were considered a "supplement" to the family budget. This defined not only the working woman's task but also her destiny. Entire sectors of production were closed to women. Furthermore, the nineteenth-century worker's identity was based on a model of virility, on the everyday, private level as well as on the public, political level. P. Stearns has noted the stress in sex relations in late-nineteenth-century English working-class couples.[20] Dorothy Thompson has shown how women withdrew from activist roles in the Chartist period. Their voices grew faint at meetings where soon even their presence came to seem incongruous, to the point where they were excluded from pubs and inns, henceforth purely male gathering places.[21] Similar developments, although with many variants, occurred everywhere. Working-class women's bodies became targets of violence in the urban jungle and often in the family, and of sexual harassment in the workplace.[22] For a woman there was no recognition except as mother or homemaker. Women had little place in the workers' movement, except as *Mère des compagnons* (the woman who ran a boarding house for journeymen workers, or *compagnons*), although the United States had its Mother Jones, an Irishwoman who organized miners. But for the most part the movement saw itself as male, even in its symbols: the naked torso, bulging biceps, powerful muscles, and stalwart solidity of the male worker replaced the basket-bearing housewife in popular imagery.[23] Demonstrations became more ritualized and respectable, and there was wariness of women's violence and fantasies. Female companions were tolerated, to be sure, and even mobilized, but in their place, as flag-carriers, ornaments, protective cover.[24] Women were even banished from memory: in the autobiographies of working-class activists, mainly men, there is little talk of wives and mothers, who are often described as tearful nuisances to be swept aside, whereas sons often made heroes of their fathers.

Women as a group withdrew from the streets with the decline in popularity of the bread riot, the major form of protest in traditional societies as well as a means of regulating the "moral economy," of which women had been the barometer. By insisting on price controls on foodstuffs, women had gained local and even national political influence. On October 5 and 6, 1789, the women of La Halle (the Paris food market), had gone to Versailles and forced the royal family to return to Paris, thereby fundamentally reshaping the "space of power." Although bread riots were still numerous across Europe in the first half of the nineteenth century, culminating in a wave of demonstrations between 1846 and 1848, their number subsequently declined with improvements in the food supply system. Demonstrations became increasingly masculine, as factory workers and, later, union workers tended to dominate. Yet when the high cost of living triggered a crisis in industrial areas of western Europe in 1910 and 1911, thousands of housewives (in France explicitly modeling themselves on their forebears of October 1789) again sacked markets and set prices in the spirit of the "Fifteen-Cent Butter International." These women organized in "leagues" and, despite severe condemnations, boycotted speculators. The unions, however, criticized "this instinctive, disorganized, blind movement" and sought to transform it into a "male revolt."[25] The script was similar during the Amsterdam Potato Riot of 1917, which was a subtle mixture of old and new forms. The leader of the Dutch Social Democratic Party urged women who had looted two barges to relinquish leadership of the action to their sons and husbands by inciting them to strike.[26] In short, trade unionists and socialists shared the view of crowd psychologists: they were afraid that mobs of women were prone to violence.[27]

Strikes, in the sense of actions undertaken by politically aware and organized producers, were more manly affairs and increasingly rational. Violence was normally limited to a specific purpose and so, therefore, was the use of women. To be sure, strikers' wives had their role to play: at the stoves in "communist soup kitchens," a form of assistance new to the early twentieth century, singing songs of solidarity around the evening fire, and in demonstrations, during which women showed themselves to be zealous hooters of factory owners and "scabs."[28] Miners' wives, more integrated into the community than the wives of most other workers, engaged in all forms of collective action, of which a fascinated Zola provided a rather epic catalogue in *Germinal* (1885). To observers such as police agents, the number of women attending meetings or marching in demonstrations indicated the degree of discontent of the group involved in the conflict.

How men and women interacted in mixed strikes is a subject that deserves special attention. Unfortunately, little is known about it, since most of the sources merge the two sexes in the pseudoneutral "they." In negotiations, women's demands were often sacrificed, and unequal wages were rarely challenged.

As for strikes involving women alone, they were another matter entirely: to employers accustomed to docile female employees, such strikes were an intolerable form of rebellion; to families, they were an irritating annoyance, compounded by the fact that the strikers were usually young; for the public at large, they were indecent, and opinion varied from tolerant condescension ("those poor, crazy women") to sexual innuendo. Because such strikes disrupted the posture of customary female submission, they were scandalous. Workers did not like their wives, much less their daughters, to strike and often urged them to go back to work, sometimes brutally: one irate husband took his wife back to the factory where she worked and publicly reprimanded her at the gate (strike of the Lebaudy Sugar Works, Paris, 1913). Unions were hesitant about supporting women. Union rules generally allowed lower strike benefits for female workers on the grounds that they were not the sole support of their families and in any case ate less than men. Strikes by women were a threat to patriarchal society, which was no more eager to grant them the right to strike than it was to grant them the right to work.

Society's powers of dissuasion are readily appreciated. To dare to go on strike was to brave public opinion, and for a woman to parade outside the factory was to behave like a prostitute. It took the courage of a fine spring day and special circumstances: the outrage provoked by a special disciplinary action, say, or the instigation of an "agitator" who would invariably be branded a "harpy" or "shrew." In *Mary Macarthur* (1925), for example, Mary Hamilton describes a fat woman leading an army of striking women on an August morning in 1911: the women smell bad and are covered with vermin and dressed in outlandish getups of feather-boas and fur jackets.

Women were not likely to strike except in certain industries, tobacco processing, for example. In France between 1870 and 1890 women accounted for only 4 percent of strikers even though they constituted 30 percent of the work force. Their strikes, generally defensive, spur-of-the-moment affairs, disorganized and poorly prepared, were more apt to be protests against working hours that were too long or a pace that was too fast or working conditions that were intolerable or a discipline that was too harsh or arbitrary. In 1869 the silk throwers of Lyons declared that they had been suffering "for a long time." These short-lived coalitions frequently collapsed.

Yet they were escapes, unique opportunities to "step out" and express grievances that the participants would remember far longer than the workers' movement. Some did rank as events: the Lyons silk throwers' strike was taken over by the First International, which then refused to allow the strike leader, Philomène Rosalie Rozan, to sit as a representative at its Basel Congress. The London matchmakers' strike of 1888 marked the first time that women had gone on strike without appealing to a men's trade union; instead, they called on Annie Besant to organize a union and communicate their demands to the public, and they won. The female typographers of Edinburgh issued a remarkable memorandum, "We Women," in which they asserted, on grounds of equality and competence, their right to be in the printing trade. And 20,000 shirtmakers went on strike in New York in 1909, an event of which we possess particularly detailed knowledge thanks to the journal-reportage of Theresa Malkiel.[29]

Male workers disapproved of some of the more exuberant street behavior of their female coworkers—their chants, dances, bonfires—forms of expression associated with their youth and culture. In closed meetings working women discovered the intoxicating power of language and shared beliefs. They glued posters to walls and published manifestoes in the press, thereby conquering a piece of public space. Inexperienced at first, women sought the assistance of their male companions, but gradually they grew impatient with their meddling and turned to other women, often socialists, less frequently feminists: Annie Besant, Eleanor Marx, Beatrice Webb, Louise Otto, Clara Zetkin, Paule Minck, Louise Michel, Janet Addams, Emma Goldman, and others took part in their struggles. In some cases a women's "common front" began to emerge, and union leaders were particularly worried by any sign that this might become a more or less permanent feature of the workers' movement.

The trade unions were not at all receptive to women. The collection of dues, the reading of newspapers, participation in evening meetings in cafés—all these were obstacles to women's participation. But the right to work and the right of representation also stood in the way. How—in the name of what—could women vote? And for whom? Weren't men the natural representatives of the family community to which women supposedly belonged?

In trades that employed mainly men (tailors and printers, for example), women were prevented from forming unions, particularly in Germany, where the influence of Lassalle, who was hostile to women in the workplace, was dominant. Elsewhere, male unions welcomed women, with reluctance at first but more enthusiastically later on, around the turn of the century, by which time they even went so far as to deplore the passivity of women workers, an attitude they had done everything in their power to create. The unions had done nothing to promote women's right to speak (in the Nord in 1880 a woman who wished to speak at a union meeting had to submit a written request signed by her father or husband) or to foster in them a sense of responsibility. A few decorative women were allowed to take the podium, but few became union officials and still fewer served as delegates to the national conventions where the real power lay. Even in the tobacco and matchmaking industries, where women constituted two-thirds of the work force, most union officials were men. Consequently, the rates of unionization for women were low (seldom above 3 percent).

The early initiatives came in many cases from women outside the working class, activists in the cooperative movement who saw solidarity and cooperation as opportunities for education as well as for pressing demands. Louise Otto and her Allgemeiner Deutscher Frauenverein (Leipzig, 1865), Emma Paterson and the Women's Trade Union League (1874), Janet Addams and the New Women's Trade Union League (Boston, 1903), Marguerite Durand and the unions that supported La Fronde, Marie-Louise Rochebillard, Cécile Poncet, and the "free unions" of the Lyons region—all were women conscious of the specific ways in which women workers were exploited and of the urgent need for unions that did not include men. Although these leaders may have been guilty of "maternalism," they encouraged the emergence of militant female workers with the qualities needed to win their independence.

But victory did not come without struggle. Conflict was inevitable, not just with men but with women as well. "Gender consciousness" encountered rivalries for power and the social hierarchy. Working women complained that "bourgeois" women did not understand them or appreciate what they wanted in the way of social legislation. In France at the turn of the century working women favored a form of protection that feminists criticized as discriminatory.[30] In the New York strike women working on behalf of the shirtmakers, such as Rose Schneiderman and Pauline Newman, charged wealthy suffragettes Ava Belmont-Vanderbilt and Anne Morgan with taking a voyeuristic interest in poverty and publicity. The Mink Brigade was bluntly reminded of its place. As Emma Goldman said, would it make any difference to the condition of the working woman if Anne Morgan could run for the presidency?

The elegant ladies rarely considered working women as their equals; instead they looked upon them as possible servants. During the Crimean War the "ladies" constantly bickered with the "nurses" in Florence Nightingale's small band. The nurses, who considered themselves professionals, refused to clean up after the ladies, who attempted to control everything, including even how the nurses spent their off-duty hours. Florence was compelled to issue a warning: "They must understand that they will remain in exactly the same position they were in in England, that is, under the authority of the superintendent and her assistants."[31] Domestic service was always a contentious issue among women, as was evident at the Congress of 1907 in France.[32]

These social tensions were further heightened by issues of race and ethnicity. The Women's Trade Union League was troubled by antagonism between Protestants, Italians, and Jews, and cultural contrasts in the New York garment industry strike were glaring.

The workers' movement (trade unions and socialists) exploited these differences in denying women the right to represent female workers. In France it was argued that women were agents of the Church and that feminism was essentially "bourgeois." This was a useful argument for blocking any "sex front," accused as usual of potential betrayal of the working class. This was the origin of the vehement antifeminism and antisuffragism of certain socialist women (such as Louise Saumoneau in France or Clara Zetkin versus Helene Lange and Lily Braun in Germany). The conflict was particularly bitter in France and Germany.[33] In Great Britain, where social contacts among women were more developed and where suffragism had greater influence, the situation was different. The female cotton workers of Lancashire were not only highly unionized but also militant suffragettes. Using the philanthropic methods of the Bible Women to their own advantage, they waged a diligent petition campaign and collected the signatures of some 30,000 female workers, which their delegates laid before Parliament (1893–1900).[34]

The Expansion of Space: Migrations and Journeys

"Any woman who shows herself dishonors herself," Rousseau wrote to d'Alembert. The statement was even more true of the woman who traveled. Any woman traveler was suspect, particularly if she was single. Flora Tristan, who suffered from this prejudice during her "tour of France" (where many hotels in the southern part of the country refused to give rooms to single women for fear of abetting prostitution), wrote a pamphlet on the "Need to Welcome Foreign Women" (1835), in which she proposed a society to assist female visitors to France. The organization would maintain a building with a library and reading room where one could read newspapers; its motto was to be "Virtue, Prudence, Publicity." Members would wear green ribbons with red edges as a recognition signal, but their identities would remain secret, to safeguard their privacy. This proposed "home" for female travelers was the forerunner of many others that would be promoted in the second half of the century by various groups and organizations, most of them Protestant.[35]

Yet women inevitably shared in the increased mobility made possible by the development of new means of transportation, particularly after 1850. Though some were migrants by virtue of economic or political necessity, women traveled not only out of obligation but also by their own choice, and their travels inevitably influenced their view of the world.

Migrants at Home

In the back-and-forth movements typical of internal migrations in a country like France, men customarily left their home towns for urban workshops and construction sites while women remained in the village, taking care of the farm and preserving age-old traditions to the point where they appeared old-fashioned to men returning home from the city. In Martin Nadaud's Creuse village, the old woman Fouénouse falls silent as the young masons, freshly returned from the big city, captivate listeners with their stories.[36] But eventually the rural exodus uprooted whole families. The middle classes needed more servants, and the garment and service industries enticed young women to leave the countryside to look for work. In some urban neighborhoods the ratio of males to females was severely out of balance, so that it was not always easy to meet someone of the opposite sex. Dance halls filled the need to some extent, and so did prostitution.

Female migrants, at first subject to close scrutiny by the people back home and by the support networks that welcomed them to their destinations, gradually acquired greater freedom, for better and for worse. Seduced and abandoned, they crowded the maternity wards, called upon abortionists, and resorted to minor crime, mainly theft, usually of fabric from large department stores. But they also saved, accumulating a dowry for an eventual marriage while getting used to the city, whose possibilities they were clever enough to assess. The need for the young women's services made them more demanding. The big-hearted servant of the past gave way to the cheeky chambermaid, like Octave Mirbeau's Juliette,[37] or to the "insolent" servant always "ready to turn in her apron." Before finally settling with Arthur Munby, her employer, Hannah Cullwick recounts in her journal that she was constantly on the move. As a married servant subject to the sexual whims of "Massa" and never recognized by his family, she exemplifies the limits of servile emancipation.[38] Jeanne Bouvier, who moved to Paris with her mother in 1879, was surprisingly mobile, as was Adelaide Popp in Vienna. Of course women who "made something" of themselves were movers by definition (Bouvier organized her memoirs around her three "careers" of trade unionist, writer, and feminist). Moving—a necessary though not sufficient condition of change, not to say liberation—indicated a desire to break with the past in order to create possibilities for the future.

Rural migrants, especially those who became servants, carried urban fashions, consumer goods, and other habits, including contraceptive practices, back to the countryside. By the end of the nineteenth century families were increasingly reluctant to allow daughters to leave home. Too independent, they were lost forever to the countryside, where the celibacy rate was on the rise, while the number of young women (aged twenty to thirty-nine) exceeded the number of comparably aged men in the cities by 20 percent (in France, at any rate).[39]

Governesses made up another important group of migrant workers. Whether they were born into families that had come down in the world or to bourgeois intellectuals who wanted their daughters to profit from travel in the same way as sons (as in the case of the Protestant Reclus family), their horizons were broad, and many traveled across Europe.[40] Henriette Renan spent several years in Poland in order to earn the money needed for her brother's studies. Conversely, Russian women came to Paris, among them Nina Berberova, who amassed treasures of observation for her writing. Exploited by virtue of their foreign birth, governesses did not always enjoy good reputations. They were accused of being scheming seductresses. For the love of a governess the Duc de Choiseul-Praslin murdered his wife: this scandal from the waning years of Louis-Philippe's reign unfortunately strengthened the stereotype.

Long-Distance Migrants

The ratio of men to women among emigrants to foreign countries evolved in a similar fashion. At the beginning of the period men clearly predominated. Then families began leaving together, and the rates equalized. The men went ahead, and the women followed. The frontier was a place for fighters and pioneers, a virile world in which women were scarce, and in which the extremes of the blonde "lady" and the more colorful prostitute stood out. This situation would later be reflected in the misogyny of the Westerns.

The United States offers a fascinating laboratory for the study of these questions, and both feminist and nonfeminist historians have begun to explore this rich terrain. Migration had contradictory effects. Sometimes it strengthened the power of the family, which was not only the heart of the economy but the central element in ethnic solidarity, and at the same time accentuated sex-role differentiation. In New England between 1780 and 1835 intense "bonds of womanhood" developed in the "women's sphere," according to Nancy Cott, and these became the basis of "gender consciousness." Among prairie farmers and in Irish and Italian working-class families the mother was a powerful figure, like the epic mother figure in Steinbeck's *Grapes of Wrath*. According to Elinor Lerner, in New York the greatest support for feminist and suffragist causes came from the Jewish community, both bourgeois and working-class. The most vehement and tenacious opposition came from the Irish, while the Italians were divided: the southern Italians, more used to dealing with forceful women, were more favorably disposed than the northerners.[41]

In some cases the availability of space and a concomitant loosening of the constraints imposed by crowding contributed to affirmation of the self. When Tocqueville visited America in 1832, he was struck by the American woman's freedom of movement and behavior. Under Louisiana law women were granted the right to conduct a private correspondence. Many American women were great travelers, and some visited Europe in the late nineteenth century. In love with Italy, they vied with men as art critics (Lee Vernon followed in Bernard Berenson's footsteps in Tuscany, and Edith Wharton also wrote about art). In Paris they colonized the Left Bank. Natalie Clifford Barney, the "Amazon of the rue Jacob," and Gertrude Stein, of the rue de Fleurus, embodied the New Woman, intellectually and sexually liberated and accepted all the more readily because they came from elsewhere and lived on the fringes of the intelligentsia.[42]

Russian and Jewish women, often mistakenly grouped together, deserve particular attention. They were more apt than other women to rebel, and their influence was considerable, as Nancy Green shows in her essay in this volume. "I don't want just work and money. I want freedom," said one Jewish immigrant on arriving in New York.[43] Emma Goldman's memoirs are an exemplary account of how travel could lead to emancipation.[44]

In the Colonies[45]

Initially associated with forced deportation, colonial emigration later kept its bad reputation. In France after 1854 female prisoners condemned to forced labor could choose to be sent to a prison colony abroad, but few did: 400 women were sent to New Caledonia between 1870 and 1885. In 1866 there were only 240 women in Cayenne, compared with 16,805 men.[46] This failed experiment was ended in 1900. Deported for her activities during the Commune, Louise Michel wrote a sensitive account of the Kanaks and dreamed of returning to New Caledonia as a free woman so as to reacquaint herself with the island's natives under different circumstances.

Free women did not go to the colonies voluntarily. The French army discouraged them. The few officers' wives adventurous enough to accompany their husbands found themselves rather isolated. The women's auxiliary was not respected, as we learn from Isabelle Eberhardt's plans for a novel about these forgotten women *(Femmes du Sud)*. Philanthropic organizations made some attempt to entice women to settle in the colonies. The Société Française d'Emigration des Femmes aux Colonies, founded in 1897 by J.-C. Bert and the Comte d'Huassonville, published an appeal for women in the *Revue des Deux Mondes* and the *Quinzaine coloniale:* 400 to 500 candidates answered the call, mostly cultivated but impoverished women whose letters tell us a great deal about female fantasies of the colonies, compounded of exoticism, missionary zeal, and a desire for social advancement. But nothing came of the project. Great Britain was much more active in populating its colonies. Between 1862 and 1914 several dozen organizations sponsored more than 20,000 female settlers. Some of these were promoted by feminists, who saw colonial life as an opportunity for "redundant women" languishing in mediocrity at home. One example was the Female Middle Class Emigration Society (1862–1866), run by Maria S. Rye and Jane Lewin, the former interested in finding young women to work as domestics, the latter more concerned with advancement for the middle class. But this feminist attempt to promote emigration ended in failure (only 302 women actually departed for the colonies), and in 1881 the FMCES merged with the Colonial Emigration Society, which was much more effective but only as a placement bureau filling the needs of colonials.

Colonial customs included strict rules against mixed marriages, and the migration of women from the mother country did little to broaden views in this regard, although it did reduce the incidence of interracial marriage of the sort typified by the Signares of Senegal, black women who married the earliest white colonizers. A very few exceptional women were able to achieve a fresh view of such matters, among them Hubertine Auclert in Algeria (*Les Femmes arabes en Algérie,* 1900) and the writers listed by Denise Brahimi.[47]

A few other women took advantage of the expansion of empire to satisfy their curiosity about Africa and the Orient.

Travelers

Alongside these one-way migrations, often undertaken in dramatic circumstances, a boom in travel linked to the rise of tourism and thermal cures offered well-to-do women the opportunity to get out and see the world. True, doctors poured cold water on their enthusiasm by pointing out the damage the sun could do to the complexion and observing that chaotic transportation could be hard on the internal organs. Women were also burdened with loads of baggage and worries about timetables, sickness, and unsavory encounters—enough to dissuade many from traveling. Coastal resorts and spas reinforced sexual and social segregation. Women never got to enjoy the pleasures of swimming or the sublime sights of the coast, whose raptures were reserved for their male companions.[48] Yet escape was possible, escape in which the eyes, sharpened by innumerable taboos, became the primary organ for touching and taking hold of new places. Women made sketches of scenic spots and soon were taking snapshots. And in the distance they may have glimpsed the young female cyclists on the beach at Balbec, as Proust described them in *A l'ombre des jeunes filles en fleur* (In a Budding Grove).

Among Protestants, and to a lesser extent and somewhat later among Catholics, travel became an accepted component of the final phase of a girl's education. The study of foreign languages enabled them to do translations, an acceptable line of work for women. Some traveled to contemplate the art treasures of Italy and Flanders, which offered any number of models for patient copyists. Didn't Baudelaire say that museums were the only public place where women could decently appear? In them, however, a young lady could learn a great deal about male anatomy, so Catholic educators preferred churches. By the turn of the twentieth century the "grand tour," long a staple in the education of young men, became available to their sisters as well. Marguerite Yourcenar (1903–1988) profited greatly from the opportunity.[49] A traveler, translator, and writer, she was a product of the new women's culture, at once classical and European, and she would take it to new heights of creativity. Henceforth travel would be a part of the female imagination, stimulated by the texts, objects, and illustrations in magazines such as *Tour du Monde* and *Harper's Bazaar* as well as by visits to world fairs. The Mediterranean, the Near and Far East, and later Africa became part of the mental geography of European women, giving content to generally vague dreams of the exotic *à la* Madame Bovary. But what dramatic breaks might one day stem from this desire to leave home?

Here I am interested not so much in travel for the purpose of cultural consumption as I am in travel as action, travel in which women truly attempted to "break out" of their assigned spaces and roles. To accomplish this one had to have a desire to escape, experience suffering, repudiate an intolerable future; it took conviction and a spirit of discovery or mission like that which drove the Saint-Simonian Suzanne Voilquin to Egypt, Princess Belgioioso from oppressive Italy to liberated France, the Russian students toward "the people," and female investigators into poor urban neighborhoods (where the People lived, the Worker embodying for many the sublime figure of the Other).[50] And philanthropists, feminists, and socialists traveled to attend their conferences, whose importance for the political education of women cannot be overestimated. Delegates learned to speak to large audiences, to manage relations with the public and the press, and to deal with international affairs. In her memoirs Emma Goldman noted what travel meant to the political activist. Her journeys set the pace of her life. She was always on the road, going from meeting to meeting, making the rounds of various conferences—typical of the well-traveled militant to whom people and ideas mattered more than landscapes, and the very antithesis of the kind of tourism that Marx himself reviled. Jeanne Bouvier, who in October 1919 served as a delegate to the International Congress of Working Women in Washington, has left an admiring account of her transatlantic voyage and friendly welcome as well as a description of the organization of the National Women's Trade Union League, which she dreamed of replicating in France.[51] Women had always enjoyed working in the theater even though they were excluded from directing;[52] in this sense the congress was a spectacular revenge, an opportunity for a legitimate voyage. The seriousness of these women is obvious; their secret pleasure has to be imagined.

That pleasure was intensified by writing, for which travel provided the opportunity or the pretext. The German Sophie von La Roche (1730–1807) would have been passionate about travel if she had had the opportunity. On a trip through Switzerland she climbed Mont Blanc, and the account she gave of it in her *Journal of a Trip through Switzerland* is considered to be the first report on women's sports. The twice-divorced Russian Lydia Alexandra Pachkov worked as a correspondent for newspapers in Saint Petersburg and Paris and made travel-writing her profession. In 1872 she toured Egypt, Palestine, and Syria, waxed enthusiastic about Palmyra, and gave a richly detailed account to the *Tour du Monde*. Her story nurtured a "desire for the East" in Isabelle Eberhardt (1877–1904), who would eventually out-travel her mentor. The illegitimate daughter of a Russian noblewoman living in exile in Switzerland, Eberhardt converted to Islam and fought in North Africa in the guise of a young rebel, Mahmoud, who fascinated the French general Lyautey. Dead at twenty-seven, she left an unpublished body of work dedicated to the humble people of the Maghreb.[53]

Alexandra David-Néel (1868–1969), an explorer and orientalist turned Buddhist, has left an account of her travels in the Far East in the form of letters written to her husband until his death in 1941. After more than thirty years in Asia, she returned to Europe in 1946 at the age of seventy-eight, bringing with her an extraordinary record of her journey, much of it in photographs that can be viewed today in her house in Digne, which has been turned into a museum.

Traveling from one lamasery to another with an escort of porters, she crossed the Tibetan highlands in search of documentation for her orientalist researches as well as of inner peace: "Yes," she wrote her husband, Philippe, "when one has been up there, there is nothing more to see or do: life—a life like mine, which was nothing but one long wish to travel—is over; it has achieved its ultimate goal" (August 8, 1917).[54]

As for Jane Dieulafoy (1851–1916), born to a good family and raised in the Convent of the Assumption, nothing would seem to have predestined her to become the "lady who dressed as a man" and one of the first female archaeologists. She married Marcel, a graduate of the Ecole Polytechnique and an engineer, because she shared his interest in Algeria and the Orient as well as his belief that husband and wife should be companions in life. She saw herself as his collaborator (and she insisted on using the masculine form of the word in French, *collaborateur* rather than *collabora-*

trice). Working at first as an assistant, she kept travel notes and took responsibility for the photography and cooking, but later she took an increasing part in the archaeological work as well. Together, they discovered in Persia the celebrated frieze of Assyrian warriors, on display today in a room in the Louvre that bears their names. Her special interest was Persian society, particularly the private lives of Persian women. And she became a writer. Upon returning to France after two expeditions to Persia, she found it difficult to accept the conventions, and braving public mockery she refused to wear anything but men's clothing. With her short hair and slender figure she looked like an adolescent—that figure of the androgyne that haunted the imagination of the Belle Epoque. A feminist more in the way she lived than in the ideology she espoused, she opposed divorce, which offended her Catholic beliefs. Travel did not abolish all frontiers; on the contrary, it revealed contradictions.[55]

Travel in itself settled nothing. But what an experience! It allowed women to become familiar with other cultures. Some went on to do creative work, to experiment with new techniques: the affinity of women for photography is striking. Initially photography was considered a minor art. It required a great deal of fussy preparation and long hours in the darkroom and could therefore be left to women. Before long some had distinguished themselves: Julia Margaret Cameron, Margaret Bourke-White, and Gisela Freund, to name a few. Women also moved into new fields such as archaeology and orientalism, not without encountering misogynist prejudices that would have kept them confined to minor roles. In Alexandra David-Néel's words: "You do not move in these circles, so you cannot suspect what certain men are capable of, men whose hatred of feminism grows with each passing day."[56]

Above all women asserted their freedom as individuals: in their dress and life-styles, in their religious, intellectual, and amorous choices. In one way or another, and often at great cost to themselves, they broke the circle of confinement and pushed back the frontiers of sex.

Breaks in Time

What kinds of changes encouraged women to emerge into public space and, in particular, the political arena in the nineteenth century? How were relations between the sexes modified to that end?

Here, I am not concerned with the "condition" of women, whose history must take account of all those things usually placed under the head of "modernization," including the history of technology (the sewing machine, the vacuum cleaner) and the history of medicine (bottle feeding, contraception).[57] I am interested, rather, in women as *actresses*. In particular, what was the impact of what we generally refer to as "events"? Just what constituted an "event" in this area? Shouldn't the notion be broadened or modified? Shouldn't it be extended to culture or biology?

Book-events too shaped the consciousness of readers and by stimulating conversation, contacts, and exchanges gave ideas physical embodiment. Among them were Mary Wollstonecraft's *Vindication of the Rights of Woman,* John Stuart Mill's *The Subjection of Women,* August Bebel's *Die Frau und der Sozialismus,* and, later, Simone de Beauvoir's *Le Deuxième Sexe*. Novels should also be included in the list: Mme de Staël's *Corinne* and George Sand's *Indiana* provided many new models with which women could identify. In her life as much as in her work George Sand seems to have transcended boundaries to become a liberating figure, especially in Germany. There is still a great deal to learn about influences of this kind.

What effects did changes in educational systems have on women's groups (boarding schools in England and America were social gathering places and bases of action, for instance) or on women's pioneering in male professions (such as that of schoolteacher, everywhere—even in remote Salonika—a beacon as well as a target of criticism)? In the 1880s medical studies were first opened to women in Russia and then closed again. But this new beginning played a crucial role in the formation of a particularly dynamic group, the female students of medicine.[58] Of course an educational event often reflected or crystallized a political conjuncture.

In view of the importance of the body and health it seems reasonable to allow that there could be biological events as well. The cholera epidemic of 1831–32 (and to a lesser extent that of 1859) mobilized women. By forcing them to explore poor neighborhoods, these epidemics changed their way of seeing the world and equipped them with expertise. Bettina Brentano and her German friends saw the failure of standard medicine and advocated homeopathic remedies and preventive hygiene. Social plagues such as tuberculosis, alcoholism, and syphilis were battlefronts where women fought in the front lines with a sense that they were defending the cause of women as victims of these scourges. In the spirit in which Josephine Butler criticized the Contagious Diseases Act, women sometimes voiced a radical critique of "male civilization," against which they held up an ideal of "purity."

Broadly speaking, public health, nursing, and medicine, particularly in the areas of gynecology and obstetrics, became battlegrounds everywhere from the Urals to the Appalachians. Midwives vanished from the birthing room. Denied the right to perform cesarean sections or to use forceps, they clashed bitterly with physicians and increasingly became the butt of hostility to abortion. Worries over population made birth control an affair of state in the late nineteenth century. Increased repression of abortion and other neo-Malthusian population-limitation methods led women to view their bodies in political terms, as Judith Walkowitz has shown.

Concerning the Father: Changes in the Law

The creation of legislators elected by exclusively male suffrage, the law was at this time the uncompromising expression of a patriarchal power that governed relations between the sexes—not in an "arbitrary" manner (for it conformed to a strict logic of its own), but in ways that sometimes seemed arbitrary. The debates that went on in these male debating societies were replete with choice specimens for any anthology of misogyny. In general there was little legislation concerning women: why bother, since it was all in the codes, which simply had to be preserved. Unless of course legislation was needed to "protect" women, in the workplace, for example, where they were at first classed together with children. This, by the way, explains the reluctance of many feminists to support the sort of laws that might turn out to be discriminatory measures. Truly egalitarian laws were less common, and their origins were always problematic: what was the legislature's real motive? Nicole Arnaud-Duc has called attention to the ambiguity of the French law of 1907 that granted married women control over their own wages so as to allow them to manage the family budget more effectively. Similarly, it was the spectacle of the condition of the poor that impelled the British Parliament to reform the laws concerning women and property. Social utility mattered more than sexual equality.

Many women were conscious of the legal obstacles they encountered every day, which continually reminded them of their inferiority. On occasion a court case revealed some flagrant injustice to women and thus crystallized public opinion. The Norton case in England, for example, led to the reform of laws governing divorce laws and the property of married women. Separated from her husband in 1836, Caroline Norton became a celebrated woman of letters. But since she had married under the community property regime, all her earnings belonged to her husband, who, to make sure of them, accused her of adultery with the Prime Minister and then secured custody of their three children. She protested in a stinging pamphlet that led to the Act of 1839, which spelled out the rights of separated mothers with respect to their children. But she did not stop there: in 1853 she published *English Law for Women in the Nineteenth Century,* and in 1855 she brought out a *Letter to the Queen on Lord Cranworth's Marriage and Divorce Bill.* Her actions were seconded by Barbara Leigh Smith (1827–1891), the daughter of a liberal M.P., who enlisted both public opinion and the support of Lord Brougham's Law Amendment Society. The Divorce Act was passed in 1857. Its provisions concerning women's property were important but insufficient. Many more battles were necessary, and many additional acts were passed (in 1870, 1882, and 1893), before women gained the right to dispose of their property as they wished; much of the opposition came from the House of Lords. It took the joint efforts of feminists and democrats (such as John Stuart Mill and Russel Gurney), coupled with an outcry by women outraged by the case of Suzannah Palmer and other women who were driven into poverty. At the height of the legislative battle, petitions bearing thousands of signatures were submitted to Parliament, and one member, an important industrialist, reported that he could not set foot inside his factory gate without being assailed by questions from his female employees concerning the progress of the reform.[59] The situation was similar in France in the period 1831–1834: liberal efforts in favor of divorce were supported by innumerable petitions in which women called upon lawmakers to heed their suffering.[60] Feminists insisted that the slow pace of reform proved the need to grant women the right to vote so that they could make their wishes heard. By linking civil rights and political rights, they showed that the right to divorce was fundamentally a recognition of women as individuals, "the first step along the road to citizenship for women."[61] Fierce resistance was therefore only to be expected from the traditionalists. "Do not touch the French family," Monsignor Freppel warned in 1882 in the course of debates of unprecedented vehemence, "for along with religion it is our one remaining strength."[62] An alliance of republicans of every stripe—including Freemasons, Protestants, and Jews—was necessary to secure final passage of the Naquet Law in 1884.

Because of its fundamental importance, divorce is an excellent issue for demonstrating the true nature of law as a constantly shifting field of forces, a battleground on which competing groups test their strength, measure the extent of the obstacles they face, assess their alliances, and assay changes in public opinion. For feminists, the mediators between the political process and women at large, the legal struggle is a confrontation in a continuing combat, a place where they can test their representativity. In the many varieties of nineteenth-century feminism, the legal dimension was essential because the Law symbolized the Father.

Concerning God: Religious Ruptures

The intensity of the bond between women and religion bestowed particular importance on religious events. Religion, with its dense associations of discipline and duty, sociability and law, custom and language, weighed on women's shoulders like a leaden cape. But it also brought consolation and aid. Thus the feminization of religion in the nineteenth century can be interpreted in two ways: as a form of regimentation and as an acquisition of influence.[63] But not of power: that remained male, as did politics.

This was especially true in the Catholic Church, turned more rigid than ever under the counter-revolution and the twin dogmas of papal infallibility and Immaculate Conception. There were few breaches in this fortress, which frequently mobilized its troops and dispatched them on crusades. When the Church encouraged women to move into politics through such organizations as the Ligue Patriotique des Francaises, it was to defend an uncompromisingly conservative model of the family.[64] It praised the woman who stayed at home and sewed or went to church and prayed. Social Catholicism loosened things up a bit, but its effects on sexual relations were more indirect than direct.

There was much more innovation among Protestants, as Jean Baubérot showed earlier. Pietism encouraged the German women of Goethe's day to speak out. Revivals in England and America produced cracks in the old monolith that gave women a toehold. In late-eighteenth-century New England Esther Burr and Sarah Prince, cultivated Bostonians whose letters reveal their friendship as well as their fervor, and Sarah Osborne and Suzanne Anthony, Newporters of humble background, founded female societies with radical religious and social agendas.[65] In the first third of the nineteenth century the second Great Awakening witnessed a proliferation of sects led by inspired women preachers such as Jemima Wilkinson and Anna Lee, the founder of Shakerism. In a temporary equality of the sexes, women, often allied with marginal social sectors, subverted religious symbols, rites, and messages. Others were critical of the injustice and licentiousness of the new urban society: the Female Reform Society, founded in New York in 1834, attacked the hypocrisy of the "double standard" and sought without much success to convert prostitutes.[66]

In Great Britain, the religious revival, chiefly Methodist, was far more conservative with respect to sexual roles, yet it did encourage women to resist. Some embraced a rationalist agenda in which social issues took the place of sacred ones. Among them was Emma Martin (1812–1851), who, after being reduced to silence and treated like a pariah, decided to become a midwife, as did the Saint-Simonian Suzanne Voilquin. Others poured their energies into a chiliastic socialism suffused with a belief in salvation through women. Joanna Southcott (1750–1814), a Devonshire servant, heard voices telling her that she was the "Woman clothed with the Sun" and thereupon embarked on a crusade of preaching that attracted more than 100,000 converts, 60 percent of them women. Owenism, a mixture of highly rational social science and millenarian rhetoric, also exalted "woman's mission."[67]

French Saint-Simonism was in some ways similar, though it lacked any specific religious reference. It was, however, an extraordinary brew of moralistic, apostolic feminism and love of freedom. It looked to the East for its Mother of Salvation, and drew an enthusiastic response from women, who were called to "testify in equality with men."[68] Désirée Véret, Jeanne Deroin, Eugénie Niboyet, and Claire Démar spoke, acted, and wrote with messianic faith. What a disappointment it must have been when the Father rejected in a quite clerical fashion the women he had called to himself. Resignations and even suicides were common.

All these sects, associated with a common archaeology and

possibly even with the revolutionary earthquake, were experiments in public expression and responsibility, and their legacy would bring life-giving sustenance to the remainder of the century.

The Motherland: Wars and Struggles for National Independence

War—the virile act *par excellence*—tended to consolidate traditional roles. In an atmosphere of heightened discipline and a rhetoric calculated to induce guilt, particularly in women, both sexes are mobilized in service of the fatherland, men at the front, women in the rear, where we find them sewing, making bandages, cooking, and above all tending the wounded. Associations of patriotic German women did this kind of work in 1813, and it took the enlightened spirit of a Rahel Varnhagen to call for caring for the enemy as well. Princess Belgioioso, who aspired to a political role, was entrusted by Mazzini with organizing hospitals and clinics in Rome in 1849. She hired women of the lower classes, courageous but uninhibited, and sought to discipline them. "Unbeknownst to myself I had formed a seraglio," she said, but she would defend it against bitter criticism.[69] When volunteers became professionals and offered their advice, conflicts arose: this happened with Florence Nightingale in Crimea and with female medical students in Russia, who tried, amid the confusion of the Russo-Turkish War of 1878, to win recognition of their qualifications, without much success.

Many women would have liked to fight, to follow in the footsteps of Clorinde, Joan of Arc, or the Grande Mademoiselle, to step into the breach brandishing a sword. But they were not allowed to use weapons: "Would it be appropriate or even decent for girls and women to stand guard and go out on patrol?" asked Sylvain Maréchal.[70] And, he might have added, "to feminize the soldiers," for it was also a question of sexuality. The law of April 30, 1793, ordered women who had joined the revolutionary armies back to their homes and prohibited any further military service by women. A few remained in the ranks in disguise, however.[71] But women who tried to join up were henceforth stigmatized. In 1848 obscene mockery greeted not only German women but even more the Vésuviennes of Paris, lower-class women who had the audacity to insist on a "political constitution for women," the right to wear male clothing, and access to all public positions, "civil, religious,

[and] military." Daumier, Flaubert, and even Daniel Stern (Marie d'Agoult) herself met their demands with derision.[72]

Elsewhere in Europe, the participation of women in the war for Greek independence—in armed defense as well as in resupply efforts—caught the attention of the international public. There were even staff-level female commanders on the revolutionary side, and they enjoyed equality with their male counterparts: they were wealthy women, daughters or widows of Greek shipowners, who had placed their fortunes and prestige at the service of the cause. Two became well known: Lascarina Bouboulina (1783–1825), the patroness of the Society of Friends, who laid the groundwork for the uprising and played a major role in the siege of Tripoli, where she managed to negotiate for the safety of the women in Hourchit Pasha's harem, commanded three ships against the Turks, and was killed in action; and Mado Mavrogenous (1797–1838), who persuaded the leading men of Mykonos, her island, to join the insurrection. After the massacre of Chio (1822), she organized a militia and commanded it arms in hand. She sent a letter to the "ladies of Paris," whom she urged to support the cause of Greek Christians against the threat of Islam: "I desire a day of battle, much as you long for the moment of a ball." Renounced by her family for having squandered her inheritance on the war, she would die alone and in poverty.[73] The image of the woman soldier, which had been compatible with an aristocratic and religious world view, was untenable in a bourgeois century, for which violence by women (whether criminals, warriors, or terrorists) was a scandal that criminologists attempted to naturalize in order to neutralize (see Lombroso, *The Criminal Woman*).

Women's support for national struggles was obliged to take other acceptable forms. Queen Louise of Prussia, Polish countesses in exile, Countess Markievicz in Ireland, Princess Cristina Belgioioso—all used their influence to serve their countries. Princess Belgioioso, a journalist, historian, and friend of Augustin Thierry and Mignet, did all she could to win the support of French intellectuals and the French government in the cause of Italian unification. She frequently regretted her banishment: "Forced labor was what I needed, not just work with a pen, but action. But where is a woman to find such a thing?"[74] The hospitals were her prize, but then came the quarrel with Mazzini, ruin, exile in Turkey. Women who aspired to play a political role were suspect. The experience of the Irish Ladies' Land League offers yet another example, this one collective rather than individual.

Parnell and the leaders of the Land League, which championed the cause of the Irish farmer, called upon women to support their struggle. At the behest of Parnell's sisters Ann and Fanny an independent Ladies' Land League was established on the American model. Refusing to limit their activity to charity work, they urged resistance to tenant evictions and provided shelter to tenants thrown off their land. Radicalizing the movement, they advocated withholding rent payments, which earned them the ire of landlords and wealthy farmers. Despite their fundraising efforts, their budget was in deficit, and this was used to deride their lack of managerial ability. Public opinion, roused by Catholic and Protestant bishops, was critical of such a salient role for women. In meetings women who timidly gathered in the back of the hall mounted the podium to speak, and this was considered unacceptable, despite their reserve (Ann Parnell always dressed in black and spoke slowly and calmly). Families disapproved of women who dishonored their names by going out at night. And were they not thrown into jail along with common criminals? Mary O'Connor served six months alongside prostitutes. In December 1881 the Ladies' Land League was banned, as were women's meetings in general, and women were excluded from the Irish National League. Fanny Parnell died at age thirty-three. Ann quarreled with her father and went to live in an artists' colony under an assumed name. In 1911 she drowned while swimming in a rough sea. She left an account of her experiences, *The Land League: Story of a Great Shame,* which long remained unpublished; in it she says nothing about herself.[75]

Women who lent their services or filled in for men during wartime were expected to disappear when peace returned. Struggles for national independence did nothing to change sex relations; the twentieth century teaches the same lesson. Yet women who met in the course of war-related activities found it difficult simply to return home. The German generation of 1813 found an outlet for its energies in the private sphere. After the Civil War women in the United States brought their abolitionist enthusiasm to philanthropy and feminism.

Revolution, Sister?

Revolutions—as we have seen in the case of the French Revolution with which the century and this book began—pose a threat to existing power structures and daily routines and therefore have the potential to disrupt gender relations. The history of feminism has been marked, as Anne-Marie Käppeli has shown, by a series of revolutions. Whereas war imposes silence on individuals in the name of the national interest, revolution, at least initially, legitimates the expression of the desires and discontents from which it arose. And why not the desires and discontents of women? Yet women have never been as deeply caught up in these "great vacations from life" as men have been, in part because their job, as always, is to provide for the material needs of their family, a job that the circumstances of revolution only make more difficult. Nevertheless, revolutionary upheaval does offer women opportunities to get around and meet other people.

Women are no more of one mind about revolution than men. The counter-revolutionary camp has had its heroines and its loyal female adepts. Women supported priests who refused to take the oath of loyalty to the Republic, and this was always advanced as an argument against granting women the right to vote. But here I am concerned not so much with that issue as with the larger question of "rights," whose proclamation is always accompanied by conditions ("universal" rights implying certain limitations and exclusions). From this same contradictory space emerged a feminism that, in France at any rate, was at first more legal than social. Classed with foreigners, minors, serfs, and paupers, women on occasion derived a power of representation from this proximity.

Women were not in the forefront of the French Revolution. At first their place was in the shadows, their role the traditional one of auxiliary: the women of the bread march to Versailles (October 5 and 6, 1789), for example, or those who participated in the Festival of the Federation, whose unifying and maternal role Michelet lauded. Later they suffered because they were ignored. They sought allies: Condorcet and a few Girondins in 1789; Saint-Simonians in 1830; workers in 1848; freethinkers, Freemasons, and democrats later on. Everywhere the alliance with socialism was the most common and the most problematic, especially in the second half of the nineteenth century, because party socialism thought "class" first and rejected any independent organization of women. But integration with men spelled silence for women who were not free to choose their spokespersons. When they tried to meet, they were greeted with obscene catcalls. In June 1848, Eugénie Niboyet, tired of confronting this "racket," declared that "henceforth no man will be admitted without a recommendation from his mother or sister" (*La Liberté,* June 8, 1848), an ironic turning of the tables. Women who did not wish to be stifled had to have their own associations, clubs, meetings, and newspapers. We know what invariably came of such demands.

Restorations followed revolutions. From King Otto's Greece to Biedermeier Germany, from the France of Charles X to Victorian England, traditionalists attempted to restore order and banish the decadence they blamed for political anarchy. The subjugation of women was usually one element of such attempts at restoration. Was not the Civil Code worse than customary law? Some jurists thought so, as did some women: "Women are more deprived of all rights than under the Ancien Régime," one could read in the *Journal des Femmes* in 1838. Where optimists saw progress, militant women saw regression (and socialists pauperization). They consoled themselves with the anthropological theory of a "primitive matriarchy," and Marxists approved this theory with its corollary that women had suffered a "historical defeat." Abandonment by allies, repression by the authorities, and vast indifference combined to create a profound sense of disappointment, which encouraged the formation of a gender consciousness, of women who thought of themselves as "we."

Gender relations thus appear in history as a dynamic process, sustained by conflicts stemming from ruptures of varying types and degrees of importance. Does history lurch by fits and starts? That is the way it is generally presented, indeed invariably presented in male accounts indifferent to or scornful of women's issues. In fact there is probably a tissue of invisible connections among these various disturbances. A kind of transmission takes place through the press, through memory, through direct contact between mothers and daughters, and this helps to shape the kind of self-conscious groups that are the basis of opinion-making. And it goes without saying that the job of writing a gendered history of public opinion remains to be done.

TRANSLATED FROM THE FRENCH BY ARTHUR GOLDHAMMER

18

Feminist Scenes

Anne-Marie Käppeli

FEMINISM HAS MANY FACES, so there is no point looking for the moment of origin.[1] We can examine its various guises by focusing at times on ideas and discourses, at other times on social practices.

In the nineteenth century a small number of women forged a feminist public identity for themselves through their writing and organizational talents. Some invoked the rights of man while championing the cause of their own sex. Others asserted themselves through religious dissidence. Changes in the law eventually accorded them a recognized civil status. The suffragettes looked forward to a new political identity. Breaking the silence surrounding sexuality, they argued in favor of a new morality. Their struggle for access to jobs laid the groundwork necessary for achieving financial independence.

Between the French Revolution and the First World War feminism in Europe and the United States manifested itself in a variety of women's movements, publications, and organizations, each with its own tactics and alliances. Their claims and the hostility they provoked demonstrate that the "woman question" had become an issue of broad public debate and figured in a variety of social and political struggles. While men of the nineteenth century organized on the basis of class, women too organized, but on the basis of sex, thereby disrupting existing political patterns.

The Emergence of Feminisms

Enlightenment philosophy supplied the feminist cause with an arsenal of weapons: the ideas of reason and progress, natural rights, individual fulfillment, the positive influence of education, the social utility of freedom, and the axiom of equal rights. In 1791 Olympe de Gouges asked that the rights of man be extended to include women, and Mary Wollstonecraft based her *Vindication of the Rights of Woman* (1792) on the ideas of the Enlightenment and the French Revolution. The soil of feminism was further enriched by Protestant social ideas: like rationalist individualism, religious individualism applied to both sexes.[2] But the ideas of the enlightened bourgeoisie had a hard time finding a social and political base. Feminism relied more on the separation of the two spheres of life, a legacy in part of the liberal evangelical tradition, which emphasized the specific qualities of women and their role in public life,[3] and in part of the bourgeois polarization of male and female characteristics.[4] Women thus learned how to take advantage of their power in the private sphere as well as how to subvert the boundaries of that sphere by raising ostensibly private issues in the public arena.

Egalitarian and Dualist Currents

The theoretical support for nineteenth-century feminism was based largely on two distinct representations of woman: one, based on the idea of common humanity, supported an egalitarian current; the other, derived from the idea of the eternal feminine, gave rise to a dualist current. Paradoxically, women were asking for equality of the sexes while insisting on their difference from men. Hence feminists were caught in the conflict between the general and the particular: which qualities mattered more in determining woman's political status, the human ones or the female ones?[5]

The bourgeois egalitarians looked upon the legislator as the central motor of change and the state as a partner to be called in to settle conflicts of interests. The demand that women be recognized as citizens and the repeated campaigns for political equality were the forms in which the humanist/egalitarians expressed themselves. Invoking Locke, Mary Wollstonecraft declared her opposition to the idea that women have specific virtues or belong in a specific sphere of their own. At mid-century John Stuart Mill insisted that the promises of the American Declaration of Independence should extend to women. His essay on *The Subjection of Women* (1869) was translated into all the European languages and became a basic reference for liberal egalitarian feminists.[6] Throughout the century isolated feminists continued to invoke the rationalism of the Enlightenment, not only in connection with the issue of women's suffrage but also in the fight against a double standard in sexual mores: for example, the Italian Luisa Tosco invoked both Jenny d'Héricourt and John Stuart Mill in her book, *La Causa delle donne* (1876).[7]

By contrast, the dualist representation, which steadily gained ground, emphasized woman's maternal capacities—capacities defined not only physically but also psychically and socially. Special attention was paid to the cultural contributions of women. A contemporary of Stuart Mill, Ernest Legouvé, rehabilitated femininity in his *Histoire morale des femmes* (1849), which was widely read in Europe; he used maternity as an argument to justify educational and legislative reform. In opposition to the egalitarian view, here the fundamental sociopolitical unit was not the individual but the couple and the family.[8]

This difference in the interpretation of equality led to two distinct views of women, as "female citizens" and as "wives and mothers." The feminist problem seemed at times to be one of politics and legislation, at times one of society and ethics. Championing abstract rights having little to do with the everyday realities of women's lives tended to paralyze the feminist movement, whereas the dualist conception had greater potential as cultural critique but masked conflicts of interest between men and women in a patriarchal society.

Periods of Feminist Effervescence

Periods of feminist effervescence mark the entire nineteenth century. Sometimes the ferment was confined to a single generation, sometimes it was carried over from one generation to the next. In France the early attempts to organize women in patriotic clubs during the Revolution withered after the authoritarianism of the

Napoleonic years halted all efforts toward the liberation of women. The Civil Code of 1804, which influenced the legal status of women throughout Napoleonic Europe, embodied the idea that a woman is man's property and that her first task is to make children. During this reactionary phase, feminism metamorphosed from an intellectual movement into a socialist one. The utopian socialist circles that flourished in France and England between 1820 and 1840 concluded their analysis of the subjugation of women with a vehement attack on marriage.[9] The utopians' commitment to sexual equality went hand in hand with a belief in the moral superiority of women. Anne Wheeler brought Saint-Simon's ideas to England, thereby forging bonds between the first French and English socialists. The two theorists of the English cooperative movement, William Thompson and Robert Owen, provided a crucial intellectual framework for the elaboration of socialist feminism. In their *Appeal on Behalf of Women* (1825) Wheeler and Thompson argued in utilitarian terms for a transformation of the competitive economic structure so as to favor women. Ten years later, Owen criticized the established social order and in a series of ten lectures *(On the Marriages of the Priesthood of the Old Immoral World)* condemned existing sexual and family arrangements. In response to the writings and lectures of such Owenist disciples as Frances Wright and Frances Morrison, small social communities were formed. Following the Owenist model, Chartist women, who were organized on a national level, lectured in public at a time when the right of middle-class women to speak out publicly was still new and tenuous.

In many other European countries early feminists linked up with democratic and nationalist movements. What had happened in France at the end of the eighteenth century—women joining the Revolution and forming political clubs—happened to a lesser extent in Germany in the Revolution of 1848. Young Louise Otto expressed her patriotic sentiments in the *Lieder eines deutschen Mädchens* (1847). In Poland a circle of "Enthusiasts" formed around Narcyza Zmichowska. Impelled by their enthusiasm for liberty and equality, they worked to bring better education to the people and to abolish serfdom. In Italy, the political influence of the "illustrious women" of the Risorgimento spread from their salons, where nationalist leaders were frequent guests: the best known was that of Clara Maffei in Milan. The ambassadress of Italian national unity, Cristina Trivulzio Belgioioso, established

Fourierist-inspired institutions in Lombardy between 1842 and 1846, and in Rome in 1849 she operated hospitals and clinics in service of the cause. Also in Lombardy, Ester Martini Currica was one of the leading organizers of Mazzini's movement.[10] In Czechoslovakia after 1860 bourgeois salons became the center of patriotic Prague, most notably those of Karolina Svetlá and Augusta Braunerová. Anna Lauermannová's literary salon helped Czech women free themselves from the grip of Austro-German culture and look to France for a possible intellectual emancipation.[11]

Feminists drew support not only from political movements but also from centers of religious dissidence. Quaker prayer meetings in the United States and England in the early and middle part of the century and charity organizations that sprang up in Switzerland and Holland during the Awakening of 1830–1840 allowed middle-class women to break out of their traditional roles.[12] A highly developed social consciousness prompted women to speak out and organize. In Germany in the 1840s adepts of Free Protestantism (Freiprotestantismus) and German Catholicism (Deutschkatholizismus) raised radical questions about "woman's fate." A Catholic theorist named Rupp working in Königsberg developed a model communal constitution that guaranteed women the right to vote and be elected to office.[13] It is not surprising that Louise Otto saw the German Catholic movement as one of the most important factors favoring the emancipation of women. Although feminist organizing was slowed by counter-revolution, it became active again in 1872 after the Franco-Prussian War. Progress toward industrialization, the formation of political parties, and the bourgeois predilection for organization played the role of catalyst in the consolidation and diversification of feminism from then until the eve of World War I.

If European feminism in the first half of the nineteenth century benefited from the spirit of revolution and religious dissidence, feminism in the United States bore the stamp of the pioneer spirit. Daughters of Liberty such as Abigail Adams remained isolated theorists like the women writers of the Enlightenment, the French Revolution, and the German *Vormärz*. In the 1830s the women of the American middle class, who had learned to express themselves in the religious revivals that followed the American Revolution, found their "school of politics" in the antislavery movement. By the end of the nineteenth century, however, feminisms on both sides of the Atlantic seemed to be moving closer together.

An excellent barometer of feminist successes can be found in the growth of the women's press and women's organizations. Mid-century feminists were quite well aware of this. In England Frances Power Cobbe observed that "the advancement of a sex in the civilized world is certainly a unique fact in history, which should immediately have important repercussions."[14]

The Feminist Press

The general pattern was that the creation of a feminist journal went hand in hand with the foundation of an organization. The paper or journal became a focal point of various battles, and the contents allows us to distinguish among different feminist positions.

Journals

One of the most important of the new publications was the *Englishwoman's Journal.* It began publication in 1859 and was linked to the feminists who met at Langham Place, which became the headquarters of groups such as the Society for Promoting the Employment of Women. One of its editors, Emily Davies, used the journal as a platform in her battle to improve girls' education. Susan B. Anthony used the editorial offices of *The Revolution* (1868–1870) to organize the working women of New York. In these and other ways a journal was often much more than a mere instrument for influencing public opinion. *La Fronde* (daily from 1897 to 1903, monthly from 1903 to 1905) was a true organ of French feminist culture and represented a whole way of life for Parisian women. Its editor, Marguerite Durand, was a pioneer in opening journalism as a profession for women. Her coworker, Caroline Rémy, known as Séverine, was the first woman journalist to live on the income generated by her columns.[15] Hélène Sée attended all parliamentary debates and became the first female political columnist. *La Fronde* also set up a free employment office for women. This feminist republican daily figured among the leading French and for that matter European papers of its day.[16]

During the same period Clara Zetkin left her stamp on a paper that aimed at raising the political consciousness of female workers. Out of the *Arbeiterin,* published in Hamburg in 1891, she created the journal of German, indeed international, socialist women, *Gleichheit,* which steadily attracted new readers and numbered leading socialist women among its collaborators: Angelica Balabanoff, Mathilde Wibaut, and H. Roland-Holst (Holland), Hilja Parssinen (Finland), Adelheid Popp (Austria), Ines Armand (Russia), Laura Lafargue, Käthe Duncker, Louise Zietz, and others. At the turn of the century Lily Braun and Clara Zetkin launched the reformist controversy in the pages of the journal. Lenin admired *Gleichheit* and adapted its articles for the Russian press.[17]

Beginnings

Women found their voices in different ways at various key points in the history of feminism. The first known feminist journals were published in the early nineteenth century by English freethinkers and French Saint-Simonians. Female members of organizations whose goal was the reform of the British Parliament openly questioned the tyranny of church and state. The best known of these women, Elizabeth Sharples, an adept of Carlyle's freethinking rationalism, published her own journal, *Isis,* and wrote about "superstition and reason, tyranny and freedom, morality and politics." In July 1832 the Saint-Simonians launched *La Femme libre,* which was followed by *La Femme nouvelle, la tribune des femmes.*[18] Gifts, expressions of support, and congratulations flowed in from all over France. The journal discussed economics, politics, and education as well as issues of women's work and free love. Authors signed articles with their first names, not only in order to hide their identities but also in repudiation of the names forced on them by marriage.

The Revolution of 1848 was the spur to the founding of several women's journals: in France, *La Voix des femmes* and *L'Opinion des femmes;* in Leipzig, Louise Otto's *Frauenzeitung,* which took as its slogan "Dem Reich der Freiheit werb'ich Bürgerinnen" (I recruit citizens for the realm of freedom). These journals soon became targets of political repression. In Switzerland too the feminist press emerged in this period. Joséphine Stadlin, a follower of Pestalozzi, edited *Die Erzieherin* from 1845 to 1849. In the United States it was also in 1849 that the first feminist journal, *The Lily,* was published at the behest of Amelia Bloomer—the woman who also advocated clothing reform (she gave her name to "bloomers").

A third wave of feminist publication began in 1868. In Geneva

Marie Goegg-Pouchoulin published *La Solidarité,* the first international forum for feminists, for ten years. In the United States, after the failure of an attempt to amend the Constitution to protect women's rights, Susan B. Anthony and Elizabeth Cady Stanton launched their *Revolution* (1868). In the same year *La Donna,* a cosmopolitan newspaper that published news of feminist activities abroad, appeared in Italy thanks to the efforts of Anna Maria Mozzoni.[19] In 1869 Léon Richer brought out *Le Droit des femmes* in France, while in England the Ladies' National Association launched its campaign against regulated prostitution with *The Shield.*

The Fate of Journalism

As feminist organizations multiplied and diversified, an independent and varied press grew up alongside, even if most of the publications were short-lived. Many feminists dreamed of becoming journalists: Elizabeth Cady Stanton, for example, aspired to work for the *New York Tribune* but with seven children was never to see her dream come true. But others did realize their ambitions. Margaret Fuller, for instance, was named the *Tribune*'s chief literary critic in 1845, the first woman to hold that post. It would be some time yet, however, before feminists would have an impact on the official press: Emma Goldman served an apprenticeship on the German anarchist paper *Freiheit* before starting *Mother Earth,* her "pampered child," in 1906.

Learning to write for the public was a crucial element of feminism and one that turned out to be essential in the battle against indifference: "Then we would get out our pens and write articles for the papers or a petition to the legislature; indite letters to the faithful, here and there; call on *The Lily, The Una, The Liberator, The Standard* to remember our wrongs as well as those of the slave," Stanton remembered.[20]

The degree to which the women of a particular society are liberated and the level of tolerance for feminism in that society can be gauged in terms of the growth and acceptance of the feminist press. Consider the long-subordinate position of Swiss women. The first journal to champion political rights for women, *Le Mouvement féministe,* was founded by Emilie Gourd as recently as 1912, at which time it took over the feminist column that Auguste de Morsier published in the *Signal de Genève.*[21] Poland, too, was inhospitable to feminism. The only nineteenth-century women's movement in the country was connected with the Positivist Circle of Warsaw, which was receptive to the ideas of John Stuart Mill, and with *Truth*, a newspaper published by Alexander Swietochowski.[22] Even in France and Germany the feminist press ran afoul of repressive laws aimed at various political groups. It did not always fare better in the twentieth century than in the nineteenth, moreover. As late as 1914, Margaret Sanger was arrested when she published a plea for birth control in the first issue of *The Woman Rebel*.[23]

Organizations

Once the issue of women's liberation had been broached in philosophical, literary, and educational debate, it was essential for men and women to join together in organizations for the purpose of developing strategies and approaches for dealing with women as a social question. Some of these organizations counted on private initiative, while others lobbied for state support.

In Europe the first half of the nineteenth century saw only sporadic action, during periods of social and political crisis, in favor of women's liberation: the women's clubs of the French Revolution, the Saint-Simonian women of 1830, the French feminist clubs and associations of German democratic women in 1848. By contrast, more sustained efforts toward national organization were already under way in the United States: as early as 1837 feminist demands were expressed through the National Female Antislavery Association. This group served as a model for the first organizers of female textile workers, foremost among them Sarah Bagley, in 1845–46 leader of the fight as head of the Female Labor Reform Association. Out of the Seneca Falls Convention of 1848 came the Equal Rights Association, which survived for more than ten years. Nineteenth-century American women demonstrated the political lucidity and organizational skills they had acquired in the antislavery struggle.

As the nations of Europe shaped their forms of government in the second half of the century, many feminists tried to link their groups to efforts to promote egalitarian and republican political systems. In France the advent of the Third Republic in 1870 allowed women to associate their struggle for liberation with the long-term struggle over the nature of French society; feminists meanwhile formed numerous groups.[24]

Liberal and Socialist Groups

In Germany in 1865–66 the women's movement began organizing around two rival centers, one liberal, the other independent and created by women themselves.[25] The Berlin Lette-Verein, backed by the Protestant liberal bourgeoisie, drew its inspiration from the London-based association for the promotion of women's labor as well as from Parisian experiments with training the daughters of the upper classes for professional careers. Through an appeal published in the newspapers the Lette group founded the Verein zur Förderung des weiblichen Geschlechts (1866) (Union for the Advancement of the Female Sex), which would always be chaired by a man. The group had only a limited conception of women's liberation. In Saxony, an industrialized region, Louise Otto organized a meeting of local groups involved in women's education and training. This convention, called Frauenschlacht von Leipzig (1865), received a great deal of publicity because women for the first time claimed the right to speak and organize in public. They organized the Allgemeinen Deutschen Frauenverein (General Union of German Women) as an independent women's self-help group. From then until World War I local women's groups multiplied in Germany. Some of these organizations were professional, others charitable. Their goals ranged from the reform of women's clothing to the control of alcoholism to winning the vote for women, all under the umbrella of Frauenverein.[26]

The third European country to witness large-scale efforts to organize women after mid-century was England. Here we see clearly how women's groups came into being in response to political measures hostile to women. In 1866 John Stuart Mill presented to Parliament a petition asking that women be granted the right to vote; although approved by the Parliament, it was rejected by Prime Minister Gladstone. As a result, the National Society for Women's Suffrage was formed under the chairmanship of Lydia Becker. A few years later Josephine Butler chose not to compromise the struggle for the vote by waging war on a taboo evil, the sexual exploitation of women, under the aegis of that organization. She formed an independent group, the Ladies' National Association, for that purpose.

In a small country such as Switzerland, late-nineteenth-century feminist groups represented a realignment of interests within a pluralist society. To help it deal with specific symptoms of social misery, the government subsidized women's self-help groups. Feminism of this kind appealed essentially to the social conscience of women and remained dependent on the political authorities.[27]

The campaigns for women's suffrage and against regulated prostitution contributed to the growth of many organizations and publications. They mobilized thousands of women, not only in the countries that played key roles in Western feminism, namely, the United States, England, France, and Germany, but also in other European countries as well as at the international level.[28] Clearly, one of these campaigns saw itself as a struggle *for* rights, while the other saw itself as a struggle *against* an abuse of the law. Excluded from suffrage, women joined associations in order to forge a public identity for themselves. They used the whole arsenal of democratic expression on behalf of their organizations: the press, petitions, conferences, meetings, parades, banquets, expositions, and national and international congresses which heightened exchange among feminists and created a trans-European network.

In parallel with this liberal network, a second network of socialist women organized on the basis of a class alliance. It was in Germany that class antagonisms were most marked: long inhibited by antisocialist laws, associations of women workers forged ties with the socialist party as soon as the restrictions were lifted in 1890. When bourgeois women, both liberal and conservative, formed the Alliance of German Women's Groups in 1894, the associations of women workers were excluded. In 1896 the split between socialist and bourgeois women burst into the open at the International Feminist Congress in Berlin. Socialist women organized their own congress and refused to collaborate with the bourgeois women's movement even in pursuing their common goal, the right to vote. They maintained their own organization within the socialist party and regularly held women's conferences.[29]

International Effort

As feminists shared experiences through the press, visits, and international congresses, some began to move toward a federational model on both the national and international levels.[30] Feminist consciousness was also carried across national boundaries by the translation into numerous European languages of such classics as John Stuart Mill's *The Subjection of Women* (1869) and August Bebel's *Die Frau und der Sozialismus* (1883, often translated in the original 1879 version, whose title was *Die Frau in der Vergangenheit, Gegenwart und Zukunft;* Woman in the Past, Present, and Future).

The first effort of international organization was associated with democratic pacifism in Europe: it was in 1868 that Marie Goegg-Pouchoulin published an appeal for a Women's International Association in the journal *Les Etats-Unis d'Europe.* Three years later she fell victim to the repression that followed the destruction of the Paris Commune.[31]

Josephine Butler enjoyed greater success in Geneva. Thanks to the support of men in the Protestant aristocracy and the organizing talents of Freemason politician Aimé Humbert, she founded the British, Continental and General Federation for the Abolition of the State Regulation of Vice in 1875; the organization still exists today under the name of the International Abolitionist Federation.[32]

Another international initiative was launched by American women. The arrival in Europe of Elizabeth Cady Stanton and Susan B. Anthony, as well as the success of the World's Woman's Christian Temperance Union, led to the founding of the International Council of Women in Washington in March 1888, on the fortieth anniversary of the Seneca Falls Declaration.[33] In the beginning this was simply an American organization. It would take time for other countries to set up their own national women's councils. When the Countess of Aberdeen was elected president of the International in 1900, it was a sign not only of growing independence from American influence but also of the political establishment's control over moderate feminism. Numerous national councils were formed right up to the eve of World War I: Canada (1893), Germany (1894), England (1895), Sweden (1896), Italy and Holland (1898), Denmark (1899), Switzerland (1900), France (1901), Austria (1902), Hungary and Norway (1904), Belgium (1905), Bulgaria and Greece (1908), Serbia (1911), and Portugal (1914). The one consensus issue at the international level was legitimation of women's participation in politics and, therefore, strict observance of parliamentary procedure. Those who wished to work toward the more specific goal of women's suffrage felt hampered by the International Council of Women. There was talk of forming a separate organization as early as 1899, and the split became manifest at the Berlin Congress of 1904. The International Woman Suffrage Alliance, with the radical American Carrie Chapman Catt as president, won the allegiance of suffragist organizations in a variety of countries. The Alliance proved to be a dynamic group but representative of only a minority of women.[34]

These two organizations turned out to be important not only for bringing feminist groups in different countries into contact with one another but also for encouraging the formation of new groups. Whether they issued general demands or focused on specific issues—temperance, abolition of prostitution, socialism—these international groups enabled members to feel that they were part of a vast current of world opinion. The organizations strengthened their members' confidence in themselves and faith in the inevitability of victory.

Current events provided new organizing themes. For example, the first international demonstration of pacifist women, organized by Margarethe Selenka, a German, with the support of Bertha von Suttner, an Austrian, was held in The Hague in 1899. Speakers proclaimed that the "woman question" and the "peace question" were inseparable: "Both are in essence a struggle for the power of law and against the law of power."[35]

Intercultural Dynamics: Journeys and Exiles

The intercultural dynamic engendered by nineteenth-century feminism was not limited to the institutionalization of international bonds, and it should not be underestimated. Travel by isolated feminists and emigration spurred the formation of feminist consciousness. For example, the Swedish writer Frederika Bremer (1801–1865) visited the United States regularly from 1849 on. Her short story "Hertha," published in 1856, shows clear traces of American feminist experience.[36] The reputation and symbolic power of American feminism are similarly reflected in the Norsk Kvinnesaksforening (Norwegian Feminist Society) and its journal *Nylaende* (New Frontiers), which came into being in 1887.

Cross-border contacts were facilitated not only by emigration but also by exile. Angelica Balabanoff promoted feminist socialism among Italian and Swiss workers through the journal *Su Compagne!* which she published in 1904 in exile in Lugano. In Switzerland Russian medical students came into contact with feminist groups in Zurich.

A less spectacular but nonetheless significant form of intercultural communication was the practice of medicine. Muslim female patients were early treated by female physicians such as Anna Bayerova in Bosnia[37] and the women doctors of Russia.[38]

Demands

The feminist press and organizations engaged in much discussion of emancipation, liberation, and equal rights—democratic values in contradiction with the representation of woman as a legal minor and with sexual slavery. Feminist battles on the field of law were aimed at bringing about fundamental changes in legal and political conditions.

The Law

Feminist critics attacked marital dependency: the husband's right to decide matters concerning the couple, his right to administer and enjoy the fruits of his wife's property, and the exclusive parental rights of the father; they also criticized unjust treatment of unwed mothers and their children and legalized, regulated prostitution. Feminists advocated the right to higher education, the right to vote, and equal pay for equal work.

Giving priority to legal matters had a radicalizing effect.[39] Anita Augspurg, the legal advisor to the radical wing of the German women's movement, was convinced that "the women's issue is largely an economic one, and it may be even more a cultural one . . . but it is above all an issue of law, for it is only on the basis of written laws . . . that we can claim to find a reliable resolution."[40] Repressive laws aimed at political activity restricted the available means of carrying on the fight, limiting expression to what Clara Zetkin called the "heroism of petitions" *(Petitionsheldentum)*.

At the turn of the century the right to vote became the centerpiece of the feminist struggle. For radicals, this was not simply a question of equality but a *sine qua non* for achieving equal rights in public and private life. For moderates, suffrage remained a distant goal, one that would crown all their efforts: they would first have to earn the right by acquiring a better education and proving that they could render useful public service. They would first have to cross the threshold of "competence."[41] Unlike the German and English suffragettes radicalized at the turn of the century, the Americans found that suffragism, the heir to the revolutionary tradition, utopian socialism, and the battle against slavery, lost its political capacity to transform society at the end of the nineteenth century.[42] It was not enough, apparently, for women to achieve legal status equal to that of men. Women's legal demands made sense only when they called the whole structure of power into question.

Education and Training

In most European countries education received first priority among feminist demands. Those who advocated better education for girls and women pointed out that knowledge is indispensable in life.[43] Women, it was argued, play a key role in civilization, since they are responsible for educating their children. Nor could they achieve economic independence without acquiring professional skills. The psychology of woman had been under discussion since the end of the eighteenth century: intellectuals such as Mary Wollstonecraft and Germaine de Staël examined Rousseau's views. Other contributors to the debate included republicans such as the Marquis de Condorcet and Theodor Gottlieb von Hippel. In the first half of the nineteenth century, education was conceived in terms of woman's social role, a role that feminists redefined with each new revolution. In the second half of the century, the issue gradually became one of women's access to secondary and higher education and occupational training. Various experiments in bringing education to women of all classes were attempted throughout the century, from Elizabeth Jesse Reid's pioneering Bedford Ladies' College (1849)[44] to the humanitarian socialist Sibilla Aleramo's Union of Roman Women (1904), which offered night courses to illiterate peasant women.[45] Women did not wait for the state to give them satisfaction. On the contrary, they founded private institutions on their own initiative and set up their own curricula. At the beginning of the twentieth century, many European feminists, inspired by American initiatives, became advocates of coeducation and sexual education.[46] Thus each generation reformulated the question of the content of feminist education.

There is food for thought in the permanent need of feminists to become educators. It is as if the omission of a political and economic status for women from the bourgeois social plan left feminists only one realm in which to take their revenge: education. They thereby exploited the power conferred on them "by nature" and made education their first professional labor. The unmarried schoolteacher who managed to live without depending financially on a husband became a typical sort of feminist model. The many teachers among the third generation of feminist leaders represent all segments of the political spectrum: Germans Helene Lange (1848–1930), Minna Cauer (1842–1922), Clara Zetkin (1857–1933), Anita Augspurg (1857–1943), Gertrud Bäumer (1873–1954); the Austrian Augusta Fickert (1855–1910); the Swiss Emma Graf (1881–1966); Italians Maria Giudice (1880–1953), Adelaide Coari (1881–1966), and Linda Malnati (1885–1921); and countless others. Schoolteachers' organizations also formulated the first demands for "equal pay for equal work" and provided large numbers of activists to support the cause of women's suffrage. They played a major role in spreading feminism beyond the major European cities.[47]

Self-Determination of the Body

Feminists found it difficult to place issues concerning the female body on the public agenda. They began by focusing on matters of civil law, such as the right to divorce.[48] Later, utopian socialists in the 1830s and anarchists at the turn of the twentieth century launched more radical attacks on the institution of marriage.[49] In 1913 Alexandra Kollontai celebrated *The New Woman:* unmarried, proud of her inner strength, unwilling to sacrifice her life for love or passion. At the time, most feminists, regardless of which wing of the movement they belonged to, were unmarried by choice. While some considered being called "Miss" a tribute to their physical and moral integrity, many feminists insisted that every woman over the age of eighteen be addressed as "Mrs."[50]

Many married women with families came to agree on a feminist position concerning birth control, which was worked out in the context of a new image of sexuality. In the United States the Moral Education societies that emerged in the 1870s promoted the concepts of "self-ownership" and rationalization of sexual desire. Lucinda Chandler was one of the most insistent voices in this legal and educational campaign.

At around the same time Josephine Butler launched a campaign against state regulation of prostitution in England. The question of sexuality was examined not only from the moral angle but also in terms of science, politics, and economics.[51] By insisting on the dangers of sexuality, activists hoped to force men and women to look to sexual continence as the antidote to the double standard. "Social purity" thus became the feminist watchword of the last quarter of the nineteenth century. By the beginning of the twentieth century it had become possible for women to take a more positive attitude toward sexuality. In part this was because a first generation of women physicians had shown how women could regain control of their bodies through scientific knowledge, and their teaching encouraged women to overcome fear and ignorance of their physical nature. In part, too, it was because a variety of neo-Malthusian organizations had begun to publicize various methods of contraception. But this was still slippery terrain. Annie Besant, a member of the English Malthusian League, was arrested when she published a book on population control in 1877.[52]

Separating sexual pleasure from procreation aroused fears. Alette Jacobs, who, along with her husband, founded the Dutch Neo-Malthusian League in 1881, resigned from the organization because she felt that its analysis of the situation was based too exclusively on economics. A feminist physician, she continued to give free medical consultations in a working-class neighborhood of Amsterdam. She talked to women about contraceptive methods and taught them to use the pessary, which earned her the condemnation of most of her male colleagues.[53]

Thirty years after neo-Malthusianism came to England, Paul Robin introduced it in France, where it met with a hostile reception from repopulationists. As early as 1902 Nelly Roussel, Madeleine Pelletier, Gabrielle Petit, and Claire Galichen were defending Robin's ideas. Dr. Pelletier, however, was the only one who, with perfect logical consistency, advocated the right to abortion.[54] Meanwhile, a neo-Malthusian group in Geneva promoted the distribution of *La Vie intime* (1908–1914) in a trilingual edition and championed planned parenthood. The only Swiss feminist journals to discuss contraception and abortion in the early part of this century were *L'Exploitée* (1907–1908) and its German counterpart *Die Vorkämpferin* (1906–1920), both edited by Marguerite Faas-Hardegger, secretary of the Swiss Syndical Union.[55]

In the United States Margaret Sanger and Emma Goldman broke the law to promote contraception, and they were among the few feminists to give the issue priority before World War I.[56] English feminists involved in the birth-control and abortion campaigns such as Stella Browne and Marie Stopes became associated with the movement for sexual reform. They also dared to discuss female homosexuality in a scientific context.[57] In Germany, a few isolated feminist voices pointed out the stigmatization of homosexuality, but no political organization of lesbians was possible in the conservative climate of prewar evangelical and "maternalist" feminism.[58]

It was easier to mount an opposition to the tyranny of fashion and the corset. Some feminists proposed a new dress code for women. The struggle for freedom of the body was one aspect of a feminist culture that was also influenced by vegetarianism and the animal protection movement. In the United States the Free Dress League was organized in 1878. The idea spread to Europe at the end of the century. In 1899 Dutch women founded the Vereeniging voor Verbetering van Vrouwenkleding (Organization for the Improvement of Women's Clothes).[59] The goal of liberating the female body from cumbersome dress generally went hand in hand with the promotion of women's athletics.

Morality

Courage and virtue mattered more to nineteenth-century feminists than the body did. The spiritual and social maternalism advocated by educators, the humanitarian efforts of the first nurses, the philanthropic attitudes at the origin of professional social work all of these things appealed to women's courage and virtue and spurred their social mission. Discontent and rebellion invariably began with experiences of injustice and suffering. Florence Nightingale put it this way in *Suggestions for Thought to Searchers after Religious Truth* (1859): "Why do women exhibit passion, intellect, and moral action . . . yet have a place in society where none of these qualities can be used to advantage? . . . I must aspire to a better life for women."[60]

Her experiences as a nurse during the Crimean War led her to found nursing schools. For some feminists, the mission to "save the world," deeply rooted in the evangelical tradition, took the form of a campaign to promote civilized values. This was succinctly expressed by the Protestant feminist Emilie de Morsier, who convoked the Congrès International des Oeuvres et Institutions Féminines in Paris in 1899. She proposed a counterweight to political feminism and redefined the feminist field of action vis-à-vis men: "We would never dispute a shred of your glory . . . if we took our place alongside you to work for the betterment of society . . . because for us women, the fatherland is wherever anyone is suffering."[61] Historically, the professionalization of social work inscribed philanthropic action in the process of women's liberation. By the end of the century bonds were being forged between certain philanthropists and suffragist groups.[62]

If philanthropy as practiced in England and the United States was a way of overcoming the conflict between feminism and bourgeois society, the German concept of spiritual maternity *(geistige Mütterlichkeit)* proved even more effective. Without any overt conflict, sexual dualism subtly supplanted the egalitarian interpretation. Thus in 1882 Henriette Goldschmidt brushed aside the feminist critique and placed the women's movement at the service of political stabilization: "The spiritual elevation of woman's natural profession does not lead solely to conscious comprehension of family duties; it leads also to the discovery that it is woman's cultural mission to awaken the 'maternal heart' in our lower classes and thus to transform an instinctive and passive role into a conscious role equal in importance to that of men."[63] Thus a woman's maternal virtue was confounded with civic virtue. Fifteen years later, Helene Lange developed a concept of cultural emancipation quite removed from the concept of human rights. Invoking the name of Georg Simmel, she revived spiritual maternity as an ideal of women's education and as a critique of cultural alienation.[64] In its conservative version, which mythologized maternity, this form of cultural resistance was symptomatic of society's permanent exclusion of the feminine.[65]

Feminists also reverted to morality to deal with sexual relations inside and outside marriage. The early parts of both the nineteenth and twentieth centuries seemed propitious moments, moreover, for the definition of new ethical codes: at the beginning of the nineteenth century Fourier's psychology of the human passions proposed a new morality that diversified the possibilities for amorous liaison.[66] At the beginning of the twentieth century radical

German and Austrian feminists championed a new sexual ethic that rehabilitated unwed motherhood. In the meantime moral virtue was celebrated by women who favored the abolition of legalized prostitution. In their struggle against the sexual double standard, they insisted that men take female continence as a model. "Ethical" feminists believed that society could achieve a higher moral level through cooperation between men and women. Josephine Butler's French collaborators claimed that "the law is not the whole of justice; morality is the whole of justice," and they sought to influence public opinion through articles in the *Revue de Morale progressive* (1887–1892) and the *Revue de Morale sociale* (1899–1903).[67]

Rosa Mayreder (1858–1938) in Vienna and Helene Stöcker (1869–1943) in Berlin also attacked the double standard. Unlike the abolitionists, however, they attempted to rehabilitate female sexuality and eroticism.[68] Mayreder developed what she called a "secular ethics" in the Wiener Ethische Gesellschaft (founded in 1894). Starting in 1905 Stöcker used the Bund für Mutterschutz und Sexualreform and the journal *Die Neue Generation* as her propaganda platforms. She emphasized the need for improvement in the condition of unwed mothers and illegitimate children and worked for legal and social recognition of extramarital sexual relations. In 1910, however, the Bund's application for membership in the Alliance of German Women's Groups was rejected. Even radicals who had previously supported the "new ethics" repudiated Stöcker's position on free love. The sublimation of sexuality as moral virtue precluded any utopian move toward sexual freedom.

Economic Independence

The feminist struggle for economic autonomy proceeded in several stages. With the support of male legal experts and politicians, bourgeois women fought for the married woman's right to administer her own property as she saw fit. Laws to that effect were passed in the United States in 1848 and in England in 1882. The Swiss jurist Louis Bridel wrote his doctoral thesis on marital power (1879). In Italy the Convegno Femminile Nazionale included this issue in its minimal feminist program in 1907.

In seeking the right to work, the unmarried bourgeois woman first had to fight against prejudice. In some countries the bourgeois women's movement demanded emancipation before working women did. In 1865 the Alliance of German Women's Groups coupled its demand for emancipation with a demand for occupational training. In France the first public feminist meetings at Vaux-Hall in 1868 were concerned with the issue of women's labor. In Switzerland the right of women to work was not included among the demands of liberal Protestant groups until the turn of the century. It was not until the Second National Congress on Women's Interests in 1921 that Swiss feminists ratified the principles of a woman's right to work and "equal pay for equal work."[69] In the United States the economic argument in favor of the right to vote replaced arguments based on natural law and dualism (Charlotte Perkins Gilman, *Women and Economics,* 1898). Major expositions were organized for the purpose of enhancing the prestige of female labor. These were held at different times in different countries: in Berlin the Lette-Verein organized a women's industrial exposition in 1868; the Nationale Tentoonstelling van Vrouwenarbeid was inaugurated at The Hague in 1893;[70] in Paris an International Exposition of Women's Arts and Trades opened its doors in 1902; in Switzerland it was not until 1928 that a Swiss Exposition of Women's Labor (SAFFA) was organized. Toward the end of the century professional women's groups began to represent the interests of particular groups.

Great emancipatory powers were ascribed to work: "The whole evolution of women's labor . . . shows clearly to all who are not and do not pretend to be blind that no other phenomenon in the modern world has produced such revolutionary effects."[71] For working-class women, however, the central issue was not the right to work but their exploitation as workers. Among their demands were a ban on night work, the eight-hour day, employment of factory inspectors, a ban on child labor, an end to the exploitation of domestic help, an end to prostitution, and so on.

Little attention was devoted to housework. Invoking the name of Fourier, only early socialist feminists still looked on housework as productive labor. Hubertine Auclert voiced a lonely demand for remuneration for housework at the Marseilles workers' congress of 1879. A German socialist, Lily Braun, proposed a rationalization of housework in *Frauenarbeit und Hauswirtschaft* (1901). It was a man who proposed that Czech women organize their movement around the issue of housework: Vojta Fingerhut-Narpstek, the founder of the Prague Industrial Museum, waged a major campaign in favor of labor-saving household appliances and recommended that women look to the American home as a model. In 1862 he called upon engineers to devote "their abilities and their genius not only to the needs of heavy industry but also to the needs of the home."[72]

Housework returned to the feminist agenda early in the twentieth century because of a shortage of household help. The Swedish feminist Ellen Key again proposed the idea of wages for housework.

The battle for economic independence is never-ending. Even as women won a place for themselves in the economy, they found themselves victims of the "double day" (the workday plus housework at home) and the absence of social policy. Early in the twentieth century the struggle for the right to work therefore became confused with battles over sexual discrimination.

Strategies and Alliances

Strategies and alliances ranged from reformism to radicalism. In the United States in the middle of the nineteenth century feminism was part of a reformist bourgeois strategy aimed at reconstructing American institutions along rationalist, egalitarian lines.[73] The "vital issues" for this reform movement were issues of civil society. Feminists sought and obtained a certain power in the private sphere. In the late nineteenth and early twentieth century some American feminists moved to a separatist political strategy that emphasized difference; this strategy was rooted in middle-class women's culture. Women's clubs adopted civic reform agendas and encouraged women to define themselves as citizens and not just as wives and mothers. This strategy turned out to be so far-reaching that the decline of American feminism after women obtained the right to vote in the 1920s has been attributed by some to a general devaluation of women's culture.[74] Lesbian feminism also drew inspiration from this separatist tendency.

In Europe tactics wavered between liberal reformism and Social Protestant moralism. The rise of socialism with its organizing tactics and propaganda methods encouraged a more aggressive approach by feminists.[75] Activists focused on four areas: propaganda, civil disobedience, active nonviolence, and physical violence. In the early twentieth century the most radical feminists adopted proven socialist tactics—street demonstrations, banners, slogans, colors, attacks on adversaries—which earned them the name "militants." Modern propaganda techniques were passed around by word of mouth and traveled widely (Rosiska Schwimmer and her followers used them in the suffragist movement in Hungary). Only a minority practiced civil disobedience: the Women's Freedom League and the Vote for Women Fellowship in England, along with a few isolated feminists such as Anita Augspurg and Lida Gustava Heymann in Germany, and Hubertine Auclert and Madeleine Pelletier in France, refused to pay taxes as long as women were not represented in the legislature.

Militancy could also take the active form of a nonviolent challenge to the government: questioning of politicians, interruption of legislative sessions, refusal to pay fines, prison hunger strikes. In England as well as in France a number of unusual provocations attest to the inventiveness of the feminist imagination.[76] In April 1901, when France issued a postage stamp celebrating the Declaration of the Rights of Man, Jeanne Oddo-Deflou proposed a negative replica of the stamp with a man holding the tables of the "Rights of Woman." This met with great success. When the Napoleonic Code was honored in 1904, Hubertine Auclert ripped up a copy of it during a feminist demonstration. In the midst of a banquet held in connection with the same celebration, Caroline Kauffman, the secretary of Solidarité des Femmes, released a number of large balloons bearing the slogan, "The Code oppresses women, it dishonors the Republic!"

Some English suffragettes turned to physical violence, arson, and vandalism, extreme forms of militant action that their leader, Emmeline Pankhurst, claimed to have borrowed from the Irish nationalist movement.[77]

Democratic Alliances

Alliances formed where political and religious forces came together. The experiences of a group or even of a single feminist could modify them. All across Europe feminists and democrats often joined forces. In Germany members of the free churches formed ties with democrats and the workers' movement. Through these dissidents the women's movement made contact with democratic-republican internationalism and pacifism in the 1860s. Apparently the attitude of the secular democratic opposition was similar to that of the free church communities as well as of the women grouped around Louise Otto.[78]

In France feminists and republicans were allied in the democratic struggle. Between 1870 and 1890 French feminism was influenced by Léon Richer (1824–1911), a Freemason, and Maria Deraismes (1828–1894), also a freethinker. The rights to sue for paternity and divorce figured on the radical agenda. But the two leaders were not in favor of immediately granting women the right to vote for fear that the Catholic Church would profit from it. In Holland freethinkers made common cause with feminists from the literary and theatrical worlds, particularly in the circle of De Dageraad ("The Dawn").[79] The alliance between French feminists and freethinkers and Masons did not yield much in the way of tangible progress, however. Its impact was mainly symbolic, influencing statements in favor of equality and political rights for women. French feminists, weary of such statements of principle, drew back from their unsatisfactory allies and adopted more independent tactics.[80]

Alliances with liberals took shape all across Europe, from England to Russia. In the birthplace of liberalism a powerful bond was established between feminism and John Stuart Mill's utilitarianism.[81] Lydia Becker, the leader of the National Society for Women's Suffrage, was a Manchester liberal. She enjoyed the support of the Lancashire liberals, proponents of free trade. In Parliament left-wing liberals spoke regularly in favor of granting women the right to vote right up to the turn of the century. In Sweden as well as Denmark the suffragettes of 1900 profited greatly from their alliance with the liberal party.[82] In Austria and Germany liberals encouraged the formation of groups to promote jobs for women. The Wiener Frauen-Erwerbsverein (1866) served as a model for similar groups in Prague and Brünn.[83] In Holland Helene Mercier's efforts on behalf of social work were financed by wealthy left-wing liberals.[84] And even in Russia, where feminism came into its own after 1905, feminists benefited from the support of the Kadet liberal party.[85] By contrast, feminists in Latin countries failed to forge alliances with liberals. The situation in Italy was similar to that in France: Anna Mozzoni worked closely in the 1880s with Italian Freemasons, republicans, and liberals, who together formed a sort of independent left. But she became disappointed by the republican, anticlerical left's economic failure and indifference to democracy and turned toward socialism, although she never joined the socialist party.[86]

Socialist Alliances

From the beginning of the nineteenth century feminism and socialism were closely associated. The publication of Engels's *Origin of the Family, Private Property, and the State* (1884) and Bebel's *Woman and Socialism* (1883) gave the alliance a solid theoretical base. But when socialist feminists attempted to prod their male comrades to put their promises into practice, ambivalences and conflicts arose. At times socialist feminists were reluctant to proclaim their feminist aims for fear of injuring the proletarian cause. The 1890s saw a major organizing effort: the feminists of the first European socialist party, the Dutch Social-Democratic Union, opted for autonomy. After seven years of common experience they left the party to found the Vrije Vrouwen Vereeniging (1889) in the hope of giving the "woman question" its proper due. When a new social-democratic workers' party was formed in 1894, women were of necessity incorporated into the party structure, but they organized separately: for instance, Mathilde Wibaut-Berdenis van Berlekom organized the working women of the southwest as the Samen Sterk (Together Strong, 1902). When she saw that party propaganda was failing to reach the women of Amsterdam, she founded women's propaganda clubs there. Although the party insisted on incorporating these clubs as formal affiliates, it did not finance the women's journal *Proletarische Vrouw*.[87]

In Italy, Anna Kuliscioff (1854–1925), an eclectic socialist, at first treated socialism and feminism as a single cause in articles published in the *Rivista internazionale del socialismo* (1880). But later the needs of the socialist party took precedence. When a law on female and child labor that Kuliscioff sponsored was passed in 1902, she regarded the victory as more significant for socialism than for feminism. Similarly, she looked upon agitation in favor of women's right to vote as an "indispensable and useful necessity" for the interests of the party.[88] In the end, Kuliscioff may have done more for Italian women than the so-called feminist groups.[89]

During the two decades prior to World War I, relations between socialist women and the party and trade unions were marked by the conviction that the formal equality that bourgeois women were demanding perpetuated social inequalities. The International Workers' Congress held in Zurich in 1893 endorsed the principle of special laws for the protection of women workers, and thereafter any coalition between socialist and bourgeois women became impossible.[90] The rupture was more pronounced in some countries than in others. In Austria relations with the bourgeois women's movement were more relaxed than in Germany. For example, Theresa Schlesinger not only participated in the workers' movement but also wrote for the independent feminist journal *Dokumente der Frauen* (1899), founded by suffragettes Augusta Fickert, Rosa Mayreder, and Marie Lang. Nevertheless, the loyalty of Austrian socialist women to their party was absolute. In 1905 they abandoned, for tactical reasons, their demand that women be granted the right to vote; the more immediate goal was to obtain the suffrage for men.[91]

English women working in the textile industry met the same fate at the end of the nineteenth century as the Chartists did some fifty years earlier. When they asked for the right to vote and placed their faith in the new Labor Party, they were told to be patient. Unlike their Austrian counterparts, these British women turned their backs on the party. Emmeline Pankhurst, having already been disappointed once by the Liberals under Gladstone, attempted to promote women's suffrage through the Independent Labor Party of Manchester. After her husband's death she quit this party as well and gathered her energies to found, together with her two daughters, the Women's Social and Political Union (1903), which soon was taking a radical approach to the battle for the vote.[92]

Like Europe, the United States witnessed two distinct phases in the socialist-feminist alliance. A product of the utopian socialist tradition, Frances Wright collaborated with Robert Owen in the New York workers' movement in the 1830s, their goal being a society without oppression on account of class, race, or sex. But her national education plan drew little response within the movement, because education outside the home frightened working-class families. Late in the nineteenth century, Charlotte Perkins Gilman, influenced by American sociology and its notion of class harmony, developed her own personal brand of socialist feminism.[93] The California Federation of Trades awarded her a medal and sent her as a delegate to the Second International in London in 1896. Her book *Women and Economics* (1898) was extremely well received at the London Congress of the International Council of Women (1899). She set herself apart from the suffragettes in these terms: "The political equality demanded by the suffragettes has not proved sufficient to bring true freedom. Women who work as servants or not at all, who are fed and clothed and given their pocket money by men, cannot obtain freedom or equality through the ballot box."[94] For Gilman socialism meant first of all socialization of production. The implementation of socialism mattered more to her than membership in any party. Furthermore, she looked upon elements of the enlightened bourgeoisie as more progressive than the working class.

Anarchist Alliances

If the relation between socialism and feminism was one of conflict, the opportunity to make contact with anarchism was missed altogether.[95] No feminist anarchist movement came into being. But the idea of individual autonomy, with its implication of autonomy for women, was honored in libertarian circles. Isolated anarchist women were sensitive to this issue. In France, in particular, Anna Mahé, cofounder of the journal *Anarchie,* set forth the principles of anarchist education in a way that took account of the unique role of the mother and the ideal of autonomy alike. Her series of articles on the subject was collected in a brochure entitled *L'Hérédité et l'education* (1908). Libertarians rejected both suffragism and the effort to reform the Civil Code but made common cause with feminists on neo-Malthusian issues thanks to the efforts of Nelly Roussel, Madeleine Pelletier, and Madeleine Vernet. In the United States Emma Goldman gave numerous lectures on abortion, contraception, and vasectomy.[96]

In Switzerland Margarethe Faas-Hardegger stressed women's social and political rights as well as contraception and abortion in her union-organizing work between 1905 and 1909.[97] She was inspired by French revolutionary syndicalism and its methods of direct action, strikes, boycotts, and the formation of cooperatives. She also took an antimilitarist stand that cost her her position as union secretary.

In general, feminist alliances with liberals, socialists, and anarchists were only as strong as women's support for the positions of allied groups. Each party had its own hobbyhorse: for liberals, work and suffrage; for socialists, worker protection and education; for anarchists, birth control.

Antifeminisms

Antifeminist reactions crystallized around two main issues. In France the working class was influenced by Pierre-Joseph Proudhon, whose ideas opposed those of Fourier. Feminists were critical of the Proudhonian notion that women must be either "housewives or whores," which was influential in both socialist and syndicalist circles. Among the most notable critiques were Juliette Lamber's *Idées anti-proudhoniennes sur l'amour, la femme et le mariage* (1858) and Jenny d'Héricourt's *La Femme affranchie* (1860). The Couriau Affair, which erupted in Lyons in 1913, offers a striking example of syndicalist antifeminism: when Emma Couriau, a typographer, asked to join the union, not only was she refused but her husband was expelled from the same union for having failed to keep his wife from entering the trade. This scandal had enormous repercussions in the syndicalist and feminist press.[98] In Germany followers of Ferdinand Lassalle, the first president of the Allgemeinen Deutschen Arbeiterverein (1863) union, defended women working at home but not in factories. Proletarian antifeminism and misogyny thus relegated women to the "domestic sphere."[99]

In the academic world, antifeminism declared itself vehemently, particularly in the areas of medicine and law. In Vienna, for example, women asked to be admitted to the faculty of medicine in the 1890s. Professor Albert, a surgeon, expressed his opposition in a notorious pamphlet that stirred up a lengthy controversy and elicted a riposte from Marianne Hainisch: *Seherinnen, Hexen und die Wahnvorstellungen über das Weib im 19. Jahrhundert* (1896).[100] The first European woman to study law, Emilie Kempin-Spyri, enrolled in the University of Zurich in 1883; she was first denied her law degree, and later her candidacy for the chair in Roman law was rejected. Of necessity she emigrated to New York and there founded the first women's law college. Upon her return to Zurich in 1891 she failed in a second attempt to join the faculty of law. She then tried to make it in Berlin as an expert on international private law, without much success. In 1899, her spirit broken, she sought employment as a member of the staff of a Basel psychiatric clinic.[101]

An interesting debate around "feminist antifeminism" developed in Sweden, involving both August Strindberg and the feminist

Ellen Key.[102] Strindberg criticized Swedish feminism for being too provincial and too closely allied with Pietist moralists. In the preface to *Giftas* (Married, 1884) he criticized Ibsen and attacked marriage and the family, but he was also critical of the new reformisms, which to him seemed just as repressive as the established order of things. Like Strindberg, Key, an innovative educator, refused to accept the norm of sexual abstinence promoted by the feminists of the Frederike Bremer Association. But she was above all critical of the egalitarianism favored by middle-class women insofar as their ambitions were the same as those of men. In *Missbrukad kvinnokraft* (Women's Misuse of Power, 1896) and *Kvinnopsykologi och kvinnliglogik* (Women's Psychology and Feminine Logic, 1896), she attempted to refocus attention on what was unique about women. Her defense of maternity was linked to a defense of individualism and liberty.

At the other extreme we find "masculinist antifeminism": the emancipated woman who opposed any feminist demands. This paradoxical position was taken by the Victorian writer Eliza Lynn Linton (1822–1898), who chose to counter the concept of femininity created by the Victorian patriarchy by denying her own sex.[103]

Historical Figures

The feminists of the nineteenth century, whether solitary or members of groups, had something heroic about them. Their uncommon achievements allow us to experience the spark of their time of provocation; they reveal something essential and communicate a "pride in being women."

Let us mention a few of the solitary feminists, women often in advance of their age, their class, and their country. The Victorian feminist Harriet Martineau (1802–1876) refused marriage and earned her living by writing. She developed a technique of sociological and political observation well before the institutionalization of the social sciences. Celebrated at age thirty for her works on political economy, she shrewdly analyzed the role and political status of women in Europe and the United States. Her writings stimulated the birth of several progressive movements in England, most notably to improve women's education, to abolish legalized prostitution, and to win for women the right to vote.[104]

The Swiss aristocrat Meta von Salis-Marschlins (1855–1929)

held ideas antithetical to the liberal politics of her day: she championed not democratization but aristocratization in the Nietzschean sense. In *Die Zukunft der Frau* (1886) she boldly sketched out a utopian "woman-humankind" *(Frauenmenschentum)*, where men and women could be soulmates without conforming to the confining framework of the "household machine."[105] At a time when Swiss feminism slumbered in philanthropic work, she studied philosophy and law and made lecture tours to plead the case for equal rights for women.

Another aristocrat, the Austrian Bertha von Suttner (1843–1914), lived for a single idea: peace in Europe and in the world. It was no small thing to fight for peace in the colonialist kingdom of Wilhelm II or in the Hapsburg empire with its expansionist policy toward the Balkans. She was mocked as the "shrew of peace" and the "hysterical bluestocking," yet her novel, *Die Waffen nieder!* (1889), was translated into a dozen languages. She organized hundreds of pacifist meetings and tried to persuade politicians and diplomats at a time when women had no political rights, not even the right to belong to a political group. Her singular emancipation was all the more striking given her background, in which politics was a taboo subject for young ladies.[106]

Rather than preach emancipation the Dutch singer and actress Mina Kruseman (1839–1922) wanted to live it. Her first published story, *Een huwelijk in Indië* (1873), was about a young woman compelled to marry against her will. This realistic critique of the subjugation of women contrasts sharply with other Dutch fiction. Mina taught young women to write and act and showed them how to discipline themselves and negotiate with publishers to win respect as artists. For her, an emancipated woman was both single and active.[107]

The Englishwoman Olive Schreiner (1855–1920) was an unrivaled feminist. Born in South Africa, a friend of Eleanor Marx, she was for years a central figure in the life of Havelock Ellis, one of the first English theorists of sexuality. At a time when neither feminists nor socialists in Britain were questioning the country's colonial relations with South Africa, she provided a lucid analysis of the racial issue (published posthumously in *Thoughts on South Africa*, 1923). For her, life, politics, and writing formed a seamless whole, captured in the now-famous phrase, "The personal is political."[108]

The Berliner Hedwig Dohm (1833–1919) was an impassioned

feminist theorist. Her situation as a Jew may have helped to make her an unusually acute observer. With her pen she did battle on a broad front of feminist issues. Her first pamphlet attacked the clergy: *Was die Pastoren von Frauen denken* (1872). It was followed by an analysis of the oppression of women within the family: *Der Jesuitismus im Hausstande* (1873). Although it was still too early to confront the suffrage issue in Germany, even in the women's movement, she published *Der Frauen Natur und Recht, Eigenschaften und Stimmrecht der Frau* (1876). She refuted recent anatomical, physiological, and medical theories of women's inferiority in *Die wissenschaftliche Emanzipation der Frau* (1874) and further elaborated her analysis in *Die Antifeministen* (1902). Hedwig Dohm counted Nietzsche and Moebius among the antifeminists she attacked. Throughout her life she opposed the sexual, financial, and psychological oppression of women.[109]

These solitary feminists stand out for their singular strength. Others derived their energy from lifelong friendships. The Americans Elizabeth Cady Stanton (1815–1902) and Susan B. Anthony (1820–1906)—one a mother, the other single by political choice—were inseparable in the battle against slavery and for women's suffrage, even if Anthony became more conservative with age and Stanton more radical, especially in matters of religion and sexuality. It was Anthony who encouraged Stanton to get out of the house and enter public life. Their relationship was vital, both for emotional support and intellectual stimulus, and it accentuated the eccentricity of both women. Together they not only founded numerous groups, spoke on countless tours, and organized feminist congresses but also edited the immense *History of Woman Suffrage* (1881).[110]

The Germans Helene Lange (1848–1930) and Gertrud Bäumer (1873–1954), both daughters of Protestant pastors, formed a similar "couple." Lange, the founder of the Allgemeinen Deutschen Lehrerinnenvereins, influenced the intellectual and political development of the younger Bäumer, a schoolteacher. The fruit of their collaboration can be found in the *Geschichte der Frauenbewegung in den Kulturländern* (1901), a summing up of their cultural mission.[111]

Two Swiss feminists, Helene von Mülinen (1850–1924) and Emma Piecynska-Reichenbach (1854–1927), moved in together in 1890. Their thirty years of living together liberated vast quantities of energy. The two women founded the Alliance of Swiss Feminine

Societies. Their house in Berne became a sort of pilgrimage site for feminists from around the world. They worked closely with Josephine Butler in the abolitionist struggle and in the creation of women's charities in Switzerland.[112]

Some feminist families extended over generations. Among the most remarkable of these were the Pankhursts in England and the de Morsiers in Switzerland. Emmeline Pankhurst (1858–1928) founded the Woman's Social and Political Union along with her daughters Christabel (1880–1948) and Sylvia (1882–1960). All three were involved in the battle for woman's suffrage.[113] And three generations of de Morsiers from the Swiss Social Protestant milieu—Emilie de Morsier (1843–1896), her son Auguste de Morsier (1864–1923), and her granddaughters Valérie Chevenard de Morsier (1891–1977) and Emilie Droin de Morsier (born 1898), along with their spouses—worked with the International Abolitionist Federation.[114]

Whether by brilliance of personality or painstaking persistence, whether through brief, not to say scandalous, notoriety or long and patient effort, all of these women left their mark on the consciousness of the century.

The Historians of the Women's Movement

Some feminists eager to recount their experiences undertook to write the history of Western feminism in the nineteenth century. Two standard references reflect different approaches to the subject. One—American—was the six-volume *History of Woman Suffrage* edited by Elizabeth Cady Stanton, Susan B. Anthony, and Matilda Gage between 1881 and 1887. The other—German—was the result of collaboration between feminists in Europe and the United States and reflected an interest in organizations and struggles. Edited by Helene Lange and Gertrud Bäumer, this work took the form of a manual, the *Handbuch der Frauenbewegung* (Handbook of the Women's Movement, 1901).

Kaethe Schirmacher (1865–1930) drew on her travel experiences in writing *Féminisme aux Etats-Unis, en France, dans la Grande-Bretagne, en Suède et en Russie* (1898). She also chose to present five different types of feminism in the form of a manual. In 1909 Ellen Key (1849–1926) published *Kvinnorörelsen* (Women's Movement) in Sweden. The book analyzed the influence of feminism on men and women of different ages and social backgrounds.

After World War I feminists continued to take an interest in the nineteenth-century feminist tradition. When Ray Strachey (1887–1940) published *The Cause* (1928), she drew on a variety of materials including her own recollections to present the struggles of English feminists in all their variety. Johanna Naber (1859–1941), president of the National Council of Dutch Women, retraced the progress of the women's movement in her country in *Chronologisch Overzicht* (1937).

At the beginning of the twentieth century the third generation of feminists was therefore confronted, much like feminists today, with the question of influences. The portrait of nineteenth-century feminism emerged from what was remembered and likewise from what was forgotten; from identification and distance. It bore the marks of rebellion, repression, and reform, which shaped a variety of discourses and practices. But glory seldom survived the battle. Each generation of feminists seems to have had to resume the struggle toward an end that has yet to be definitively achieved.

TRANSLATED FROM THE FRENCH BY ARTHUR GOLDHAMMER

19

The New Eve and the Old Adam

Annelise Maugue

THERE IS NO NEED TO look to literature for proof of dramatic changes in the condition of women: plenty of evidence is to be found elsewhere. Literature does, however, help to pinpoint how the phenomenon was perceived by contemporaries, and obviously that perception was not without influence on the pace and direction of the movement.

To say that the issue interested writers is to put it mildly: it excited them. The subject gave rise to many works—all too many. It found its way into oeuvres not essentially concerned with it. In short, to judge by literature, contemporaries were quite well aware of the importance of the process. What is more, although it was by no means a foregone conclusion that male writers would take much of an interest in the fate of the second sex—in the problems of women traumatized by the wedding night or obsessed with dreams of diplomas—the subject proved an almost inexhaustible source of inspiration to at least as many men of letters as women.

Yet enthusiasm did not figure on the agenda—and that too is surprising. For in the end it was a question of rights. Given the situation of women in the nineteenth century, no matter how one approached the subject, whether through issues arising from labor, morals, education, or the couple, whether in the form of an essay or in fiction, at one point or another the question of rights was bound to come up: a right to be granted, a right to be denied. Now, writers, as good intellectuals, obedient to the principle of bastardy so dear to Sartre, frequently put their pens to the service of those who had been denied their rights, of the oppressed of every variety. They mobilized on behalf of the Other: the proletarian, the black, the Jew. But woman? No—in every country the emulators of John Stuart Mill could be counted on the fingers of one hand: torrents of words poured out, but they were anxious words, reticent words, hostile words. Thus we find as convinced a democrat as Anatole France solemnly declaring in 1899 that "the emancipation of women has today gone far enough."[1]

A sticking point had been reached, a sticking point so serious that it required some remarkable inconsistencies on the part of writers otherwise compelled by the clarity of reason and the logic of their humanist commitments to concede on all points. No sooner had Emile Zola described the ideal society in which "a woman was free not to marry, to live as a man, to fill the man's role in every way and everywhere" than he added: "But what is the good of mutilating oneself, denying desire, setting oneself apart from life? . . . Thus the natural order soon reasserted itself and peace was made between reconciled sexes, each one finding its happiness in the happiness of the couple."[2]

Zola could not imagine the socially free woman, the woman actually exercising her rights (and what was the good of having rights without exercising them?), as anything other than celibate, chaste, sexless, and "mutilated"; she was free, but no longer a woman. The success of the expression "new Eve," which recurs in text after text, which served as the title of a short story by D. H. Lawrence and of a novel by Jules Bois, can be interpreted in a similar way: no, contemporaries did not underestimate the importance of the process, for they believed they were witnessing not a simple evolution but a true mutation, a mutation in the strict sense of the word.

Eve was dying, Eve was dead. In her place arose a new kind of creature, something different and strange. What could be more troubling? Because the change was perceived in this way, it is easy to understand why it aroused so much interest and apprehension. Yet our astonishment remains: how strange it was, after all, to ascribe such radical effects to such simple actions as obtaining a diploma or a divorce, riding a bicycle or entering a voting booth?

Humble Daring

The women who most spectacularly embodied the new Eve nevertheless gave reassuring signs of continuity. Many famous feminists, such as Emmeline Pankhurst in England and Dr. Edwards-Pilliet in France, were duly married and had families. Neither the Saint-Simonian Pauline Roland nor the feminist Regina Terruzzi, both unwed mothers, placed their offspring in state orphanages, as Rousseau did. As for George Sand, not only did she fight for the custody of her children, she made plum pudding for Jules Sandeau, cared for Chopin when he was ill, and made slippers for a husband from whom she had already separated. How could it have been otherwise? Immersed in the family, social, and cultural environment of the nineteenth century, all these women, however radical they may have become, had been imbued in their formative years with the traditional model—they had "become women," as Simone de Beauvoir would have it. So they were reassuring in their behavior, and for that matter even the feminist discourse of the day was reassuring. Take this interview in the French feminist weekly *La Française* with the mother of Thérèse Robert, a candidate for an advanced degree in the natural sciences: "Don't imagine that her science has turned her into a pedant. She never turns up her nose at helping me out with the housework, and you can see her every morning shopping in the neighborhood. And so affectionate."[3] And this, about Marie Curie: "Simple and sweet, she held her daughter by the hand, little Irène, as she walked her to school the way she did every day."[4] And this, on the remarkable progress made by the feminist cause in Sweden: "But one mustn't think on that account that Swedish women have lost their taste for family life or the duties of motherhood."[5]

These texts, though not literary as such, are nevertheless worth quoting because they define the new Eve as she was imagined by her most convinced apologists. The leitmotif that runs through issue after issue is clear, and it was by no means the monopoly of *La Française*. Marie d'Agoult offered her assurance that "the duties of maternity are compatible with great thoughts."[6] The journalist Séverine, describing the participants in the 1900 Congress on the Rights of Women, noted: "Beneath their gloves, more than one delicate index finger might have shown, by imperceptible prick marks, that the needle had preceded the pen in homely combat."[7]

This distressing promise of continuity cannot be dismissed as a mere tactical decision, so that there is no point in asking today whether it might not have been an erroneous one. And there is no point in worrying about an equally distressing absence. Well may Thérèse Robert combine "masculine" qualities (intellectuality) with "feminine" ones (domestic skills): she is not being presented to her male colleagues as the prototype of a new human being harmoniously combining all the potential capabilities of the species in a single individual. Feminists may have gone about demanding crèches and "wages for motherhood," but with few exceptions they never envisioned sharing household chores with their husbands. Avant-garde rhetoric, as detached as it was from the concrete and immediate contradictions with which every contemporary woman had to contend, and as general and future-oriented as it may have been, never once suggested that the new Eve represented the ineluctable fate of the species.

Fate is a big word, and one that ill suits such prosaic, everyday matters as childcare and household chores—in any case, women have since amply demonstrated that they could continue to take care of such things even while conquering new social terrain. If, however, we take the trouble to examine them closely (and is it an accident that for centuries no one thought of doing this?), we discover that these burdens vary widely and are apt to be assumed in different ways by women of different social stations. To be sure, they require a broad range of technical aptitudes, but what establishes their unity is an aptitude of another order, to which Thérèse Robert's mother refers naïvely when she associates her daughter's enthusiasm for housework with her "affectionate" temperament: a disposition to serve others that is shared even by the wealthiest upper-class woman when she organizes receptions to promote her husband's career.

There are one-time sacrifices, heroic and splendid, in which the ego annihilates itself for its greater glory. The devotion that manifests itself in (though without being limited to) the performance of ephemeral as well as repetitive household chores (every morning, every day) is of a different nature. Here the ego is lost, buries itself, gives itself up without recompense. Men are no longer expected to practice this specific form of altruism. It remains a feminine virtue, and not just one virtue among others: by cultivating it the new Eve is supposed to prove that she is still a woman. In the final analysis it is this virtue that continues to define the feminine, which is still looked upon as distinct from and complementary to the masculine (the distinction going far beyond the *petite différence* established by biology).

Devotion, abnegation, self-effacement: with these cardinal virtues the rupture does not occur. Even as she thought she was repudiating them, even as she asked a journalist to write "in capital letters" that "self-development is a higher duty than self-sacrifice," the American feminist Elizabeth Cady Stanton still honored them.[8] Why a duty? Why not simply a right? Why not treat self-fulfillment as a form of pleasure or happiness? No: duty remains preeminent, a concept that stems from irrepressible concern for the well-being of the other. The generic identity that women have inherited is not just ill suited to the affirmation of the feminine ego; based as it is on forgetting oneself for the sake of another, it precludes that affirmation, makes it the ultimate taboo. Apparently even feminists find it supremely difficult to free themselves from this insistent apprenticeship in humility, and that is what leads them, paradoxically, to fight for the right to work a double shift, to multiply their burden.

Curious Contradictions

Women writers were not unaware how peculiar it was to be a full-fledged individual only part of the time. They were continually obliged to confront the difficulties and contradictions inherent in what they were doing: "Sometimes, when I am teaching or sewing, I would rather be reading or writing," Charlotte Brontë confessed.[9] But time was not the only issue. Eugénie de Guérin complained of the thousand preoccupations that grew out of concern for the needs of others, "those household chores that claim all my moments and all of myself,"[10] that dispersed and diluted an ego that, in its creative ambition, aspired with peculiar intensity to concentrate itself so as to display its uniqueness. Women who wished to write, publish, and win recognition undeniably faced difficulties that men did not have to confront. Yet not all women writers became feminists, despite such daily experience and despite their status as intellectuals. The content of their work goes some way toward explaining this: do we not find in the work an odd persistence of the very taboo that these women so spectacularly violated?

In *Histoire de ma vie* George Sand attributed her development to a stroke of luck, an unusual circumstance that freed her of all "external influence" for an entire year of her adolescence: "If my destiny had taken me directly from the domination of my grandmother to that of a husband, it is possible that I should never have been myself."[11]

She thus called attention to both the destructive aspects of the traditional female upbringing and the extreme difficulty of escaping their effects. It is hardly surprising that the female characters in her work are sweet, humble, and devoted: realism demanded it. It is surprising, on the other hand, that far from limiting herself to the representation of female self-denial, she often exalted it. To be sure, she created Lélia and Consuelo, figures of strength and rebellion. But she also created "little Marie" of *La Mare au diable* and "little Fadette" (the eponymous heroine of *La Petite Fadette*). Is it necessary to summarize the plots of these two novels? The names of the characters speak for themselves. There is Marie, as persistently mothering a figure as her name suggests. But more than that, she is "little Marie," the adjective guaranteeing that she will never derive any power from her role. And there is "little Fadette," who is triply diminished: she is little, and she is condemned for life by the diminutive attached to her name, whose root, *fade,* means insipid. These are the women that Sand presents as positive figures, as ideals of femininity. Was this merely to please an audience? No: it was with Lélia and Consuelo that she enjoyed success and fame. What obscure feelings of guilt led her to hold up as exemplary characters who are, as it were, a negation of herself?

George Eliot's relations with her heroines were perhaps even more unusual. Neither Maggie Tulliver in *The Mill on the Floss* nor Dorothea Brooke in *Middlemarch* remotely resembles little Fadette. "One expects few ideas from women," the author notes at the beginning of *Middlemarch*. Her heroine is sufficiently in her own image that no reader can fail to recognize it. The ideal of which Dorothea is enamored, a compound of Christianity, altruism, and mysticism, leads her throughout the novel, and with her creator's approval, to reject the traditional feminine model. Neither jewels nor clothes interest her; she rejects a young and attractive suitor; she is less ecstatic than she ought to be about her sister's baby; and so on. Yet she puts her intellectual and moral independence to strange use. Having married Reverend Casaubon, whom she does not love but whose lofty views she admires, she discovers that the work of scholarship to which he has devoted his life is without value. But when he feels his strength waning, he asks Dorothea to devote her widowhood to his project, and only his sudden death prevents her from giving him her promise, from "acquiescing in her own condemnation." When she later remarries, this time for love, the marriage is once again placed under the sign of renunciation: renunciation, first, of her fortune, which she gives up to spare the pride of her penniless suitor, and, above all, renunciation of herself, as marriage returns her to the conventional mold: "Among her friends, several regretted that so independent and original creature should have been absorbed by the life of another and known only in a small circle as wife and as mother."

Dorothea, Eliot explained, is "a Saint Theresa, foundress of nothing," the materialism of modern society preventing her from achieving self-fulfillment. Was it society or George Eliot who prevented her from pouring her altruism into the charity work that interests her so much at the beginning of the novel? Some women, after all, managed to do just that in real life. Was it society or George Eliot who prevented her from writing in order to persuade others to share her convictions, as George Eliot herself did? Through a strange paradox, Dorothea devotes her freedom to coercing her singular self voluntarily to rejoin the flock: it is by denying herself of her own free will while other women do so unwittingly or unwillingly that she, "cygnet" among "ducklings," manifests her superiority. In her own life, of course, George Eliot never resigned herself to the sublime martyrdom of deliberate self-annihilation: Casaubon was twenty-seven years older than Dorothea, but the novelist at age sixty married a man twenty years her junior. She had already lived for nearly thirty years in a free union with George Lewes, married to another woman and a father: how can one help but think of the very different fate she reserved for Maggie Tulliver, who, just as sacrificial as Dorothea, refuses to marry the man she loves and who loves her on the grounds that he was not the husband or even the fiancé but in a rather vague way the suitor of a friend of hers? To what extent was she asking forgiveness for having dared, through love and literature, *to be*, by portraying heroines who devote all their energy *not to be*?

Colette did the same thing, and the coincidence is all the more significant in that the pagan and sensual world of the French novelist was radically different from the world of George Eliot. Colette became famous by writing, under the aegis of her husband, Willy, the *Claudine* series, whose heroine, in love with love, bold, and nonconformist, was not unlike her. Colette's break with Willy logically led to her washing her hands of the character. The last novel in the series was entitled *Claudine s'en va* (Claudine Goes Away): Claudine left because Colette did, for other books and other men. But the character proved less bold than her creator. Claudine retired to the country to devote herself totally to her aging husband: what could be more edifying? In the novel another woman, Annie, long stifled by an authoritarian husband, leaves him in the end. But as if it were somehow necessary to soften this story of emancipation, Claudine metamorphoses into a sick nurse.

There is evidence of continuity in this tendency of women writers to redeem their own audacities by condemning their heroines to self-denial, much as feminists saw in needle-pricks absolution for the sin of educational ambition. The same continuity is illustrated *a contrario* by the fact that *A Doll's House* was written by a man. Henrik Ibsen's play, written in 1879, was translated, read, performed, commented on, and in various ways plagiarized throughout Europe well after 1900. Such success is in some ways surprising, since the dénouement borders on the improbable. Nora leaves a husband who is by no means a despot. No lover awaits her, and she leaves behind three children whom she loves. In order to survive she will have to seek a job for which she has neither vocation nor training. Financial insecurity and emotional distress: how many women in the real world could resolve to bring both down upon themselves at a single stroke? But the abstract nature of Ibsen's play, far from being a weakness, no doubt accounts for its impact: by boldly banishing concrete reality, the playwright laid bare a central issue that the thousand and one vicissitudes of daily life both reflected and obscured. His Nora leaves without "good" reason—other than her wish no longer to be the plaything, the possession, the creature of another person, a man, whether father or husband: "I have been your wife-doll here, just as I was papa's child-doll."

It was impossible, according to Nora and to Ibsen, for a woman to construct an authentic identity without destroying her learned identity, her generic identity, which defined the feminine ego only in relation to the other, to his needs and his desires—in other words, without ceasing to treat the other as one's primary concern. Nora's action, her improbable departure, symbolized this necessary change in attitude. But this was precisely the step that real women could not altogether imagine, let alone take.

Curious Demands

To believe men, however, women had already taken it. Nothing that women could do—neither in word or deed—could calm male fears, and what we find in the dialogue between the two sexes up to 1914 is a rather incredible case of men and women talking past one another.

Literature portrayed nothing but devastated homes, adulterous and alcoholic husbands, tuberculous and injured children—all pathetic victims of Nora's cruel emulators. This bizarre vision, though refuted in real life by the facts, is worth pausing over. The systematic dramatization is first of all a measure of the degree of fear aroused by the women's movement. It also reflects a strikingly broad notion of how women had failed in their duties. Indeed, it was not necessary for a woman actually to leave home to provoke effects as disastrous as if she had done so: if a few heroines followed Nora out the door, others who remained at their posts nevertheless precipitated identical disasters either because they worked (the line of work made no difference) or because they liked to go out or even simply because they liked to read. Neglected children, a precarious family budget, and ultimately the suicide of the husband—all these dire consequences lay in the offing the moment "Madame went to her room to read the latest Maeterlinck or Ibsen."[12] She who stole a few moments of her time and claimed a piece of her self, who did not give fully of herself, was already dangerous, already guilty. Real-life husbands were no doubt less vulnerable and less worried, but literature, the realm of fantasy, shows that they were not happy about agreeing to certain arrangements, for their fantasies are invariably tinged with regret and anxiety.

The expectation of unlimited devotion went hand in hand, as was only logical, with a desire for absolute domination, perceptible in, among other things, a curious pedagogical obsession. Theorists of the couple seemed to take it for granted that every husband was competent to teach his wife the fine points of cooking, ethics, household economics, and metaphysics: "Do not forget that in taking her for your helper, you pledge to be her husband, friend, brother, father, and priest."[13]

Priest: that ultimate and strange avatar of the ideal husband pointed to the paradoxical increase of masculine demands. Men now dreamed of controlling not only woman's body and heart but also her mind, which Strindberg likened to "a little blackboard"[14] on which a husband was free to write whatever he pleased, since "woman is man's child." Interestingly, one figure recurred regularly in works of literature: the little sister, like Soeurette in Zola's *Travail,* yet another prisoner of the diminutive. Following the premature death of their parents, an older brother finds himself left in complete charge of his younger sister's education, and he discharges his responsibility with oppressive generosity. He treats her as his double, but an inferior double, incapable of the slightest critical distance with which to judge him and doomed to unconditional adoration. As a result, she is worthy of being held up as an example to a wife or fiancée: "Oh! To love a woman as I love this one, you have to have known her since she was a child, a little baby, and to have raised her year after year like a sister."[15]

Little sisters: Verena in Henry James's *Bostonians,* who, having the interesting peculiarity of being a medium, must demonstrate her exquisite receptiveness to the influence of her future husband Basil Ransom; or Hadaly the android, Villiers de l'Isle-Adam's "future Eve"; or Eliza Doolittle, a social cipher delivered into the zealous, demonic hands of the cultivated Professor Higgins, George Bernard Shaw's Pygmalion. To have a woman entirely molded by and for oneself: there was a dream that truly obsessed the male imagination of the time. Of course even the most timid feminine forwardness could seem exorbitant to anyone who cultivated such fantasies. But why cultivate these particular fantasies in a period that at first sight does not appear to have been especially receptive to absolutist daydreams?

Adam's Woes

Yet what a period it was! It was an age that was experienced and perceived as being as new as Eve herself, a century radically different from its predecessors and pitiless in casting aside ancient landmarks. If hymns to progress and democracy were chanted lustily on all sides, a plaintive counterpoint could also be heard, a counterpoint that became more wrenching and sorrowful as the century passed: the brilliant young men in Maurice Barrès's *Les Déracinés* (1905) were "rootless" and ultimately doomed to failure, and Robert Musil's hero was *The Man Without Qualities*. To borrow the Austrian novelist's own words, "What has been lost?" In fact Musil's hero Ulrich does not lack qualities. He tries first the military, then engineering, before devoting himself successfully to mathematics, although this third enterprise proves as abortive as its predecessors: "A genius of a racehorse confirmed Ulrich's sense of being a man without qualities." The problem is that Ulrich pursued mathematics not for itself so much as to use it to prove his superiority. When the "spirit of the times" leads a journalist to bestow genius on a horse, nothing makes sense: "At the very moment when, after much effort, he might have felt close to the goal of his aspirations, the horse, which had preceded him there, hailed him from below."

Ulrich's renunciation illustrates the divorce between a spirit in quest of power and the modern era, the era of anonymity and leveling. Economic transformation takes control of the labor process out of the hands of those who once would have been peasants and artisans but who now toil mechanically in huge factories, while others work in the rapidly growing service sector. Even their supervisors are affected, and the engineers whom Ulrich imagined "shuttling back and forth between the Cape and Canada" turn out to be "firmly attached to their drafting tables." The process even reaches the owners: as the century progresses, corporations begin to supplant captains of industry, those heroes of capitalism who had left their personal stamp on the world. Meanwhile, in politics, the vote of "the hobo in the street"[16] counts as much as that of the most gifted inventor or poet. And in a consumer-entertainment society the inventor or poet has to vie with the racehorse and the courtesan for celebrity and prestige. As early as 1857 Flaubert in *Madame Bovary* identified modernism with mediocrity through the figure of the pharmacist Homais, the fool who sings the praise of progress: by the end of the century writers from Paris to Vienna to Stockholm were mournfully following in Flaubert's footsteps. Did not Zola himself, a writer whose enthusiasm for the miracles of technology was of a rather different kind from that of Flaubert, ultimately dispatch the utopian heroes of *Fécondité* and *Travail* to live out their lives in the country?

All this no doubt illustrates how over the decades intellectuals distanced themselves from bourgeois society—the society of the Useful, commercial and alienating. But there is more to it than that, for the representation of the crisis of the individual confronting the modern world is, more often and more clearly than one might expect, gendered. Ulrich's aspiration to become a great man stems, according to Musil, from an ancient "type of virility," lately become "an ideological phantom."[17] Nothing is more insistent than a phantom, and this one more than most: biologists, poets, historians, playwrights, philosophers, and novelists continued to perceive and define the masculine in the most glowing terms as a form of competitiveness, conquest, and domination and to identify it with those "polemical and martial instincts of command, firmness, and personality" that Proudhon had so ardently hailed while elsewhere celebrating the virtues of equality.[18] Reinforced by centuries of acceptance, this image proved powerful, influential, gratifying, and sufficiently normative that even those men tortured by their inability to live up to it never dreamed of challenging its authority.

No, it was not the image that was inadequate, it was the age: an age of ease, comfort, security, bureaucracy—a limp, castrating time. A "hermaphrodite world," cried Barbey d'Aurevilly,[19] populated by "demi-males," sighed Barrès,[20] a world "whose virility is flagging," lamented Zola.[21] Although D. H. Lawrence's novella, *New Eve and Old Adam,* focused on marriage, the malaise of Peter Moest, the husband, is not limited to the realm of love. The most modern aspects of the environment also play a role: "This central heating irradiated the entire building. It imposed a uniformity in which rooms became like incubation chambers. What could be more detestable?"

What was lost? Control, domination, power—even over heating. There was no longer any way to assert the value or preeminence of a unique individual: it was back to the anonymity, passivity, and sexlessness of early childhood. And Lawrence is clear that it is Adam's plaint we are hearing here: "He felt invaded by an elemental masculine force, choked by unsuspected instincts. It felt unbearable to be shut up this way inside this vast, overheated building."

Peter/Adam can find no place that suits him. He has come home from France and is soon to leave London again for Italy, where he will not find peace either. Lawrence gives no social explanation for this instability: Peter's work is only vaguely mentioned. But this virtual omission is in fact significant: no matter what kind of work he does, the hero is apparently unable to bring his "elemental masculine force" to bear in any useful way. And so he turns to his wife: "He had based his entire existence on this marriage."

This is an astonishing sentence, given that it refers to a male character. Has the hierarchy of virile values been so disrupted that love now takes precedence over ambition? Yes—and no: by way of compensation, love is more than ever imagined in terms of power. Peter dreams "that there is a woman in the world whose vocation—and not profession—[is] to take care of him."

If the world eludes Adam's sovereignty, his home at least should be a refuge (a "haven of peace," a "shelter") and last kingdom, his wife combining maternal idolatry with childish malleability. The pedagogical obsessions and "anachronistic" fantasies of absolute appropriation stem from the desire, the need, to use the wife to quench a thirst for power that can be satisfied nowhere else. Often, alas, the new Eve resists and responds with Paula Moest: "In your eyes a woman ought to be an extension of yourself, or, worse yet, your Adam's rib, devoid of the slightest autonomy. You cannot understand that I am a separate person."

But the quest continues. Lawrence for a time subscribed to an interesting variety of feminism born of the male revolt against the modern world and developed in Munich, Heidelberg, and Vienna under the auspices of Otto Gross. Because harmful progress was identified with the patriarchy, a positive image of woman emerged to counter it. Imbued with specific values, indeed, according to Georg Simmel, with the values of a counterculture, woman was able to remain closer to nature than man, closer to the freedom and joy of primitive existence, and thus she could point the way to survival. Yet beneath this feminism of difference it is impossible not to perceive the eternal return of the eternal Eve, identified with the nurturing and loving Mother Earth. Both Otto Gross and Lawrence saw this ideal woman in Frieda von Richthofen. And in Gross's letters to her, as it happens, the inevitable leitmotif of self-sacrifice reappears: "You know how to give happiness. With nobility, with grandeur, you give yourself passionately, completely."[22]

Sex Changes

Woman thus remained trapped in otherness, in good as in evil relative to man and always generically defined. When representation of the new Eve moved beyond her monstrous, unspeakable novelty, it was not to depict a full-fledged individual, a human being of the female sex. Often the role she was assigned was none other than that of the racehorse whose "genius" devalues the very idea of genius in Ulrich's eyes. Her successes prove nothing about her possibilities; on the contrary, they illustrate the degradation of a world so determined to level all identities that it becomes the accomplice of this creature with no identity: "The vast majority of civilian professions are routines that the most mediocre of feminine brains can learn in a few years."[23]

In a backhanded way, however, an immense significance came to be attached to woman's success. Men, reasoning in terms of their own model and experience, apparently never distinguished between self-assertion and domination of others. If women no longer intended to endure the power of men, then they necessarily aspired to wield power on their own. When Tekla, in Strindberg's play *The Creditors,* tires of simply paying rapt attention to her husband's grammar lessons and actually uses what she has learned to write better and develop her talent as a novelist, her husband, Strindberg naively remarks, forgets about grammar: sharing knowledge is impossible, because the power that it confers cannot be shared. And what happens when the new Eve, taking "cannibalism" to the limit, actually manages to dominate in some area? She becomes a man, according to our writers, thus confirming, with superb simplicity, that power constitutes the essence of masculinity.

So, for example, George Sand was a man owing to her power in the realm of the spirit. It is difficult today to measure the incredible impact of her work throughout Europe and the United States. Chateaubriand compared her to Byron, Henry James to Goethe: such compliments made her metamorphosis inevitable. Soon she was no longer being compared to men but was instead ranged among them, and that mutation did not take place only at a distance, through laudatory articles: Sand became a man for men even in the proximity of friendship. "I chatted with a comrade," Balzac assures us after a stay with her,[24] while Flaubert throughout their correspondence addresses her as "*cher maître.*" On her death he declared: "You had to know her as I knew her to know what was feminine in this great man."[25]

This striking reversal of perspective is also evident in Henry James's characterization of Sand's greatness in terms not of "the extension she gives to feminine nature" but of "the richness she brings to masculine nature."[26] Was Sand androgynous? Perhaps, but because she had genius, she was first of all a man, essentially a man.

But power could also be seized in love, and when that happened the same metamorphosis occurred at once. Barbey d'Aurevilly, describing his passionate fictional couple, Hauteclaire and the Comte de Savigny, called her "the man of the pair in their relations as lovers."[27] Few fictional clichés were more in vogue at the time: one finds virtually the same formula in Flaubert regarding relations between Emma Bovary and Léon; in Zola's *La Curée;* and in such best-selling authors of the day as Paul Bourget, Marcel Prévost, and Maurice Donnay. Are we to view this reference to the masculine as nothing more than a mechanical metaphor for power, since the women described here are after all women whose seduction seems to prove their femininity? No: the exercise of power impregnates woman with a masculinity that has nothing rhetorical about it. Smoking a cigarette, wearing short hair, practicing a sport, wearing a jacket or tie—all these are symptoms that betray, beneath a hypocritically feminine mask, the troubling presence of a man. Everything is a sign, even anatomy. The absence of those opulent curves that so spectacularly reveal the otherness of the female is also a sign: the slender woman is a boy, a lad, a handsome youth. So when thinness became fashionable late in the century as women adopted a less sedentary way of life, legions of androgynes suddenly seemed to haunt streets and cities.

To man, woman is never anything but a mirror. The startling ease with which the daughters of Eve were allegedly able to perform the operation of sex change—which was at the very least hazardous—reflected the depth of the masculine crisis more than anything else. Unworthy of his model, modern man is incapable of satisfying all of its fierce requirements, and it is therefore as if he has been stripped of his identity. The image that women dare not evoke, that of the man at home, the male "Cinderella," as George Orwell put it,[28] the feminized man, haunted the male imagination in symmetry with the image of the androgyne. If George Sand were to be admitted to the Académie Française, Barbey d'Aurevilly exclaimed, "we men will be making jams and pickles."[29]

Masculinity was there for the taking: how could women pass up the opportunity to seize hold of it? Yet the inability to imagine how women could conceive of liberation and use their freedom in a new way attests to the continuing hegemony of the model: the ego always seems to be understood in terms of power, and power in terms of the masculine. Either you're a man or you're not.

Doubling

From the other side, the women's side, it was not so easy to see things differently either. What principles did women possess for giving substance and content to that part of themselves that refused to dissolve and vanish into generic identity? Like Nora, they were stepping into the unknown, travelers without baggage on uncharted routes. They had no models to follow other than the unique model of the subject already occupying the terrain: the male model.

At least their relation to that model was external. Because distance gave them a vantage point that was not given to men, women laid claim *a priori* to more ample means for analyzing man's relation to the world. After all, they were not the last to endure the consequences of man's hegemony, as they searched for its origins and tried not to view it as an immutable given but to situate it in the context of the history of the species. And of course they did not fail to turn a critical regard on man—their "other." Thus George Sand, in *Dialogues imaginaires avec le docteur Pifföel,* pulled no punches: he "is perfectly contemptuous of devotion because he believes he has a natural right to it for no other reason than that he emerged from his dear mother's womb. . . . Dominating, possessing, and engrossing are merely the conditions under which he consents to be worshipped like a God."[30]

This remark establishes an interesting connection between a man's identity and his relation to his mother, but Sand, even though she dreamed of being "the Spartacus of female slavery,"[31] never placed it in a theoretical context, nor did any other nineteenth-century woman. If, referring to their own oppression, they evoked the opposite sex's tyrannical predilections and thirst for power, they usually were content simply to state this as fact without making the masculine the central object of a systematic theory: patriarchy never found its female Bachofen. The asymmetry is worth noting.

Victorian though the century may have been, the female body was on display in prostitution, literature (where the theme of prostitution was prominently featured), painting, sculpture, and even the anatomical illustrations in Larousse that left Michelet entranced. The "feminine" mind was equally on display in Charcot's staged representations of hysteria, invariably played by female actresses, and in countless texts that probed, scrutinized, and bared its contents. Conversely, Marie Laurencin did not paint male nudes or bare the masculine essence any more than feminist theorists did. Humility could not be unlearned that quickly; objective distance could not compensate for all the inhibitions created by a millennium of identifying the human with the masculine. Women themselves believed that it was up to women to make progress, to raise themselves up—so far as possible—toward the only known and acknowledged way of being an individual.

Thus they willingly played the role of androgynes. To a degree George Sand wanted to be the man that her friends saw in her, enough at any rate to assume the appearance of a man in striking fashion, with her pseudonym, her trousers, her cigarettes, and the provocative freedom of her love life. And she believed sufficiently in her pose to speak of herself sometimes as though she were a man. Why did so many other women writers take male pen names: Marie d'Agoult (Daniel Stern), Delphine Gay (the Vicomte de Launay), Mary Ann Evans (George Eliot), Jeanne Lapauze (Daniel Lesueur)? At first sight the explanation might seem to lie in a wish to avoid sexist prejudice, to preserve their work from the condescending attention accorded to "ladies' books." But once the secret got out—and it always did—what was the good of preserving the disguise? And was it really a disguise? Marie d'Agoult was forthright about hers: "To male genius, the solution of scientific problems, the organization of freedom and social equality. To female genius, the divine labor of the heart, the reconciliation of classes wedded to one another."[32]

And what was *she* concerned with in these *Lettres républicaines?* Or in her *Essai sur la liberté?* Or in her *Esquisses morales et politiques?* As the titles suggest, she dealt with the very subjects over which she granted a monopoly to male genius. No, "Daniel Stern" was by no means a mere signature intended to deceive others. Daniel Stern existed, Marie d'Agoult was Daniel Stern, and she needed to be him in order to legitimate her ambitions in her chosen field in her own eyes. A liberating device? Of course. Audacious enough to venture into the realm of political theory, Marie d'Agoult was nevertheless too timid to frequent these heights without the mediation of a male figure: starting from such premises, did she dare to follow to the end the bold thinking of a double which, as she knew only too well, was not altogether a man? Or, conversely, did she bring to the "virile" subjects treated by Daniel Stern the benefits of a woman's experience? In female androgyny men saw a savage and aggressive usurpation. But when women made the choice it appears, rather, to have reflected the contradiction with which they had to struggle, the "fissure in the center of the heart" that Virginia Woolf speaks of in *A Room of One's Own* when contemplating woman's relation to writing. Behind this need for doubling, as well as behind their exaltation through certain of their heroines of a kind of female sacrifice that women writers themselves avoided merely by the act of writing, there lurks, once again, humility, a persistent and painful sense of a fundamental illegitimacy: does one truly have the right to exist if one is not a man?

Given the persistent confusion by both men and women of the human with the masculine, a confusion that exempted the masculine from critical examination, one crisis fed another. Anxious about seeming too bold, women set limits to their own enthusiasm to protect themselves from mockery, pressure, threat, and rejection. Yet they crossed enough boundaries and swept away enough landmarks to heighten anxieties kindled in men by modernity, thereby reinforcing the fear that eats away at each and every male that he, as an individual, may not be up to the grandiose ambitions that his sex condemns him to conceive for himself. And men reacted to the humble daring of the other half of humankind with bellowing, febrile aggression.

We do not know what light might have come of this crisis, for war came instead, and reshuffled the cards. Consider two images: women driving ambulances and machining howitzers, doing work at last valued by society, alone and independent of necessity, yet surviving; men, wearing helmets, dogfaces, battered, dying (but their very death resurrecting the warrior image). Which of these would prove more influential in the years that followed?

Translated from the French by Arthur Goldhammer

five

Women's Voices

Of Women's Happiness

These important women are not the heroines—the emblems—that some histories of women are fond of representing, but they are celebrated women—very celebrated indeed. They are extraordinary, and in more ways than one. Fortunate enough to be financially independent, they were clever enough to take advantage of their freedom: to travel through Germany, Switzerland, England, and Italy; to throw off any number of prejudices that can be summed up in a single one, namely, the dictum that a woman above all must not assert her independence; and, not being timid, to see themselves almost naturally as women capable of conversing on a footing of equality with great men. They were both in their time and of it.

G.F.—M.P.

Germaine de Staël
"On Women Who Cultivate Letters"

Geneviève Fraisse and Michelle Perrot

MME DE STAËL WAS BROUGHT UP under the Ancien Régime, during which a few women achieved "dominion" over their salons and enjoyed an exceptional status, at times with grandeur. But in her maturity under the Revolution and Napoleonic Empire the status of the independent woman she was came to be viewed with suspicion. It is easy to see why she missed the Age of Enlightenment and hoped that one day enlightenment would be the possession of all. This was a woman who spoke of her suffering, of her difficulty in moving from one world to another, from monarchy to republic; but she also knew that "the pleasures of the mind are made to calm the tempests of the heart." The lucidity of her thought is striking in the excerpt quoted here, where she makes a comparison of two societies, neither of which was willing to give her a place. Through her reflections we also glimpse the essence of her life as a woman, apart from her loves: her passion for using her intelligence to participate in the intellectual life of her time, and her certainty that what is truly important, even for a woman, is public life. Mme de Staël was not in her place in her own time, yet she was willing to stake her all on playing her role. If she is hard on her contemporaries, it is without treachery. Though aware that she was exceptional, she never gave up on the idea that women's lives could be better or that their lack of solidarity was solely the result of ignorance and prejudice.

The existence of women in society is still in many respects insecure. The desire to please excites their minds; reason counsels obscurity; and everything is arbitrary in their successes as in their reverses.

There will come a time, I believe, when philosophical lawmakers will give serious attention to the upbringing that women ought to receive, to the civil laws that protect them, to the duties that ought to be imposed on them, and to the happiness that may be guaranteed them. But in the present state of things they belong for the most part neither to the order of nature nor to the order of society. What brings success to some ruins others. Their qualities sometimes do them harm, their defects sometimes do them good. Now they are everything, now they are nothing. Their destiny is similar in some respects to that of freedmen under the emperors. If they attempt to gain influence, they are accused of the crime of seizing a power not granted them by law; if they remain slaves, their futures are oppressed.

Of course it would be much better, in general, if women were to devote themselves solely to the domestic virtues, but what is bizarre in men's judgments of them is that they forgive them sooner for failing of their duties than for attracting attention through distinguished talents; men tolerate in women degradation of the heart in favor of mediocrity of mind, while the most unblemished decency could scarcely gain pardon for true superiority.

I shall examine the several causes of this singular state of affairs. I begin by examining the fate of women who cultivate letters in monarchies and in republics. I am concerned first to characterize the principal differences that these two political situations must produce in the destiny of women who aspire to literary celebrity, and then to consider in a general way what happiness fame may promise women who wish to claim it.

In monarchies, they must fear ridicule; in republics, hatred. . . .

Since the Revolution, men have thought that it was politically and morally useful to reduce women to the most absurd mediocrity. They have addressed them only in the most wretched terms, lacking both delicacy and wit. Women no longer have topics on which to hone their reason; their mores have not improved in consequence. By limiting the scope of ideas, it has been possible to restore the simplicity of the most primitive ages. The only result, however, is that less intelligence has brought with it less delicacy, less respect for public esteem, and fewer resources for enduring solitude. What has happened applies to everything in the current state of mind: people still believe that Enlightenment causes harm, and to repair the damage they wish to drive reason into retreat. The harm of Enlightenment cannot be corrected except by acquiring still more enlightenment. Either morality is a false idea, or it is true that the more enlightened one is, the more devoted to it one becomes. . . .

Men in France can never be republican enough to do entirely without women's natural independence and pride. No doubt women had too much influence on affairs under the Ancien Régime, but they were not less dangerous when they were deprived of enlightenment and consequently of reason. Their influence was then directed toward obtaining immoderate fortunes, toward making undiscerning choices, toward giving indelicate recommendations; they debased the men they loved rather than exalting them. Did the State benefit? The danger of meeting a woman whose superiority is disproportionate to the destiny of her sex is very rare: should it deprive the republic of the celebrity that France enjoyed with respect to the art of giving pleasure and living in society? Without women, however, society can be neither pleasant nor stimulating. And women devoid of wit, or of that conversational grace that only the most distinguished education can bestow, spoil society rather than embellish it. They introduce a kind of foolish talk, a cliquish slander, an insipid gaiety that can only drive away all truly superior men, and that would reduce Paris's brilliant gatherings to young men with nothing to do and young women with nothing to say.

One can find disadvantages to anything in human affairs. There are some, no doubt, in the superiority of women, indeed in that of men, in the conceit of intelligent people, in the ambition of heroes, in the imprudence of great souls, in the irritability of independent characters, in the impetuosity of courage, etc. Must one therefore combat natural qualities with all one's might and instruct all our institutions to diminish our faculties? It is not even certain that such diminution would strengthen the authority of the family or of the government. Women without a flair for conversation or literature ordinarily have greater skill in evading their duties; and nations without enlightenment know not how to be free, yet change masters quite frequently.

To enlighten, instruct, and perfect women as well as men, nations as well as individuals—this is still the best secret for achieving all reasonable ends, for securing durable social and political relations.

One cannot fear the intelligence of women except out of delicate concern for their happiness. It is possible that in fostering their reason, one may enlighten them as to the misfortunes that often afflict their destiny. But the same arguments would apply to the effect of Enlightenment in general on the happiness of the human race, and that question seems to me settled.

If the situation of women in the civil order is highly imperfect, one must work to improve their condition and not to degrade their intelligence. It is useful to society's enlightenment and happiness that women should carefully develop their intelligence and their reason. Only one truly unfortunate consequence could result from the cultivated education they ought to receive: this would be if some number of them were to acquire faculties distinguished enough to feel the need of glory; but even this accident would not harm society, and would be unfortunate only for the very small number of women whom nature may consign to the torment of an importunate superiority.

Should a woman be attracted by the celebrity of intelligence and wish to obtain it, how easy it would be to dissuade her while there is still time. One could show her the horrible fate she was about to bring down upon herself. Examine the social order, one might tell her, and you will soon see that it is fully armed against any woman who tries to raise herself up to compete for reputation with men. . . .

Glory can even be reproached in a woman, because it contrasts with her natural destiny. Austere virtue condemns even the celebrity of that which is good in itself, as if celebrity somehow interfered with the perfection of modesty. Men of intelligence, astonished to find rivals among women, do not know how to judge them, whether with the generosity of an adversary or the indulgence of a protector; and in this new combat, they obey neither the laws of honor nor those of kindness.

If, to make matters worse, it is in the midst of political dissensions that a woman acquires a notable celebrity, one might easily believe that she wielded unlimited influence when in fact she possessed none; one might blame her for all the actions of her friends; one might hate her for all that she loves, and one might choose to attack first the defenseless object before coming to those possibly still to be feared. . . .

And that is not all: public opinion seems to relieve men of any duties toward a woman acknowledged to possess a superior mind: one can be unpleasant, vicious, or mean to her without incurring public wrath. *Is she not an extraordinary woman?* Nothing more needs to be said. She is left to her own devices, left to struggle on in pain. Often she lacks both the interest that a woman inspires and the power that a man guarantees. She carries her singular existence, like the Pariahs of India, among all the classes to which she cannot belong, all the classes that consider her obliged to exist on her own: an object of curiosity, of envy perhaps, and in effect deserving nothing but pity. (From *De la littérature*, 1802.)

TRANSLATED FROM THE FRENCH BY ARTHUR GOLDHAMMER

Lou Andreas-Salomé "The Humanity of Woman"

Geneviève Fraisse and Michelle Perrot

THE END OF THE CENTURY FOUND Lou Andreas-Salomé in full maturity, much more certain of her ability to live freely and enjoy her capacities than was Mme de Staël. It is astonishing to see how clever she was at exploring possibilities, from being a traditional muse to doing creative work in her own right as a new intellectual. The men she encountered—Nietzsche, Rilke, Freud—saw this and liked debating with her. At the same time, she became the apostle of the self-fulfillment of women as women, allowing for their differences from men. There are two distinct worlds, she believed, one for each sex, and in her eyes it was not a foregone conclusion that the woman's world was the less agreeable to live in. She redefined the sphere of women's activity in terms of sex itself, hence of the body. For her, a woman's mind did not exist in isolation from her body. She was certain, therefore, that woman, unlike man, was never alienated from herself. The conclusions she draws from this notion of sexual difference are sometimes difficult to follow: to her, women's liberation seemed like a sad attempt to imitate men, and mimicry was a trap. And even though she saw clearly why women were tempted to break out of the domestic circle, she nevertheless believed that that was where woman's vocation lay. But obviously not hers: because of this exclusion it is embarrassing to read her. Who is speaking in this text, or, rather, which woman is speaking?

In her manner of being intellectual as in all the rest of her being, a woman is bound and determined by her physical existence, far more than a man. This point is frequently neglected in the name of the tritest conventions, and women are more prone than anyone else to commit this error because they like to pretend that only sickly female creatures are sensitive to their inner organic variations. Nevertheless, what inevitably influences even the healthiest and most developed of women, as a law imposed on her entire physical existence, what differentiates her from man, is by no means something that should make her feel inferior to man; on the contrary, it is what enables her to assert herself, and all that is specifically feminine in her gifts, alongside man. It is an extraordinarily important fact, and one pregnant with consequences: the natural rhythm, both physiological and psychic, of a woman's life. That life conforms to a secret rhythm, with regular highs and lows, which subject a woman to a never-ending cycle, within which her entire being, with all its manifestations, feels harmoniously sheltered. Thus physically as well as intellectually, the line that stretches out toward infinity with subtle and increasingly complex ramifications does not belong to the woman's domain: it seems that, by the simple fact of living, she traverses circle after circle. It is strange that this vital rhythm is always passed over in silence or presented as something of no importance whatsoever, whereas in fact, and precisely in the absolutely healthy creature sure of her own body, it recalls the feast and solemn meditation, the Sundays that dot the years, the hours of profound and serene peace that continually control, illuminate, and order everyday existence, and that call for flowers on the table and in the soul; because what is repeated, in the most narrowly physical sense of the word, in her is what also constitutes the intimate being of woman, in its grandeur and totality. Although the time is no doubt slowly disappearing when women believed it necessary to imitate men in any area in which they wished to prove their worth—and therefore worked under male pseudonyms, and not only when they were writers—we are still a long way from respecting all that is unique in women. As long as women do not do this, as long as they do not attempt to understand themselves as passionately and as profoundly as possible in those ways in which they *differ* from men—*and at first exclusively in those ways*—to that end using, scrupulously, the slightest evidence of their bodies as well as their souls, they will never know how broadly and powerfully they may blossom by virtue of the structure unique to their essence, and indeed how vast the boundaries of their world are. Woman is not always sufficiently in touch with herself, and therefore she has yet to become sufficiently woman—as she lives, at any rate, in the dreams of the best men of their time and in her own dreams. Once she lacked—indeed all human beings lacked—the practical knowledge of herself and the freedom from deeply ingrained prejudices necessary to attain this goal. She did not know all the treasures and rooms that were rightfully hers and so settled in whatever space was available and fixed it up as best she could. But later, giving in to intimidation and with singular stupidity she heeded the call that wrenched her from her own dwelling and cast her out upon the main road. Unfortunately, that call has become, for many women who shut their ears to it, finding in it not a wooing but a threat, an imperative of fate, as for the others: for the simple reason that understanding a social necessity, whether or not it happens to be an imperative of society, thrust them into the midst of a free-for-all where they were forced to jab with their elbows and deliver blows unrelentingly and unceasingly, while scattering their efforts every which way, just like men. That is a fact that cannot be wished away with mere words, and which I haven't time to emphasize here. One thing is certain in any case: that in just such a struggle for life it is to be hoped first and foremost that women show they have stomachs solid enough to digest even the toughest morsels without losing any of their inherent beauty. Let women place their seal on circumstances rather than surrender their femininity to them, even if in so doing they must sacrifice some of their competitive advantage. Women must put a little feminine soul, family warmth, and harmony wherever those things are lacking yet might operate discreetly. Which will prove stronger? Woman or what she can draw out of herself that is nonfeminine? Only time will tell.

Yet another circumstance is also driving armies of women out of the narrowness of the family circle: their spontaneous, profound, and undeniable eagerness for experience, their hunger for a more solid and varied diet than they are able to find easily at home. The two situations should not be confused: for as long as a young woman appears to yearn ardently for her emancipation alone, she may be looking for nothing other than her self and her own individual development. She may even find a job outside the house even though it does not attract her in any way, while in all her experiences she is simply feeling her way along various paths that she follows in the sole hope that they may lead her to herself, so that she might at last embrace herself, possess herself entirely, and therefore be ready to give everything that she has in her. How many young women temporarily disgusted, to the dismay of their families, by petty household chores, unwittingly desire nothing other than to develop a rich and precious female soul, within whose compass everyone will feel enveloped by the peace of the birth world—and if she is forbidden to try the experiment, if her most prominent qualities atrophy, she will be condemned to an eternal disharmony, crooked and ill proportioned, paying in her old age with bitter waves of bile for the gold coins she was not permitted to give away long before. In this respect, then, one can do nothing other than preach freedom, and freedom again, and we must overturn every barrier, smash every artificial bottleneck, for it is wiser to trust in the voices of desire that rise in the human bosom, even when they express themselves in untoward ways, than in preconceived and falsified theories. Whatever brings splendor and joy to a woman is the right way for her, however crooked her path may seem, and in the end the goal is to guide to maturity the woman within, in other words, to reveal her most secret gift of life. (From "The Humanity of Woman: An Outline of a Problem," 1899.)[1]

TRANSLATED FROM THE FRENCH BY ARTHUR GOLDHAMMER

Notes

Bibliography

Contributors

Illustration Credits

Index

Notes

Orders and Liberties

GENEVIÈVE FRAISSE AND MICHELLE PERROT

1. See Geneviève Fraisse, *Muse de la raison, la démocratie exclusive et la différence des sexes* (Aix-en-Provence: Alinéa, 1989), to be published in English by the University of Chicago Press in 1993); Joan B. Landes, *Women and the Public Sphere in the Age of the French Revolution* (Ithaca: Cornell University Press, 1988).

Chapter 1. Daughters of Liberty

DOMINIQUE GODINEAU

1. Arlette Farge, "Protesters Plain to See," in Natalie Zemon Davis and Arlette Farge, eds., *A History of Women,* vol. 3: *Renaissance and Enlightenment Paradoxes,* trans. Arthur Goldhammer (Cambridge, Mass.: Harvard University Press, 1993).
2. D. Godineau, *Citoyennes tricoteuses. Les Femmes du peuple à Paris pendant la Révolution* (Aix-en-Provence: Alinéa, 1988).
3. R. Dekker, L. Van de Pol, W. Tebrake, "Women and Political Culture in the Dutch Revolutions," in Harriet B. Applewhite and Darlene G. Levy, eds., *Women and Politics in the Age of the Democratic Revolution* (Ann Arbor: University of Michigan Press, 1990).
4. L. Kerber, *Women of the Republic: Intellect and Ideology in Revolutionary America* (Chapel Hill: University of North Carolina Press, 1980).
5. Ibid.
6. Hannah Adams, *Women Invited to War* (Boston, 1790).
7. Marcel Gauchet, *La Révolution des droits de l'homme* (Paris: Gallimard, 1989).

Chapter 2. The French Revolution

ELISABETH G. SLEDZIEWSKI

1. Louis de Bonald, *Théorie du pouvoir politique et religieux,* vol. 2 (Paris, 1796).

2. Edmund Burke, "First Letter on the Regicide Peace," 1796.

3. Declaration of the Rights of Man and the Citizen, article 2.

4. *Septième Lettre bougrement patriotique de la Mère Duchêne,* March 22, 1791.

5. Joachim Campe, *Lettres d'un Allemand à Paris,* August 9, 1789, trans. into French by J. Ruffet (Paris, 1989).

6. Chaumette, speech to the Commune of Paris, *Révolutions de Paris,* 27 *brumaire,* Year II (November 17, 1793).

7. Talleyrand, *Rapport sur l'Instruction publique,* Constituent Assembly, September 10, 11, and 19, 1791.

Chapter 3. A Philosophical History of Sexual Difference

Geneviève Fraisse

1. The following works are quoted in this essay in order of citation:

J. G. Fichte, *Foundations of Natural Law,* 1796–1797.

Emmanuel Kant, *Metaphysics of Morals,* 1796; *Anthropology,* 1798.

G. W. F. Hegel, *The Phenomenology of Spirit,* 1807; *Encyclopedia of Philosophical Sciences,* 1817; *The Principles of the Philosophy of Law,* 1821.

Friedrich Schlegel, *Lucinde,* 1799; *On Philosophy,* 1799.

Friedrich Schleiermacher, *Confidential Letters on Lucinde,* 1800.

Charles Fourier, *Oeuvres complètes,* especially *Théorie des quatre mouvements et des destinées générales,* 1808; *Théorie de l'unité universelle,* 1822.

P. J. G. Cabanis, *Rapports du physique et du moral de l'homme,* 1802.

Jeremy Bentham, *Constitutional Code,* 1830.

James Mill, "On Government," 1820; *Encyclopaedia Britannica,* 1824.

W. Thompson, *Appeal of One-Half the Human Race, Women, against the Pretensions of the Other Half, Men,* 1825.

Arthur Schopenhauer, "Metaphysics of Love," *The World as Will and Idea,* 1819; "On Women," *Parerga and Paralipomena,* 1850.

Søren Kierkegaard, *Works,* especially *Either/Or,* 1843.

Ludwig Feuerbach, *The Essence of Christianity,* 1841.

Auguste Comte, *Oeuvres complètes,* especially *Système de politique positive,* 1851–1854; *Catéchisme positiviste,* 1909.

Pierre Leroux, *L'Egalité,* 1848.

Max Stirner, *L'Unique et sa propriété,* 1844.

Karl Marx, *1844 Manuscripts; The German Ideology,* 1845–1846; *Capital,* Book 1, 1867.

P.-J. Proudhon, *Système des contradictions économiques, ou Philosophie de la misère,* 1846; *De la Justice dans la Révolution et dans l'Eglise,* 1858; *La Pornocratie ou les femmes dans les temps modernes,* 1875.

John Stuart Mill, *Letters to Auguste Comte;* "Enfranchisement of Women," *The Westminster Review,* 1851 (in collaboration with Harriet Taylor); *Subjection of Women,* 1869.

Charles Secrétan, *Le Droit de la femme,* 1886.

J. J. Bachofen, *Das Mutterrecht,* 1861.

Friedrich Engels, *The Origin of the Family, Private Property, and the State,* 1884.

Herbert Spencer, *The Principles of Sociology,* 1869; *The Principles of Ethics,* 1891.

Charles Darwin, *The Descent of Man and Sexual Selection,* 1871.

Friedrich Nietzsche, *Human, All Too Human,* 1878; *The Joyful Science,* 1882; *Beyond Good and Evil,* 1886.

Emile Durkheim, *Textes,* vols. 2 and 3.

Sigmund Freud, *Complete Works,* especially *Three Essays on the Theory of Sexuality,* 1905.

Otto Weininger, *Sex and Character,* 1903.

Chapter 4. The Law's Contradictions

NICOLE ARNAUD-DUC

The abbreviations in the notes to this section are as follows:

Sirey 1898.143, *Cass.*, 18 July 1898, refers to a decree of the French Cour de Cassation, Chambre Civile. The Chambre Criminelle is indicated by *Cass. crim.* These decrees are reported in the *Recueil général des lois et des arrêts,* compiled by J.-B. Sirey. The notes may also indicate the year of the volume, the part, page, type of court, and date of decree.

Dalloz 1898.1.43, *Cass.*, 18 July 1898, refers to a decree reported in *Recueil Dalloz.* The abbreviation D.P. refers to the *Dalloz périodique.*

Sirey 1898.3, Paris, 13 May 1898, refers to a decree of the Cour d'Appel of Paris.

Sirey 1898.3. C.E., 1 March 1898, refers to a decree of the French Conseil d'Etat.

1. *Moniteur universel, Journal officiel de la République,* 22 November 1851, no. 326, p. 2917 ff.

2. Dalloz 1885.1.105, *Cass.*, 16 March 1885; Sirey 1839.1.384, *Cass.*, 21 March 1893; Sirey 1913.3.89, C.E., 20 January 1910.

3. Sirey 1910.1.600, *Cass. crim.*, 17 February 1910.

4. Sirey 1879.1.433, *Cass. crim.*, 11 July 1879.

5. Maurice Hauriou, note under Sirey 1913.3.89, C.E., 26 January 1912.

6. *Le Figaro,* October 27, 1884, quoted by G. Breuillac, *De la condition civile et politique de la femme* (Aix-en-Provence, 1886), p. 98.

7. See N. Chambelland-Liebeault, "La Durée et l'aménagement du temps de travail des femmes de 1892 à l'aube des conventions collectives," Ll.D. diss., Nantes, 1989.

8. Sirey 1910.3.54, C.E., 24 January 1908.

9. Sirey 1890.4.25, Brussels, 11 November 1889.

10. Sirey, *Lois annotées,* 1901, p. 1.

11. Sirey 1885.1.487, *Cass.*, 8 July 1884.

12. Quote by Alain Corbin, *Les Filles de noce* (Paris: Aubier Montaigne, 1978), p. 343, n. 88.

13. Sirey 1877.2.297, note under Bourges, 17 August 1877.

14. See M. Bordeaux, B. Hazo, S. Lorvellec, *Qualifié viol,* Report 1154 (Paris: Klincksieck, 1990), especially pp. 1–61. On female "psychology" in regard to rape, see, for example, *Le Traité de médecine légale,* quoted by A. W. Bouché, *Etude sur l'adultère au point de vue pénal* (Paris, 1893), p. 208.

15. See F. Ronsin, *La Grève des ventres* (Paris: Aubier, 1979).

16. See A. MacLaren, *Sexuality and Social Order* (New York: Holmes and Meier, 1983).

17. Portalis, *Discours préliminaire,* in Fenet, *Recueil des travaux préparatoires du Code civil* (Paris, 1836), vol. 1, p. 522, and in *Naissance du Code civil* (Paris: Flammarion, 1989), p. 35 ff. See also J. Bart, "La Famille bourgeoise héritière de la Révolution?" in M.-F. Lévy, ed., *L'Enfant, la famille et la Révolution française* (Paris: Olivier Orban, 1989), pp. 357–372.

18. C. B. M. Toullier, *Le Droit civil français suivant l'ordre du Code,* 3rd ed. (Paris, 1821), vol. 1, p. 15.

19. Sirey 1868.2.65, Paris, 3 January 1868.

20. J. de Maleville, *Analyse raisonnée de la discussion du Code civil au Conseil d'Etat,* 2nd ed. (Paris, 1807), vol. 1, p. 235.

21. Quoted by Marcadé, *Explication théorique et pratique du Code Napoléon* (Paris, 1807), vol. 1, no. 726, pp. 581–582.

22. Toullier, *Le Droit civil,* vol. 1, p. 96.

23. Sirey 1897.1.304, *Cass. crim.,* 2 April 1897.

24. F. Basch, "La Femme en Angleterre de l'avènement de Victoria (1837) à la Première Guerre mondiale," in *Histoire mondiale de la femme* (Paris: Nouvelle Librairie de France, 1966), vol. 4, p. 199.

25. Sirey 1877.2.161, Brussels, 28 April 1875.

26. Sirey 1881.2.54, Nîmes, 6 January 1880; Sirey 1879.2.80, Rouen, 13 November 1878.

27. Sirey 1877.2.161, Brussels, 28 April 1875, note. Decision of the court of Louisville, Kentucky, reported in *Le Droit,* 28 December 1867.

28. Sirey 1830.1.99, *Cass.,* 20 January 1830.

29. Sirey 1827.1.88, *Cass.,* 9 August 1826. See also Sirey 1808.2.196, Paris, 29 May 1808; Sirey 1812.2.414, Turin, 17 July 1810; Sirey 1840.2.291, Dijon, 25 July 1840.

30. Sirey 1834.1.578, *Cass. crim.,* 18 May 1834.

31. Sirey 1839.1.817, *Cass. crim.,* 21 November 1839.

32. Sirey 1896.2.142, Nîmes, 5 June 1894.

33. Sirey 1900.2.143, Caen, 26 December 1899.

34. Sirey 1910.1.7, *Cass.,* 19 July 1909.

35. Sirey 1829.1.205, *Cass. crim.,* 17 January 1829.

36. But fifteen days in 1902: Sirey 1904.2.81, Algiers, 18 July 1902.

37. Sirey 1868.1.421, *Cass. crim.,* 28 February 1868.

38. Sirey 1848.1.731.

39. *Dictionnaire Dalloz,* 1790–1835, under *Adultère,* no. 48.

40. See M. Bordeaux, "Le Maître et l'infidèle: Des relations personnelles entre mari et femme de l'ancien droit au Code civil," in I. Théry and C. Biet,

eds., *La Famille, la loi, l'Etat* (Paris: Imprimerie Nationale, 1989), pp. 432–446.

41. Sirey 1827.2.17, Paris, 13 March 1826. See J. Mulliez, "*Pater is est* . . ., la source juridique de la puissance paternelle du droit révolutionnaire au Code civil," in *La Famille, la loi, l'Etat,* pp. 412–431.

42. Sirey 1868.2.65, Paris, 3 January 1868.

43. Sirey 1851.1.103, *Cass.,* 10 February 1851.

44. See Nicole Arnaud-Duc, "Le Droit et les comportements, la genèse du titre V du Livre III du Code civil: les régimes matrimoniaux," in *La Famille, la loi, l'Etat,* pp. 183–195.

45. See the discussion of the law in Sirey, *Lois annotées,* 1891–1895, p. 473 (law of 6 February 1893).

46. See Michelle Perrot, "La Femme populaire rebelle," in Michelle Perrot, ed., *L'Histoire sans qualités* (Paris: Galilée, 1979), pp. 131–132.

47. Sirey, *Lois annotées,* 1906–1910, p. 597.

Chapter 5. Artistic and Literary Idolatries

STÉPHANE MICHAUD

1. William Blake, *The Marriage of Heaven and Hell.*

2. Yves Bonnefoy, *La Vérité de la parole* (Paris: Mercure de France, 1988).

3. "Die Frauen sind silberne Schalen, in die wir goldene Apfel legen. Meine Idee von den Frauen ist nicht von den Erschenungen der Wirklichkeit abstrahiert, sondern sie ist mir anbegoren oder in mir entstanden."

4. "Die Welt, sie wird dich schlecht begaben, glaube mir's! Sofern du willst ein Leben haben: raub dir's!"

5. "Nun liegt es mir eigentlich ferner, von Tugenden und Leistungen zu reden, als von dem, worin ich mich kompetenter fühle: vom Glück." From "Zum Typus Weib," *Imago* 3, 1 (1914), p. 7.

6. "Ich kann weder Vorbildern nachleben, noch werde ich jemals ein Vorbild darstellen können für wen es auch sei, hingegen mein eigenes Leben nach mir selber bilden, das werde ich ganz gewiss, mag es nun gehen wie es mag. Damit habe ich ja kein Prinzip zu vertreten, sondern etwas viel Wundervolleres, etwas das in Einem selber steckt und ganz heiss vor Lauter Leben ist und jauchzt heraus will. . . . Glücklicher als ich jetzt bin, kann man bestimmt nicht werden." Letter to Hendrik Gillot, May 26, 1882, quoted in Lou Andreas-Salomé, *Lebensrückblick,* 5th ed., Ernst Pfeiffer, ed. (Frankfurt: Insel), p. 78.

7. See Nicole Savy's preface to the catalogue of the show *Les Petites Filles modernes* (Paris: Réunion des Musées Nationaux, 1989).

Chapter 6. Reading and Writing in Germany

MARIE-CLAIRE HOOCK-DEMARLE

1. Louise Ackerman, *My Life,* in *Works* (Lemerre, 1885), quoted in Christine Planté, *La Petite Soeur de Balzac* (Paris: Editions du Seuil, 1989).

2. For the French case, see François Furet and Jacques Ozouf, *Lire et écrire: L'Alphabétisation des Français de Calvin à Jules Ferry* (Paris, 1977), vol. 1. For a comparative study of literacy in France and Germany, see Etienne François, "Alphabetisierung und Lesefähigkeit in Frankreich und Deutschland um 1800," in H. Berding, E. François, and H.-P. Ullmann, eds., *Deutschland und Frankreich im Zeitalter der Französischen Revolution* (Frankfurt: Suhrkamp, 1989).

3. For the controversy between the "German school" represented by Rolf Engelsing, Ernst Hinrichs, Wilhelm Norden, and Rudolf Schenda and the "French school" of Louis Maggiolo, François Furet, and Jacques Ozouf, see Furet and Ozouf, *Lire et écrire,* p. 4.

4. Furet and Ozouf, *Lire et écrire,* p. 44.

5. See Wilhelm Norden, "Die Alphabetisierung in der oldenburgischen Küstenmarsch im 17. 18. Jht," in Ernst Hinrichs and Wilhelm Norden, eds., *Regionalgeschichte. Probleme und Beispiele* (Hildesheim, 1980).

6. Rolf Engelsing, *Analphabetentum und Lektüre. Zur Sozialgeschichte des Lesens in Deutschland zwischen feudaler und industrieller Gesellschaft* (Stuttgart, 1973).

7. Bettina von Arnim, *Dies Buch gehört dem König,* in *Werke und Briefe,* G. Konrad, ed. (Cologne, 1963), vols. 3 and 4.

8. Fanny Lewald-Stahr, *Für und wider die Frauen* (Berlin: Otto Janke, 1870), p. 68.

9. One autodidact who became an author was Christiane Sophie Ludwig; her novels of the turn of the century dealt with such subjects as the condition of blacks and Jews.

10. W. von Kügelgen, *Jugenderinnerungen eines alten Mannes* (Munich, 1867), p. 32.

11. Christa Wolf, *Lesen und Schreiben* (Darmstadt: Luchterhand, 1980), p. 281.

12. Wolfgang von Goethe, *Wilhelm Meisters Lehrjahre.*

13. Karl Ferdinand von Klöden, *Jugenderinnerungen* (Leipzig, 1874), p. 19.

14. Elisa von der Recke, *Briefe und Tagebücher,* C. Träger, ed. (1984), p. 86.

15. Wilhelm Fleischer, *Plan und Einrichtung eines neuen Lese Instituts im Frankfurt-am-Main,* 1796.

16. Marie-Claire Hoock-Demarle, *La Rage d'écrire. Les femmes allemandes face à la Révolution française (1790–1815)* (Aix-en-Provence: Alinéa, 1990), pt. 2, chaps. 1 and 2.

17. Caroline Schlegel-Schelling's letter to her sister Lotte Michaelis, March 22, 1786, in Sigrid Damm, ed., *Caroline Schlegel-Schelling in ihren Briefen* (Darmstadt, 1980), p. 90.

18. Ibid., pp. 152–153.

19. Barbey d'Aurevilly, *Les Bas-Bleus* (Brussels, 1878). On the origin of the term "bluestocking," see Planté, *La Petite Soeur de Balzac,* p. 28.

20. Catharina Elisabeth Goethe's letter to her son, February 15, 1798, in C. E. Goethe, *Briefe an ihren Sohn* (Stuttgart: Reclam, 1971), p. 131.

21. J. J. Ersch, *Allgemeines Repertorium der Literatur für die Jahre 1785–90, 1791–95, 1796–1800.*

22. The terms "intensive" and "extensive" are used by Engelsing in *Analphabetentum,* and in other works.

23. Marlies Prüsener, "Lesengesellschaften im 18. Jahrhundert," *Archiv für Geschichte des Buchwesens,* no. 13, 1973.

24. Ibid. Prüsener cites the case of a doctor from the Hamburg region who opened his library to neighbors. It contained thirteen books, nine of them dealing with the French Revolution.

25. Henriette Herz, *Erinnerungen,* ed. R. Schmitz (Frankfurt, 1984), p. 50.

26. Johanna Schopenhauer, *Jugendleben und Wanderbilder* (1839; reprinted Munich: Winkler, 1958), p. 267.

27. Adolf von Knigge, *Über den Umgang mit Menschen,* 1790, pt. 2, chap. 5.

28. Terms used in 1853 by the founder of *Gartenlaube,* quoted in Renate Möhrmann, *Die andere Frau. Emanzipationsansätze deutscher Schriftstellerinnen im Vorfeld der 48-Revolution* (Metzler, 1977), p. 167.

29. Von Knigge, *Über den Umgange mit Menschen,* pt. 2, chaps. 5, 10.

30. P.-J. Proudhon, quoted in Planté, *La Petite Soeur de Balzac,* p. 216. See also the biological theories of Paul Möbius, whose *Über den physiologischen Schwachsinn des Weibes* caused a sensation in 1900.

31. Letter of Clemens Brentano to Emilie von Niendorf, Munich, 1844.

32. *Literaturblatt,* March 15, 1839.

33. *Allgemeine deutsche Biographie,* article on Theresa Forster-Huber, excerpts from her *Memoirs* (1803).

34. Sophie Mereau translated the letters of Ninon de Lenclos in 1797; Theresa Huber translated those of Mme Roland.

35. Written in 1867, Marie von Ebner-Eschenbach's tragedy *Marie Roland* was performed only once, by amateurs in Weimar.

36. According to the academician Auger, quoted in Jean Larnac, *Histoire de la littérature féminine en France* (Paris, 1929).

37. Marie-Claire Hoock-Demarle, "Bettina Brentano-von Arnim ou la mise en oeuvre d'une vie," Ph.D. diss., 1985.

38. Among the many women's autobiographies published between 1830 and 1850 notable are those by Henriette Herz (written in 1823 and published in 1850), Elisa von der Recke (1804 and 1830), and Johanna Schopenhauer (published by her daughter in 1839), as well as the edited correspondence of Rahel Varnhagen (published by her husband in 1833) and Bettina von Arnim (referring to 1807 in a text written in 1843).

39. Louise Aston, *Meine Emanzipation, Verweisung und Rechtfertigung* (Brussels, 1846), quoted in Möhrmann, *Die andere Frau,* p. 146.

40. *Vormärz* (literally: pre-March) refers to the period 1840–1848 prior to the eruption of the Revolution of 1848 in March of that year.

41. Fanny Lewald, *Meine Lebensgeschichte Berlin* (1863), vol. 1, p. 260.

42. On the literature of these pioneers, see Marianne Walle, "Contribution à l'histoire des femmes allemandes entre 1848 et 1920 (Louise Otto,

Helene Lange, Clara Zetkin, et Lily Braun)," Ph.D. diss., University of Paris VII, 1989.

43. Adelheid Popp, *Die Jugendgeschichte einer Arbeiterein,* preface by August Bebel (Munich, 1909).

44. *Neue Bahnen* (new directions) was the title Louise Otto-Peters gave to the newspaper she founded in 1875.

45. Hedwig Dohm, *Die wissenschaftliche Emanzipation der Frau* (Berlin, 1893), pp. 45 and 185.

Chapter 7. The Catholic Model

MICHELA DE GIORGIO

1. A. M. Mozzoni, *Un passo avanti nella cultura femminile: tesi e progetto* (Milan, 1866), pp. 27–28.

2. R. P. G. Ventura, *La donna cattolica* (Milan and Genoa, 1855), vol. 3, pp. 249–259.

3. G. Fraisse, *Muse de la raison* (Paris: Alinéa, 1989).

4. G. d'Azambuja, *Ciò che per la Donna ha fatto il Cristianesimo* (Rome, 1912). Italian translation of the 6th French ed.

5. R. Deniel, *Une image de la famille et de la société sous la Restauration* (Paris: Editions Ouvrières, 1965), p. 125.

6. M. Bernos, "De l'influence salutaire ou pernicieuse de la femme dans la famille et la société," *Revue d'histoire moderne et contemporaine* (July-September, 1982).

7. G. Leopardi, *Dei costumi italiani,* ed. A. Placanica (Venice: Marsilio, 1989), p. 132.

8. S. Bertelli, G. Calvi, *Rituale, cerimoniale, etichetta nelle corti italiane,* in S. Bertelli and G. Grifò, eds., *Rituale, Cerimoniale, Etichetta* (Milan: Franco Angeli, 1985), p. 11 and following.

9. I. Porciani, "Il Plutarco femminile," in S. Soldani, ed., *L'educazione delle donne. Scuole e modelli di vita femminile nell'Italia dell'Ottocento* (Milan, 1989).

10. A. Scattigno, "Letture devote," in Porciani, ed., *Le donne a scuola, L'educazione femminile nell'Italia del Ottocento.* Catalog for documentary and iconographic show (Siena, 1987).

11. F. Lebrun, ed., *Histoire des catholiques en France* (Toulouse, 1980), pp. 321–330.

12. E. Saurer, "Donne e preti. Colloqui in confessionale agli inizi dell'Ottocento," presented at the Centro di Documentazione delle Donne di Bologna, in L. Ferrance, M. Palazzi and G. Pomata, eds., *Ragnatele di rapporti. Patronage e reti di relazione nella storia delle donne* (Turin: Rosenberg and Sellier, 1988), pp. 253–281.

13. *Civiltà Cattolica* ser. I, 10 (1852): 381.

14. I owe to the courtesy of Philippe Boutry this rare quantitative fact on the religious habits of Italy in the nineteenth century.

15. Ph. Boutry, *Prêtres e paroisses au pays du curé d'Ars* (Paris: Le Cerf,

1986), p. 19. An "Italian" (Hapsburgian, really) example: L. Pesce, ed., *Thesaurus Ecclesiarum Italiae Recentoris Aevi,* III, 9, *La visita pastorale di Sebastiano Soldati nella Diocesi di Treviso (1832–1838)* (Rome: Edizioni di Storia e Letteratura, 1979).

16. G. d'Azambuja, *La giovane e l'evoluzione moderna* (Rome, 1911), Italian translation of the 2nd French ed. (1880).

17. D'Azambuja, *Ció che per la Donna ha fatto il Cristianesimo.*

18. *Historia della Madre Barat fondatrice dell'Istituto del Sacro Cuore di Gesù* by Abbate (sic) Baunard (Rome, 1877), vol. 1, p. 510.

19. L. Colet, *L'Italie des Italiens* (Paris, 1862), p. 142.

20. J. W. Goethe, *Viaggio in Italia,* in *Opere,* Vittorio Santoli, ed. (Florence, 1970), pp. 356–357.

21. M. D'Azeglio, *I miei ricordi* (Milan, 1932), p. 20.

22. N. Tommaseo, *La donna, scritti vari* (Milan, 1872; 1st ed., 1833), p. 237.

23. Abbé J. Gaume, *Histoire de la société domestique* (Paris, 1844), p. 472.

24. M. L. Trebiliani, "Modello Mariano e immagine della donna nell'esperienza educativa di don Bosco," in Francesco Traniello, ed., *Don Bosco nella storia della cultura popolare* (Turin: Società Editrice Internazionale, 1987), pp. 187–207.

25. Leo XIII (Gioacchino Pecci), *Arcanum,* in *Il problemma femminile* (Rome, 1962), p. 13.

26. Some examples: E. Nevers, *L'età del marito* (Turin, 1891); T. Guidi, *L'amore dei quarant'anni* (Milan and Palermo, 1902).

27. L. Scaraffia, *La Santa degli Impossibili. Vicende e significati della devozione a S. Rita* (Turin: Rosenberg and Sellier, 1990), pp. 55–56.

28. J. Vincent, *Le Livre d'amour* (Paris: Brouwer, 1960).

29. C. Langlois, *Le Catholicisme au feminin. Les congrégations françaises à Supérieur Générale au XIX siècle* (Paris: Le Cerf, 1987), pp. 307–323.

30. S. Franchini, *Gli educandati nell'Italia postunitaria,* in Soldani, *L'educazione delle donne,* pp. 57–86.

31. S. Sighele, *Eva moderna* (Milan, 1910), p. 182.

32. G. Rocca, "Le nuove fondazioni religiose femminili in Italia dal 1800 al 1860," in *Problemi di storia della Chiesa dalla Restaurazione all'unità d'Italia* (Naples, 1985), pp. 107–192.

33. E. Caracciolo, *Misteri del chiostro napoletano* (1864; rpt. Florence, 1986).

34. M. Petrocchi, *Storia della spiritualità italiana* (Rome: Edizioni di Storia e Letteratura, 1979), vol. 3.

35. A. Gambasin, *Religiosa magnificenza e plebi in Sicilia nel XIX secolo* (Rome: Edizioni di Storia e Letteratura, 1979), pp. 163–221.

36. Sant'Alfonso de Liguori, *La vera sposa di Gesù Cristo, cioè la Monaca Santa* (Turin, 1862), p. 120.

37. O. Arnold, *Le Corps et l'âme. La Vie des religieuses au XIX siècle* (Paris: Le Seuil, 1984).

38. S. O'Brien, "Terra Incognita: The Nun in Nineteenth-Century England," in *Past and Present* 121 (1988).

39. B. Welter, "The Feminization of American Religion, 1800–1860," in L. W. Banner and M. Hartman, eds., *Clio's Consciousness Raised: New Perspectives on the History of Women* (New York: Harper and Row, 1974).

40. C. Langlois, "'Je suis Jeanne Jugan.' Dépendence sociale, condition féminine et fondation religieuse," *Archives de Sciences Sociales des Religions* 52 (1981): 21–35.

41. M. De Giorgio, *Les Demoiselles catholiques italiennes,* in Y. Cohen, ed., *Femmes et contre-pouvoirs* (Montreal: Boréal-Express, 1987), pp. 101–126.

42. J. Pitt-Rivers, *The Fate of Sechem, or the Politics of Sex: Essay in the Anthropology of the Mediterranean* (Cambridge: Cambridge University Press, 1977).

43. L. Guidi, "La 'Passione governata dalla virtù': benefattrici nella Napoli ottocentesca," in L. Ferrante, M. Palazzi, and G. Pomata, eds., *Ragnatele di rapporti,* pp. 148–165.

44. G. Cholvy and Y.-M. Hilaire, *Histoire religieuse de la France contemporaine, 1880–1930* (Paris: Privat, 1986), p. 363.

45. M. De Giorgio and P. Di Cori, "Politica e sentimenti: le organizzazioni femminili cattoliche dall'età giolittiana al fascismo," *Rivista di storia contemporanea* 3 (1980).

46. A. Pavissich, S.J., *Donna antica e donna nuova. Scene di domani* (Rome, 1909).

47. C. Dau Novelli, "Alle origini dell'esperienza cattolica femminile: rapporti con la Chiesa e gli altri movimenti femminili (1908–1912)," *Storia contemporanea* 22, 4/5 (1981).

48. J. W. Goethe, *Viaggio in Italia,* p. 481.

49. P. Macry, "La Napoli dei dotti. Lettori, libri e biblioteche di una excapitale (1870–1900)," *Meridiana* 4 (1988).

50. E. Raimondi, *Il romanzo senza idillio* (Turin, 1974), pp. 129–130.

51. M. Berengo, *Intellettuali e librai nella Milano della Restaurazione* (Turin: Einaudi, 1980).

52. Madame Bourdon (Mathilde Froment), *Souvenirs d'une institutrice* (Paris, 1869), 8th ed., pp. 22–23.

53. D. Maldini Chiarito, "Lettrici ed editori a Milano tra Otto e Novecento," *Storia di Lombardia* 2 (1988).

54. J. L. Desbordes, "Les Écrits de Mgr. Dupanloup sur la haute éducation des femmes," in F. Mayeur and J. Gadille, eds., *Education et images de la femme chrétienne en France au début du XXème siècle* (Grenoble: Editions Hermès, 1980).

55. M. J. Rouet de Journel, S.J., *Une russe catholique. Madame Swetchine* (Paris, 1929), pp. 16–17.

56. R. Ricci, *Memoria della Baronessa Olimpia Savio* (Milan, 1911), pp. 4–5.

57. M. L. Trebiliani, "Santità femminile e società a Lucca nell'Otto-

cento," in S. Boesch Gajano and L. Sebastiani, *Culto dei Santi, istituzioni e classi sociali in età preindustriale* (Aquila/Rome, 1984), pp. 959–995.

58. P. Ramon Ruiz Amado, *La educación femenina* (Barcelona, 1912), p. 115.

59. G. Thuillier, *L'Imaginaire quotidien au XIXe siècle* (Paris: Económica, 1985), p. 42.

60. A.-M. Thiesse, *Le Roman du quotidien* (Paris: Chemin vert, 1984), pp. 125–127.

61. "La biblioteca di una sposa," in *Fiamma viva* (April 1927): 251–253.

62. C. Savart, *Les Catholiques en France au XIX siècle: le témoignage du livre religieux* (Paris, 1985).

63. P. Camaiani, "La donna, la morte, e il giovane Vittorio Emanuele," in F. Traniello, ed., *Dai Quaccheri a Gandhi. Studi di storia religiosa in onore di Ettore Passerin d'Entrèves* (Bologna: Il Mulino, 1987), p. 169.

64. M.-F. Lévy, *De mères en filles* (Paris: Calmann-Lévy, 1984).

65. Ph. Boutry, M. Cinquin, *Deux pèlerinages au XIXe siècle: Ars et Paray* (Paris: Beauchesne, 1980), p. 22.

66. Thuillier, *L'Imaginaire,* pp. 44–45.

67. C. Brâme, *Journal intime. Enquête de M. Perrot e G. Ribeill* (Paris: Montalba, 1985).

68. Jolanda, *Eva Regina. Consigli e norme di vita femminile contemporanea* (Florence, 1907), p. 7.

69. P. Macry, *Ottocento. Famiglia, élites e patrimoni a Napoli* (Turin: Einaudi, 1988), p. 70.

70. *Journal de Marie Bashkirtseff* (Paris: Mazarine, 1980), p. 45.

71. L. Accati, "La politica dei sentimenti. L'Immacolata Concezione fra '600 e '700," *Atti del Primer Coloqui di Historia de la Dona* (Barcelona, 1986, forthcoming).

72. M. Segalen, J. Charmarat, "La Rosière et la 'Miss': les 'reines' des fêtes populaires," *L'Histoire* 53 (1983).

73. A. Marro, *La pubertà studiata nell'uomo e nella donna (in rapporto all'Antropologia alla Psichiatria ed alla Sociologia)* (Turin, 1897).

74. L. Guidi, *L'onore in pericolo. Carità e reclusione femminile nell'Ottocento napoletano* (Naples: Guida, 1991).

75. R. Betazzi, *La giovine e la moralità* (Turin, 1915), p. 19.

76. M. Turi, "La costruzione di un nuovo modello di comportamento femminile. Maria Goretti tra cronaca nera e agiografia," *Movimento operaio e socialista* 3 (1987).

77. A. Buttafuoco, *Le Mariuccine. Storia di un'istituzione laica. L'Asilo Mariuccia* (Milan: Franco Angeli, 1985).

78. *Bollettino Unione Donne Cattoliche d'Italia,* May 1911.

79. Benedetto XV (Giacomo Della Chiesa), *Allocuzione alle donne italiane,* 21 October, 1919.

80. "La virtù mal vestita," in *Fiamma viva,* October 1922, p. 579.

81. J. C. Flugel, *The Psychology of Clothes* (London, 1930).

82. G. Thuillier, *L'Imaginaire,* pp. 14–16.

83. N. Ginzburg, *La famiglia Manzoni* (Turin: Einaudi, 1989), pp. 37–38.

84. Madame Mathilde Bourdon, *Giornata Cristiana della giovinetta* (Turin, 1888, Fr. ed., 1867), p. xiv.

85. B. G. Smith, *Ladies of the Leisure Class. The Bourgeoises of Northern France in the Nineteenth Century* (Princeton, 1981), pp. 14–16.

86. Ph. Perrot, "Pour une généalogie de l'austérité des apparences," *Communications* 46 (1987): 157–179.

87. N. Ginzburg, *La famiglia Manzoni,* pp. 132–135.

88. *Historia della Madre Barat,* p. 517.

89. Ph. Ariès, *L'Homme devant la mort* (Paris, 1977).

90. *Récit d'une soeur, souvenirs de famille,* collected by Madame Augustus Craven née La Ferronays (Paris, 1911) (52nd ed.), vol. 1, p. 199.

91. E. Legouvé, *Padri e figli nel secolo che muore* (Florence, 1899).

92. M. Gioja, *Il primo e il nuovo galateo,* p. 258.

93. M. L. Trebiliani, *Don Bosco nella storia della cultura popolare.*

94. R. Deniel, *Une image de la famille,* p. 194.

95. G. Leopardi, *Zibaldone,* vol. 1, pp. 353–356.

96. D. Maldini Chiarito, "Trasmissione di valori e educazione famigliare: le lettere al figlio di Costanza D'Azeglio," *Passato e presente* (January-April 1987): 35–62.

97. J. Maître, "Idéologie religieuse, conversion mystique e symbiose mère-enfant; le cas de Thérèse Martin (1873–1897)," *Archives de Sciences Sociales des Religions* 51 (1981): 65–99.

98. M. Milan, *Donna, famiglia, società. Aspetti della stampa femminile cattolica in Italia tra '800 e '900* (Istituto di Studi Storico-Politici, Università di Genova, 1983).

99. J. Michelet, *La Femme* (Paris, 1860), p. 118.

100. G. Lombroso, *L'anima della donna* (Florence, 1918), and *L'anima della donna, II:Qualità e difetti* (Florence, 1918).

Chapter 9. The Making of the Modern Jewish Woman

NANCY L. GREEN

1. Lilly Scherr, cited in Judith Friedlander, "The Jewish Feminist Question," *Dialectical Anthroplogy* 8, 1–2 (October 1983), p. 113.

2. Rachel Biale, *Women and Jewish Law: An Exploration of Women's Issues in Halakhic Sources* (New York: Schocken, 1984), pp. 6–7; Moshe Meiselman, *Jewish Women in Jewish Law* (New York: KTAV, 1978).

3. Barbara Myerhoff, *Number Our Days* (New York: Simon and Schuster, 1980), pp. 234–235.

4. Deborah Hertz, *Jewish High Society in Old Regime Berlin* (New Haven: Yale University Press, 1988).

5. Hannah Arendt, *Rahel Varnhagen: The Life of a Jewish Woman*, rev. ed. (New York: Harcourt Brace Jovanovich, 1974), p. 57.

6. Jacob Katz, *Out of the Ghetto: The Social Background of Jewish Emancipation, 1770–1870* (New York: Schocken Books, 1978), chap. 4.

7. Marion Kaplan, *The Jewish Feminist Movement in Germany: The Campaigns of the Jüdischer Frauenbund, 1904–1938* (Westport, Conn.: Greenwood Press, 1979), pp. 19–20. See also her "Tradition and Transition: Jewish Women in Imperial Germany," in *Jewish Women in Historical Perspective*, Judith R. Baskin, ed. (Detroit: Wayne State University Press, 1991), pp. 202–221.

8. Arendt, *Rahel*, p. 8.

9. Lucy S. Dawidowicz, *The Golden Tradition: Jewish Life and Thought in Eastern Europe* (Boston: Beacon Press, 1967), p. 31; Michael Stanislawski, *Tsar Nicholas I and the Jews* (Philadelphia: Jewish Publication Society, 1983).

10. Steven J. Zipperstein, *The Jews of Odessa: A Cultural History, 1794–1881* (Stanford: Stanford University Press, 1985), pp. 129–130.

11. Edward J. Bristow, *Prostitution and Prejudice: The Jewish Fight against White Slavery, 1870–1939* (New York: Schocken Books, 1983), p. 51n6.

12. Sydney Stahl Weinberg, *The World of Our Mothers: The Lives of Jewish Immigrant Women* (Chapel Hill: University of North Carolina Press, 1988), pp. 76 and 276n33.

13. Elizabeth Hasanovitz, *One of Them* (New York: Houghton Mifflin, 1918), pp. 6–9.

14. Nancy Green, "L'Émigration comme émancipation: Les Femmes juives d'Europe de l'Est à Paris, 1881–1914," *Pluriel* 27 (1981): 56–58.

15. Bristow, *Prostitution*, pp. 51, 229; Kaplan, *The Jewish Feminist Movement*, pp. 37–38, 110–112; Polly Adler, *A House Is Not a Home* (New York: Rinehart, 1953).

16. Charlotte Baum, Paula Hyman, Sonya Michel, *The Jewish Woman in America* (New York: New American Library, 1975), p. 87.

17. Paula E. Hyman, "Culture and Gender: Women in the Immigrant Jewish Community," in *The Legacy of Jewish Immigration*, David Berger, ed. (New York: Brooklyn College Press, 1983), pp. 157–168.

18. Weinberg, *World of Our Mothers*, pp. 76 and 276n33.

19. Ibid., p. 281n55; Paula E. Hyman, "Gender and the Immigrant Jewish Experience in the United States," in Baskin, ed., *Jewish Women*, pp. 222–242.

20. Mary Antin, *The Promised Land*, 2d ed. (Princeton: Princeton University Press, 1969), p. 223.

21. Weinberg, *World of Our Mothers*, p. 174. Compare Selma Berrol, "Education and Economic Mobility: The Jewish Experience in New York City, 1880–1920," *American Jewish Historical Quarterly* 65, 3 (March 1976): 263; Sherry Gorelick, *City College and the City Poor: Education in New York, 1880–1924* (New Brunswick, N.J.: Rutgers University Press, 1981), pp. 121–123.

22. Berrol, "Education"; Gorelick, *City College,* pp. 113, 124 and passim.

23. Stephen E. Brumberg, "Going to America, Going to School: The Jewish Immigrant Public School Encounter in Turn-of-the-Century New York City," *American Jewish Archives* 36, 2 (November 1984): 99; Weinberg, *World of Our Mothers,* p. 117.

24. Jacob R. Marcus, ed., *The American Jewish Woman: A Documentary History* (New York: KTAV; and Cincinnati: American Jewish Archives, 1981), p. 137.

25. Gorelick, *City College,* p. 31.

26. Hasanovitz, *One of Them,* p. 81.

27. Ellen Schiff, "What Kind of Way Is That for Nice Jewish Girls to Act? Images of Jewish Women in Modern American Drama," *American Jewish History* 70, 1 (September 1980): 112.

28. Alice Kessler-Harris, "Organizing the Unorganizable: Three Jewish Women and Their Union," in *Class, Sex, and the Woman Worker,* Milton Cantor and Bruce Laurie, eds. (Westport, Conn.: Greenwood Press, 1977), pp. 144–165; Theresa S. Malkiel, *The Diary of a Shirtwaist Striker,* Françoise Basch, ed. (Ithaca: Cornell University Press, 1990); Susan A. Glenn, *Daughters of the Shtetl: Life and Labor in the Immigrant Generation* (Ithaca: Cornell University Press, 1990).

29. Paula E. Hyman, "Immigrant Women and Consumer Protest: The New York City Kosher Meat Boycott of 1902," *American Jewish History,* 70, 1 (September 1980): 91–105; Elizabeth Ewen, *Immigrant Women in the Land of Dollars: Life and Culture on the Lower East Side, 1890–1925* (New York: Monthly Review Press, 1985), pp. 126–127, 176–183.

30. Ewen, *Immigrant Women,* p. 245.

31. Weinberg, *World of Our Mothers,* p. 151.

32. Baum, Hyman, and Michel, *The Jewish Woman,* p. 184; compare Berrol, "Class or Ethnicity: The Americanized German Jewish Woman and Her Middle-Class Sisters in 1895," *Jewish Social Studies* 47, 1 (Winter 1985): 21–32.

33. Kaplan, *The Jewish Feminist Movement,* p. 50.

Chapter 10. The Secular Model of Girls' Education

FRANÇOISE MAYEUR

1. Martine Sonnet, *L'Education des filles au temps des Lumières* (Paris: Le Cerf, 1987).

2. See Françoise Mayeur, *L'Enseignement secondaire des jeunes filles sous la Troisième République* (Paris: Presses de la Fondation Nationale des Sciences Politiques, 1977), p. 489. See also Mayeur, *L'Education des filles en France au XIXe siècle* (Paris: Hachette, 1979), p. 207.

3. David Wardle, *English Popular Education, 1780–1970* (Cambridge: Cambridge University Press, 1970), p. 118.

4. Jean Dulck, *L'Enseignement en Grande-Bretagne* (Paris: Armand Colin, 1968).

5. Elie Halévy, *Histoire du peuple anglais au XIXe siècle* (Paris: Hachette, 1926–1932, rpt. 1975), 2 vols.

6. According to A. Couvreur, a layman, quoted in Yolande Mendes da Costa and Anne Morelli, eds., *Femmes, libertés, laïcité* (Brussels: Université libre, 1989).

7. Jacques Lory, *Libéralisme et instruction primaire 1842–1879* (Louvain: Nauwelaerts, 1979).

8. Mendes da Costa and Morelli, *Femmes*, p. 18.

9. J. Bartier, *Eglise et enseignement* (Brussels: Université libre, 1977).

Chapter 11. Images—Appearances, Leisure, and Subsistence

ANNE HIGONNET

1. P. G. Hubert, Jr. "Art and Art Industries," *The Woman's Book* (New York: C. Scribner's Sons, 1894), vol. 1, p. 4.

2. The source for this entire case is Charlotte Yeldham, *Women Artists in Nineteenth-Century France and England*, 2 vols. (New York: Garland, 1984).

3. Abigail Solomon-Godeau, "The Legs of the Countess," *October* 39 (Winter 1986): 96.

4. Ibid., p. 93.

5. Anna Jameson, *Legends of the Madonna as Represented in the Fine Arts, Forming the Third Series of Sacred and Legendary Art*, 2nd ed. (London: Longman, Brown, Green, Longman, and Roberts, 1857), p. 58.

Chapter 12. Representations of Women

ANNE HIGONNET

1. Wellesley College archives, Wellesley, Mass.

2. Lisa Tickner, *The Spectacle of Women: Imagery of the Suffrage Campaign, 1907–1914* (London: Chatto and Windus, 1987), p. 71.

3. Ibid., pp. 74–75, 80–81, 93–95, 122–123.

Family Is Women's Work

G.F.–M.P.

1. Anne-Marie Sohn, "Les Attentats à la pudeur sur les fillettes en France (1870–1939) et la sexualité quotidienne," *Mentalités* 3 (1989). The same issue contains articles by Amy Gilman Srebnick, "L'assassinat et le mystère de Mary Rogers," and Judith Walkowitz, "Jack l'éventreur et les mythes de la violence masculine," also published in *Feminist Studies* 8:3.

2. Anne-Louise Shapiro, "Love Stories: Female Crimes of Passion in Fin de Siècle Paris," to appear in 1991.

Chapter 13. Bodies and Hearts

YVONNE KNIBIEHLER

1. Paola Di Cori, "Rosso e bianco. La devozione al Sacro Cuore di Gesù nel primo dopoguerra," *Memoria* 5 (Turin) (November 1982); see also "Sacro e profano" in the same issue, pp. 82–107.

2. Yannick Ripa, "L'Histoire du corps, un puzzle en construction," *Histoire de l'éducation* 37 (January 1988): 47–54.

3. Odile Arnold, *Le Corps et l'âme: la vie des religieuses au XIXe siècle* (Paris: Editions du Seuil, 1984), chap. 3.

4. Yvonne Knibiehler, Marcel Bernos, Elisabeth Ravoux-Rallo, Eliane Richard, *De la pucelle à la minette. Les Jeunes Filles de l'âge classique à nos jours* (Paris: Messidor, 1989), pp. 97–99.

5. Catalogue, *Les Petites Filles modernes,* edited by Nicole Savy, Les Dossiers du Musée d'Orsay, 33 (Paris, 1989).

6. Agnès Fine, "A propos du trousseau: Une culture féminine?" in Michelle Perrot, ed., *Une Histoire des femmes est-elle possible?* (Marseilles and Paris: Editions Rivages, 1984), pp. 155–188.

7. Emile Zola, *Les Quatre Evangiles. Fécondité* (Paris: Bibliothèque Charpentier, 1899), p. 50.

8. *Dictionnaire des sciences médicales,* 60 vols. (Paris: Panckoucke, 1812–1822), article "Grossesse."

9. Edward Shorter, *A History of Women's Bodies* (New York: Basic Books, 1982).

10. Carl Degler, *At Odds: Women and the Family in America from the Revolution to the Present* (New York: Oxford University Press, 1980).

11. Jean-Paul Bardet, K. A. Lynch, G.-P. Mineau, M. Hainsworth, M. Skolnick, "La Mortalité maternelle autrefois, une étude comparée (de la France de l'Ouest à l'Utah)," *Annales de démographie historique,* 1981, *Démographie historique et condition féminine* (Paris: Mouton, 1981), pp. 31–48.

12. Françoise Leguay and Claude Barbizet, *Blanche Edwards-Pilliet, femme et médecine, 1858–1941* (Le Mans: Editions Cenomanes, 1988).

13. Louis Henry, "Mortalité des hommes et des femmes dans le passé," *Annales de démographie historique,* 1987, pp. 87–118; Arthur Imhof, "La Surmortalité des femmes mariées en âge de procréation: un indice de la condition féminine au XIXe siècle," *Annales de démographie historique,* 1981, pp. 81–87.

14. *Dictionnaire des sciences médicales,* 1812–1822, article "Fille."

15. Michel Poulain and Dominique Tabutin, "La Surmortalité des petites filles en Belgique au XIXe siècle et début du XXe siècle," *Annales de démographie historique,* 1981, pp. 105–139.

16. Amédée Dechambre, ed., *Dictionnaire encyclopédique des sciences médicales* (Paris: Asselin et Masson, 1864–1889), article "Syphilis."

17. Laura Kreyder, *L'Enfance des saints et les autres. Essai sur la Comtesse de Ségur* (Biblioteca della Ricerca, 1987), chap. 4.

18. Bonnie G. Smith, *Ladies of the Leisure Class: The Bourgeoises of Northern France in the Nineteenth Century* (Princeton: Princeton University Press, 1981), p. 48.

19. Edmondo De Amicis, *Amore e ginnastica;* transl. into French, *Amour et gymnastique* (Paris: Editions Philippe Picquier, 1988).

20. Jacques Thibault, "Les Origines du sport féminin," in Pierre Arnaud, ed., *Les Athlètes de la République. Gymnastique, sport et idéologie républicaine 1870–1914* (Toulouse: Privat, 1987).

21. The quoted phrase was the title of a celebrated work by Dr. Georges Cabanis, published in Paris in 1803.

22. *Hygiène et physiologie du mariage,* published by the author (Paris, 1848), 1853 ed., chap. 12.

23. *The Functions and Disorders of the Reproductive Organs in Youth, in Adult Age, and in Advanced Life: Considered in Their Physiological, Social and Psychological Relations* (Philadelphia, 1865).

24. Michelle Perrot, ed., *A History of Private Life,* vol. 4: *From the Fires of Revolution to the Great War,* trans. Arthur Goldhammer (Cambridge, Mass.: Harvard University Press, 198?).

25. Quoted in Degler, *At Odds,* p. 267.

26. Havelock Ellis, *Studies in the Psychology of Sex* (New York: Random House, 1936), vol. 1, p. 464.

27. Madeleine Pelletier, *La Femme vierge* (Paris: Editions Bresle, 1933), quoted in Claude Maignen, ed., *L'Education féministe des filles* (Paris: Syros, 1978), p. 9.

28. Knibielher et al., *De la pucelle,* p. 147.

29. Jean-Louis Flandrin, *Les Amours paysannes (XVIe–XVIIe siècles)* (Paris: Gallimard/Julliard, 1975), pp. 114–115.

30. Jeffrey Weeks, *Sex, Politics, and Society: The Regulation of Society since 1800* (New York: Longman, 1981), p. 60.

31. Marie Dugard, *La Société américaine* (Paris: Hachette, 1895), pp. 170–171.

32. Degler, *At Odds,* pp. 20–21.

33. *Récit de vie, Denise S., bourgeoise d'Anvers,* interviewed by Edith R. (Brussels: Université des femmes, 1988), p. 46.

34. Louise Weiss, *Mémoires d'une Européenne* (Paris: Payot, 1970), vol. 1, p. 58.

35. Perrot, ed., *Histoire de la vie privée,* vol. 4, p. 546.

36. Thierry Eggerickx and Michel Poulain, "Le Contexte et les connaissances démographiques de l'émigration des Brabançons vers les Etats-Unis au milieu du XIXe siècle," in *Annales de démographie historique,* 1987.

37. *Annales de démographie historique,* 1981 and 1984.

38. Louis Bergeret, *Des fraudes dans l'accomplissement des fonctions*

génératrices (Paris: J.-B. Baillière et fils, 1868); English trans. by P. de Marmon, *The Preventive Obstacle, or Conjugal Onanism* (New York: Turner and Mignard, 1870).

39. Jean-Pierre Bardet and Hervé Le Bras, "La Chute de la fécondité," *Histoire de la population française, de 1789 à 1914* (Paris: Presses Universitaires de France, 1990), vol. 3, p. 361.

40. Degler, *At Odds,* p. 273; Weeks, *Sex, Politics and Society,* p. 71; Carroll Smith-Rosenberg, *Disorderly Conduct: Visions of Gender in Victorian America* (New York: Oxford University Press, 1985), p. 219.

41. Shorter, *A History of Women's Bodies,* pp. 182–190.

42. Joëlle Guillais, *La Chair de l'autre. Le Crime passionnel au dix-neuvième siècle* (Paris: Olivier Orban, 1986).

43. Degler, *At Odds,* pp. 279–297.

44. Jules Michelet, *L'Amour* (Paris: Calmann-Lévy, n.d.), p. 246.

45. Pierre Garnier, *Le Mariage dans ses devoirs, ses rapports et ses effets conjugaux* (Paris: Garnier frères, 1879), p. 540.

46. Quoted in Fanny Fay-Sallois, *Les Nourrices à Paris au XIXe siècle* (Paris: Payot, 1980), p. 237.

47. Valérie Fildes, *Wet Nursing: A History from Antiquity to the Present* (Oxford: Blackwell, 1988), pp. 207, 221–241.

48. Catherine Rollet-Echalier, *La Politique à l'égard de la petite enfance sous la troisième République,* Works and Documents, notebook 127, Institut National d'Etudes démographiques (Paris: Presses Universitaires de France, 1990).

49. François Bigot, "Les Enjeux de l'assistance à l'enfance," Ph.D. diss., University of Tours, 1988, 2 vols., typescript, pp. 138–139.

50. Agnès Fine, "Enfant et normes familiales," in Jacques Dupâquier, ed., *Histoire de la population française* (Paris: Presses Universitaires de France, 1988), vol. 3, p. 437.

51. Weeks, *Sex, Politics and Society,* pp. 61–62.

52. Perrot, ed., *Histoire de la vie privée,* pp. 61–62. See also Michèle Bordeaux, Bernard Hazo, Soizic Lorvellec, *Qualifié viol* (Paris: Klincksieck, 1990).

53. Brian Juan O'Neill, *Social Inequality in a Portuguese Hamlet: Land, Late Marriage and Bastardy (1870–1978)* (Cambridge: Cambridge University Press, 1987), p. 334.

54. Gianna Pomata, "Madri illegitime tra ottocento e novecento: Storie cliniche e storie di vita," in *Quaderni Storici,* 44 (August 1980), pp. 506–507.

55. Perrot, ed., *Histoire de la vie privée,* pp. 455–460.

56. See Marie Bashkirtseff, *Journal* (Paris: Mazarine, 1985); Eugénie de Guérin, *Journal et Fragments* (Paris: Lecoffre, 1884); Alphonse de Lamartine, *Le Manuscrit de ma mère* (Paris: Hachette, 1924).

57. Erna Olafson Hellestein et al., eds., *Victorian Women: A Documentary Account of Women's Lives in Nineteenth-Century England, France, and the United States* (Stanford: Stanford University Press, 1989).

58. Adrienne Necker de Saussure, *Education progressive ou étude du cours de la vie* (Paris: Garnier, n.d.; 1st ed. 1828), vol. 2, p. 478.

59. Caroline Brame, *Journal intime* (Paris: Montalba, 1985).

60. Hellestein et al., eds., *Victorian Women,* p. 144.

61. Quote in Geneviève Fraisse, *Clémence Royer, philosophe et femme de sciences* (Paris: La Découverte, 1985).

62. Ginette Raimbaut and Caroline Eliacheff, *Les Indomptables, figures de l'anorexie* (Paris: Editions Odile Jacob, 1989); Joan J. Brumberg, *Fasting Girls: The Emergence of Anorexia Nervosa as a Modern Disease* (Cambridge, Mass.: Harvard University Press, 1988).

63. Steve M. Stowe, "'The Thing, Not Its Vision': A Woman's Courtship and Her Sphere in the Southern Planter Class," *Feminist Studies* 9, 1 (Spring 1983): 113–130. See also Hellestein et al., eds., *Victorian Women,* p. 88.

64. Smith Rosenberg, *Disorderly Conduct,* pp. 52–76.

65. Arnold, *Le Corps et l'âme. La Vie des religieuses au XIXe siècle.*

66. Jacques Leonard, "Femmes, religion et médecine. Les religieuses qui soignent en France au XIXe siècle," *Annales, Economie, Société, Civilisation* (September-October 1977), pp. 897–907.

67. Flaviana Zanolla, "Suocere, nuore et cognate nel primo '900 a P. nel Friuli," in *Parto e maternita, momenti della biografia femminile.* Special issue of *Quaderni Storici* 44(August 1980):429–450.

68. Smith, *Ladies of the Leisure Class.*

69. Ibid., chap. 3.

70. Perrot, ed., *Histoire de la vie privée,* p. 128.

71. Weiss, *Mémoires d'une Européene,* vol. 1, pp. 93–94.

72. Evelyne Berriot-Salvadore, "'L'Effet 89' dans le journal intime d'une jeune fille de la Belle Epoque," Proceedings of the colloquium *Les Femmes et la Révolution française* (Toulouse: Presses Universitaires du Miral, 1989–1990).

73. Perrot, ed., *Histoire de la vie privée,* pp. 516–517; Degler, *At Odds,* pp. 107–108; Knibiehler et al., *De la pucelle,* p. 102.

74. Robert Musil, *The Man Without Qualities* (London: Picador, 1979).

75. Jacques Poumarède, "L'Inceste et le droit bourgeois," in Poumarède and J. P. Royer, eds., *Droit, histoire et sexualité* (Paris: Publications de l'espace juridique, 1987), pp. 213–228.

76. Weeks, *Sex, Politics and Society,* p. 31.

77. Yvonne Knibiehler and Catherine Fouquet, *L'Histoire des mères, du Moyen Age à nos jours* (Paris: Hachette, 1982), pp. 186–193.

78. Will Aeschimann, *La Pensée d'Edgar Quinet. Etude sur la formation de ses idées avec essais de jeunesse et documents inédits* (Paris: Editions Anthropos, 1986).

79. H.-A. Dideriks, "Le Choix du conjoint à Amsterdam au début du 19e siècle," *Annales de démographie historique,* 1986, pp. 183–194.

80. Paul Lachance, "L'Effet du déséquilibre des sexes sur le comportement matrimonial: Comparaison entre la Nouvelle France, Saint-Domingue

et la Nouvelle Orléans," *Revue d'histoire de l'Amérique française* 39, 2 (Autumn 1985).

81. Julie Dunfey, "'Living the Principle' of Plural Marriage: Mormon Women, Utopia, and Female Sexuality in the Nineteenth Century," *Feminist Studies* 10, 3 (Fall 1984): 523–536.

82. Stowe, "'The Thing, Not Its Vision': A Woman's Courtship and Her Sphere in the Southern Planter Class," pp. 113–130.

83. Yvonne Knibiehler, "Fanny Reybaud," *Provence historique* (October 1991).

84. Degler, *At Odds*, pp. 31–32.

85. Bernard Schnapper, "La Séparation de corps de 1837 à 1914: Essai de sociologie juridique," *Revue historique* (April-June 1978).

86. Michelet, *L'Amour*, pp. 358–359.

87. Jean Estebe, *Les Ministres de la République, 1871–1914* (Paris: Presses de la Fondation Nationale des Sciences Politiques, 1982), p. 91.

88. Smith-Rosenberg, *Disorderly Conduct*, pp. 190–195.

89. Hellestein et al., eds., *Victorian Women*, pp. 453–508.

90. Eliane Richard, "Des veuves riches au 19e siècle," Proceedings of the colloquium *Les Femmes et l'argent*, Centre d'Etudes Féminines of the Université de Provence (Aix-en-Provence: 1985), pp. 21–35.

Chapter 14. Dangerous Sexualities

Judith R. Walkowitz

1. Kathy Peiss and Christina Simmons, "Passion and Power: An Introduction," in Peiss and Simmons, with Robert A. Padgug, eds., *Passion and Power: Sexuality in History* (Philadelphia: Temple University Press, 1989), p. 3.

2. Abraham Flexner, *Prostitution in Europe* (New York: Century, 1920), p. 64.

3. *Downward Paths: An Inquiry into the Causes which Contribute to the Making of the Prostitute, with a Foreword by A. Maude Royden* (London, 1913), p. 48.

4. Cited in Ronald Pearsall, *The Worm in the Bud: The World of Victorian Sexuality* (Toronto: Macmillan, 1969), p. 283.

5. Cited in John D'Emilio and Estelle Freedman, *Intimate Matters: A History of Sexuality in America* (New York: Harper and Row, 1988), p. 182.

6. Ellen Ross, "'Fierce Questions and Taunts': Married Life in Working-Class London, 1870–1914," *Feminist Studies* 8, 3 (Fall 1982): 575–576.

7. Cited in Jill Harsin, *Policing Prostitution in Nineteenth-Century Paris* (Princeton: Princeton University Press, 1980), p. 22.

8. William Acton, *Prostitution*, ed. Peter Fryer (1870; abridged ed. New York: Praeger, 1968), p. 23.

9. *Daily Chronicle* (London), 10 November 1888.

10. Alain Corbin, "Commercial Sexuality in Nineteenth-Century France:

A System of Images and Regulations," trans. Katherine Streip, *Representations* 14 (Spring 1986):212–213.

11. "Report of the Royal Commission on the Administration and Operation of the Contagious Diseases Acts 1866–69 (1871)," *Parliamentary Papers*, 1871 (C.408), p. xix.

12. Cited in Judith R. Walkowitz, *Prostitution and Victorian Society: Women, Class and the State* (New York: Cambridge University Press, 1980), p. 177.

13. Cited in Alain Corbin, *Les Filles de noce: Misère sexuelle et prostitution (19e et 20e siècles)* (Paris: Aubier Montaigne, 1978), p. 134.

14. Cited in Henry Mayhew and Bracebridge Hemyng, "The Prostitute Class Generally," in Henry Mayhew, ed., *London Labour and the London Poor* (4 vols., London, 1861; rpt. New York: Dover, 1968), vol. 4, p. 205.

15. Cited in Walkowitz, *Prostitution*, p. 170.

16. Cited in Judith R. Walkowitz, "Male Vice and Female Virtue: Feminism and the Politics of Prostitution in Nineteenth-Century Britain," in Ann Snitow et al., eds., *Powers of Desire: The Politics of Sexuality* (New York: Monthly Review Press, 1983), p. 423.

17. Cited in ibid., p. 186.

18. Jeffrey Weeks, *Coming Out: Homosexual Politics in Britain from the Nineteenth Century to the Present* (London: Quartet, 1977), p. 18.

19. Cited in Flexner, *Prostitution in Europe*, p. 190.

20. Ibid., p. 197.

21. Ibid.

22. Cited in Ute Frevert, *Women in German History: From Bourgeois Emancipation to Sexual Liberation*, trans. Stuart McKinnon-Evans (Oxford: Berg, 1989), pp. 133–134.

23. Elizabeth Cobb to Karl Pearson, 17 July 1885. Pearson Papers, 663/1. University College, London.

24. Maria Sharpe, "Autobiographical Notes," p. 1, Pearson Papers, 10/1.

25. Emma Brooke, "Notes on a Man's View of the Woman Question," Pearson Papers, 10/2.

26. Rachel Bernstein, "Boarding-Housekeepers and Brothel Keepers in New York City, 1880–1910," Ph.D. diss., Rutgers University, 1984, pp. 144–145.

27. Mrs. G., Interview, Dame Colet House, East London, July 1983.

28. Mrs. M., Interview, Toynbee Hall, East London, July 1983.

29. Cited in Josephine Butler, "The Garrison Towns of Kent," *The Shield* (London), 25 April 1870.

30. Bracebridge Hemyng, "Prostitution in London," in Mayhew, ed., *London Labour*, vol. 4, p. 250.

31. Cited in D'Emilio and Freedman, *Intimate Matters*, p. 137.

32. Cited in W. T. Stead, Diary Entries, 3 March 1886. Stead Papers. I am grateful to Professor J. O. Baylen for access to these papers.

33. Rosalind Pollak Petchesky, *Abortion and Woman's Choice: The State, Sexuality and Reproductive Freedom* (Boston: Longman, 1984), p. 78.

34. Cited in Angus McLaren, "Abortion in France: Women and the Regulation of Family Size, 1800–1914," *French Historical Studies* 10, 3 (1878): 476.

35. Cited in Peter Gay, *The Bourgeois Experience: Victoria to Freud.* Volume 1. *Education of the Senses* (Oxford: Oxford University Press, 1984), p. 254.

36. Cited in Carroll Smith-Rosenberg, *Disorderly Conduct: Visions of Gender in Victorian America* (New York and Oxford: Oxford University Press, 1985), pp. 236–237.

37. Petchesky, *Abortion and Woman's Choice,* p. 45.

38. Cited in ibid., p. 55.

39. Cited in McLaren, "Abortion in France," p. 476.

40. Petchesky, *Abortion and Woman's Choice,* p. 54.

41. Cited in Margaret Hunt, "Girls Will Be Boys," *The Women's Review of Books* 6, 12 (September 1989): 11.

42. Cited in Anna Clark, "Cross-Dressing." Unpublished paper, 1986, p. 9.

43. Cited in D'Emilio and Freedman, *Intimate Matters,* pp. 124–125.

44. Cited in Smith-Rosenberg, *Disorderly Conduct,* p. 58.

45. Christine Stansell, "Revisiting the Angel in the House: Revisions of Victorian Womanhood," *New England Quarterly* 60 (1987): 474.

46. Ibid., p. 482.

47. Jeannette Marks, cited in Lillian Faderman, *Surpassing the Love of Men: Romantic Friendship and Love Between Women from the Renaissance to the Present* (New York: William Morrow, 1981), p. 229.

48. Emma Willard, "Companionships," reprinted in Jonathan Katz, *Gay/Lesbian Almanac: A New Documentary* (New York: Harper and Row, 1983), pp. 216–218.

49. Jeffrey Weeks, *Sexuality and Its Discontents: Meanings, Myths, and Modern Sexualities* (London: Routledge and Kegan Paul, 1985), p. 67.

50. Cited in Katz, *Gay/Lesbian Almanac,* p. 189.

51. Cited in ibid., p. 144.

52. Cited in ibid., p. 270.

53. Carroll Smith-Rosenberg, "Discourses of Sexuality and Subjectivity: The New Woman, 1870–1936," in Martin Bauml Duberman, Martha Vicinus, and George Chauncey, Jr., eds., *Hidden from History: Reclaiming the Gay and Lesbian Past* (New York: New American Library, 1989), p. 270.

54. "'The Truth about Myself': Autobiography of a Lesbian" (1901), in Eleanor Riemer and John C. Fout, eds., *European Women: A Documentary History 1789–1945* (New York: Schocken, 1980), pp. 235–236.

55. Cited in Faderman, *Surpassing the Love,* p. 229.

56. Cited in Gudrun Schwarz, "'Virago' in Male Theory in Nineteenth-Century Germany," in Judith Friedlander et al., eds., *Women in Culture and Politics: A Century of Change* (Bloomington: Indiana University Press, 1986), p. 139.

57. Cited in Katz, *Gay/Lesbian Almanac*, p. 137.

58. Leila J. Rupp, "'Imagine My Surprise': Women's Relationships in Mid-Twentieth Century America," in *Hidden from History*, p. 410.

Chapter 15. The Woman Worker

Joan W. Scott

1. Jules Simon, *L'Ouvrière*, 2nd ed. (Paris: Hachette, 1861), p. v.

2. Maurice Garden, *Lyon et les Lyonnais au XVIIIe siècle* (Paris: Flammarion, 1975), p. 139.

3. Dominique Godineau, *Citoyennes tricoteuses: Les Femmes du peuple à Paris pendant la Révolution française* (Paris: Alinea, 1988), p. 67.

4. John Burnett, ed., *Annals of Labour; Autobiographies of British Working-Class People, 1820–1920* (Bloomington: Indiana University Press, 1974), p. 285.

5. Eileen Yeo and E. P. Thompson, eds., *The Unknown Mayhew* (New York: Schocken Books, 1972), pp. 122–123.

6. Karl Marx and Friedrich Engels, *The Communist Manifesto*, ed. D. Ryazanoff (New York: Russel and Russel, 1963), p. 35. The argument continues: "Differences of age and sex no longer have any social significance for the working class. All are now mere instruments of labor, whose price varies according to age and sex."

7. Cited in Ava Baron, "Questions of Gender: Deskilling and Demasculinization in the U.S. Printing Industry, 1830–1915," *Gender and History* 1, 2 (Summer 1989): 164.

8. Ramsay MacDonald, ed. *Women in the Printing Trades: A Sociological Study* (London: P. S. King and Son, 1904), p. 36.

9. Cited in Michelle Perrot, "Le Syndicalisme français et les femmes: histoire d'un malentendu," *Aujourd'hui* 66 (March 1984): 44.

10. Adam Smith, *The Wealth of Nations*, 2nd ed. (Oxford: Clarendon Press, 1880), vol. 1, p. 71.

11. Jean-Baptiste Say, *Traité de l'économie politique*, 6th ed., 2 vols. (Paris, 1841), vol. I, p. 324.

12. Eugène Buret, *De la misère des classes laborieuses en France et en Angleterre*, 2 vols. (Paris, 1840), vol. I, p. 287, cited in Therese Moreau, *Le Sang de l'histoire: Michelet, l'histoire, et l'idée de la femme aux XIXe siècle* (Paris, Flammarion, 1982), p. 74.

13. *L'Atelier*, 30 December 1842, p. 31.

14. Sidney Webb, "The Alleged Differences in the Wages Paid to Men and to Women for Similar Work," *Economic Journal* 1 (1891): 657–659.

15. Ivy Pinchbeck, *Women Workers and the Industrial Revolution, 1750–1850* (New York: G. Routledge, 1930; rpt. A. Kelley, 1969), p. 185.

16. Cited in John C. Holley, "The Two Family Economies of Industrialism: Factory Workers in Victorian Scotland," *Journal of Family History* 6 (Spring 1981): 64.

17. Cited in Louise A. Tilly and Joan W. Scott, *Women, Work and Family* (New York: Holt, Rinehart and Winston, 1978; rpt. Methuen, 1987), p. 79.

18. Jill K. Conway, "Politics, Pedagogy, and Gender," in Jill K. Conway, Susan C. Bourque, and Joan W. Scott, eds., *Learning About Women: Gender, Politics, and Power* (Ann Arbor: University of Michigan Press, 1987), p. 140.

19. Samuel Cohn, *The Process of Occupational Sex-Typing: The Feminization of Clerical Labor in Great Britain* (Philadelphia: Temple University Press, 1985).

20. Cited in Susan Bachrach, "Dames Employées: The Feminization of Postal Work in Nineteenth-Century France," *Women and History* 8 (Winter 1983): 33.

21. Ibid., p. 35.

22. Ibid., p. 42.

23. Cited in Jane Lewis, *Women in England, 1870–1950: Sexual Divisions and Social Change* (Sussex: Wheatsheaf Books, 1984), p. 175.

24. Michelle Perrot, "L'Éloge de la ménagère dans le discours des ouvriers français au XIXe siècle," in *Mythes et représentations de la femme au XIXe siècle* (Paris: Champion, 1977), p. 110.

25. Ute Frevert, *Women in German History: From Bourgeois Emancipation to Sexual Liberation,* trans. by Stuart McKinnon-Evans (Oxford: Berg, 1989), p. 99.

26. Ava Baron, "Questions of Gender," p. 164.

27. Cited in Mary Lynn Stewart, *Women, Work and the French State: Labour Protection and Social Patriarchy, 1879–1919* (Montreal: McGill-Queen's University Press, 1989), p. 51.

28. Ibid., p. 175.

29. Ibid., p. 14.

30. Ibid., p. 119.

31. Jeanne Bouvier, *Mes mémoires: ou 59 années d'activité industrielle, sociale et intellectuelle d'une ouvrière* (Paris: L'Action Intellectuelle, 1936).

32. Margaret Lleweleyn Davies, ed., *Life as We Have Known It by Cooperative Working Women* (New York: Norton, 1975).

33. Cited in Stewart, *Women, Work and the French State,* p. 177.

34. Jane Lewis, *Women in England,* p. 146.

Chapter 16. Single Women

Cécile Dauphin

1. Dora Greenwell, "Our Single Women," *North British Review* 26 (February 1862):63.

2. See the bibliography in Martha Vicinus, *Independent Women: Work and Community for Single Women, 1850–1920* (Chicago: University of Chicago Press, 1985), and the special issue on "Spinsters" of the *Journal of Family History* (Winter 1984), Susan Cotts Watkins, ed. Between 1840 and

1847 the painter Richard Redgrave exhibited a series of paintings on the theme of the "redundant woman" at the Royal Academy; this fashionable subject was also treated by George Frederick Watts.

3. W. R. Gregg, "Why Are Women Redundant?" *National Review* 14 (April 1862):436.

4. Emile Levasseur, *La Population française: Histoire de la population avant 1789 et démographie de la France comparée à celle des autres nations au 19e siècle* (Paris: A. Rousseau, 1889–1892), vol. 1, p. 333.

5. Jacques Dupâquier, *La Population française aux 17e et 18e siècles* (Paris: Presses Universitaires de France, 1979), p. 84.

6. Honoré de Balzac, *La Vieille Fille* (1837) (Paris: Albin Michel, 1955), p. 65.

7. *Annales de démographie historique,* 1981, section A: "La Mortalité différentielle des femmes," pp. 23–140.

8. Patrice Bourdelais, "Le Poids démographique des femmes seules en France," in ibid., pp. 215–227.

9. John Hajnal, "European Marriage Patterns in Perspective," in D. V. Glass and D. E. C. Eversley, eds., *Population in History* (London: Arnold, 1965), pp. 101–143.

10. Jack Goody, *The Development of the Family and Marriage in Europe* (New York: Cambridge University Press, 1983).

11. Louis Henry and Jacques Houdaille, "Célibat et âge au mariage aux 18e et 19e siècles en France. I-Célibat définitif. II-Age au premier mariage," *Population* 1 and 2 (1979).

12. Patrice Bourdelais, "Femmes isolées en France, 17e-19e siècles," in Arlette Farge and Christiane Klapisch-Zuber, eds., *Madame ou Mademoiselle? Itinéraires de la solitude féminine, 18e-20e siècles* (Paris: Arthaud-Montalba, 1984), pp. 66–67.

13. M. Anderson, "Marriage Patterns in Victorian Britain: An Analysis Based on Registration District Data for England and Wales 1861," *Journal of Family History* 2 (1976):55–78; John Knodel and Mary Jo Maynes, "Urban and Rural Marriage Patterns in Imperial Germany," ibid., pp. 129–168.

14. Léon Abensour, *La Femme et le féminisme avant la Révolution* (1923), (rpt. Geneva: Slatkine, 1977), p. 206.

15. Knodel and Maynes, "Urban and Rural Marriage Patterns."

16. To North Africa, America, and the Pacific. See Y. Turin, *Femmes et Religieuses au XIXe siècle. Le Féminisme "en religion"* (Paris: Nouvelle Cité, 1989).

17. S. Dryvik, "Remarriage in Norway in the Nineteenth Century," in J. Dupâquier et al., eds., *Marriage and Remarriage in Populations of the Past* (San Diego: Academic Press, 1981), p. 305.

18. *Fraser's Magazine* 66 (1862):594–610.

19. Maurice Garden, "L'Evolution de la population active," in Jacques Dupâquier, ed., *Histoire de la population française* (Paris: Presses Universi-

taires de France, 1988), vol. 3, p. 267.

20. Theresa McBridge, "Social Mobility for the Lower Classes: Domestic Servants in France," *Journal of Social History* (Fall 1974):63–78.

21. Abel Chatelain, "Les Usines internats et les migrations féminines dans la région lyonnaise," *Revue d'histoire économique et sociale* 3 (1970):373–394; Louis Reybaud, *Etudes sur le régime des manufactures, condition matérielle et morale des ouvriers en soie* (Paris: Michel-Lévy Frères, 1859).

22. Françoise Parent, "La Vendeuse de grand magasin," in Klapisch-Zuber and Farge, eds., *Madame ou Mademoiselle?* p. 97.

23. Pierrette Pézerat et Danièle Poublan, "Femmes sans maris, les employées des postes," in ibid., pp. 117–162; Maurizio Gribaudi, "Procès de mobilité et d'intégration. Le monde ouvrier turinois dans le premier demi-siècle," Ph.D. diss., Ecole des Hautes Etudes en Sciences Sociales, 1986.

24. Gro Hagemann, "Class and Gender during Industrialization," in *The Sexual Division of Labour, 19th and 20th Centuries,* Uppsala Papers in Economic History, 7 (1989), pp. 1–29; Ursula D. Nienhaus, "Technological Change, the Welfare State, Gender and Real Women: Female Clerical Workers in the Postal Services in Germany, France and England 1860 to 1945," in ibid., pp. 57–72.

25. *Statistique des familles,* Statistique Générale de la France, 1906.

26. Marlène Cacoualt, "Diplôme et célibat, les femmes professeurs de lycée entre les deux guerres," in Klapisch-Zuber and Farge, *Madame ou Mademoiselle?* p. 177; Françoise Mayeur, *L'Enseignement secondaire des jeunes filles sous la 3e République* (Paris: Fondation Nationale des Sciences Politiques, 1977), p. 256.

27. Claude Langlois, *Le Catholicisme au féminin. Les Congrégations françaises à supérieure générale au 19e siècle* (Paris: Editions du Cerf, 1984); Vicinus, *Independent Women;* Lucia Ferrante et al., eds., *Patronage e reti di relazione nelle storia delle donne* (Turin: Rosenberg and Sellier, 1988).

28. *Les Enseignements pontificaux. Le Problème féminin,* introduction and tables by the monks of Solesmes (Paris: Desclée Brouwer, 1953).

29. Jacques Bertillon, *Etude démographique du divorce et la séparation de corps dans les différents pays de l'Europe* (Paris: G. Masson, 1883).

30. Barbey d'Aurevilly, *Les Bas-Bleus* (Paris: V. Palmé, 1878).

31. V. Chambers-Schiller, *Liberty, a Better Husband: Single Women in America: The Generation of 1780–1840* (New Haven: Yale University Press, 1984).

32. Ibid., p. 10, quoting Louisa May Alcott in 1868: "The loss of liberty, happiness and self-respect is poorly repaid by the barren honor of being called 'Mrs' instead of 'Miss.' Spinsters, she assured her readers, were as a class 'composed of superior women . . . remaining as faithful to and as happy in their choice as married women with husbands and homes'."

33. The expression was actually coined by Shakespeare to ridicule the solitude of women who refused marriage: *A Midsummer Night's Dream* I.i.67.

34. Edith Thomas, *Pauline Roland: Socialisme et féminisme au 19e siècle*

(Paris: Marcel Rivière, 1956). On Nightingale and Pankhurst, see Sheila Jeffreys, *The Spinster and Her Enemies: Feminism and Sexuality, 1880–1930* (London: Pandora, 1985).

35. Carroll Smith-Rosenberg and Esther Newton, "Le Mythe de la lesbienne et la Femme nouvelle," in *Stratégies des femmes* (Paris: Tierce, 1984), pp. 274–311.

36. Gudrun Schwarz, "L'Invention de la lesbienne par les psychiatres allemands," ibid., pp. 312–328.

37. Jean Borie, *Le Célibataire français* (Paris: Le Sagittaire, 1976).

38. Cécile Dauphin, "La Vieille Fille, histoire d'un stéréotype," in Klapisch-Zuber and Farge, *Madame ou Mademoiselle?* pp. 207–231.

39. Yvonne Knibiehler, "Les Médecins et la nature féminine au temps du Code civil," *Annales Economie, Société, Civilisation* 4 (1976), pp. 824–825; Arlette Farge, "Les Temps fragiles de la solitude des femmes à travers le discourse médical du 18e siècle," in Klapisch-Zuber and Farge, *Madame ou Mademoiselle?* pp. 251–263.

40. Serge Moscovici, "L'Individu et ses représentations," *Magazine littéraire* 264 (April 1989):28–31.

41. According to anthropologist Louis Dumont, a holistic society is one that favors the totality of a group over its component parts or members.

The Great Enterprise of Feminism

1. Claude Quiguer, *Femmes et machines de 1900. Lecture d'une obsession Modern Style* (Paris: Klincksieck, 1979).

2. See Stella Georgoudi, "Creating a Myth of Matriarchy," in Pauline Schmitt Pantel, ed., *A History of Women,* vol. 1 (Cambridge, Mass.: Harvard University Press, 1992).

3. Jacques Le Rider, *Le Cas Otto Weininger. Racines de l'antiféminisme et de l'antisémitisme* (Paris: Presses Universitaires de France, 1982).

Chapter 17. Stepping Out

MICHELLE PERROT

1. *La Tribune des Femmes,* second year, quoted in Michèle Riot-Sarcey, "Parcours de femmes à l'époque de l'apprentissage de la démocratie," Ph.D. diss., University of Paris I, 1990.

2. Nancy F. Cott, *The Bonds of Womanhood: "Woman's Sphere" in New England, 1780–1835* (New Haven: Yale University Press, 1977); Bonnie G. Smith, *Ladies of the Leisure Class: The Bourgeoises of Northern France in the Nineteenth Century* (Princeton: Princeton University Press, 1981); Eleni Varikas, "La Révolte des dames. Genèse d'une conscience féministe dans la Grèce du XIXe siècle," Ph.D. diss., University of Paris VII, 1988, to be published in Paris by Klincksieck.

3. B.-C. Pope, Renate Bridenthal, and Claudia Koonz, eds., *Becoming Visible: Women in European History* (Boston: Houghton Mifflin, 1977).

4. Catherine Duprat, "Charité et philanthropie à Paris au XIXe siècle," Ph.D. diss., University of Paris I, 1991.

5. Quoted in Geneviève Fraisse, *Muse de la raison. La Démocratie exclusive et la différence des sexes* (Aix-en-Provence: Alinéa, 1989), p. 36.

6. Ute Frevert, *Women in German History: From Bourgeois Emancipation to Sexual Liberation* (Oxford: Berg, 1989).

7. F. K. Prochaska, *Women and Philanthropy in 19th Century England* (London: Oxford, 1980); Françoise Barret-Ducrocq, "Modalités de reproduction sociale et code de morale sexuelle des classes laborieuses à Londres dans la période victorienne," Ph.D. diss., University of Paris IV, 1987; Carroll Smith-Rosenberg, *Religion and the Rise of the American City* (Ithaca: Cornell University Press, 1971).

8. Rosalind H. Williams, *Dream Worlds: Mass Consumption in Late Nineteenth-Century France* (Berkeley: University of California Press, 1982).

9. Martha Vicinus, *Independent Women: Work and Community for Single Women, 1850–1920* (London: Virago Press, 1985).

10. Sylvie Fayet-Scribe, "Les Associations féminines d'éducation populaire et d'action sociale: De *Rerum Novarum* (1891) au Front Populaire," Ph.D. diss., University of Paris VII, 1988.

11. Marie-Claire Hoock-Demarle, "Bettina Brentano von Arnim ou la mise en oeuvre d'une vie," Ph.D. diss. 1985; M. Perrot, "Flora Tristan enquêtrice," in Stéphane Michaud, ed., *Flora Tristan: Un fabuleux destin* (Dijon: Presses Universitaires, 1985).

12. Marie-Antoinette Perret, "Enquête sur l'enfance 'en danger moral,'" M.A. diss., University of Paris VII, 1989.

13. Yvonne Knibiehler, *Nous les assistantes sociales* (Paris: Aubier-Montaigne, 1981); Yvonne Knibiehler et al., *Cornettes et blouses blanches* (Paris: Hachette, 1984).

14. Duprat, "Charité et philanthropie."

15. Bonnie G. Smith, *Changing Lives: Women in European History since 1700* (Lexington: Heath, 1989), p. 218; Anne Summers, "Pride and Prejudice: Ladies and Nurses in the Crimean War," *History Workshop Journal* 16 (Autumn 1983):33–57; Martha Vicinus and Bea Nergaard, eds., *Ever Yours, Florence Nightingale: Selected Letters* (London: Virago, 1990).

16. Smith, *Ladies.*

17. Quoted by Riot-Sarcey, "Parcours de femmes" (text of 1831).

18. Mary P. Ryan, "The Power of Women's Networks," in Judith L. Newton, Mary P. Ryan, and Judith R. Walkowitz, eds., *Sex and Class in Women's History* (London: Routledge and Kegan Paul, 1985), pp. 167–186.

19. Carroll Smith-Rosenberg, *Disorderly Conduct: Visions of Gender in Victorian America* (Oxford: Oxford University Press, 1985), pp. 176–177.

20. Peter Stearns, "Working-class Women in Britain, 1890–1914," in Martha Vicinus, ed., *Suffer and Be Still: Women in the Victorian Age* (Bloomington: Indiana University Press, 1972), pp. 100–120.

21. Dorothy Thompson, "Women and Nineteenth-Century Radical Politics: A Lost Dimension," in Juliette Mitchell and Ann Oakley, eds., *The*

Rights and Wrongs of Women (New York: Penguin Books, 1976), pp. 112–139.

22. Nancy Tomes, "A Torrent of Abuse: Crimes of Violence Between Working-class Men and Women in London (1840–1875)," *Journal of Social History* 11, 3 (Spring 1978):328–345.

23. Eric Hobsbawm, "Sexe, vêtements et politique," *Actes de la recherche en sciences sociales* 23 (1978).

24. Ludwig-Uhland Institut of the University of Tübingen, *Quand les Allemands apprirent à manifester. Le Phénomène culturel des "manifestations pacifiques de rue" durant les luttes pour le suffrage universel en Prusse,* Catalog of Exposition of May-June 1989 (Paris, 1989).

25. Jean-Marie Flonneau, "Crise de vie chère et mouvement syndical (1900–1914)," *Le Mouvement social* (July-September 1970).

26. Rudolf M. Dekker, "Women in Revolt: Popular Protest and Its Social Basis in Holland in the Seventeenth and Eighteenth Centuries," *Theory and Society,* 16 (1987):337–362; Malcolm I. Thomis and Jennifer Grimmett, *Women in Protest 1800–1850* (London: Croom Helm, 1982); Louise A. Tilly, "Paths of Proletarianization: Organization of Production, Sexual Division of Labor, and Women's Collective Action," *Signs* 7 (1981):401–417; Temma Kaplan, "Female Consciousness and Collective Action: The Case of Barcelona, 1910–1918," *Signs* 7 (Spring 1982):564.

27. Suzannah Barrows, *Distorting Mirrors: Visions of the Crowd in Late Nineteenth-Century France* (New Haven: Yale University Press, 1981).

28. Michelle Perrot, *Les Ouvriers en grève (1871–1900),* vol. 1 (Paris: Mouton, 1974).

29. Claire Auzias and Annick Houel, *La Grève des ovalistes. Lyon, juin-juillet 1869* (Paris: Payot, 1982); Sian F. Reynolds, *Britannica's Typesetters: Women Compositors in Edinburgh* (Edinburgh: Edinburgh University Press, 1989); Françoise Basch, ed., *Theresa Malkiel. Journal d'une gréviste* (Paris: Payot, 1980).

30. Nathalie Chambelland-Liebault, "La Durée et l'aménagement du temps de travail des femmes de 1892 à l'aube des conventions collectives," Ll.D. diss., Nantes, 1989.

31. Letter (XII 1855) quoted in Summers, "Pride and Prejudice," p. 48.

32. Geneviève Fraisse, *Femmes toutes mains. Essai sur le service domestique* (Paris: Editions du Seuil, 1979), pp. 3 ff.

33. Charles Sowerwine, *Les Femmes et le socialisme* (Paris: Presses de la Fondation Nationale des Sciences Politiques, 1978); Marianne Walle, "Contribution à l'histoire des femmes allemandes entre 1848 et 1920, à travers les itinéraires de Louise Otto, Helene Lange, Clara Zetkin et Lily Braun," Ph.D. diss., University of Paris VII, 1989.

34. Jill Liddington, "Women Cotton Workers and the Suffrage Campaign: The Radical Suffragists in Lancashire, 1893–1914," in Sandra Burman, ed., *Fit Work for Women* (London: Croom Held, 1979), pp. 98–112.

35. Reprinted by Denys Cuche and Stéphane Michaud (Paris: L'Harmattan, 1988).

36. Martin Nadaud, *Mémoires de Léonard ancien garçon maçon,* ed. Maurice Agulhon (Paris: Hachette, 1976).

37. Octave Mirbeau, *Le Journal d'une femme de chambre* (Paris, 1900).

38. Leonore Davidoff, "Class and Gender in Victorian England," in *Sex and Class in Women's History* (London: Routledge and Kegan Paul, 1983), pp. 17–71; L. Stanley, ed., *The Diaries of Hannah Cullwick* (New Brunswick: Rutgers University Press, 1984).

39. J. Dupâquier, *Histoire de la population française* (Paris: Colin, 1989), vol. 3, pp. 133 and 184.

40. M. Jeanne Peterson, "The Victorian Governess: Status Incongruence in Family and Society," in Martha Vicinus, ed., *Suffer and Be Still: Women in the Victorian Age* (Bloomington: Indiana University Press, 1972).

41. Elinor Lerner, "Structures familiales, typologie des emplois et soutien aux causes féministes à New York (1915–1917)," in Judith Friedlander, ed., *Stratégies des femmes* (Paris: Tierce, 1984), pp. 424–443. English ed.: *Women in Culture and Politics: A Century of Change* (Bloomington: Indiana University Press, 1986).

42. Carroll Smith-Rosenberg and Esther Newton, "Le Mythe de la lesbienne et la Femme nouvelle," in *Stratégies des femmes,* pp. 274–312; Shari Benstock, *Femmes de la Rive Gauche, Paris, 1900–1914* (Paris: Editions des Femmes, 1987).

43. Quoted in Lerner, "Structures familiales," p. 429.

44. Emma Goldman, *Living My Life* (New York: Knopf, 1932).

45. Yvonne Knibiehler and Régine Goutalier, *La Femme au temps des colonies* (Paris: Stock, 1985); A. J. Hammerton, "Feminism and Female Emigration, 1861–1886," in Martha Vicinus, ed., *A Widening Sphere: Changing Roles of Victorian Women* (Bloomington: Indiana University Press, 1977), pp. 52–72.

46. Odile Krakovitch, *Les Femmes bagnardes* (Paris: Olivier Orban, 1990).

47. Denise Brahimi, *Femmes arabes et soeurs musulmanes* (Paris: Tierce, 1984).

48. Alain Corbin, *Le Territoire du vide. L'Occident et le désir du rivage, 1750–1840* (Paris: Aubier, 1988).

49. Marguerite Yourcenar, *Quoi? L'Eternité* (Paris: Gallimard, 1988), pp. 98 ff.

50. Jacques Rancière, *Courts Voyages au pays du Peuple* (Paris: Editions du Seuil, 1990). Frequently women embodied "the people" for writers.

51. Jeanne Bouvier, *Mes mémoires. Une syndicaliste féministe (1876–1935)* (Paris: Maspero, 1983), pp. 123–136.

52. Marie-Claire Pasquier, "'Mon nom est Persona.' Les femmes et le théâtre," in *Stratégies des femmes,* pp. 259–273.

53. Edmonde Charles-Roux, *Un désir d'Orient. La Jeunesse d'Isabelle Eberhardt* (Paris: Grasset, 1988).

54. Alexandra David-Néel, *Journal de voyage (11 août 1904–26 décembre 1917)* (Paris: Plon, 1975).

55. Eve and Jean Gran-Aymeric, *Jane Dieulafoy, une vie d'homme* (Paris: Perrin, 1990).

56. Ibid., p. 101, letter of February 12, 1912.

57. Compare Edward Shorter, *A History of Women's Bodies* (New York: Basic Books, 1982).

58. Christine Fauré, *Terre, Terreur, Liberté* (Paris: Maspero, 1979); Nancy Green, "L'Emigration comme émancipation: Les Femmes juives d'Europe de l'Est à Paris, 1881–1914," *Pluriel* 27 (1981):51–59.

59. Lee Holcombe, "Victorian Wives and Property: Reform of the Married Women's Property Law, 1857–1882," in Vicinus, ed., *A Widening Sphere,* pp. 3–28.

60. Francis Ronsin, *Le Contrat sentimental. Débat sur le mariage, l'amour, le divorce, de l'Ancien Régime à la Restauration* (Paris: Aubier, 1990); and especially Riot-Sarcey, thesis cited.

61. Fraisse, *Muse de la Raison,* p. 107.

62. Francis Ronsin, "Du divorce et de la séparation de corps en France au XIXe siècle," Ph.D. diss., University of Paris VII, 1988 (unpublished portion).

63. Barbara Welter, "The Feminization of American Religion, 1800–1860," in Mary Hartman and Lois W. Banner, eds., *Clio's Consciousness Raised: New Perspectives on the History of Women* (New York: Harper and Row, 1974), pp. 137–158.

64. Anne-Marie Sohn, "Les Femmes catholiques et la vie publique en France (1900–1930)," in Friedlander, ed., *Stratégies des femmes,* pp. 97–121.

65. Lucia Bergamasco, "Condition féminine et vie spirituelle en Nouvelle-Angleterre au XVIIIe siècle," Ph.D. diss., Paris, Ecole des Hautes Etudes, 1987; and Cott, *The Bonds of Womanhood.*

66. Carroll Smith-Rosenberg, "The Cross and the Pedestal: Women, Antiritualism, and the Emergence of the American Bourgeoisie," in her *Disorderly Conduct: Vision of Gender in Victorian America* (New York: Oxford, 1985), pp. 129–165.

67. Barbara Taylor, *Eve and the New Jerusalem: Socialism and Feminism in the Nineteenth Century* (London: Virago Press, 1983).

68. Jacques Rancière, *Courts Voyages au pays du Peuple* (Paris: Le Seuil, 1991) and *La Nuit des Prolétaires* (Paris: Fayard, 1981); Claire Démar, *Ma loi d'avenir* (1831), reprinted (Paris: Maspero, 1981).

69. Beth Archer Brombert, *Cristina, Portraits of a Princess* (New York: Knopf, 1977).

70. Quoted in Fraisse, *Muse de la Raison,* p. 31.

71. Rudolf M. Dekker and Lotte C. Van de Pol, "Republican Heroines: Cross-Dressing Women in the French Revolutionary Armies," in *History of European Ideas* 10, 3 (1989):353–363.

72. Lucette Czyba, *La Femme dans les romans de Flaubert* (Lyon: Presses Universitaires de Lyon, 1983), pp. 193 and 366.

73. Information provided by Eleni Varikas.

74. Quoted in Brombert, *Cristina,* p. 174.

75. Margaret Ward, *Unmanageable Revolutionaries: Women and Irish Nationalism* (London: Pluto Press, 1983).

Chapter 18. Feminist Scenes

ANNE-MARIE KÄPPELI

1. Geneviève Fraisse, "Droit naturel et question de l'origine dans la pensée féministe au XIXe siècle," in Judith Friedlander, ed., *Stratégies des femmes* (Paris: Tierce, 1984), pp. 375–390.

2. Richard J. Evans, *The Feminists: Women's Emancipation Movement in Europe, America and Australia, 1840–1920* (New York: Barnes and Noble, 1979).

3. Nancy F. Cott, *The Bonds of Womanhood: "Woman's Sphere" in New England, 1780–1835* (New Haven: Yale University Press, 1977).

4. Karin Hausen, "Die Polarisieung der 'Geschlechtscharakter'" in Werner Conze, ed., *Sozialgeschichte der Familie in der Neuzeit Europas* (Stuttgart, 1976), pp. 363–393.

5. Bärbel Clemens, *"Menschenrechte haben kein Geschlecht": Zum Politikverständnis der bürgerlichen Frauenbewegung* (Pfaffenweiler: Centaurus, 1988), p. 71.

6. Diana H. Coole, "J. S. Mill: Political Utilitarian and Feminist," in her *Women in Political Thought* (Sussex, 1988), pp. 133–153.

7. Giovanna Biadne, "Primato della ragione e doppia morale, 'La causa della donna' di Luisa Tosco," *Memoria* 1 (1981):87–93.

8. Karen Offen, "Ernest Legouvé and the Doctrine of 'Equality in Difference' for Women," *Journal of Modern History* 58 (June 1986):452–484.

9. Elke Kleinau, *Die freie Frau: Soziale Utopien des frühen 19. Jhd* (Düsseldorf: Schwann, 1987).

10. Rachele Farina and Maria Teresa Sillano, "Tessitrici dell'Unità escluse dal Risorgimento," in N. Bortolotti, ed., *Esistere come donna* (Milan, 1983).

11. Helena Volet-Jeanneret, "La Femme bourgeoise à Prague: 1860–1895: De la philanthropie à l'émancipation," Ph.D. diss., Faculty of Letters, University of Lausanne, 1987, p. 92.

12. Tineke de Bie and Wantje Fritschy, "De 'wereld' van Reveilvrouwen, hun liefdadige activiteiten en het outstaan van het feminisme in Nederland," *De eerste feministische golf* (1985), pp. 30–58.

13. Herrad-Ulrike Bussemer, *Frauenemanzipation und Bildungsbürgertum, Sozialgeschichte der Frauenbewegung in der Reichsgründungszeit* (Weinheim: Beltz, 1985), p. 81.

14. Frances Power Cobbe (1869), in *The History of Women Suffrage II,* quoted by Barbara Verena Schnetzler, *Die frühe amerikanische Frauenbewegung und ihre Kontakte mit Europa (1836–1869)* (Berne: Lang, 1971), p. 113.

15. Laure Adler, *A l'aube du féminisme, les premières journalistes (1830–1850)* (Paris: Payot, 1979); "Les Femmes et la presse, France XVIIIe-XXe siècles," *Pénélope* 1 (June 1979); *Séverine, Choix de papiers,* annotated by

Evelyne Le Garrec (Paris: Tierce, 1982); Irène Jami, "*La Fronde,* quotidien féministe et son rôle dans la défense des femmes salariées," M.A. diss., University of Paris I, 1981.

16. Simone Schürch, "Les Périodiques féministes. Essai historique et bibliographique" (Geneva: Ecole de Bibliothécaire, 1942), p. 23.

17. Fritz Staude, "Die Rolle der 'Gleichheit' im Kampf Clara Zetkins für die Emanzipation der Frau," *Beiträge zur Geschichte der Arbeiterbewegung* 16 (1974):427.

18. Michelle Perrot, "Naissance du féminisme en France," *Le Féminisme et ses enjeux* (Paris: FEN-Edilig, 1988), p. 41.

19. Franca Alloatti and Mirella Mingardo, "'L'Italia Femminile.' Il florire della stampa delle donne tra Ottocento e Novecento," in Bortolotti, ed., *Esistere,* pp. 153–158; Maria Pia Bigaran, "Mutamenti dell'emancipazionismo all vigilia della grande guerra—I periodici femministi italiani del primo novecento," *Memoria* 4 (1982):125–132.

20. Elizabeth Cady Stanton, *Eighty Years and More* (New York, 1898), pp. 165–166, quoted in Eleanor Flexner, *Century of Struggle: The Woman's Rights Movement in the United States* (Cambridge, Mass.: Harvard University Press, 1959), p. 89.

21. Anne-Marie Käppeli, "Le Féminisme protestant de Suisse romande à la fin du XIXe et au début du XXe siècle," Ph.D. diss., University of Paris VII, 1987, p. 281.

22. J. Moszczenska, "Die Geschichte der Frauenbewegung in Polen," in Helene Lange and Gertrud Bäumer, eds., *Handbuch der Frauenbewegung,* pt. 1 (Berlin: Moeser, 1901), pp. 350–360.

23. Margaret Forster, *Significant Sisters: The Grassroots of Active Feminism, 1839–1939* (New York: Penguin Books, 1984), p. 255.

24. Laurence Klejman and Florence Rochefort, "Les Associations féministes en France de 1871 à 1914," *Pénélope* 11 (Autumn 1984):147–153.

25. Bussemer, *Frauenemanzipation,* p. 94.

26. Ute Frevert, *Frauen-Geschichte: Zwischen bürgerlicher Verbesserung und neuer Weiblichkeit* (Frankfurt: Suhrkamp, 1986), p. 110.

27. Beatrix Mesmer, *Ausgeklammert—Eingeklammert, Frauen und Frauenorganisationen in der Schweiz des 19. Jhd.* (Basel: Helbling and Lichtenhahn, 1988), p. 150.

28. Evans, *The Feminists.*

29. Herrad Schenk, *Die feministische Herausforderung, 150 Jahre Frauenbewegung in Deutschland* (Munich, 1988), p. 52.

30. Richard J. Evans, "Appendix: International Feminist Movements," in Evans, *The Feminists,* p. 52.

31. Franca P. Bortolotti, *La Donna, la pace, l'Europa, l'Associazione internationale delle donne dalle origini all prima guerra mondiale* (Milan: Franco Angeli, 1985), p. 39.

32. Käppeli, "Le Féminisme protestant de Suisse romande."

33. Marie-Hélène Lefaucheux, *Women in a Changing World* (London, 1966).

34. Evans, *The Feminists,* p. 252.

35. Gisela Brinker-Gabler, "Einleitung," in Gisela Brinker-Gabler, ed., *Frauen gegen den Krieg* (Frankfurt: Fischer, 1980), pp. 19–20.

36. Janet E. Rasmussen, "Sisters across the Sea: Early Norwegian Feminists and Their American Connections," *Women's Studies International Forum* 5, 6 (1982):647–654.

37. Volet-Jeanneret, "La Femme bourgeoise à Prague," p. 244.

38. M. Bessmertny, "Die Geschichte der Frauenbewegung in Russland," in Lange and Bäumer, eds., *Handbuch der Frauenbewegung* (1895), p. 345.

39. Ute Gerhard, "Bis an die Wurzeln des Uebels," *Feministische Studien* 3, 1 (May 1984):77.

40. Anita Augspurg, "Gebt acht, solange noch Zeit ist!" in *Die Frauenbewegung,* p. 4.

41. Maria Pia Bigaran, "Progetti e dibattiti parlamentari sul suffragio femminile: da Peruzzia Giolitti," *Rivista di Storia Contemporanea* 1(1985):50–82.

42. Ellen Carol Du Bois, ed., *Elizabeth Cady Stanton, Susan B. Anthony, Correspondence, Writings, Speeches* (New York: Schocken, 1981), p. 193.

43. Ilse Brehmer et al., *Frauen in der Geschichte,* IV, "Wissen heisst leben" (Düsseldorf: Schwann, 1983).

44. Philippe Levine, "Education: The First Step," in Philippe Levine, *Victorian Feminism 1850–1900* (London: Hutchinson, 1987), pp. 26–56.

45. Sibilla Aleramo, *La donna e il femminismo* (Rome: Riuniti, 1978), p. 26.

46. Madeleine Pelletier, *L'Education féministe des filles et autres textes* (Paris: Syros, 1978).

47. Laurence Klejman and Florence Rochefort, "La Province à l'heure du féminisme," in Klejman and Rochefort, eds., *L'Egalité en marche: Le féminisme sous la troisième République* (Paris: Presses de la Fondation Nationale des Sciences Politiques et des Femmes, 1989), pp. 175–182.

48. Susan Groag Bell and Karen M. Offen, *Women, the Family, and Freedom,* vols. 1 and 2 (Stanford: Stanford University Press, 1983).

49. Kleinau, *Die freie Frau.*

50. Klejman and Rochefort, *L'Egalité,* p. 314.

51. Judith R. Walkowitz, *Prostitution and Victorian Society: Women, Class, and the State* (Cambridge: Cambridge University Press, 1980).

52. Sheila Rowbotham, *Hidden from History* (London: Pluto Press, 1980).

53. Wantje Fritschy, Floor Van Gelder, and Ger Harmsen, "Niederlande," in Ernest Bornemann, ed., *Arbeiterbewegung und Feminismus, Berichte aus vierzehn Ländern* (Frankfurt: Ullstein, 1981), pp. 132–133.

54. Klejman and Rochefort, *L'Egalité,* p. 327.

55. Ursula Gaillard and Annik Mahaim, *Retards de règles* (Lausanne, 1983).

56. Forster, *Significant Sisters,* p. 241.

57. Sheila Jeffreys, *The Spinster and Her Enemies: Feminism and Sexuality, 1880–1930* (London: Pandora, 1985), p. 102.

58. Ilse Kokula, *Weibliche Homosexualität um 1900 in zeitgenössischen Dokumenten* (Munich: Frauenoffensive, 1981), p. 42.

59. Carin Schnitger, "'Ijdelheid hoeft geen ondeugd te zijn.' De Vereeniging voor Verbetering van Vrouwenkleeding," in *De eerste feministische golf*, pp. 163–185.

60. Florence Nightingale, *Suggestions for Thought to Searchers after Religious Truth*, quoted in Ray Strachey, *The Cause* (London: Virago, 1979), p. 27; Martha Vicinus and Bea Nergaard, *Ever Yours, Florence Nightingale: Selected Letters* (London: Virago, 1989).

61. Käppeli, "Le Féminisme protestant de Suisse romande," p. 225.

62. Françoise Ducrocq, "Les Associations philanthropiques en Grande-Bretagne au XIXe siècle: Un facteur d'émancipation pour les femmes de la bourgeoisie?" *Pénélope* 11 (Autumn 1984):71–77.

63. Bussemer, *Frauenemanzipation*, p. 246.

64. Barbara Brick, "Die Mütter der Nation: Zu Helene Lange Begründung einer 'weiblichen Kultur,'" in Brehmer et al., *Frauen in der Geschichte*, pp. 99–132; Marianne Ulmi, *Frauenfragen-Männergedanken. Zu Georg Simmels Philosophie und Soziologie der Geschlechter* (Zürich: efef-Verlag, 1989); Suzanne Vromen, "Georg Simmel and the Cultural Dilemma of Women," *History of European Ideas* 8, 4 and 5 (1987):563–579.

65. Ulrike Hass, "Zum Verhältnis von Konservatismus, Mütterlichkeit und dem Modell der neuen Frau," in Barbara Schaeffer-Hegel and Barbara Wartmann, eds., *Mythos Frau* (Berlin: Publica, 1984), pp. 81–87.

66. Kleinau, *Die freie Frau*, p. 50.

67. Käppeli, "Le Féminisme protestant de Suisse romande," p. 289.

68. Ann Tylor Allen, "Mothers of the New Generation: Adele Schreiber, Helene Stöcker, and the Evolution of a German Idea of Motherhood, 1900–1914," *Signs* 3, 10 (1985):418–438.

69. Elisabeth Joris and Heidi Witzig, eds., *Frauengeschichte(n)* (Zürich: Limmat-Verlag, 1986), pp. 189–190.

70. Mirjam Elias, *Drie Cent in het urt* (Amsterdam: FNV Secretariaat, 1984).

71. Lily Braun, *Die Frauenfrage. Ihre geschichtliche Entwicklung und ihre wirtschaftliche Seite* (Leipzig, 1901), p. 278.

72. Volet-Jeanneret, "La Femme bourgeoise à Prague," p. 167.

73. William Leach, *True Love and Perfect Union: The Feminist Reform of Sex and Society* (New York: Basic Books, 1980), p. 9.

74. Estelle Freedman, "Separation as Strategy: Female Institution Building and American Feminism 1870–1930," *Feminist Studies* 5, 1 (Spring 1979):524.

75. Evans, *The Feminists*, p. 189.

76. Klejman and Rochefort, *L'Egalité*, p. 256.

77. Evans, *The Feminists*, p. 194.

78. Bussemer, *Frauenemanzipation*, p. 87.

79. Fritschy et al., "Niederlande," in Bornemann, ed., *Arbeiterbewegung und Feminismus*, p. 129.

80. Klejman and Rochefort, *L'Egalité*, p. 61.

81. Coole, *Women in Political Thought,* p. 149.

82. Evans, *The Feminists,* pp. 73 and 79.

83. Marianne Hainisch, "Die Geschichte der Frauenbewegung in Oesterreich," in Lange and Bäumer, *Handbuch der Frauenbewegung,* pp. 170–171.

84. Inge de Wilde, "The Importance of Hélène Mercier for the Women's Movement," in *De eerste feministische golf,* p. 204.

85. Richard Stites, *The Women's Liberation Movement in Russia: Feminism, Nihilism and Bolshevism 1860–1930* (Princeton: Princeton University Press, 1977), p. 198.

86. Donald Meyer, *Sex and Power: The Rise of Women in America, Russia, Sweden, Italy* (Middletown: Wesleyan University Press, 1987), p. 124.

87. Fritschy et al., "Niederlande," p. 132.

88. Marilyn J. Boxer and Jean H. Quataert, eds., *Socialist Women: European Socialist Feminism in the 19th and Early 20th Century* (New York: Elsevier, 1978), p. 159.

89. Ibid., p. 175.

90. Jean H. Quataert, *Reluctant Feminists in German Social Democracy, 1885–1917* (Princeton: Princeton University Press, 1979).

91. Herta Firnberg, "Oesterreich," in Bornemann, *Arbeiterbewegung und Feminismus,* p. 83.

92. Ray Strachey, *The Cause* (London: Virago, 1979), p. 288.

93. Sigbert Kluwe, *Weibliche Radikalität* (Frankfurt: Campus, 1979), p. 41.

94. *The Living of Charlotte Perkins Gilman: An Autobiography* (1935), reprinted (New York: Harper, 1975), p. 235.

95. Marie-Jo Dhavernas, "Anarchisme et féminisme à la Belle Epoque," *La Revue d'en face* 13 (Winter 1983):74.

96. Claire Auzias-Gelineau et al., eds., "Preface," to Emma Goldman, *La Tragédie de l'émancipation féminine* (Paris: Syros, 1978), p. 31.

97. Monica Studer, "Schweiz," in Bornemann, ed., *Arbeiterbewegung und Feminismus,* p. 62.

98. Klejman and Rochefort, *L'Egalité,* p. 245.

99. Walter Thönnessen, *Frauenemanzipation: Politik und Literatur der deutschen Sozialdemokratie zur Frauenbewegung 1863–1933* (Frankfurt, 1969).

100. Evans, *The Feminists,* pp. 175–176.

101. Susanna Woodtli, *Du féminisme à l'égalité politique—un siècle de luttes en Suisse 1868–1971* (Lausanne: Payot, 1977), p. 53.

102. Meyer, *Sex and Power,* p. 176.

103. Nancy Fix Anderson, *Women Against Women in Victorian England: A Life of Eliza Lynn Linton* (Bloomington: Indiana University Press, 1986).

104. Gaby Weiner, "Harriet Martineau: A Reassessment," in Dale Spender, *Feminist Theorists* (London: Women's Press, 1983).

105. Meta von Salis, "The Position of Women in Europe," *The Postgraduate and Wooster Quarterly* 2, 1 (October 1887):39; Doris Stump, *Sie töten uns—nicht unser Ideen, Meta von Salis-Marschlins* (Thalwil: paeda media, 1986).

106. Gisela Brinker-Gabler, *Bertha von Suttner* (Frankfurt: Fischer, 1982), pp. 11–12.

107. Fia Dieteren, "Mina Kruseman and Her Circle, a Network of Dutch Women Artists in the Nineteenth Century," in *Language, Culture and Female Future*. Workshop, Utrecht, April 1986, pp. 11–18.

108. Liz Stanley, "Olive Schreiner: New Women, Free Women, All Women (1855–1920)," in Spender, ed., *Feminist Theorists*, pp. 229–243.

109. Renate Duelli, "Hedwig Dohm: Passionate Theorist," in ibid., pp. 165–183.

110. Spender, *Feminist Theorists*, p. 198.

111. Marie Luise Bach, *Gertrud Bäumer* (Weinheim: Beltz, 1988).

112. Woodtli, *Du féminisme à l'égalité politique*, pp. 76–78.

113. Spender, *Feminist Theorists*, pp. 397–408.

114. Käppeli, "Le Féminisme protestant de Suisse romande," pp. 184–248 and 350–359.

Chapter 19. The New Eve and the Old Adam

ANNELISE MAUGUE

1. Anatole France in *L'Estafette*, July 24, 1899.

2. Emile Zola, *Travail* (1901) (Paris: Fasquelle, 1906), vol. 2, p. 487.

3. *La Française* 3 (November 1906).

4. *La Française* 4 (November 1906).

5. *La Française* 5 (November 1906).

6. Quoted by Barbey d'Aurevilly, *Les Bas-Bleus* (Brussels: Victor Palmé, 1878), p. 70.

7. Séverine (pseud.), in *La Chevauchée* 2 (October 15, 1900).

8. Quoted in Carol Gilligan, *In a Different Voice* (Cambridge, Mass.: Harvard University Press, 1982), p. 129.

9. Quoted in Mrs. Gaskell, letter of March 16, 1837.

10. Eugénie de Guérin, *Journal*, March 22, 1836, pp. 113–114.

11. George Sand, *Histoire de ma vie*, in *Oeuvres autobiographiques* (Paris: Pléiade, 1970–71), vol. 1.

12. Théodore Joran, *Le Mensonge du féminisme* (Paris: Jouve, 1905), p. 184.

13. Alexandre Dumas fils, *L'Homme-Femme* (Paris: Lévy Frères, 1872), p. 174.

14. August Strindberg, *The Creditors*, 1888.

15. Marcel Prévost, *Les Demi-Vierges* (Paris: Lemerre, 1894), p. 87.

16. Emile Faguet, *Le Féminisme* (Paris: Boivin, 1906), p. 16.

17. Musil, *The Man Without Qualities*.

18. P.-J. Proudhon, *La Pornocratie* (Paris: Lacroix, 1875), p. 29.

19. Barbey d'Aurevilly, *Les Bas-Bleus*, preface.

20. Barrès, *Les Déracinés*, p. 86.

21. Emile Zola, *Fécondité* (Paris: Fasquelle, 1906), p. 39.

22. Otto Gross, letter to Frieda, quoted in Martin Green, *The Von Richthofen Sisters* (New York: Basic Books, 1974).

23. Faguet, *Le Féminisme,* p. 11.

24. Honoré de Balzac, letter to Mme Hanska, *Correspondance* (Paris, 1967–1970), vol. 1, p. 584.

25. Gustave Flaubert, *Correspondance,* vol. 15, pp. 181–182.

26. Henry James, *Notes on Novelists* (New York, 1914), pp. 220–221.

27. Barbey d'Aurevilly, *Les Diaboliques* (1874), in *Oeuvres complètes* (Geneva: Slatkine Reprints, 1979), vol. 2, p. 176.

28. George Orwell, *Collected Essays, Journalism and Letters* (New York: Penguin Books, 1970), vol. 1, p. 222.

29. Barbey d'Aurevilly, *Les Bas-Bleus,* p. 82.

30. Sand, *Oeuvres autobiographiques,* vol. 2, pp. 987–988 (entry for June 13, 1837).

31. Sand, *Correspondance,* vol. 3, pp. 18–19.

32. Daniel Stern, *Lettres républicaines* (1848), quoted by B. Slama in *Misérable et glorieuse, la femme du XIXe siècle* (Paris: Fayard, 1980), p. 239.

Lou Andreas-Salomé

GENEVIÈVE FRAISSE AND MICHELLE PERROT

1. This article was published in 1899 in *Neue deutsche Rundschau;* it was reprinted in *Die Erotik* (Munich: Patthes und Seitz Verlag, 1979). French translation by Henri Plard, published in *Eros* (Paris: Minuit, 1984), pp. 27–30. Here retranslated from the French.

Bibliography

Abel, Elizabeth, ed. *Writing and Sexual Difference.* Chicago: University of Chicago Press, 1982.

Accati, Luisa. "La politica dei sentimenti: L'Immacolata Concezione fra 600 e 700." *Atti del Primer Coloqui di Historia de la Dona.* Barcelona, 1986 (forthcoming).

Addis Saba, Marini, et al. *Storia delle donne, una scienza possibile.* Rome: Edizione Felina Libri, 1986.

Adler, Laure. *A l'aube du féminisme: Les premières journalistes (1830–1850).* Paris: Payot, 1979.

——— *Secrets d'alcôve: Histoire du couple de 1830 à 1930.* Paris: Hachette, 1983.

——— *La Vie quotidienne dans les maisons closes, 1830–1930.* Paris: Hachette, 1990.

Adler, Polly. *A House Is Not a Home.* New York: Rinehart, 1953.

Agulhon, Maurice. *Marianne au combat: L'imagerie et la symbolique républicaines de 1789 à 1880.* Paris: Flammarion, 1979.

——— *Marianne au pouvoir: L'imagerie et la symbolique républicaines de 1880 à 1914.* Paris: Flammarion, 1989.

Aimer en France, 1760–1860. *Actes du Colloque International de Clermont-Ferrand,* 2 vols., collected and presented by Paul Villaneix and Jean Ehrard. Faculté des Lettres et Sciences Humaines de Clermont-Ferrand, 1980.

Albistur, Maïté, and Daniel Armogathe. *Histoire du féminisme français.* Paris: Editions des Femmes, 1977.

Allen, Ann T. "Spiritual Motherhood: German Feminists and the Kindergarten Movement, 1848–1911," in *History of Education Quarterly* 22, 3 (Autumn 1982).

Amoros, Celia. *Hacia una crítica de la razón patriarcal.* Madrid, 1985.

Amsden, Alice H., ed. *The Economics of Women.* New York: Penguin Books, 1980.

Anderson, Gregory, ed. *The White-Blouse Revolution: Female Office Workers since 1870.* Manchester: Manchester University Press, 1988.

Anderson, Michael. *Family Structure in Nineteenth-Century Lancashire.* Cambridge: Cambridge University Press, 1971.

Annales de démographie historique, "La Femme seule," section C (1981): 207–317.

Antin, Mary. *The Promised Land,* 2nd ed. Princeton: Princeton University Press, 1969.

Applewhite, Harriet B., and Darline G. Levy, eds. *Women and Politics in the Age of the Democratic Revolution.* Ann Arbor: University of Michigan Press, 1990.

Ardener, Shirley, ed. *Women and Space.* London: Croom Helm, 1981.

Arendt, Hannah. *Rahel Varnhagen: La vie d'une juive allemande à l'époque du romantisme.* Paris: Tierce, 1986; English rev. ed.: *Rahel Varnhagen.* New York: Harcourt Brace Jovanovich, 1974.

Ariès, Philippe, and Georges Duby, eds. *A History of Private Life,* vol. 4: *From the Fires of Revolution to the Great War,* Michelle Perrot, ed. Trans. Arthur Goldhammer. Cambridge, Mass.: Harvard University Press, 1990.

Arnaud, Pierre, dir. *Les Athlètes de la République: Gymnastique, sport, et idéologie républicaine, 1870–1914.* Bibliothèque historique. Toulouse: Privat, 1987.

Arnaud-Duc, Nicole. *Droit, mentalités et changement social en Provence occidentale: Une étude des stratégies et de la pratique notariale en matière de régime matrimonial.* Aix-en-Provence: Edisud, 1985.

Arnold, Odile. *Le Corps et l'âme: La vie des religieuses au XIXè siècle.* Paris: Le Seuil, 1984.

Ascoli, Giulietta, et al., eds. *La questione femminile in Italia dal '900 ad oggi.* Milan: Franco Angeli, 1977.

Asher, Carol, Louise De Salvo, and Sara Ruddick. *Between Women: Biographers, Novelists, Critics, Teachers, and Artists Write about Their Work on Women.* Boston: Beacon Press, 1984.

Association internationale pour l'histoire de l'education. Service d'histoire de l'education, Paris. *L'Offre d'école.* Paris: Publications de la Sorbonne, INRP, 1983.

Atti del Primer Coloqui di Historia de la Dona. Barcelona, 1986 (forthcoming).

Audoux, Marguerite. *Marie-Claire,* Les Cahiers rouges. Paris: Bernard Grasset, 1910.

——— *L'Atelier de Marie-Claire,* Les Cahiers rouges. Paris: Bernard Grasset, 1920.

Bacci, Massimo Levi. *A History of Italian Fertility during the Last Two Centuries.* Princeton: Princeton University Press, 1977.

Badinter, Elisabeth. *L'Un et l'autre sexe.* Paris: Odile Jacob.

Baldassari, Aldo. *La capacità patrimoniale della donna maritata nel diritto civile dei principali Stati d'Europa, e i conflitti di leggi.* Rome, 1910.

Ballestrero, Maria Vittoria. "Sorelle di fatiche e di dolori" and "Madri di pioneri e di soldati," in Giovanni Tarello, *Studi materiali per una storia della cultura giuridica,* vol. 7. Bologna: Il Mulino, 1977.

Banks, Olive. *Becoming a Feminist: The Social Origins of "First Wave" Feminism.* Brighton: Wheatsheaf Books, 1986.

Banner, Lois W., and Mary Hartman, eds. *Clio's Consciousness Raised: New Perspectives on the History of Women.* New York: Harper and Row, 1974.

Baron, Ava. "Women and the Making of the American Working Class: A Study of the Proletarianization of Printers," *The Review of Radical Political Economics* 14 (1982): 23–42.

Barret-Ducrocq, Françoise. *L'Amour sous Victoria.* Paris: Plon, 1989.

——— "Modalités de reproduction sociale et code de morale sexuelle des classes laborieuses à Londres dans la période victorienne." Thesis, Paris IV, 1987. Published in part under the title *Pauvreté, charité et morale à Londres au XIXè siècle: Une sainte violence.* Paris: Presses Universitaires de France, 1991.

Barrett, Michèle, and Mary McIntosh. "The 'Family Wage': Some Problems for Socialists and Feminists," *Capital and Class* 11 (1980): 51–72.

Barry, Joseph. *Infamous Woman: The Life of George Sand.* New York: Doubleday, 1977.

Basch, Françoise. *Les Femmes victoriennes, roman et société, 1837–1867.* Collection "Le Regard de l'histoire." Paris: Payot, 1979.

——— *Rebelles américaines au XIXè siècle.* Paris: Méridiens-Klincksieck, 1990.

——— *Theresa Malkiel: Journal d'une gréviste.* Paris: Payot, 1980.

Basch, Norma. *In the Eyes of the Law: Women, Marriage, and Property in Nineteenth-Century New York.* Ithaca: Cornell University Press, 1982.

Bashkirtseff, Marie. *Journal.* Paris: Mazarine, 1887.

Baubérot, Jean. *Un Christianisme profane?* Paris: Presses Universitaires de France, 1978.

——— *Le Retour des huguenots: La vitalité protestante XIXe-XXème s.* Paris and Geneva: Cerf-Labor and Fides, 1985.

Bauer, Karin. *Clara Zetkin und die Proletarische Frauenbewegung.* Berlin: Oberbaum, 1978.

Baum, Charlotte, Paula Hyman, and Sonya Michel. *The Jewish Woman in America.* New York: New American Library, 1977.

Baxandall, Roselyn. "Women in American Trade Unions: An Historical Analysis," in Judith Mitchell and Ann Oakley, eds., *The Rights and Wrongs of Women,* pp. 256–270. New York: Penguin Books, 1976.

Beck, C. H., and Arthur E. Imhof. *Der Mensch und sein Körper von der Antike bis Heute,* ed. Arthur E. Imhof. Munich: Verlag C. H. Beck, 1983.

Belle, Susan, and Karen M. Offen, eds. *Women, the Family, and Freedom,* 2 vols. Stanford: Stanford University Press, 1983.

Bennent, Heidemarie. *Galanterie und Verachtung: Eine philosophiegeschichtliche Untersuchung zur Stellung der Frau in Gesellschaft und Kultur.* Frankfurt, 1985.

Benstock, Shari. *Femmes de la rive gauche: Paris, 1900–1914.* Paris: Editions des Femmes, 1987.

Berding, Helmut, Etienne François, and Hans Peter Ullmann. *Deutschland und Frankreich im Zeitalter der Französischen Revolution.* Frankfurt: Suhrkamp, 1989.

Berg, Maxime. "Women's Work, Mechanization, and the Early Phases of Industrialization in England," in Patrick Joyce, ed., *The Historical Meanings of Work,* pp. 64–98. Cambridge: Cambridge University Press, 1987.

Berkeley, Ellen Perry, ed. *Architecture: A Place for Women.* Washington: Smithsonian Institution Press, 1989.

Berrol, Selma. "Class or Ethnicity: The Americanized German-Jewish Woman and Her Middle-Class Sisters in 1895," *Jewish Social Studies* 47, 1 (Winter 1985).

——— "Education and Economic Mobility: The Jewish Experience in New York City, 1880–1920," *American Jewish Historical Quarterly* 65, 3 (March 1976): 257–271.

Bertin, Célia. *La Femme à Vienne au temps de Freud.* Paris: Stock, 1989.

Besombes, Amédée. "Condition juridique de la femme mariée espagnole." Law thesis. Toulouse, 1927.

Biale, Rachel. *Women and Jewish Law: An Exploration of Women's Issues in Halakhic Sources.* New York: Schocken Books, 1984.

Bidelman, Patrick Kay. *Pariahs Stand Up! The Founding of the Liberal Feminist Movement in France (1858–1889).* Westport, Conn.: Greenwood Press, 1982.

Bigot, François. "Les Enjeux de l'assistance à l'enfance." Sociology thesis, 2 vols., Université de Tours, 1988.

Birkett, Dea. *Spinsters Abroad: Victorian Lady Explorers.* Oxford: Basil Blackwell, 1989.

Black, Clementina, ed. *Married Women's Work.* London: G. Bell and Sons, 1915.

Blackburn, Helen, and Nora Vynne. *Women under the Factory Act.* London: Williams and Norgate, 1903.

Blanc, Olivier. *Olympe de Gouges.* Paris: Syros, 1989.

Blewett, Mary H. *Men, Women, and Work: Class, Gender, and Protest in the New England Shoe Industry, 1780–1910.* Urbana: University of Illinois Press, 1988.

Blom, Ida. *Den haarde Dyst: Birth and Birth Help in Norway since 1800.* Oslo: Cappelen, 1988.

——— "'Real Excellent Men Do Not Grow on Trees': Breadwinning and Structures of Authority in Bourgeois Marriage around the Turn of the Century," *Deutsch-Norwegischen Historikertreffen* (May 28–31, 1987).

Blunden, Katherine. *Le Travail et la vertu. Femmes au foyer: Une mystification de la Révolution industrielle.* Paris: Payot, 1982.

Boesch Gajano, Sofia, and Lucia Sebastiani. *Culto dei santi: Istituzioni e classi sociali in étà preindustriale.* Aquila and Rome: Japadre Editore, 1984.

Bois, Jean-Pierre. *Les Vieux: De Montaigne aux premiers retraités.* Paris: Fayard, 1989.

Bonnefoy, Yves. *La Vérité de la parole*. Paris: Mercure de France, 1988.
Bonnet, Marie-Jo. *Un Choix sans équivoque: Recherches historiques sur les relations amoureuses entre les femmes, XVIè-XXè siècles*. Paris: Denoël-Gonthier, 1981.
Bordeaux, Michèle. "Droit et femmes seules: Les pièges de la discrimination," in Arlette Farge and Christiane Klapisch-Zuber, *Madame ou Mademoiselle? Itinéraires de la solitude féminine, XVIIIè-XXè siècles*, pp. 19–57. Paris: Montalba, 1984.
Bordeaux, Michèle, Bernard Hazo, and Soizic Lorvellec. *Qualifié viol*. Collection "Déviance et société." Paris: Méridiens Klincksieck, 1990.
Borie, Jean. *Un Siècle démodé*. Paris: Payot, 1989.
——— *Le Tyran timide: Le naturalisme de la femme au XIXè siècle*. Paris: Klincksieck, 1973.
Bornemann, Ernest, ed. *Arbeiterbewegung und Feminismus: Berichte aus vierzehn Ländern*. Frankfurt: Ullstein, 1982.
Bortolotti, Franca P. *La donna, la pace, l'Europa: L'associazione internationale delle donne dalle origini alla prima guerra mondiale*. Milan: Franco Angeli, 1985.
——— *Alle origini del movimento femminile in Italia, 1848–1892*. Rome: Einaudi, 1963.
Boston, Sarah. *Women Workers and the Trade Unions*. London: Lawrence and Wishart, 1987.
Bourgade, Germaine. *Contribution à l'étude d'une histoire de l'éducation féminine à Toulouse de 1830 à 1914*. Toulouse: Association des Publications de l'Université de Toulouse le Mirail, 1980.
Bouvier, Jeanne. *Histoires des dames employées dans les postes, télégraphes et téléphones de 1714 à 1929*. Paris: Presses Universitaires de France, 1930.
Bovenschen, Sylvia. *Die imaginierte Weiblichkeit: Exemplarische Untersuchungen zu Kulturgeschichtlichen und literarischen Präsentationsformen des Weiblichen*. Frankfurt: Suhrkamp, 1979.
Bowlby, Rachel. *Just Looking: Consumer Culture in Dreiser, Gissing, Zola*. London: Methuen, 1985.
Boxer, Marilyn J., and Jean H. Quataert, eds. *Socialist Women: European Socialist Feminism in the Nineteenth and Early Twentieth Century*. New York: Elsevier, 1978.
Boyd, L. A., and R. D. Brackenridge. *Presbyterian Women in America*. Westport, Conn.: Greenwood Press, 1983.
Branca, Patricia. *Silent Sisterhood: Middle-Class Women in the Victorian Home*. London: Croom Helm, 1975.
Brehmer, Ilse, et al., eds. *Frauen in der Geschichte*, vol. IV: *Wissen heisst leben*. Düsseldorf: Schwann, 1983.
Bridel, Louis. *Los derechos de la mujer y el matrimonio*. Madrid, 1894.
——— *La Femme et le droit*. Lausanne, 1884.
Bridenthal, Reina, and Claudia Koonz, eds. *Becoming Visible: Women in European History*. Boston: Houghton Mifflin, 1987.

Brinker-Gabler, Gisela. *Deutsche Literatur von Frauen,* 2 vols. Munich: Beck, 1988.

Bristow, Edward J. *Prostitution and Prejudice: The Jewish Fight against White Slavery, 1870–1939.* New York: Schocken Books, 1983.

Brive, Marie-France, ed. *Les Femmes et la Révolution française,* 3 vols. *Actes du Colloque de Toulouse,* April 12–14, 1989. Université Internationale de Toulouse le Mirail, 1989–1992.

Brombert, Beth A. *Cristina: Portrait of a Princess.* New York: Alfred A. Knopf, 1977; French ed.: *La Princesse Belgiojoso ou l'engagement romantique.* Paris: Albin Michel, 1989.

Brumberg, Joan J. *Fasting Girls: The Emergence of Anorexia Nervosa as a Modern Disease.* Cambridge, Mass.: Harvard University Press, 1988.

Brumberg, Stephen E. "Going to America, Going to School: The Jewish Immigrant Public School Encounter in Turn-of-the-Century New York City," *American Jewish Archives* 36, 2 (November 1984): 86–135.

Buhle, Mari Jo. *Women and American Socialism, 1870–1920.* Urbana: University of Illinois Press, 1981.

Burguière, André, Christiane Klapisch-Zuber, Martine Segalen, and Françoise Zonabend, eds. *Histoire de la famille,* vol. 2: *Le Choc des modernités.* Paris: Armand Colin, 1986.

Burman, Sandra, ed. *Fit Work for Women.* London: Croom Helm, 1979.

Bussemer, Herrad-Ulrike. *Frauenemanzipation und Bildungsbürgertum: Sozialgeschichte der Frauenbewegung in der Reichsgründungsszeit.* Weinheim: Beltz, 1985.

Buttafuoco, Annamarita. *Le mariuccine: Storia di un' istituzione laica. L'Asilo Mariuccia.* Milan: Franco Angeli, 1985.

Cantor, Aviva. *The Jewish Woman, 1900–1985: A Bibliography.* Fresh Meadows, N.Y.: Biblio Press, 1987.

Capia, R. *Les Poupées françaises.* Paris: Hachette, 1979.

Caplan, Jane. "Women, the Workplace, and Unions in International Perspective," in *International Labor and Working Class History* 35 (Spring 1989).

Cassin, René. *L'Inégalité entre l'homme et la femme dans la législation civile.* Marseilles: Barlatier, 1919.

Catalogue de l'exposition, "L'Education des jeunes filles il y a cent ans." Rouen: Musée National de l'Education, 1983.

Chafe, William H. *The American Woman: Her Changing Social, Political, and Economic Roles, 1920–1970.* New York: Oxford University Press, 1972.

Chambelland-Liebault, Noëlle. "La Durée et l'aménagement du temps de travail des femmes en France de 1892 à l'aube des conventions collectives." Law thesis, Nantes, 1989.

Chambers-Schiller, Lee V. *Liberty, a Better Husband: Single Women in America: The Generation of 1780–1840.* New Haven: Yale University Press, 1984.

Charles-Roux, Edmonde. *Un Désir d'Orient: La jeunesse d'Isabelle Eberhardt.* Paris: Grasset, 1988.

Charlot, Monica. *Victoria: Le pouvoir partagé.* Paris: Flammarion, 1989.

Chauvin, Jeanne. *Des professions accessibles aux femmes en droit romain et en droit français: Evolution historique de la position économique de la femme dans la société.* Paris: Ginard and Brière, 1892.

Chew, Doris Nield. *Ada Nield Chew: The Life and Writings of a Working Woman.* London: Virago, 1982.

Citron, Pierre. *Dans Balzac.* Paris: Le Seuil, 1986.

Clark, Alice. *The Working Life of Women in the Seventeenth Century.* London: G. Routledge and Sons, 1919 (reissued by Frank Cass, 1968).

Clark, Linda L. *Schooling the Daughters of Marianne: Textbooks and the Socialization of Girls in Modern French Primary Schools.* Albany: State University of New York Press, 1984.

Claverie, Elisabeth, and Pierre La Maison. *L'Impossible Mariage: Violence et parenté en Gévaudan, 17è, 18è and 19è siècles.* Paris: Hachette, 1982.

Clemens, Bärbel. *"Menschenrechte haben kein Geschlecht": Zum Politikverständnis der bürgerlichen Frauenbewegung.* Pfaffenweiler: Centaurus, 1988.

Cohen, Yolande. *Femmes et contre pouvoirs.* Montreal: Boréal-Express, 1987.

Collet, Clara E. "Women's Work," in Charles Booth, ed., *Life and Labour of the People in London,* vol. 4, first series. London: Macmillan, 1902.

Condorcet, *Ecrits sur l'instruction publique,* vol. 1: *Cinq mémoires sur l'instruction publique,* presented by Charles Coutel and Catherine Kintzler. Paris: Edilig, 1989; vol. 2: *Rapport sur l'instruction publique,* presented by Charles Coutel. Paris: Edilig, 1989.

Conti, Odorisio G. *Storia dell'idea femminista in Italia.* Turin: ERT, 1980.

Coole, Diane H. *Women in Political Theory: From Ancient Misogyny to Contemporary Feminism.* Brighton: Wheatsheaf Books, 1988.

Corbin, Alain. *Les Filles de noce: Misère sexuelle et prostitution (19è and 20è siècles).* Paris: Aubier-Montaigne, 1978.

Cott, Nancy F. *The Bonds of Womanhood: "Woman's Sphere" in New England, 1780–1835.* New Haven: Yale University Press, 1977.

——— *The Grounding of Modern Feminism.* New Haven: Yale University Press, 1987.

——— "Passionlessness: An Interpretation of Victorian Sexual Ideology, 1790–1850," in Nancy F. Cott and Elizabeth H. Pleck, eds., *A Heritage of Her Own,* pp. 162–181. New York: Simon and Schuster, 1979.

Dall'Ava-Santucci, Josette. *Des Sorcières aux mandarines: Histoire des femmes médecins.* Paris: Calmann-Lévy, 1989.

Damez, Albert. *Le Libre Salaire de la femme mariée et le mouvement féministe.* Paris: Rousseau, 1905.

Daric, Jean. *L'Activité professionnelle des femmes en France. Etude statistique: Evolution et comparaisons internationales,* I. N. E. D., Cahier 5. Paris: Presses Universitaires de France, 1947.

Daudet, Mme. Alphonse. *L'Enfance d'une parisienne: Enfants et mères*. Paris, 1892.

Daumard, Adeline. *La Bourgeoisie parisienne de 1815 à 1848*. Paris: Sevpen, 1963.

Dauphin, Cécile, et al. "Culture et pouvoir des femmes: Essai d'historiographie." *Annales Economie, Société, Civilisation* 41 (1986).

Davidoff, Leonore, and Catherine Hall. *Family Fortunes: Men and Women of the English Middle Class, 1780–1850*. London: Hutchinson, 1987.

Davin, Anna. "Imperialism and Motherhood," *History Workshop* 5 (1978).

Degler, Carl. *At Odds: Women and the Family in America from the Revolution to the Present*. New York: Oxford University Press, 1980.

Dekker, Rudolf. "Republican Heroines: Cross-Dressing Women in the French Revolution Armies," *History of European Ideas* 10, 3 (1989): 353–363.

——— "Women and Political Culture in the Dutch Revolutions," in Applewhite and Levy, *Women and Politics*, pp. 109–146.

——— "Women in Revolt: Collective Protest and Its Social Basis in Holland, 1600–1795," *Theory and Society* 16 (1987).

D'Emilio, John, and Estelle Freedman. *Intimate Matters: A History of Sexuality in America*. New York: Harper and Row, 1988.

Deniel, Raymond. *Une Image de la famille et de la société sous la restauration*. Paris: Les Editions Ouvrières, 1965.

Derrida, Jacques. *Eperons: Les styles de Nietzsche*. Paris: Flammarion, 1978.

De Saive, J. P. "Le nu hurluberlu," *Ethnologie française* 3–4 (1976).

Dessertine, Dominique. *Divorcer à Lyon sous la Révolution et l'Empire*. Lyon: PUL, 1981.

Dhavernas, Odile. *Droits des femmes: Pouvoir des hommes*. Paris: Le Seuil, 1978.

Doray, Marie-France. *Une Étrange Paroissienne: La Comtesse de Ségur*. Marseilles: Rivages, 1990.

Doux de Labro, Yvonne. *Journal d'une jeune fille à la Belle Epoque*. Paris: Le Cerf, 1991.

Drake, Barbara. *Women in Trade Unions*. London: Allen Unwin, 1920.

Drees, Annette. *Die Ärzte auf dem Weg zu Prestige und Wohlstand: Sozialgeschichte der würtembergischen Ärzte im 19. Jahrhundert*. Collection *Studien zur Geschichte des Alltags*. Münster: Coppenrath, 1988.

Duberman, Martin Bauml, Martha Vicinus, and George Chauncey, Jr., eds. *Hidden from History: Reclaiming the Gay and Lesbian Past*. New York: New American Library, 1989.

Dublin, Thomas. *Women at Work: The Transformation of Work and Community in Lowell, Massachusetts, 1826–1860*. New York: Columbia University Press, 1979.

Dubois, Ellen C. *Feminism and Suffrage: The Emergence of an Independent Women's Movement in America, 1848–1869*. Ithaca: Cornell University Press, 1978.

Duhet, Paule-Marie. *Les Femmes et la Révolution, 1789–1794*. Paris: Julliard, 1971.

Dumont-Johnson, Micheline, and Nadia Fahmy Eid. *Les Couventines: L'education des filles au Québec dans les congrégations religieuses enseignantes (1840–1960).* Quebec: Boréal, 1986.
Dupaquier, Jacques, ed. *Histoire de la population française,* vol. 3: *De 1789 à 1914.* Paris: Presses Universitaires de France, 1988.
Duprat, Catherine. "Charité et philanthropie à Paris dans la première moitié du XIXè siècle." Thesis, Paris I, 1991.
"Écriture, féminité, féminisme," *Revue des Sciences humaines* 168, 4 (1977).
Elshtain, Jean Bethke. *Public Man, Private Woman: Women in Social and Political Thought.* Princeton: Princeton University Press, 1981.
Emilie, 1802–1872, presented by Bernard de Freminville. Paris: Le Seuil, 1985.
Engelsing, Rolf. *Analphabetentum und Lektüre: Zur Sozialgeschichte des Lesens in Deutschland (1500–1800).* Stuttgart: Metzler, 1973.
——— *Der Bürger als Leser.* Stuttgart: Metzler, 1974.
——— *Zur Sozialgeschichte deutscher Mittel- und Unterschichten.* Göttingen: Vanderhoeck and Rupredd, 1973.
Ertel, Rachel. *Le Shtetl: La bourgade juive de Pologne.* Paris: Payot, 1982.
Escher, Nora. *Entwicklungstendenzen der Frauenbewegung in der deutschen Schweiz, 1850–1918/19.* Zurich: ADAG, 1985.
Evans, Richard J. *Comrades and Sisters: Feminism, Socialism, and Pacifism in Europe, 1870–1945.* New York: St. Martin's, 1987.
——— *The Feminist Movement in Germany, 1894–1944.* London: Sage, 1976.
——— *The Feminists: The Women's Emancipation Movement in Europe, America, and Australia, 1840–1920.* New York: Barnes and Noble, 1979.
——— "Prostitution, State, and Society in Imperial Germany," *Past and Present* 70 (1976): 106–129.
——— *Sozialdemokratie und Frauenemanzipation im deutschen Kaiserreich.* Berlin: Dietz, 1979.
Evans, Sara. *Born for Liberty: A History of Women in America.* New York: The Free Press, 1989.
——— *Personal Politics: The Roots of Women's Liberation in the Civil Rights Movement and the New Left.* New York: Vintage Books, 1980.
Ewen, Elizabeth. *Immigrant Women in the Land of Dollars: Life and Culture on the Lower East Side, 1890–1925.* New York: Monthly Review Press, 1985.
Eyquem, Marie-Thérèse. *La Femme et le sport.* Paris: Ed. Susse, 1944.
Faderman, Lillian. *Surpassing the Love of Men: Romantic Friendships between Women from the Renaissance to the Present.* New York: William Morris, 1981.
Farge, Arlette, and Christiane Klapisch-Zuber, eds. *Madame ou Mademoiselle? Itinéraires de la solitude féminine, 18è-20è siècles.* Paris: Arthaud-Montalba, 1984.
Farina, Rachele, et al., eds. *Esistere come donna.* Milan: Mazzotta, 1983.
Fauré, Christine. *Terre, Terreur, Liberté.* Paris: Maspero, 1979.

Fay-Sallois, Fanny. *Les Nourrices à Paris au XIXè siècle.* Paris: Payot, 1980.

Fayet-Scribe, Sylvie. *Associations féminines et catholicisme: De la charité à l'action sociale (XIXè-XXè siècle).* Paris: Les Editions Ouvrières, 1990.

Feminist Studies, 9, 1 (Spring 1983); 9, 2 (Summer 1983); 9, 3 (Fall 1983); 10, 3 (Fall 1984).

Feministische Studien, 3, 1 (1984): "Die Radikalen in der alten Frauenbewegung."

La Femme, Recueil de la Société Jean Bodin pour l'Histoire comparative des institutions, XII. Brussels: Librairie Encyclopédique, 1962.

"La Femme soignante," *Pénélope* 5 (Autumn 1981).

Femmes, libertés, laïcité. Centre d'action laïque, Editions de l'Université Libre de Bruxelles, under the direction of Yolande Mendes da Costa and Anne Morelli. Brussels: Editions de l'Université, 1989.

Ferando, Lloyd. "George Eliot, Feminism, and Dorothea Brooke," in *Review of English Literature* (January 1963).

Ferrante, Lucia, Maura Palazzi, and Gianna Pomata. *Ragnatele di rapporti: Patronage e reti di relazione nella storia delle donne.* Turin: Rosenberg and Sellier, 1988.

Ferrero, Pat, Elaine Hedges, and Julie Silber. *Hearts and Hands: The Influence of Women and Quilts on American Society.* San Francisco: The Quilt Digest Press, 1987.

Fildes, Valérie. *Wet Nursing: A History from Antiquity to the Present.* Oxford: Basil Blackwell, 1988.

Les Filles de Marx: Lettres inédites. Presented by Michelle Perrot. Paris: Albin-Michel, 1979.

Flandrin, Jean-Louis. *Les Amours paysannes (XVIè-XIXè siècles).* Collection Archives, Gallimard, Julliard, 1975.

Flexner, Eleanor. *Century of Struggle: The Woman's Rights Movement in the United States.* Cambridge, Mass.: Harvard University Press, 1973.

Folguera, Pilar, ed. *El feminismo en España: Dos siglos de historia.* Madrid: Ediciones de la Fundación Pablo Iglesias, 1988.

Forster, Margaret. *Significant Sisters: The Grassroots of Active Feminism, 1839–1939.* New York: Penguin Books, 1984.

Foucault, Michel. *La Volonté de savoir,* vol. 1: *Histoire de la sexualité.* Paris: Gallimard, 1976.

Fout, John C., ed. *German Women in the Nineteenth Century: A Social History.* New York: Holmes and Meier, 1984.

Fox-Genovese, Elizabeth. *Within the Plantation Household: White and Black Women in American Slave Society.* Chapel Hill: University of North Carolina Press, 1988.

Fraisse, Geneviève. *Clémence Royer: Philosophe et femme de sciences.* Paris: La Découverte, 1985.

——— *Femmes toutes mains: Essai sur le service domestique.* Paris: Le Seuil, 1979.

——— *Muse de la raison: La démocratie exclusive et la différence des sexes.* Aix-en-Provence: Alinéa, 1989.

——— "La Rupture révolutionnaire et l'histoire des femmes," in *Actes du Colloque "Femmes et pouvoirs"* held in Paris, Reid Hall, December 1989. Marseilles: Rivages, 1991.

Francheo, Marianne. "La Femme allemande au XIXè siècle: Statut juridique et condition sociale." Thesis (Nouveau Régime), Paris IV, 1986–1987.

Franchini, Sylvia. "L'Instruzione femminile in Italia dopo l'Unita: Percossi di una ricerca sugli educandati pubblici di elite," *Passato e Presente* 10 (1986): 53–94.

François, Etienne. "Alphabetisierung und Lesefähigkeit in Frankreich und Deutschland um 1800," in Berding, François, and Ullmann, *Deutschland und Frankreich im Zeitalter der Französischen Revolution*. Frankfurt: Suhrkamp, 1989.

Frank, Louis. *Essai sur la condition politique de la femme: Etude de sociologie et de législation*. Paris: Rousseau, 1892.

——— *La Loi sur l'enseignement supérieur et l'admission des femmes dans les facultés belges*. Brussels, 1889.

Fraser, Harrison. *The Dark Angel: Aspects of Victorian Sexuality*. Sheldon Press, 1977. 2nd ed., Glasgow: Fontana/Collins, 1979.

Frei, Annette. *Rote Patriarchen: Arbeiterbewegung und Frauenemanzipation in der Schweiz um 1900*. Zurich: Chronos, 1987.

Frevert, Ute. *Frauengeschichte: Zwischen bürgerlicher Verbesserung und neuer Weiblichkeit*. Frankfurt: Suhrkamp, 1978.

——— *Krankheit als politisches Problem, 1770–1880: Soziale Unterschichten in Preussen zwischen medizinischer Polizei und staatlicher Sozialversicherung*. Göttingen: Vandenhoeck and Ruprecht, 1984.

——— *Women in German History: From Bourgeois Emancipation to Sexual Liberation*. Oxford: Berg, 1989.

———, ed. *Bürgerinnen und Bürger—Geschlechterverhältnisse im 19. Jhd.* Göttingen: Vandenhoeck and Ruprecht, 1988.

Frey, L., and J. Schneider. *A Bibliography of Women in West European History*. Brighton: Harvester Press, 1986.

Frey, L., M. Frey, and J. Schneider. *Women in Western European History: A Select Chronological, Geographical, and Topical Bibliography*. Brighton: Harvester Press, 1982.

Friedlander, Judith. "The Jewish Feminist Question," *Dialectical Anthropology* 8, 1–2 (October 1983): 113–120. French ed.: "La Question féministe juive," *Nouvelles questions féministes* 1–2 (October 1983): 21–34.

———, ed. *Women in Culture and Politics: A Century of Change*. Bloomington: Indiana University Press, 1986. French ed.: *Stratégies des Femmes*. Paris: Tierce, 1984.

Furet, François, and Jacques Ozouf. *Lire et écrire: L'alphabétisation des Français de Calvin à Jules Ferry*, 2 vols. Paris: Minuit, 1977.

Gaillard, Henry. *La Condition des femmes dans la législation des Etats-Unis*. Law thesis. Paris, 1899.

Galoppini, Anna Maria. *Il lungo viaggio verso la parità: I diritti civili e politici delle donne dall'unità a oggi*. Bologna: Zanichelli, 1980.

Garrison, Dea. "The Tender Technicians: The Feminization of Public Librarianship, 1876–1905," in *Clio's Consciousness Raised,* pp. 158–178. New York: Harper and Row, 1974.

Garrisson-Estebe, J. *L'Homme protestant.* Paris: Hachette, 1980.

Gautier, Arlette. *Les Sœurs de solitude: La condition féminine dans l'esclavage aux Antilles du XVIIè au XIXè siècle.* Paris: Editions Caribéennes, 1985.

Gdalia, Janine, and Annie Goldman. *Le Judaïsme au féminin.* Paris: Balland, 1989.

"Le Genre de l'histoire," *Les Cahiers du GRIF* 37–38 (1988).

Georgel, P. *Léopoldine Hugo: Une jeune fille romantique.* Paris: Catalogue du Musée Victor Hugo, 1967.

Gerbod, Paul. "Les Métiers de la coiffure dans la première moitié du XXè siècle," *Ethnologie française* (January-March 1983).

Gerhard, Ute. *Verhältnisse und Verhinderungen: Frauenarbeit, Familie und Rechte der Frauen im 19. Jahrhundert.* Frankfurt: Suhrkamp, 1978.

Gerster, Franziska, and Ursi Blosser. *Töchter der guten Gesellschaft: Frauenrolle und Mädchenerziehung im schweizerischen Grossbürgertum um 1900.* Zurich: Chronos, 1985.

Gibson, Mary. *Prostitution and the State in Italy, 1860–1915.* New Brunswick, N.J.: Rutgers University Press, 1986.

Giddings, Paula. *When and Where I Enter: The Impact of Black Women on Race and Sex in America.* New York: Morrow, 1984.

Gide, Paul. *Etude sur la condition privée de la femme.* Paris: L. Larosse and Forcel, 1885.

Gilbert, Sandra M., and Susan Gubar. *The Madwoman in the Attic: The Woman Writer and the Nineteenth-Century Literary Imagination.* New Haven: Yale University Press, 1979.

Glassman Hersh, B. *The Slavery of Sex: Feminist-Abolitionists in America.* Urbana: University of Illinois Press, 1978.

Glickman, Rose L. *Russian Factory Women: Workplace and Society, 1880–1914.* Berkeley: University of California Press, 1986.

Godineau, Dominique. "Autour du mot *citoyenne,*" *Mots* 16 (March 1988).

——— *Citoyennes tricoteuses: Les femmes du peuple à Paris pendant la Révolution française.* Aix-en-Provence: Alinéa, 1988.

——— "Qu'y a-t-il de commun entre vous et nous? Enjeux et discours sur la différence des sexes pendant la Révolution (1789–1793)," *La Famille, la loi, l'état.* Paris, 1989.

——— "La *Tricoteuse:* Formation d'un mythe contre-révolutionnaire," in Michel Vovelle, ed., *L'Image de la Révolution française,* vol. 3. Oxford: Pergamon Press, 1990.

Goldberg, Vicki. Catalog of the "Margaret Bourke-White Retrospective." Paris: Palais de Tokyo (June-September 1989).

The Golden Tradition: Jewish Life and Thought in Eastern Europe, presented by Lucy S. Dawidowicz. Boston: Beacon Press, 1967.

Goldman, Emma. *Living My Life,* 2 vols. New York: Da Capo, 1976.

Gordon, Eleanor. *Women and the Labour Movement in Scotland.* Oxford: Oxford University Press, 1989.
Gordon, Linda. *Woman's Body, Woman's Right: A Social History of Birth Control in America.* New York: Crossman Publishers, 1976; Penguin Books, 1977.
Gorelick, Sherry. *City College and the Jewish Poor: Education in New York, 1880–1924.* New Brunswick, N.J.: Rutgers University Press, 1981.
Goren, Arthur. *New York Jews and the Quest for Community: The Kehillah Experiment, 1908–1922.* New York: Columbia University Press, 1970.
Grafteaux, S. *Mémé Santerre: Une vie.* Paris: Marabout, 1978.
Gran-Aymeric, Eve and Jean. *Jane Dieulafoy: Une vie d'homme.* Paris: Perrin, 1991.
Greard, Octave. *Education et instruction: Enseignement secondaire,* vol. 1. Paris: Hachette, 1987.
Greaves, R. L., ed. *Triumph over Silence: Women in Protestant History.* London: Greenwood Press, 1985.
Green, Martin. *The Von Richthofen Sisters.* New York: Basic Books, 1974; French ed., Paris: Le Seuil, 1979.
Green, Nancy. "L'Emigration comme émancipation: Les femmes juives d'Europe de l'est à Paris, 1881–1914," *Pluriel* 27 (1981): 51–59.
Grellet, I., and C. Kruse. *Histoire de la tuberculose: Le fièvres de l'âme, 1800–1940.* Paris: Ramsay, 1983.
Greven-Aschoff, Barbara. *Die bürgerliche Frauenbewegung in Deutschland, 1894–1933.* Göttingen: Vandenhoeck and Rupprecht, 1981.
Grimal, Pierre, ed. *Histoire mondiale de la femme,* vol. 4. Paris: Nouvelle Librairie de France, 1966.
Grimmett, Jennifer, and Malcolm I. Thomis. *Women in Protest, 1800–1850.* London: Croom Helm, 1982.
Groneman, Carol, and Mary Beth Norton. *To Toil the Livelong Day: America's Women at Work, 1870–1980.* Ithaca: Cornell University Press, 1987.
Grubitzsch, Helga, et al., eds. *Grenzgängerinnen: Revolutionäre Frauen im 18. und 19. Jhd., Weibliche Wirklichkeit und männliche Phantasien.* Düsseldorf: Schwann, 1985.
Guermont, Marie-F. *La "Grande Fille": L'hygiène de la jeune fille d'après les ouvrages médicaux (fin XIXè début XXè).* Master's thesis, Université de Tours, 1981.
Guidi, Laura. *L'Onore in pericolo: Carità e reclusione femminile. Nele'ottocento napoletano.* Naples: Guida, 1991.
Guilbert, Madeleine. *Les Fonctions des femmes dans l'industrie.* Paris: Mouton, 1966.
Guilbert, Madeleine, Nicole Lowit, and Marie-Hélène Zylberberg-Hocquart. *Travail et condition feminine (bibliographie commentée).* Published with the help of Centre National de la Recherche Scientifique: Editions de la Courtille, 1977.
Guillais, Joëlle. *La Chair de l'autre: Le crime passionnel au dix-neuvième siècle.* Paris: O. Orban, 1986.

Hahn, Barbara. *"Antworten sie mir": Rahel Levin Varnhagens Briefwechsel.* Frankfurt: Stromfeld and Roterstern, 1990.

——— *Unter falschem Namen: Von der schwierigen Autorschaft der Frauen.* Frankfurt, 1991.

Hall, Jacquelyn Dowd, ed. *Like a Family: The Making of a Southern Cotton Mill World.* Chapel Hill: University of North Carolina Press, 1987.

Hamer, T. L. *Beyond Feminism: The Women's Movement in Austrian Social Democracy, 1890–1920.* Thesis, Ohio State University, 1973.

Harsin, Jill. *Policing Prostitution in Nineteenth-Century Paris.* Princeton: Princeton University Press, 1985.

Hasanovitch, Elizabeth. *One of Them.* New York: Houghton Mifflin, 1918.

Hause, Steven. *Women's Suffrage and Social Politics in the French Third Republic.* Princeton: Princeton University Press, 1984.

Hausen, Karin, ed. *Frauen suchen ihre Geschichte.* Munich: Beck, 1983.

Heller, Geneviève. *"Propre en ordre": Habitation et vie domestique, 1850–1930—L'exemple vaudois.* Lausanne: Editions d'En Bas, 1979.

Hertz, Deborah. *Jewish High Society in Old Regime Berlin.* New Haven: Yale University Press, 1988.

Hervé, Florence. *Geschichte der deutschen Frauenbewegung.* Cologne: Pahl-Rugenstein, 1982.

———, ed. *Frauenbewegung und revolutionäre Arbeiterbewegung. Texte zur Frauenemanzipation in Deutschland und in der BRD von 1848–1980.* Frankfurt: Verlag Marxistische Blätter, 1981.

Hewitt, Margaret. *Wives and Mothers in Victorian Industry.* London: Rockliff, 1958.

Higonnet, Margaret R., Jane Jenson, Sonya Michel, and Margaret G. Weitz. *Behind the Lines: Gender and the Two World Wars.* New Haven: Yale University Press, 1987.

Hilden, Patricia Jane. *French Socialism and Women Textile Workers in Lille-Roubaix-Tourcoing (1880–1914): A Regional Study.* Oxford: Clarendon Press, 1986.

Himmelfarb, Gertrude. *Marriage and Morals among the Victorians.* London: Faber, 1986.

Holcombe, Lee. *Victorian Ladies at Work.* Hamden, Conn.: Archon Books, 1973.

——— *Wives and Property: Reform of the Married Women's Property Law in Nineteenth-Century England.* Toronto: University of Toronto Press, 1983.

Hollis, Pat, ed. *Women in Public: The Women's Movement (1850–1910): Documents.* London: Allen and Unwin, 1979.

Honneger, Claudia. *Die Ordnung der Geschlechter: Die Wissenschaft vom Menschen und das Weib.* Frankfurt, 1991.

Hoock-Demarle, Marie-Claire. *La Femme au temps de Goethe.* Paris: Stock, 1987.

——— *La Rage de lire: Les femmes allemandes face à la Révolution française (1790–1815).* Aix-en-Provence: Alinéa, 1990.

Houghton, Walter E. *The Victorian Frame of Mind, 1830–1870*. Published for Wellesley College by Yale University Press: New Haven, 1957.
Hufton, Olwen. "Women in the French Revolution," *Past and Present* 53 (1971).
Hunt, Felicity, ed. *Lessons for Life: The Schooling of Girls and Women, 1850–1950*. Oxford: Basil Blackwell, 1987.
Hunt, Lynn. "L'Axe masculin/féminin dans le discours révolutionnaire," in *La Révolution française et les processus de socialisation de l'homme moderne*. Actes du Colloque de Rouen, 13–15 October 1988. Paris: Messidor, 1989.
Hyman, Paula. "Culture and Gender: Women in the Immigrant Jewish Community," in David Berger, *The Legacy of Jewish Immigration*, pp. 157–168. New York: Brooklyn College Press, 1983.
——— "Immigrant Women and Consumer Protest: The New York City Kosher Meat Boycott of 1902," *American Jewish History* 60, 1 (September 1980): 91–105.
Irigaray, Luce. *Spéculum de l'autre femme*. Paris: Minuit, 1974.
Jalland, Pat. *Women, Marriage, and Politics, 1860–1914*. Oxford: Oxford University Press, 1988.
Janiewski, Dolores E. *Sisterhood Denied: Race, Gender, and Class in a New South Community*. Philadelphia: Temple University Press, 1985.
Janz, Marlies. "Hölderlins Flamme—Zur Bildwerdung der Frau in 'Hyperion,'" *Hölderlin-Jahrbuch* (1980–1981): 122–142.
Jardine, Alice. *Gynesis*. Ithaca: Cornell University Press, 1985; French ed., Paris: Presses Universitaires de France, 1991.
Jauche, Ursula Pia. *Immanuel Kant zur Geschlechterdifferenz: Aufklärerische Vorurteilskritik und Bürgerliche Geschlechtsvormundschaft*. Vienna: Passagen, 1988.
Jeffrey, Julie Roy. *Frontier Women: The Trans-Mississippi West, 1840–1880*. New York: Hill and Wang, 1980.
Jeffreys, Sheila. *The Spinster and Her Enemies: Feminism and Sexuality, 1880–1930*. London: Pandora, 1985.
John, Angela V., ed. *Unequal Opportunities: Women's Employment in England, 1880–1918*. Oxford: Basil Blackwell, 1986.
Johnson, Barbara. *A World of Difference*. Baltimore: Johns Hopkins University Press, 1987.
Jones, Jacqueline. *Labor of Love, Labor of Sorrow: Black Women, Work, and the Family from Slavery to the Present*. New York: Basic Books, 1985.
Joris, Elisabeth, and Heidi Witzig, eds. *Frauengeschichte (n)*. Zurich: Limmat-Verlag, 1986.
Joselit, Jenna. "The Special Sphere of Middle-Class American-Jewish Woman: The Synagogue Sisterhood, 1890–1940," in J. Wertheimer, *The American Synagogue: A Sanctuary Transformed*, pp. 206–230. New York: Cambridge University Press, 1987.

Journal of Family History, 1, 2 (Winter 1976); Special no., "Spinsters," ed. Susan Cotts Watkins (Winter 1984).

Kaplan, Marion A. *The Jewish Feminist Movement in Germany: The Campaigns of the Jüdischer Frauenbund, 1904–1938.* Westport, Conn.: Greenwood Press, 1979.

Käppeli, Anne-Marie. "Le Féminisme protestant de suisse romande à la fin du XIXè et au début du XXè siècles." Thesis, Paris VII, 1987.

——— *Sublime croisade: Ethique et politique du féminisme protestant (1875–1928).* Preface by Mireille Cifali. Geneva: Editions Zoé, 1990.

Karlsen, Carol F. *"Devil in the Shape of a Woman": Witchcraft in Colonial New England.* New York: Norton, 1987.

Katz, Jacob. *Out of the Ghetto: The Social Background of Jewish Emanicipation, 1770–1870.* New York: Schocken Books, 1978; French ed.: *Hors du ghetto: L'emancipation des juifs en Europe (1770–1870).* Preface by Pierre Vidal-Naquet. Paris: Hachette, 1984.

Katz, Jonathan. *Gay/Lesbian Almanac: A New Documentary History.* New York: Harper and Row, 1983.

Katzman, David M. *Seven Days a Week: Women and Domestic Service in Industrializing America.* Urbana: University of Illinois Press, 1981.

Kelly, Joan. *Women, History, and Theory.* Chicago: University of Chicago Press, 1984.

Kennedy, E., and S. Mendus. *Women in Western Political Philosophy: Kant to Nietzsche.* Brighton: Wheatsheaf Books, 1987.

Kerber, Linda K. *Women of the Republic: Intellect and Ideology in Revolutionary America.* Chapel Hill: University of North Carolina Press, 1980.

Kessler-Harris, Alice. "Organizing the Unorganizable: Three Jewish Women and Their Union," in M. Cantor and B. Laurie, *Class, Sex, and the Woman Worker,* pp. 144–165. Westport, Conn.: Greenwood Press, 1977.

Kessner, T., and B. B. Caroli. "New Immigrant Women at Work: Italians and Jews in New York City, 1880–1905," *Journal of Ethnic Studies* (Winter 1978).

Kittler, Friedrich. *Aufschreibesysteme, 1800–1900.* Munich: Fink, 1985.

Kleinau, Elke. *Die freie Frau: Soziale Utopien des frühen 19.* Jhd. Düsseldorf: Schwann, 1987.

Klejman, Laurence, and Florence Rochefort. *L'Egalité en marche: Le féminisme sous la Troisième République.* Paris: Editions Des Femmes, 1989.

Klinger, Cornelia. "Das Bild der Frau in der Patriarchalen Philosophiegeschichte: Bibliographie," in Herta Nagl, ed., *Feminismus und Philosophie.* Munich: Oldenbourg Verlag, 1990.

Knibiehler, Yvonne. *Cornettes et blouses blanches: Les infirmières dans la société française, 1880–1980.* Paris: Hachette, 1984.

Knibiehler, Yvonne, and Catherine Fouquet. *La Beauté pour quoi faire?* Paris: Temps actuels, 1982.

——— *La Femme et les médecins.* Paris: Hachette, 1983.

——— *Histoire des mères: Du moyen age à nos jours.* Paris: Montalba, 1980; Hachette, 1987.

Knibiehler, Yvonne, and Régine Goutalier. *La Femme au temps des colonies.* Paris: Stock, 1985.
Knibiehler, Yvonne, Marcel Bernos, Richard Eliane, and Elisabeth Ravoux-Rallo. *De la pucelle à la minette: Les jeunes filles de l'âge classique à nos jours,* 2nd ed. Paris: Messidor, 1989.
Kofman, Sarah. *Le Respect des femmes.* Paris: Galilée, 1984.
Kokula, Ilse. *Weibliche Homosexualität um 1900 in zeitgenössischen Dokumenten.* Munich: Frauenoffensive, 1981.
Krug, Charles. *Le Féminisme et le droit civil français.* Paris, 1899.
Labalme, Patricia H., ed. *Beyond Their Sex: Learned Women of the European Past.* New York: New York University Press, 1984.
Lamphere, Louise. *From Working Daughters to Working Mothers: Immigrant Women in a New England Industrial Community.* Ithaca: Cornell University Press, 1987.
Landes, Joan. *Women in the Public Sphere in the Age of the French Revolution.* Ithaca: Cornell University Press, 1988.
Langlois, Claude. *Le Catholicisme au féminin: Les congrégations françaises à supérieure générale au XIXè siècle.* Preface by René Rémond. Paris: Le Cerf, 1984.
Langlois, Claude, and Paul Wagret. *Structure religieuse et célibat féminin au XIXè siècle.* Lyon: Centre d'Histoire du Catholicisme, 1972.
Laqueur, Thomas. *Making Sex: Body and Gender from the Greeks to Freud.* Cambridge, Mass.: Harvard University Press, 1990.
Leach, William. *True Love and Perfect Union: The Feminist Reform of Sex and Society.* New York: Basic Books, 1980.
Lebsock, Suzanne. *The Free Women of Petersburg: Status and Culture in a Southern Town (1784–1860).* New York: W. W. Norton, 1984.
Léger, Christine. "Le Journal des demoiselles." Thesis, Paris VII, 1989.
Lerner, Elinor. "Jewish Involvement in the New York City Women's Suffrage Movement," *American Jewish History* 70, 4 (June 1981): 442–461.
Lerner, Gerda. *De l'esclavage à la ségrégation: Les femmes noires dans l'Amérique des Blancs.* Paris: Denoël-Gonthier, 1975.
Lespine, Louis. *La Femme en Espagne: Etude juridique, sociale, économique, et de législation comparée.* Toulouse: Clémence-Isaure, 1919.
Levine, Philippa. *Victorian Feminism, 1850–1900.* London: Hutchinson, 1987.
Lévy, Marie-Françoise. *De mères en filles: L'éducation des françaises (1850–1880).* Paris: Calmann-Lévy, 1984.
Lewis, Jane. *Women in England, 1870–1950: Sexual Divisions and Social Change.* Bloomington: Indiana University Press, 1984.
———, ed. *Before the Vote Was Won: Arguments for and against Women's Suffrage, 1864–1896.* London: Routledge and Kegan Paul, 1988.
———, ed. *Labour and Love: Women's Experience of Home and Family, 1850–1940.* Oxford: Basil Blackwell, 1986.
Liddington, Jill, and Jill Norris. *One Hand Tied behind Us.* London: Virago Press, 1978.

Lloyd, Geneviève. *The Man of Reason: "Male" and "Female" in Western Philosophy*. London: Methuen, 1984.

Lory, Jacques. *Libéralisme et instruction primaire, 1842–1879: Introduction à l'étude de la lutte scolaire en Belgique,* 2 vols. Louvain: Ed. Nauvwelaerts, 1979.

Lowder Newton, Judith. *Women, Power, and Subversion: Social Strategies in British Fiction, 1778–1860*. Athens: University of Georgia Press, 1981. Rev. ed., London: Methuen, 1985.

Luker, Kristin. *Abortion and the Politics of Motherhood*. Berkeley: University of California Press, 1984.

Lundbergh, Beate. *Kom ihag att du är underlägen: Pedagogik för borgarflickor i 1880 talets Sverige*. Lund: Student Litteratur, 1986.

Lundgreen, Peter. *Sozialgeschichte der deutschen Schule im Überblick,* I, *1770–1918*. Göttingen: Vandenhoeck, 1980.

Lyon-Caen, Léon. *La Femme mariée allemande—ses droits, ses intérêts pécuniaires: Etude de droit civil et de droit international privé allemand*. Paris: Rousseau, 1903.

McCrone, Kathleen E. *Sports and the Physical Emancipation of English Women, 1870–1914*. London: Routledge and Kegan Paul, 1988.

McLaren, Angus. *Reproductive Rituals: The Perceptions of Fertility in England from the Sixteenth Century to the Nineteenth Century*. London: Methuen, 1984.

——— *Sexuality and the Social Order: The Debate over the Fertility of Women and Workers in France, 1770–1920*. New York: Holmes and Meier, 1983.

Maire, Catherine-Laurence. *Les Possédées de Morzine, 1857–1873*. Lyon: PUL, 1981.

Malkiel, Theresa. *Journal d'une gréviste,* F. Basch, ed. Paris: Payot, 1980.

Maquieira, Virginia, and Cristina y Sánchez, eds. *Violencia y sociedad patriarcal*. Madrid: Ediciones de la Fundación Pablo Iglesias, 1990.

Marcil-Lacoste, Louise. *La Raison en procès: Essais sur la philosophie et le sexisme*. La Salle and Quebec: Hurtubise, 1986; Paris: Nizet, 1986.

Marcus, Jacob R., ed. *The American Jewish Woman: A Documentary History*. New York: KTAV; Cincinnati: American Jewish Archives, 1981.

Margadant, Jo B. *Madame le professeur: Women Educators in the Third Republic*. Princeton: Princeton University Press, 1990.

Marthe (1892–1902), presented by Bernard de Fréminville. Paris: Le Seuil. Collection "Libre à elles," 1985.

Martin-Fugier, Anne. *La Bourgeoise: La femme au temps de Paul Bourget*. Paris: Grasset, 1983.

——— *La Place des bonnes: La domesticité féminine à Paris en 1900*. Paris: Grasset, 1979.

"Masculin/Féminin," *Actes de la Recherche en Sciences Sociales* 84 (September 1990).

Mattaei, Julie A. *An Economic History of Women in America: Women's*

Work, the Sexual Division of Labor, and the Development of Capitalism. New York: Schocken Books, 1982.

Maugue, Annelise. *L'Identité masculine en crise au tournant du siècle.* Marseilles: Rivages, 1987.

Max-Planck Institute for Human Development and Education. *Between Elite and Mass Education.* Education in the Federal Republic of Germany. Albany: State University of New York Press, 1983.

Mayeur, Françoise. *L'Education des filles en France au XIXè siècle.* Paris: Hachette, 1979.

——— *L'Enseignement secondaire des jeunes filles sous la Troisième République.* Paris: Presses de la Fondation Nationale des Sciences Politiques, 1977.

Mayeur, Françoise, and Jacques Gadille. *Education et images de la femme chrétienne en France au début du XXè siècle.* Lyon: L'Hermès, 1980.

Mayreder, Rosa. *Zur Kritik der Weiblichkeit: Einleitung von H. Schnedl.* Munich: Frauenoffensive, 1982.

Meiselman, Mosche. *Jewish Women in Jewish Law.* New York: KTAV, 1978.

"Métiers de femmes," *Le Mouvement social* 140 (July-September 1987).

Meyer, Donald. *Sex and Power: The Rise of Women in America, Russia, Sweden, and Italy.* Middletown: Wesleyan University Press, 1987.

Milan, Maria. *Donna, famiglia, società: Aspetti della stampa femminile cattolica in Italia tra 800 e 900.* Università degli studi di Genova, Istituto di Studi Storico-Politici, 1983.

Mill, John Stuart, and Harriet Taylor Mill. *Essays on Sex Equality.* Introduction by Alice S. Rossi. Chicago: University of Chicago Press, 1970.

Mirabel, Cecil. *Heroines in Love, 1750–1914.* London: Michael Joseph, 1974.

Mitchell, Judith, and Ann Oakley, eds. *The Rights and Wrongs of Women.* New York: Penguin Books, 1976.

Möhrmann, Renate. *Die andere Frau: Emanzipationsansätze deutscher Schrifstellerinnen im Vorfeld der 48—Revolution.* Stuttgart: Metzler, 1977.

Moller Okin, Susan. *Women in Western Political Thought.* Princeton: Princeton University Press, 1979.

Moreau, Thérèse. *Le Sang de l'histoire: Michelet, l'histoire et l'idée de la femme au XIXè siècle.* Paris: Flammarion, 1982.

Moses, Claire. *French Feminism in the Nineteenth Century.* Albany: State University of New York Press, 1984.

Myerhoff, Barbara. *Number Our Days.* New York: Simon and Schuster, 1980.

"Mythes et représentations de la femme,"*Romantisme* 13 and 14 (1976).

Nead, Lynda. *Myths of Sexuality: Representations of Women in Victorian Britain.* London: Basil Blackwell, 1987.

Neuman, R. P. "Working-Class Birth Control in Wilhelmine Germany," *Comparative Studies in History and Society* 20 (1978): 408–428.

Newton, Judith L., Mary P. Ryan, and Judith R. Walkowitz, eds. *Sex and Class in Women's History: Essays from Feminist Studies*. London: Routledge and Kegan Paul, 1985.

Niggemann, Heinz. *Emanzipation zwischen Sozialismus und Feminismus*. Wuppertal: Hammer, 1981.

Norton, Mary Beth. *Liberty's Daughters: The Revolutionary Experience of American Women, 1750–1800*. Boston: Little, Brown, 1980.

——— *Major Problems in American Women's History: Documents and Essays*. Lexington, Mass.: D. C. Heath, 1989.

Offen, Karen M., ed. *Women in European Culture and Society,* special ed., *History of European Ideas* 8, 4/5 (1987).

Offen, Karen M., Ruth R. Pierson, and Jane Rendall, eds. *Writing Women's History: International Perspectives*. Published by The International Federation for Research in Women's History (forthcoming).

Olafson Hellerstein, Erna, Leslie Parker-Hume, and Karen M. Offen, eds. *Victorian Women: A Documentary Account of Women's Lives in Nineteenth-Century England, France, and the United States*. Stanford: Stanford University Press, 1989.

Opinions de femmes, de la veille au lendemain de la Révolution française, presented by Geneviève Fraisse. Paris: Côte-Femmes Éditions, 1989.

Ortner, S., and H. Whitehead, eds. *Sexual Meanings: The Cultural Construction of Gender and Sexuality*. Cambridge, Mass.: Harvard University Press, 1981.

Outram, Dorinda. *The Body and the French Revolution: Sex, Class, and Political Culture*. New Haven: Yale University Press, 1989.

Owen, Alex. *The Darkened Room: Women Power and Spiritualism in Late Nineteenth-Century England*. London: Virago, 1989.

Palacio, Jean de. "La Curée: Histoire naturelle et sociale, ou agglomérat de mythes?" Société des Etudes romantiques, *La Curée de Zola*. Paris: SEDES, 1987.

Parker, Rozsika, and Griselda Pollock. *Old Mistresses, Women, Art, and Ideology*. New York: Pantheon, 1981; London: Pandora Press, 1986.

Paroles d'hommes, 1790–1793, presented by Elisabeth Badinter. Paris: POL, 1989.

Pateman, Carole. *The Sexual Contract*. London: Polity, 1988.

Peiss, Kathy, and Christina Simmons, eds., with Robert A. Padgug. *Passion and Power: Sexuality in History*. Philadelphia: Temple University Press, 1989.

Pellegrin, Nicole. "Chemises et chiffons: Le vieux et le neuf en Poitou et Limousin, XVIIIè-XIXè siècles," *Ethnologie française* 3–4 (1986): 283–298.

——— "Les Chiffons de la naissance (XVIè-XXè siècles)." *Actes du Colloque "L'Aventure de Naître,"* pp. 55–75. Poitiers: Le Lezard, 1989.

——— *Les Vêtements de la Liberté*. Aix-en-Provence: Alinéa, 1989.

Perrot, Michelle, ed. *Une histoire des femmes est-elle possible?* Marseilles: Rivages, 1984.

Perrot, Philippe. *Les Dessus et les dessous de la bourgeoisie.* Editions Complexe, Librairie Arthème Fayard, 1981.

——— *Le Travail des apparences ou les Transformations du corps féminin XVIIIè–XIXè siècle.* Paris: Le Seuil, 1984.

Petchesky, Rosalind Pollack. *Abortion and Women's Choice: The State, Sexuality, and Reproductive Freedom.* Boston: Northeastern University Press, 1984.

Pinchbeck, Ivy. *Women Workers and the Industrial Revolution, 1750–1850.* New York: Kelley, 1969 (original ed., 1930).

Planté, Christine. *La Petite Sœur de Balzac: Essai sur la femme auteur.* Paris: Le Seuil, 1989.

Polasky, Janet L. "Women in Revolutionary Belgium: From Stone Throwers to Hearth Tenders," *History Workshop Journal* 21 (Spring 1986): 87–104.

Popp, Adelheid. *La Jeunesse d'une ouvrière* (1909); French ed., Paris: Maspero, 1979.

Preaux, Jean, ed. *Eglise et enseignement.* Brussels: Editions de l'Université Libre de Bruxelles, 1977.

Prochaska, F. K. *Women and Philanthropy in Nineteenth-Century England.* Oxford: Clarendon Press, 1980.

Prüsener, Marlies. "Lesegesellschaften im 18. Jahrhundert: Ein Beitrag zur Lesergeschichte," in *Archiv für die Geschichte des Buchwesens* 13 (1973).

Pusch, Luise, ed. *Feminismus: Inspektion der Herrenkultur.* Frankfurt: Suhrkamp, 1983.

Quaderni storici, no. 44, *Pareto e maternità: Momenti della biografia femminile.* Rome, August 1980.

Quataert, Jean H. *Reluctant Feminists in German Social Democracy, 1885–1917.* Princeton: Princeton University Press, 1979.

Quiguer, Claude. *Femmes et machines de 1900: Lecture d'une obsession modern style.* Paris: Klincksieck, 1979.

Ravera, Camilla. *Breve storia del movimento femminile in Italia.* Rome: Ed. Riuniti, 1978.

Rendall, Jane. *Equal or Different: Women's Politics, 1800–1914.* Oxford: Basil Blackwell, 1987.

——— *The Origins of Modern Feminism: Women in Britain, France, and the United States, 1780–1860.* London: Macmillan, 1985.

Revue d'histoire de l'amérique française, special no., *Histoire de la famille* 39, 2 (Autumn 1985). Quebec: Institut d'Histoire de l'Amérique Française.

Reys, Jeske, et al., eds. *De eerste feministische golf, 6 de Jaarboek voor Vrouwengeschiedenis.* Nijmegen: SUN, 1985.

Richebächer, Sabine. *Uns fehlt nur eine Kleinigkeit: Deutsche proletarische Frauenbewegung, 1890–1914.* Frankfurt: Fischer, 1982.

Rider, Jacques le. *Le Cas Otto Weininger: Racines de l'antiféminisme et de l'antisémitisme.* Paris: Presses Universitaires de France, 1982.

Riley, Denise. *Am I That Name? Feminism and the Category of "Women" in History.* London: Macmillan, 1988.

——— *War in the Nursery: Theories of the Child and Mother.* London: Virago, 1983.

Riley, Glenda. *Frontierswomen: The Iowa Experience.* Ames: Iowa State University Press, 1981.

Riot-Sarcey, Michèle, and Marie-Hélène Zylberberg-Hocquard. *Travaux de femmes au XIXè siècle.* Paris: Musée d'Orsay-CRDP, 1987.

Ripa, Yannick. *La Ronde des folles: Femme, folie, et enfermement au 19è siècle.* Paris: Aubier, 1986.

Rollet-Echalier, Catherine. *La Politique à l'égard de la petite enfance sous la Troisième République.* Cahier de l'INED (127). Paris: Presses Universitaires de France, 1990.

Romantisme anglais et Eros. Faculté des Lettres de l'Université de Clermont-Ferrand II, 1982.

Rosa, Annette. *Citoyennes: Les Femmes et la Révolution française.* Paris: Messidor, 1988.

Rosenberg, Rosalind. *Beyond Separate Spheres: Intellectual Roots of Modern Feminism.* New Haven: Yale University Press, 1982.

Ross, Ellen. "Survival Networks: Women's Neighbourhood Sharing in London before World War I," *History Workshop Journal* 15 (Spring 1983): 4–27.

Roth, Marie-Louise, and Roberto Olmi. "Musil," *Cahiers de l'Herne,* 1982.

Rothman, Sheila M. *Woman's Proper Place: A History of Changing Ideals and Practices, 1870 to the Present.* New York: Basic Books, 1978.

Roudinesco, Elisabeth. *Théroigne de Méricourt: Une femme mélancolique sous la Révolution.* Paris: Le Seuil, 1988.

Rowbotham, Sheila. *Hidden from History.* London: Pluto Press, 1973.

——— *Women, Resistance, and Revolution.* London: Allen Lane, 1972.

Rowe, K. E., ed. *Methodist Women.* Lake Junaluska, N.C.: General Commission on Archives and History, the United Methodist Church, 1980.

Ryan, Mary P. *Cradle of the Middle Class: The Family in Oneida County, New York (1790–1865).* New York: Cambridge University Press, 1981.

Sachsse, Christoph. *Mütterlichkeit als Beruf: Sozialarbeit, Sozialreform und Frauenbewegung, 1871–1929.* Frankfurt: Suhrkamp, 1986.

Saisselin, Rémy G. *The Bourgeois and the Bibelot.* New Brunswick, N.J.: Rutgers University Press, 1984; French ed., Albin Michel, 1990.

Schenda, Rudolf. *Volke ohne Buch: Studien zur Sozialgeschichte der populären Lesestoffe, 1770–1910.* Frankfurt: Klostermann, 1970.

Schiff, Ellen. "What Kind of Way Is That for a Nice Jewish Girl to Act?: Images of Jewish Women in Modern American Drama," *American Jewish History* 10, 1 (September 1980): 106–118.

Schnapper, Bernard. "La Séparation de corps de 1837 à 1914: Essai de sociologie juridique," in *Revue Historique* 526 (April-June 1978): 453–466.

Schnetzler, Barbara V. *Die frühe amerikanische Frauenbewegung und ihre Kontakte mit Europa (1836–1869).* Bern: Lang, 1971.

Schorske, Carl E. *Vienne fin de siècle*. Paris: Le Seuil, 1983.
Schröder, Hannelore. *Die Rechtlosigkeit der Frau im Rechtsstaat*. Frankfurt: Campus, 1979.
Schuller, Marianne. *Freud und Leid: Bei Tragik und Tod*. Frankfurt, 1991.
——— *Im Unterscheid: Lesen/Korrespondieren/Adressieren*. Frankfurt, 1990.
Scott, Joan W. *Gender and the Politics of History*. New York: Columbia University Press, 1988.
——— "'L'Ouvrière! Mot impie, sordide . . .': Women Workers in the Discourse of French Political Economy, 1840–1860," in Patrick Joyce, ed., *The Historical Meanings of Work*, pp. 119–142. Cambridge: Cambridge University Press, 1987.
Scott, Joan W., and Louise Tilly. *Women, Work, and Family*. New York: Holt, Rinehart, and Winston, 1978; French ed.: *Les Femmes, le travail et la famille*. Marseilles: Rivages, 1987.
Seccombe, Wally. "Patriarchy Stabilized: The Construction of the Male Breadwinner Wage Norm in Nineteenth-Century Britain," *Social History* 2 (January 1986): 53–76.
Segalen, Martine. *Mari et femme dans la société paysanne*. Paris: Flammarion, 1980.
Seller, Maxine. "The Education of the Immigrant Woman, 1900–1935," *Journal of Urban History* 4, 3 (May 1978): 307–330.
The Sexual Division of Labour, 19th and 20th Centuries. Uppsala Papers in Economic History. Uppsala: Uppsala University, 1989.
"Sexuality and the Social Body in the Nineteenth Century," *Representations* 14 (1986).
Shanley, Mary Lindon. *Feminism, Marriage, and the Law in Victorian England, 1850–1895*. Princeton: Princeton University Press, 1989; London: Tauris, 1990.
Shorter, Edward. *A History of Women's Bodies*. New York: Basic Books, 1982. French ed.: *Le Corps de femmes*. Paris: Le Seuil, 1984.
——— *Naissance de la famille moderne*. Paris: Le Seuil, 1981.
"Silence: Emancipation des femmes entre public et privé," *Cahiers du CEDREF* 1 (Paris VII), 1989.
Singer, Isaac. "Yentl the Yeshiva Boy," in *Short Friday and Other Stories*. New York: Farrar, Straus, and Giroux, 1964. French ed.: "Yentl," in *Yentl et autres nouvelles*. Paris: Stock, 1984.
Sledziewski, Elisabeth G. *Révolutions du sujet*. Paris: Méridiens Klincksieck, 1989.
Smith, Bonnie G. *Changing Lives: Women in European History since 1700*. Lexington, Mass.: D. C. Heath, 1989.
——— *Ladies of the Leisure Class: The Bourgeoises of Northern France in the Nineteenth Century*. Princeton: Princeton University Press, 1981; French ed.: *Les Bourgeoises du nord*. Paris: Perrin, 1989.
Smith-Rosenberg, Carroll. *Disorderly Conduct: Visions of Gender in Victorian America*. New York: Oxford University Press, 1986.
——— *Religion and the Rise of the American City*. Ithaca: Cornell University Press, 1971.

Snitow, Ann, et al. *Powers of Desire: The Politics of Sexuality in America.* New York: Routledge and Kegan Paul, 1984.

Sochen, June. *Consecrate Every Day: The Public Lives of Jewish American Women, 1880–1980.* Albany: State University of New York Press, 1981.

Sohn, Anne-Marie. "Les Rôles féminins dans la vie privée: Approche méthodologique et bilan de recherches," *Revue d'histoire moderne et contemporaine* 28 (October-December 1981): 597–623.

"Solidarietà, Amicizia, Amore," Marina d'Amelia, ed., *Donnawomanfemme* 10–11 (January-June 1979).

Soldani, Simonetta, ed. *L'educazione delle donne: Scuole e modelli di vita femminile nell'Italia dell'ottocento.* Milan: Franco Angeli, 1989.

Solomon-Godeau, Abigail. "The Legs of the Countess," *October* 39 (Winter 1986): 65–108.

Sonnet, Martine. *L'Education des filles au temps des Lumières.* Paris: Le Cerf, 1987.

Sowerwine, Charles. *Les Femmes et le socialisme.* Paris: Presses de la Fondation Nationale des Sciences Politiques, 1978. English trans.: *Sisters or Citizens? Women and Socialism in France since 1876.* New York: Cambridge University Press, 1982.

Spender, Dale. *Feminist Theorists.* London: Women's Press, 1983.

——— *Women of Ideas.* London: Routledge and Kegan Paul, 1982.

Stanislawski, Michael. *Tsar Nicholas I and the Jews: The Transformation of Jewish Society in Russia, 1825–1855.* Philadelphia: Jewish Publication Society, 1983.

Stansell, Christine. *City of Women: Sex and Class in New York (1789–1860).* New York: Knopf, 1986.

Starobinski, Jean. *Le Remède dans le mal.* Paris: Gallimard, 1989.

Stefan, Inge, and Sigrid Weigel. *Die verborgene Frau.* 3rd ed. Berlin: Argument Verlag, 1988.

Stites, Richard. *The Women's Liberation Movement in Russia: Feminism, Nihilism, and Bolshevism, 1860–1930.* Princeton: Princeton University Press, 1977.

Stratton, Joanna L. *Pioneer Women: Voices from the Kansas Frontier.* New York: Simon and Schuster, 1981.

Studer, Monica. "L'Organisation syndicale et les femmes: L'action de Margarete Faas-Hardegger à l'Union Syndicale Suisse (1905–1909)." Master's thesis, Université de Genève, 1975.

Suleiman, Susan Rubin, ed. *The Female Body in Western Culture: Contemporary Perspectives.* Cambridge, Mass.: Harvard University Press, 1986.

Sullerot, Evelyne. *Histoire de la presse féminine en France des origines à 1848.* Paris: A. Colin, 1966.

Susman, Margarete. *Frauen der Romantik.* Cologne: Meltzer, 1960.

Swain, Gladys. "L'Âme, la femme, le sexe et le corps: Les métamorphoses de l'hystérie au XIXè siècle," *Le Débat* (March 1983).

Szapor, Judith. "Les Associations féministes en Hongrie XIXè-XXè siècles," in *Penelope* 11 (Autumn 1984): 169–173.

Taeger, Annemarie. *Die Kunst: Medusa zu töten*. Bielefeld: Aisthesis Verlag, 1987.

Tax, Meredith. *The Rising of the Women Feminist Solidarity and Class Conflict, 1880–1917*. New York: Monthly Review Press, 1980.

Taylor, Barbara. *Eve and the New Jerusalem: Socialism and Feminism in the Nineteenth Century*. London: Virago, 1979; Cambridge, Mass.: Harvard University Press, 1993.

Thalmann, Rita, ed. *Femmes et fascismes*. Paris: Tierce, 1986.

Théry, Irène, and Christian Biet, eds. *La Famille, la loi, l'état: De la Revolution au code civil*. Paris: Imprimerie Nationale et Centre Georges-Pompidou, 1989.

Thomas, H. F., and R. Skinner Keller. *Women in Two Worlds*, 2 vols. Nashville: Abington Press, 1981–82.

Thompson, Dorothy. "Women and Nineteenth-Century Radical Politics: A Lost Dimension," in Mitchell and Oakley, *Rights and Wrongs*.

Thumerel, Thérèse. "Maupassant ou le double saturnien de Nerval," *Romantisme* (forthcoming).

Tickner, Lisa. *The Spectacle of Women: Imagery of the Suffrage Campaign, 1907–1914*. London: Chatto and Windus, 1987.

Tomalin, Claire. *The Life and Death of Mary Wollstonecraft*. New York: Harcourt Brace Jovanovich, 1974.

"Travaux de femmes dans la France du XIXè siècle," *Le Mouvement social* 105 (October-December 1978).

Turin, Yvonne. *Femmes et religieuses au XIXè siècle: Le féminisme "en religion."* Paris: Editions Nouvelle Cité, 1989.

Twellmann, Margrit. *Die deutsche Frauenbewegung*. Ihre Anfänge und erste Entwicklung. Quellen, 1843–1889. Meisenheim-am-Glan, 1972.

Vance, Carole S. *Pleasure and Danger: Exploring Female Sexuality*. New York, 1984.

Varikas, Eleni. *"La Révolte des dames: Genèse d'une conscience féministe dans la Grèce du XIXè siècle."* Thesis, Paris IV, 1988.

Verdier, Yvonne. *Façons de dire, façons de faire: La laveuse, la couturière, la cuisinière*. Paris: Gallimard, 1979.

Viala, Robert. *L'Enseignement secondaire des jeunes filles, 1880–1940: Par ceux qui l'ont créé et celles qui l'ont fait vivre*. Sèvres: CIEP, 1987.

Vicinus, Martha. *Independent Women: Work and Community for Single Women, 1850–1920*. Chicago: University of Chicago Press, 1985.

———, ed. *Suffer and Be Still: Women in the Victorian Age*. Bloomington and London: Indiana University Press, 1972.

———, ed. *A Widening Sphere: Changing Roles of Victorian Women*. Bloomington: Indiana University Press, 1977.

"Victoria Station," *Critique* (February-March 1981): 405–406.

Vidal, Christiane. "Une Surmortalité féminine prolongée en Europe: Le cas français des Alpes du sud," *Population* 35 (1980): 698–708.

"Vieillesses des femmes," *Pénélope* 13 (Autumn 1985).

Voeltzel, R. *Service du Seigneur*. Strasbourg: Oberlin, 1983.

Volet-Jeanneret, Helena. *La Femme bourgeoise à Prague, 1860–1895: De la philanthropie à l'émancipation*. Thesis, Université de Lausanne. Geneva: Slatkine, 1988.

Waithe, Mary Ellen, ed. *A History of Women Philosophers (1600–1900)*, vol. 3. Dordrecht: Martinus Nijhoff Publishers, 1987.

Walkowitz, Judith. *Prostitution and Victorian Society: Women, Class, and the State*. New York: Cambridge University Press, 1980.

Walle, Marianne. "Contribution à l'histoire des femmes allemandes entre 1848 et 1920 (Louise Otto, Helene Lange, Clara Zetkin, Lily Braun)." Thesis, Paris VII, 1989.

Walter, Eva. *Schrieb oft, von Mägde Arbeit müde, Lebenszusammenhänge deutscher Schriftstellerinnen um 1800, Schritte zur bürgerlichen Weiblichkeit*. Düsseldorf: Schwann, 1985.

Ward, Margaret. *Unmanageable Revolutionaries: Women and Irish Nationalism*. London: Pluto Press, 1983.

Weaver, Mike. *Julia Margaret Cameron (1815–1879)*. An exhibition arranged by the John Hansard Gallery, the University, Southampton: The John Hansard Gallery, 1984.

Weber-Kellerman, Ingeborg. *Die deutsche Familie: Versuch einer Sozialgeschichte*. Frankfurt: Suhrkamp, 1974.

Weeks, Jeffrey. *Coming Out: Homosexual Politics in Britain from the Nineteenth Century to the Present*. London: Quartet Books, 1977.

——— *Sex, Politics, and Society: The Regulation of Sexuality since 1800*, vol. 13. London and New York: Longman, 1981.

——— *Sexuality and Its Discontents: Meanings, Myths, Modern Sexualities*. London: Routledge and Kegan Paul, 1985.

Weickart, Eva. "Zur Entwicklung der polnischen Frauenbewegung in der 1. Hälfte des 19. Jhd," in Jutta Dalhoff, Uschi Frey, and Ingrid Schöll, eds., *Frauenmacht in der Geschichte*. Düsseldorf: Schwann, 1986.

Weiland, Daniela. *Geschichte der Frauenemanzipation in Deutschland und Oesterreich*. Düsseldorf: Econ-Verlag, 1983.

Weinberg, Sydney S. *The World of Our Mothers: The Lives of Jewish Immigrant Women*. Chapel Hill: University of North Carolina Press, 1988.

Welsch, Ursula, and Michaela Wiesner. *Lou Andreas-Salomé*. Munich and Vienna: Verlag Internationale Psychoanalyse, 1988.

Wemyss, A. *Histoire du réveil*. Paris: Les Bergers and les Mages, 1977.

Werner, Pascale, ed. *L'Histoire sans qualités*. Paris: Galilée, 1979.

Wheelwright, Julie. *Amazons and Military Maids: Women Who Dressed as Men in Pursuit of Life, Liberty, and Happiness*. London: Pandora, 1989.

White, Cynthia. *Women's Magazines, 1693–1968*. London: Michael Joseph, 1970.

Whitelegg, Elizabeth, ed. *The Changing Experience of Women*. Oxford: Basil Blackwell, 1982.

Wilkman, Ruth. *Women, Work, and Protest: A Century of American Women's Labour History*. London: RKP, 1985.

Willemsen, Roger. *Robert Musil: Vom intellektuellen Eros*. Munich: Piper, 1985.

Williams, Rosalind H. *Dream Worlds: Mass Consumption in Late Nineteenth-Century France*. Berkeley: University of California Press, 1982.
Woodtli, Susanna. *Du féminisme à l'égalité politique: Un siècle de luttes en Suisse, 1868–1971*. Lausanne: Payot, 1977.
Woolf, Virginia. *The Common Reader; The Second Common Reader; The Death of the Moth; The Captain's Death Bed; The Moment; Granite and Rainbow*. London: Hogarth Press.
Yeldham, Charlotte. *Women Artists in Nineteenth-Century France and England*, 2 vols. New York and London: Garland, 1984.
Yezierska, Anzia. *The Bread Givers*. New York: Persea, 1975.
Zipperstein, Steven J. *The Jews of Odessa: A Cultural History, 1794–1881*. Stanford: Stanford University Press, 1985.
Zylberberg-Hocquard, Marie-Hélène. *Féminisme et syndicalisme en France*. Paris: Anthropos, 1978.

Contributors

NICOLE ARNAUD-DUC. Doctor of law, research associate of the Centre National de Recherche Scientifique. Her research focuses on criminality, deviancy, and gender relations as revealed by legal documents. She has published numerous papers. Her major work on women is *Droit, mentalités et changement social en Provence occidentale. Stratégies et pratique notariale en matière de régime matrimonial* (Aix-en-Provence, 1985).

JEAN BAUBÉROT. *Directeur d'études* at the Ecole Pratique des Hautes Etudes and chair of the Religious Sciences Section, he is a specialist in the history and sociology of Protestantism, secularism, and of religion and morality generally. Among his many works: *Histoire du protestantisme* (Paris, 1987, 1990); *Le Protestantisme doit-il mourir?* (Paris, 1988); *La Laïcité: quel héritage de 1789 à nos jours?* (Paris, 1990); *Vers un nouveau pacte laïque?* (Paris, 1990).

CÉCILE DAUPHIN. *Ingénieur d'études* at the Centre National de Recherche Scientifique. She has participated in a number of research projects under the auspices of the Centre de Recherches Historiques–Ecoles des Hautes Etudes en Sciences Sociales and is the coeditor of *Cahiers Pénélope. Pour l'Histoire des Femmes*. Her publications include "La Vieille Fille. Histoire d'un stéréotype," in Arlette Farge and Christiane Klapisch Zuber, eds., *Madame ou Mademoiselle? Itinéraires de la solitude féminine au XIXe siècle* (Paris, 1984); "L'Enquête postale de 1847"; and "Les manuels épistolaires au XIXe siècle," in Roger Chartier, ed., *La Correspondance. Les usages de la lettre au XIXe siècle* (Paris, 1991).

MICHELA DE GIORGIO. Research associate at the Gramsci Institute in Rome. She is particularly interested in the social behavior and culture of Italian women in the nineteenth and twentieth centuries. Her most recent publication in this area is "Signore et signorine italiane fra otto a novecento," in L. Ferrante, M. Palazzi, and G. Pomata, eds., *Ragnatele di rapporti* (Turin, 1988).

GENEVIÈVE FRAISSE. Research associate in philosophy at the Centre National de Recherche Scientifique, she is one of the pioneer historians of French feminism (as well as a founder of the journal *Révoltes logiques,* 1975). She is currently working on representations and philosophical understandings of gender difference. Among her published works are *Femmes toutes mains, essai sur le service domestique* (Paris, 1979); *Clémence Royer, philosophe et femme de sciences* (Paris, 1985); and *Muse de la raison, la démocratie exclusive et la différence des sexes* (Aix-en-Provence, 1989).

DOMINIQUE GODINEAU. A historian specializing in the French Revolution, she has contributed to a number of anthologies and edited the "Woman and Family" section of the French Revolution Research Collection. Her major work is *Citoyennes Tricoteuses. Les femmes du peuple à Paris pendant la Révolution française.*

NANCY GREEN. After taking a Ph.D. at the University of Chicago, she is now *maître de conférences* at the Ecole des Hautes Etudes en Sciences Sociales. A specialist in the comparative history of immigration in France and the United States, she is the author of *Les Travailleurs immigrés juifs à la Belle Epoque* (Paris, 1985). She is currently working on immigrants in the garment trade in Paris and New York (1880–1980).

ANNE HIGONNET. Assistant Professor of Art at Wellesley College and a specialist in the art of the nineteenth century, she works at the intersection of art history, social history, and women's history. Her doctoral dissertation (Yale, 1988) has been published as *Berthe Morisot: Images of Women* (Cambridge, Mass., 1993).

MARIE-CLAIRE HOOCK-DEMARLE. A specialist in German literature. Her doctoral dissertation on *Bettina Brentano von Arnim ou la mise en oeuvre d'une vie 1785–1859* was published in 1985. She is a professor at the University of Paris VII-Jussieu. Among her recent works: *La Femme au temps de Goethe* (Paris, 1987); *La Rage d'écrire. Femmes-écrivains en Allemagne de 1790 à 1815* (Aix-en-Provence, 1990). She is currently interested in European letter-writing and the role of correspondence in shaping the consciousness of nineteenth-century Europe.

ANNE-MARIE KÄPPELI A historian employed by the Fonds National Suisse de la Recherche Scientifique, she works on the history of women in Switzerland, especially Protestant feminists and teachers. Her publications include *Sublime Croisade: Ethique et politique du féminisme protestant (1875–1928)* (Geneva, 1990), and *Emancipation féminine et pédagogie (1845–1972): Les pionnières suisses de la formation des mères et de l'éducation des filles* (forthcoming).

YVONNE KNIBIEHLER. Professor emeritus at the University of Provence, she specializes in intellectual history (her thesis, *Mignet et l'histoire philosophique du XIXe siècle,* was published in 1973) and the history of women, to which she has contributed more than sixty articles and a dozen books, most notably, with Catherine Fouquet, *L'Histoire des mères* (Paris, 1980); *Nous les assistantes sociales. Naissance d'une profession,* 1980 (with Catherine Fouquet); *La Femme et les médecins* (Paris, 1983); *Cornettes et blouses blanches. Les infirmières dans la société française, 1880–1980* (Paris, 1984); (with Régine Goutalier), *La Femme au temps des Colonies* (Paris, 1985); *Les pères aussi ont une histoire* (Paris, 1987).

ANNELISE MAUGUE. A teacher at the Lycée Rabelais in Paris, her research concerns problems of sexual identity and their literary expression. Among her publications: *La Crise de l'identité masculine au tournant du siècle* (Paris-Marseille, 1987).

FRANÇOISE MAYEUR. A professor at the University of Paris IV-Sorbonne and specialist in the history of education, particularly of girls, she is the author of numerous books and articles, including *L'Enseignement secondaire des jeunes filles sous la troisième République* (Paris, 1977) and *L'Education des filles au XIXe siècle* (Lyon, 1980). She is also the author of volume three of *L'Histoire de l'enseignement et de l'éducation en France* (Paris, 1981).

STÉPHANE MICHAUD. Professor of comparative literature at the Université Jean-Monnet in Saint-Etienne and member of the editorial board of *Romantisme,* he specializes in the history of women and their representation in nineteenth-century French and German literature. He is the author of *Un fabuleux destin: Flora Tristan* (Dijon, 1985); *Flora Tristan (1803–1844)* (Paris, 1984); and *Muse et Madone. Visages de la femme de la Révolution française aux apparitions de Lourdes* (Paris, 1985).

MICHELLE PERROT. Professor of contemporary history at the University of Paris VII-Jussieu. After early work on the nineteenth-century working class (*Les Ouvriers en grève* [Paris, 1974]), she turned to the study of crime and the penal system: *L'Impossible Prison* (Paris, 1980) and *Ecrits pénitentiaires d'Alexis de Tocqueville.* She edited volume four of *A History of Private Life,* published by Harvard. But her major interest in recent years has been the history of women, with publications including *Lettres des filles de Karl Marx* (Paris, 1979); (with Georges Ribeill), *Journal intime de Caroline B.* (Paris, 1985); and *Une histoire des femmes est-elle possible?* (Marseille, 1984).

JOAN WALLACH SCOTT. After teaching at various American universities and heading Brown University's Center for the Study of Women, she is now professor of social science at Princeton's Institute for Advanced

Study. A specialist in French social history (and author of *The Glassworkers of Carmaux*), she has turned more recently to the history of women and theories of gender. She has also published *Gender and the Politics of History* (New York, 1988).

ELISABETH G. SLEDZIEWSKI. *Maître de conférences* at the Institut d'Etudes Politiques in Strasbourg and associate professor at the University of Erlangen-Nümberg in Germany, she is interested in the political culture of Eastern Europe and the role of women in politics during the French Revolution (her primary specialty) as well as in contemporary Europe. Among her publications: *Voies idéologiques de la Révolution française* (1976–1989); *Idéaux et Conflits dans la Révolution française* (Paris, 1986); *Révolutions du sujet* (Paris, 1989); and (with J.-L. Vieillard-Baron), *Penser le sujet aujourd'hui* (1988).

JUDITH WALKOWITZ. Professor of history and director of women's studies at Johns Hopkins University and a specialist in the history of feminism, sexuality, and medicine in relation to society and culture, she is the author of *Prostitution and Victorian Society: Women, Class and the State*, 1980. Her *City of Dreadful Delight: Narratives of Sexual Danger in Late-Victorian London* is forthcoming.

Illustration Credits

1. The Art Institute of Chicago
2. Archiv für Kunst und Geschichte, Berlin
3. Louvre, Paris. Photo Musées Nationaux
4. Louvre, Paris. Photo Musées Nationaux
5. Bibliothèque Nationale, Paris
6. © Neville Ollerenshaw c/o Victor Gollancz, London
7. Chatto & Windus, London
8. Tate Gallery, London
9. Bibliothèque Nationale, Paris
10. Bibliothèque Nationale, Paris
11. Bibliothèque Nationale, Paris
12. Archiv für Kunst und Geschichte, Berlin
13. Harvard University Theater Collection, Cambridge, Mass.
14. Private collection
15. Private collection
16. Private collection
17. Harvard University, Widener Library, Cambridge, Mass.
18. Underlinden Museum, Colmar
19. Musée de l'Horlogerie et de l'Emaillerie, Geneva
20. Metropolitan Museum of Art, New York
21. Penguin Books, London
22. Museum of Fine Arts, Boston
23. The Art Institute of Chicago
24. Photo André Held, Ecubens, Switzerland
25. Hermann Mayer Collection. Photo Mt. Holyoke College Art Museum, South Hadley, Mass.
26. Archiv für Kunst und Geschichte, Berlin
27. Archiv für Kunst und Geschichte, Berlin
28. *McLure's Magazine*, VII, 5 (October 1896)
29. Archiv für Kunst und Geschichte, Berlin
30. Photo Musée Carnavalet, Paris
31. Photo George Eastman House, International Museum of Photography, Rochester, N.Y.
32. Musée d'Orsay, Paris. Photo Musées Nationaux
33. Photo SIP
34. Arthur Munby Collection, Trinity College, Cambridge
35. Private collection, Paris
36. Museum of the City of New York
37. Photo Bibliothèque Charcot de la Salpêtrière, Paris
38. Gérard Lévy Collection, Paris
39. Musée Rodin, Paris
40. Musée Rodin, Paris
41. Documents Collection, College of Environmental Design, University of California, Berkeley
42. Isabella Stewart Gardner Museum, Boston
43. Isabella Stewart Gardner Museum, Boston
44. Photo Wilma Slaight, Clapp Library Archives, Wellesley College, Wellesley, Mass.
45. Archiv für Kunst und Geschichte, Berlin
46. Photo Newnham College, Cambridge University
47. Gernsheim Collection, University of Texas, Austin

Index